AF324994

40 YEARS NEW

Lisa Phillips

With Johanna Burton, Lauren Cornell, Massimiliano Gioni, Joseph Grima, Julia Kaganskiy, Ned Rifkin, Alicia Ritson, Lynne Tillman, and Brian Wallis

NEW MUSEUM

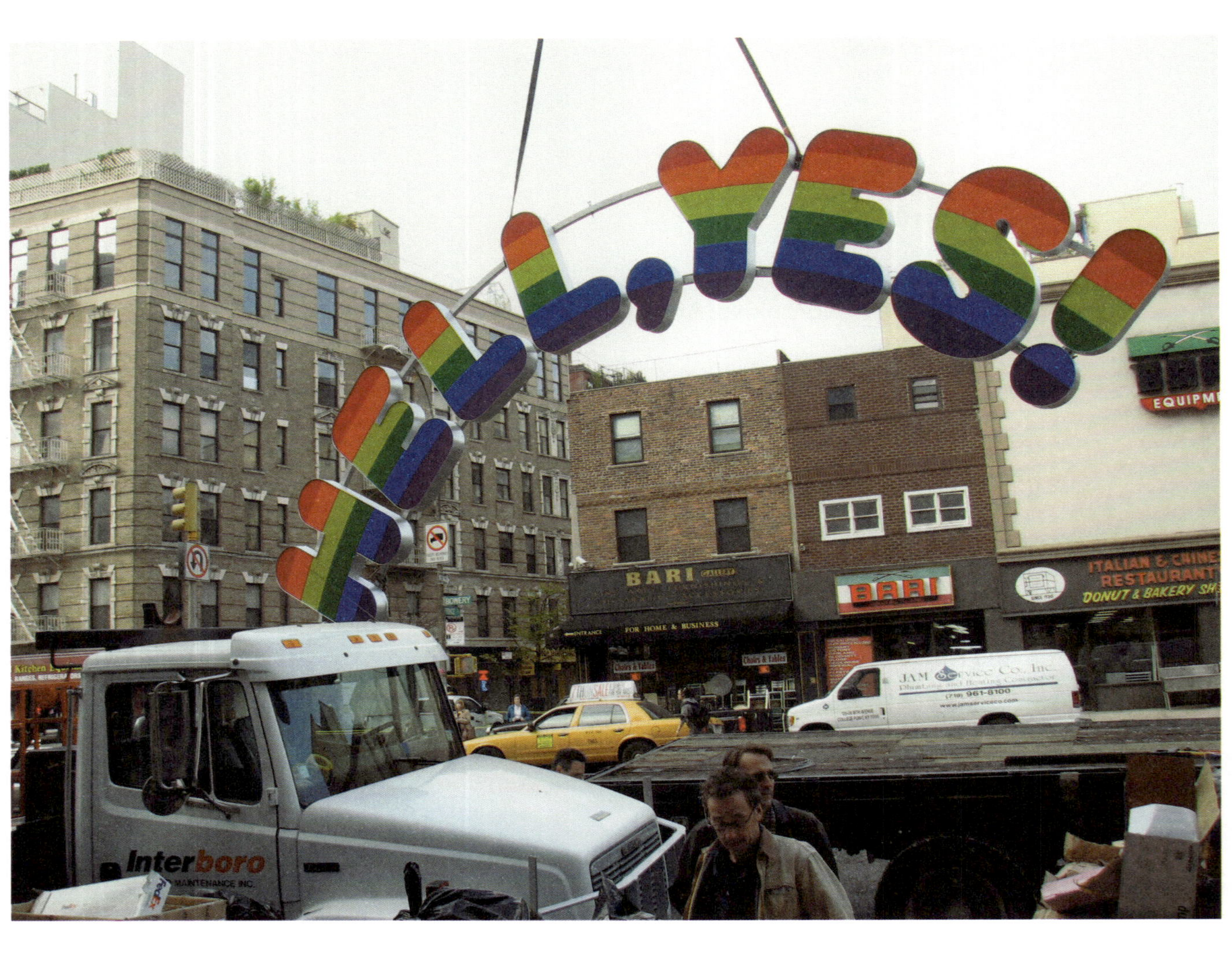

Installation of Ugo
Rondinone's *Hell, Yes!*,
2001, on the New Museum's
facade for the opening of
the new building on the
Bowery in 2007

Change Agent

Lisa Phillips

At forty, the New Museum is still a relative newcomer, and yet 1977—the year it was founded—seems light years away from the hyper-accelerated pace of our twenty-first-century networked world. The Museum was born in a very different era: there were no cell phones, no internet, no cable TV, no laptops, no ATMs, no iTunes, no FedEx, no email, and certainly no Twitter, Facebook, or Instagram. It was an analog time of Rolodexes, electric typewriters, Wite-Out, phone booths, vinyl records, mimeograph machines, and "snail mail." When we wanted to tune in to breaking news, we turned on the television or the radio. In New York, rent for a one-bedroom was $125 a month, there were plenty of loft spaces for artists, and underground culture was thriving. The city was gritty, dangerous, and economically diverse, and artists didn't expect to make a living from their work—they all had day jobs. But there was a lot of room for experimentation and reinvention fueled by the counterculture of the 1960s and the liberation movements for civil rights, women's rights, and gay rights.

It was during this period that Marcia Tucker, a young curator with a strong, independent spirit, had a vision for a new kind of cultural institution. She wasn't alone—she was part of a cohort of colleagues who were inventing new alternative arts organizations at that time—but her vision had a unique inflection. For most of her career, Tucker worked at the Whitney Museum of American Art, where she had curated pioneering shows of work by women artists (Lee Krasner, Joan Mitchell, Betye Saar, Joan Snyder) and staged daring group exhibitions of work by an emerging generation, such as "Anti-Illusion: Procedures/Materials" (1969). Her final show was a survey of the deliberately modest art of Richard Tuttle, where I happened to be a young intern, greeting the (often irate) public. At the Whitney, Tucker was a vociferous advocate for radical forms of art-making—tattooing, bodybuilding, performance—that many considered outside the boundaries of art. When a new director arrived in 1974, tensions simmered, and their personalities clashed, which led to her much-publicized firing in 1976. Tucker set out to found her own institution the very next day. She had no collection and no financial resources of her own, just a passionate belief that art can make a difference and can change lives.

Right from the start, the name "New Museum" signaled an intentional paradox: This would not be a traditional institution, and it would not be bureaucratic, hierarchical, or centered around a permanent collection. However, it would maintain the seriousness and promote the scholarship of a museum. Tucker envisioned an alternative to the conventional art institution, a place where discovery and risk-taking were encouraged, where artists could experiment, where leading-edge research would be conducted, where ever-new ideas about art were embraced, and where the character of the "museum" could be redefined. That spirit of investigation and challenge lives on in our mission and programs as an essential part of who we are.

When the New Museum was founded in 1977, few museums were showing contemporary art. According

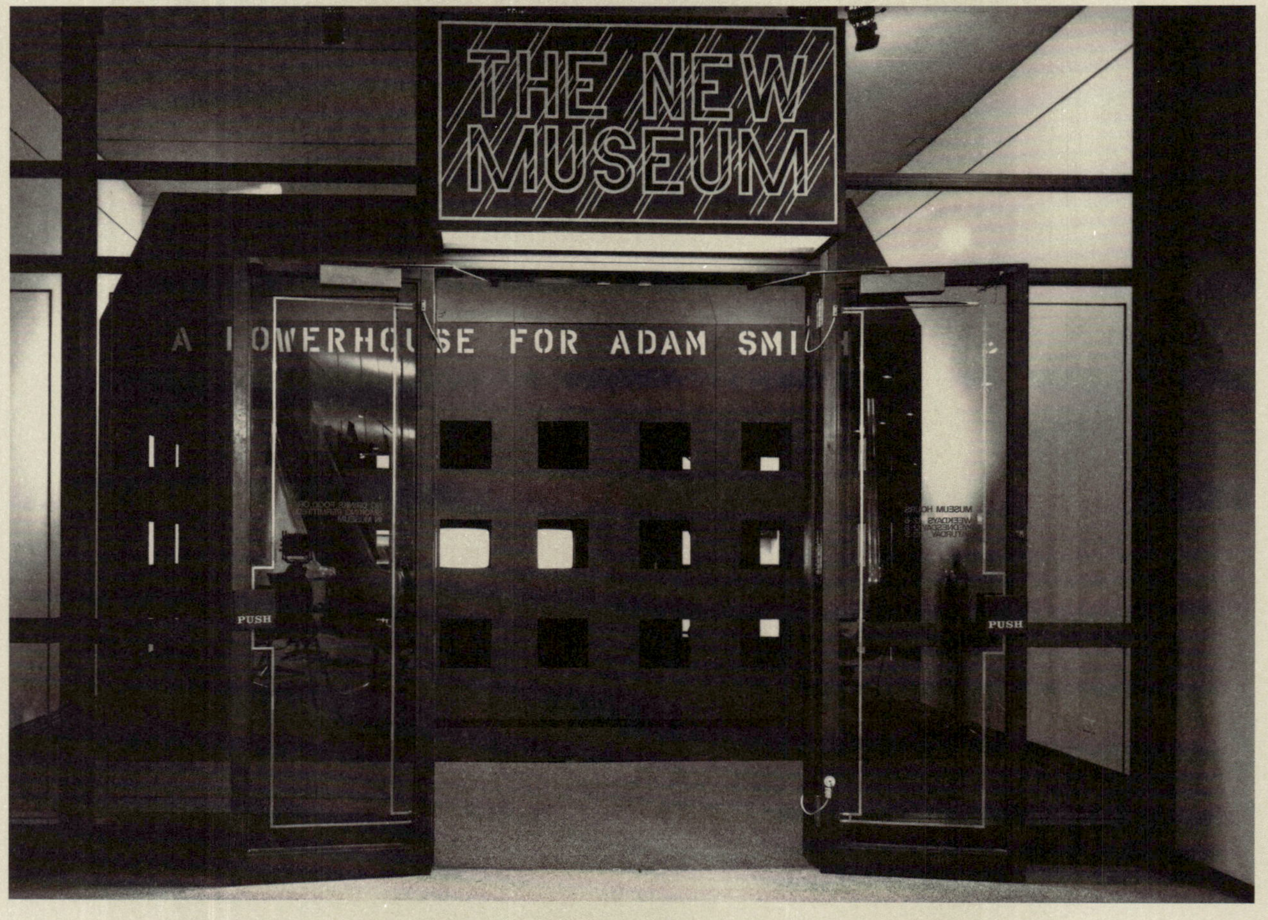

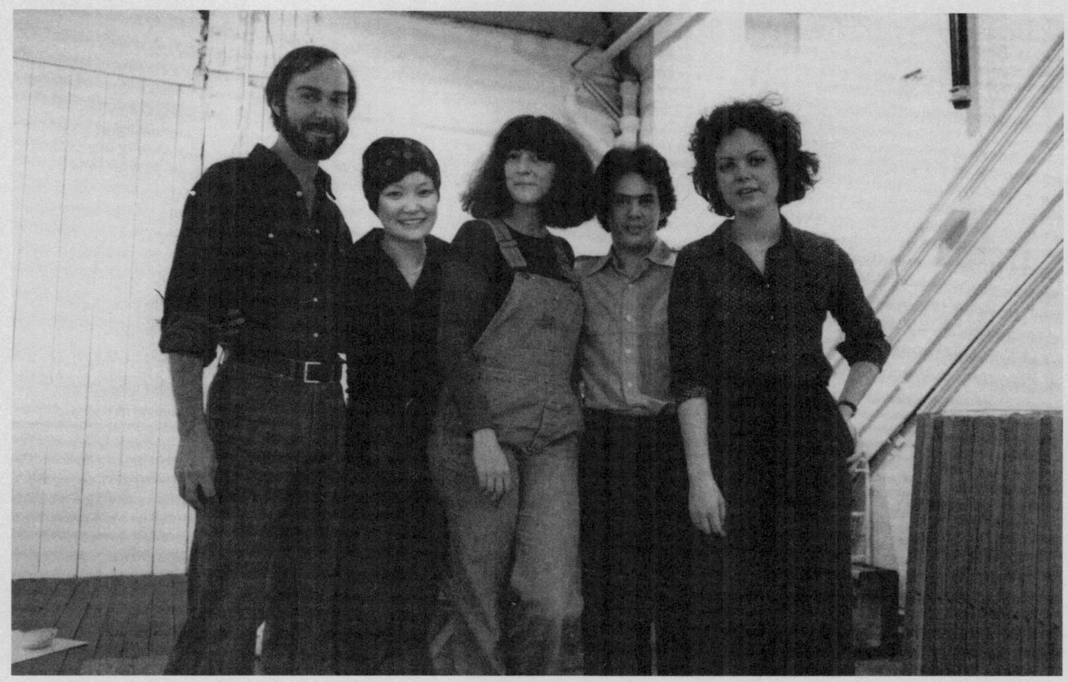

to the Museum's first prospectus, "it would be the only museum in New York to have, as its priority, living artists and the work they make."[1] This still holds true today. We've always been a *future-facing* museum—not a place for preserving and recording history, but a place where history is made.

And so began the Museum's forty-year trajectory of groundbreaking firsts, including benchmark solo exhibitions of artists who were under-recognized at the time and provocative theme shows that would go to the heart of urgent issues. Throughout that arc, it has served as an incubator for new art through exhibitions, projects, residencies, and commissions; for new ideas through conferences, scholarship, and publications; for new models of cultural exchange; for broader reach and impact through programs like Museum as Hub and Ideas City; and for cultivating new talent and leadership by nurturing a young staff who would go on to populate the field in senior positions.

For all our emphasis on exploration and trailblazing over the years, the institution's own history has been somewhat neglected and never systematically recorded.

1. The New Museum's first prospectus, cited in Marcia Tucker, "The New Museum of Contemporary Art 1977–1992: Fifteen Years of Exploration," in *15th Anniversary*, ed. Charlayne Haynes (New York: New Museum, 1992), 6. The major difference between then and now is that, forty years on, even the most traditional institutions have stretched to incorporate contemporary art. The New Museum helped to spur that change.

We rarely looked back. This volume, together with the
Museum's relaunched online archive, redresses this lack,
illuminating the Museum's restless inventiveness as it
grew from a fledgling organization to an internationally
recognized cultural destination whose outsize influence
and values of intimacy, empathy, and collaboration have
profoundly shaped the museum field.

The Rise of Alternatives

The Museum started its peripatetic life in a small office
in the Fine Arts Building at 105 Hudson Street. It was a
tiny outfit with a staff of three operating on a shoestring
budget of $30,000. The first curator, Allan Schwartzman
—who today is a principal of the advisory group Art
Agency Partners—was barely nineteen, had not yet
finished college, and knew little about curating. He refers
to this opening chapter as "the Judy and Mickey show,"
because the "Museum" was really a DIY start-up and the
young staff was learning on the job.[2]

The first New Museum exhibitions were pop-up installations in other venues, like C Space and ICA Tokyo, until
the fall of 1977, when Trustee Vera List arranged for
the nascent organization to occupy a ground-floor
gallery space in the Albert and Vera List Graduate
Center Building of the New School for Social Research
on Fourteenth Street, where it would remain for the
next six years. The New Museum was one of a crop of
alternative spaces that sprang up during the 1970s.
The rise of alternative institutions was an explosive
phenomenon that changed the artistic landscape in
our country—a chapter in cultural history that has yet
to be sufficiently explored by scholars. Several other
alternative spaces and nonprofits were founded in
New York during this decade—Anthology Film Archives,
Artists Space, the Clocktower Gallery, Creative Time,
the Drawing Center, Film Forum, Franklin Furnace, Just
Above Midtown, the Kitchen, P.S.1, and the Public Art
Fund among them—and had similarly active programs
and devoted followings. These organizations were
designed to support emerging artists, experimental art
forms, and new curators, and a number of them continue
to operate and flourish today.[3]

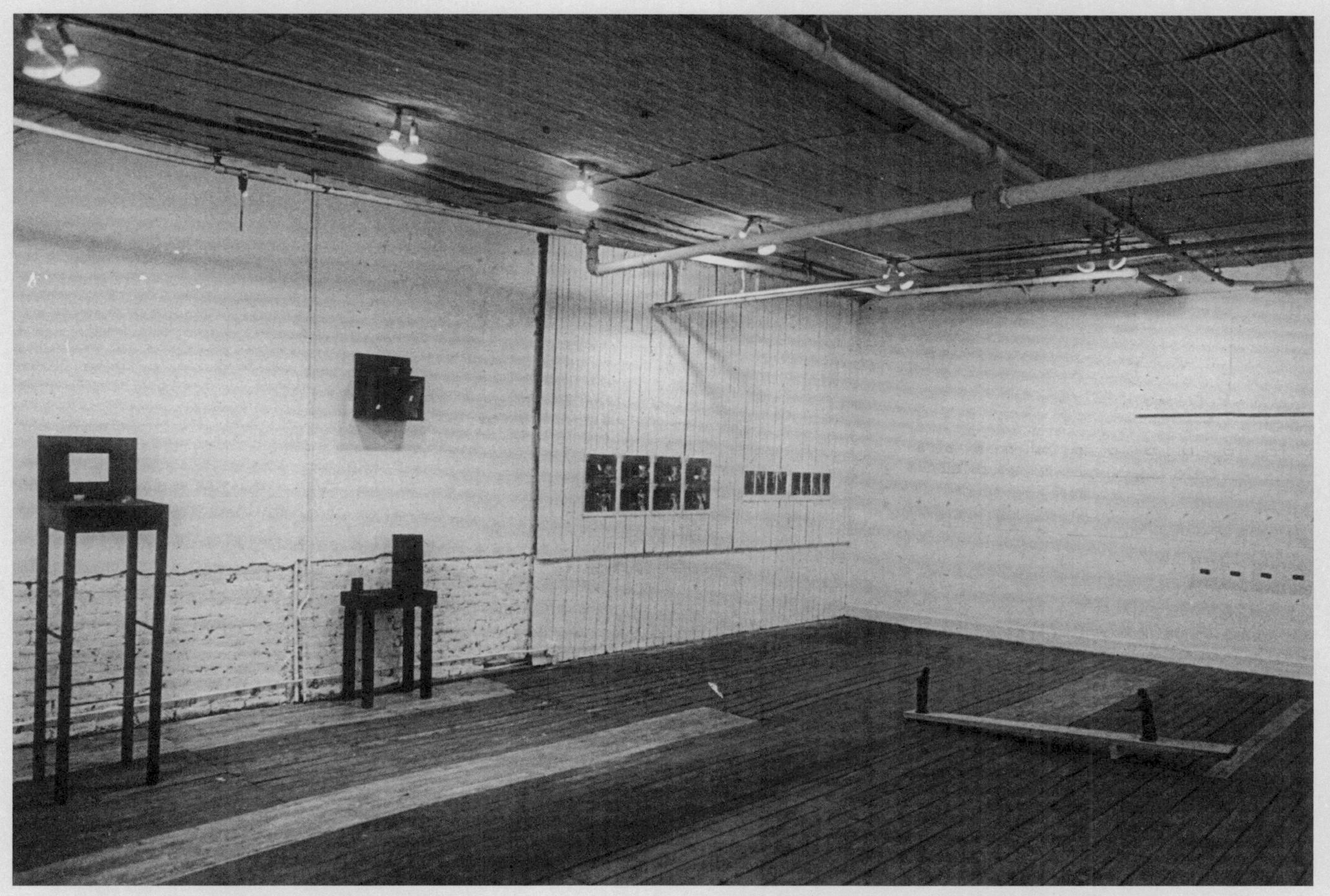

It is worth noting that many of these enterprises were founded by and/or run by women, including Martha Beck, founder of the Drawing Center; Linda Goode Bryant, founder of Just Above Midtown; Karen Cooper, Director of Film Forum; Anita Contini, Director of Creative Time; Alanna Heiss, founder of the Clocktower Gallery and P.S.1; Martha Wilson, founder of Franklin Furnace; and Helene Winer, Director of Artists Space. Facing barriers to advancement in conventional organizations and emboldened by the feminist movement, these women, like Tucker, created alternative structures that have endured as a vital counterpoint to mainstream

2. Allan Schwartzman in conversation with the author, March 30, 2017. Schwartzman was part of the first of many successive waves of curators, which also included Susan Logan and Kathleen Thomas; followed by Lynn Gumpert and Ned Rifkin; followed by Russell Ferguson, William Olander, and Brian Wallis; followed by France Morin, Gary Sangster, Laura Trippi, and Alice Yang; followed by Anne Barlow, Dan Cameron, Anne Ellegood, Yukie Kamiya, and Gerardo Mosquera; followed by Lauren Cornell, Richard Flood, Massimiliano Gioni, Jarrett Gregory, Laura Hoptman, Eungie Joo, and Jenny Moore; followed by our current cohort, Natalie Bell, Johanna Burton, Gary Carrion-Murayari, Helga Christoffersen, Gioni, and Margot Norton.

3. There were still others that had shorter life spans but were no less influential, like 98 Greene Street, 112 Greene Street (later renamed White Columns), Idea Warehouse, Apple, and C Space. Some of these organizations were featured in the New Museum's 1981 exhibition "Alternatives in Retrospect: An Historical Overview 1969–1975," which looked at the history of art spaces that had opened and closed prior to the Museum's 1977 founding.

institutions. As Tucker described it years later, she was privileged to be "one of the few women who are museum directors, and yet marginalized by virtue of having had to create the institution in order to work in it."[4] For these women, it was not about size or collections, but about ambition, collaboration, inclusion, and controlling their own destinies.

Changing and Expanding the Canon

It made sense that as an alternative space—albeit one with the professional standards of a museum—the New Museum would invite and support viewpoints and histories that both challenged and expanded the canon, countering top-down or received ideas about taste and quality. One early example of this was "'Bad' Painting" (1978), an exhibition that took an oppositional position with respect to skill and finish in general and to the geometric and industrial purity of the prevailing Minimalist aesthetic in particular by embracing excess, allegory, and folk and outsider art. "Outside New York" (1978–83) —a series that showcased artists from places such as Florida, Illinois, Ohio, and Texas who drew from and enriched regional styles and traditions—was another. Tucker steadfastly supported work that went against the grain, raising important questions about hierarchies of taste and disrupting monocultural standards of quality. She was compelled to see "bad" as its opposite, as a badge of honor, and she later proudly opened a lecture by saying, "I've had a substantial career based on really bad reviews of almost everything I've ever done. An early example: *'"Bad" Painting'—Unfortunately, most of it is really bad.*"[5]

Since the early days, the Museum has consistently been the first New York museum to present artists who were unknown or under-recognized at the time of their exhibitions. Our curators have always been prescient in their choices, helping to establish significant reputations for a number of artists whose work would soon be acknowledged, exhibited, and collected by larger institutions. This impressive history includes the first major New York museum exhibitions of the work of, among others, Alfred Jensen (1978), Barry Le Va (1978), John Baldessari

(1981), Hans Haacke (1986), Martin Puryear (1984), Leon
Golub (1984), Ana Mendieta (1987), Christian Boltanski
(1988), Nancy Spero (1989), Robert Colescott (1989),
Mary Kelly (1990), Andres Serrano (1995), Carolee
Schneemann (1996), Mona Hatoum (1997), Martin Wong
(1998), Faith Ringgold (1998), David Wojnarowicz (1999),
Cildo Meireles (1999), Adrian Piper (2000), Martha Rosler
(2000), William Kentridge (2001), Paul McCarthy (2001),
Hélio Oiticica (2002), Carroll Dunham (2002), John Waters
(2004), Andrea Zittel (2006), Elizabeth Peyton (2008),
Mary Heilmann (2008), Urs Fischer (2009), Rivane
Neuenschwander (2010), Lynda Benglis (2011), George
Condo (2011), Carsten Höller (2011), Rosemarie Trockel
(2012), Phyllida Barlow (2012), Ellen Gallagher (2013),
Chris Burden (2013), Paweł Althamer (2014), Ragnar
Kjartansson (2014), Camille Henrot (2014), Chris Ofili
(2014), Albert Oehlen (2015), Sarah Charlesworth (2015),
Jim Shaw (2016), Cheryl Donegan (2016), Nicole Eisenman
(2016), Simone Leigh (2016), Pipilotti Rist (2016), and
Raymond Pettibon (2017).

As the contemporary art market exploded in the 1980s
and a new generation of dealers opened up shop,
frequently in small establishments that resembled and
were in close proximity to unconventional alternative
spaces, even the most vanguard and critical work was
quickly embraced and absorbed by the market. This trig-
gered renewed questioning about what "acceptance,"
"mainstream," and "alternative" meant, or whether these
terms were even relevant any longer, and how alternative
institutions like the New Museum inevitably became
unwitting accomplices to the commercial system.
While the rapid pace of the art market opened up more
and more opportunities for artists, biases persisted
against women, artists of color, and artists working
outside the major United States and European cosmo-
politan centers.

4.   Marcia Tucker, "From Muse to Museum: Feminism and Artistic Practice at the End
     of the Century in the United States," unpublished lecture presented at the École
     des Beaux-Arts, Paris (March 23, 1990), 1. Marcia Tucker Papers 1957–2007, Series
     V, Writings 1957–2004, box 70, folder 11, The Getty Research Institute, Los Angeles,
     Accession no. 2204.M.13.

5.   Marcia Tucker, "Why Art Matters," unpublished lecture presented at Colgate University,
     Hamilton, NY (April 2, 2003), 1. New Museum Archive, 2017AC01TUCKER01WR.

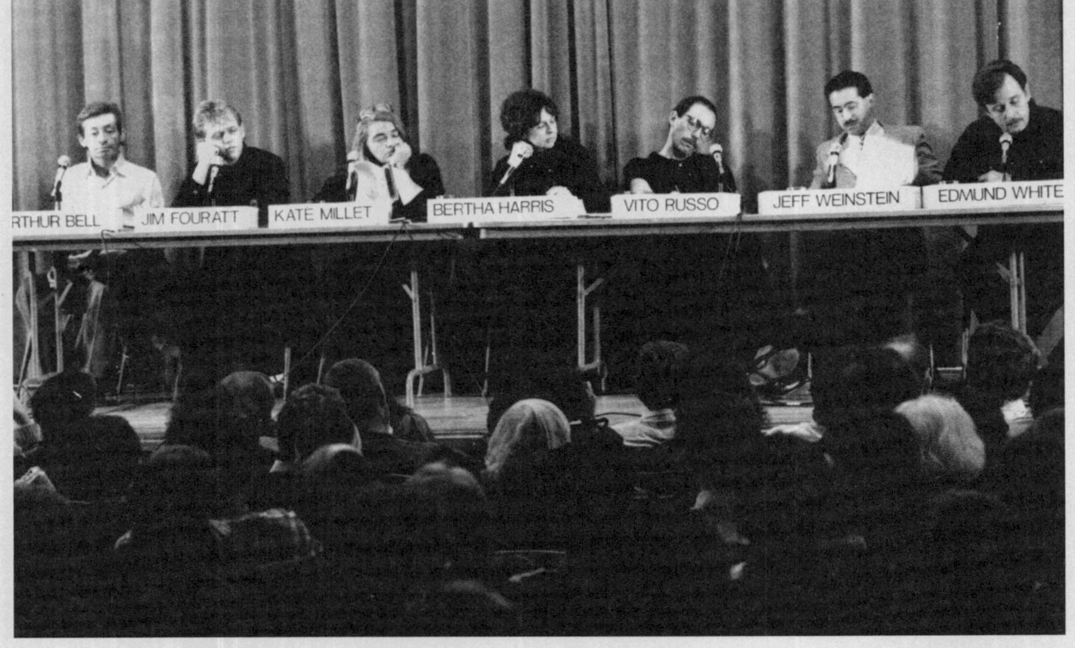

"What is the Impact of Homosexual Sensibility on Contemporary Culture?," a panel discussion organized in conjunction with the exhibition "Extended Sensibilities: Homosexual Presence in Contemporary Art," 1982. Left to right: Arthur Bell, Jim Fouratt, Kate Millett, Bertha Harris, Vito Russo, Jeff Weinstein, and Edmund White

Art and Activism

Tucker was a feminist and an activist, two values that were entwined in the New Museum's founding DNA and have remained at the core of its program. Since the Museum was established, over 50 percent of the artists shown in its exhibitions have been women. The Museum's two directors have been women, and many women have held leadership positions over the years. In recognition of this history, two years ago the Museum started Artemis, a fund to support exhibitions and projects by women that quickly attracted and galvanized a group of young women patrons.[6]

The politics of inclusion and exclusion have been the subject of a through line of exploration in our curatorial and education programs, from "Extended Sensibilities: Homosexual Presence in Contemporary Art" (1982), one of the earliest exhibitions anywhere to showcase gay subjects and aesthetics; to "Difference: On Representation and Sexuality" (1984), which looked at the politics of subject formation; "The Decade Show: Frameworks of Identity in the 1980s" (1990), an important collaboration between the New Museum, the Museum of Contemporary Hispanic Art, and the Studio Museum in Harlem, which opened up the critical debate on diversity and multiculturalism; to our current exhibition, "Trigger: Gender as a Tool and a Weapon" (2017), which heralds the multitude of gender choices and genderqueer voices today.

The New Museum has always been responsive to urgent
cultural issues and related crises—among them race,
women's rights, gay rights, AIDS awareness, censorship,
xenophobia, freedom of expression, trans rights, and
surveillance—and has often acted as a "first responder,"
as Lynne Tillman observes in her essay for this volume.
In his contribution, Brian Wallis looks at the New Museum's
position on the front lines of the culture wars. In the
last two years alone, through specific social practice
residencies, public events, and exhibitions, there have
been programs for healing black bodies in the wake of
continued police brutality against unarmed black men
and the creation of a meeting space at the Museum for
the collective Black Women Artists for Black Lives Matter
("Simone Leigh: The Waiting Room," 2016), questions
and debate about the last presidential election ("My
Barbarian: The Audience is Always Right," 2016), and an
information session on the legal rights and protections
that safeguard public protest ("A.K. Burns: Shabby but
Thriving," 2017). So many of these social impact projects
have come out of curatorial and educational collaborations and are themselves hybrid forms: part public
program (live performance), part artwork (installation),
and part research project (collaboration and pedagogy).
Johanna Burton, in her essay "An Ever-Expanding Field:
The New Museum and Cross-Disciplinary Practices,"
speaks to the Museum's long-standing embrace of
multidisciplinary and interdisciplinary forms and their
expansion of artistic parameters. She points out that many
of today's political, discursive, and activist impulses find
expression in boundary-crossing forms.

The kind of courage and activism the New Museum is
known for is needed more than ever today, as we face
renewed culture wars and mounting extremism on
both the right and the left, fueled by rapidly shifting
demographics and a growing awareness that multiculturalism is the core of the new society we are living
in. Courageous leadership requires examining deeply

6.   Artemis was formed following a conversation between entrepreneur and art patron
     Maria Baibakova and me, during which she offered to help create this special support
     group in recognition of the Museum's history in general and specifically following
     the "New Museum Triennial: Surround Audience" (2015), which had the distinction of
     including more women than men.

entrenched ethno- and gender-centric biases embedded
in our language, tools, and methodologies, all of which
are in drastic need of revision.

Thematic exhibitions present a singular opportunity for
artists and curators to experiment with just such new
tools and methodologies. Provocative and polemical
group shows—several of which have already been cited—
have been a defining feature of the New Museum's
program. These exhibitions are not easy to fund, and they
take courage, intelligence, and a willingness to fail, which
is the ultimate curatorial (and institutional) challenge.
Shows such as "Bad Girls" (1994), which featured artists
who turned that cliché into an emblem of empowerment;
"The Time of Our Lives" (1999), which looked at how artists
confront aging and the cultural representations of it; and
the "New Museum Triennial: The Ungovernables" (2012),
which spotlit artists who embrace the impermanence
and new contingencies of an unknown future, all disrupted
conventional, status quo thinking. They questioned the
relation of "margin" to "mainstream," the limitations
of binary frames of reference, and the general tyranny
of a monoculture.

Global Program/Global Network and Collaboration

A defiance of hierarchies also found expression in the
Museum's determination to present work from beyond
New York. Ned Rifkin talks about this aspect of the
Museum's program in its early days in his contribution to
this volume, "Alternative Geographies: Art in New York and
Beyond." As the Museum, its network of national and inter-
national partners, and its reputation grew, our program
expanded globally, coinciding with the emergence of the
internet, which connected cultural communities and
practitioners around the world. By the early '90s, the New
Museum had shown contemporary art from Asia, Europe,
South America, and Africa, sometimes in partnership
with other organizations. The curatorial team gradually
became more global as well, with the addition of Dan
Cameron, a well-traveled curator who, together with
Gerardo Mosquera, a Cuban curator who brought his deep
knowledge of Latin American art to the program, planned
a deliberate and focused international program.[7] Curators

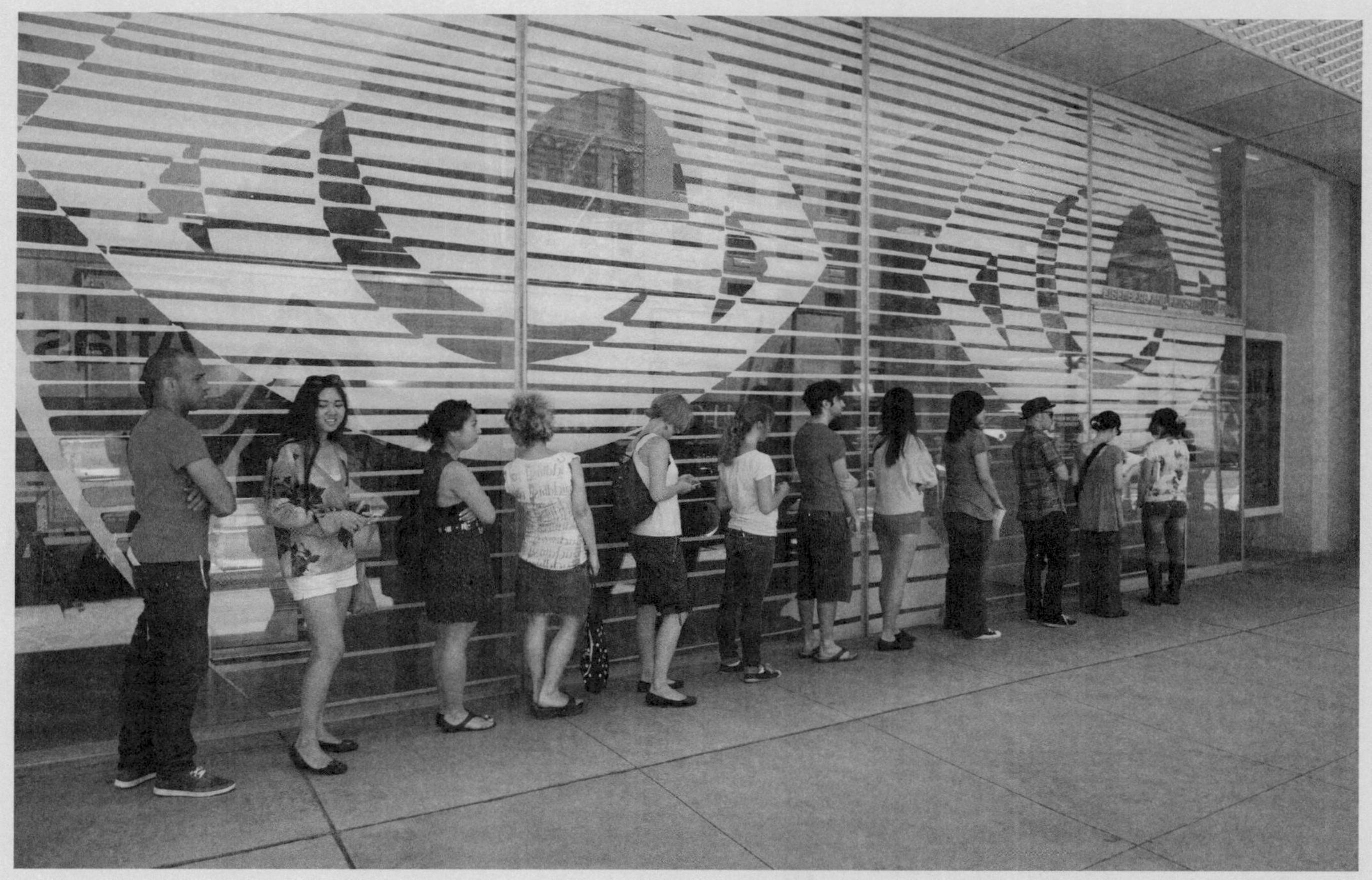

"Ostalgia," 2011.
Glass facade: Paulina
Olowska, *Alice Eyes
(after Jerzy Kolecki)*,
2011. Foreground:
participants in Roman
Ondák's performance
*Good Feelings in Good
Times*, 2003

Alice Yang, Yukie Kamiya, and Eungie Joo contributed their first-hand understanding and experience of contemporary Asian art; Anne Barlow and Helga Christoffersen, from Scotland and Denmark, respectively, brought their expertise in European art; and Massimiliano Gioni, who joined the Museum in 2006, and became Artistic Director in 2014, is one of the most widely admired international curators today, with an extensive network of colleagues and a comprehensive grasp of art from around the globe.

By the 2000s, the New Museum program had become truly global—which was and remains a real distinction among our museum peers in the United States. The reality was that after the advent of the web in 1993, the art world quickly became linked through a global network and began operating internationally as well as locally. Curators tracking breaking developments in contemporary art had to travel extensively, visit international biennials and art fairs, and work collaboratively with colleagues in other cities in order to comprehend this vast, expanding cultural

7. Beyond curatorial appointments and exhibitions, the Museum's broader scope was also reflected in publications, notably the anthologies *Out There: Marginalization and Contemporary Cultures*, ed. Russell Ferguson, Martha Gever, Trinh T. Minh-ha, and Cornel West (New York: New Museum; Cambridge, MA: MIT Press, 1990), and *Over Here: International Perspectives on Art and Culture*, ed. Gerardo Mosquera and Jean Fisher (New York: New Museum; Cambridge, MA: MIT Press, 2004).

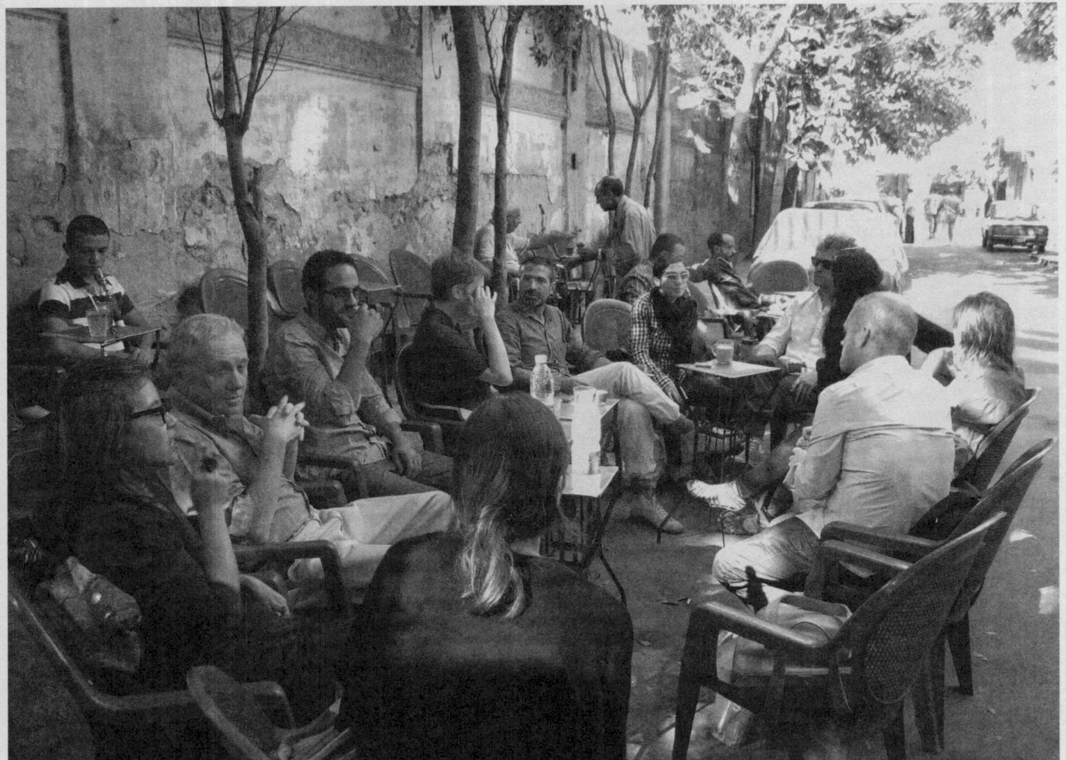

landscape that the internet and the ease of travel had helped expose. But most American museums were lagging behind with a more local and sometimes insular focus. The New Museum was well-positioned and seized the opportunity, even with its modest resources, to mount a fully international program; it began to show artists like Cildo Meireles and William Kentridge, major senior figures who were then surprisingly little known, even by many New York art world cognoscenti.

Over the past ten years, we have built a formidable international network, forged exhibition exchanges with a range of collaborating institutions around the world —in France, England, Italy, Germany, China, Brazil, Mexico, Austria, Russia, Lebanon, Turkey, Greece, Korea, Switzerland, Israel, Egypt, the Netherlands, and South Africa—and have shown artists from six continents. In 2007 we formalized an international partnership with several institutions called Museum as Hub. With founding partners in South Korea (Insa Art Space), Egypt (Townhouse Gallery), the Netherlands (Van Abbemuseum), and Mexico (Museo Tamayo), this experimental program, overseen by Joo in her role then as Keith Haring Director and Curator of Education and Public Programs, was created to foster cross-cultural dialogue through collaborations on exhibitions, public forums, and residencies.[8] This seven-year project encouraged tolerance of diverse viewpoints, productive debate, and mutual understanding, and all the partners quickly discovered the widely divergent meanings that terms like "nationalism" and "public space" could have in different cultures.[9]

Our global scope was further extended by the introduction of the Triennial in 2009; the publication of *Art Spaces Directory*, a listing of independent art institutions around the world, in 2012; and collaborative exchanges and fellowships with a range of foundations and nonprofit art spaces like Borusan Contemporary, Turkey; DESTE Foundation for Contemporary Art, Greece; the K11 Art Foundation, China; LUMA Foundation, France; and NEON Foundation, Greece. We also initiated the International Leadership Council, which now has forty-three members from eighteen countries, in 2008 and have added several new international Trustees from Brazil, China, Greece, the United Kingdom, Switzerland, Austria, Holland, and Mexico to our already culturally diverse Board.

Pioneering New Paradigms

When I succeeded Marcia Tucker as the Museum's second director in 1999, I had big shoes to fill. But the Museum was at a crossroads: on the one hand, it had outgrown its

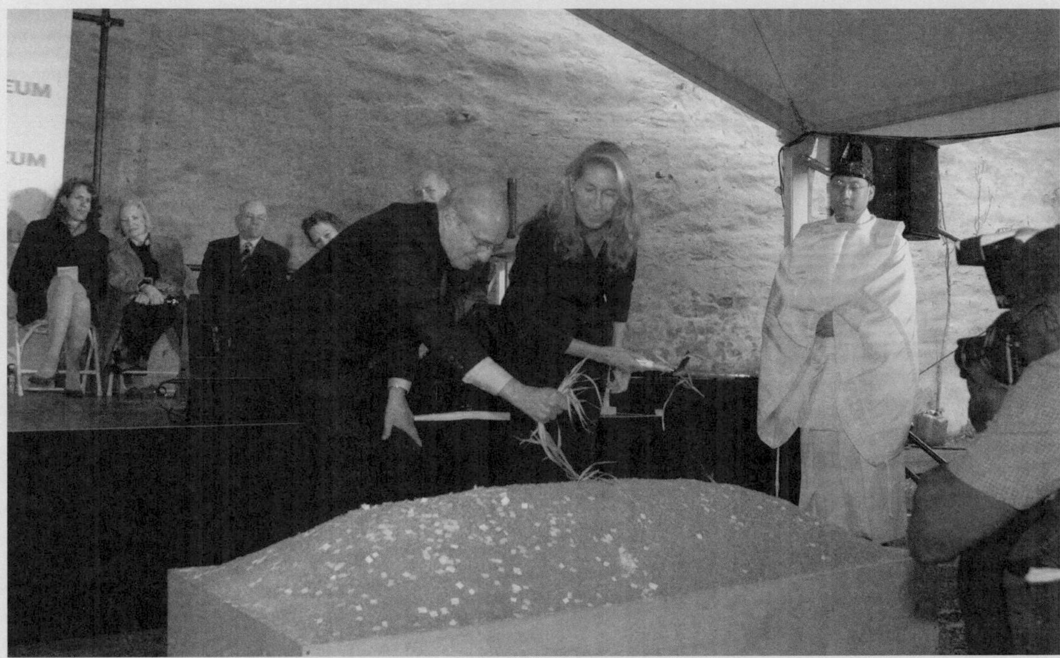

8. Subsequent participants in Museum as Hub included Art Space Pool, South Korea; the Miami Art Museum (now the Pérez Art Museum Miami); Beirut Art Center, Lebanon; and Museo Experimental el Eco and de_sitio, both in Mexico.

9. For more on the project, see *Museum as Hub* (New York: New Museum, 2016).

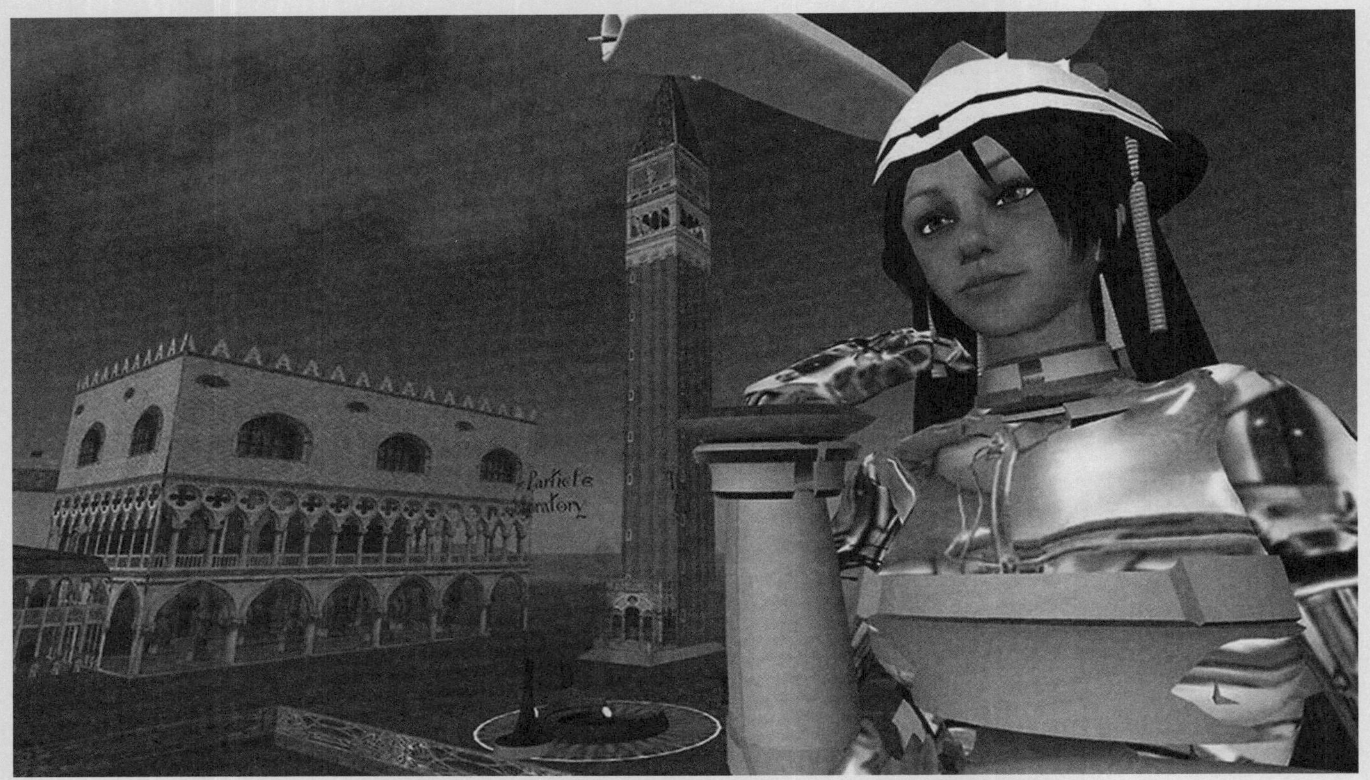

Portrait of Cao Fei's
Second Life avatar,
China Tracy, 2007.
i.Mirror, Cao Fei's
twenty-eight-
minute, three-part
documentary staged
in Second Life, was
included in "Montage:
Unmonumental
Online," curated
by Rhizome for the
multipart exhibition
"Unmonumental," 2007

space on Broadway, where it had operated since 1984, and on the other hand, it was too insider, primarily serving a small community of artists and art professionals. When I told my "non-art" friends that I was leaving the Whitney to direct the New Museum, people asked, "Oh, which *new museum?*" It was clear that the New Museum was not on the general public's radar and that we had an opportunity and a responsibility to broaden our reach. Artists were increasingly frustrated by the spatial limitations of our column-filled gallery spaces on Broadway, and it was hard for a storefront museum, located in a larger condominium building, to become a true destination for tourists and the general public.

After seven years of planning and construction, in 2007 we opened our first freestanding building on the Bowery, an eight-story structure designed by the Tokyo-based firm SANAA. Working in partnership with Board President Saul Dennison and the Board of Trustees, we raised the funding and got it done. This was the first ground-up art museum ever built downtown, and, with the support of Mayor Michael Bloomberg, we were among the first to revitalize the area in the aftermath of the dark days following 9/11. For the first time in the Museum's history, we were an international cultural destination whose architecture telegraphed our mission of change, dynamism, and openness. Attendance soared, audiences expanded fivefold, and the Bowery neighborhood boomed. Though we now have a headquarters building, our physical footprint remains relatively modest. But our impact is outsize, in part because of the excellence of our programs and in part because of the innovative platforms that we've created, leading many to assume our budget is far bigger than it really is.

If globalization and the internet went hand in hand, the New Museum was ready and willing not only to look abroad, but also to embrace the new digital mediums that were revolutionizing the world and the world of art. As early as 1994, Tucker was pondering the impact of the internet on art-making as well as the new configurations of power created by the technological age, thoughts she shared in a talk to the Association of Art Museum Directors called "Close Encounters: Defensive Driving on the Digital Highway." [10] Shortly after I arrived in 1999, we became one of the first museums to engage digital art forms through a dedicated space for new media exhibitions: the Media Lounge, designed by the architecture firm LOT-EK. We were soon deeply involved with this new community of artists and practitioners, as well as the nonprofit Rhizome, one of the earliest organizations to support born-digital art and culture.

After the dot-com bust in 2001, Rhizome was struggling financially. Together with its founding Director, Mark Tribe, we developed an unprecedented agreement by which Rhizome would take up residence at the Museum as an affiliate organization. Rhizome had the knowledge and expertise to put the Museum at the forefront of the critical conversation about technology's impact on art and culture. In her essay, Lauren Cornell, the former Executive Director of Rhizome and, later, the Associate Director, Technology Initiatives at the New Museum, traces the Museum's dynamic engagement with art and tech—which she had a big hand in shaping. New works were commissioned, important public programs were

10.   Marcia Tucker, "Close Encounters: Defensive Driving on the Digital Highway," unpublished lecture presented to the Association of Art Museum Directors, Seattle, (June 3, 1994), 1–16. Marcia Tucker papers, 1957–2007, Series V1, Lectures, 1965–2002, box 79, folder 6, The Getty Research Institute, Los Angeles, Accession no. 2004.M.13.

introduced, and Rhizome's Seven on Seven conference —an initiative that pairs seven technologists with seven artists and invites them to produce something new—was founded as part of the affiliation. Seven on Seven quickly captured the attention of small and large technology innovators from Google to Facebook and Kickstarter who were eager to work with visionary artists and think more critically about their own fields.

We also came to see our website, newmuseum.org, as a virtual extension of the institution's space, as not just a marketing vehicle to drive traffic to the Museum building, but a platform for its programs, exhibitions, and commissions. It may seem obvious now, but just a few years ago, this was a conceptual and strategic leap that not many museums were ready to make.

In 2008 we acquired the neighboring building to our south, and we are now getting ready to once again double our physical footprint in a second major expansion. Over the past seven years, we have used available space in the adjacent building to experiment with and grow several new platforms, including over fifty-eight artist residencies for research and development, as well as new productions; Rhizome and its expanding digital preservation arm; Ideas City, an international forum about the future of cities, founded in 2010; and NEW INC, the first museum-led incubator focused on art, technology, and design, which launched three years ago. These platforms, which extend the Museum out into the broader community, have exponentially increased our impact well beyond bricks and mortar.

Ideas City took shape in the aftermath of the Great Recession, when I reached out to several downtown colleagues to see if they might be interested in joining a project that would advocate for culture as key to the future vitality of our cities. Together with Karen Wong, the Museum's Deputy Director, I cofounded Ideas City, a project that immediately attracted over 150 community partners, from local universities to community groups, theaters, and other nonprofits; to city officials and city planners; to architects and artists. We had long understood the power of artistic collaboration, but now we discovered the power of community collaboration and the role the Museum could play in convening people and communities around common interests. This robust network of participants has continued to expand as we've taken Ideas City to Istanbul, São Paulo, Detroit, Athens, and Arles. Joseph Grima, now the Director of Ideas City, charts the history of this unusual museum project in "Ideas City: The Museum as a Platform for Civic Action."

Ideas City was a direct outgrowth of our experience with Museum as Hub, which led us to think further about the potential of collaboration. The power of Ideas City and all the incubation we were doing with artists and technology at Rhizome and in our exhibition program led Karen Wong and me to conclude, with the Board's unanimous support, that we should formalize that incubation activity in a dedicated space in our adjacent building. NEW INC, a curated community of art and tech entrepreneurs, was born, and, like Ideas City, it was unprecedented in the museum world. I can't count the number of times colleagues or officials have asked me, "But why is a museum doing *that*?," only to become converts a few years later. NEW INC marked a paradigm shift, taking experimentation and collaboration to a new level. It is a space for production where new tools for museums and nonprofits are developed, and where an expansive view of cultural innovation is promoted. Each year a diverse, multidisciplinary community of one hundred creators in residence experiment with leading-edge technologies from VR to AI and anti-surveillance programs. In her essay, Julia Kaganskiy, the Director of NEW INC, details this bold experiment, which has developed phenomenal momentum in just three years.

Into the Future

As Allan Schwartzman recently recalled of the Museum's early days, "Everything began and ended with artists. They built the museum, were our inspiration...our audience, spiritual guides, and judges."[11] We have always taken our cues from artists, and we work in partnership

11.   Allan Schwartzman, "Allan's Intro," *In Other Words*, April 11, 2017, http://www.artagencypartners.com/allans-intro/11-april-2017/.

with them. They show us the way forward by opening our eyes to change in the most unpredictable ways: from Wim Delvoye's *Cloaca* (2000), a giant intestinal machine that was fed twice daily and pointed to a post-human future; to Jeremy Deller's *It Is What It Is: Conversations on Iraq* (2009), a series of conversations with the public that were held beside the charred remains of a car bombed in Baghdad and were led by an array of people that included American Gulf War veterans, Iraqi citizens, and Middle East historians; to Pipilotti Rist's immersive and interactive digital dreamscape *Pixel Forest* (2016), a giant three-dimensional pixelated moving image that visitors entered. Artists continue to venture into uncharted territory, defying expectations and creating new experiences that make us see and think about the world differently.

As we enter our fifth decade, the New Museum can claim both longevity and a continued relevance that could not have been anticipated in 1977. We remain open, fearless, and alive as we keep evolving, asking the hard questions, challenging preconceptions, and embracing the role that art and culture can play in this fast-changing landscape. Without the weight of a collection, we are freer to experiment, explore, and respond to the new. At the New Museum the only constant is change. Our paradox is that change is our anchor. We are always in beta, always testing, and artists lead the way into the future, as they always have.

Lisa Phillips is *Toby Devan Lewis Director* of the New Museum. She became the Museum's second director in 1999 after twenty-two years at the Whitney Museum of American Art, where she was Curator. In addition to expanding the museum, realizing its first freestanding home, she cofounded Ideas City and NEW INC, and curated survey exhibitions of the work of Paul McCarthy (2001), Carroll Dunham (2002), John Waters (2004), and Chris Burden (2013).

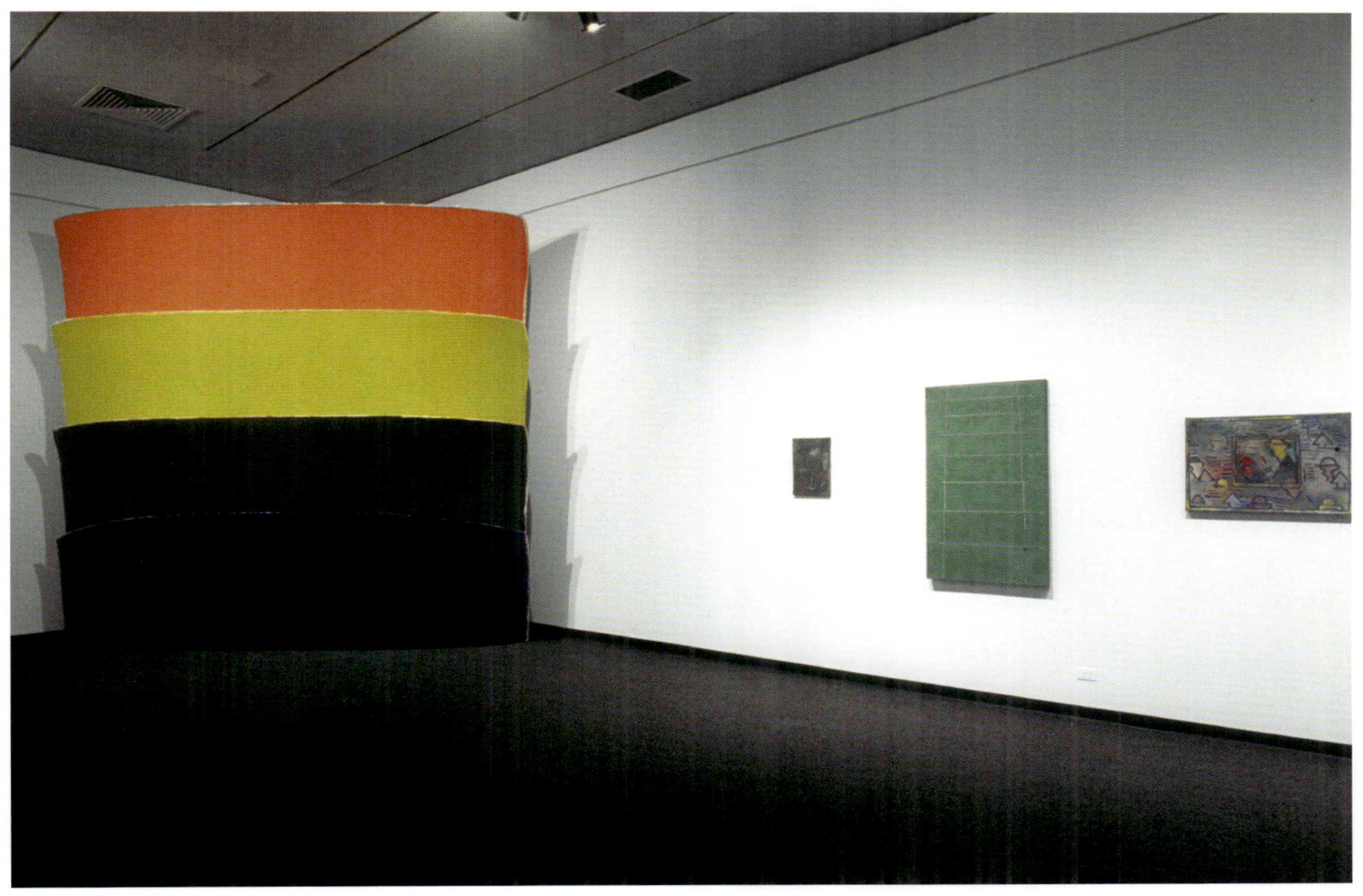

Left to right: works
by Ron Gorchov and
Elizabeth Murray

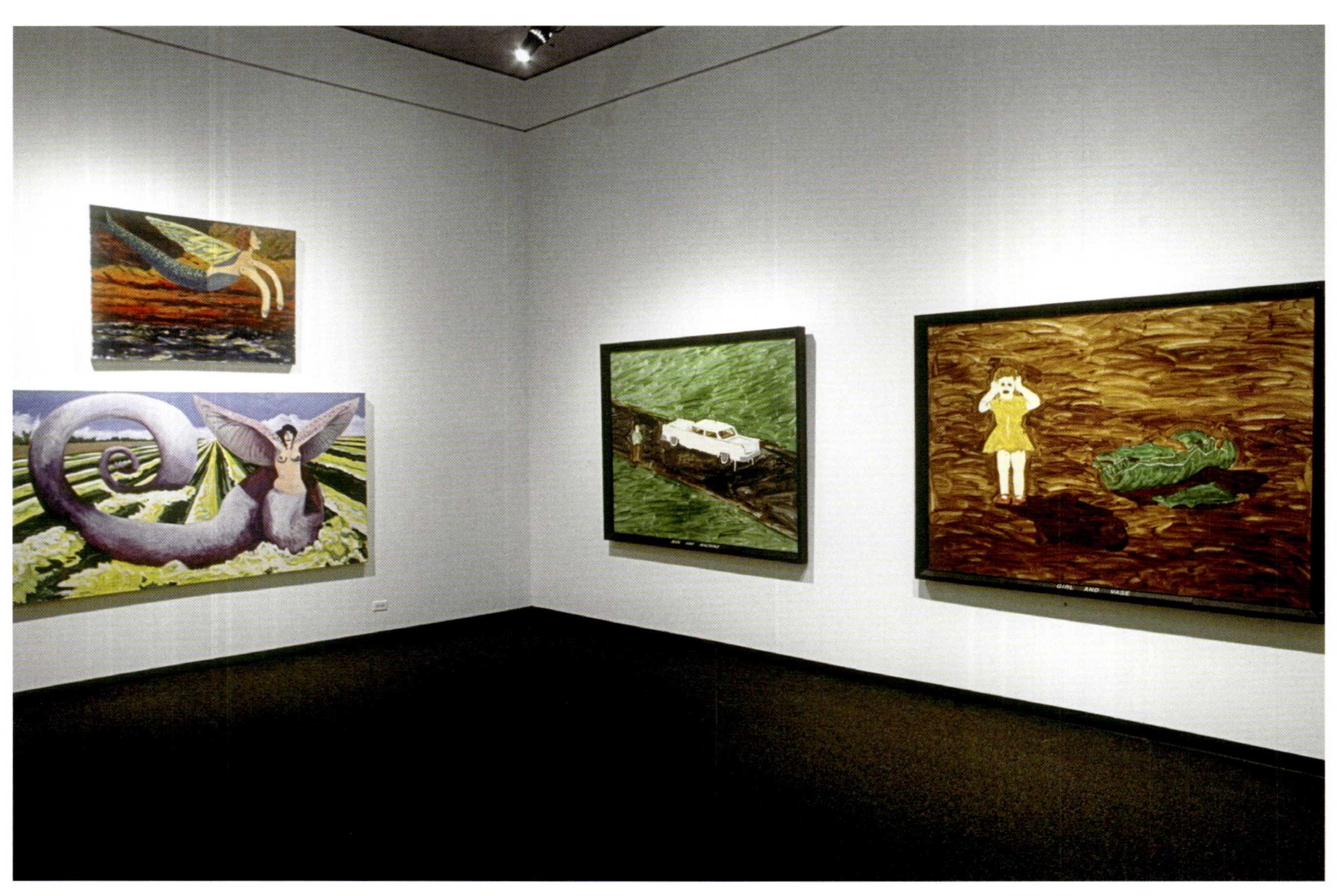

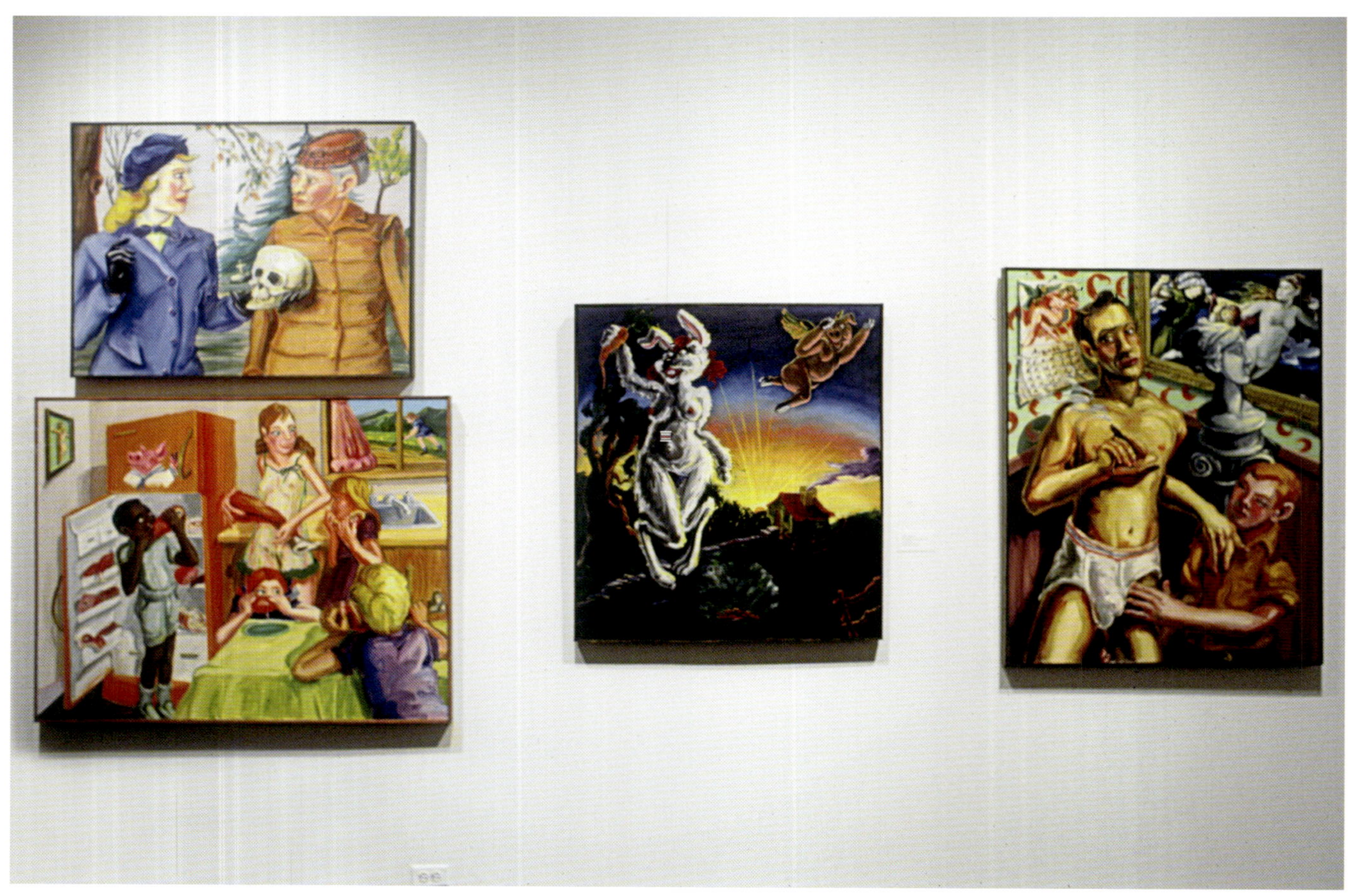

(top) Left to right:
works by Earl Staley
and Neil Jenney

(bottom) Works by
James Albertson

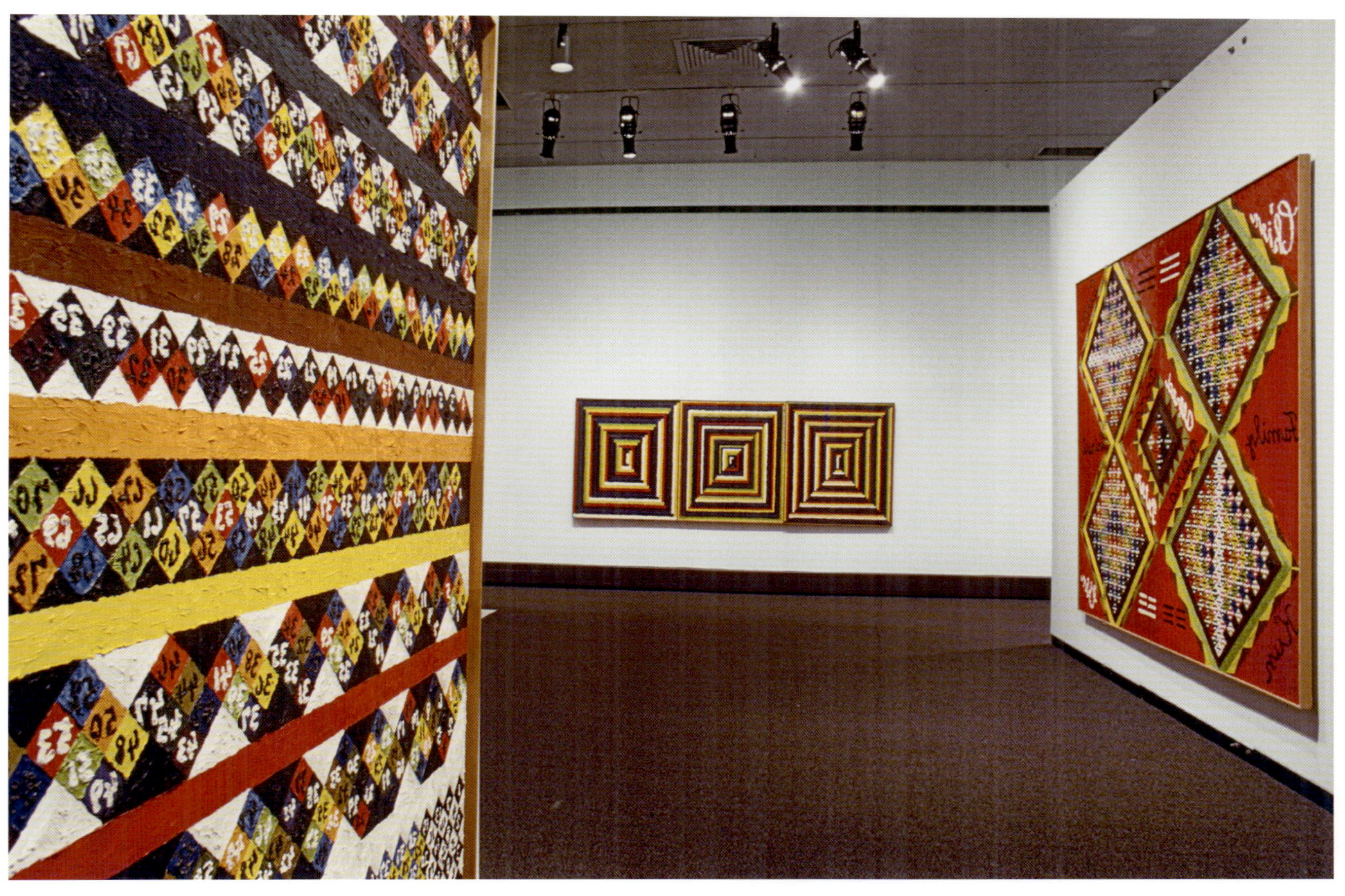

Installation view

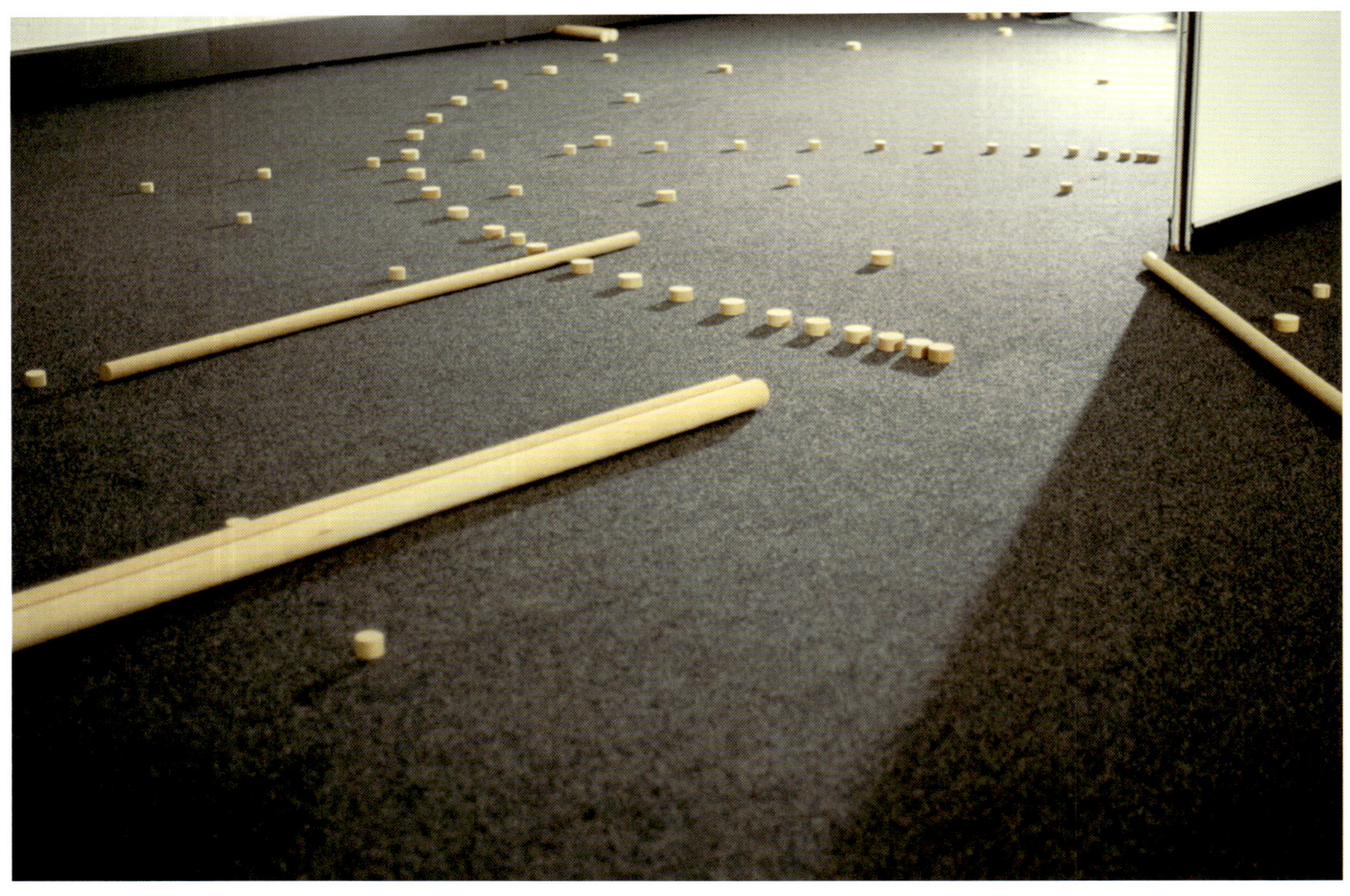

Barry Le Va,
*Unequal Length Section
in a Circular Plan: Walked
end-over-end in their own
circular path. ends touch;
ends cut, 1973*

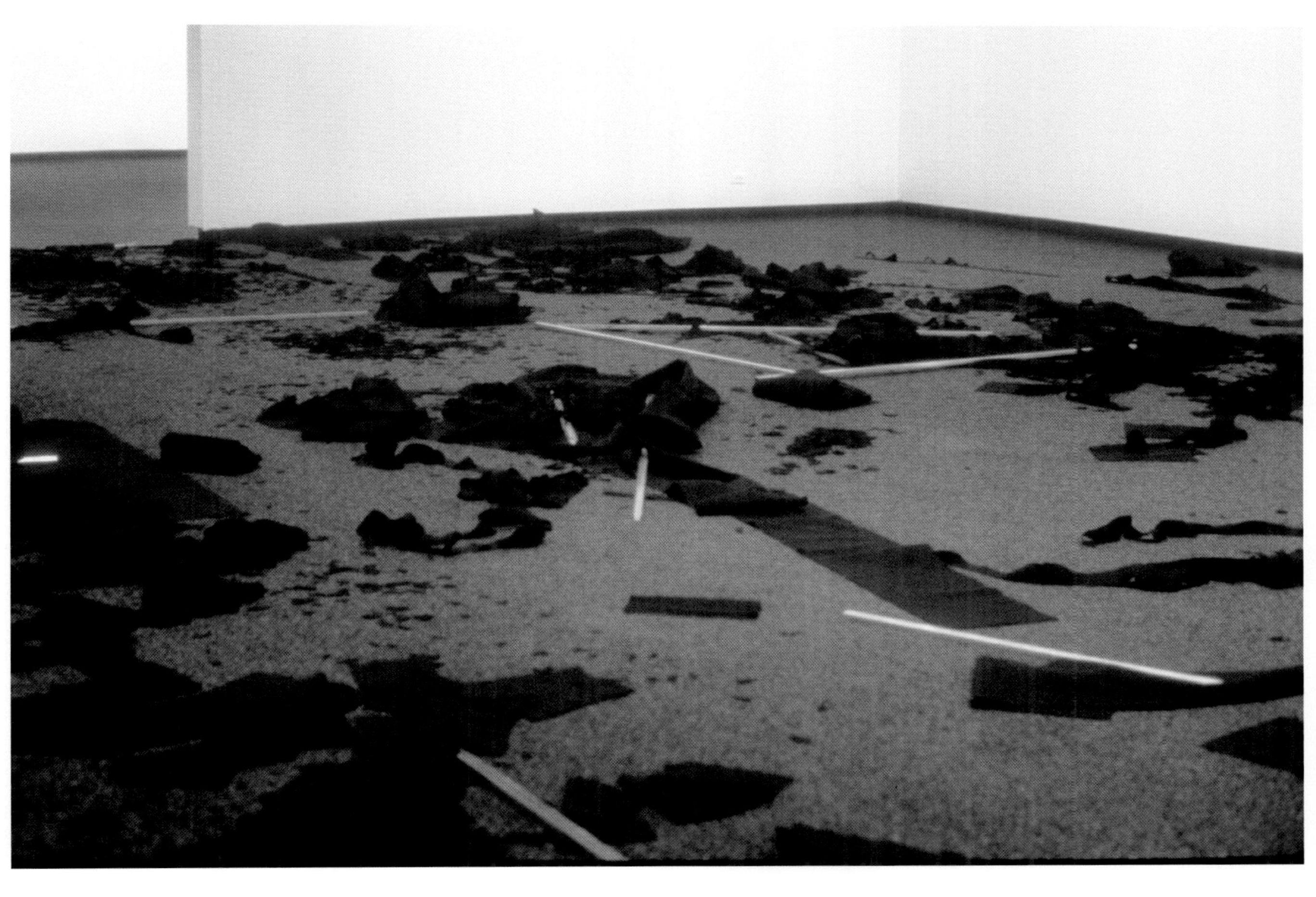

Barry Le Va,
*Equal quantities within
four equal areas:
arranged; re-arranged.
borrowed; exchanged*,
1967–68

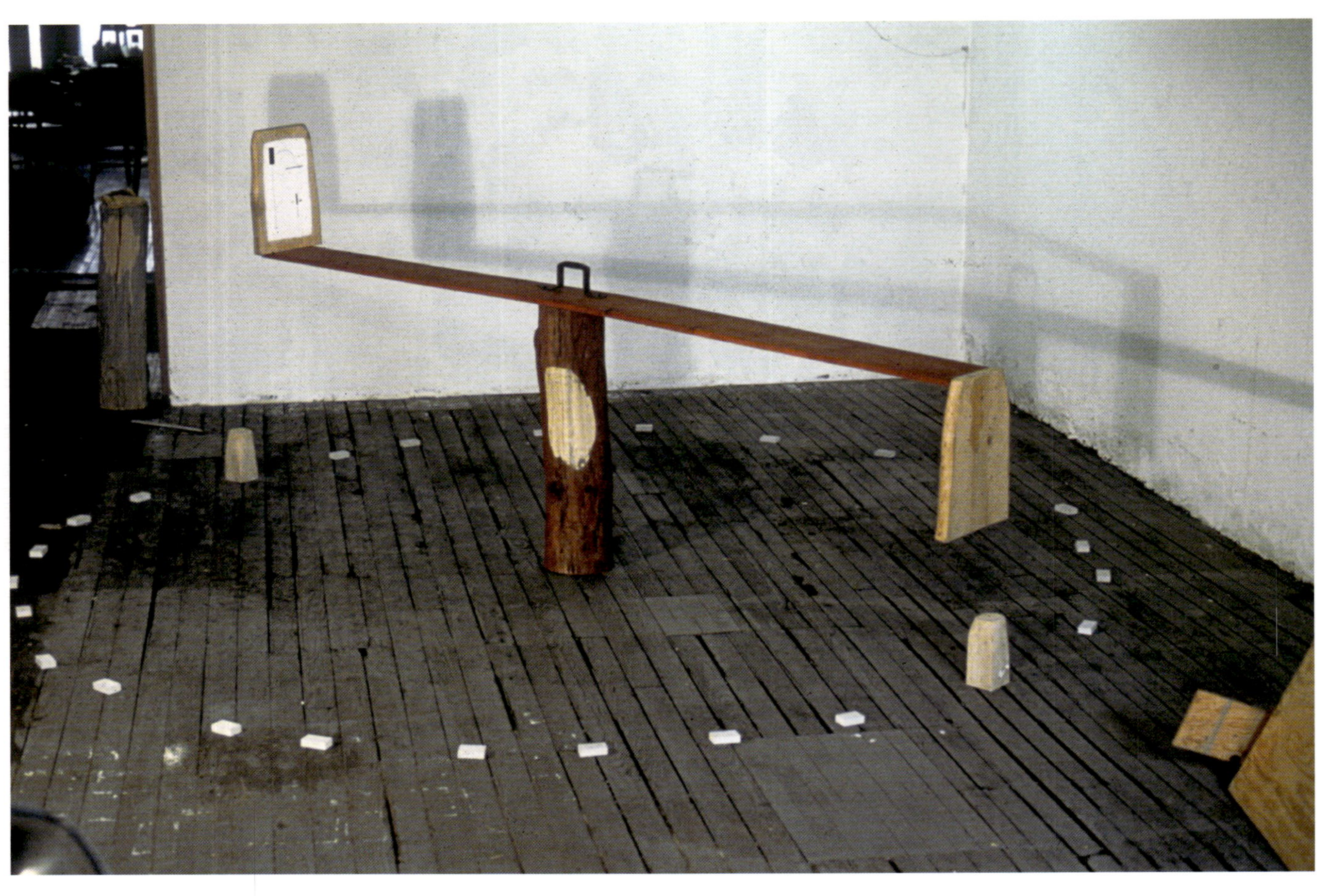

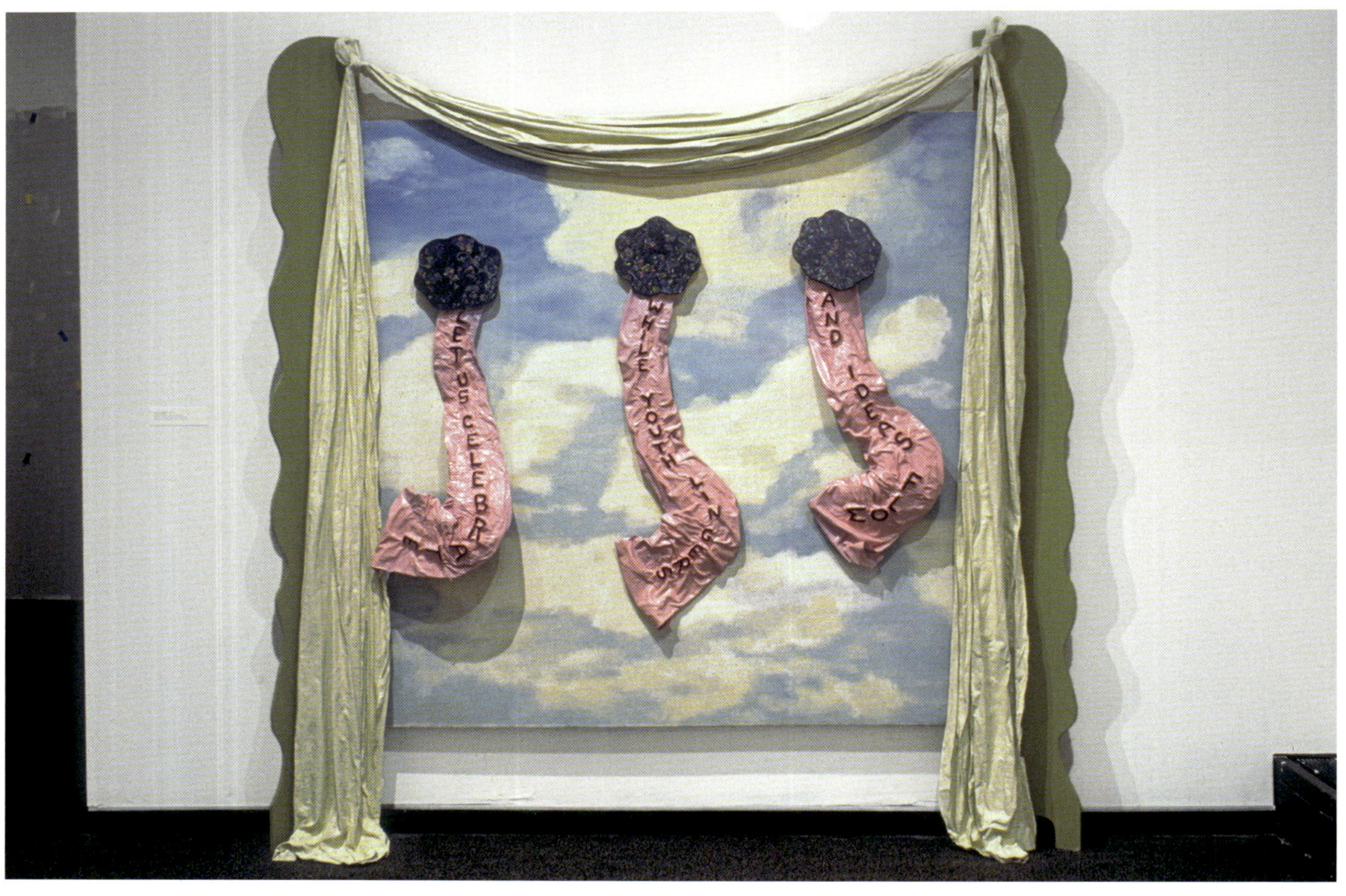

(top) Ree Morton,
See-Saw, 1974

(bottom) Ree Morton,
*Let Us Celebrate While
Youth Lingers and Ideas
Flow*, 1975

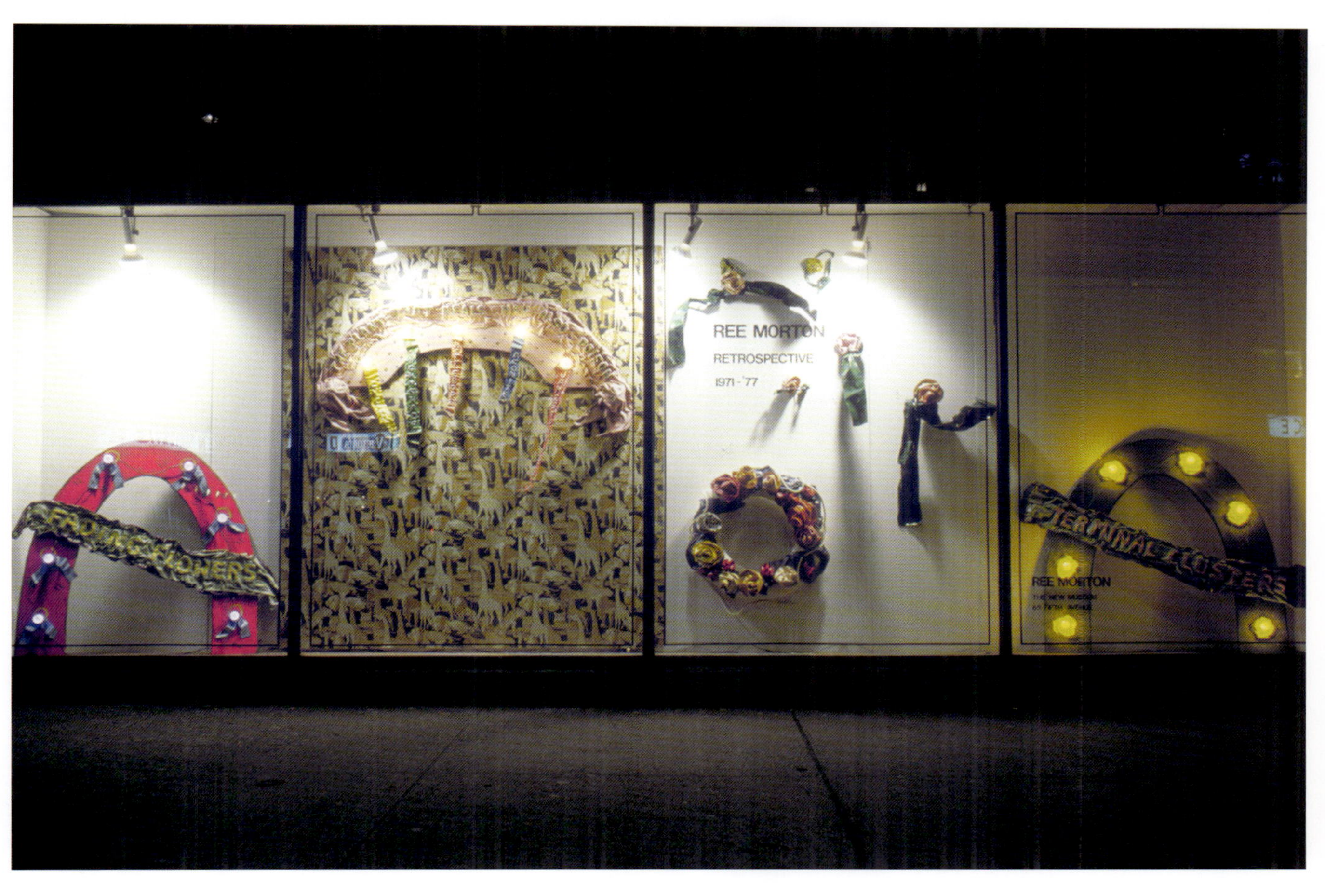

Ree Morton,
works including *Fading
Flowers*, 1974; *The Plant
That Heals May Also
Poison*, 1974; and *Terminal
Clusters*, 1974

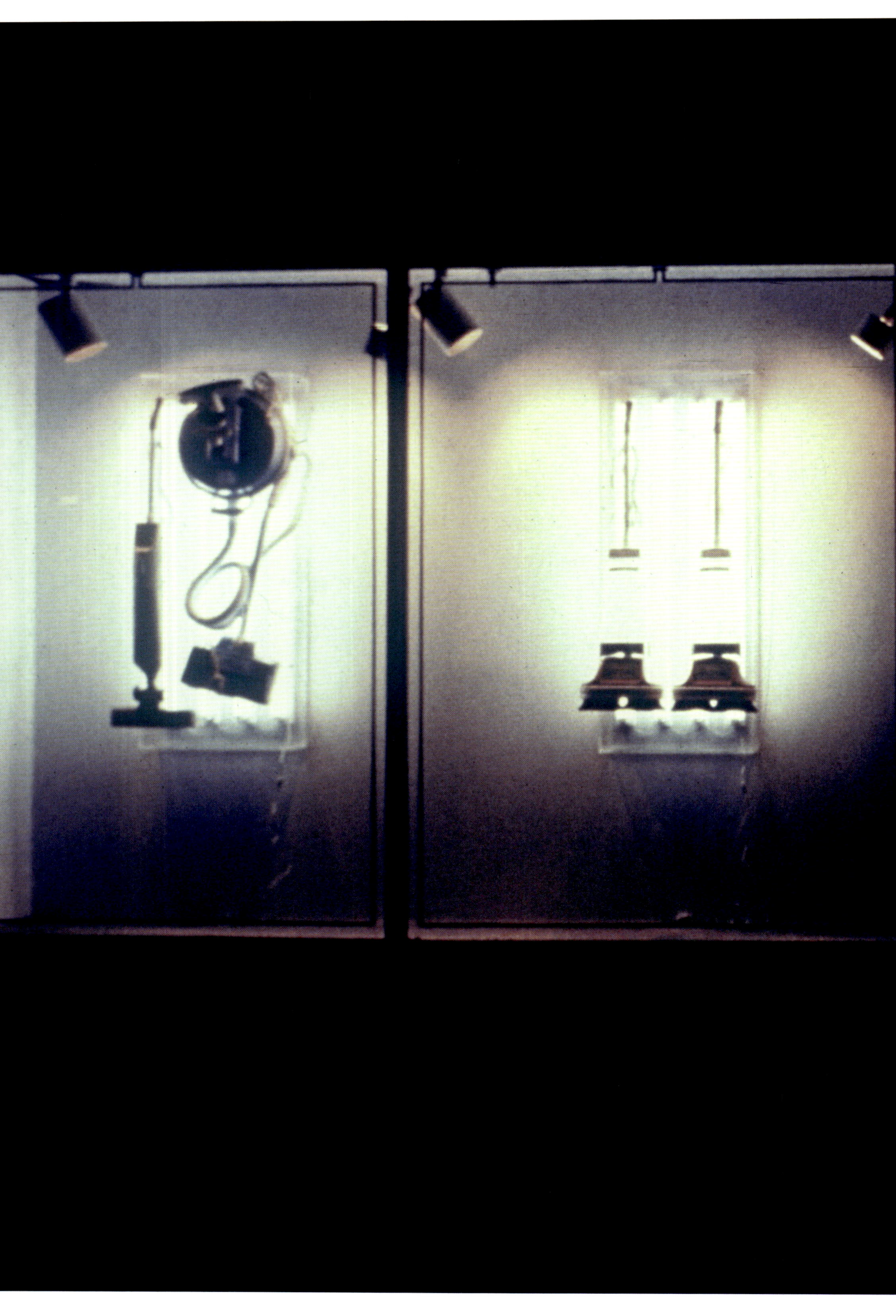

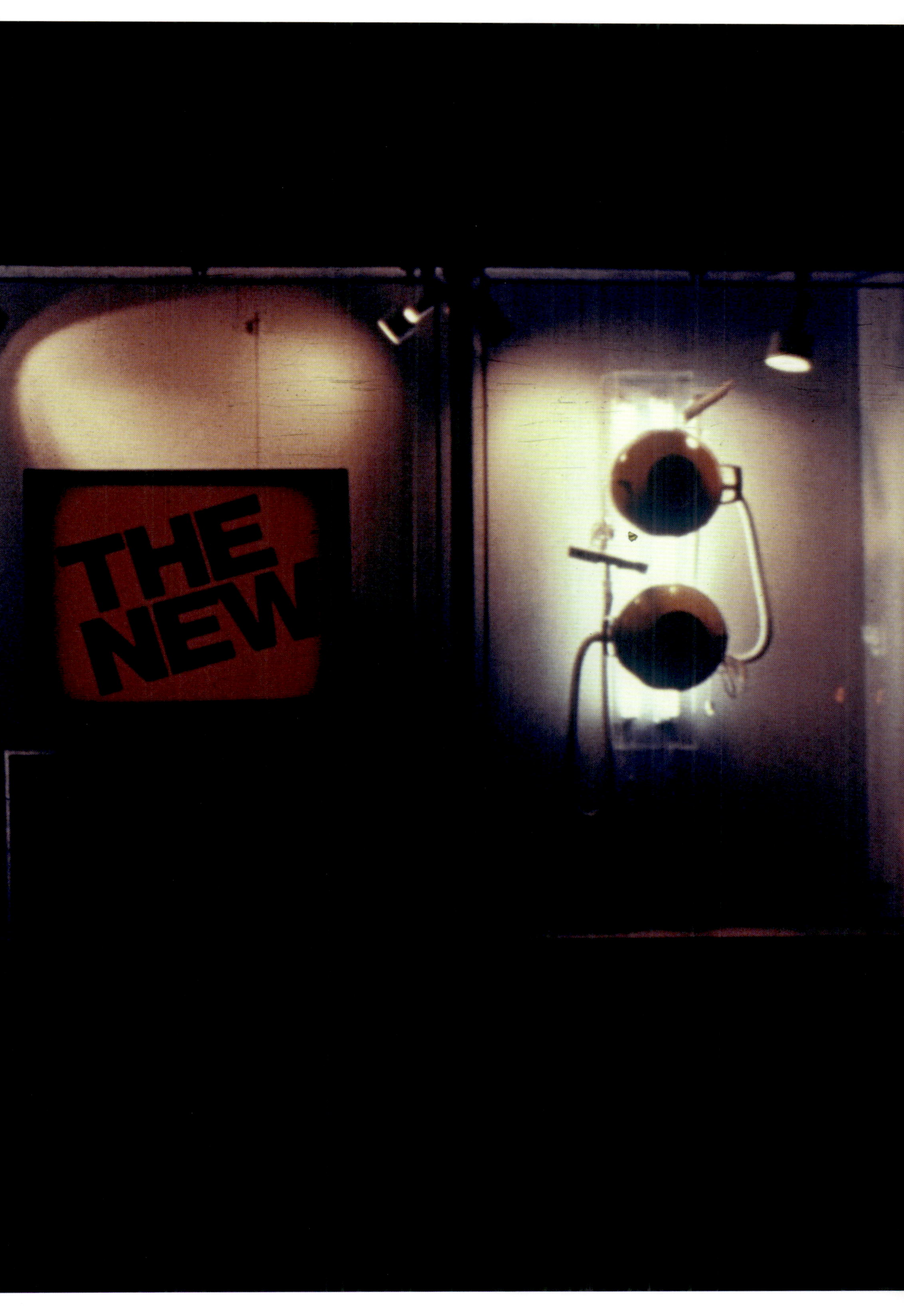
THE
NEW

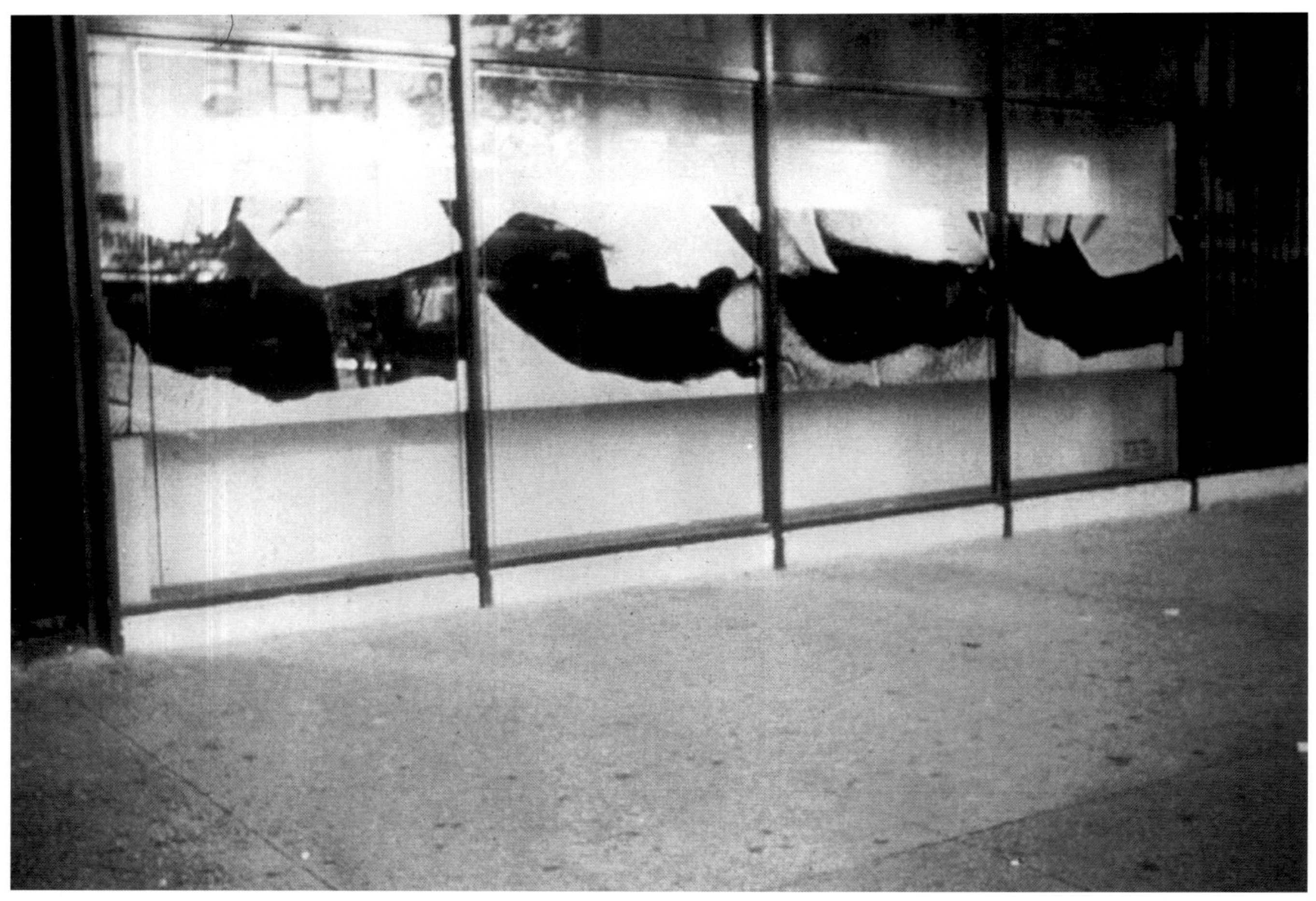

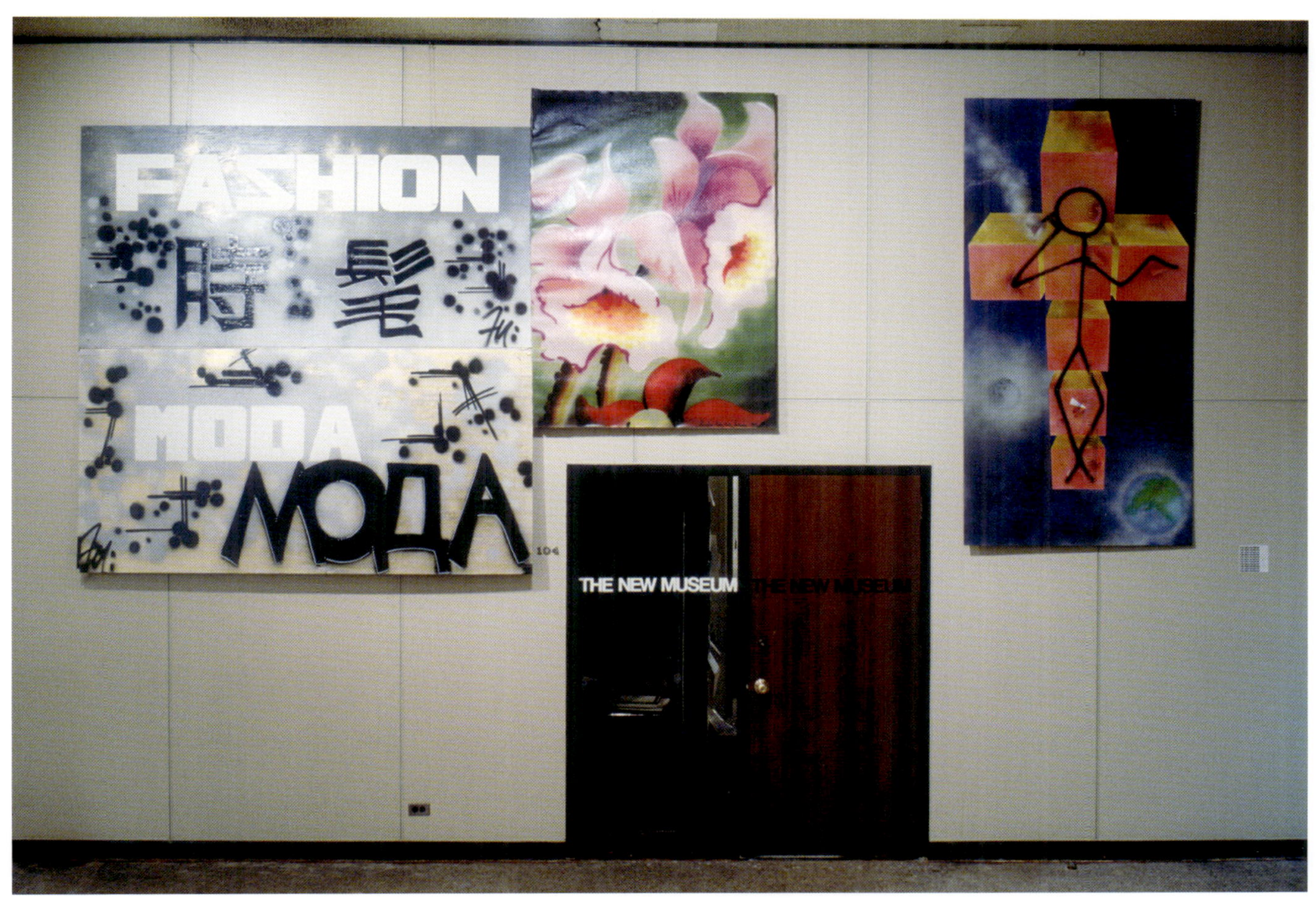

Installation view

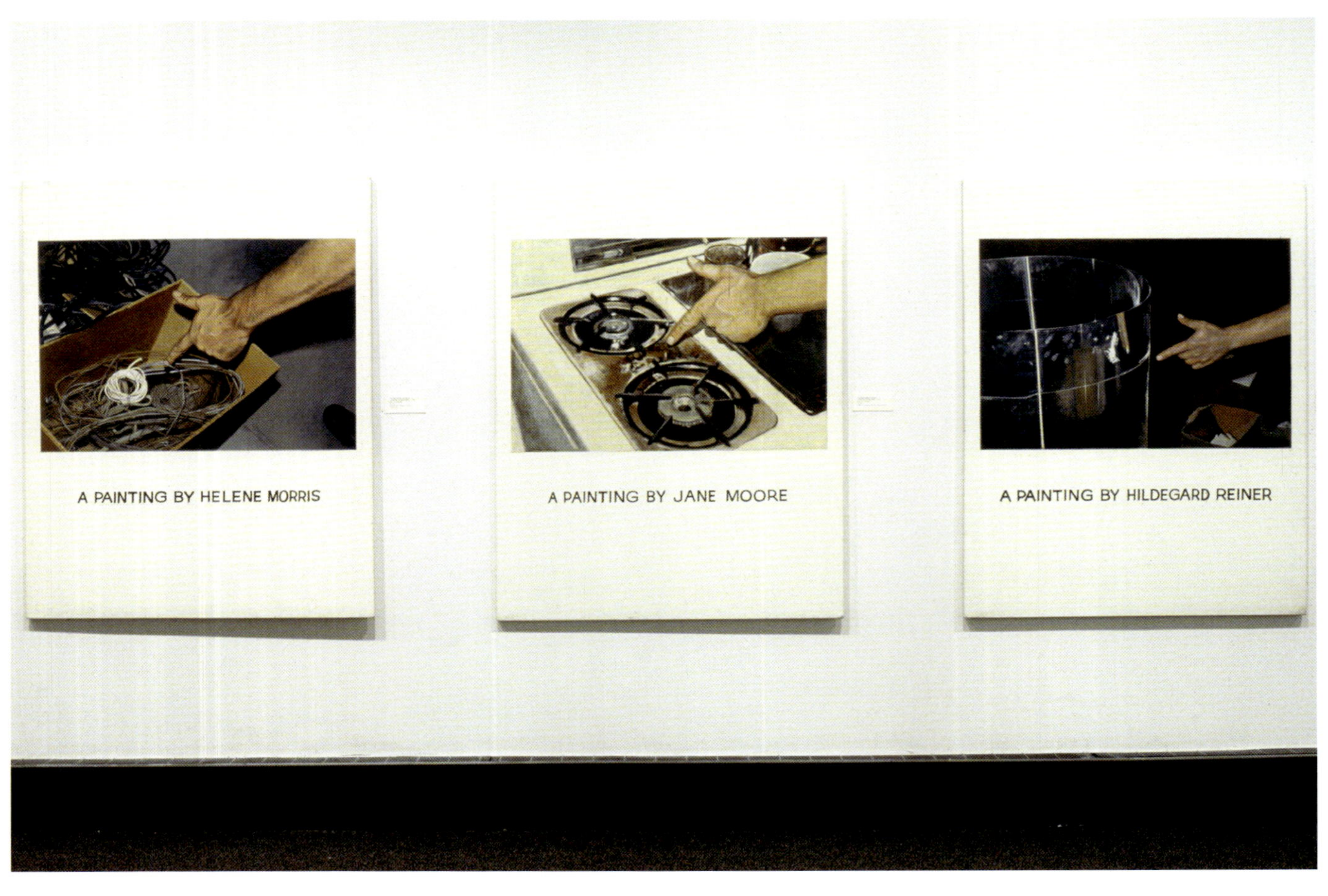

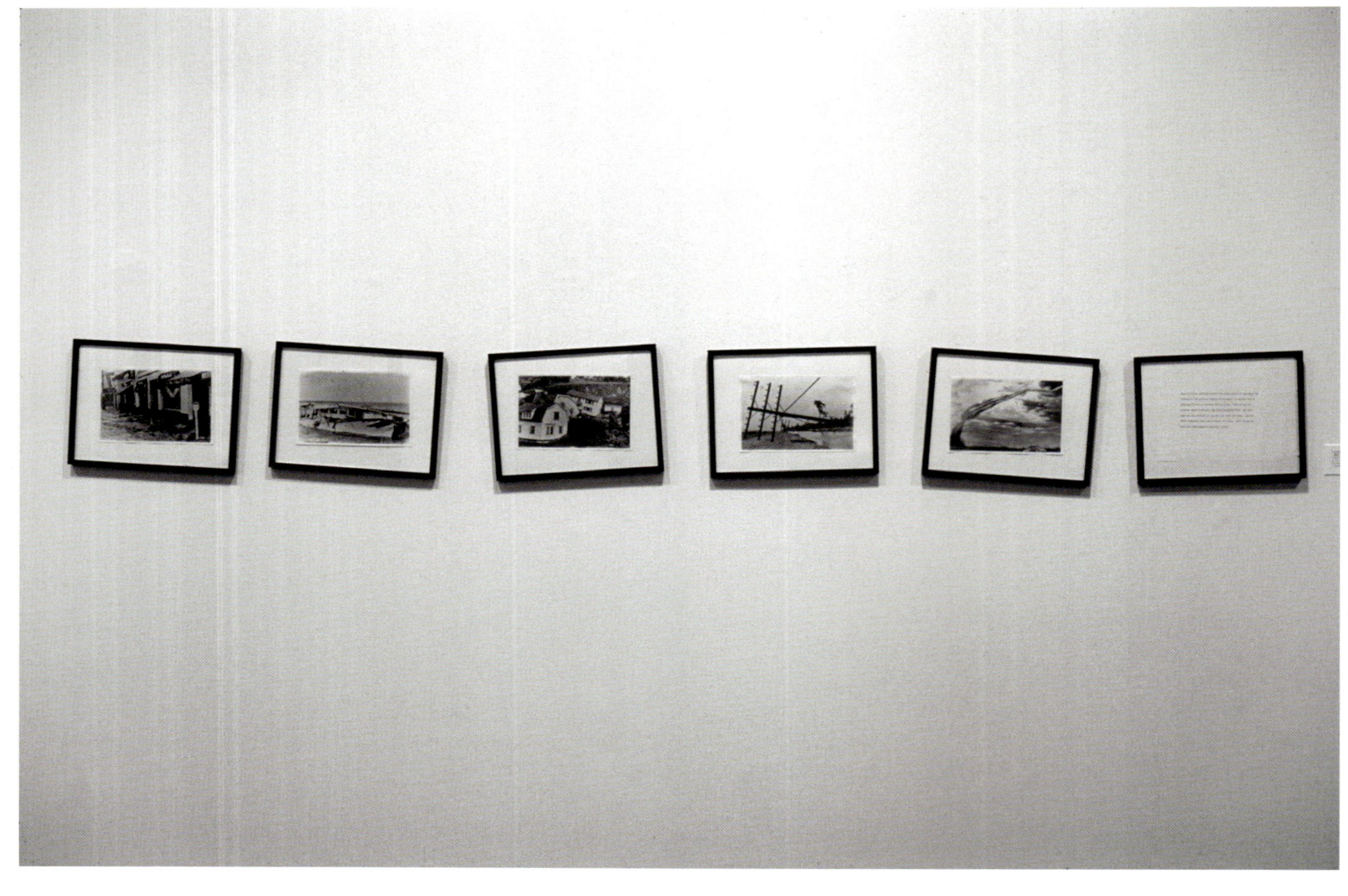

(top) Left to right: John Baldessari, *A Painting by Helene Morris; A Painting by Jane Moore;* and *A Painting by Hildegard Reiner, from the series The Commissioned Paintings,* 1969

(bottom) John Baldessari, *A Different Kind of Order (The Thelonius Monk Story),* 1972–73

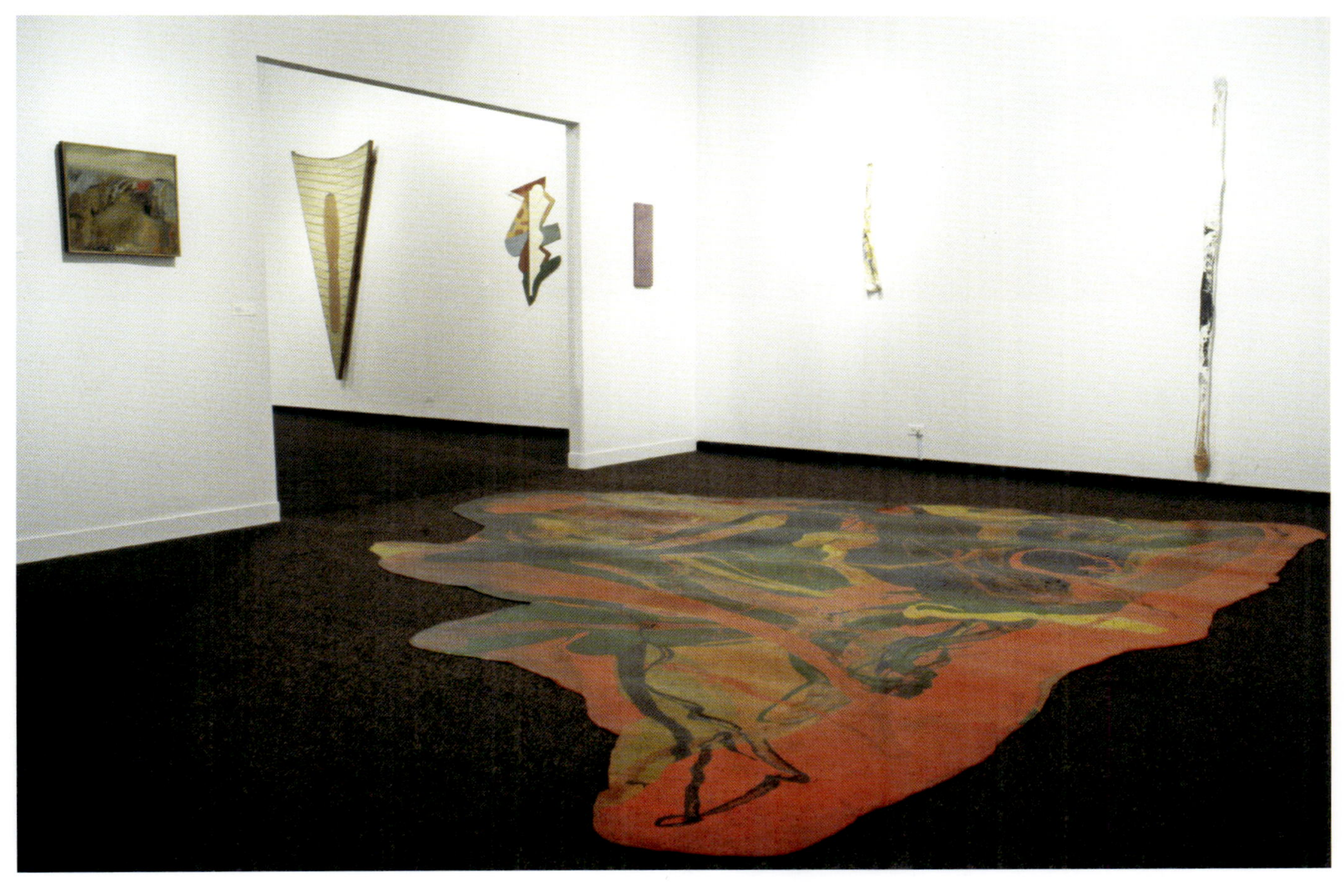

Front room: works by
Lynda Benglis.
Rear room: works by
Gary Stephan

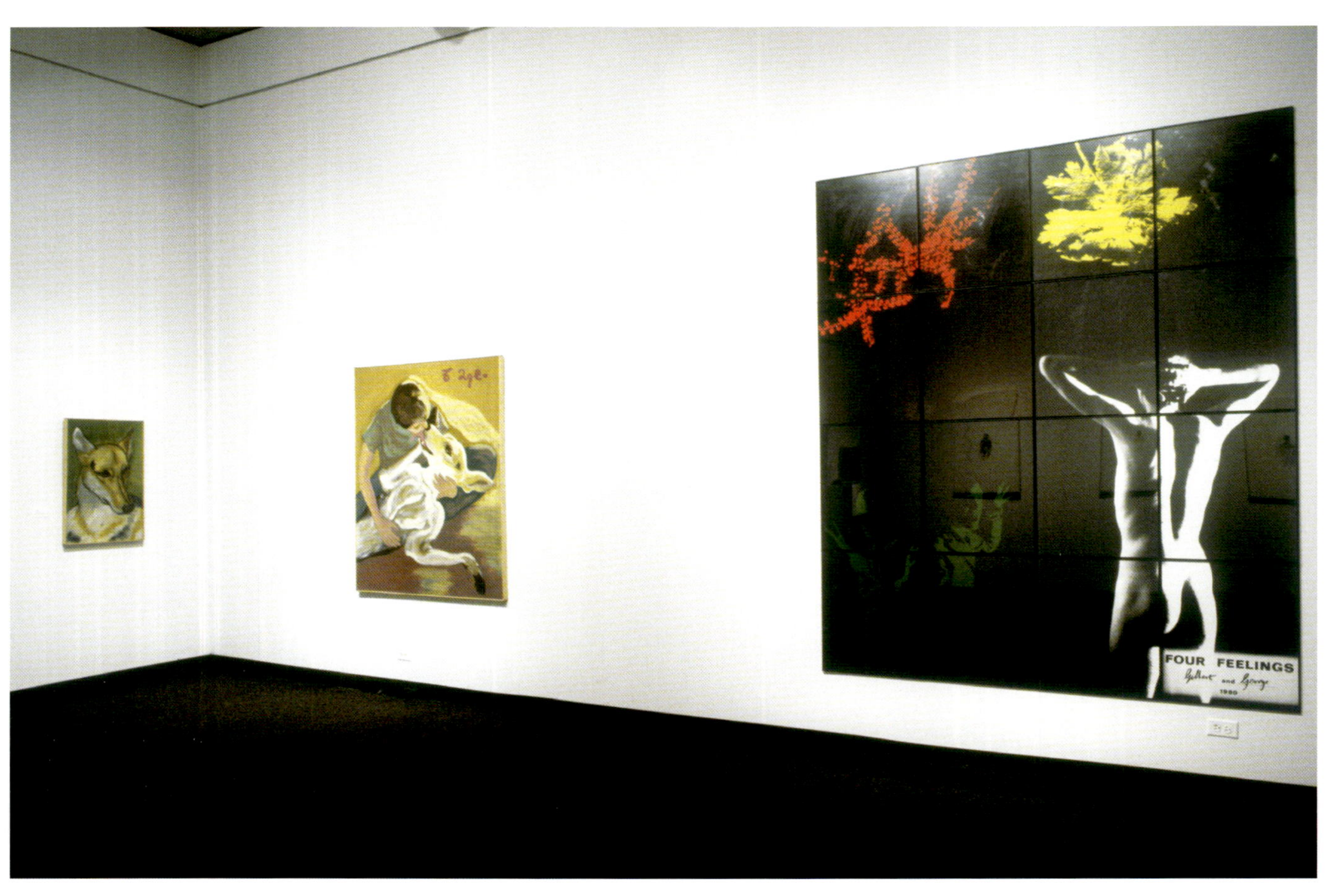

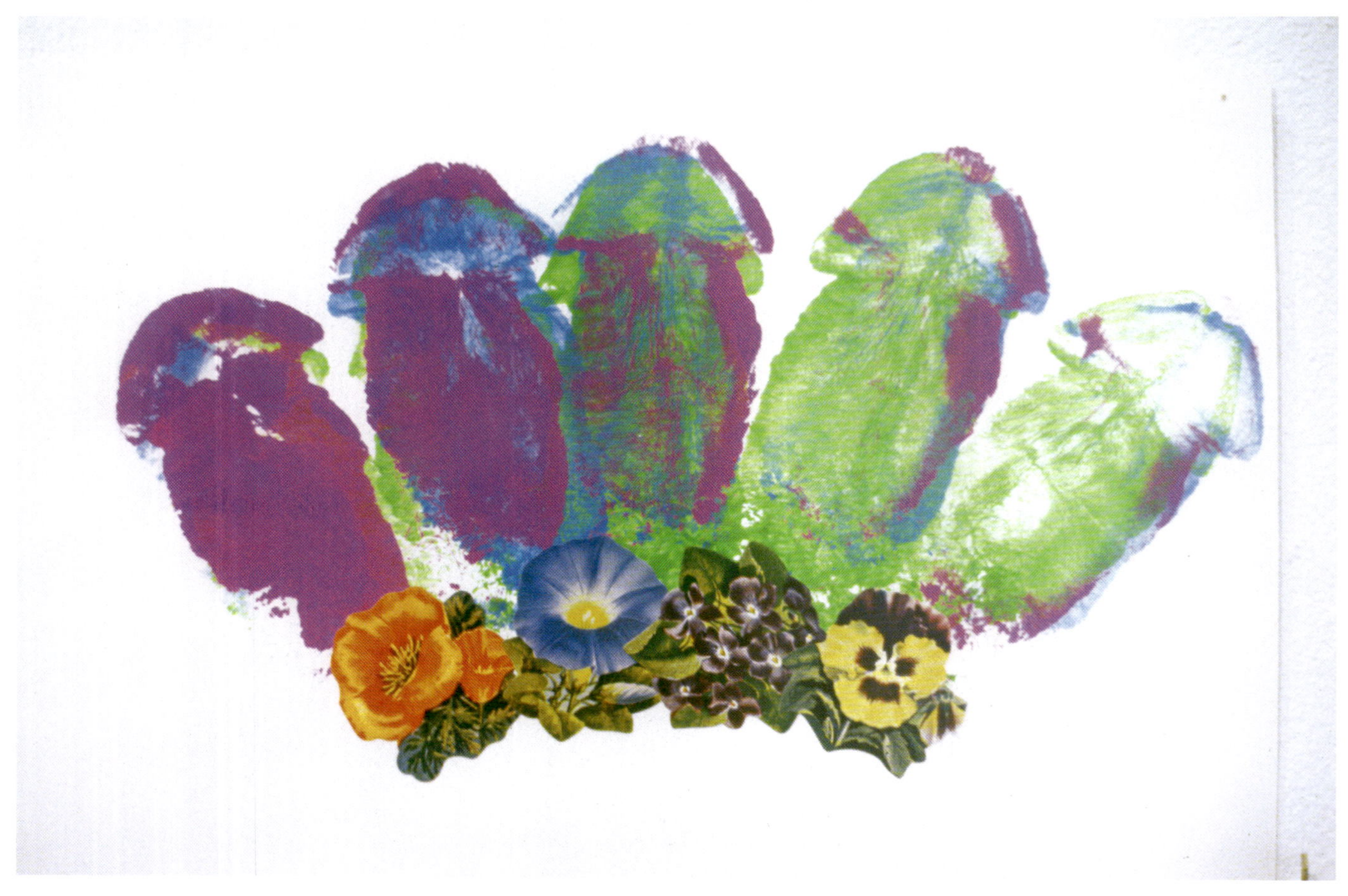

(top) Left to right:
works by Fran Winant
and Gilbert & George

(bottom) Les Petites
Bonbons, *Dayglo
Cockprint*, 1973

(right) On October 8,
1983, the New Museum
opens its new space at
583 Broadway, New York

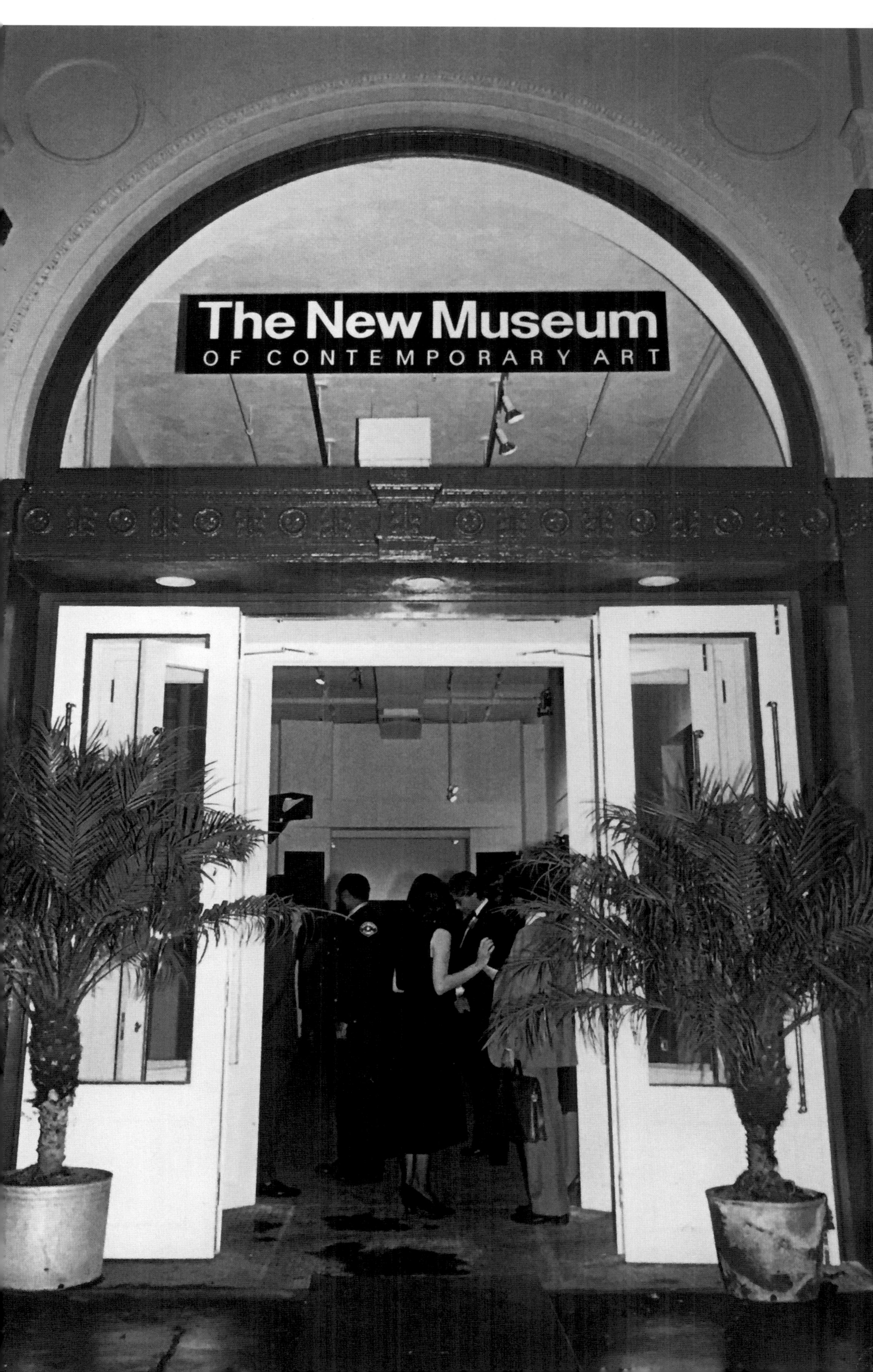
The New Museum
OF CONTEMPORARY ART

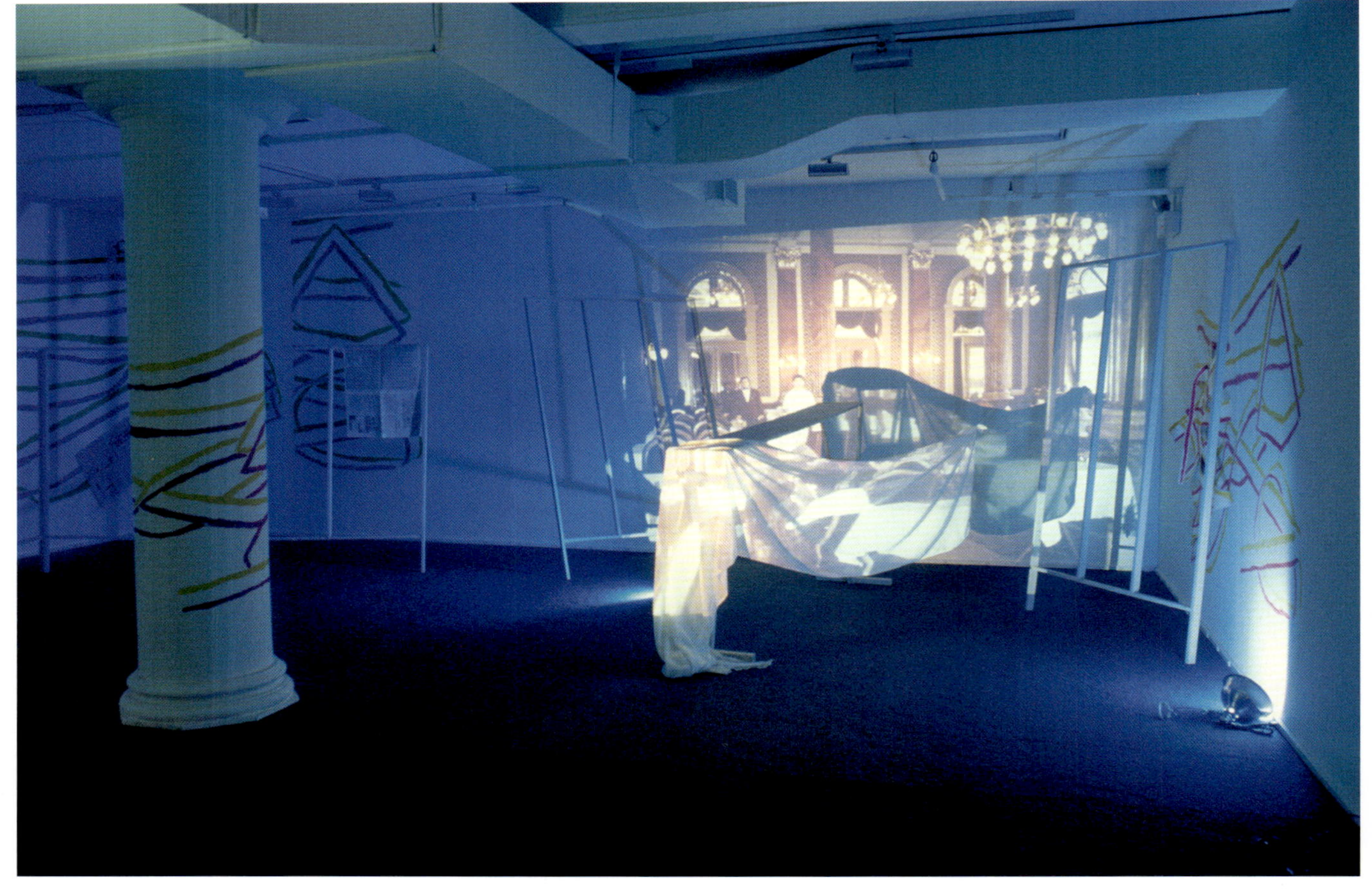

Joan Jonas,
Big Market, 1984

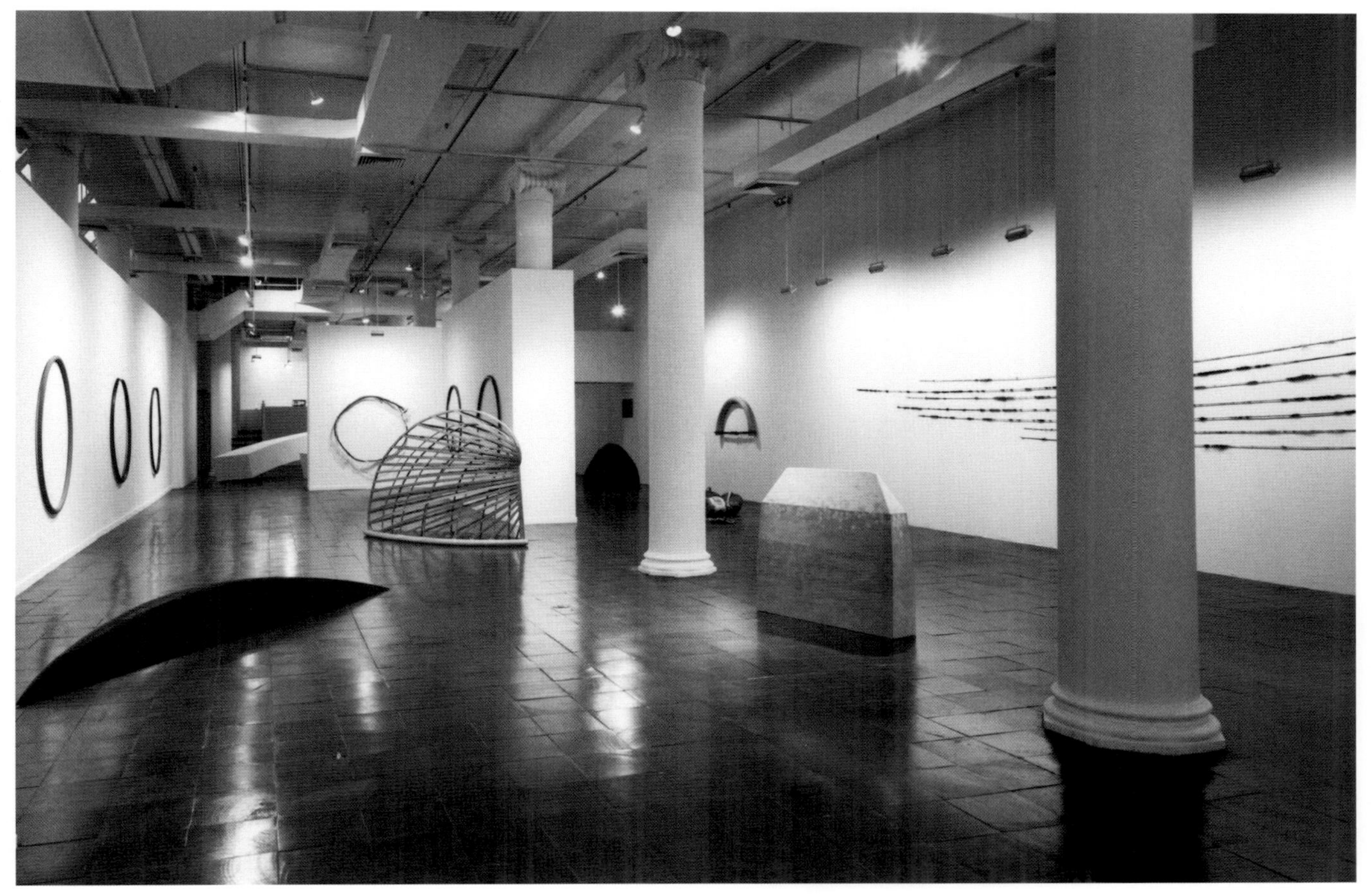

Installation view

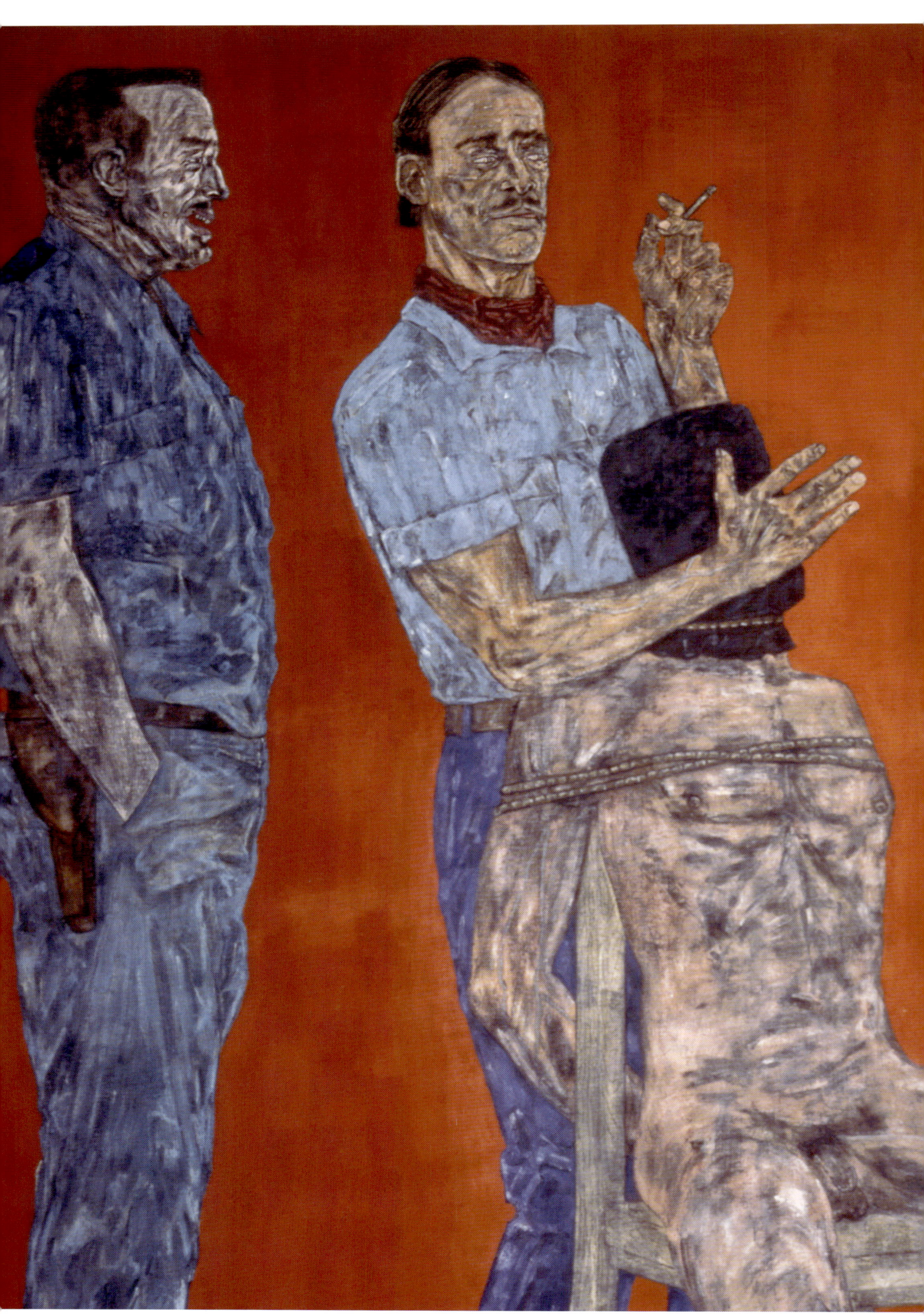

Leon Golub,
Interrogation II, 1981

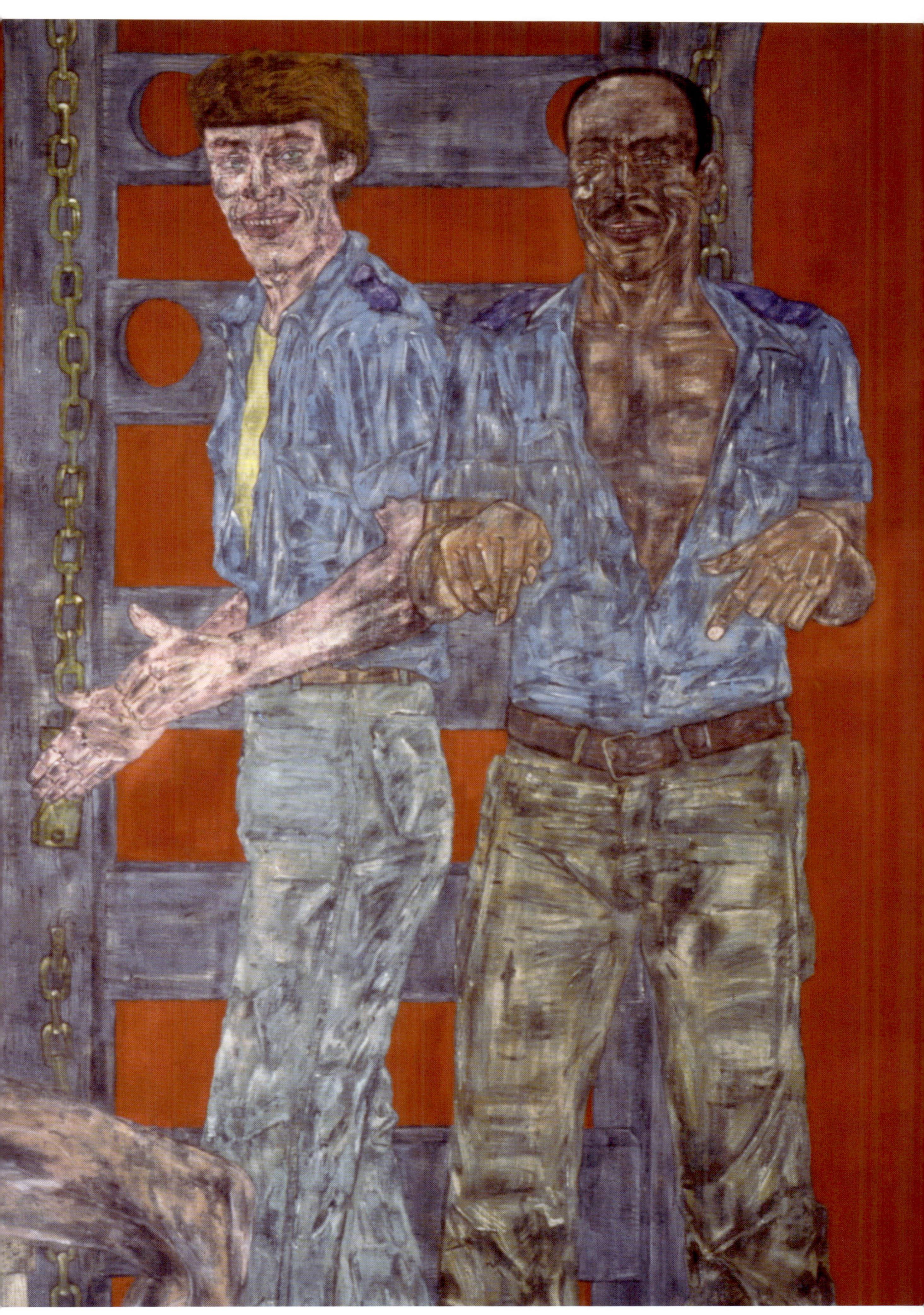

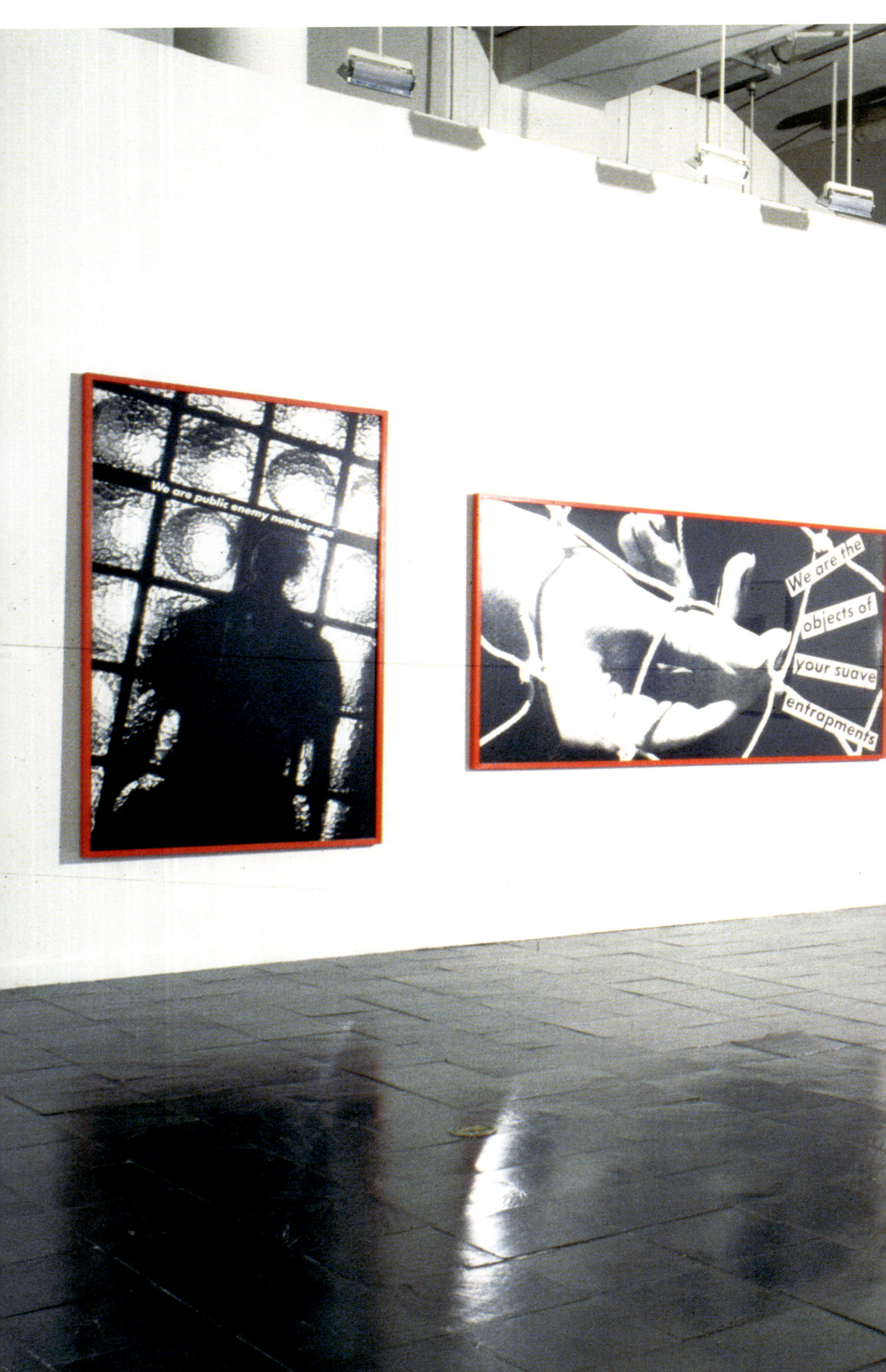
We are public enemy number one
We are the
objects of
your suave
entrapments

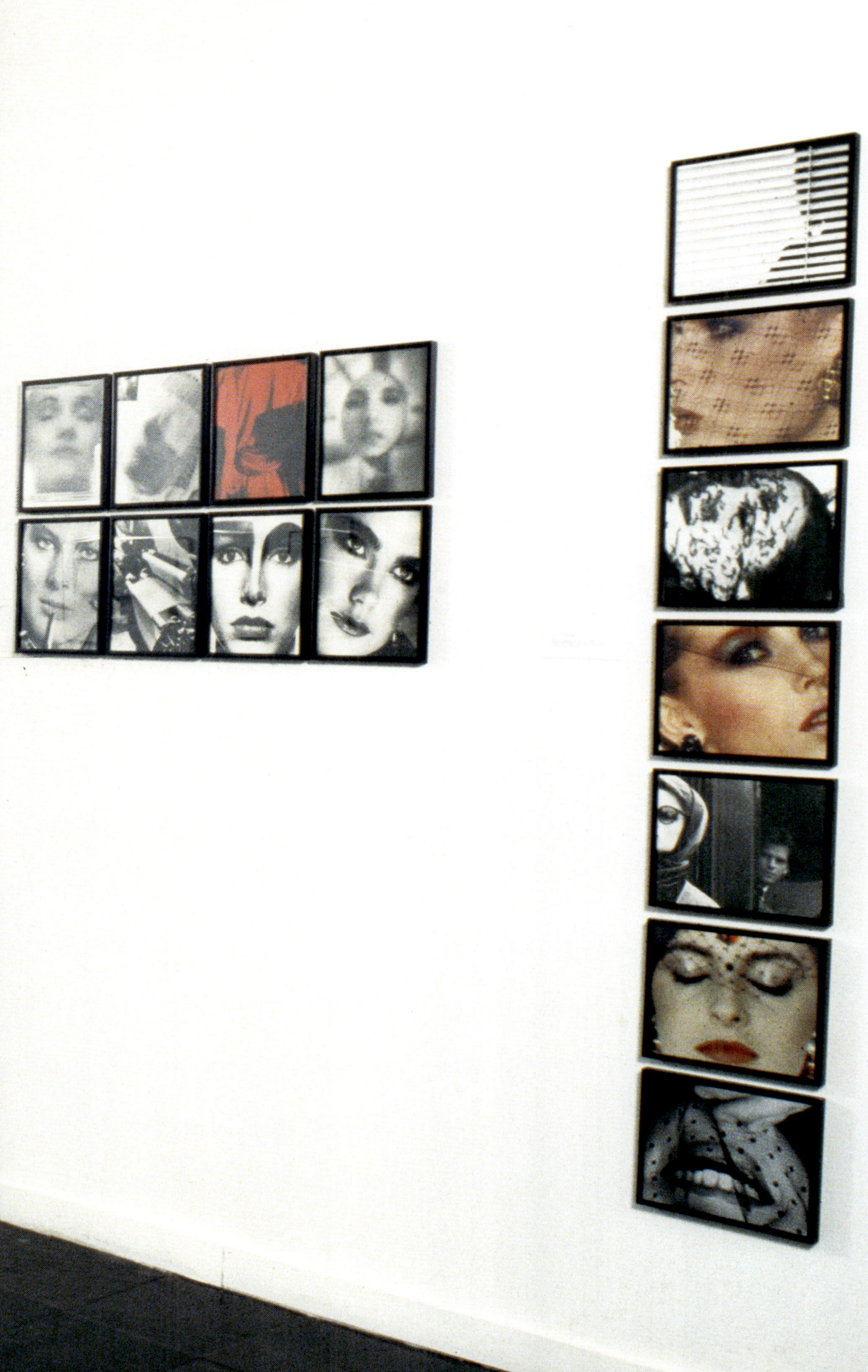

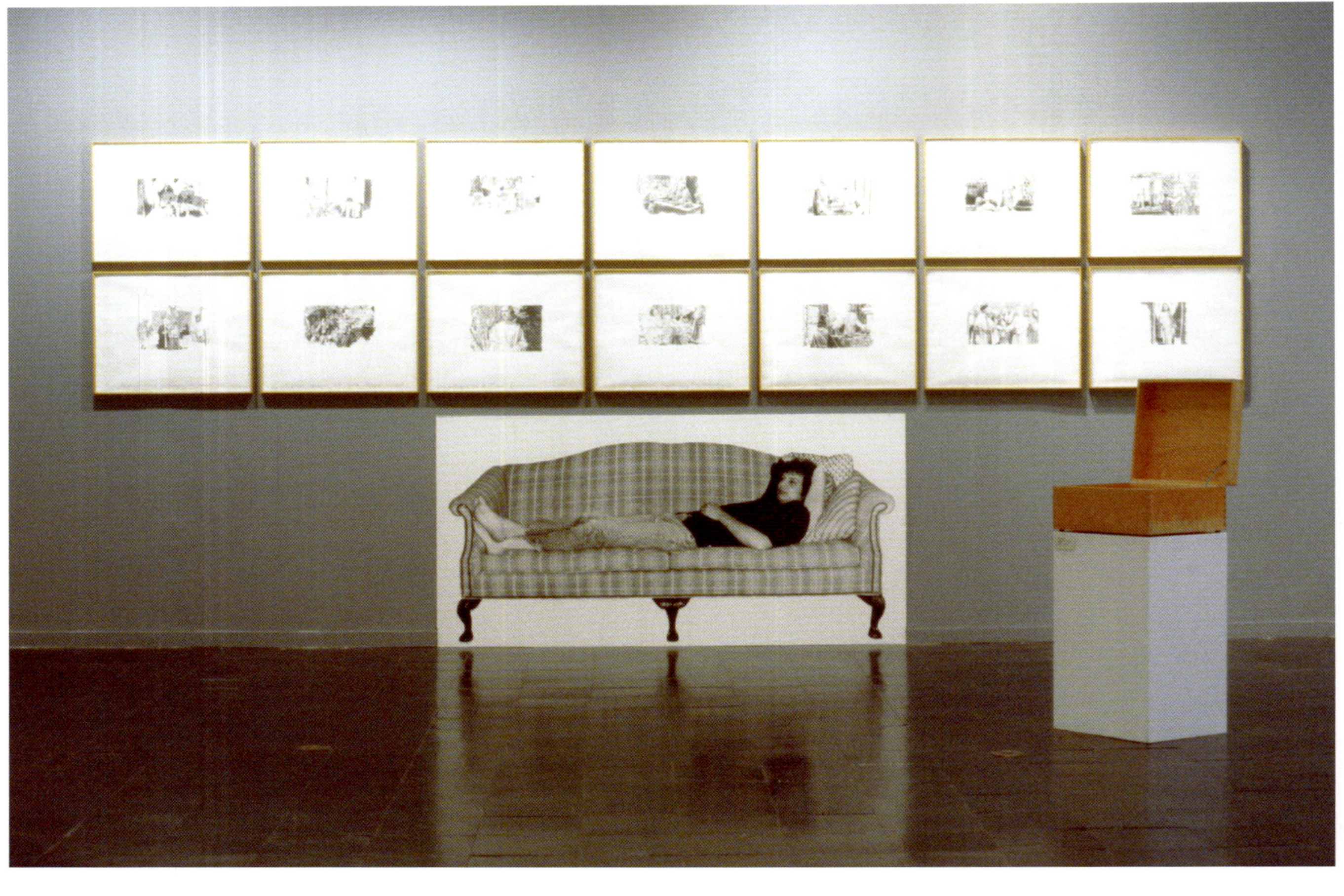

(previous spread)
"Difference: On
Representation and
Sexuality." Left to right:
works by Barbara Kruger
and Silvia Kolbowski

(above) Allen
Ruppersberg,
Men Talking, 1979

(right) Linda Montano,
*Seven Years of Living
Art*, 1984–91. Performance:
New Museum, March 1986

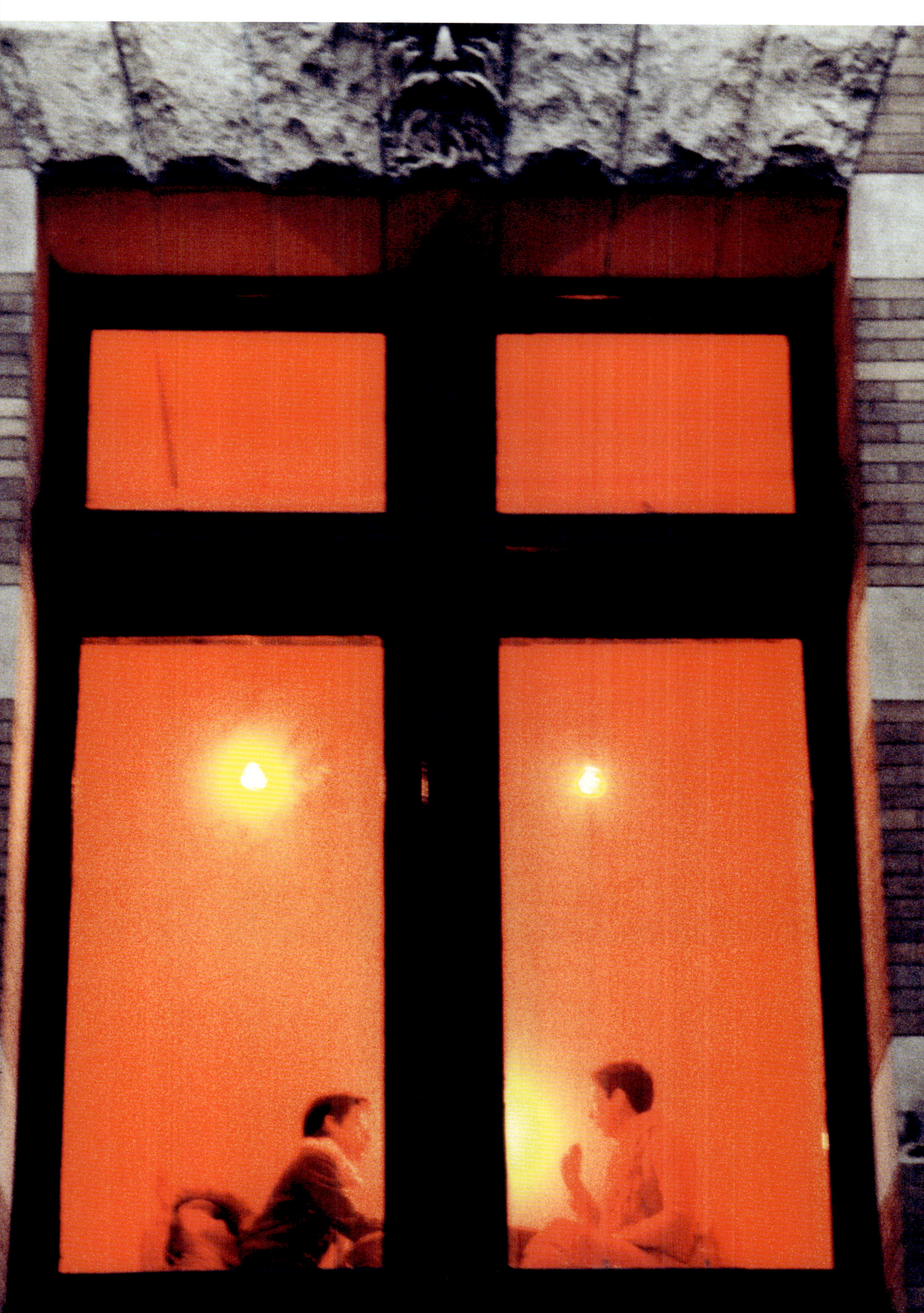

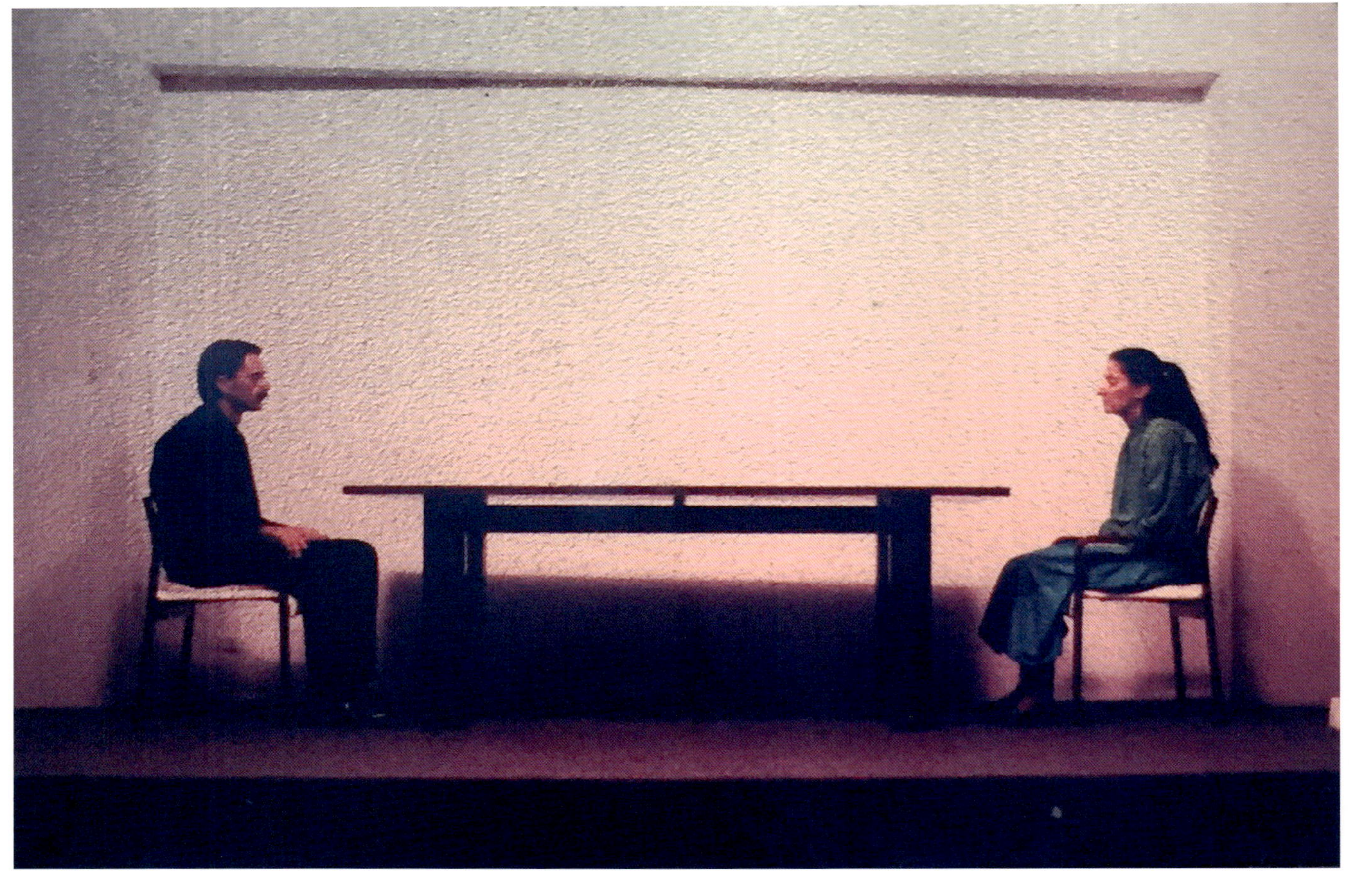

Marina Abramović and Ulay,
Nightsea Crossing, 1986.
Performance: New Museum,
March 1986

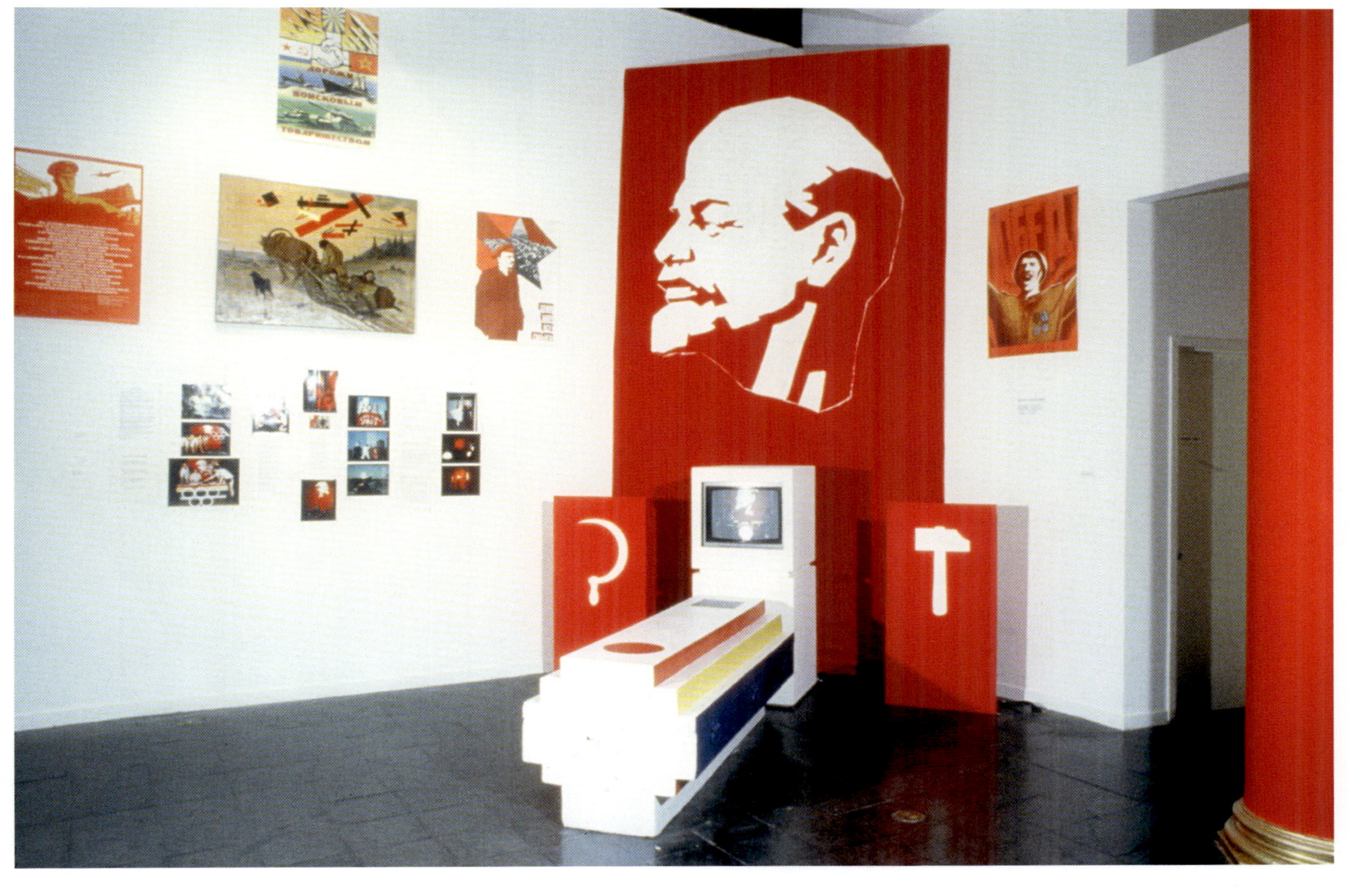

Left to right: works
by Kazimir Passion
Group, Vitaly Komar and
Alexander Melamid, and
Alexander Kosolapov

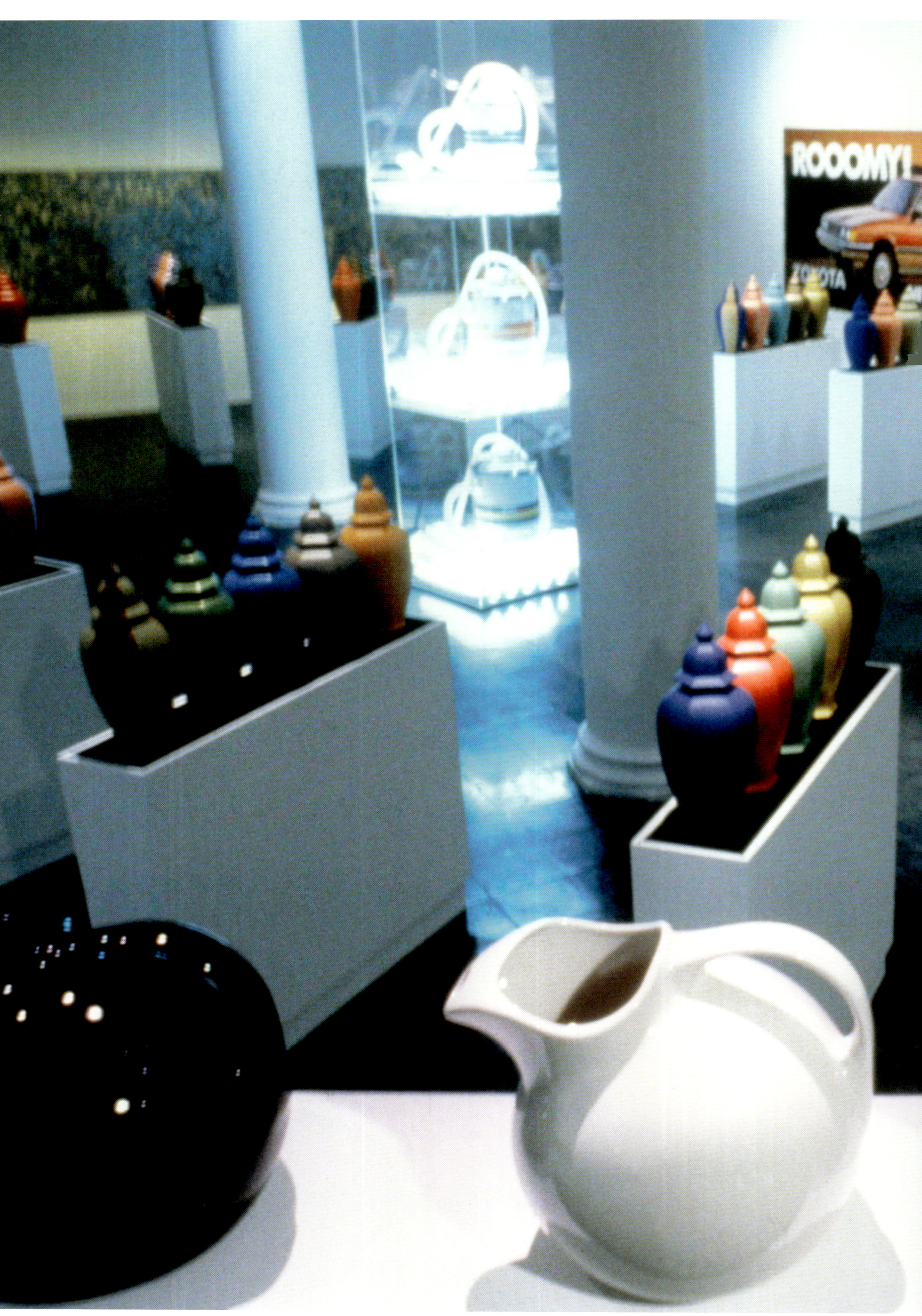

Front to back: works by
Haim Steinbach, Allan
McCollum, Jeff Koons,
and Louise Lawler

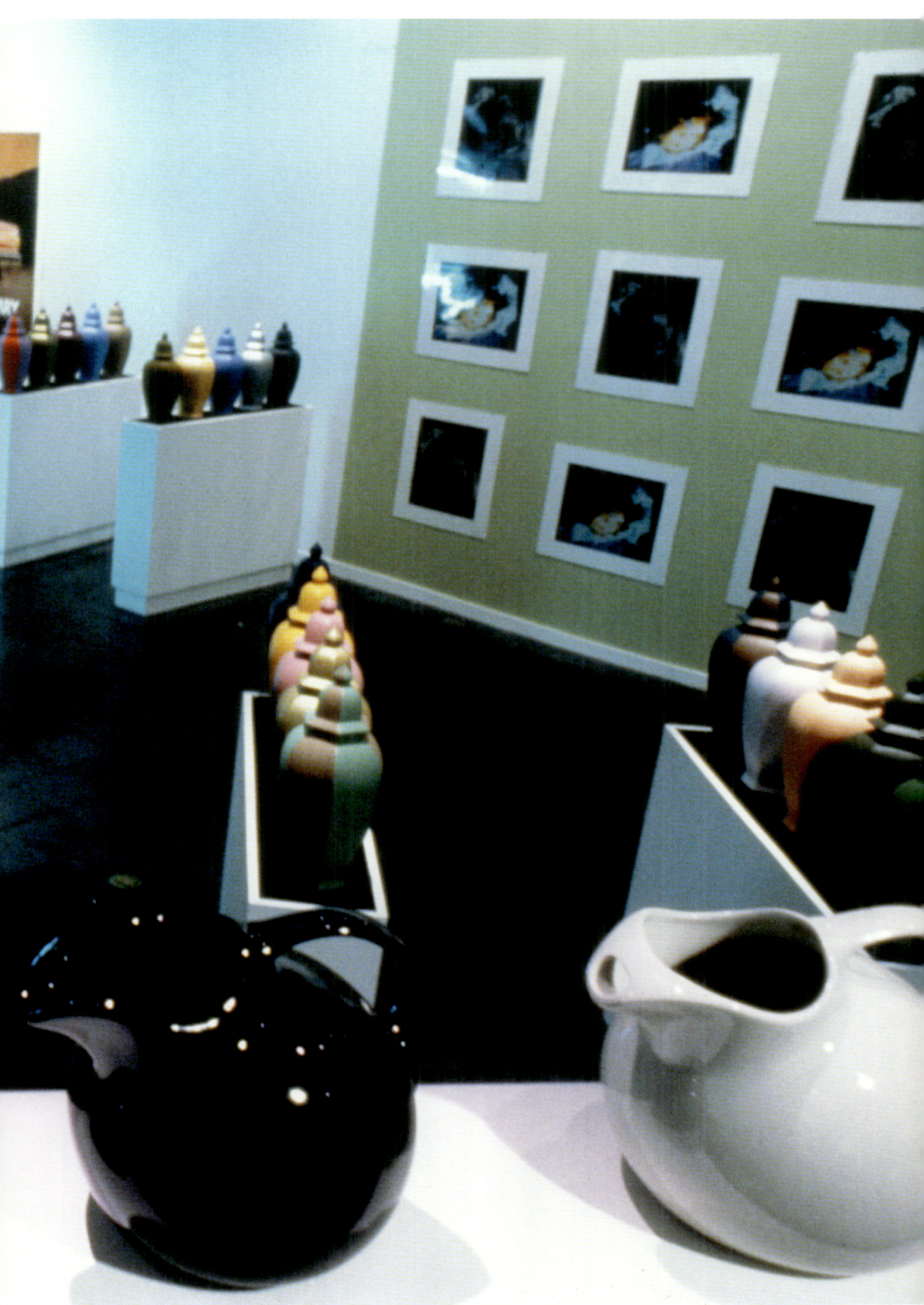

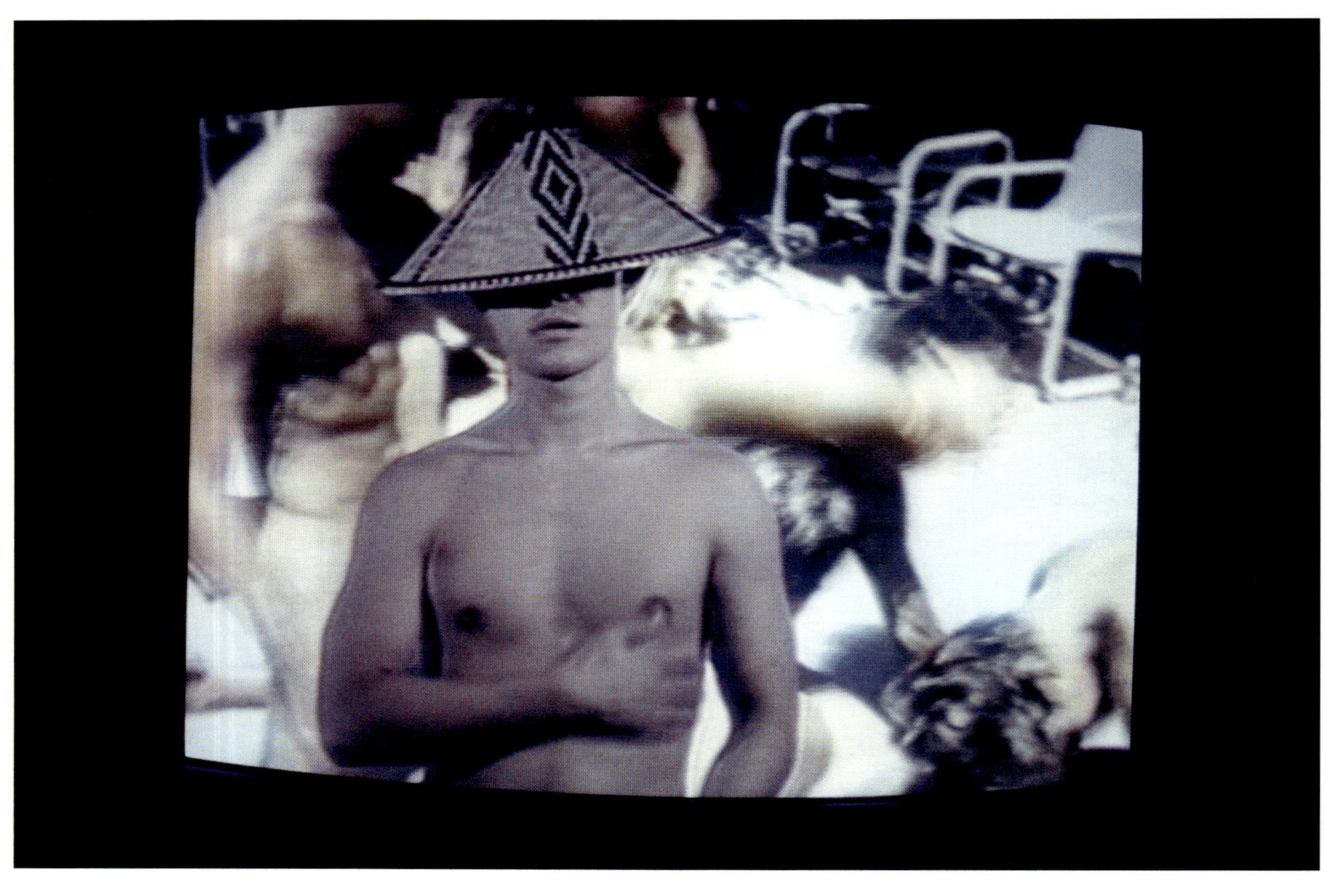

Richard Fung,
Chinese Characters, 1985

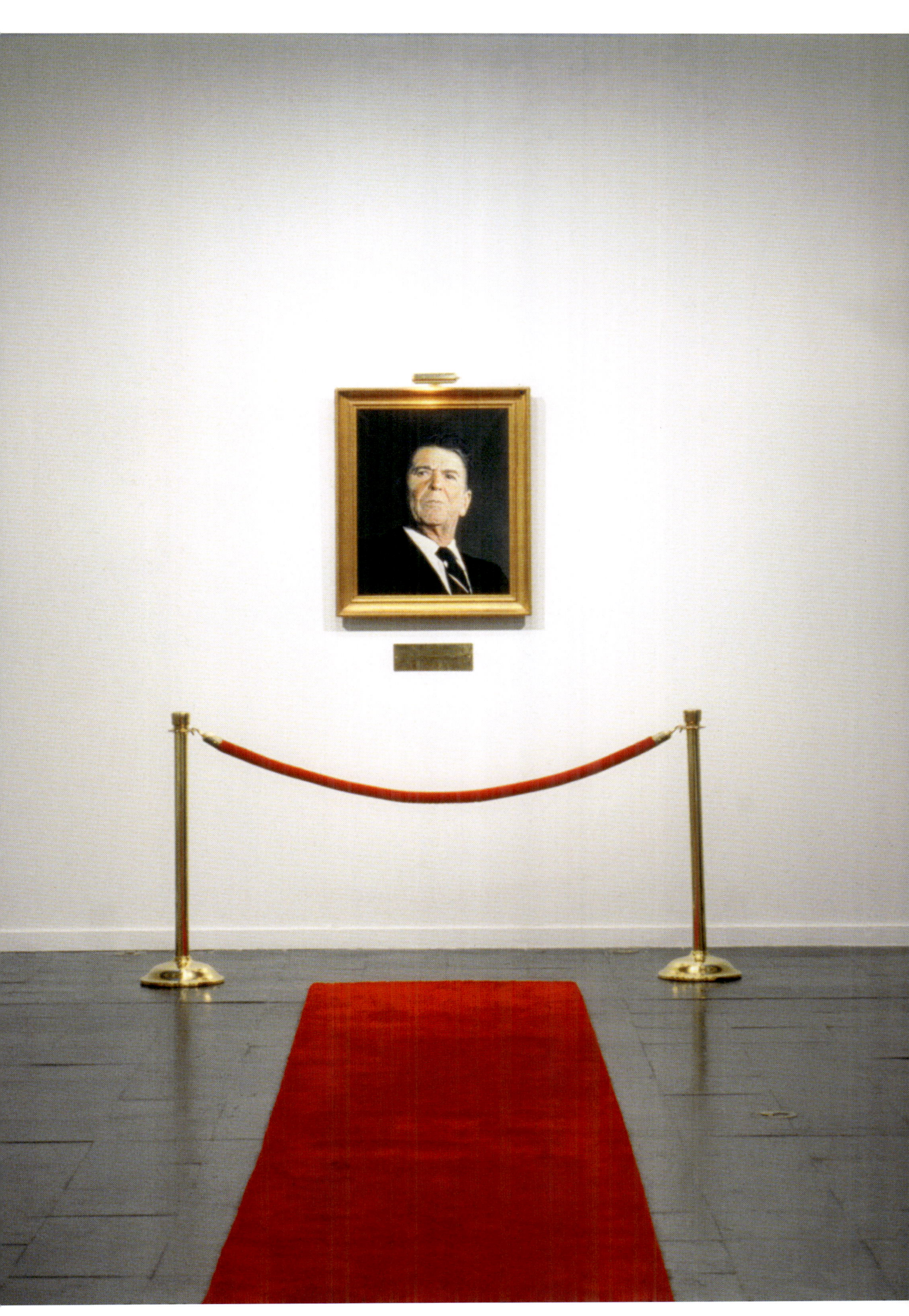

Hans Haacke,
*Ölgemälde, Hommage à
Marcel Broodthaers* [Oil
Painting, Homage to
Marcel Broodthaers], 1982
(detail)

Pat Steir: Self-Portrait: An Installation

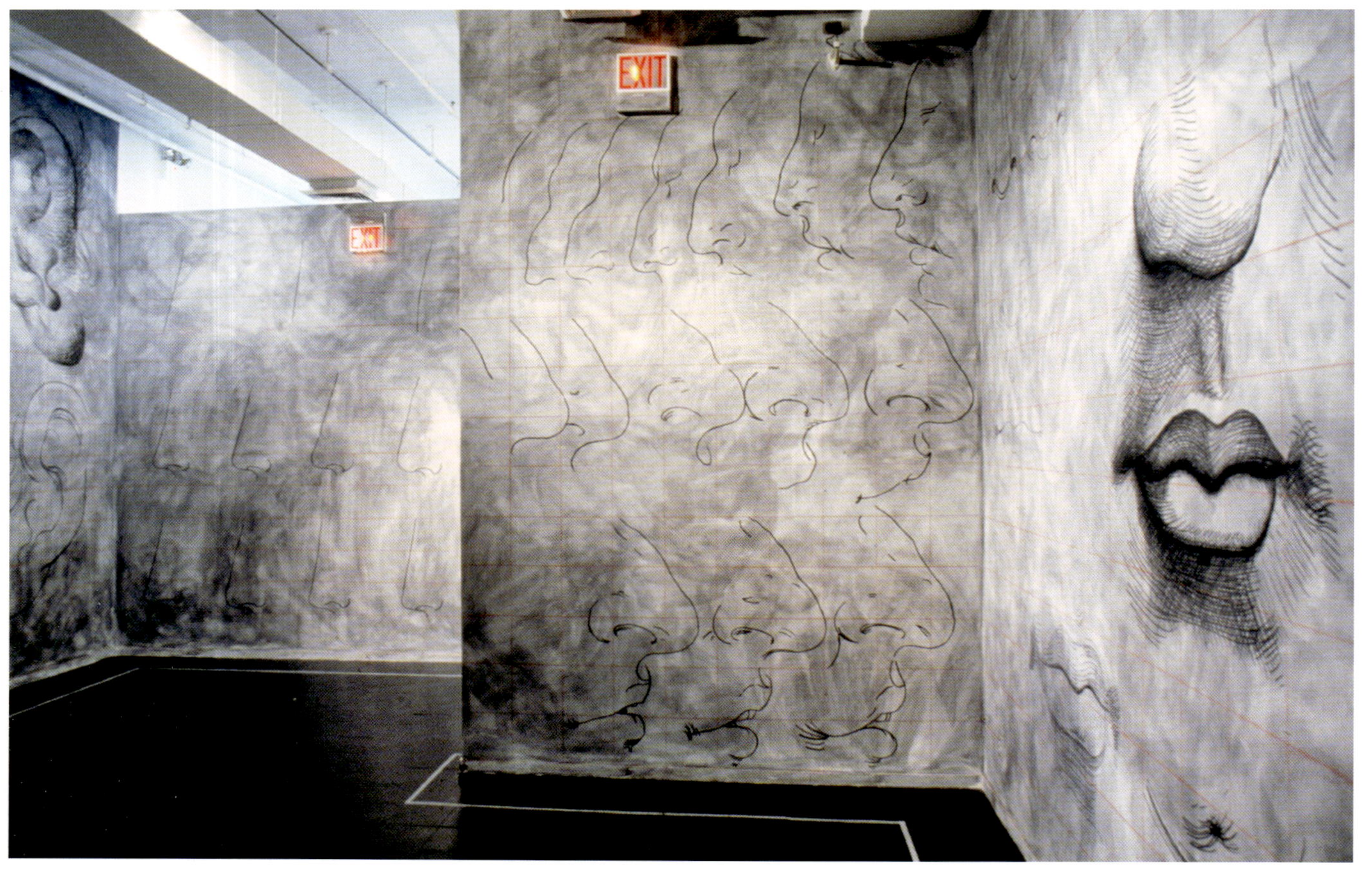

Installation view

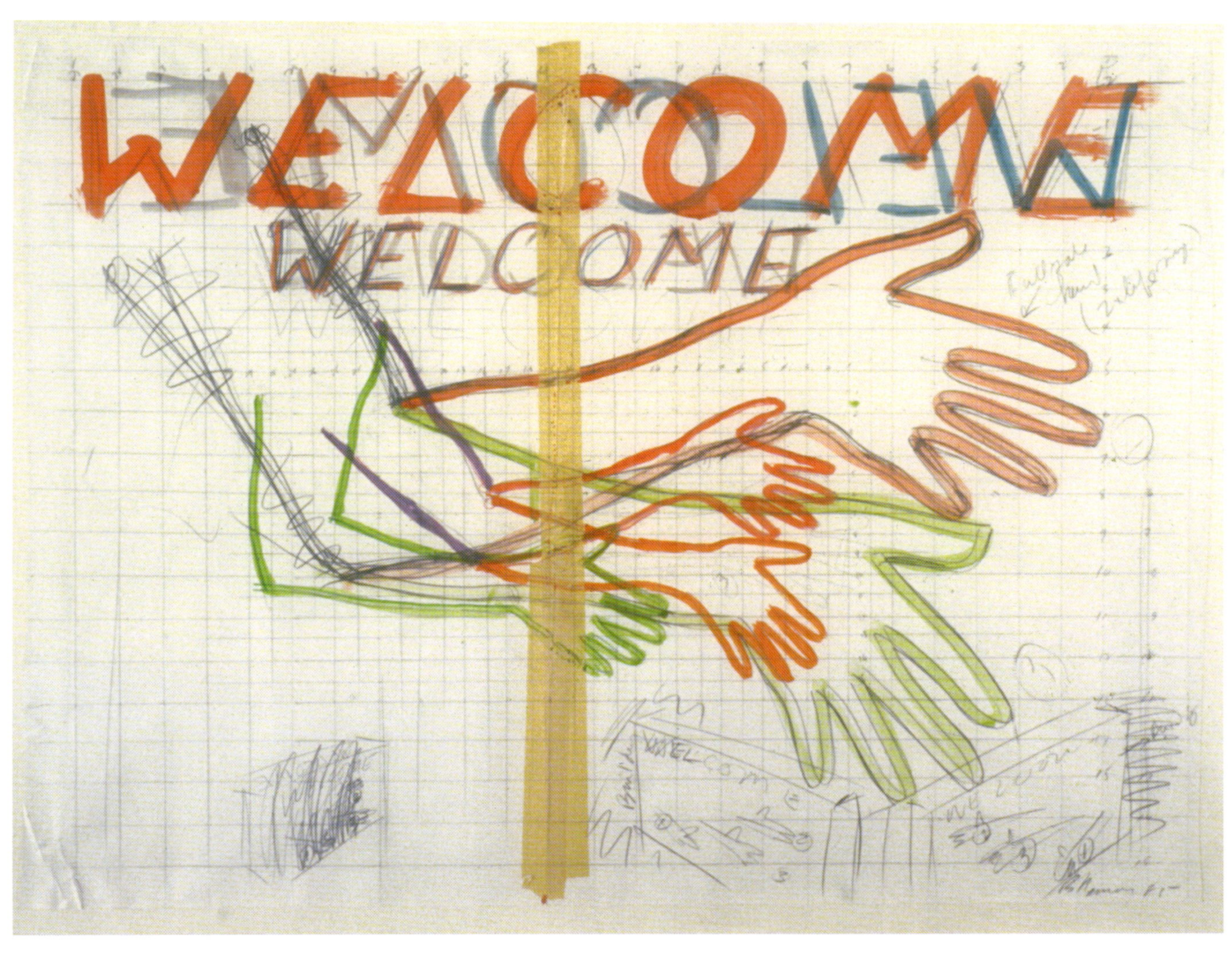

Bruce Nauman,
Welcome / Full scale /
hand / (2 x life size)
/ Building / welcome /
Welcome, 1985

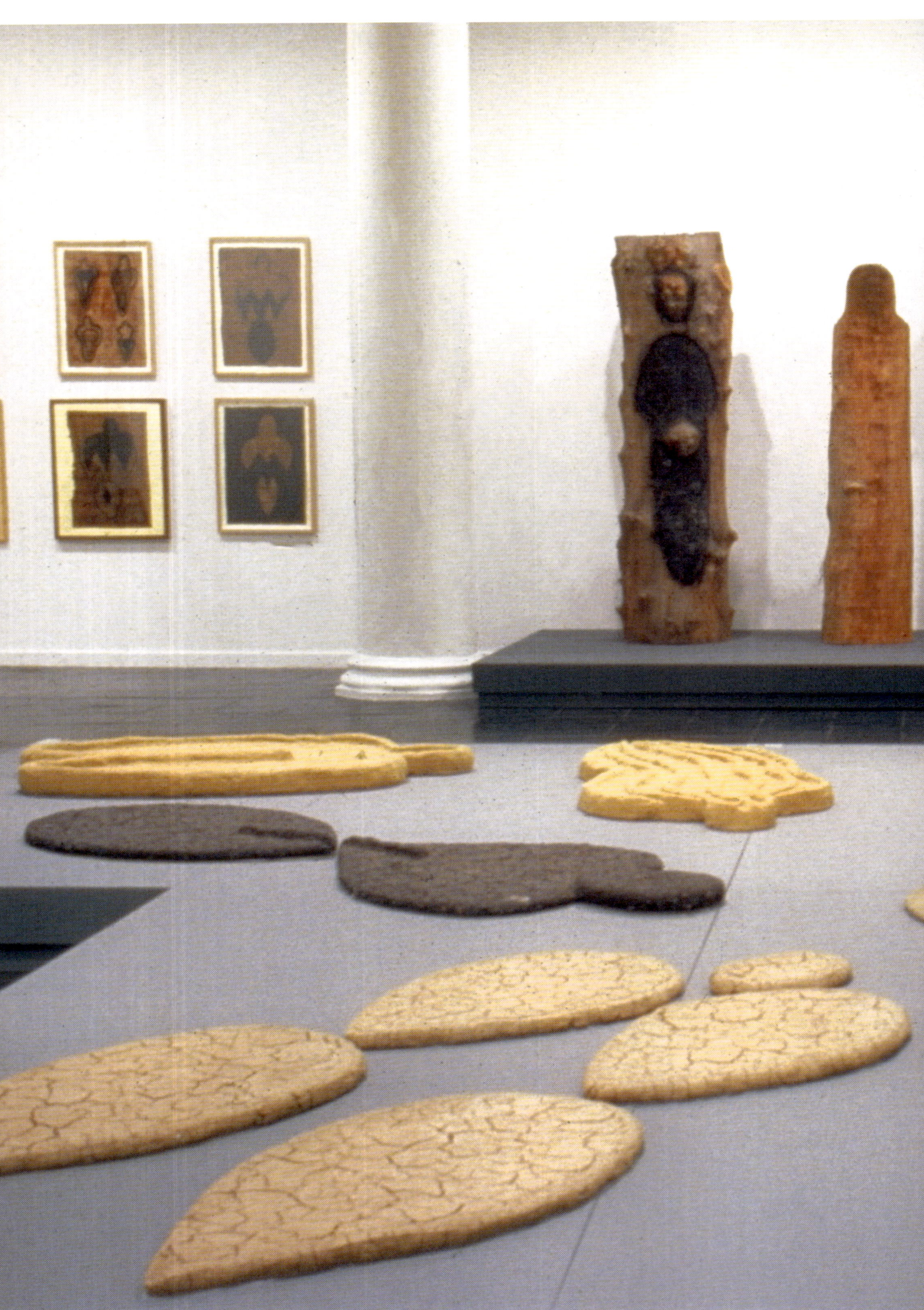

Installation view

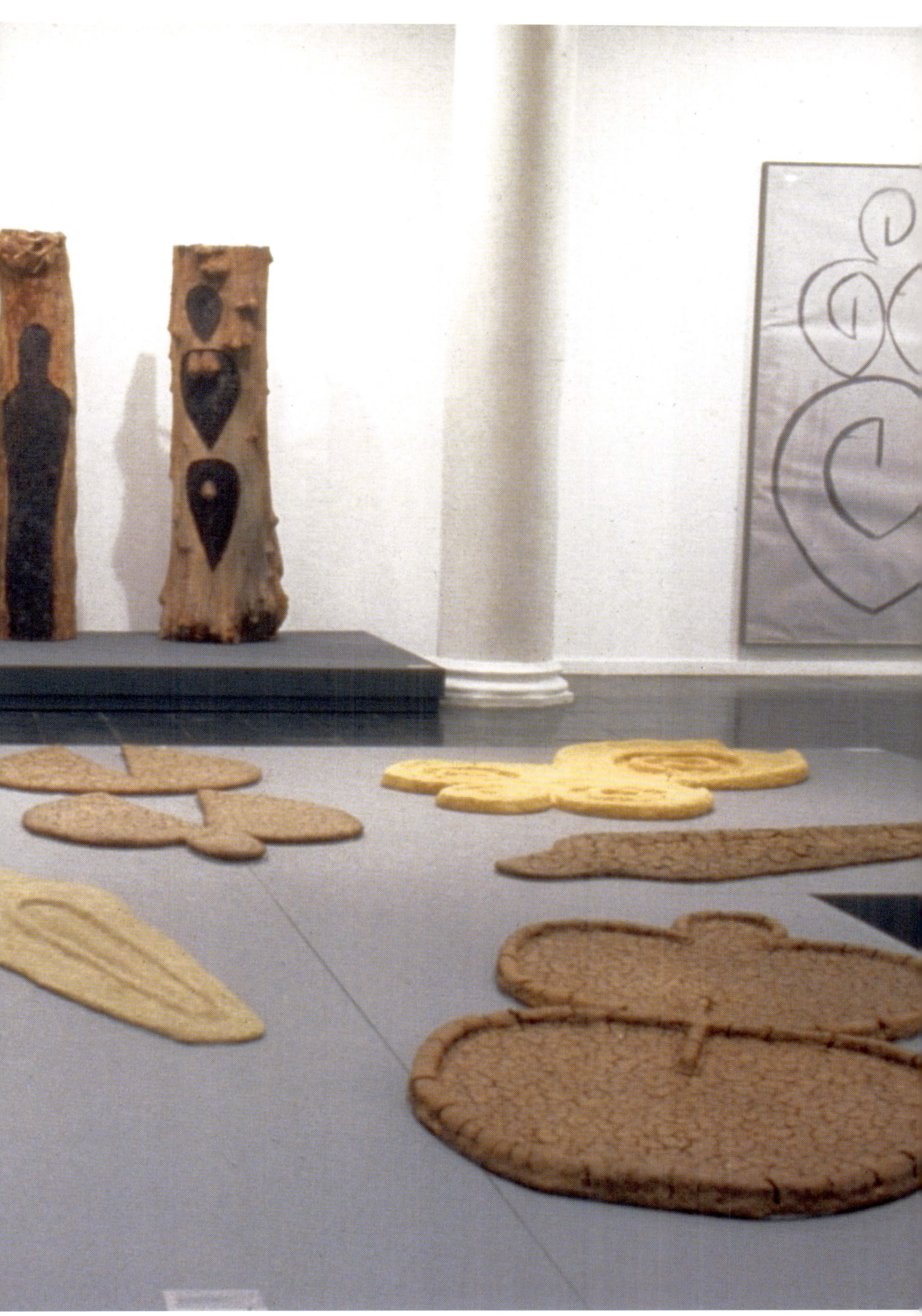

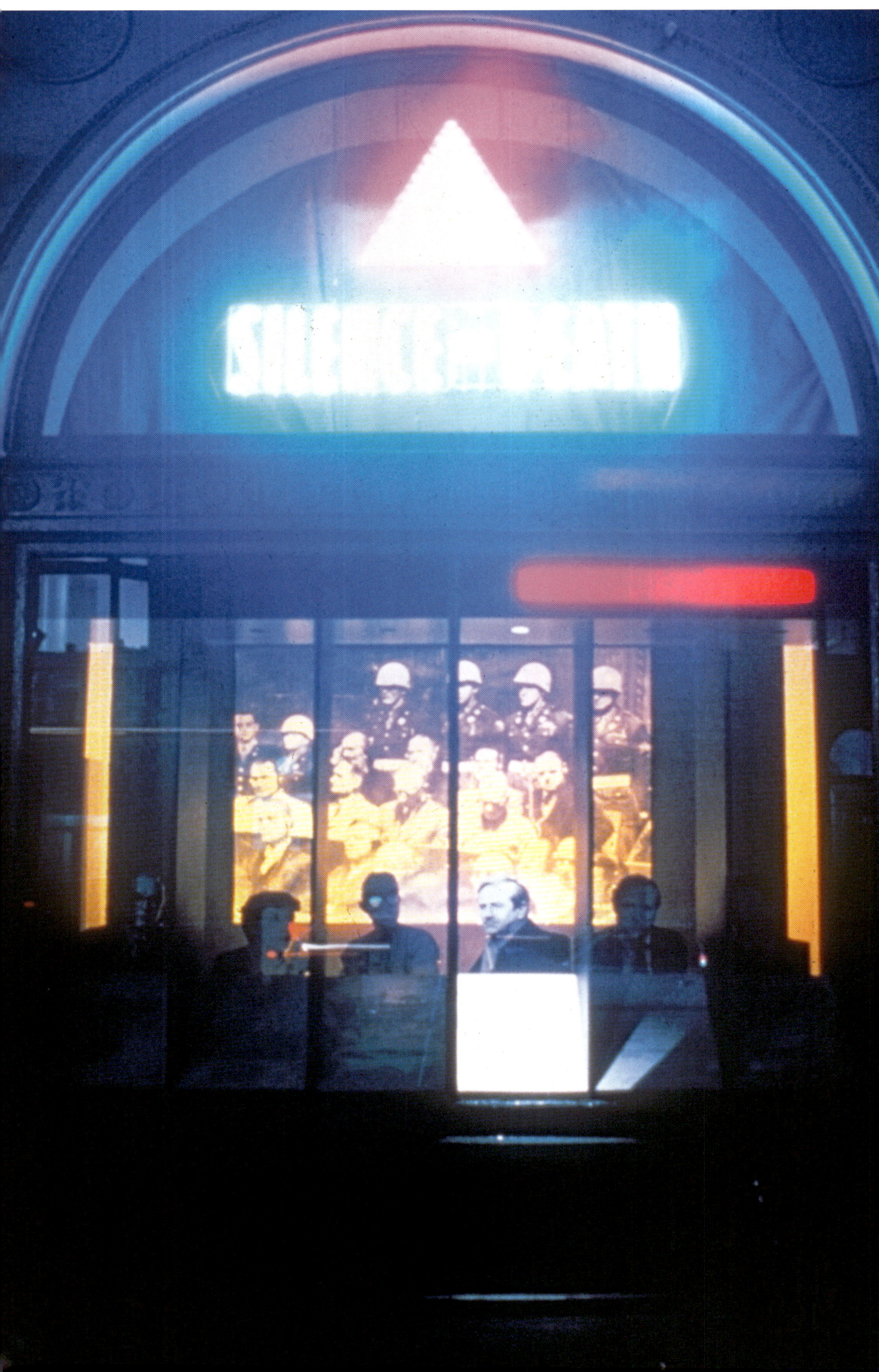
SILENCE=DEATH

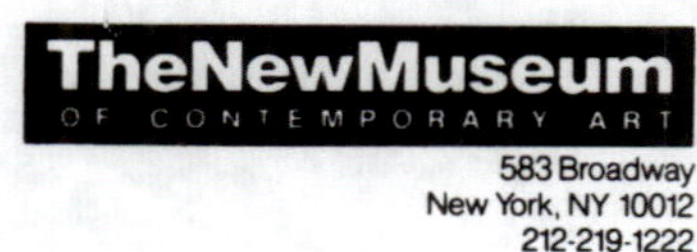

TheNewMuseum
OF CONTEMPORARY ART

583 Broadway
New York, NY 10012
212-219-1222

INSTALLATION BY FÉLIX GONZÁLEZ-TORRES
September 16 - November 20, 1988

When I was asked to write a short statement about the work in this
space I thought it would be a good opportunity to disclose and, in a
certain sense, to demystify my approach. I hope that it will guide
the viewer and will allow an active participation in the unraveling of
the meaning and the purpose of this work. Many may consider this text
redundant; an unnecessary intrusion, or even a handicap. It is
assumed that the work must "speak for itself," as if the divine dogma
of modernism were able to deliver a clear and universal message to a
uniform "family of man." Others know this is not true--that each of us
perceives things according to who and how we are at particular
junctures, whose terms are always shifting. Preferably the exhibition
gallery will function as an educational device, simple and basic,
without the mysteries of the muse, reactivating history to
affirm our place in this landscape of 1988.

This work is mostly personal. It is about those very early hours in
the morning, while still half asleep, when I tend to visualize
information, to see panoramas in which the fictional, the important,
the banal, and the historical are collapsed into a single caption.
Leaving me anxious and responsible to anchor a logical accompanying
image--scanning the TV channels trying to sort out and match sound and
sight. This work is about my exclusion from the circle of power where
social and cultural values are elaborated and about my rejection of
the imposed and established order.

It is a fact people are discriminated against for being HIV positive.
It is a fact the majority of the Nazi industrialists retained their
wealth after the war. It is a fact the night belongs to Michelob and
Coke is real. It is a fact the color of your skin matters. It is a
fact Crazy Eddie's prices are insane. It is a fact that four
colors--red, black, green and white--placed next to each other in any
form are strictly forbidden by the Israeli army in the occupied
Palestinian territories. This color combination can cause an arrest,
a beating, a curfew, a shooting, or a news photograph. Yet it is a
fact that these forbidden colors, presented as a solitary act of
consciousness here in Soho, will not precipitate a similar reaction.

From the first moment of encounter, the four color canvases in
this room will "speak" to everyone. Some will define them as an
exercise in color theory, or some sort of abstraction. Some as four
boring rectangular canvases hanging on the wall. A few experts will
interpret them as yet another minimalist ecstasy. Now that you've
read this text, I hope for a different message.

For all the PWAs.

Félix González-Torres
New York City 1988

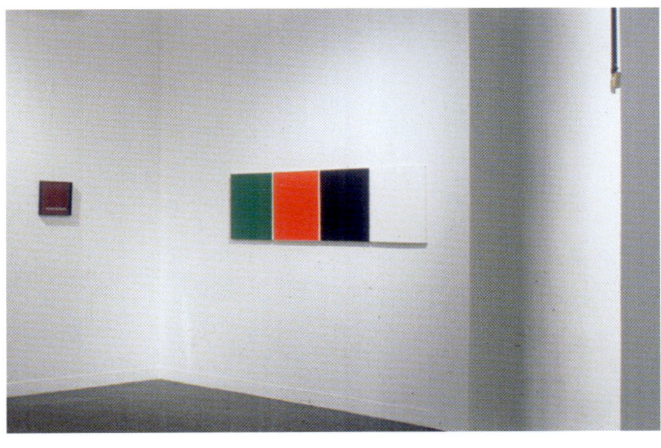

(top) Statement by
Félix González-Torres to
accompany his exhibition

(bottom) Félix
González-Torres,
Forbidden Colors, 1988

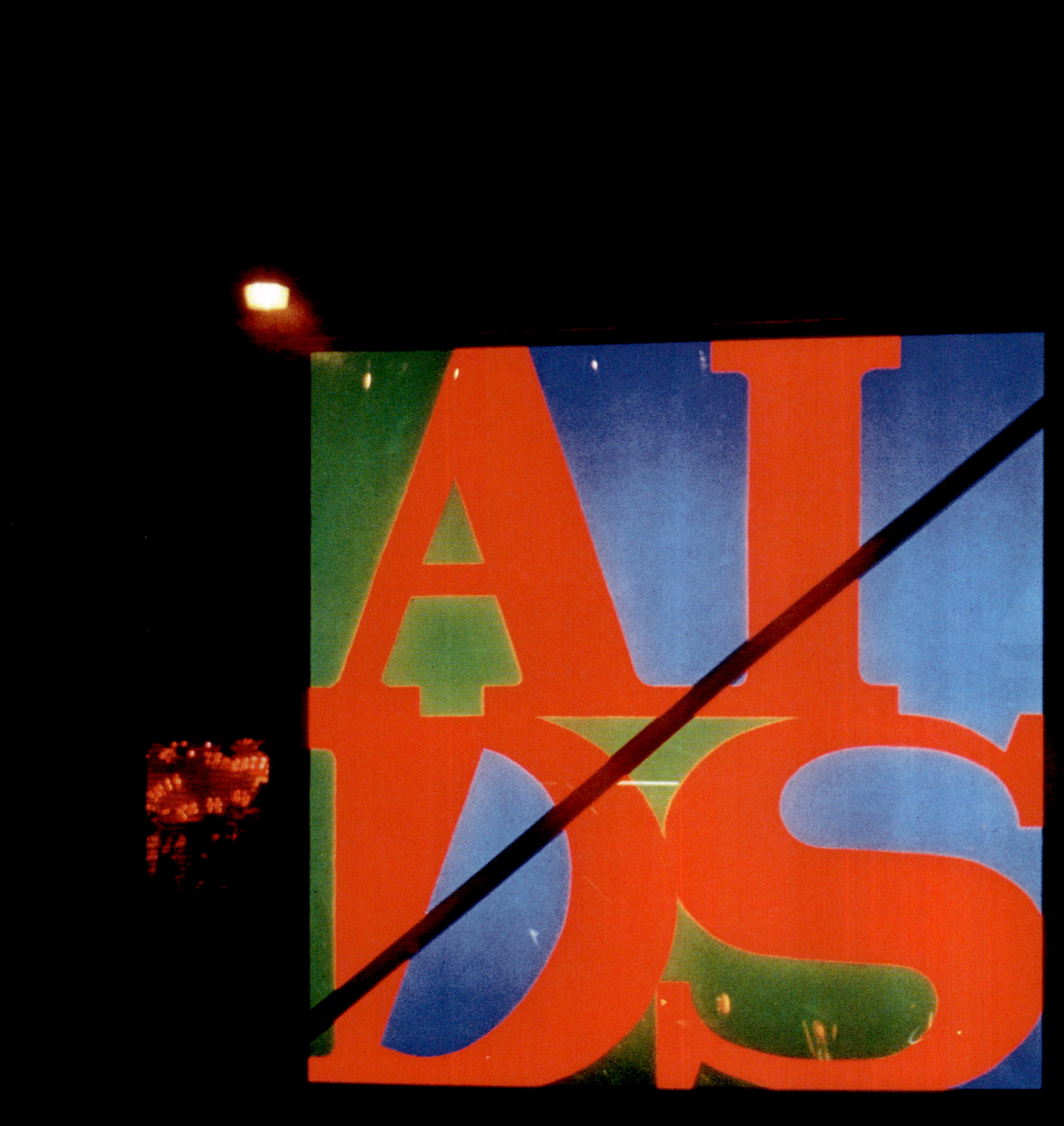

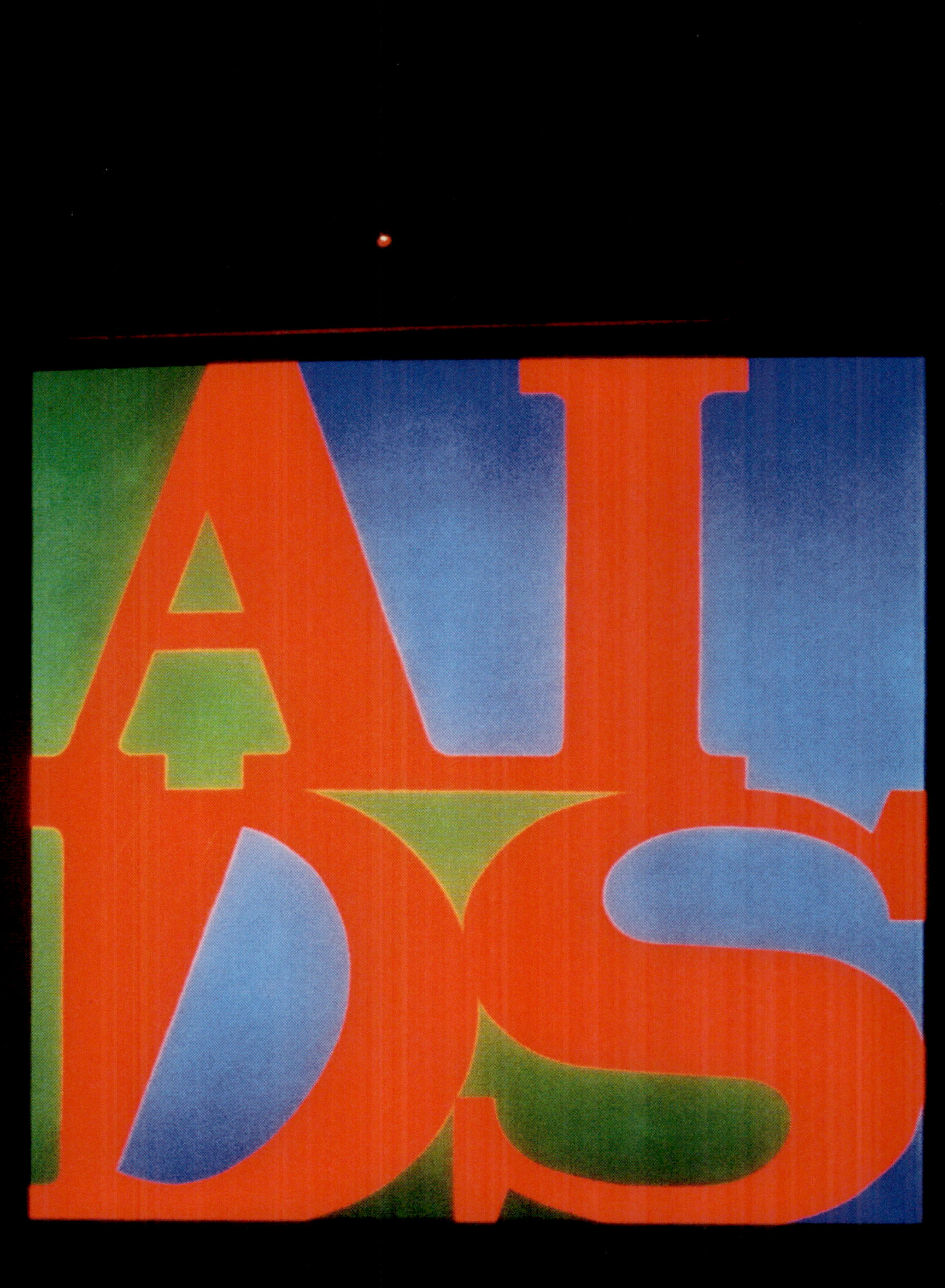
AIDS

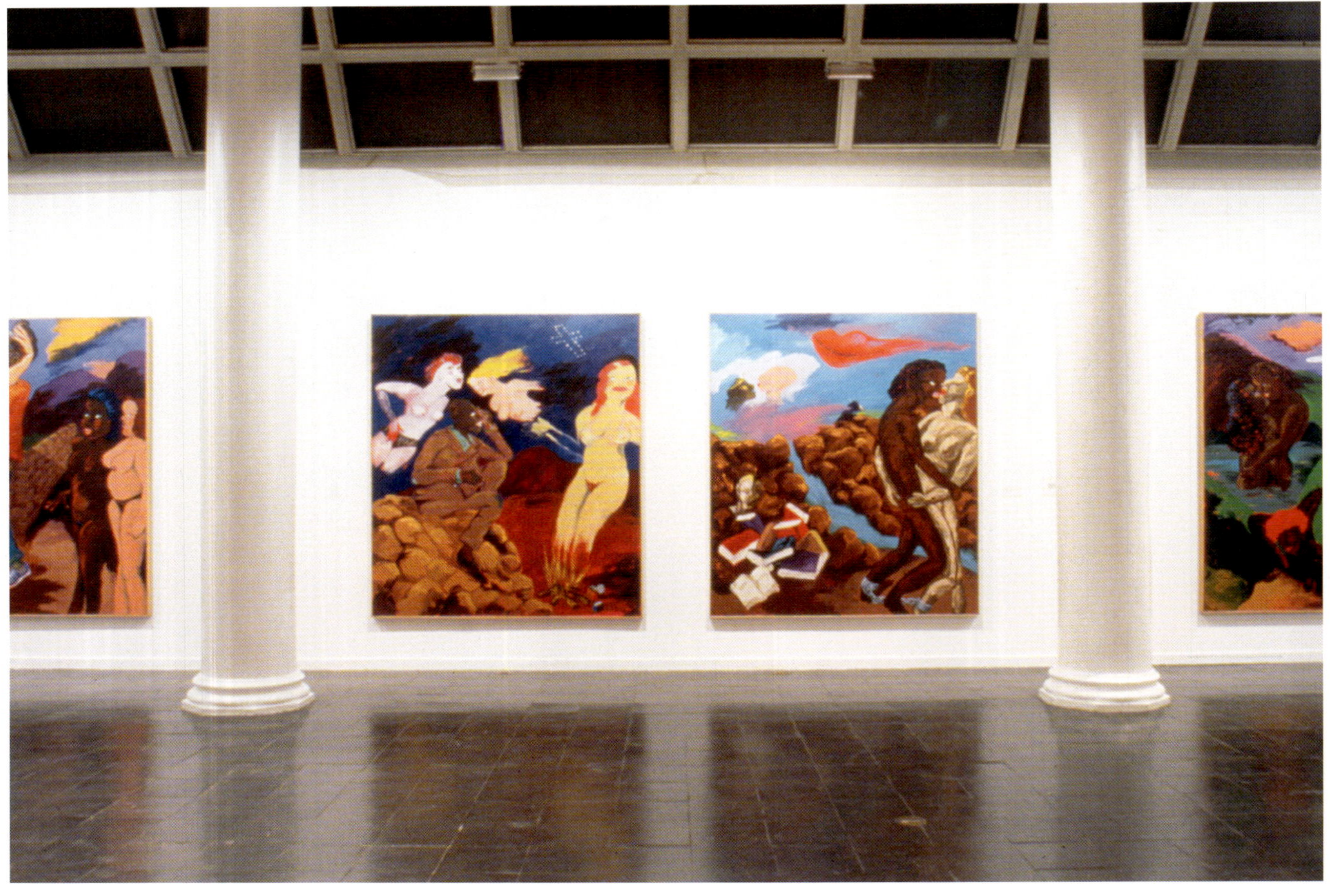

Installation view

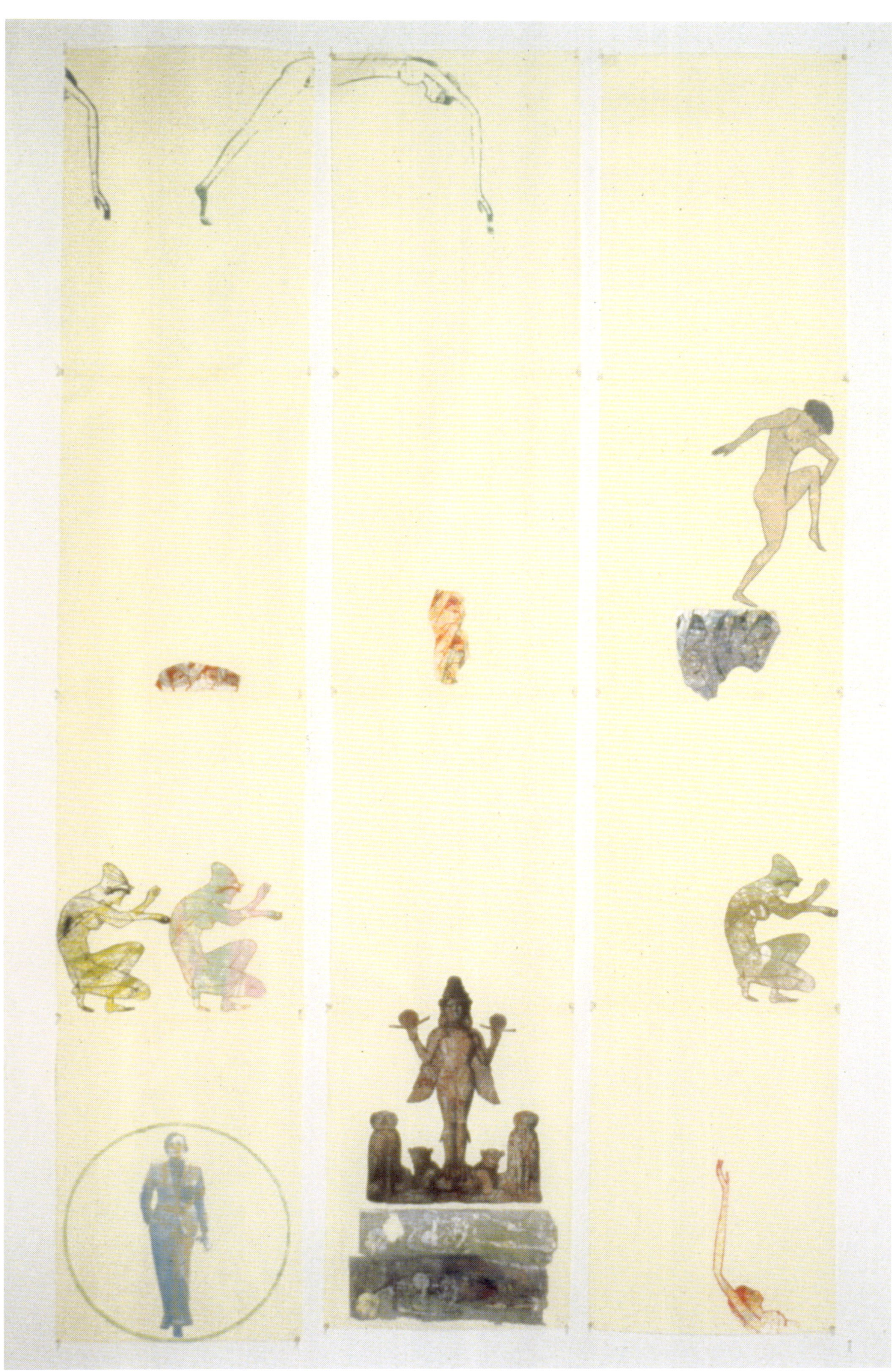

Nancy Spero,
Marlene, Sky Goddess,
Lilith (Panels 5–7), 1989

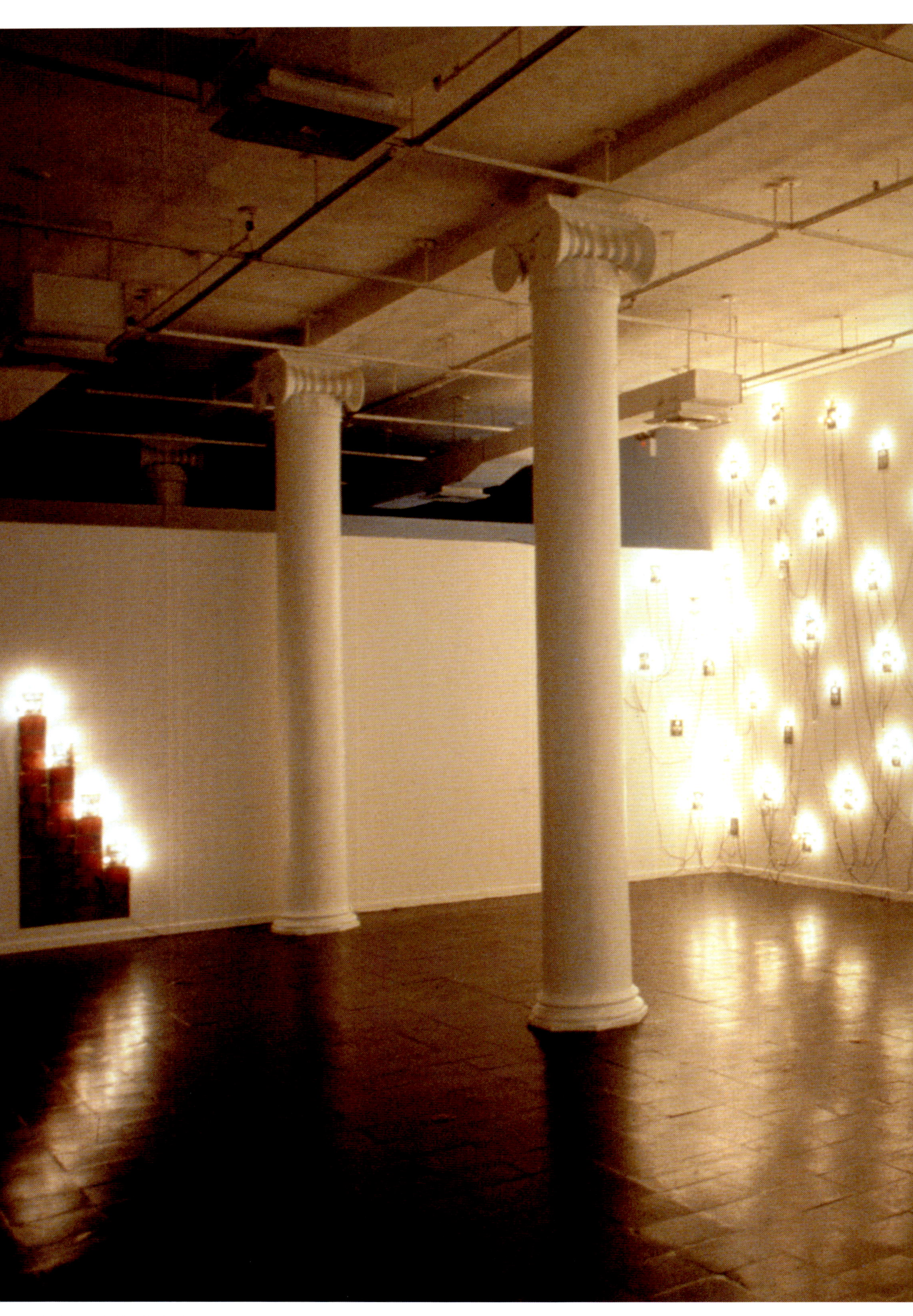

Left to right: Christian
Boltanski, *Monument*, 1985,
and *Monument: Les Enfants
de Dijon* [Monument: The
Children of Dijon], 1986

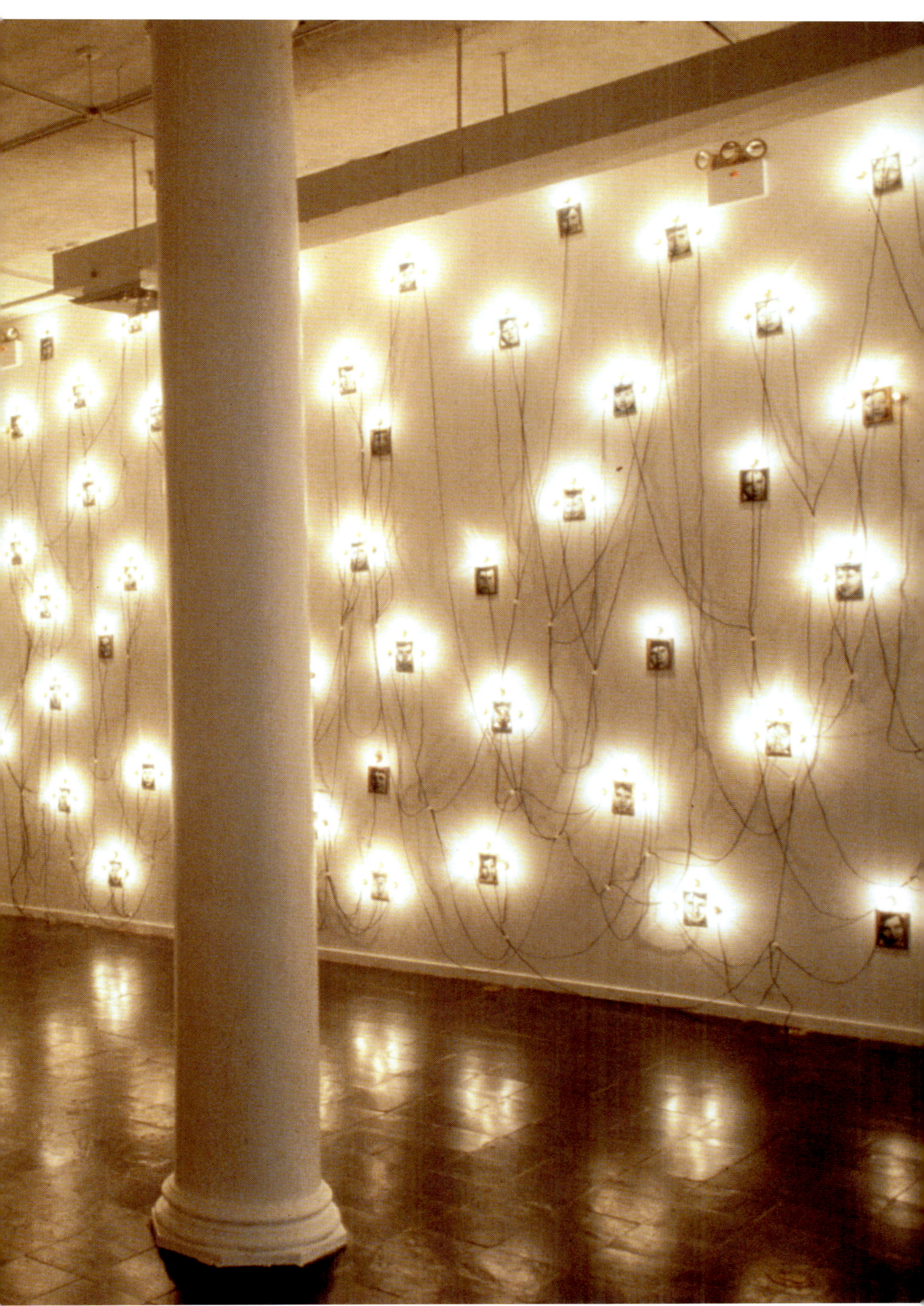

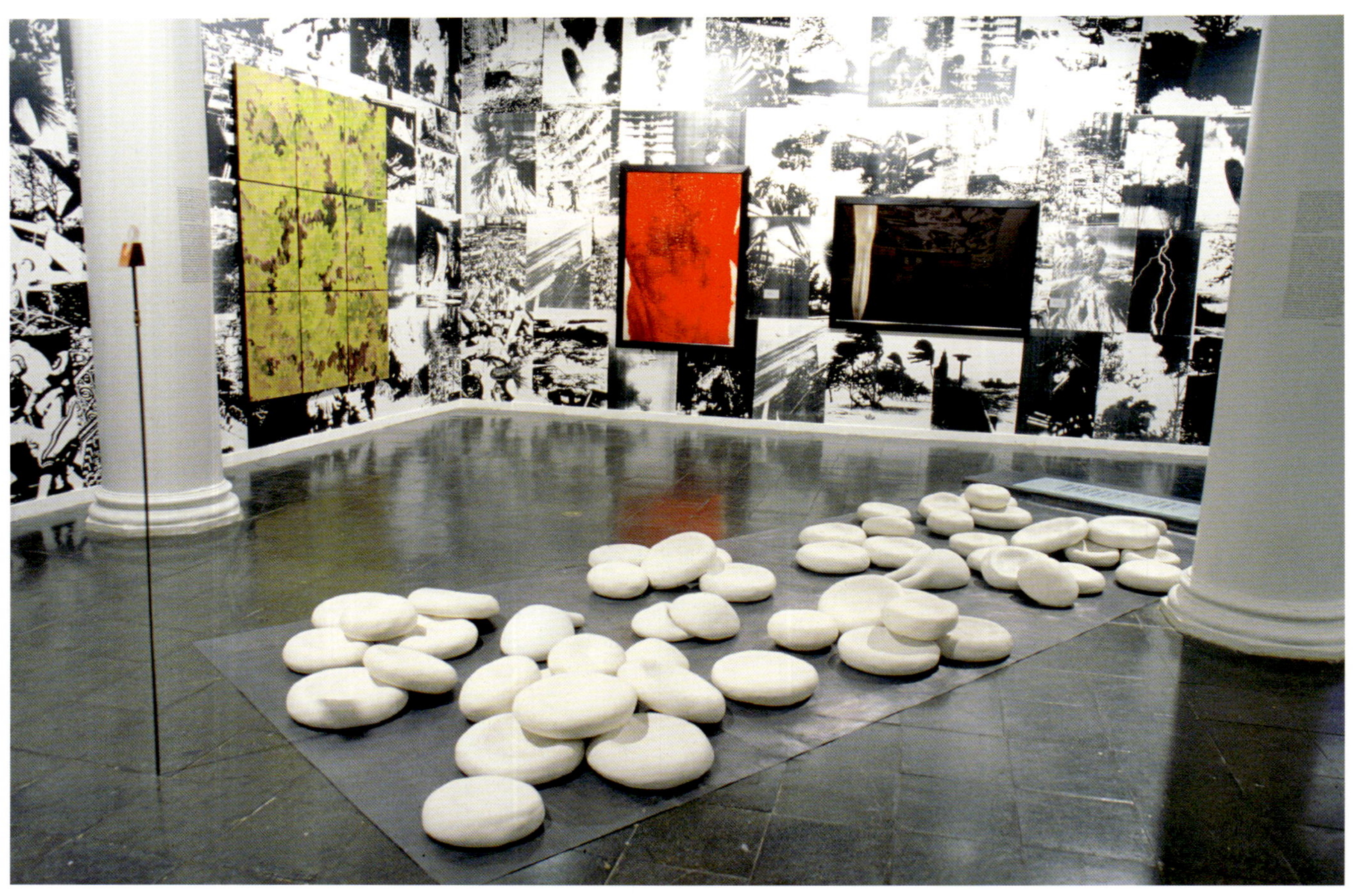

Works by Orshi Drozdik,
Andres Serrano, and
Carter Hodgkin

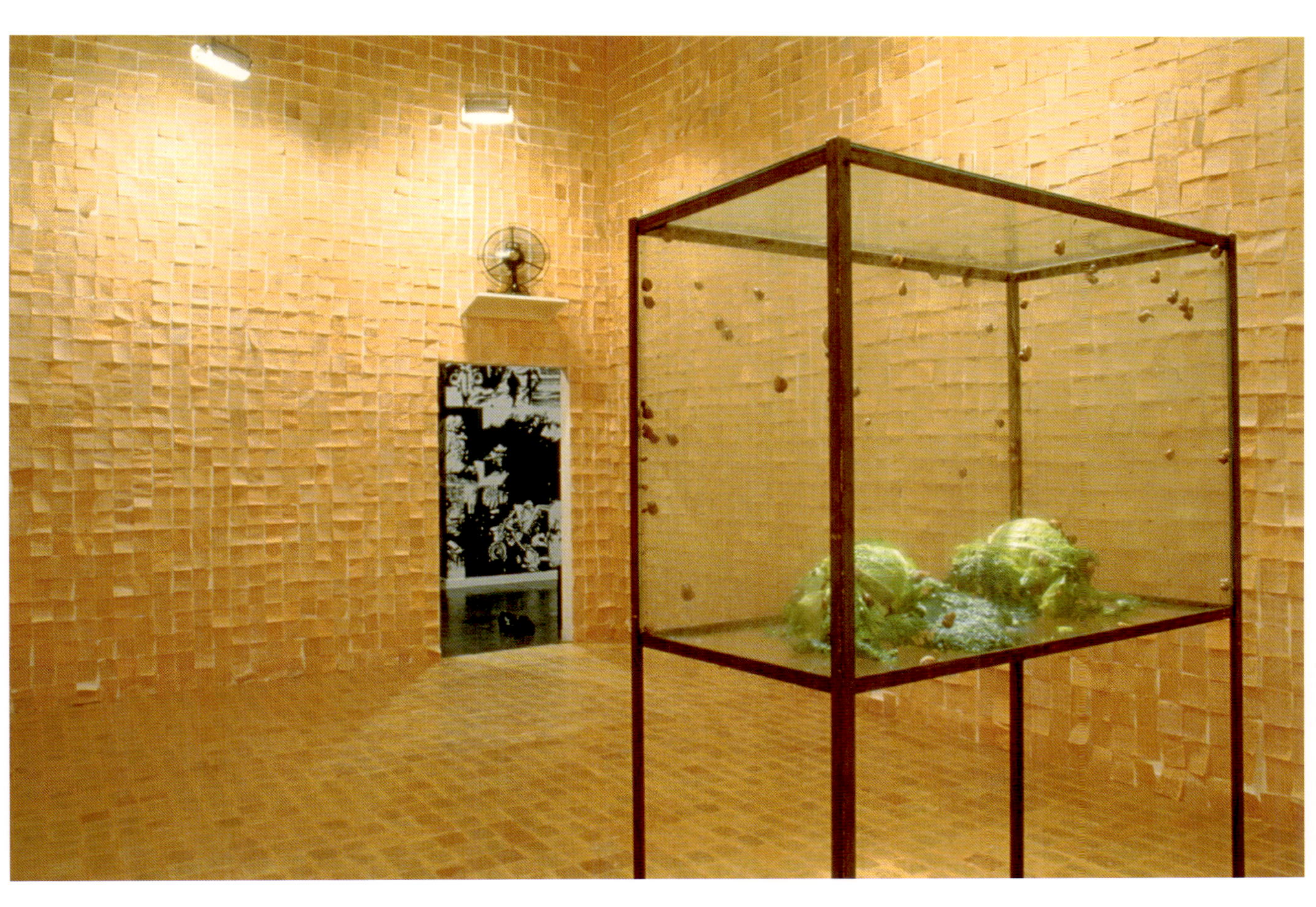

Ann Hamilton and Kathryn
Clark, *palimpsest*, 1989

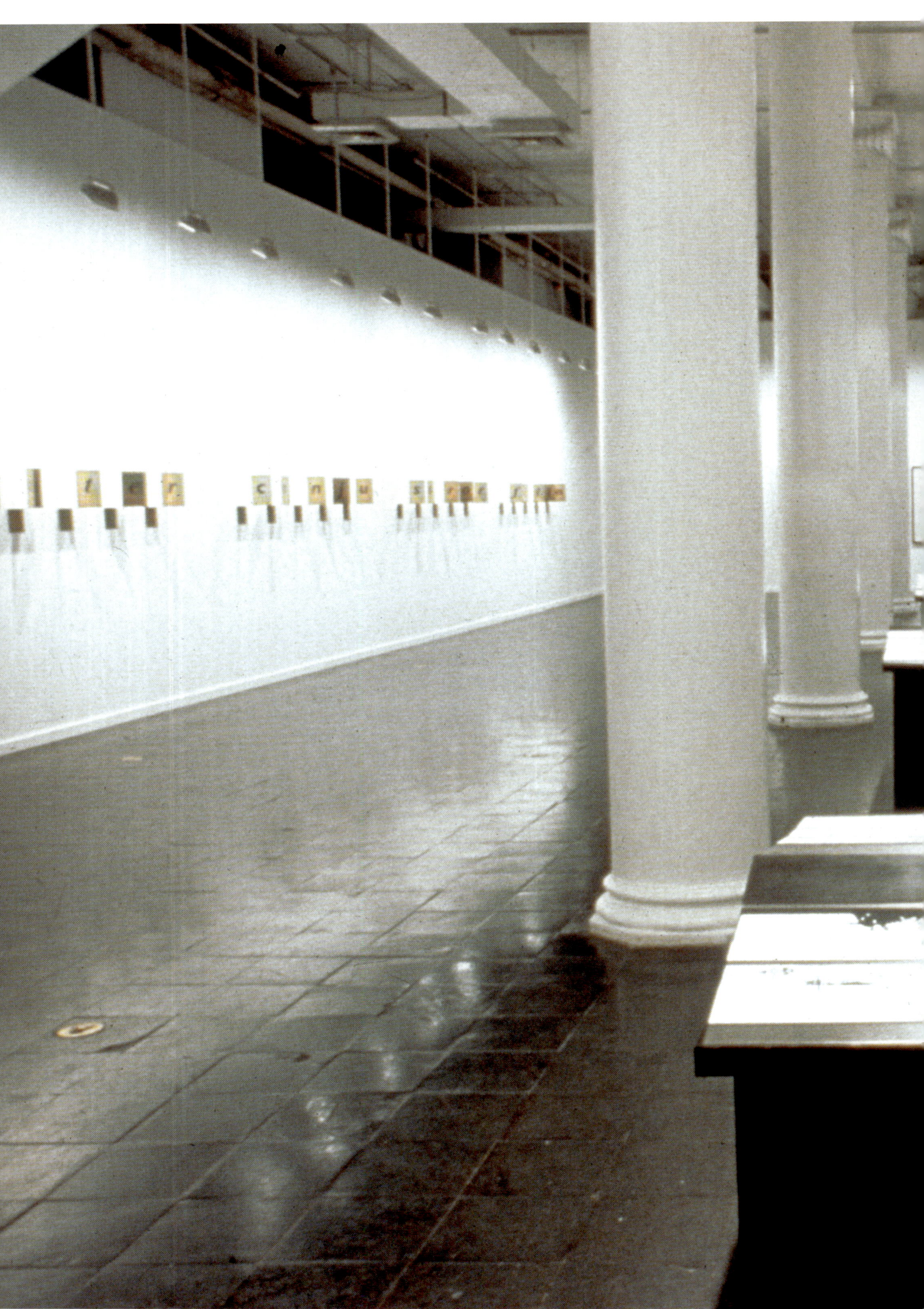

Installation view

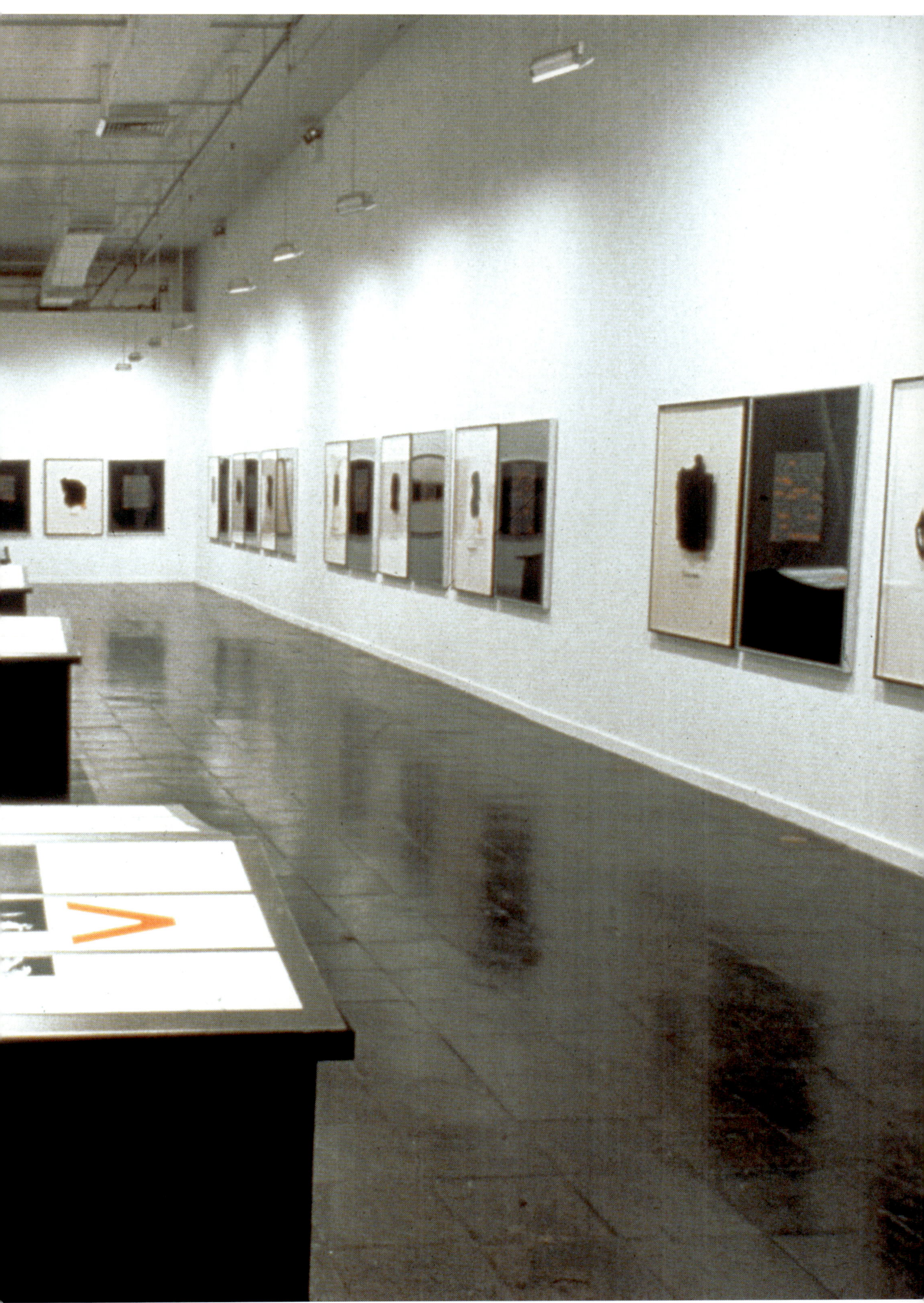

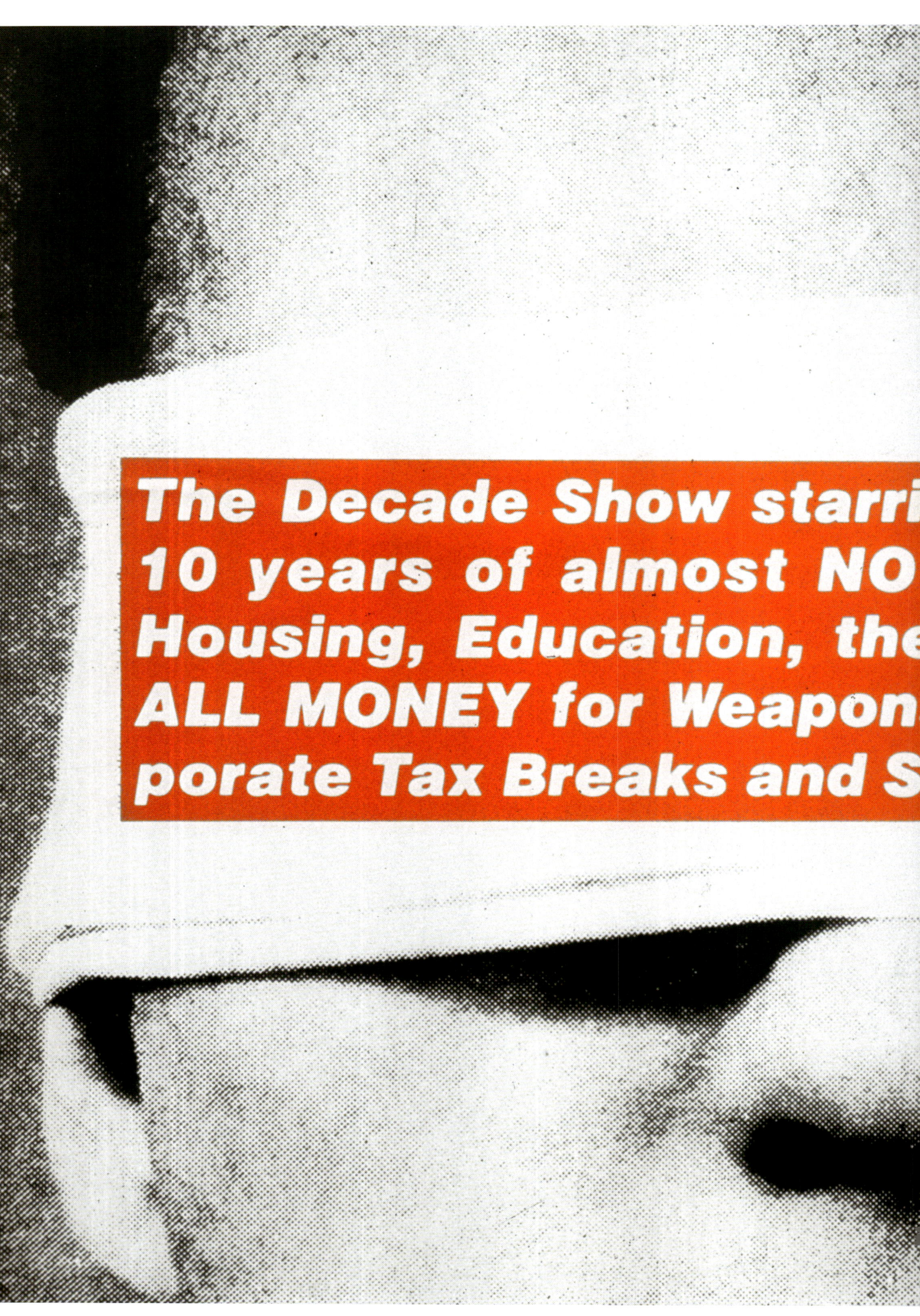

Barbara Kruger,
Untitled, 1990

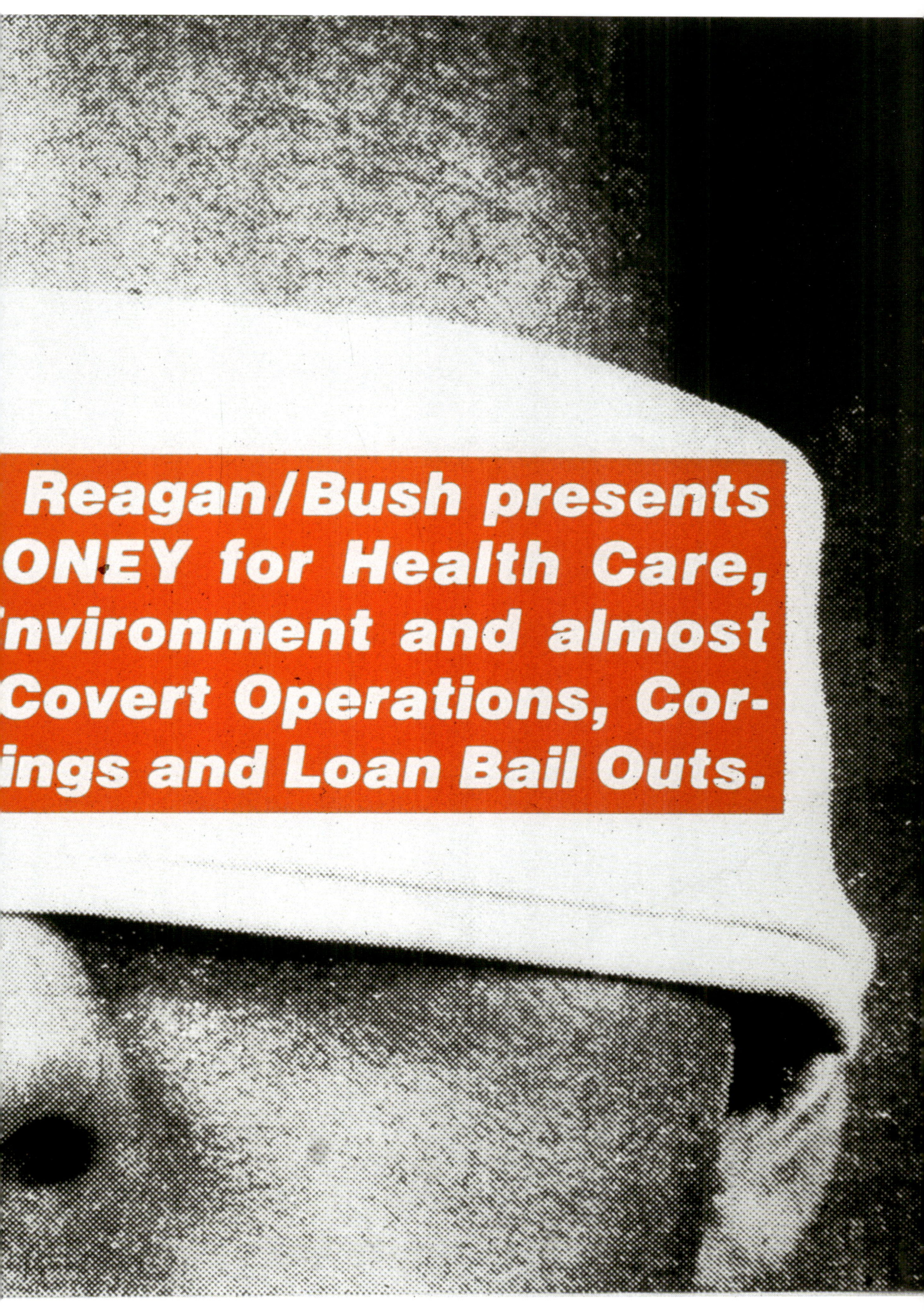

Reagan/Bush presents
ONEY for Health Care,
nvironment and almost
Covert Operations, Cor-
ings and Loan Bail Outs.

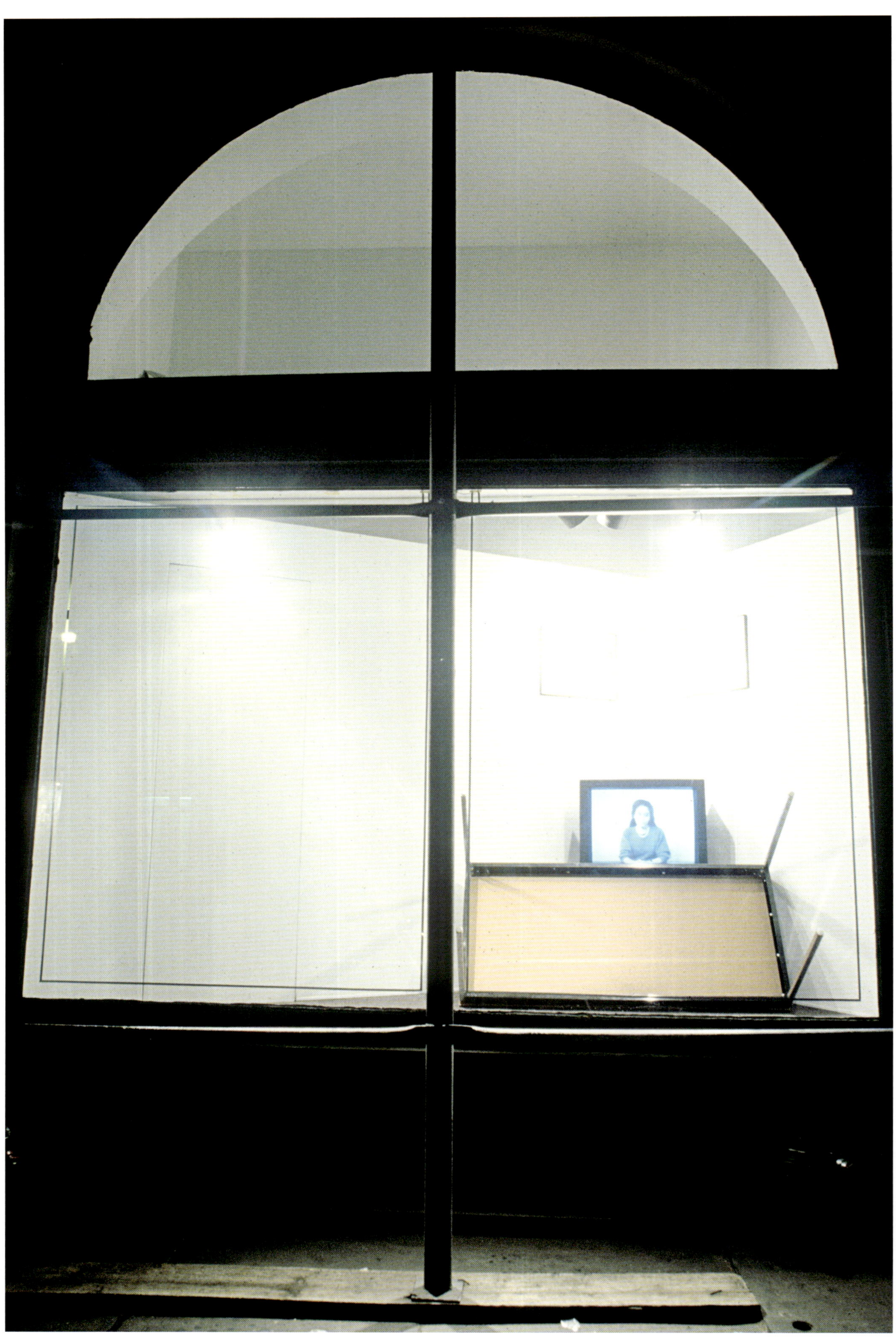

Adrian Piper,
Cornered, 1988

Alternative Geographies:
Art in New York and Beyond

Ned Rifkin

In November 1979, the Museum of Modern Art celebrated its fiftieth anniversary. Launched in temporary quarters with the unprecedented mission of presenting modern art and announcing only limited collecting plans, MoMA had become a New York landmark and an international cultural powerhouse with unparalleled holdings. That same month, a two-year-old, fledgling arts organization bluntly yet boldly calling itself the New Museum was presenting an exhibition titled "Dimensions Variable." The show included stylistically diverse works by seven relatively unknown artists from a variety of locations— artists, as described in the Museum's press release,

> whose aim is not the traditional making of art objects per se; their pieces become means rather than products which vary and/or cannot be physically bound. The artists…seek to explore the ephemeral, elusive, and undefinable by creating and utilizing specific substances and objects with little or no "art" identity…. In so doing the artists achieve phenomena not commonly visible in art and are able to express observations and ideas that resist verbalization—these means challenge the viewer to "see" what is not physically there.[1]

The founder of the New Museum, Marcia Tucker, had worked briefly as an assistant to MoMA's legendary first director, Alfred H. Barr, Jr., (she later catalogued his personal art collection) before being appointed as a curator at the Whitney Museum of American Art, where she developed a reputation as a fearless advocate of contemporary art. Marcia and fellow Whitney curator

---

1. New Museum, "Dimensions Variable," press release, 1979, https://archive.newmuseum.org/print-ephemera/7991. The exhibition was curated by Susan Logan, Allan Schwartzman, and Kathleen Thomas.

James Monte organized the exhibition "Anti-Illusion: Procedures/Materials" (1969), which included among its twenty-two artists the sculptors Carl Andre, Lynda Benglis, and Eva Hesse; painter Robert Ryman; filmmaker Michael Snow; and composer Philip Glass, all of whom would go on to be recognized as major creative figures of their day. In 1972, Marcia and Jane Livingston of the Los Angeles County Museum of Art organized the groundbreaking solo exhibition of Bruce Nauman, who would become one of the most influential visual artists of his generation. Many of the exhibitions Marcia curated were widely regarded as controversial but were respected and admired among

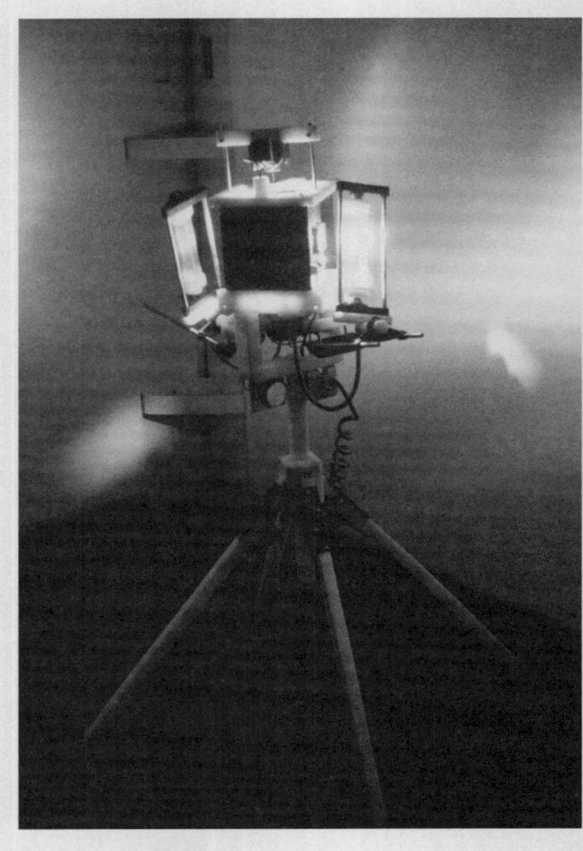

artists. In 1975, she organized the first museum exhibition devoted to the work of Richard Tuttle, a trailblazer of Post-Minimalism. The Tuttle show was widely panned by critics. Soon after this, the Whitney fired her.[2]

Rather than seek a curatorial position at another established art museum, Marcia reasoned that since other major American cities (Boston, Chicago, and Cincinnati) already had institutions exclusively devoted to the work of living artists, it was time for New York, considered the international capital of contemporary art, to have a forum for new art, ideas, and discussion. After consulting a number of close friends and devoted patrons who had been her supporters and advocates when she worked at the Whitney, she founded the New Museum at the beginning of January 1977 with a handful of young interns and associates recruited from her former department. They subsequently rented a small office at 105 Hudson Street in Tribeca and went to work organizing their inaugural exhibition, "Memory" (1977), a show of work by eight little-known artists that was presented in a borrowed space and accompanied by a modest publication of interviews with the participating artists along with the artists' statements.[3]

From the outset, the New Museum was an insistently probative organization, committed to providing a vital forum for contemporary art in its broadest definition and to opening up the contemporary art conversation to artists who typically were marginalized by virtue of their race or gender and were largely overlooked by the prevailing curatorial tastemakers at major art museums in New York. Also among those who rarely received attention were emerging artists living in New York who had not yet shown their work at a commercial gallery. This was directly addressed in the Museum's second exhibition, "New Work / New York" (1977), which included five artists, about whom Marcia wrote:

> They, and their work, remain anachronistic and idiosyncratic to the extent that neither can be polarized. This is evident in the fact that none of these artists belongs to a "school," that the work cannot be analyzed or understood in terms of a prevalent esthetic, and that each work appears as highly individualistic and resistant to interpretation.[4]

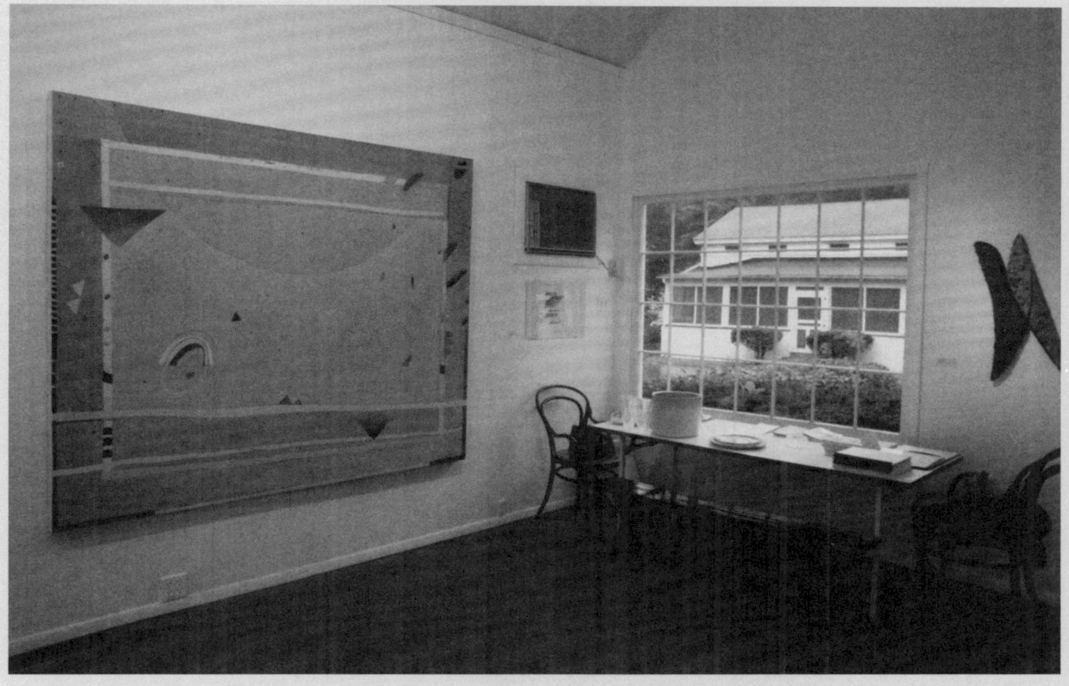

2.   There are differing accounts of Marcia Tucker's firing. She shared with me that it was over the Richard Tuttle exhibition. However, others who were present at the Whitney at that time maintain that a conflict of temperament with then-Director and other colleagues was the primary reason for her dismissal.

3.   Curated by Marcia Tucker, "Memory" was presented at C Space, located at 81 Leonard Street in Tribeca, and featured work by Sarah Canright, Brenda Goodman, Steve Gwon, Kent Hines, Ronald Morosan, Earl Ripling, Martin Silverman, and Katherine Sokolnikoff.

4.   Marcia Tucker, "New Work / New York," in *New Work / New York* (New York: New Museum, 1977), n.p., https://archive.newmuseum.org/print-ephemera/6413. The show was presented at the Gallery of July and August, in Woodstock, NY, and included work by Don Dudley, Edward C. Flood, Claudia Schwalb, D. Jack Solomon, and Marianne Stikas.

This became the model for four subsequent "New Work" group shows in 1978, 1979, 1982, and 1984.[5] For these and other exhibitions, Marcia and her staff would frequently ask better-known and more established artists to suggest compelling candidates—"artists' artists"—for studio visits.

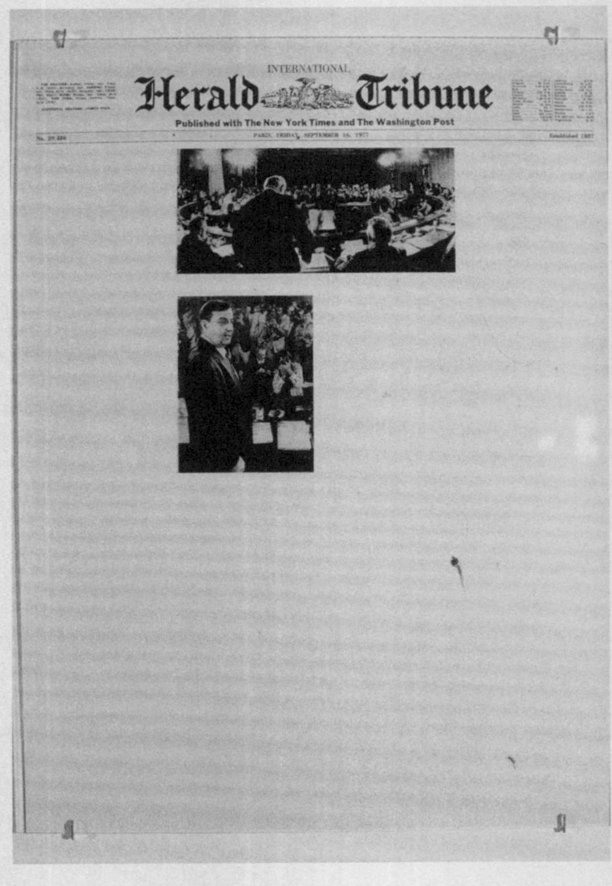

Still, it was the thematic or "idea" exhibition that became the young organization's calling card. Brandishing provocative titles—"'Bad' Painting" (1978); "In a Pictorial Framework" (1979), which was a show of installations; "The Art of Memory / The Loss of History" (1985); "Choices: Making an Art of Everyday Life" (1986); and, later, "Bad Girls" (1994)—these exhibitions were premised on identifying previously undetected affinities among selected artists that could, in turn, redirect and enlarge the current thinking of other artists, curators, critics, and even progressive collectors.

By the time I arrived as a curator in the fall of 1980, the Museum was already known as a dynamic alternative exhibition space, really a modest Kunsthalle. During those early years, Marcia effectively served as the chief curator in addition to shouldering her directorial responsibilities. Staff curators had an esprit de corps that was rare at other venues, with the exception of bona fide alternative spaces like Artists Space, Franklin Furnace, the Kitchen, and White Columns, all founded in the 1970s and located in lower Manhattan. The Museum's staff shared one small office, making a simple telephone call something of a feat. Despite the modest pay and compressed working conditions, we curators saw ourselves not only as visual art "talent scouts," but also as rigorous examiners of alternative aesthetics—the ephemeral, the temporal, and the performative, in addition to the environmental, the unconventional, the social and political, and the iconoclastic—and as contemporary art historians who were writing the initial essays about this work in a manner that would provide context for and intelligible access to what had heretofore not been approbated. Our commitment was to discover how and why artists were probing new ideas and investigating issues and approaches that were well beyond the mainstream of contemporary art.

Even as it scoured the New York art world, the New Museum quickly developed an outstanding reputation for paying attention to artists in far-flung areas of the country who had not exhibited their work in New York. In the fall of 1978, the exhibition "Outside New York" was presented at the Museum, which was by then located in a former study area in the Albert and Vera List Graduate Center Building of the New School for Social Research at 65 Fifth Avenue. The artists selected by curators Susan Logan, Allan Schwartzman, Kathleen Thomas, and Marcia Tucker were Katharine T. Carter and Alexa Kleinbard, based in Florida; Tom Hatch and Janis Provisor, based in San Francisco; and James R. Hill and Dan Rizzie, based in Texas.[6]

Another facet of the Museum's exhibition program involved examining the little-known earlier work of artists who had become widely admired and were enjoying gallery exposure and success in New York. This was the curatorial premise of "Early Work by Five Contemporary Artists: Ron Gorchov, Elizabeth Murray, Dennis Oppenheim, Dorothea Rockburne, Joel Shapiro" (1977). The approach provided important insights into contemporary art–making as a process of investigation and experimentation. A second "Early Work" exhibition followed in 1982 and featured Lynda Benglis, Joan Brown, Luis Jiménez, Gary Stephan, and Lawrence Weiner.[7]

One of the most important exhibition categories to fulfill the Museum's mission was that of the group or individual

5. The last of these exhibitions, curated by Lynn Gumpert and me, was "New Work: New York/Outside New York" (1984), which expanded the roster of artists beyond the New York metropolitan area.

6. "Outside New York" became the first of another series dedicated to emerging artists working beyond the New York metropolitan area. The Museum presented "Outside New York: The State of Ohio" in 1980 and "Outside New York: Seattle" in 1983.

7. The 1977 "Early Work" exhibition was organized by Susan Logan, Allan Schwartzman, and Marcia Tucker. The curators of the 1982 edition were Lynn Gumpert, Marcia, and me.

show dedicated to examining aspects of significant mature artists' oeuvres that had been overlooked or entirely ignored. In its third year, the Museum presented an exhibition of works by Gaylen C. Hansen, Claire Moore, and Salvatore Scarpitta under the elegantly crisp title "Sustained Visions."[8] Shows of work by individual artists in this category included a retrospective of the late Chicago-based artist Ree Morton (1980), a midcareer survey of crucial conceptual and narrative work by the Los Angeles artist John Baldessari (1981), and an exhibition of work by the painter of highly charged political scenes Leon Golub (1984), which traveled to museums in La Jolla, Chicago, Montreal, and Washington, DC.

With its move to the New School in 1977, the Museum had acquired access to a ground-floor display window on Fourteenth Street, just east of Fifth Avenue. Beginning in late 1979, artists were invited to create site-specific, ephemeral installations in the window that would supplement the exhibitions housed in the very limited gallery space. The "Window" series was launched by the artist Mary Lemley; during the following year, then-little-known artists John Ahearn, David Hammons, Jeff Koons, and Richard Prince each took a turn at displaying work in the window. With the Museum's relocation to SoHo in 1983, two windows—one adjacent to the Broadway entrance and a second in the Museum's Mercer Street facade—offered artists the opportunity to directly engage the public.

(bottom) "Sustained Visions," 1979. Left to right: Works by Gaylen C. Hansen and Salvatore Scarpitta

(right) "Outside New York," 1978. Works by Alexa Kleinbard

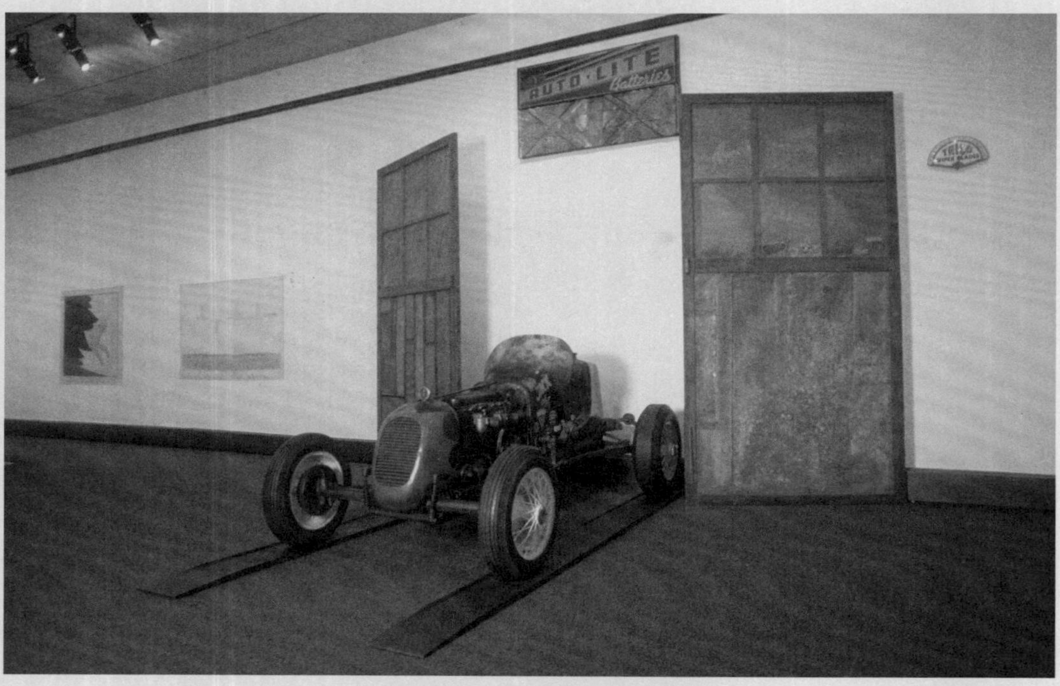

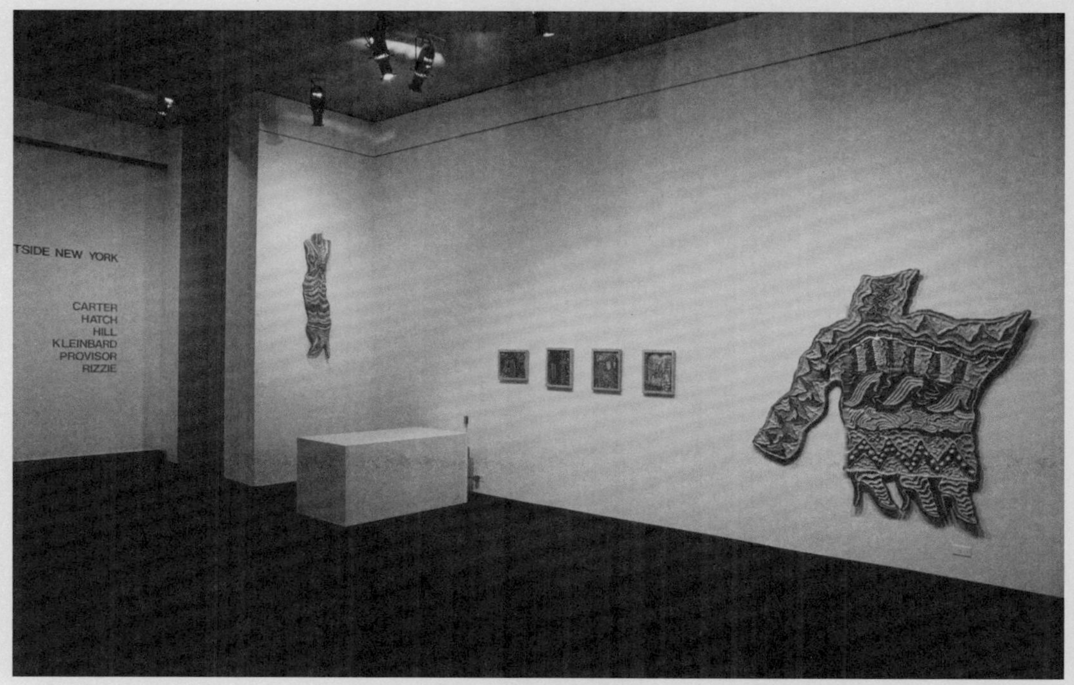

Certainly, the culmination of my tenure at the New Museum (first as Curator and then as Assistant Director) followed upon Marcia's appointment as the Commissioner for the US pavilion at the 1984 Venice Biennale. Bucking the precedent of showcasing individual artists in the pavilion, Marcia, Lynn Gumpert, and I organized the exhibition "Paradise Lost/Paradise Regained: American Visions of the New Decade." We chose two paintings by each of twenty-four contemporary American artists. At that time, the best-known figures on the roster were the New York–based artists Richard Bosman, Louisa Chase, Eric Fischl, Jedd Garet, April Gornik, and David True. But in keeping with the Museum's decentralized vision of contemporary art, fifteen of the twenty-four did not live in New York City—among them Roger Brown, the Reverend Howard Finster, Charles Garabedian, and Judith Linhares. Although the exhibition was largely reviewed unfavorably by American art critics, "Paradise Lost/Paradise Regained" became one of the most highly attended shows at that year's Biennale.

In some ways, the experience of the Venice Biennale led to Lynn's exhibition "A Distanced View: One Aspect of Recent Art from Belgium, France, Germany, and Holland" (1986), the Museum's first foray into presenting contemporary European art. Katharina Fritsch and Jan Vercruysse were among the thirteen young artists selected. From that time

8.   "Sustained Visions" was curated by Susan Logan and Kathleen Thomas.

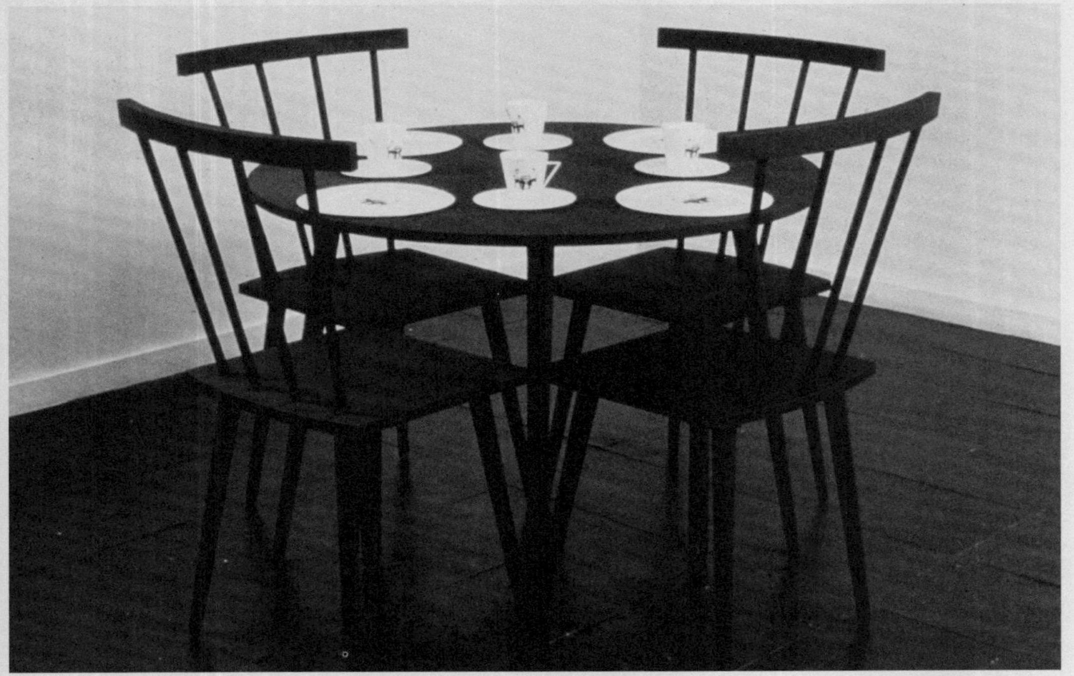

on, the Museum has tracked and exhibited new art within an ever-expanding geographic range.

Since 1999, with the passing of leadership from founding Director Marcia Tucker to Lisa Phillips, then a well-known and highly respected curator at the Whitney, the New Museum has continued to enlarge upon the radical disposition of what a contemporary art museum can and should be. This audacious legacy can be traced to the guiding principles established during the Museum's infancy. When an art organization has thrived and prospered over four decades, when it has grown from an aspirational "alternative" into a globally admired and respected institution, then the succession of administrators, curators, and trustees can only be seen as an enormous success for art and artists worldwide. The persistence and constancy with which the Museum has heralded significant artists working outside of conventional parameters serve to remind those of us interested in such things that we must always consider what we are not seeing when we evaluate what is assumed to be the art of our time.

Ned Rifkin was Curator and Assistant Director at the New Museum from 1980 to 1984. His subsequent appointments include Director, the High Museum of Art, Atlanta (1991–2000); Director, the Menil Collection and Foundation, Houston (2000–02); Director, the Hirshhorn Museum and Sculpture Garden, Washington, DC (2003–05); Under Secretary of Art, the Smithsonian Institution, Washington, DC (2004–08); and Director, the Blanton Museum of Art, the University of Texas at Austin (2009–10). He currently teaches cinema studies at the State University of New York at Purchase.

Early Years of the New Museum:
An Intellectual Reminiscence or Pieces from a Consciousness

Lynne Tillman

If I were writing a history of the New Museum, and I'm not, the first sentences would include Marcia Tucker's name. Tucker was the unique, essential element, the sine qua non, of its birth and existence. Her vision for a new museum evolved during a time when the institution of the museum was undergoing serious criticism. Did it shape art and how we see it? How do politics, of all kinds, inflect canon-building; how do important galleries and collectors affect museum collections and exhibitions? Who is excluded?

Not surprisingly, this investigation occurred in the same long breath that many American institutions underwent rigorous scrutiny. From the 1950s on, in America's postwar decades, the denial of almost any right, and any minority its rights, the denial of any group's inclusion, was fought. Exuberance and optimism after winning the war in Europe, whose emphasis was freedom and democracy, turned into disillusionment at home. A clamorous, human surge for justice, for civil and human rights, resulted, convulsing and transforming American society and culture.

Since World War II, civil and cultural wars have been constant. And inclusion has been central to them. Inclusion in a museum, also.

I'm not sure when I first visited the New Museum in SoHo. I'm not sure which show I first saw. What I remember striking me, first, was its large picture window onto Broadway. The Museum seemed instantly less grand and more like a place to drop by and browse, like a retail store. That may not be a great way to describe a museum, but window-shopping has its glories, as Walter Benjamin wrote. The Museum's designers made the space feel familiar, and approachable, which encouraged me. Over the years, the picture window was used differently by artists and groups. Anyone on the street might get a sense of what was happening in the Museum, and also catch a glimpse of contemporary art and its conversations. The New Museum became one of "my museums," just as St. Mark's Bookshop in the East Village was one of "my bookstores." Some of the museum guards were there for years, and we always said hello and talked, and that made it homey.

History/histories are made by individuals inside larger historical movements, and written about by individuals. Marcia Tucker acted as an individual, and she also acted in concert with others who supported her goals and recognized the same inequities and discriminations. They sought inclusion for "underserved" artists. So, the New Museum was both an effect of and an agent of change in the politics of representation.
     The New Museum staked a claim in the "new." The adjective may even be definitive, since its mandate would be to present new art, to address the contempo- rary quickly. But presenting the contemporary could mean that what was exhibited might be only of "tempo- rary" interest, something most museums avoided. The Museum took risks.

My two intelligent, creative, and unusual older sisters, considerably older when we were all younger, schooled my feminism. I called myself a feminist when I was eight. My mother was not quite a good-enough mother, but I didn't doubt her intelligence. So I never bought the canards—women weren't as smart as men—never bought the vague and explicit dismissals of a class called women. I knew they were wrong, but the prejudices affected me, first, psychologically. Sexual prejudice affects the ways that my writing, say, is received or read: "written by a woman." Or, by a gay writer, black artist, woman artist, black woman artist, black male writer, et al. An adjective works to limit the noun, which belongs to "the majority," and little headway has been made to break this down. In my book, I am a writer, first. Qualifiers follow.

The impact and import of feminism, sexuality, and gender on and for artists and art-making were urgent to New

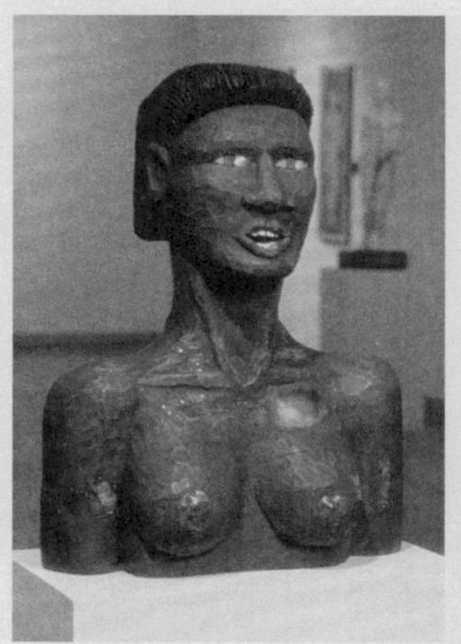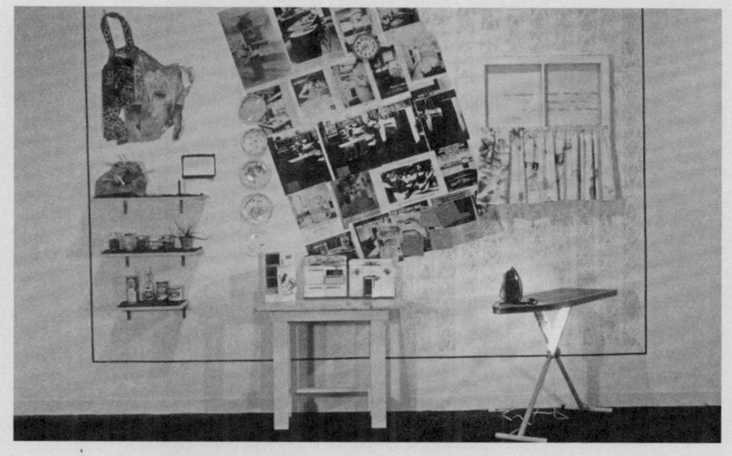

Museum founder Marcia Tucker. Mounting exhibitions under those categories and their vicissitudes, the Museum would distinguish itself with its thematic shows—"Classified: Big Pages from the Heresies Collective" (1983), "Difference: On Representation and Sexuality" (1984), "HOMO VIDEO: Where We Are Now" (1986), "Girls Night Out (Femininity as Masquerade)" (1988), "Bad Girls" (1994), "Picturing the Modern Amazon" (2000)—and major solo shows by Carolee Schneemann, Mary Kelly, Rosemarie Trockel, Ana Mendieta, and David Wojnarowicz, among others.[1]

By the mid- to late 1970s, the discourse around so-called feminist art was divided, roughly, between two addresses: essentialism versus anti-essentialism, which included the Great Mother, Goddess, or spiritual feminism, and the theoretical and/or politics of representation feminism. Within these divisions, another: pro-sex and anti-pornography feminists. The New Museum played a role in exhibiting or staging their differences.

Again, roughly, the exhibitions "Girls Night Out (Femininity as Masquerade)" and "Difference: On Representation and Sexuality" represented work that was feminist in intention, might obliquely refer to "women," used appropriated or mediated images, and engaged with other art forms, for example, conceptualism. The art recognized non-essentialist differences between men and women, proposing theoretical, especially psycho-analytical and deconstructive, approaches to imaging women, to gender generally.

1.   I chose to cite only a few names of curators, artists, participants on panels, and writers in catalogues. I have mentioned some group and solo shows from the New Museum's earlier years to indicate its program's direction and engagement with feminism, sexuality, and gender. I have had to leave out many more names than I could cite. So I'm erring on the other side, and I urge intrigued readers to use a search engine.

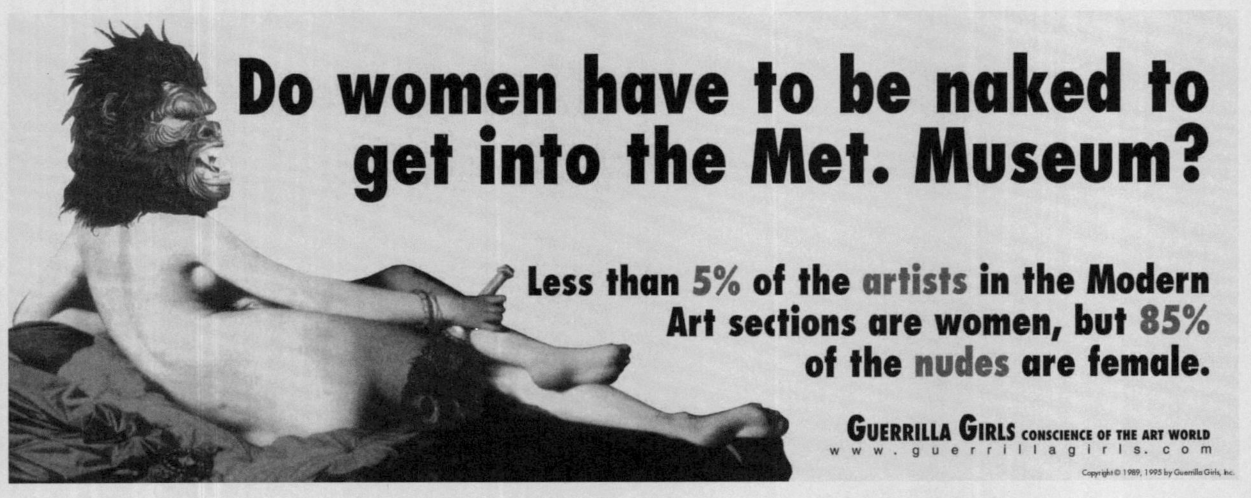

The "Bad Girls" and "Picturing the Modern Amazon" exhibitions displayed art with a focus on the body, often actual bodies, and physically powerful female ones; some of the art encouraged a contemporary identification with prehistorical and mythical female figures and imagery. "Bad Girls" did not necessarily show work made by declared feminists, because, as Marcia Tucker wrote, and I paraphrase, there wasn't agreement as to what that meant. The art was in your face, sometimes tongue-in-cheek, and allowed, Tucker suggested, the anarchic and comedic into those questions.[2]

The title "Bad Girls" was meant to embrace and, by doing so, defang a term of opprobrium. But a pejorative, even used "positively" about minorities, almost never depletes its sting. Instead, it can reinstate it.

The burden of slippery language is heavy, and any descriptions, my descriptions, of these arguments and exhibitions won't be definitive or adequate; instead, they serve as briefs for further elaboration. In writing a ten-page essay referring to "history" or "histories," brevity is a requirement, ironically, even when discussing the need for inclusion.

Framing the past for the present, without reducing its complexities, is fraught: all interpretations get shaded by the predilections of their authors. That is, the subjectivity of the language user. Words have associations and carry attitudes, and words connote more than they denote.

Memory is the single most unreliable narrator. You might remember a panel discussion differently from me, and who is right, if "right" is the right word? Can this be adjudicated? More, what will count in the historical record? I read versions of events I attended twenty years ago that I don't recognize. It's weird.

Looking back, as the New Museum asked me to do, I face another irony: many of the debates during the period were predicated as binaries, which reiterated a Western mind/body dualism that poststructuralist thinkers on "both sides" hoped to efface. Debates about pornography, pro and con; actual women versus mediated images; what was or wasn't feminist art: they were invigorating, intense, frustrating, confusing, and sometimes confused.

Still, one would not be discussing intersectionality (an ungainly new word that Virginia Woolf wouldn't entertain), wrestling with what hadn't been a dominant factor in those debates, if those earlier dialogues hadn't happened.

I was mostly a viewer/spectator at the New Museum, but my work was included in two exhibitions.

The feature film I wrote and codirected and coproduced with Sheila McLaughlin, *Committed* (1984), was among the films shown in the "Difference" exhibition. *Committed* was based on Frances Farmer's life (a 1930s movie star; a defiant, free-thinking woman; a Communist; an alcoholic, whose mother committed her to a mental institution). It wasn't a biography, but a narrative of "fact" and fiction, an imagined and interpretive work, treating historical conditions—attitudes toward mental health, defiant women, Communism, etc.—through the vector of a forgotten woman.

Committed is considered a feminist film, one of a wave of independent and artist films of the early 1970s into the mid-1990s, I'd ascertain, whose new narratives spoke to those who had been excluded, marginalized, or designated unimportant to history. Filmmakers tried, in various ways, to create cinematic treatments that would align with (form and content) "difference," about gender, sexual orientation, sexuality. People worked "against" the classic Hollywood film or used it differently, and Laura Mulvey's now familiar concept, "woman as object of the gaze," was seminal.

2.   Marcia Tucker, "Introduction and Acknowledgments," in *Bad Girls* (New York: New Museum; Cambridge, MA, and London: MIT Press, 1994), 4.

I wrote "Madame Realism's Imitation of Life" because
curator William Olander asked me to write a Madame
Realism story for the catalogue to his exhibition "Fake:
A Meditation on Authenticity" (1987).

My fictional character Madame Realism reports (thinks):

One of the women [at an opening, in the ladies' room]
said, "This isn't a good mirror," and Madame Realism
relaxed a little, the idea of a perfect mirror terrifying,
anyway, and besides she didn't like the way she
looked just then. Still, she thought, if there is no
inner life or self, and I'm not being conduited, this
physical presence, this facade, might be all one really
did have.[3]

The subtitle "Femininity as Masquerade" for "Girls
Night Out" drew on psychoanalytic theorist Joan Riviere's
1929 essay "Womanliness as Masquerade," whose
notions about a self as a pose, a presentation, gender as
performance, were of extreme importance to this story
and my thinking at the time.

Among the subjects in the various aesthetic and cultural
debates of the 1980s and 1990s, "authenticity" reared its
head. The idea, to some an ideal, confused many already
confusing issues, especially around identity politics.
It was a variation on essentialism.

The authenticity of an art object, in a sense its sincerity,
even that of its artist, was scrutinized: it became, and
still is, a difficult, critical subject. Fake or fakery is the
other side of authenticity; if one is not "authentic," whatever that is, if one's art is not, then one is fraudulent.
These are ongoing, persistent questions: Who has the
right to do or say this, to write or make art about this; who
can name themselves what; who has the right to speak,
and for whom?

Art historian and critic Craig Owens, who died of AIDS
in 1990, suggested that "we" do not speak for others but
to them.

An authentic self? Even a self… Identifications and
behaviors vary so much from people's supposed
"essences" and "roots." Whatever their origins, human
beings are generated by highly combustible fantasy

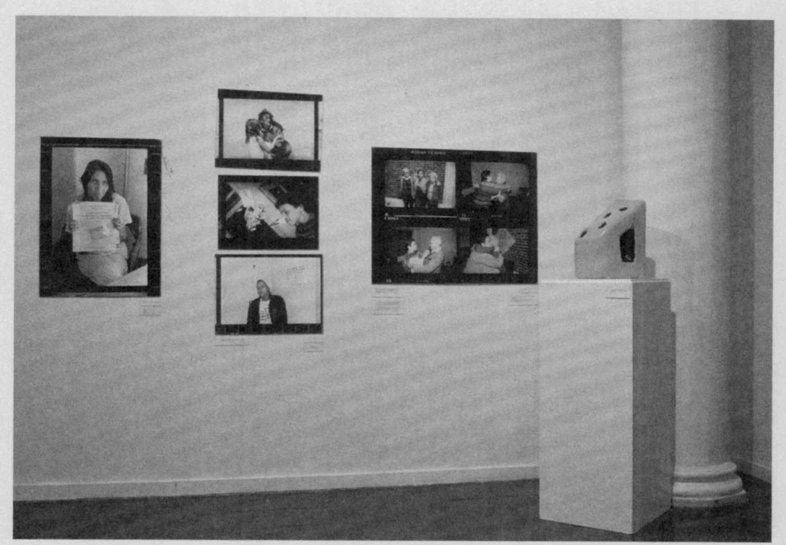

engines. (How else, in 2016, could a preponderance of white American women have voted for Donald Trump?)

I follow Kafka, who wrote, and I paraphrase: "My people, if I have one."

Andy Warhol wrote: "I don't know where the artificial stops and the real starts." Some or more of the world might consider Warhol a fake, inauthentic. I don't. For one, performing gender fits his succinct statement perfectly.

Installing the art of its time, the New Museum mounted exhibitions that were almost like exposés, foregrounding art that reflected on prejudices and stereotypes about women, races, ethnicities, nationalities, and sexual orientations. That was fundamental to its stake as a truly new institution. Its curatorial program demonstrated an institutional awareness that art can be a form of consciousness, of consciousness in process.

Some shows were better, more coherent than others. That was my sense of them, my experience. But even if I took exception to some, I usually appreciated the organizing principle, the curatorial project, because, for one thing, consciousness is always partial, which means that knowing what good art is, and how to install it, especially in its moment, can only be partial, too, in both senses of the word.

Mistakes. Wrong moves. How does learning occur? As a species, Homo sapiens's greatest faults: the wishes to appear faultless, to be right, and to win. Those wishes obscure doing wrong, being wrong. Most people hate being wrong, and won't admit it. Pointless arguments follow. (If nothing else, googling a question of fact—what year was that movie?—settles dinner table arguments fast.)

3. Lynne Tillman, "Madame Realism's Imitation of Life," in William Olander, *Fake: A Meditation on Authenticity* (New York: New Museum, 1987), 45–48; repr. in Lynne Tillman, *The Complete Madame Realism and Other Stories* (Los Angeles: Semiotext(e), 2016), 42–45.

The overarching tragedy of the 1980s into the mid-1990s was AIDS. The disease was a constant terrorism. New York City was mined with the disease.

Curator William Olander died of AIDS, and many, many artists, editors, writers, filmmakers, actors, directors, designers, and on and on. And an entire audience for art, dance, music, theater, and film was decimated, as writer Fran Lebowitz noted. Those who lived through those years will probably never forget how, one day, daily life changed into daily death.

The New Museum was like a first responder in art; there was an urgency to its exhibitions, such as "Let the Record Show…" (1987), "Until That Last Breath: Women With AIDS" (1989), and "Love for Sale… Free Condoms Inside" (1991). The ferociousness of the disease produced an extraordinary activist movement in which, for one thing, lesbians and gay men acted together, in common cause. A grave purpose effected greater solidarity, many members of various groups have reported over the years.

What does it take to bring about common cause, I often wonder. Only the fear of death?

Shifts and modulations in attitudes and positions have emerged by making, doing, thinking, unthinking, and by working through, that is, by working toward an understanding of motives, say, by compassion, through trial and error. There are always mistakes, often damaging ones.

Artists know how much they learn by accident and through mistakes. A museum does that, and presents their "mistakes," also.

When I walked into the lobby of the new New Museum on the Bowery, and entered a huge elevator, I had to adjust to a very different place, to its many floors, and much more space. It's taken me time to get used to it. But, fortunately, two of the guards were the same.

Lynne Tillman is a writer and critic. In 2017, she wrote the essay "Playing Both Sides" for the catalogue to the New Museum exhibition "Raymond Pettibon: A Pen of All Work." Her most recent books are the collection of stories *Someday This Will be Funny* (2011) and the essay collection *What Would Lynne Tillman Do?* (2014), a finalist for the National Book Critics Circle Award in Criticism. Her sixth novel, *Men and Apparitions*, will be published by Soft Skull Press in March 2018.

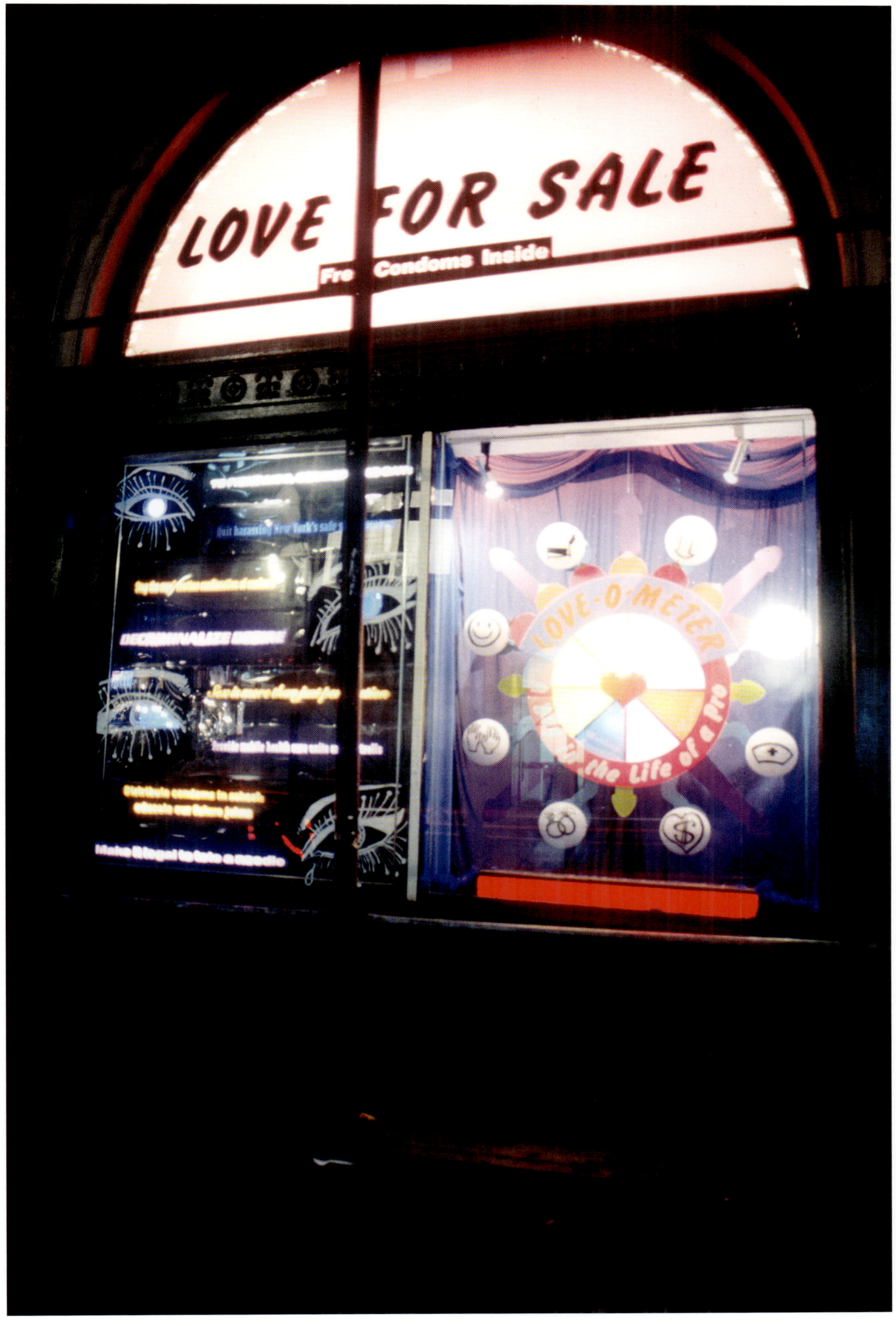
LOVE FOR SALE
Free Condoms Inside
LOVE·O·METER
the Life of a Pro

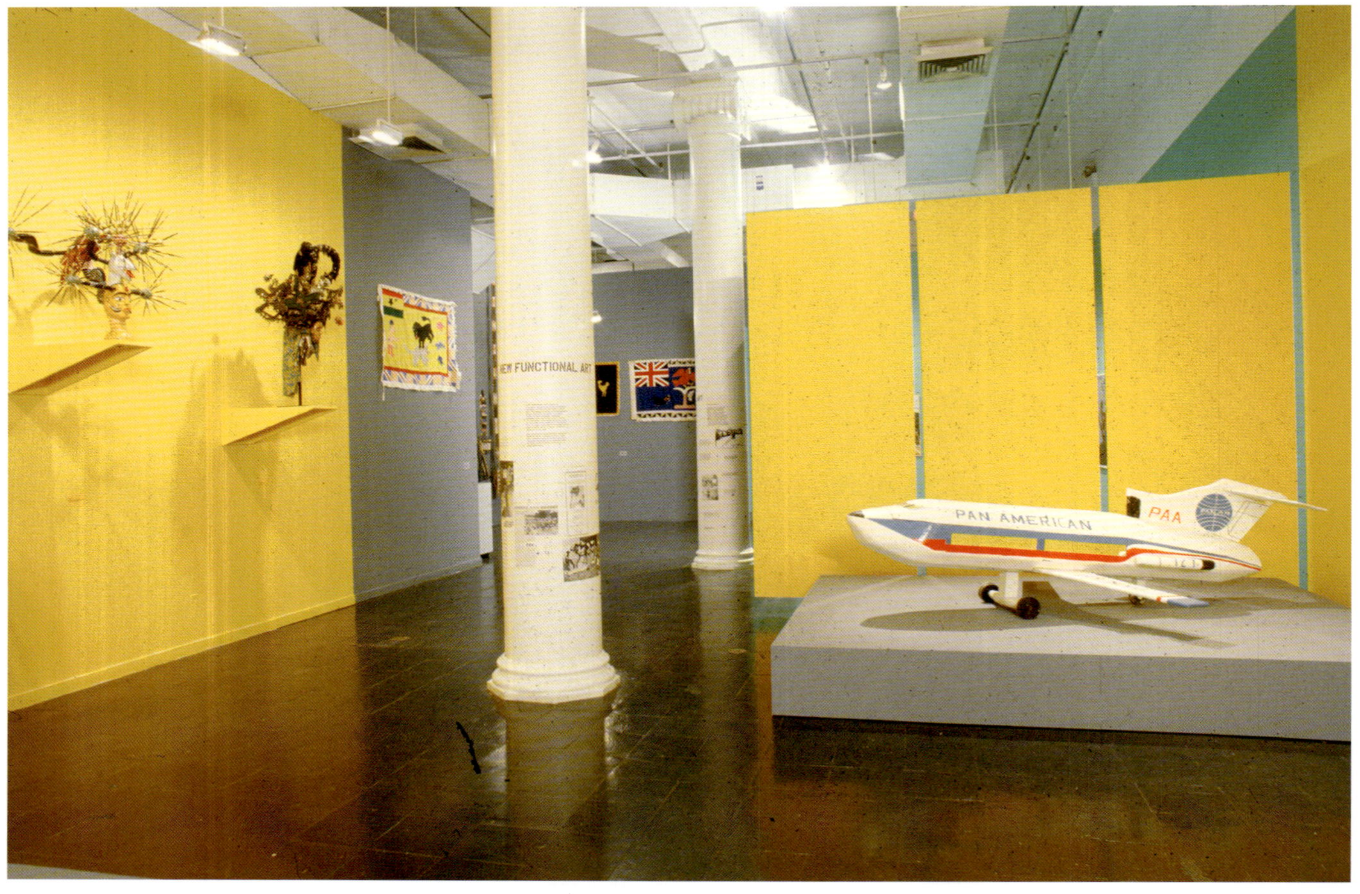

Installation view

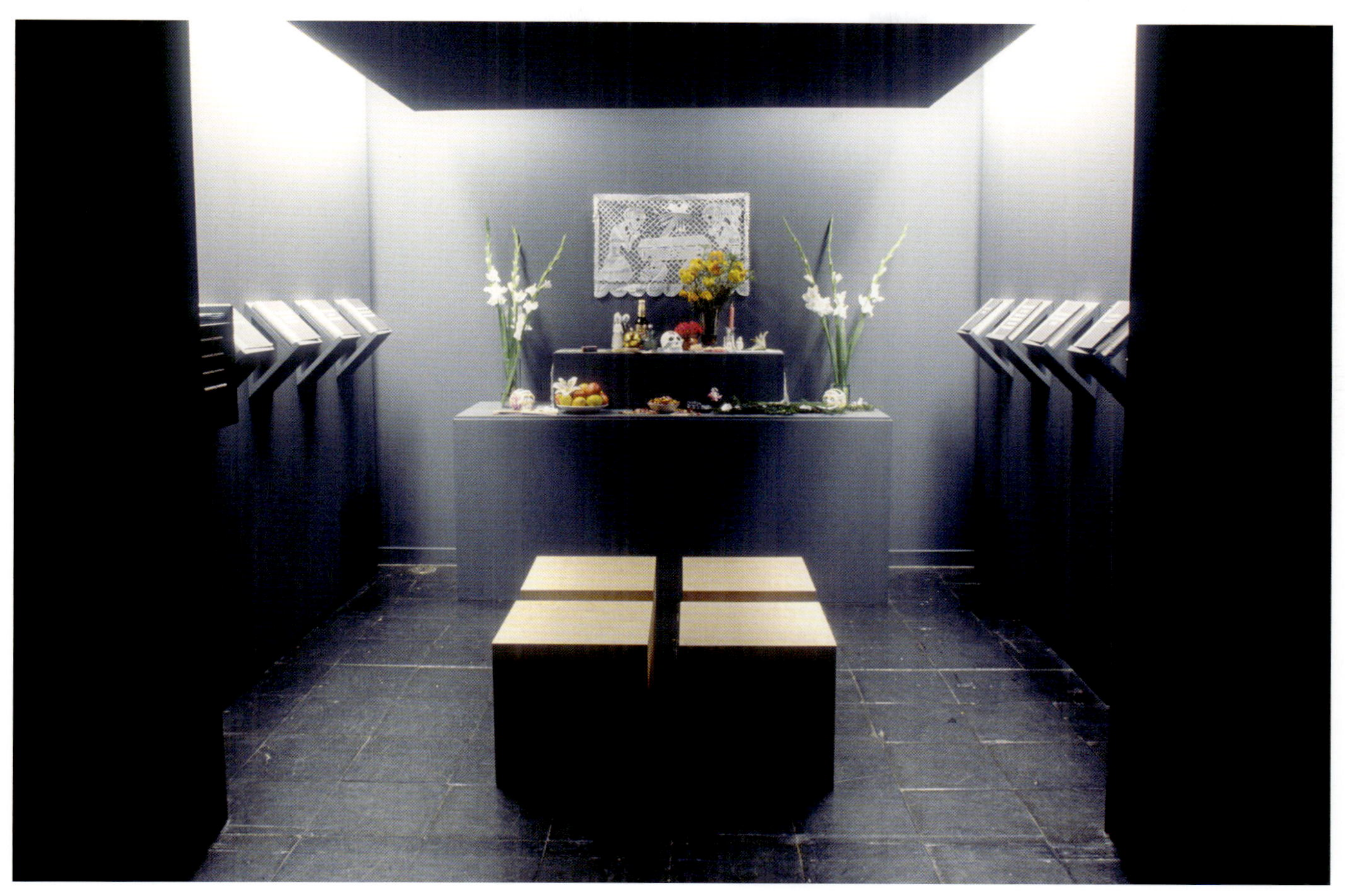

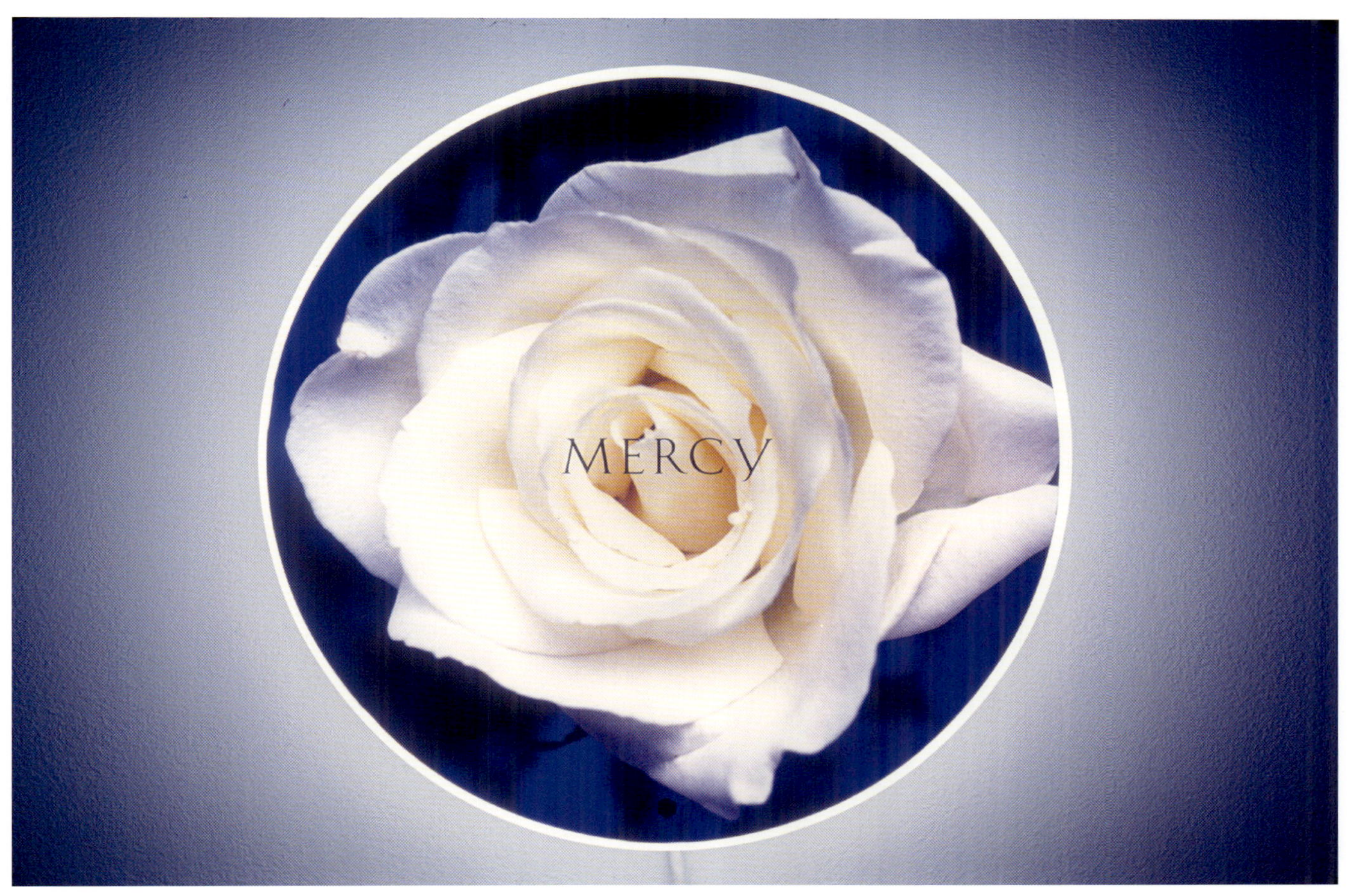

(top) Amalia Mesa-Bains,
The Living Altar, 1991

(bottom) Donald Moffett,
Mercy, 1991 (detail)

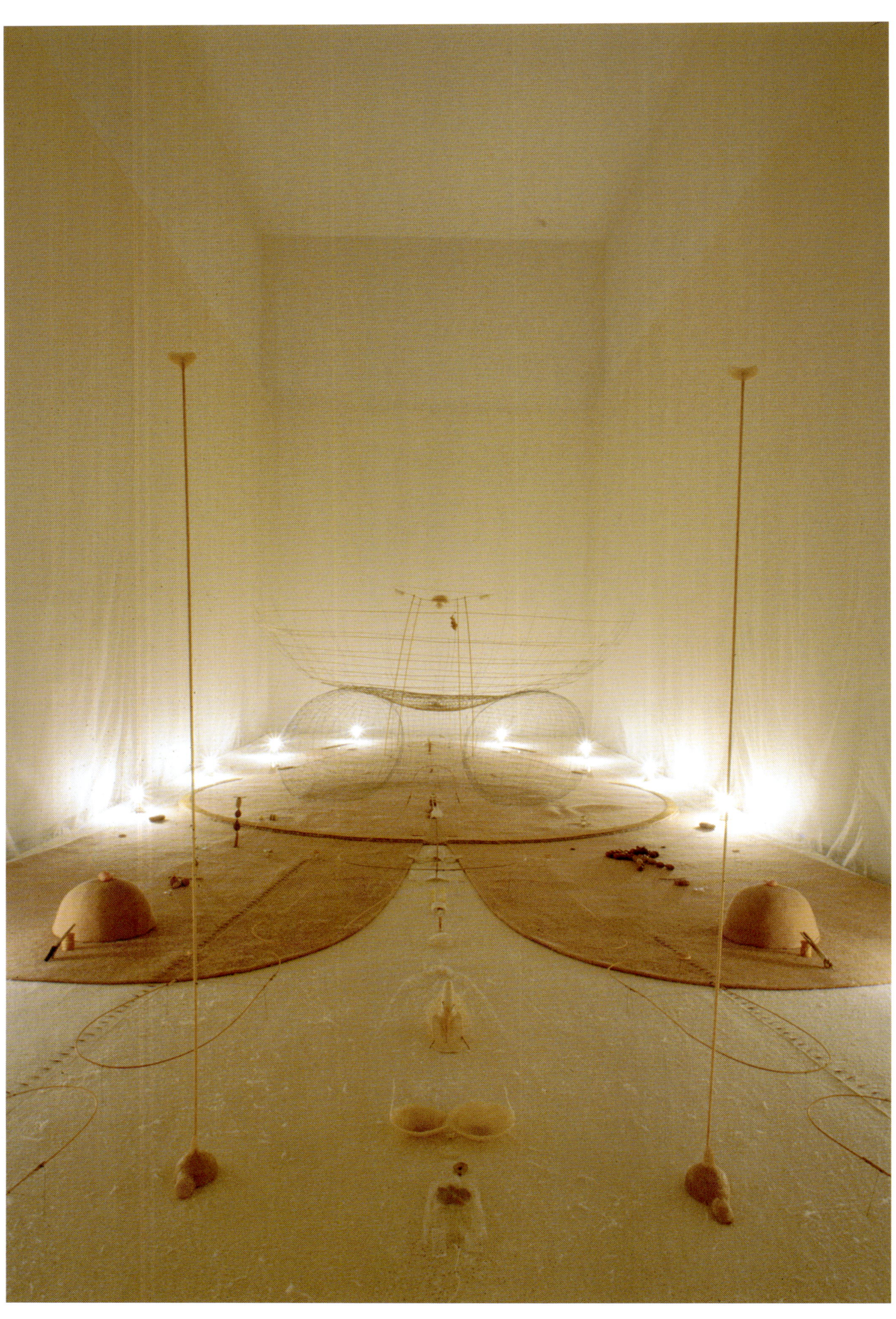

Rei Naito,
une place sur la Terre
[A Place on Earth], 1992

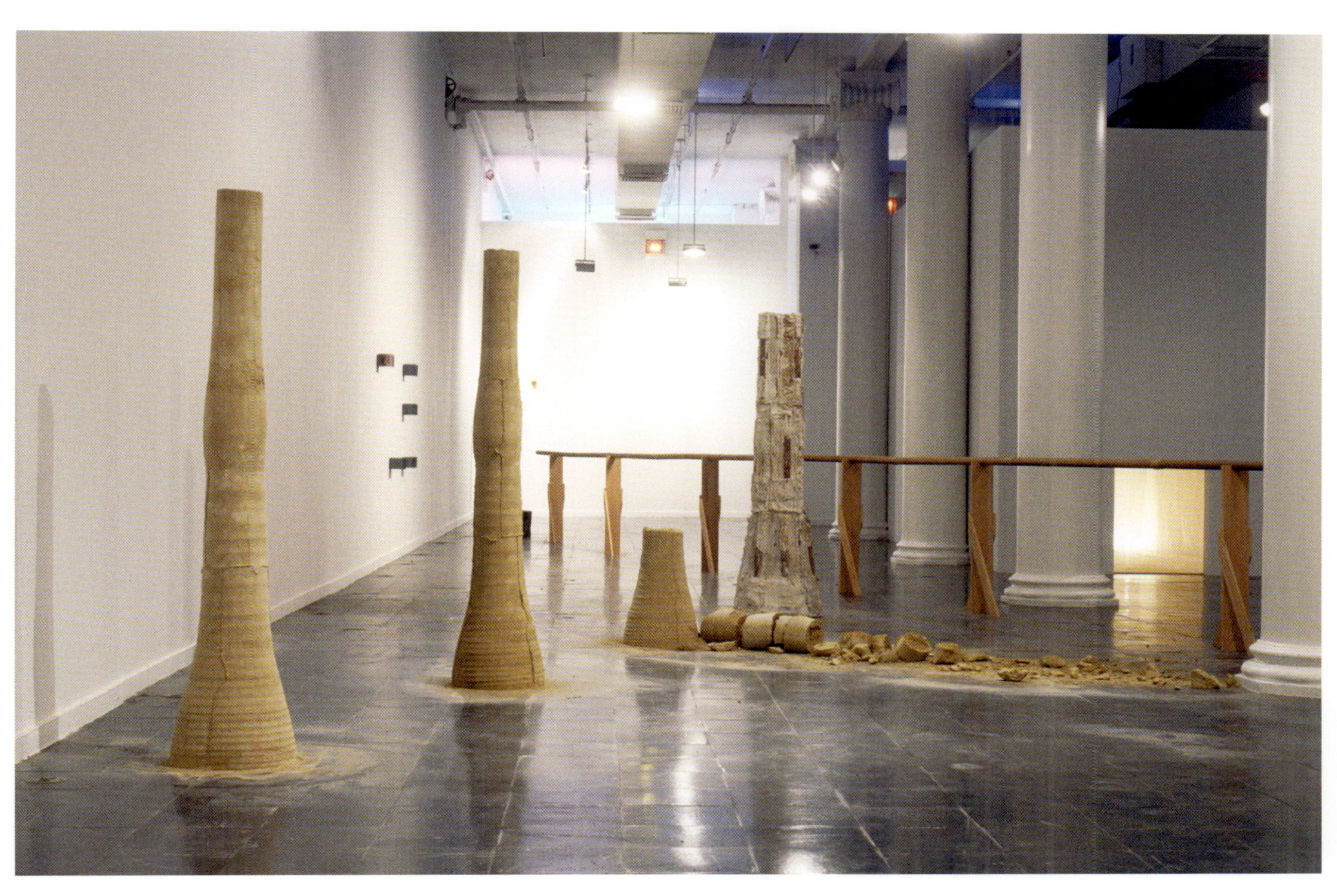

Sonia Labouriau,
Colonata [Colonade], 1992

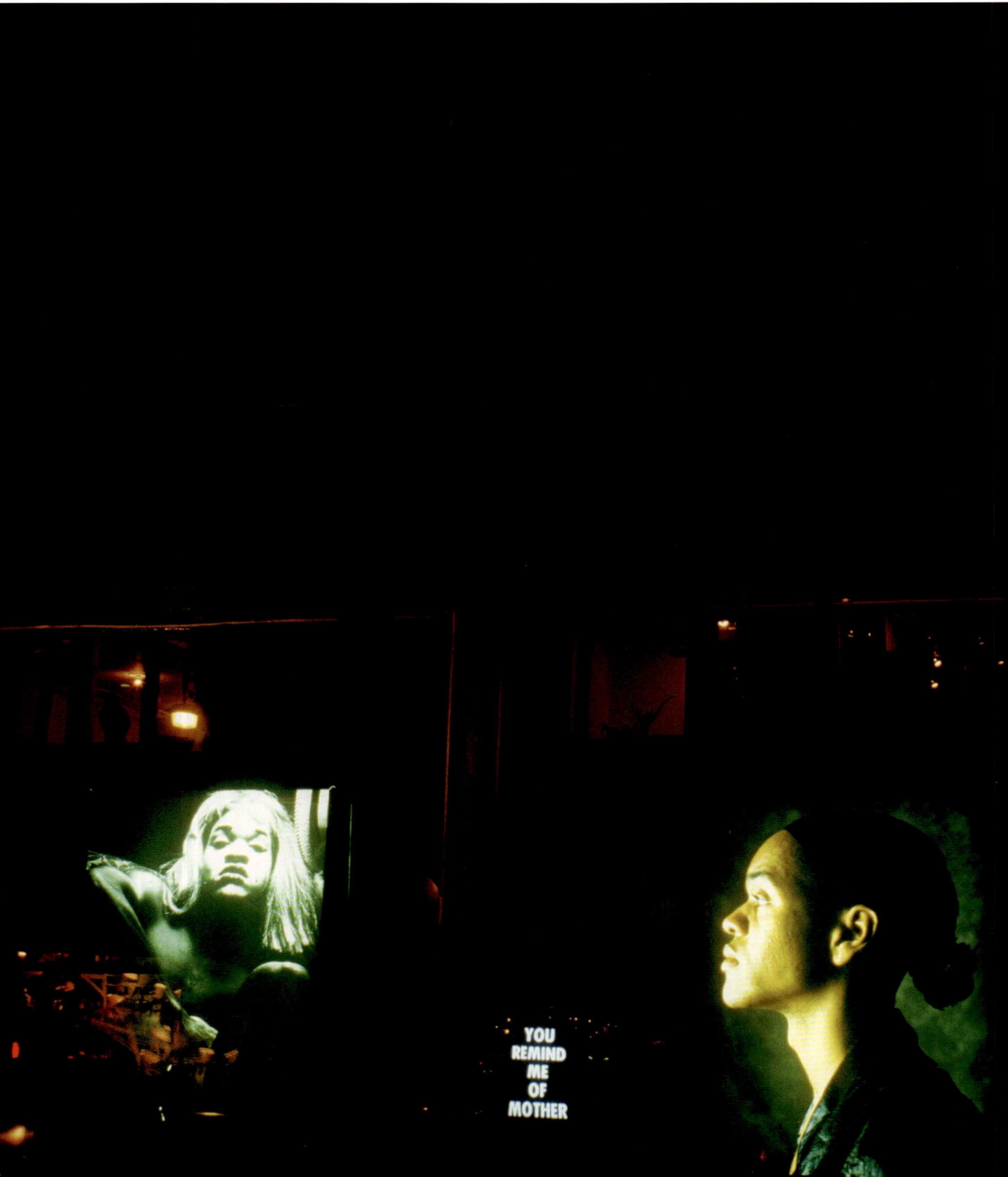
YOU
REMIND
ME
OF
MOTHER

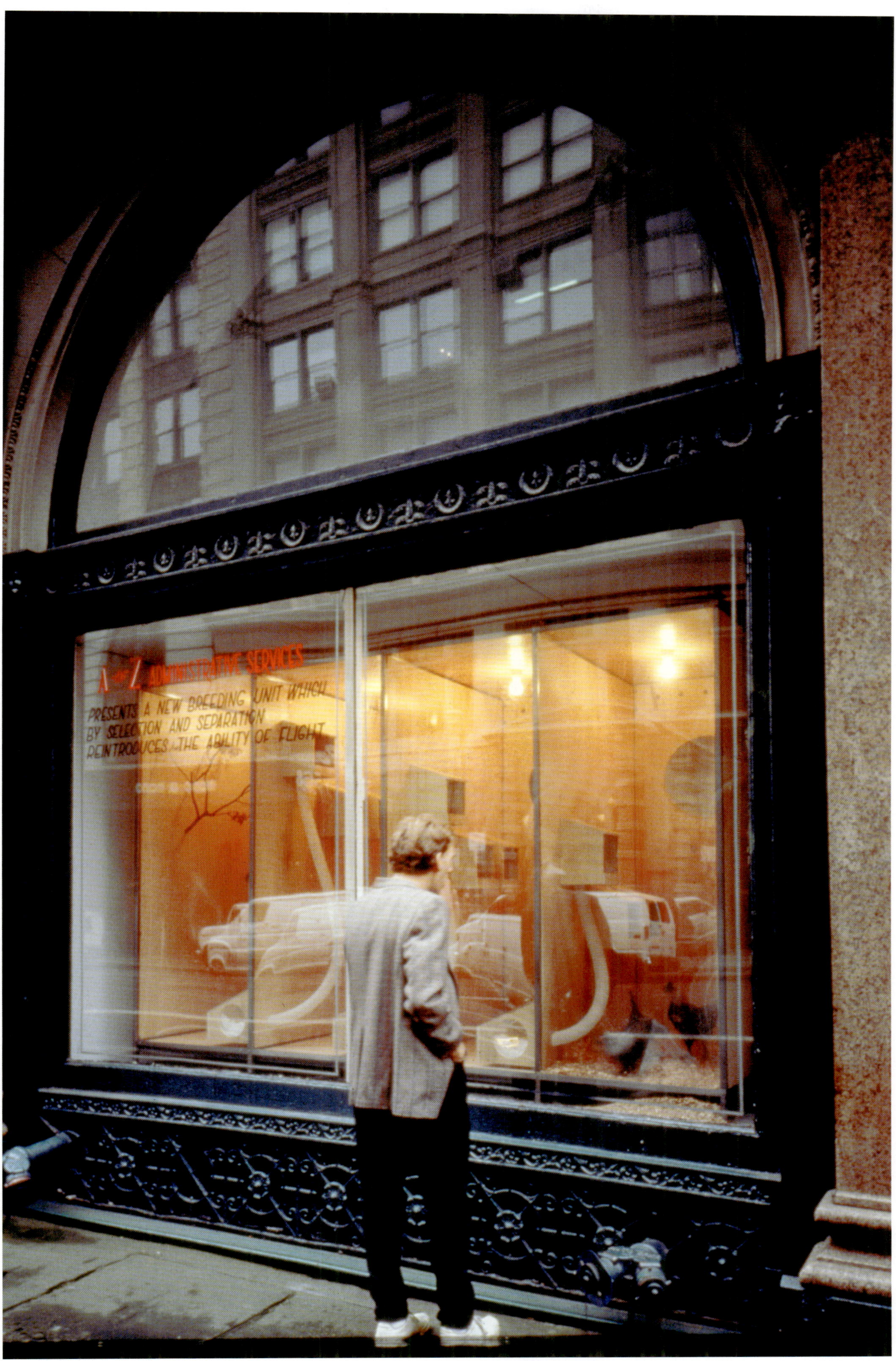

Organized in conjunction
with "The Final Frontier"

Bad Girls (Part I)

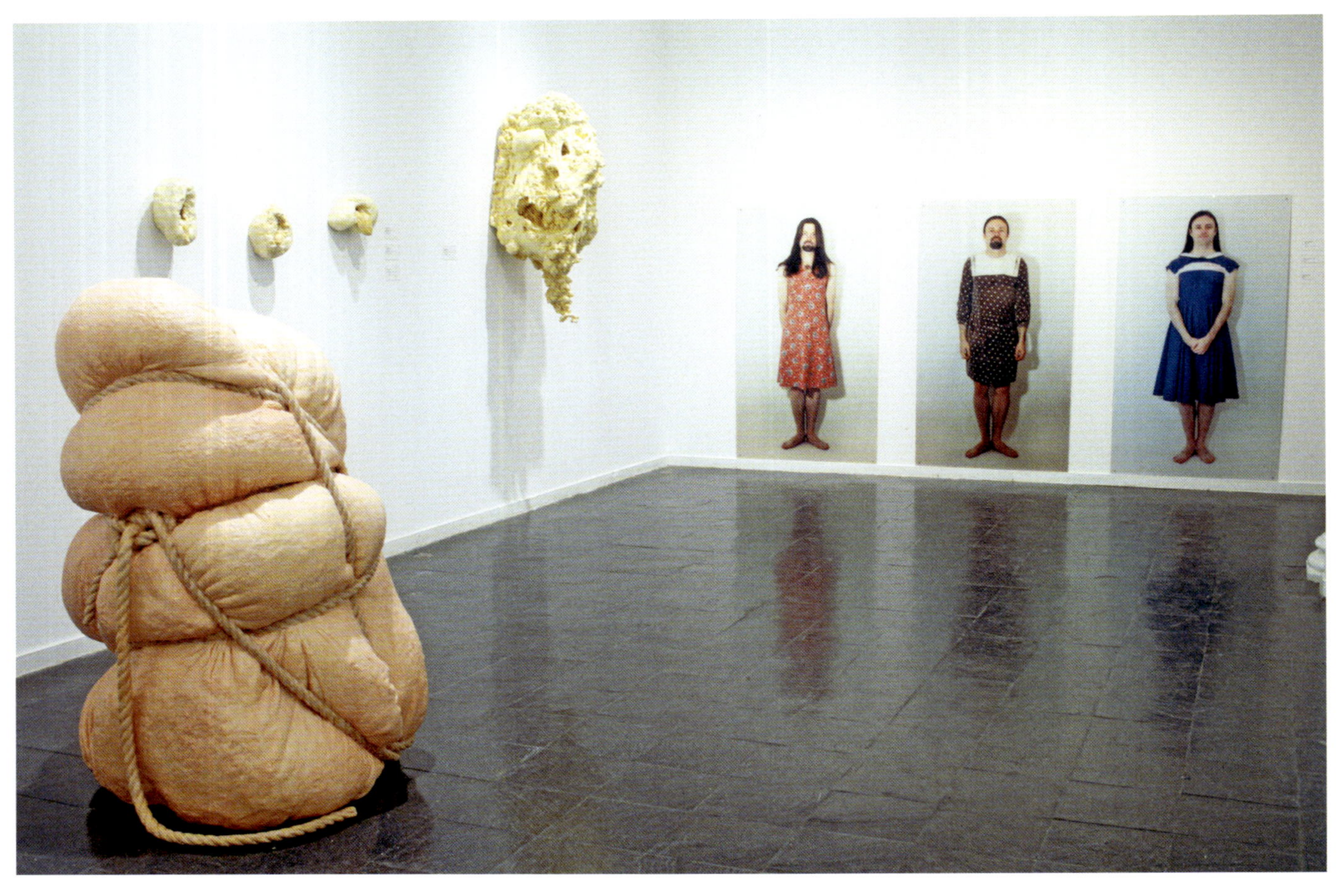

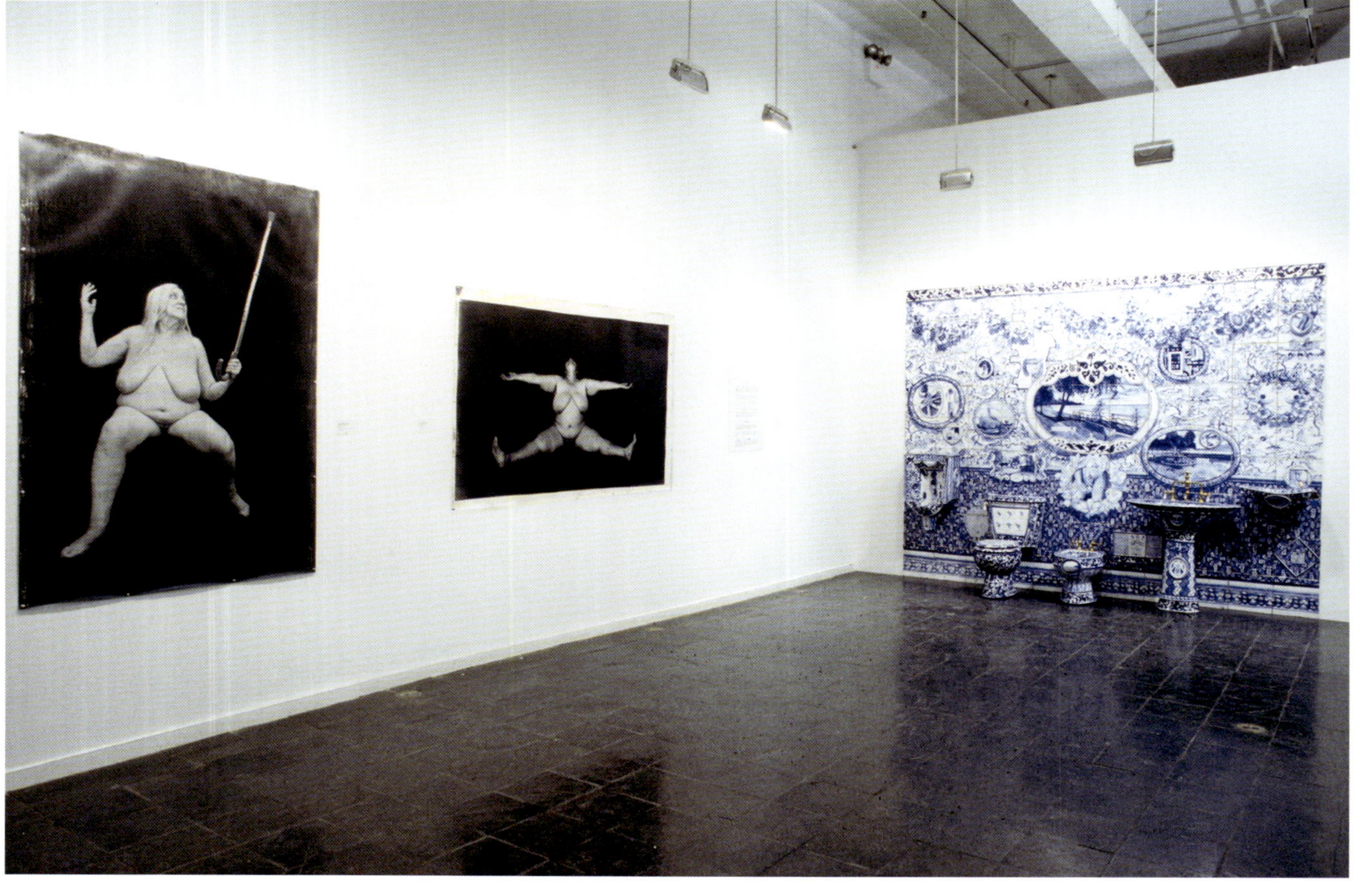

(top) Left to right:
works by Maxine Hayt
and Chuck Nanney

(bottom) Left to right:
works by Jacqueline
Hayden and Ann Agee

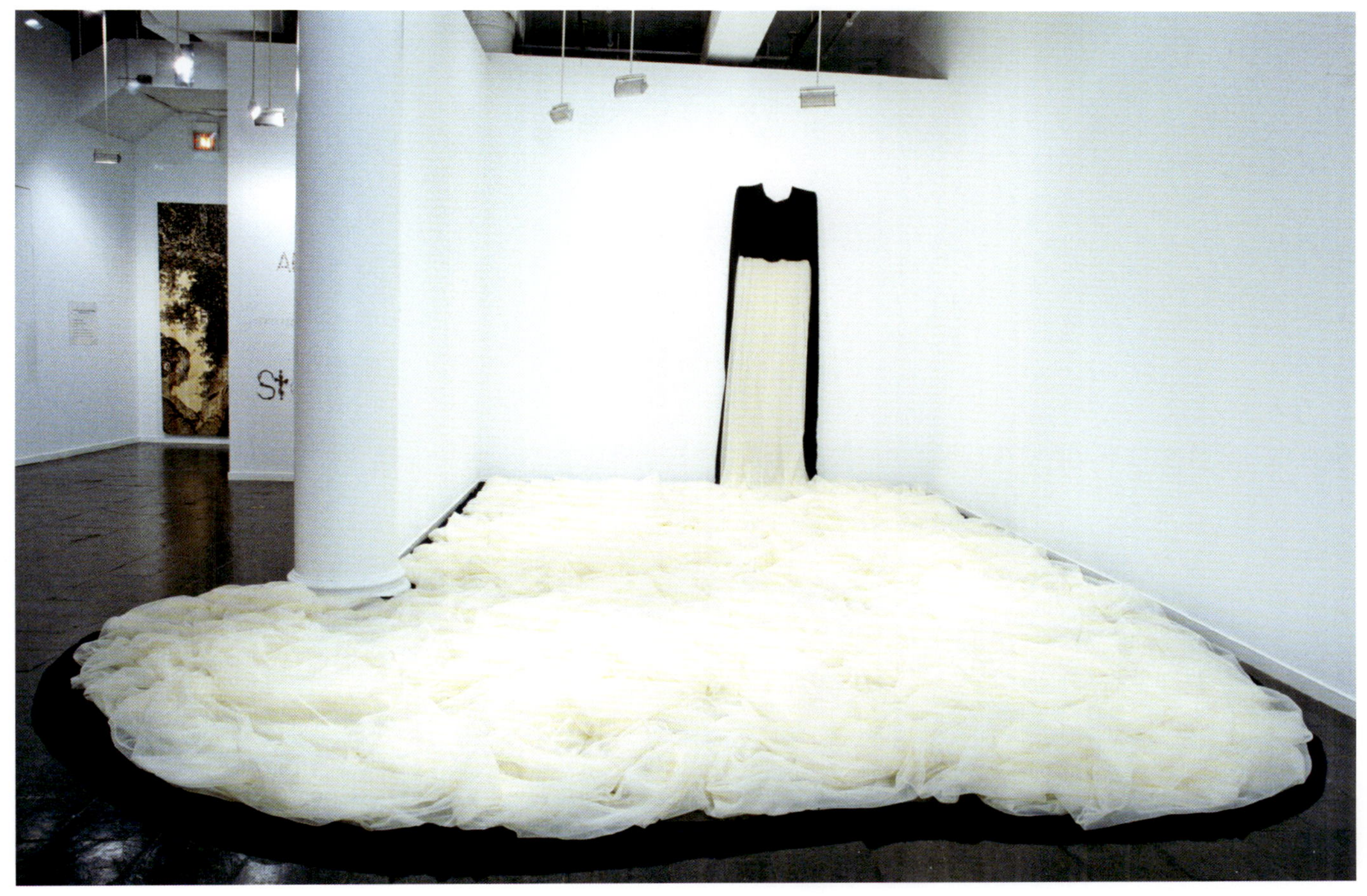

Beverly Semmes,
Yellow Pool, 1993

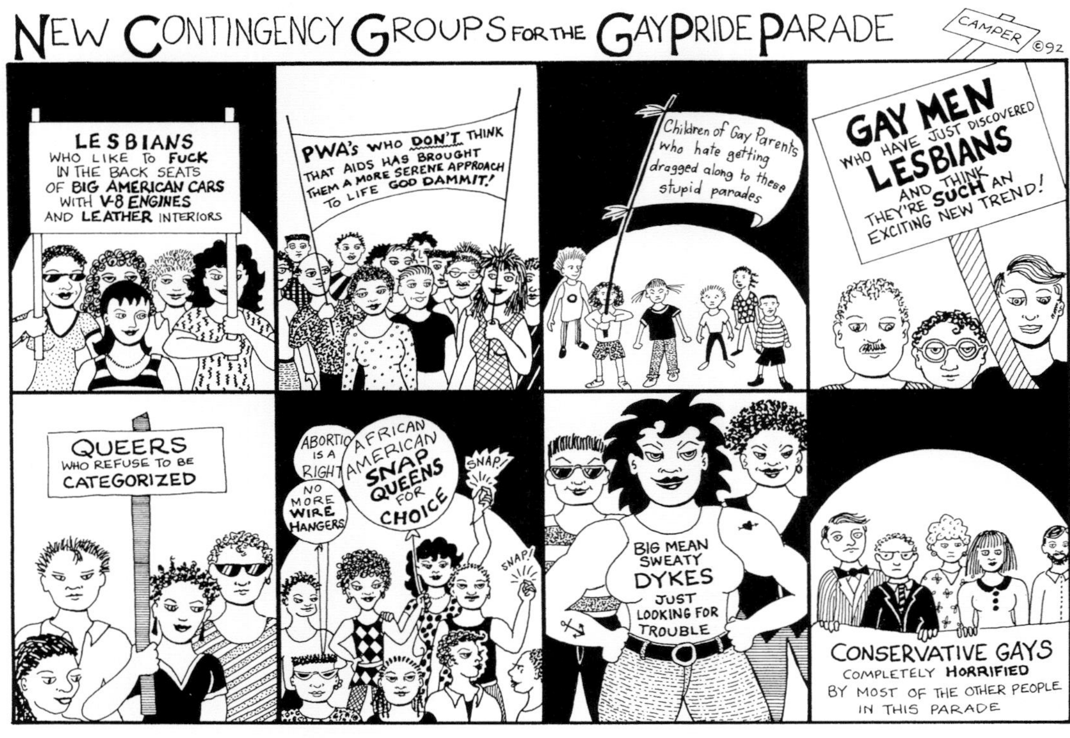

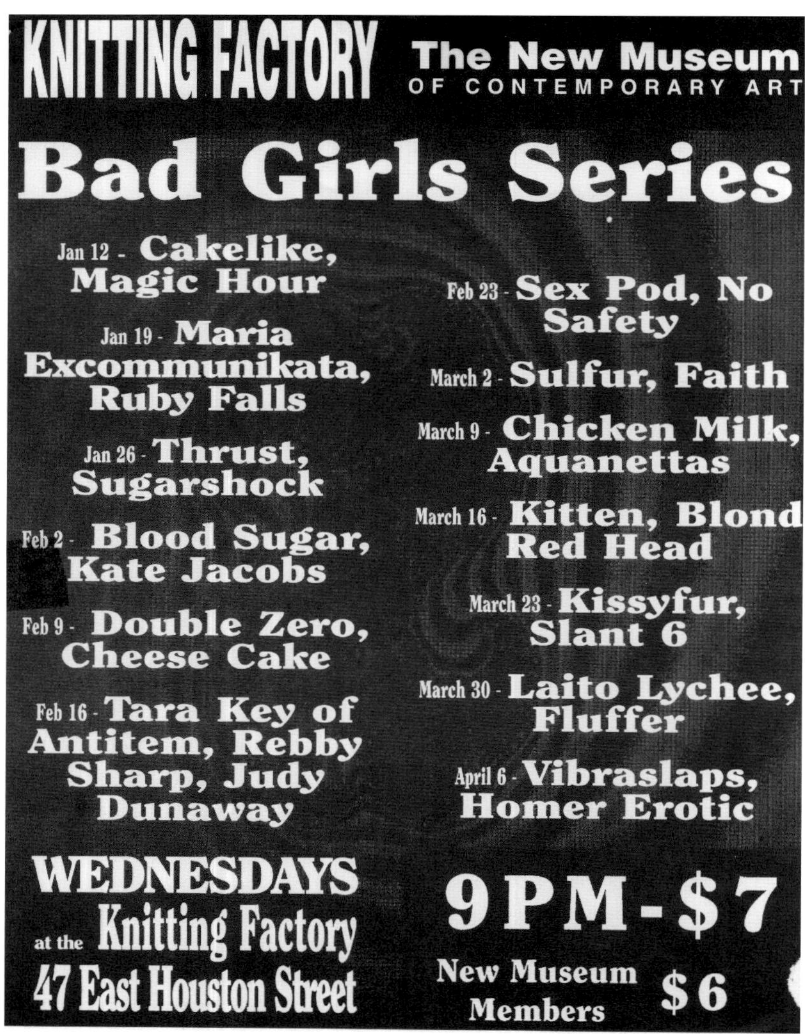

(top) Jennifer Camper,
*New Contingency Groups
for the Gay Pride
Parade*, 1992

(bottom) Flyer for
"Bad Girls Music at the
Knitting Factory," a music
series organized
in conjunction with
"Bad Girls"

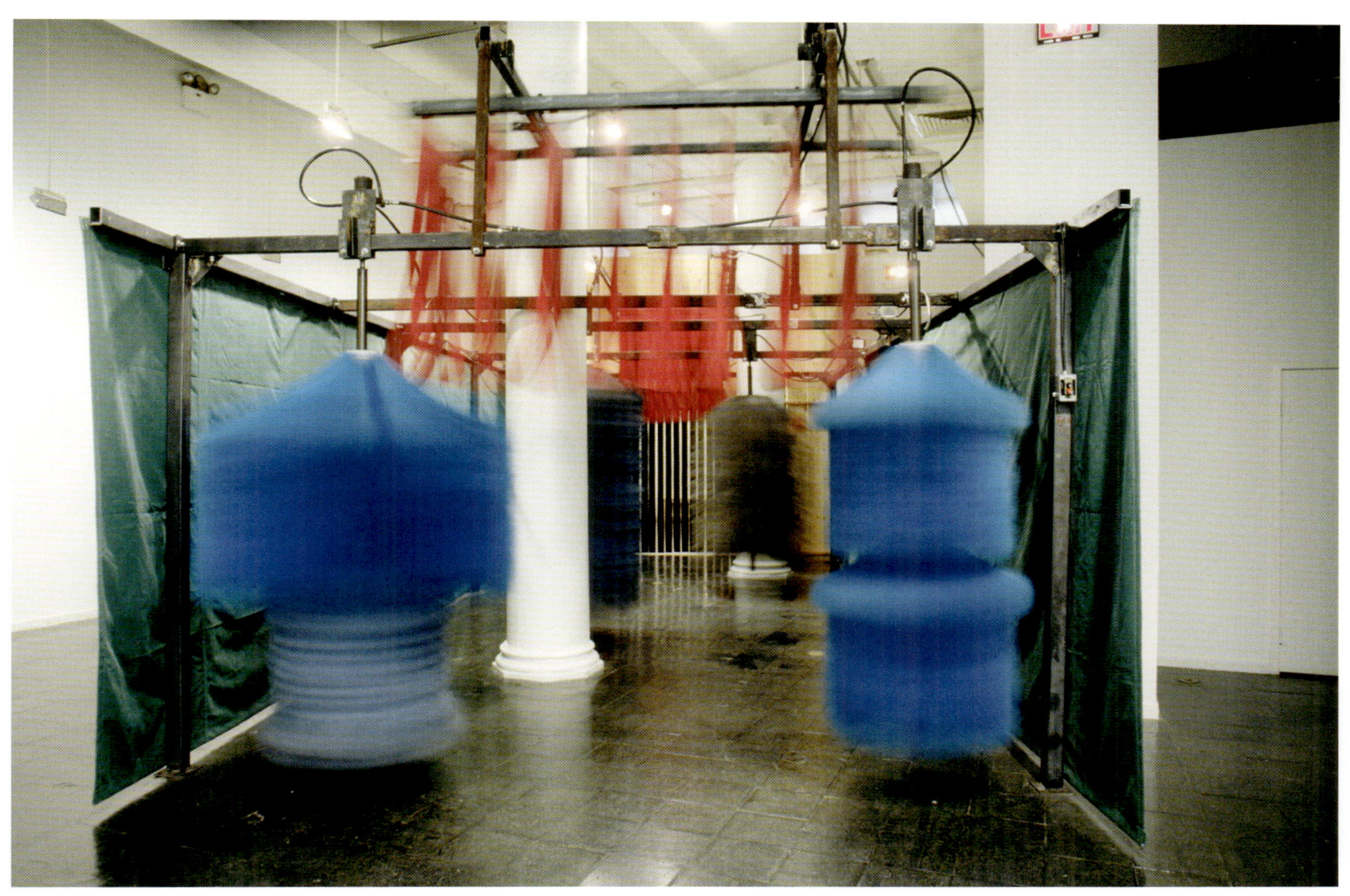

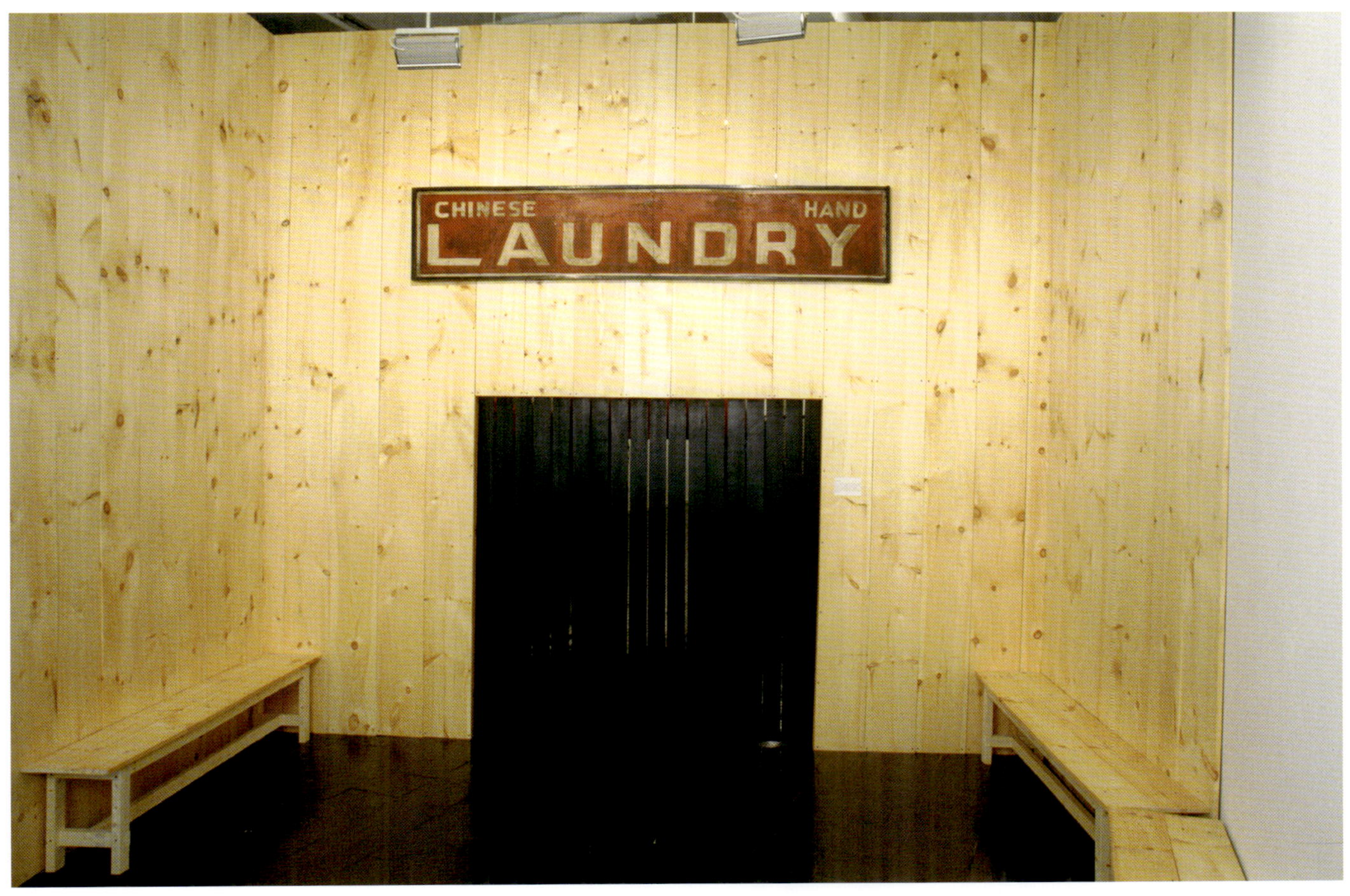

(top and bottom)
"Chinese Hand Laundry:
Huang Yong Ping"

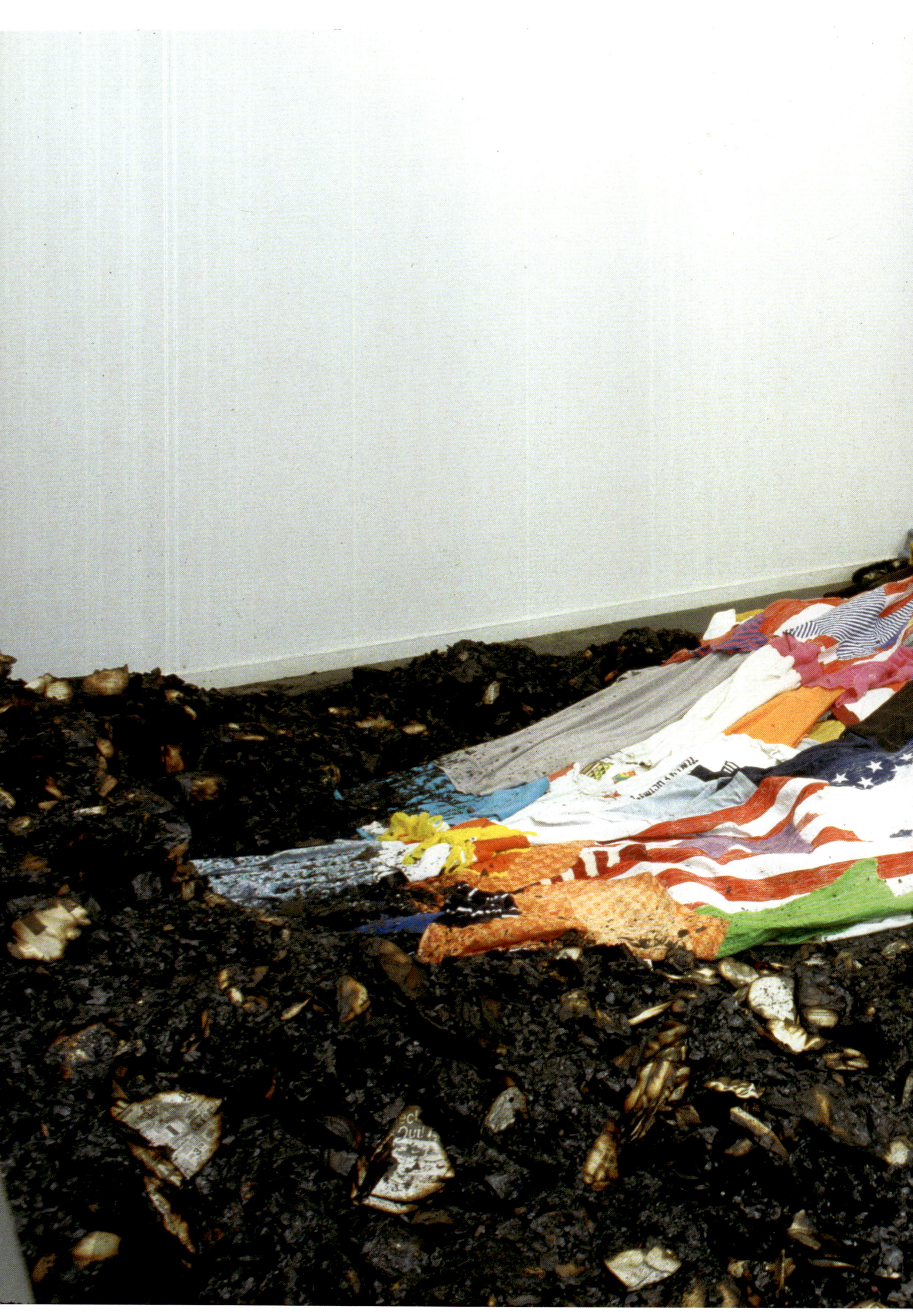

Chen Zhen,
Field of Waste, 1994

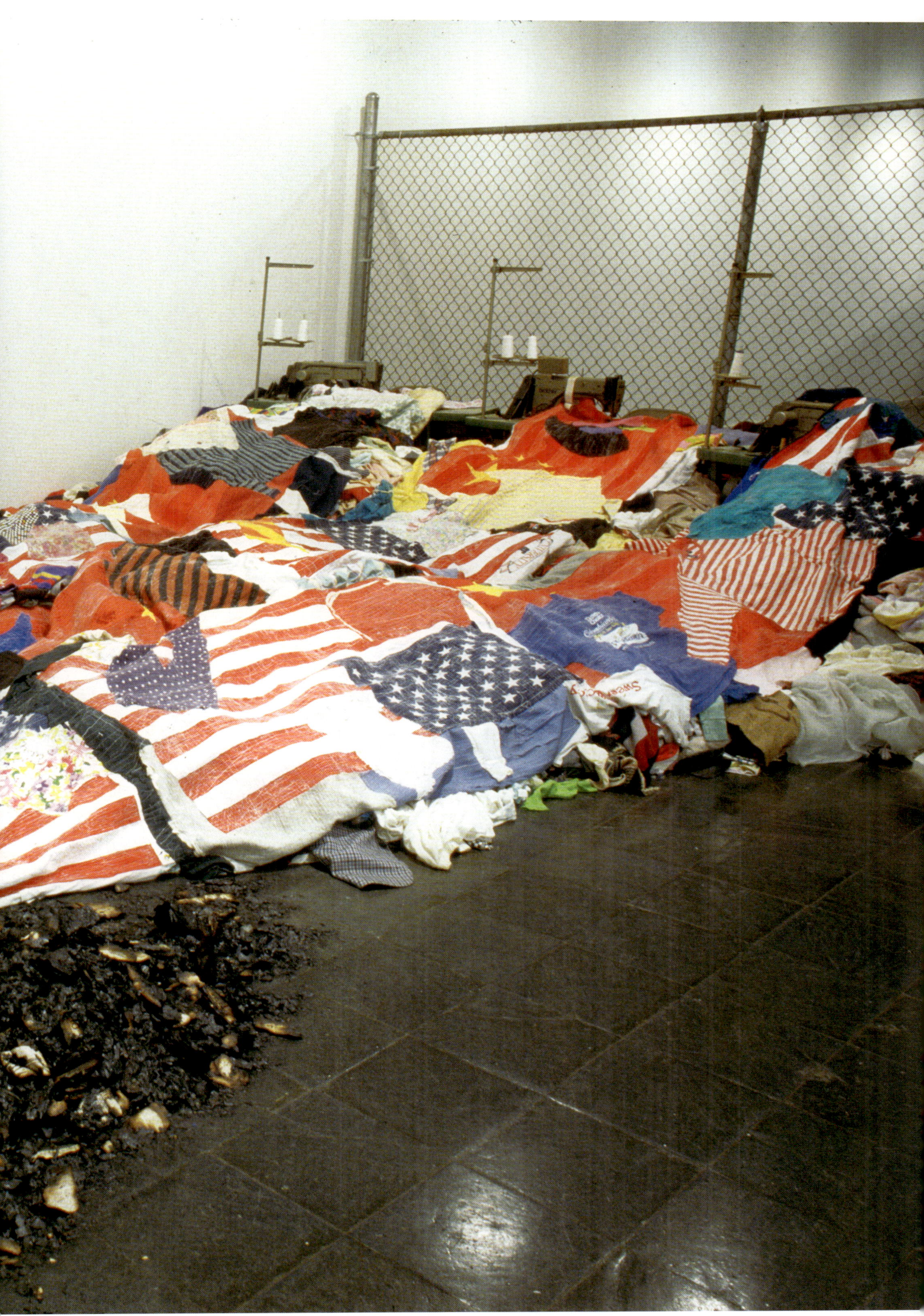

Window on Broadway: *Who Are We? What Are We? Where Did We Come From?*: Rita Ackermann

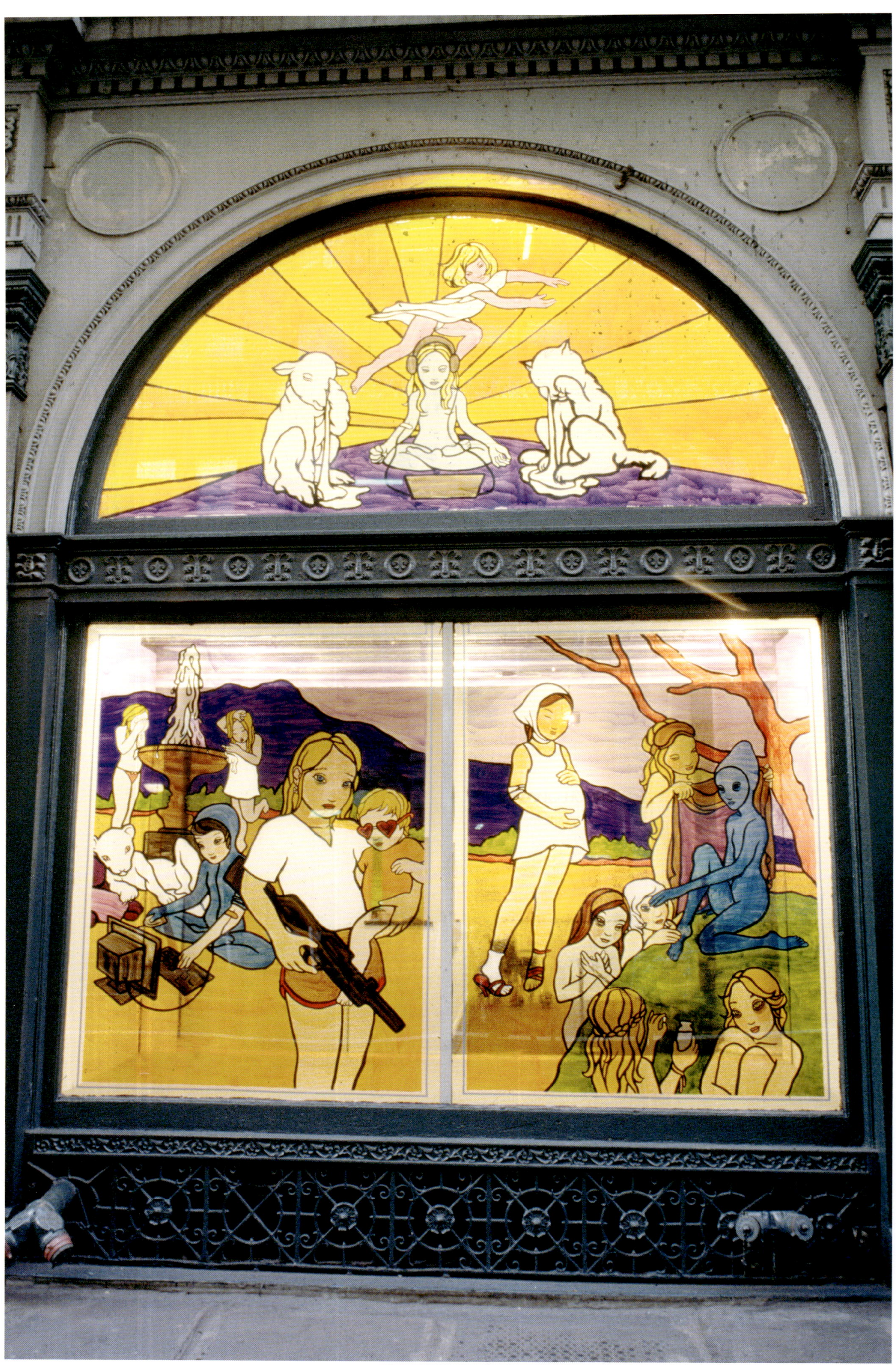

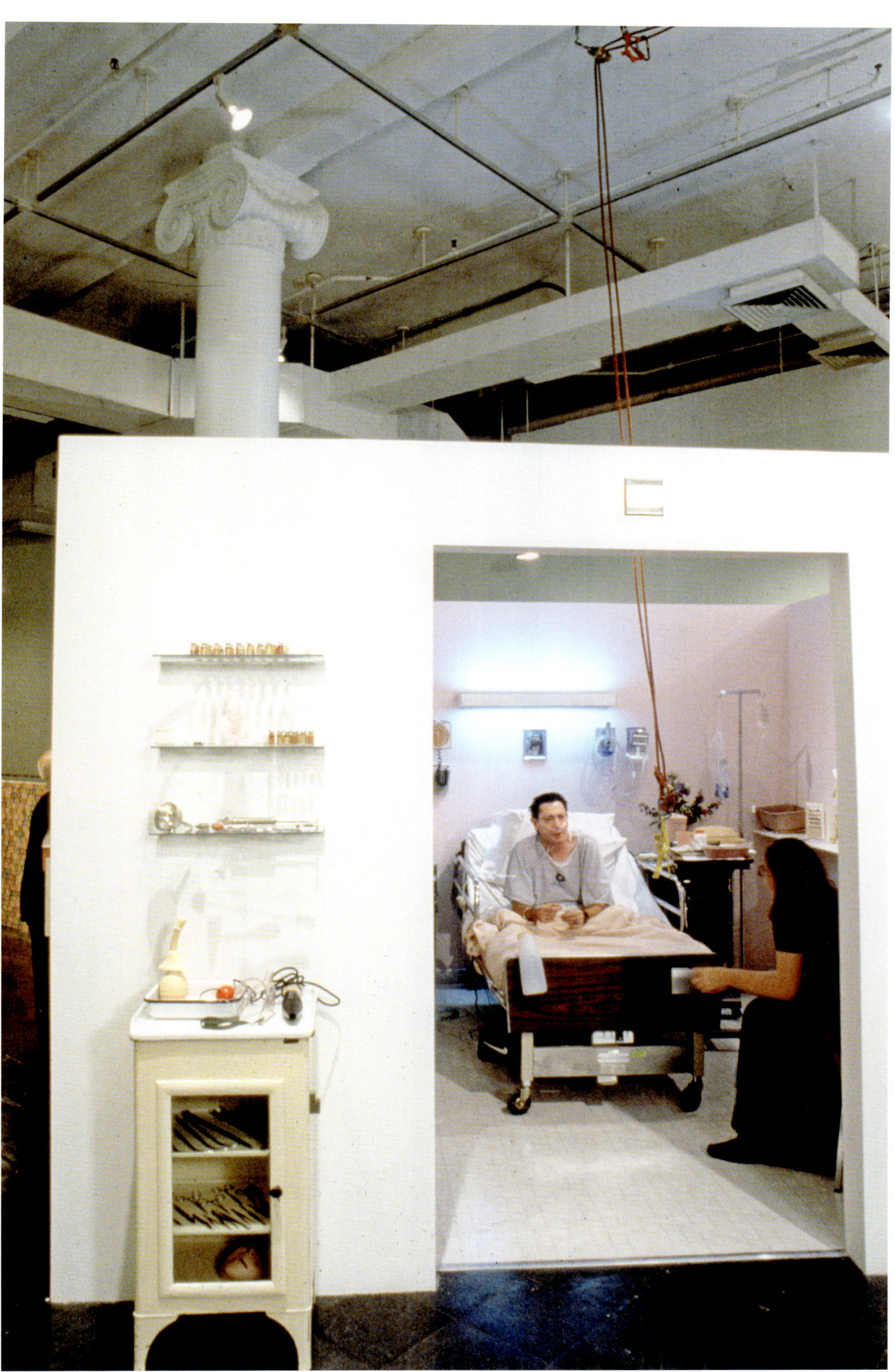

Bob Flanagan,
Hospital Room, 1992

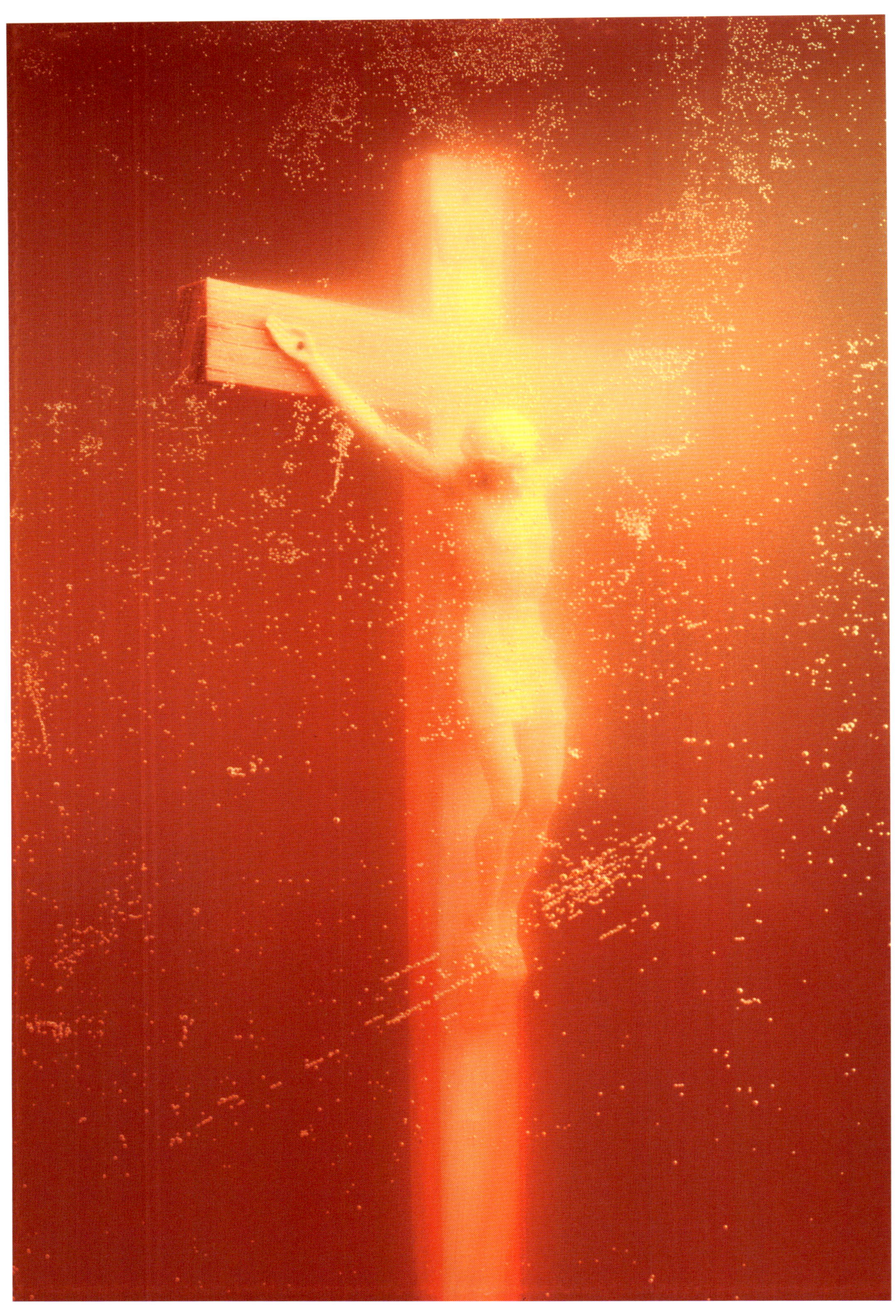

Andres Serrano,
Piss Christ, 1987

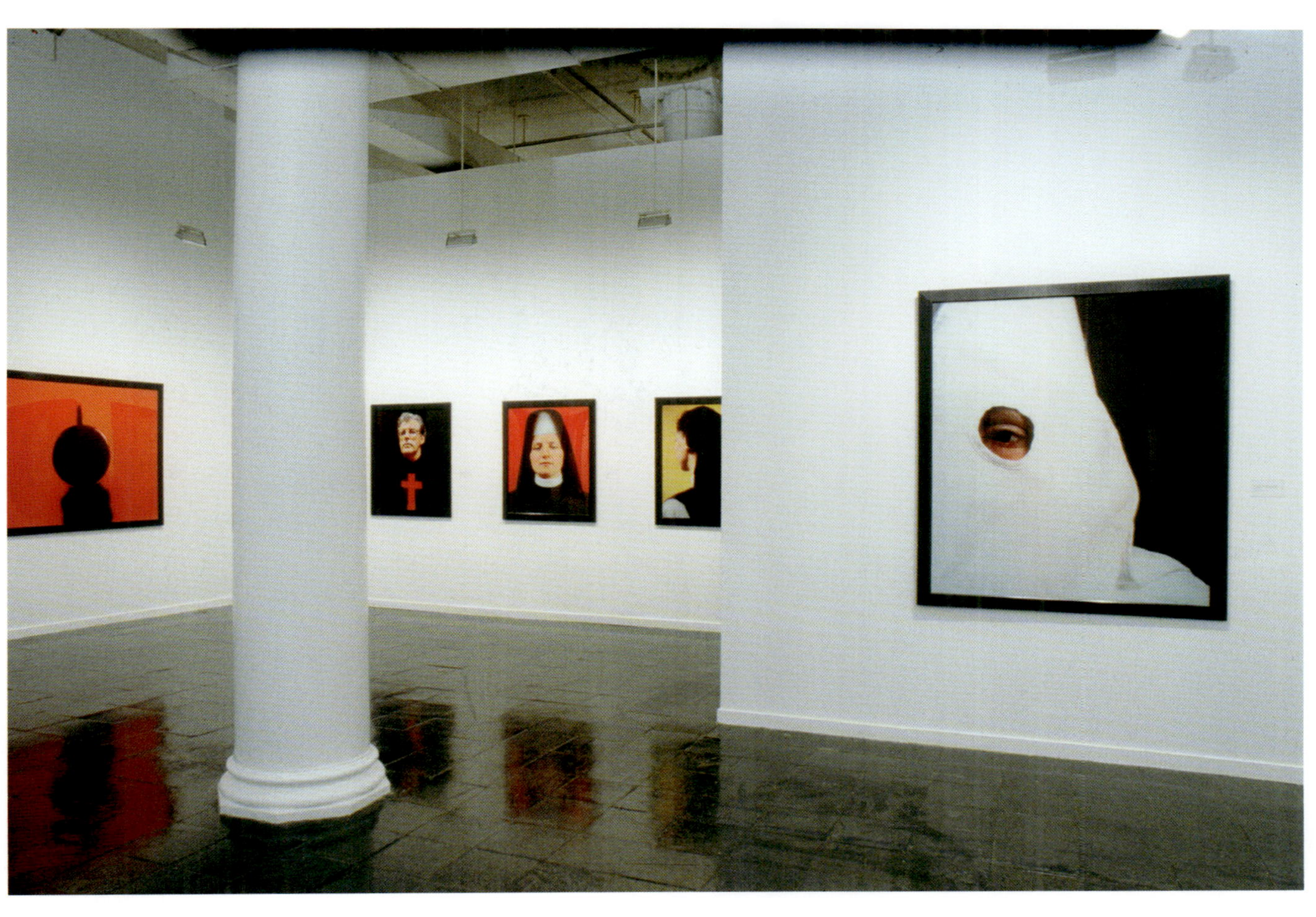

Installation view

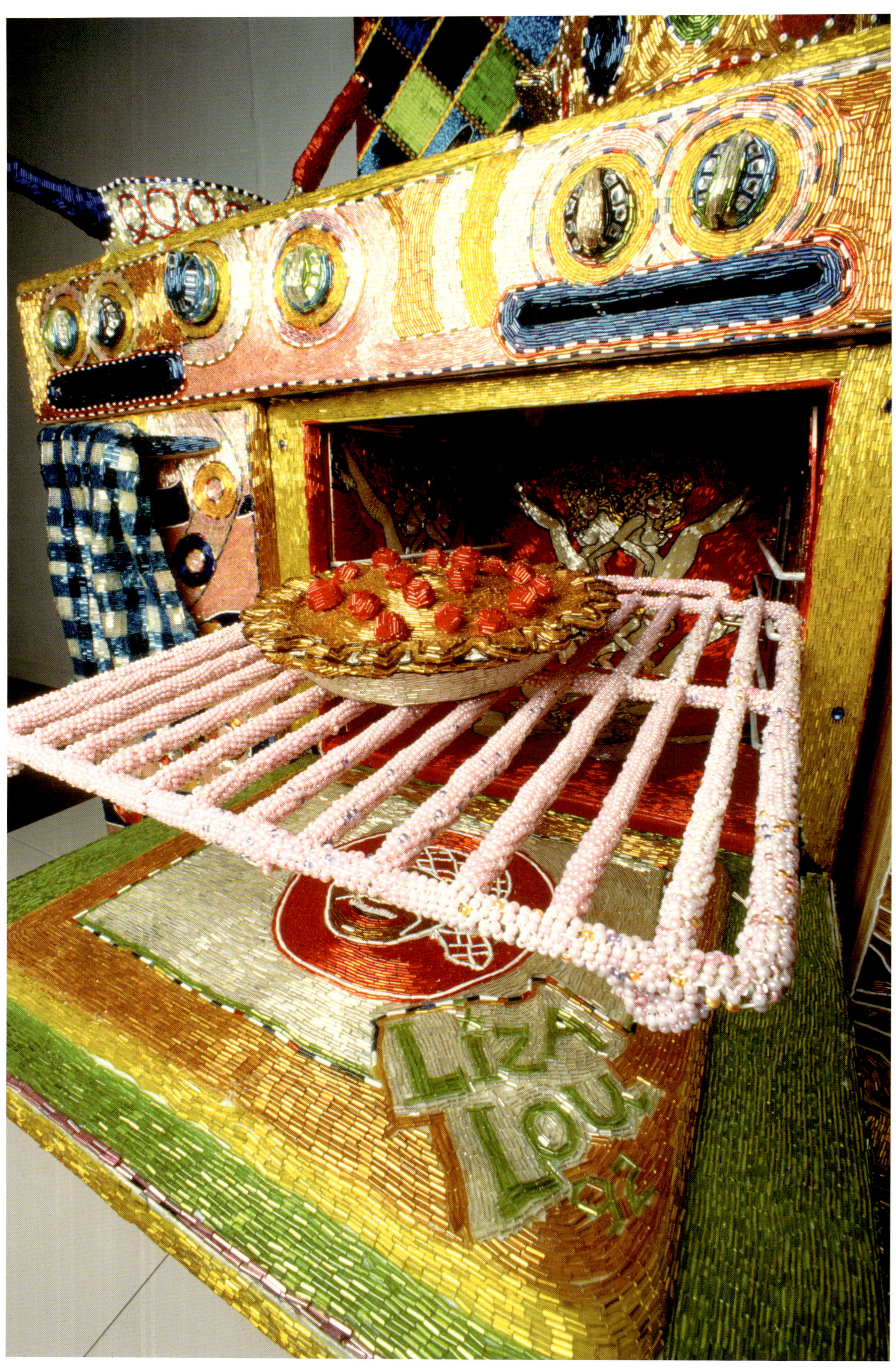

Liza Lou,
Kitchen Installation,
1991–94

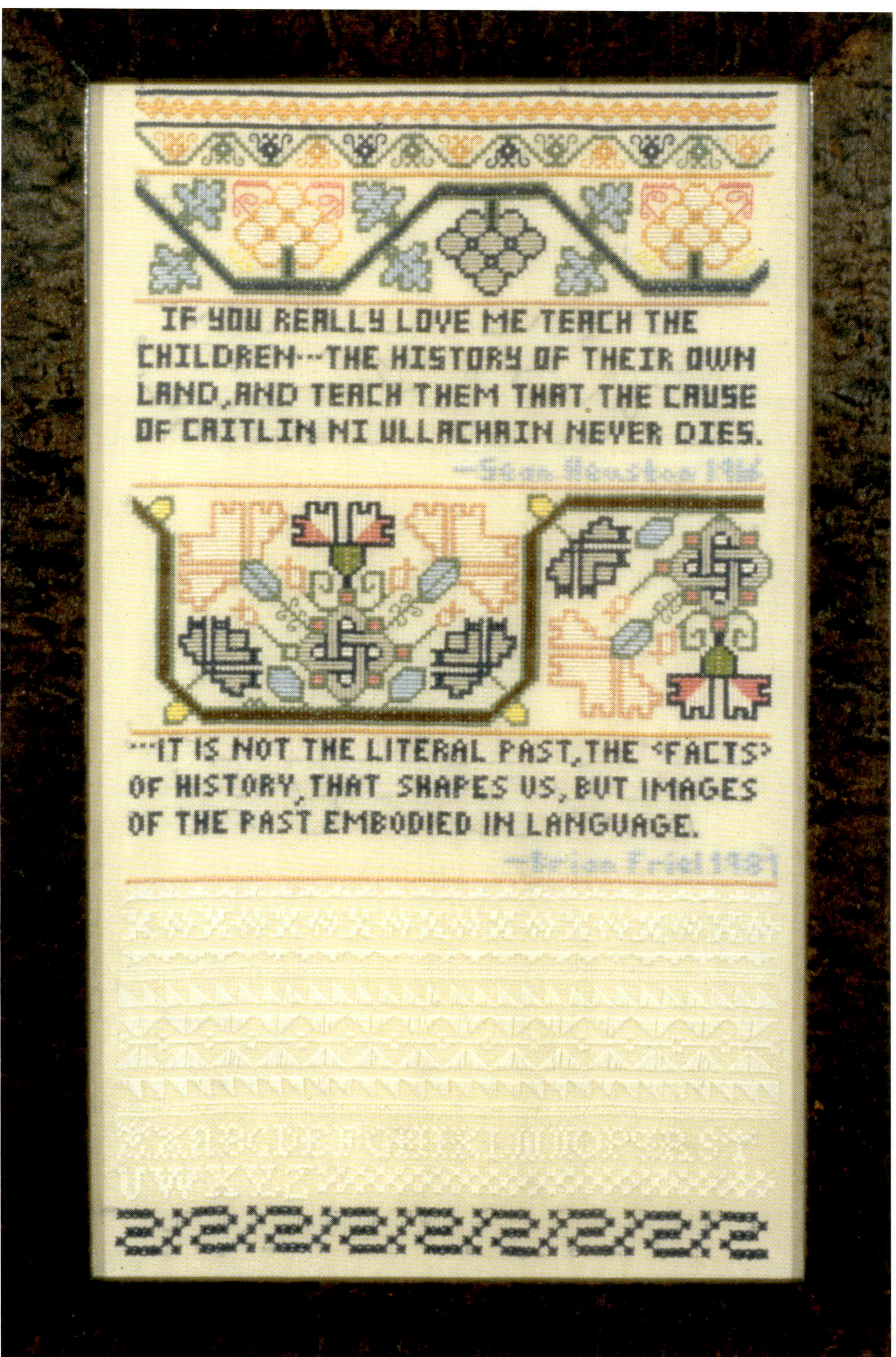

Elaine Reichek,
*Sampler (If You Really
Love…)*, 1993

Carolee Schneemann,
*Up To And Including
Her Limits*, 1976

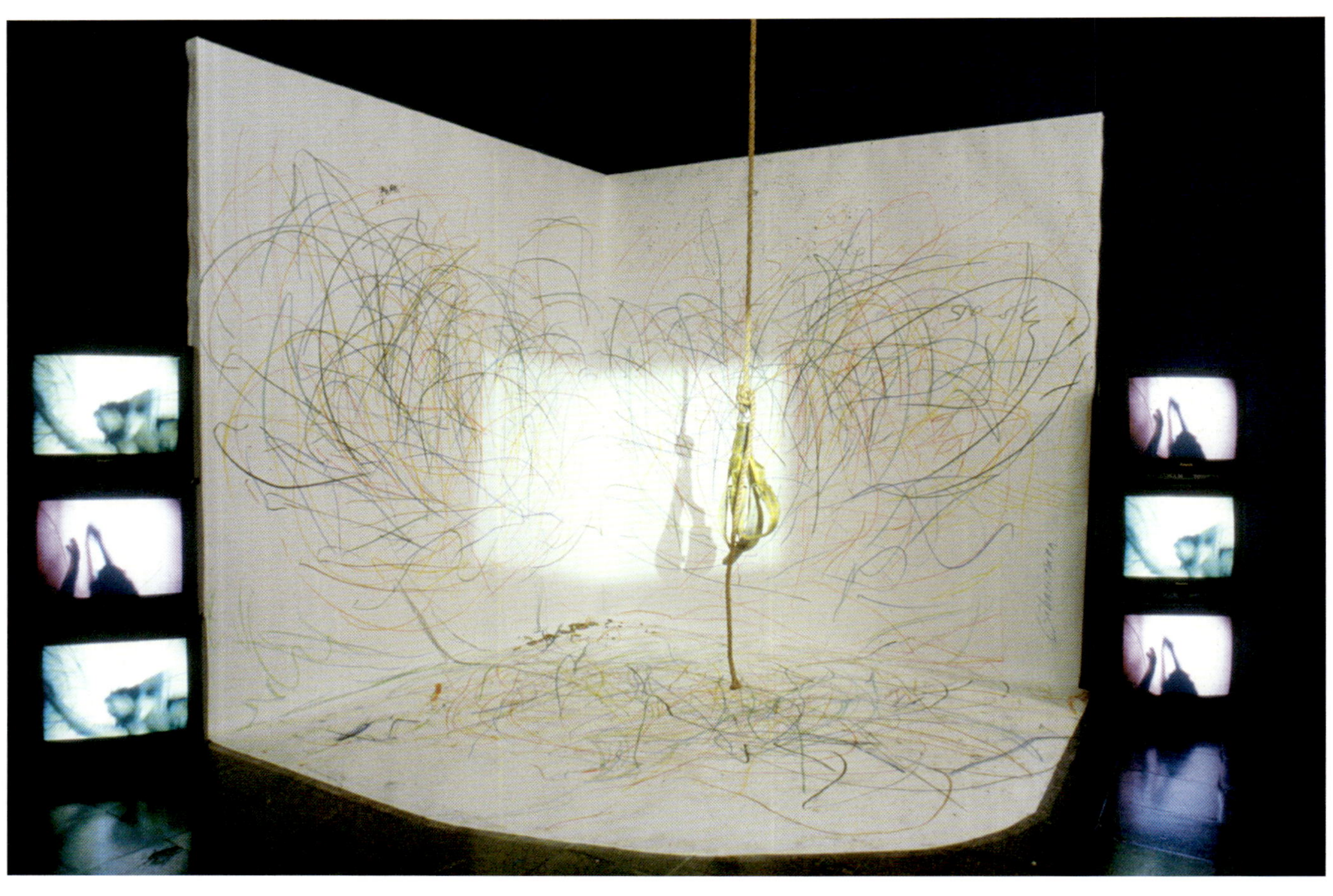

Carolee Schneemann,
*Up To And Including
Her Limits*, 1976

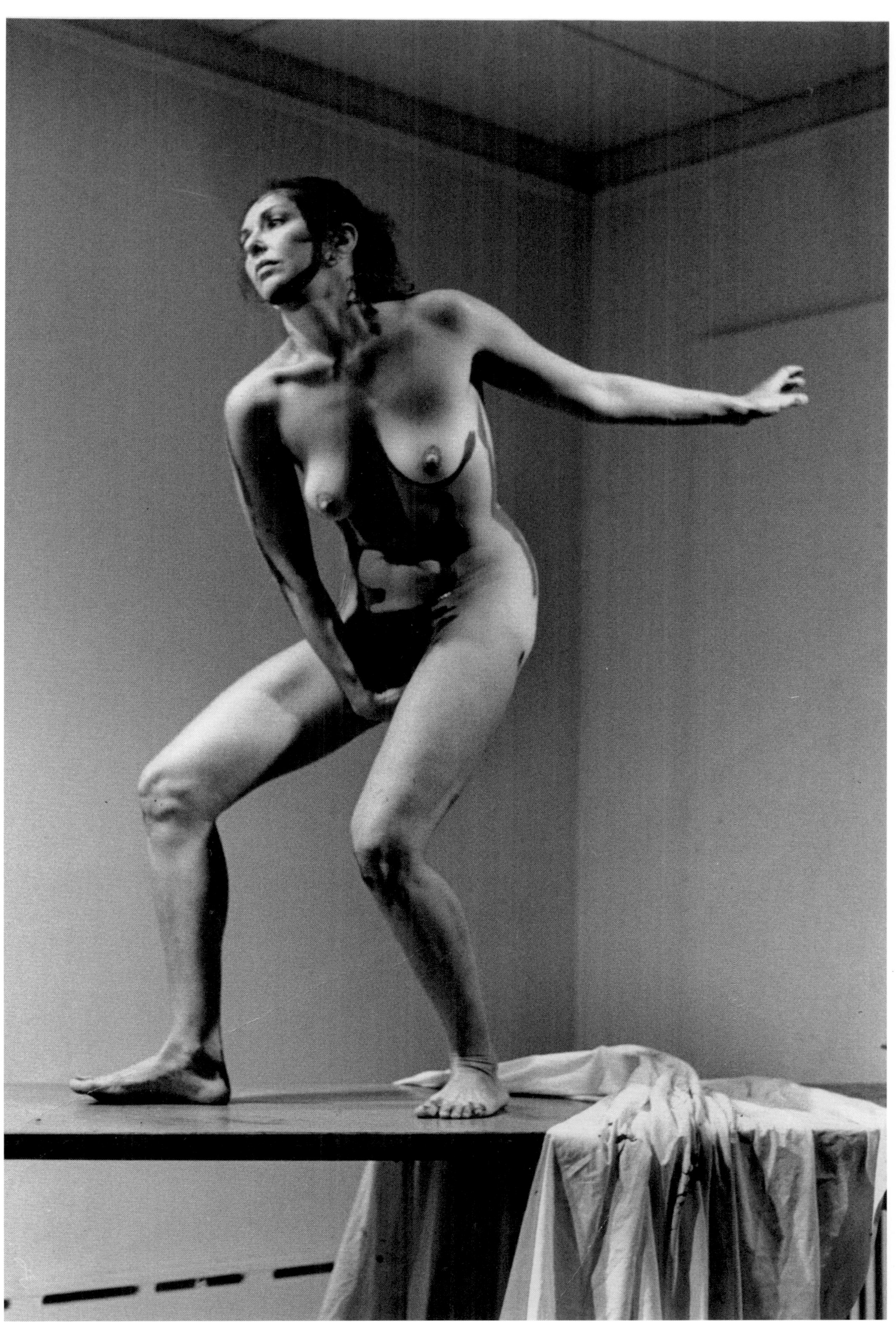

Carolee Schneemann,
Interior Scroll, 1975

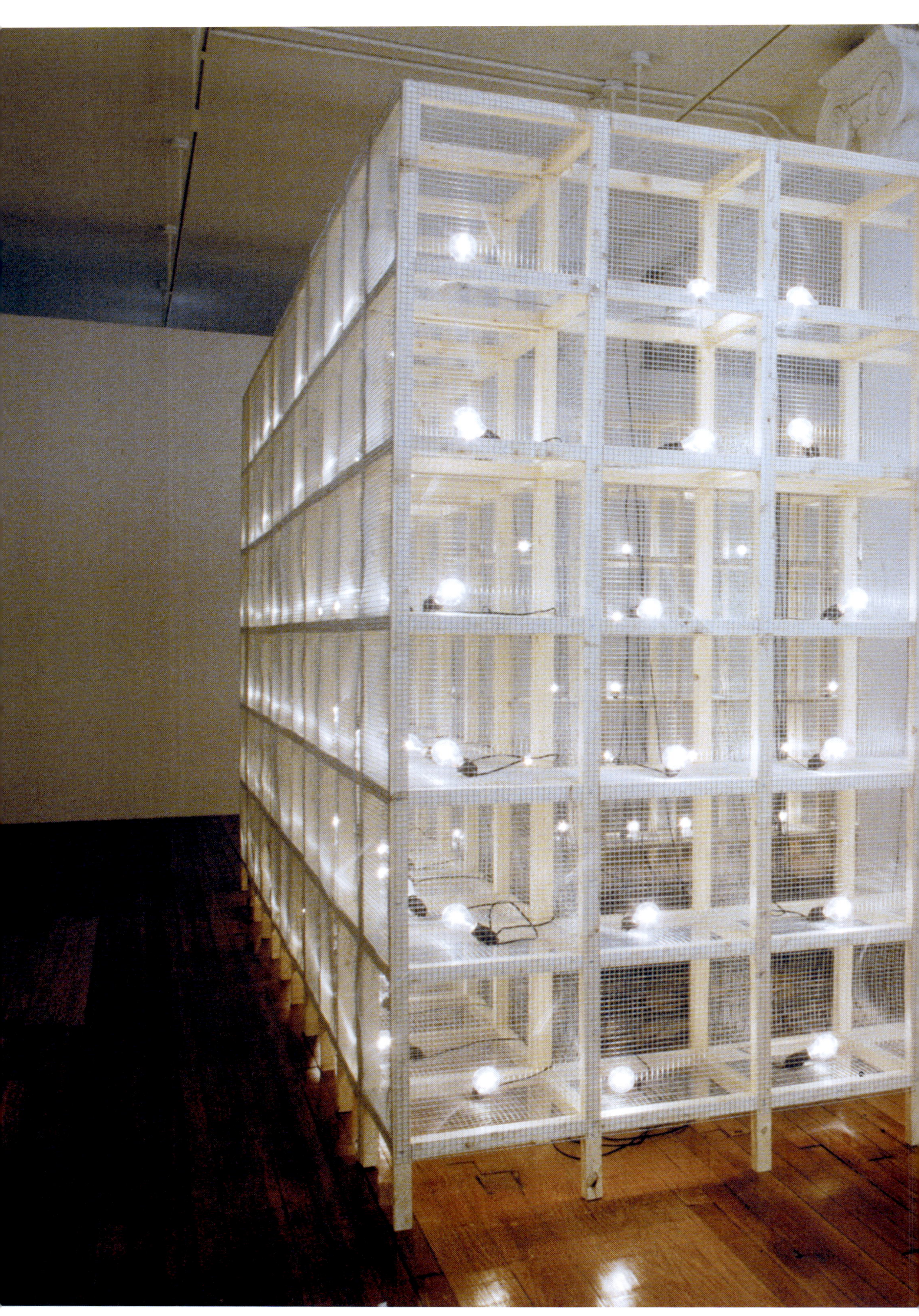

Mona Hatoum,
Current Disturbance, 1996

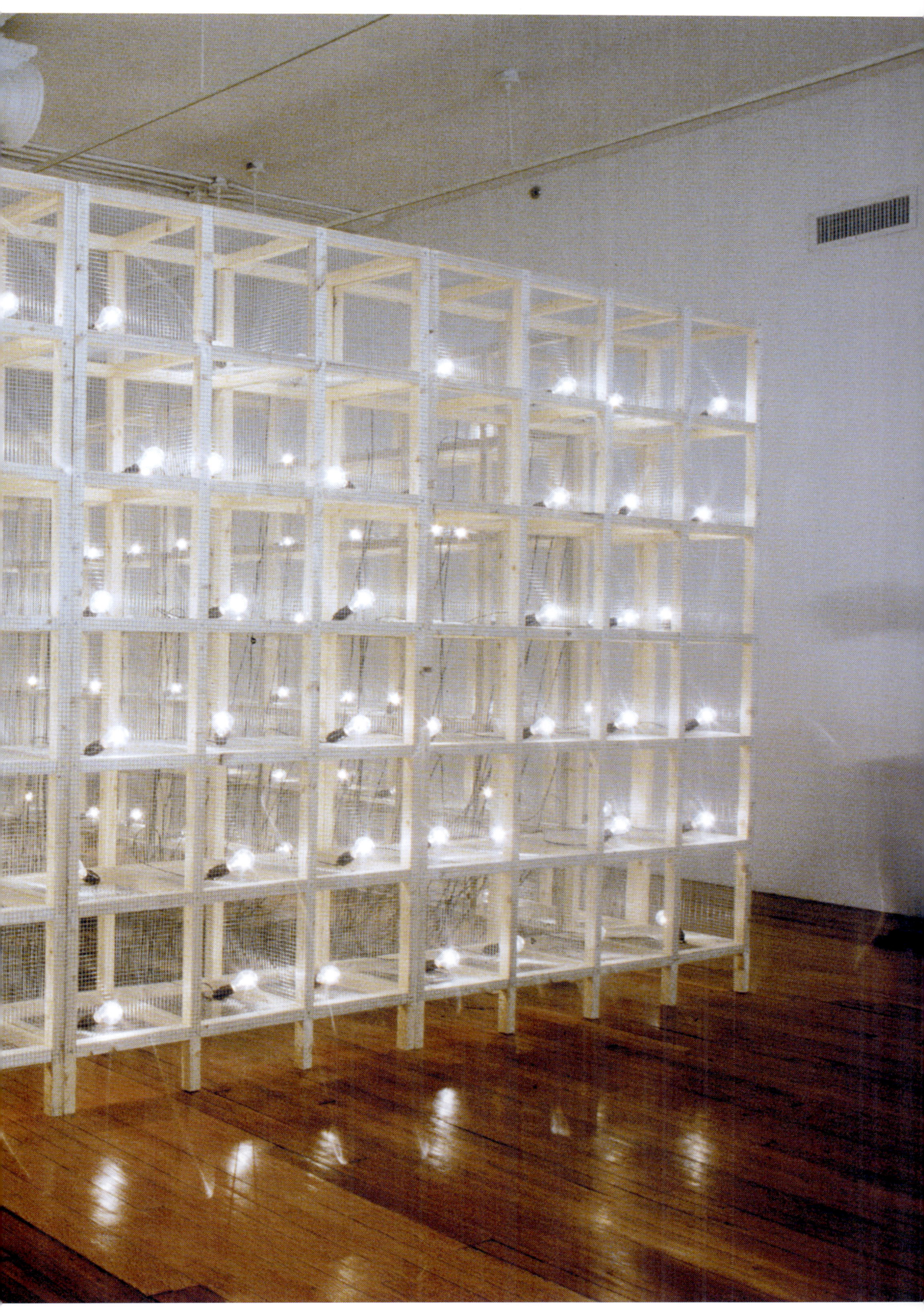

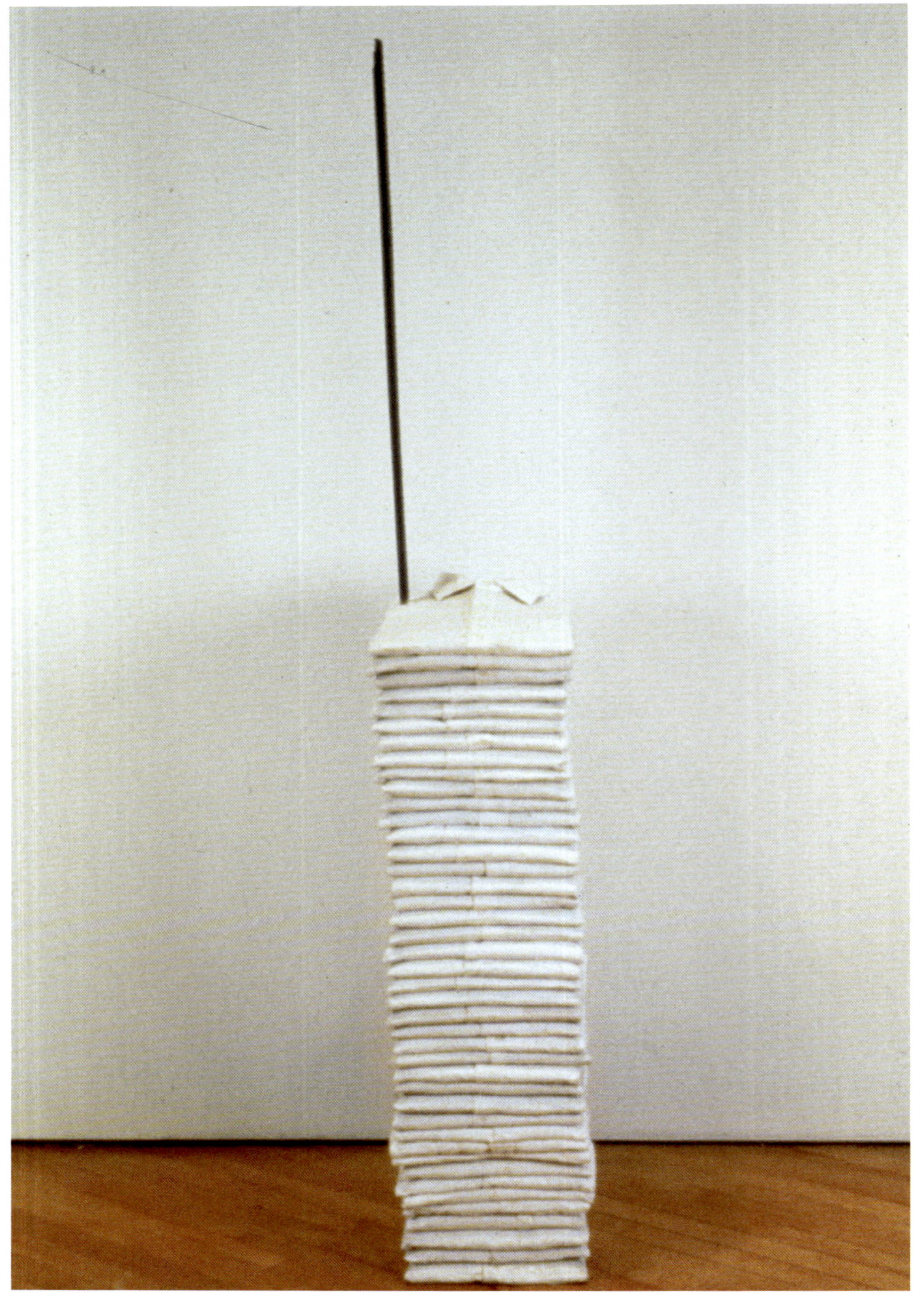

(above) Doris Salcedo,
Untitled, 1989-93

(right) Doris Salcedo,
Atrabiliarios, 1992-93

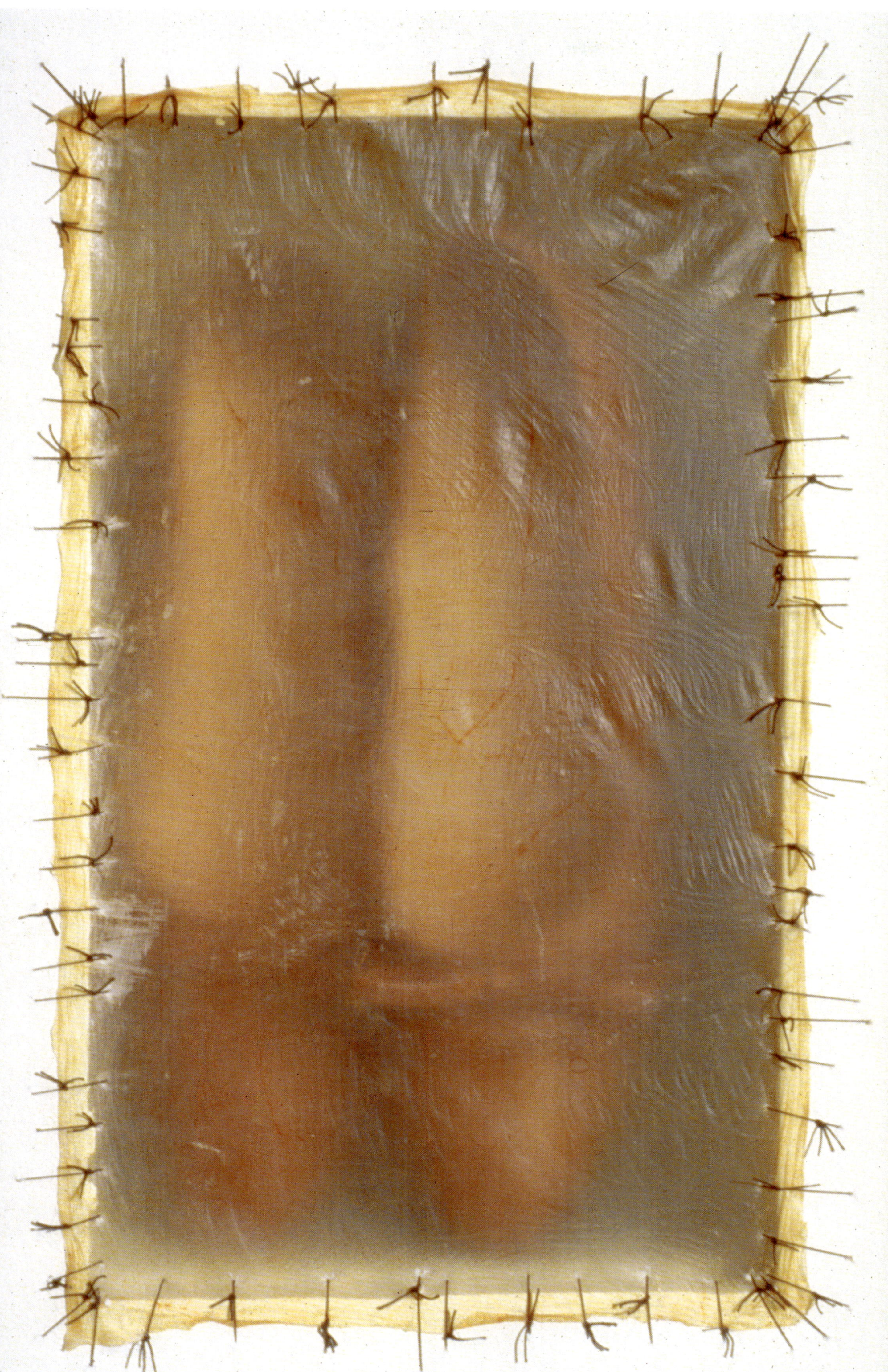

Sweet Oblivion: The Urban Landscape of Martin Wong

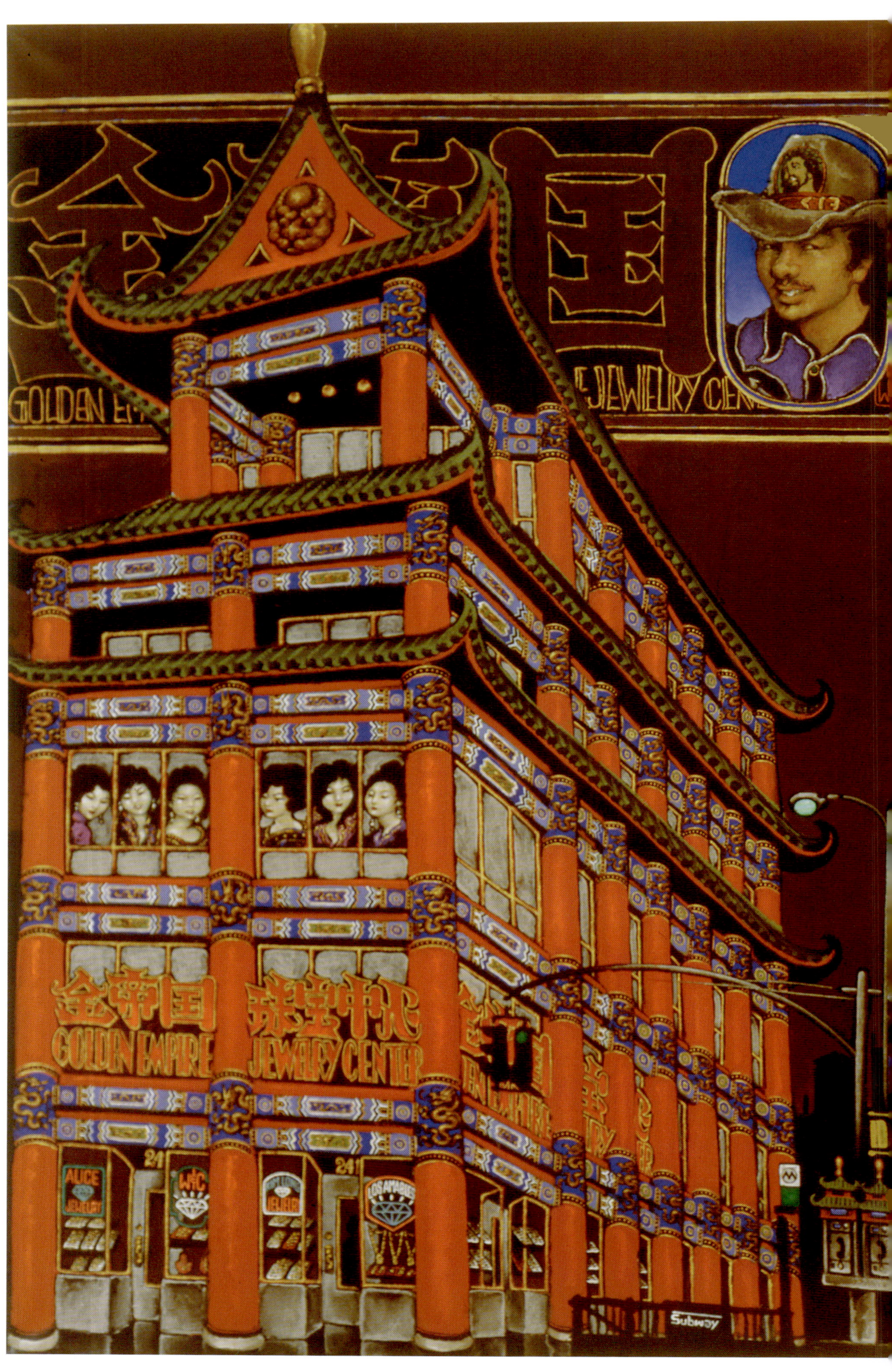

Martin Wong,
Canal Street, 1992

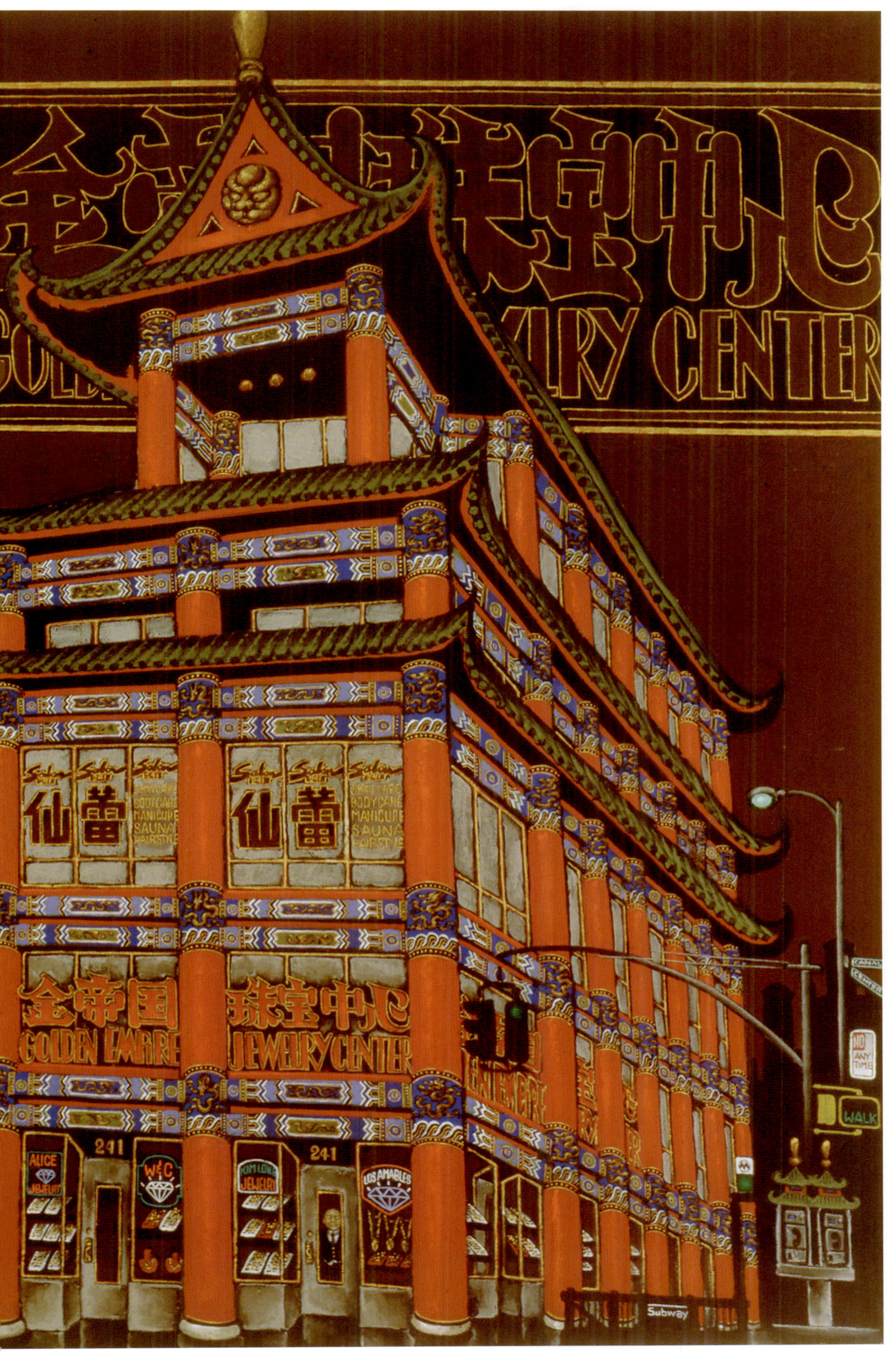

金帝国
珠宝中心
GOLDEN EMPIRE
JEWELRY CENTER
Subway
ALICE JEWELRY
W.C.
KIM LONG JEWELRY
LOS AMIGOS
241
241
CANAL CENTER
NO ANY TIME
WALK

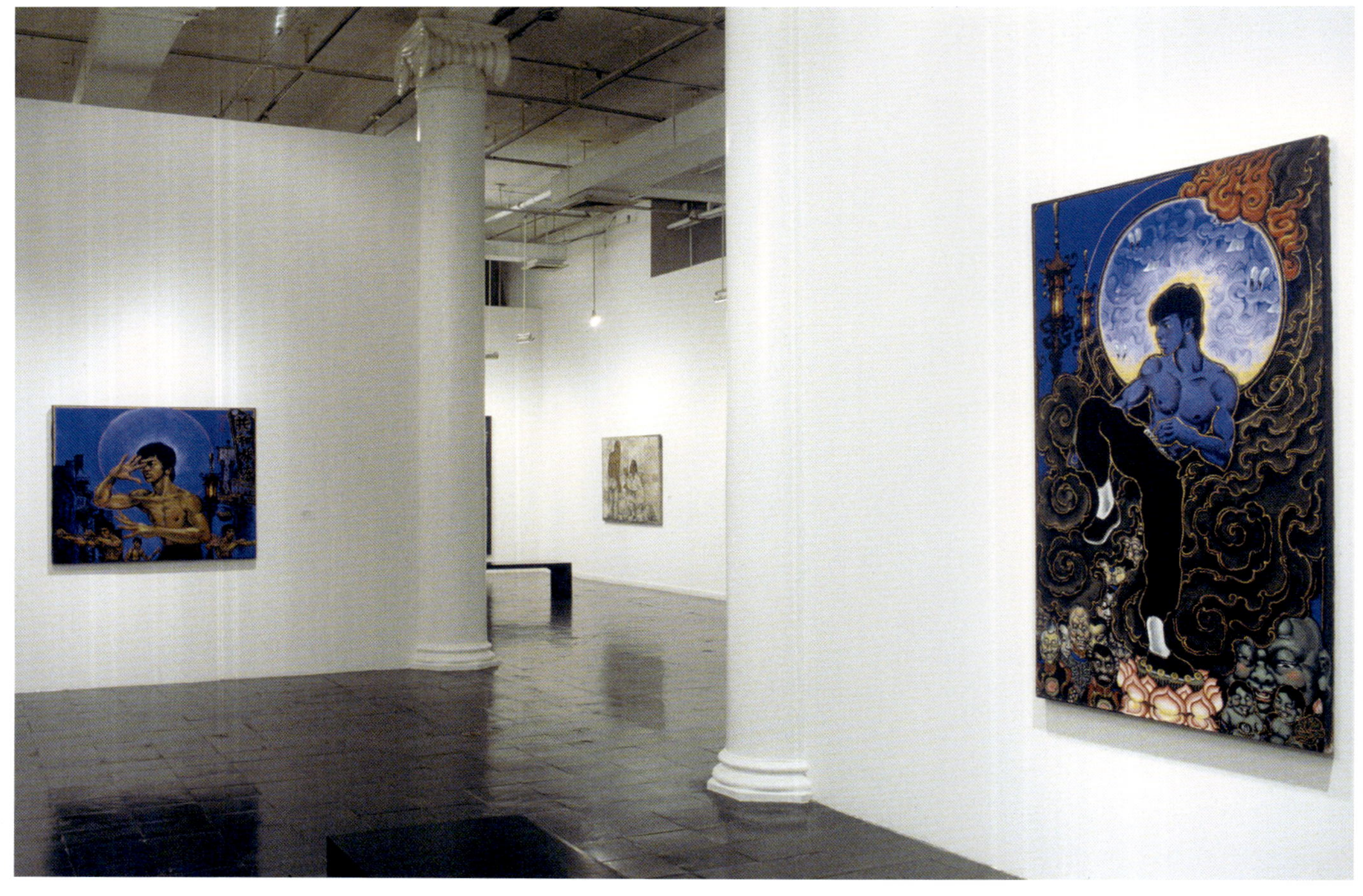

Left to right: Martin
Wong, *Clones of Bruce
Lee*, 1992, and *Bruce Lee
in the Afterworld*, 1991

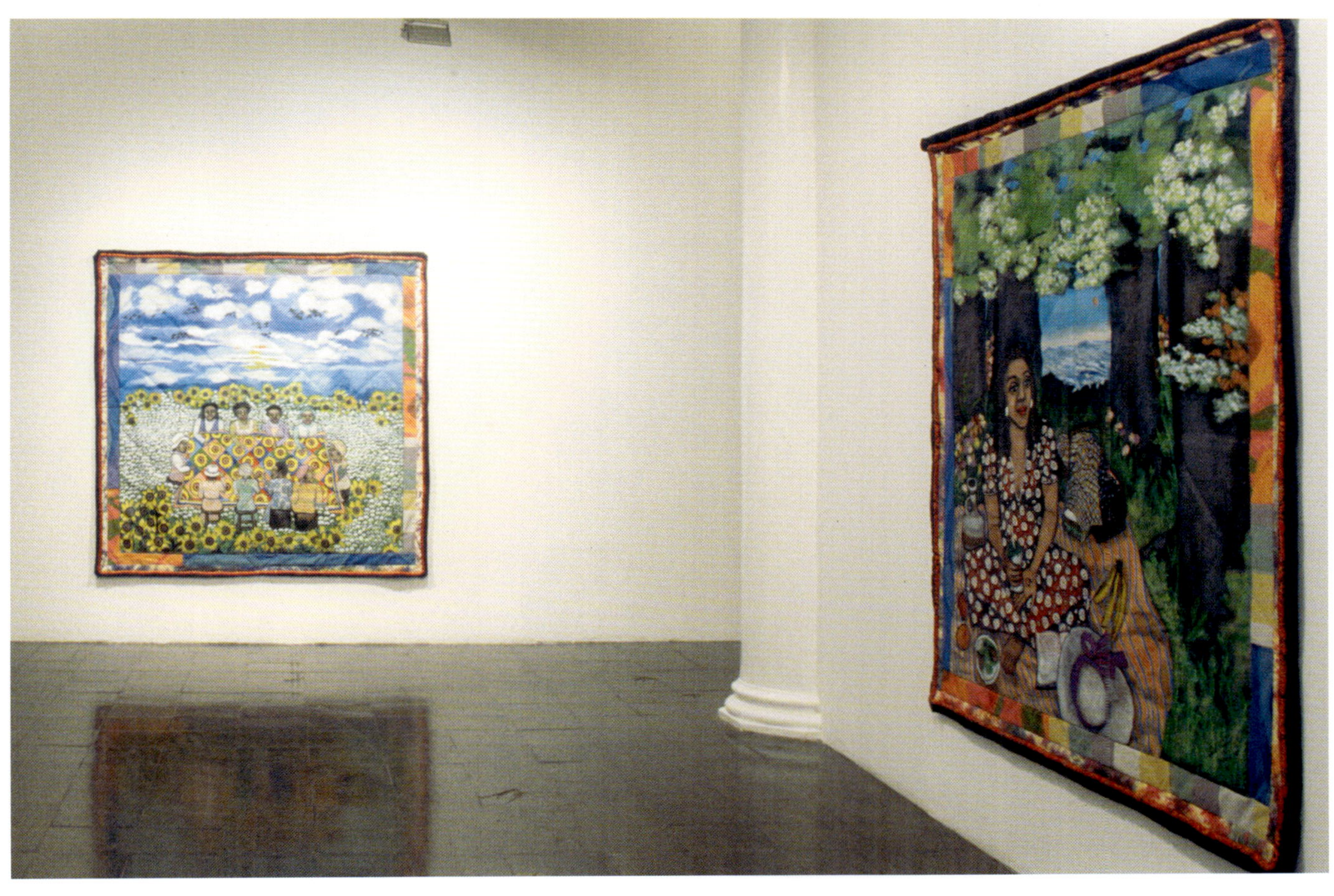

Left to right: Faith
Ringgold, *Cotton Fields,
Sunflowers, Blackbirds
and Quilting Bees,*
1997, and *Picnic on the
Grass… Alone,* 1997

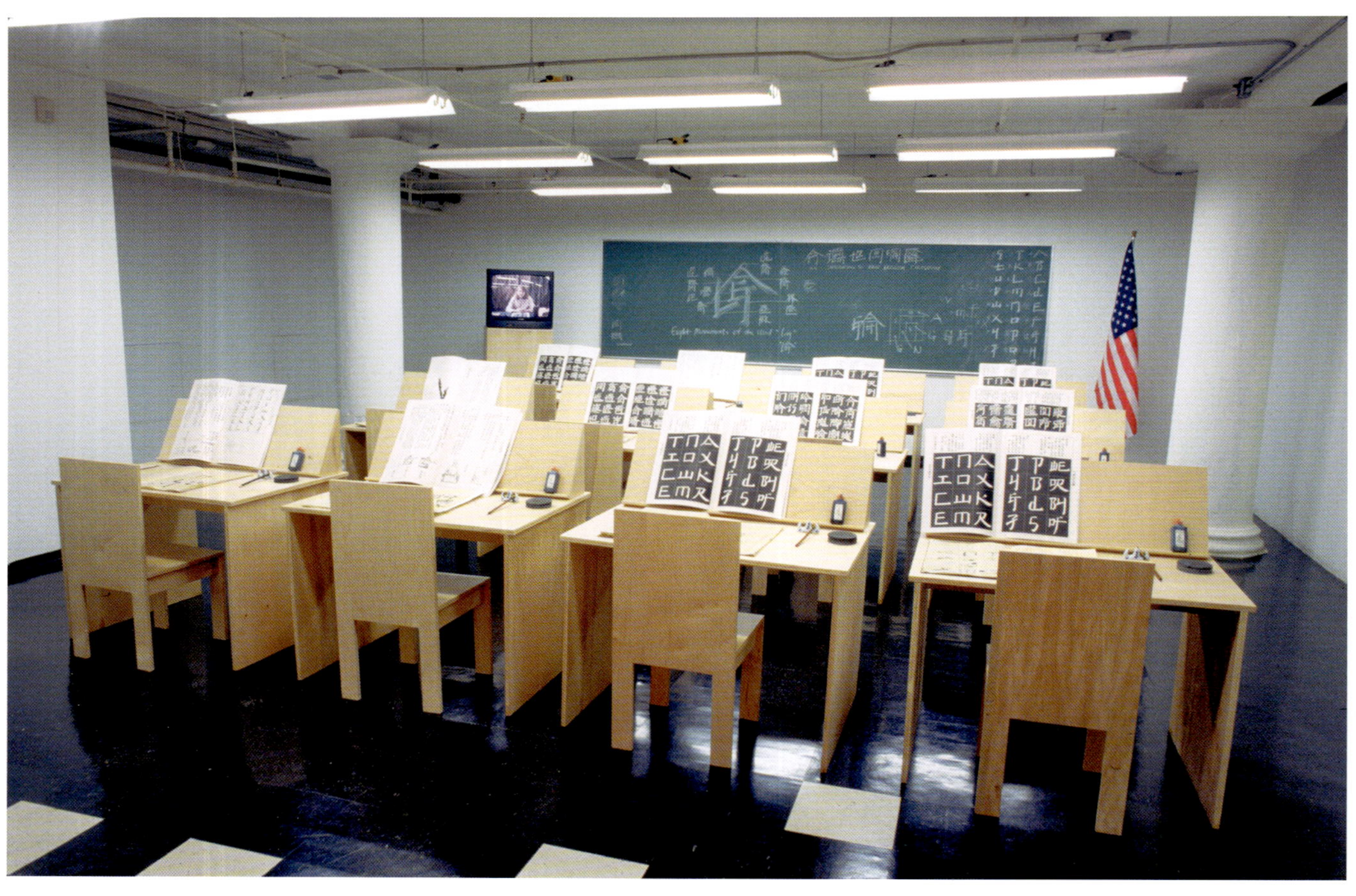

Installation views

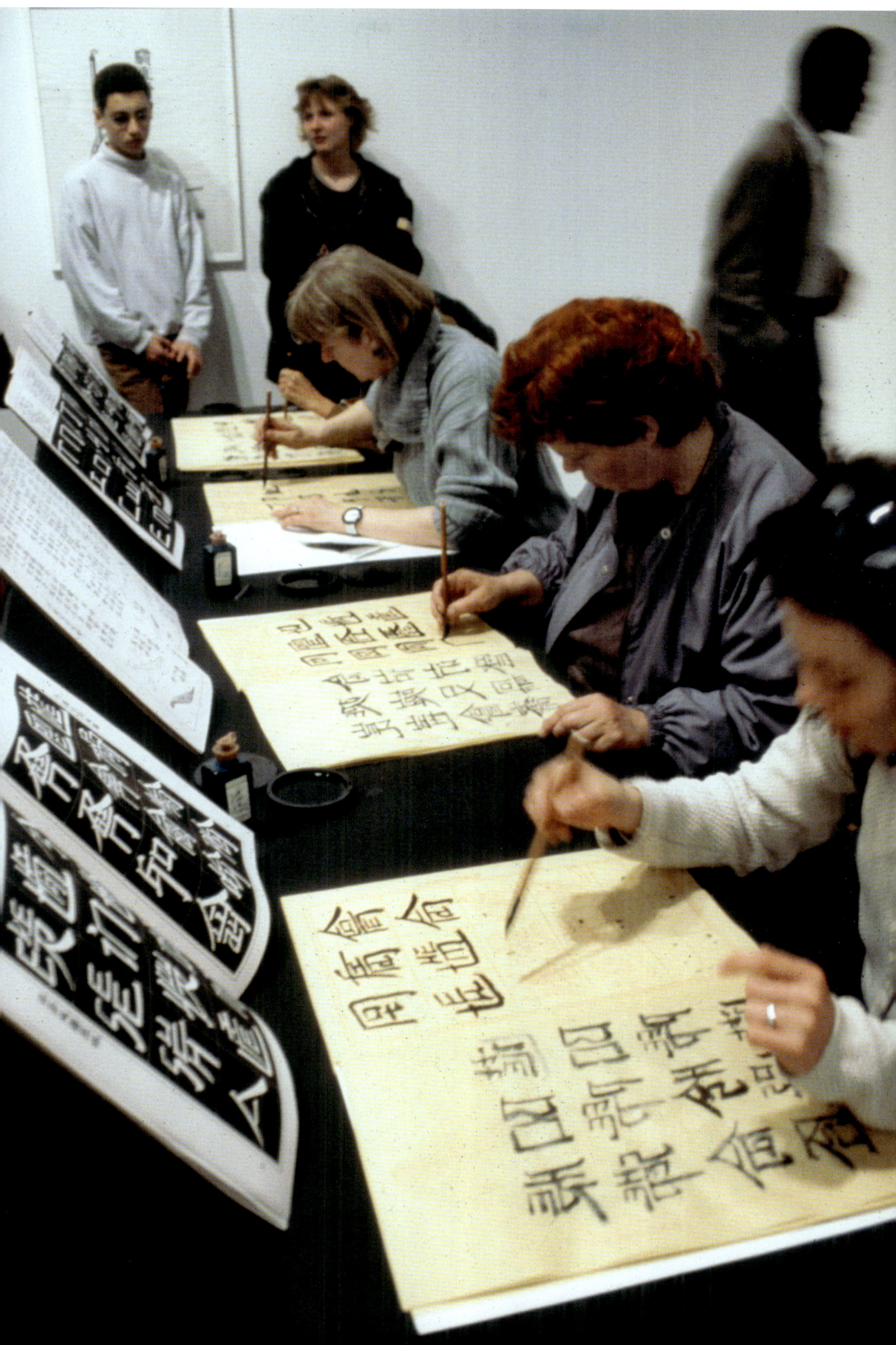

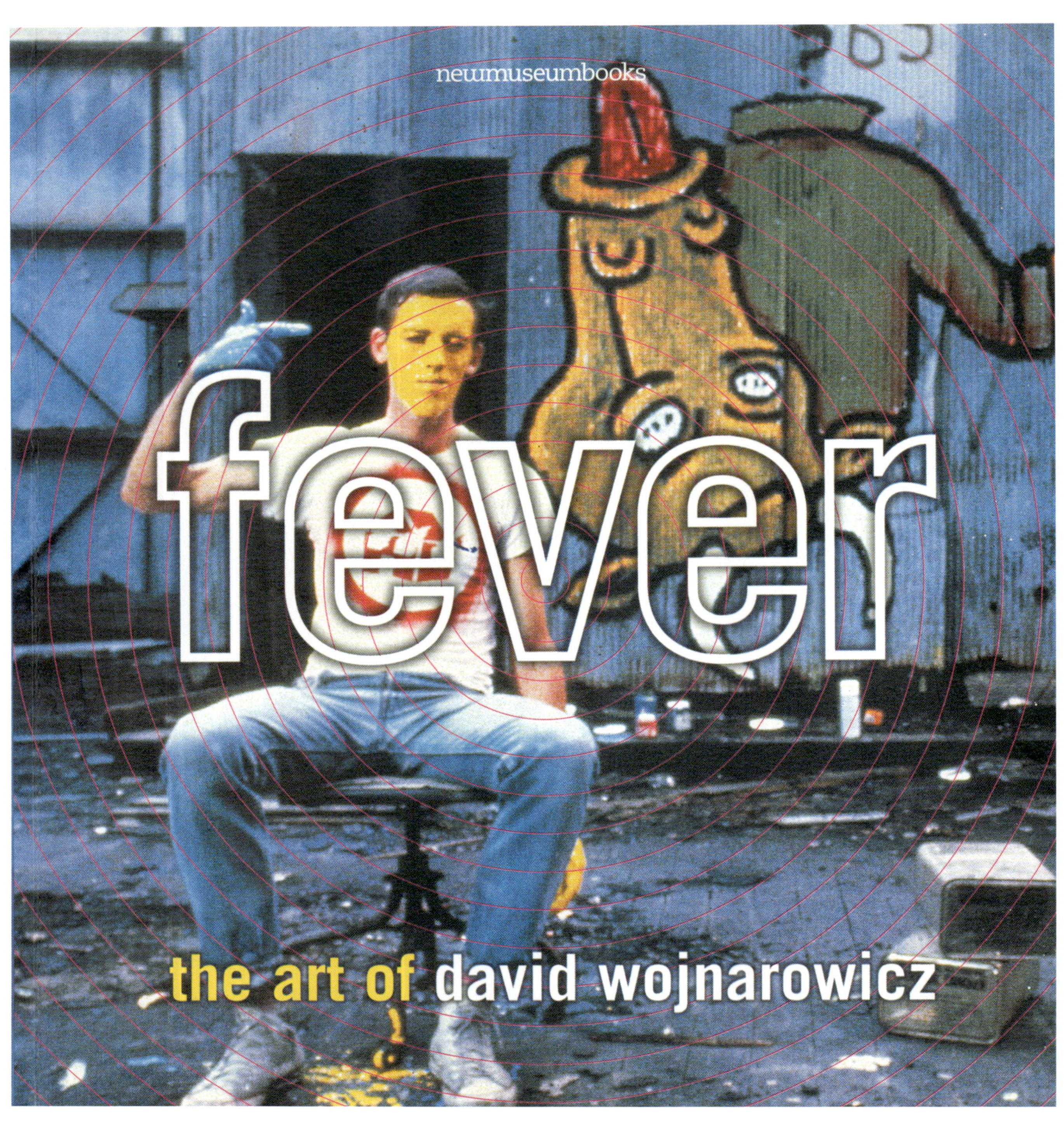

Catalogue for "Fever: The
Art of David Wojnarowicz,"
published by the New
Museum in 1999. Cover
photo by Ivan Dalla Tana

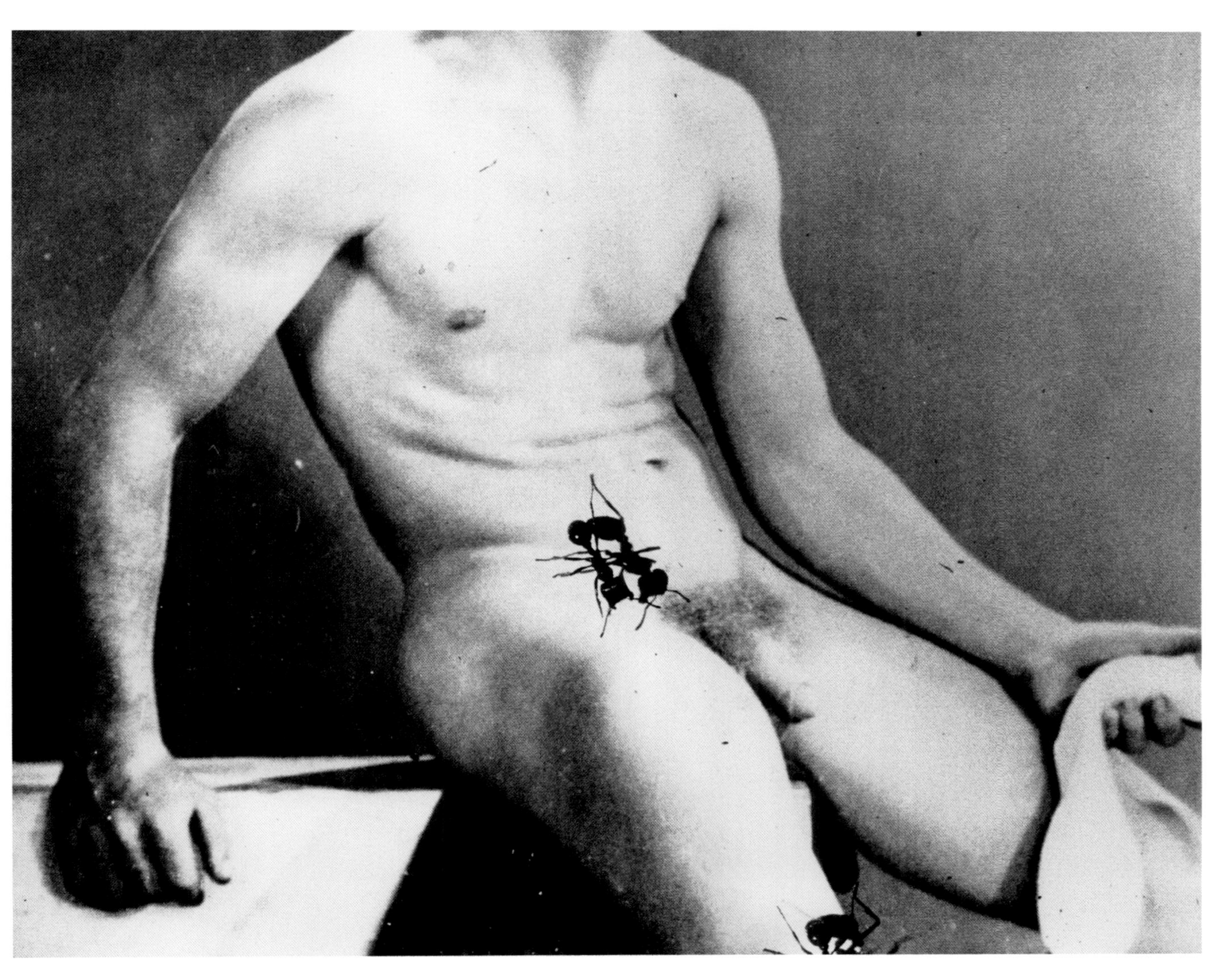

David Wojnarowicz,
Untitled (Desire),
from *Ant Series*, 1988

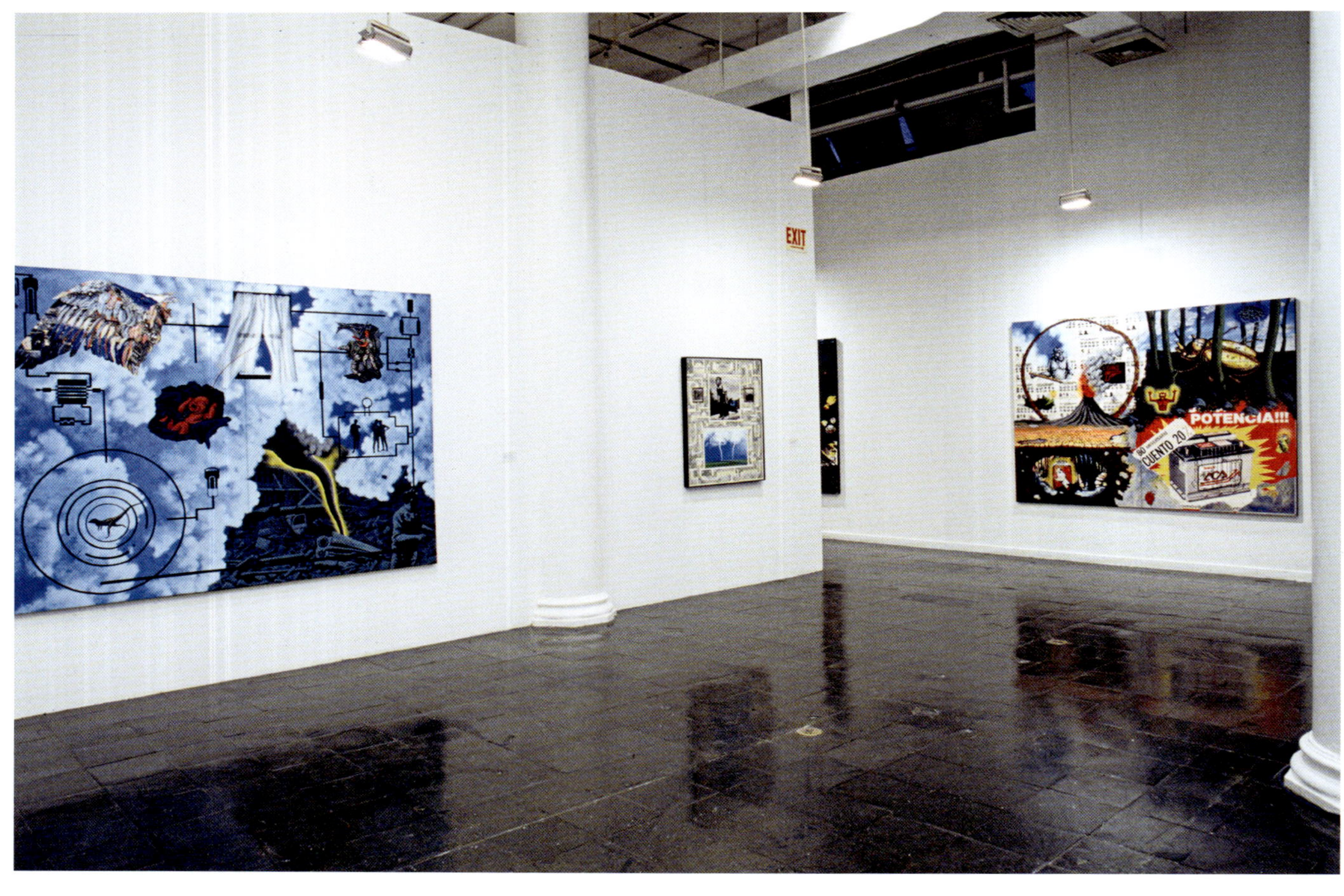

Left to right: David
Wojnarowicz, *Wind (for
Peter Hujar)*, 1987;
Fear of Evolution,
1988–89; and *Fire*, 1987

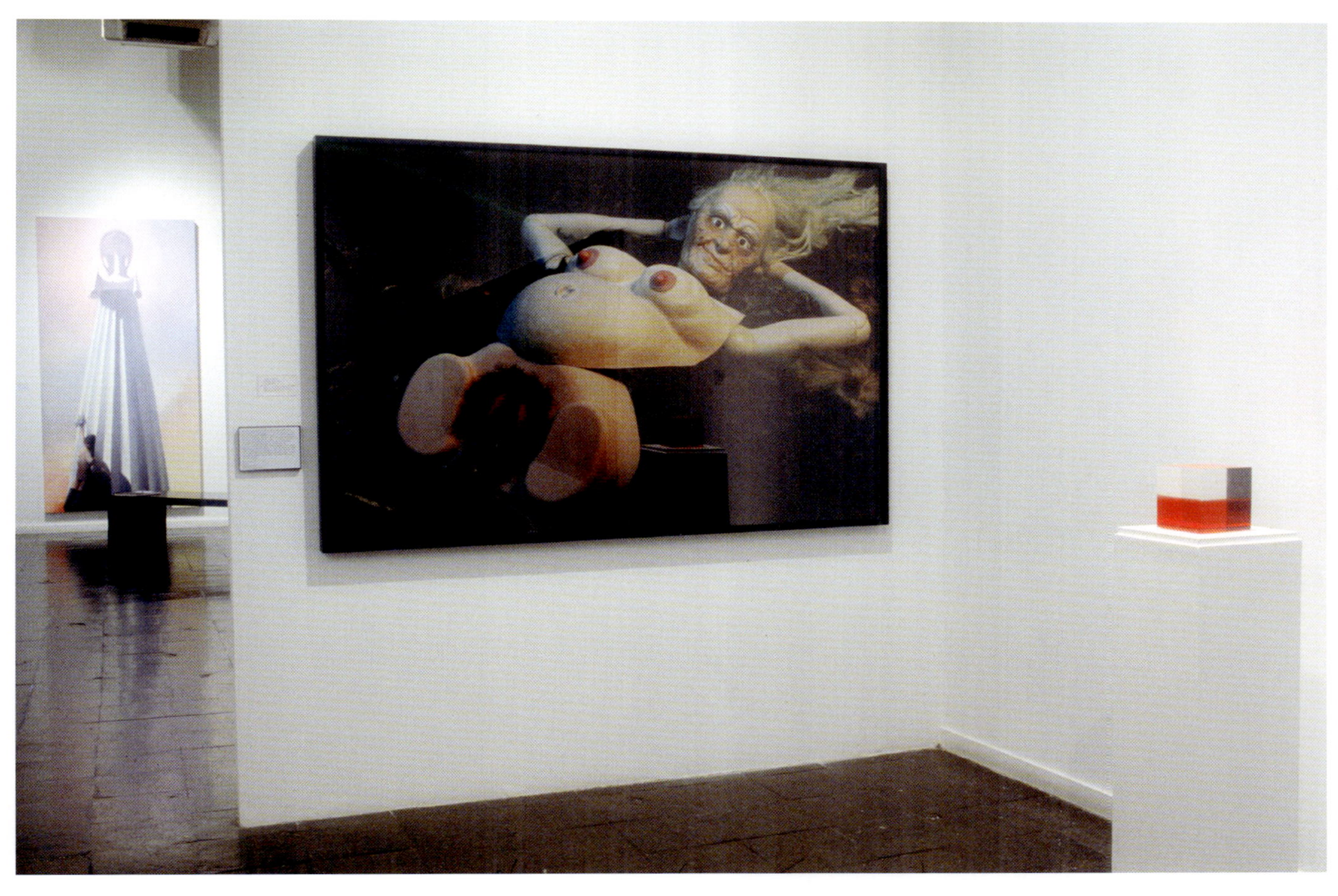

Left to right: works by
Lisa Yuskavage, Cindy
Sherman, and Micah Lexier

Cildo Meireles

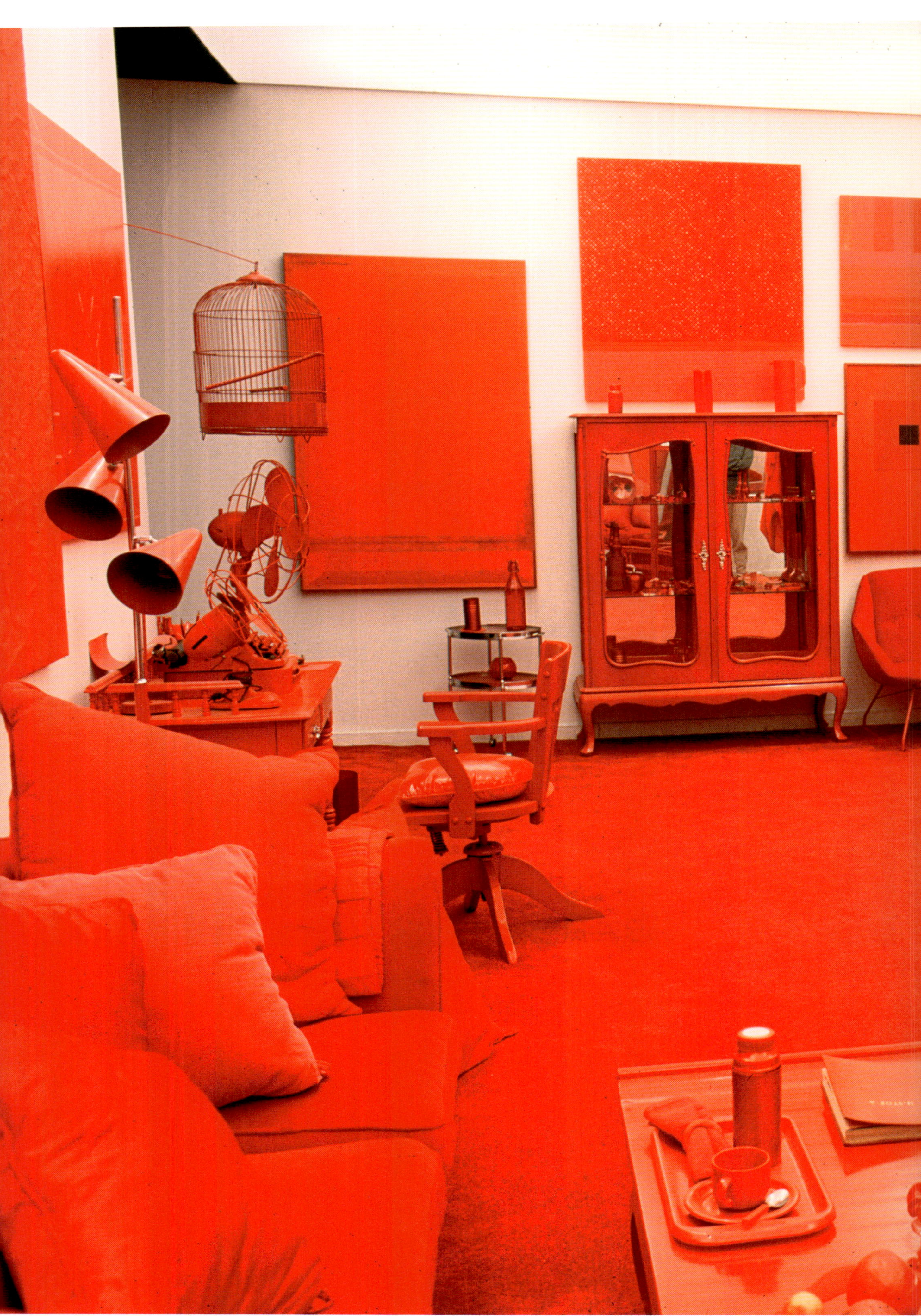

Cildo Meireles,
*Desvio para o Vermelho:
Impregnação, Entorno,
Desvio*, 1967–84

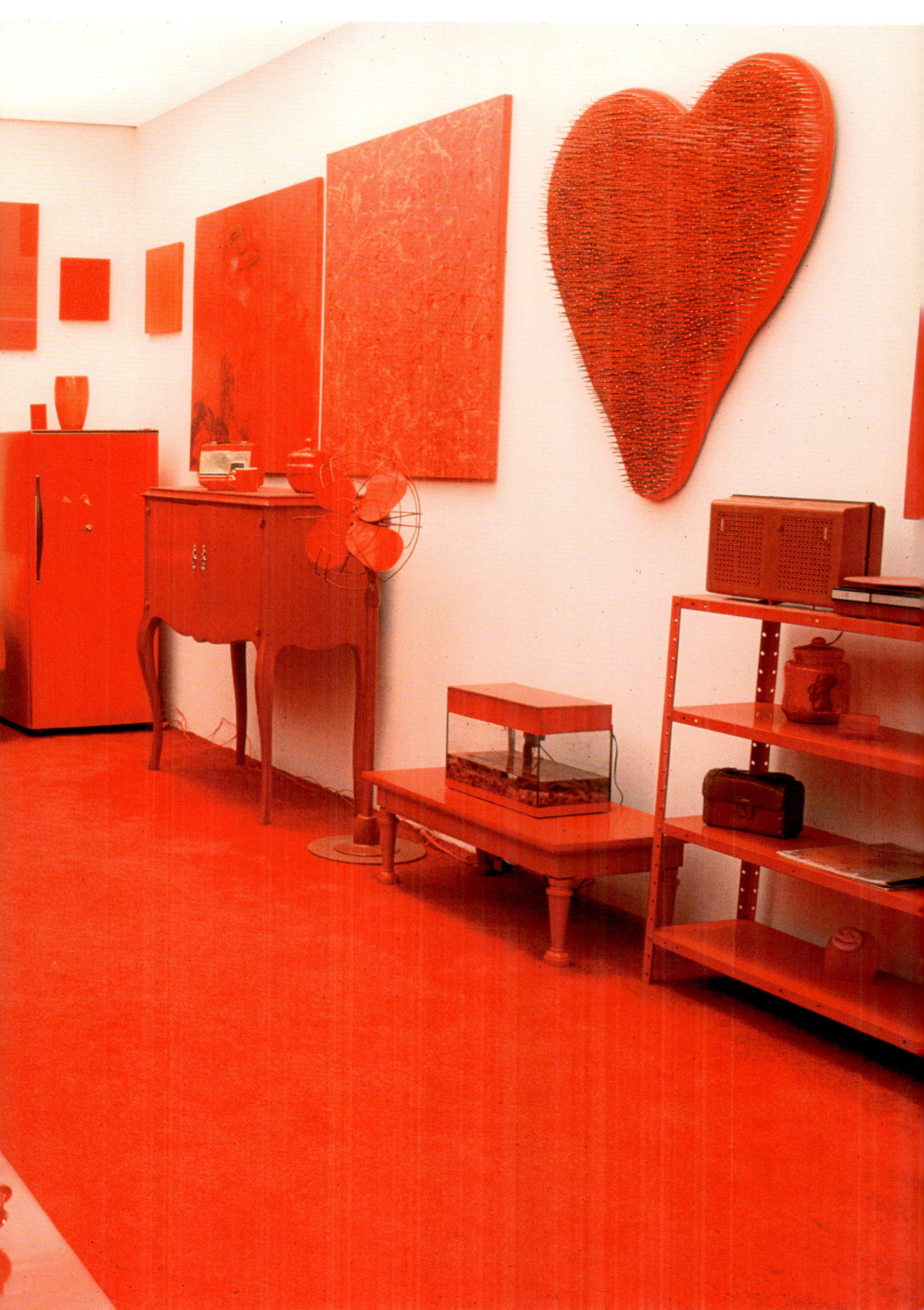

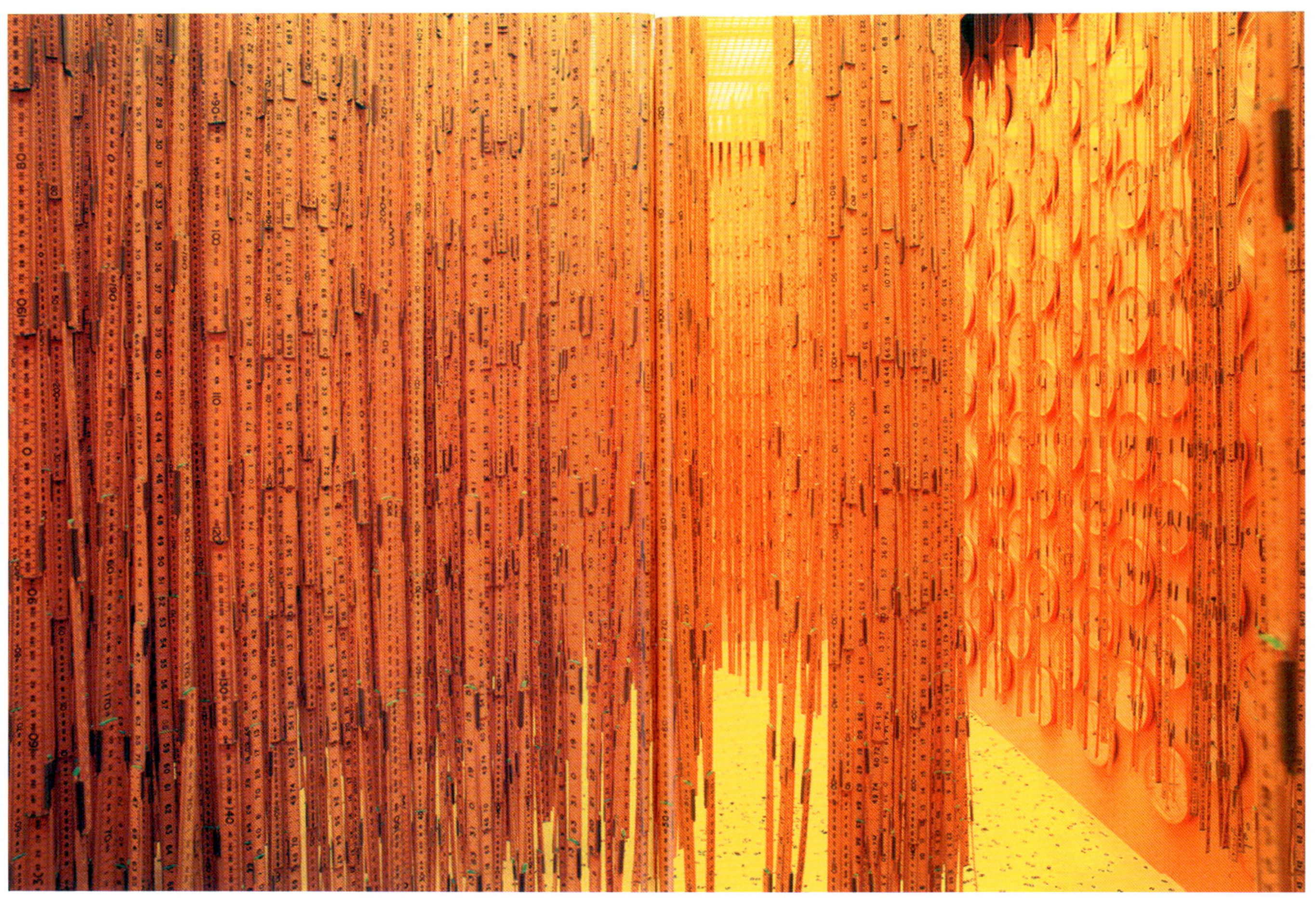

Cildo Meireles,
Fontes, 1992 (detail)

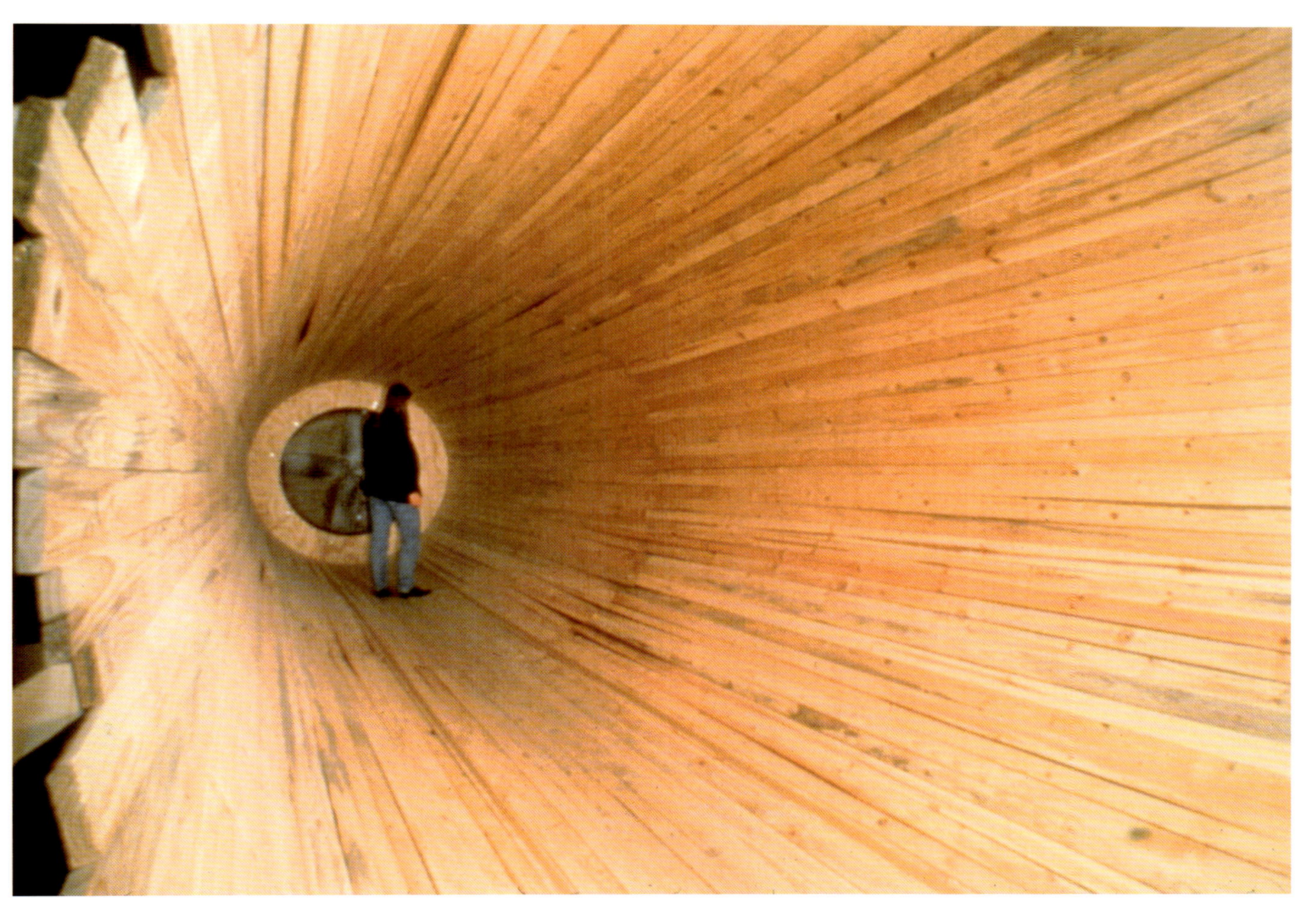

Cildo Meireles,
Entrevendo [Glimpsing],
1970–94

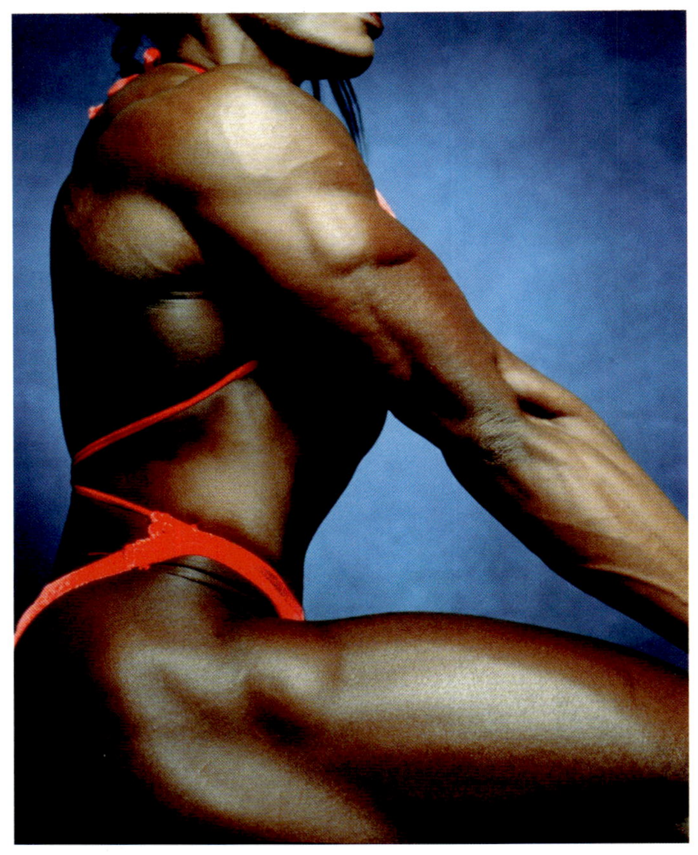

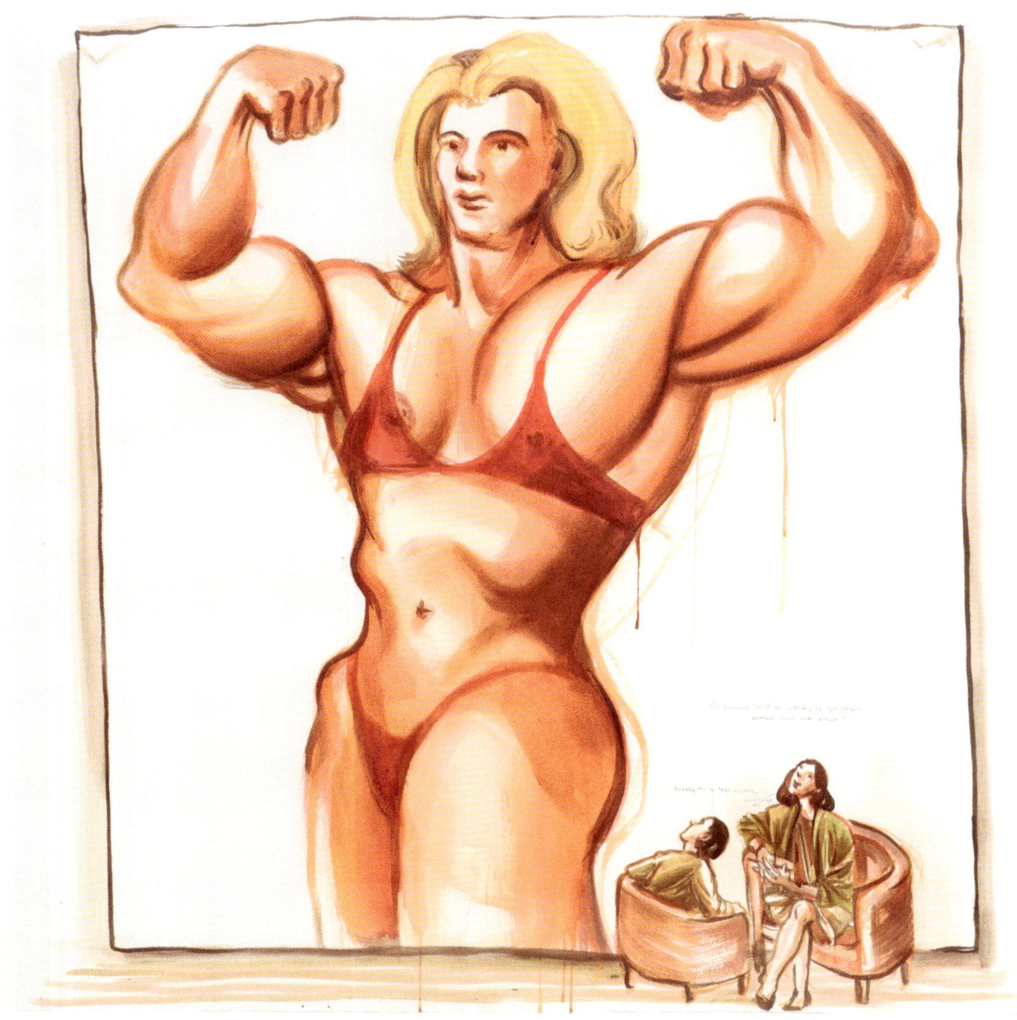

(top) Andres Serrano,
*Lisa Lewis (from Big
Women)*, 1999

(bottom) Nicole Eisenman,
The Largest Woman, 1994

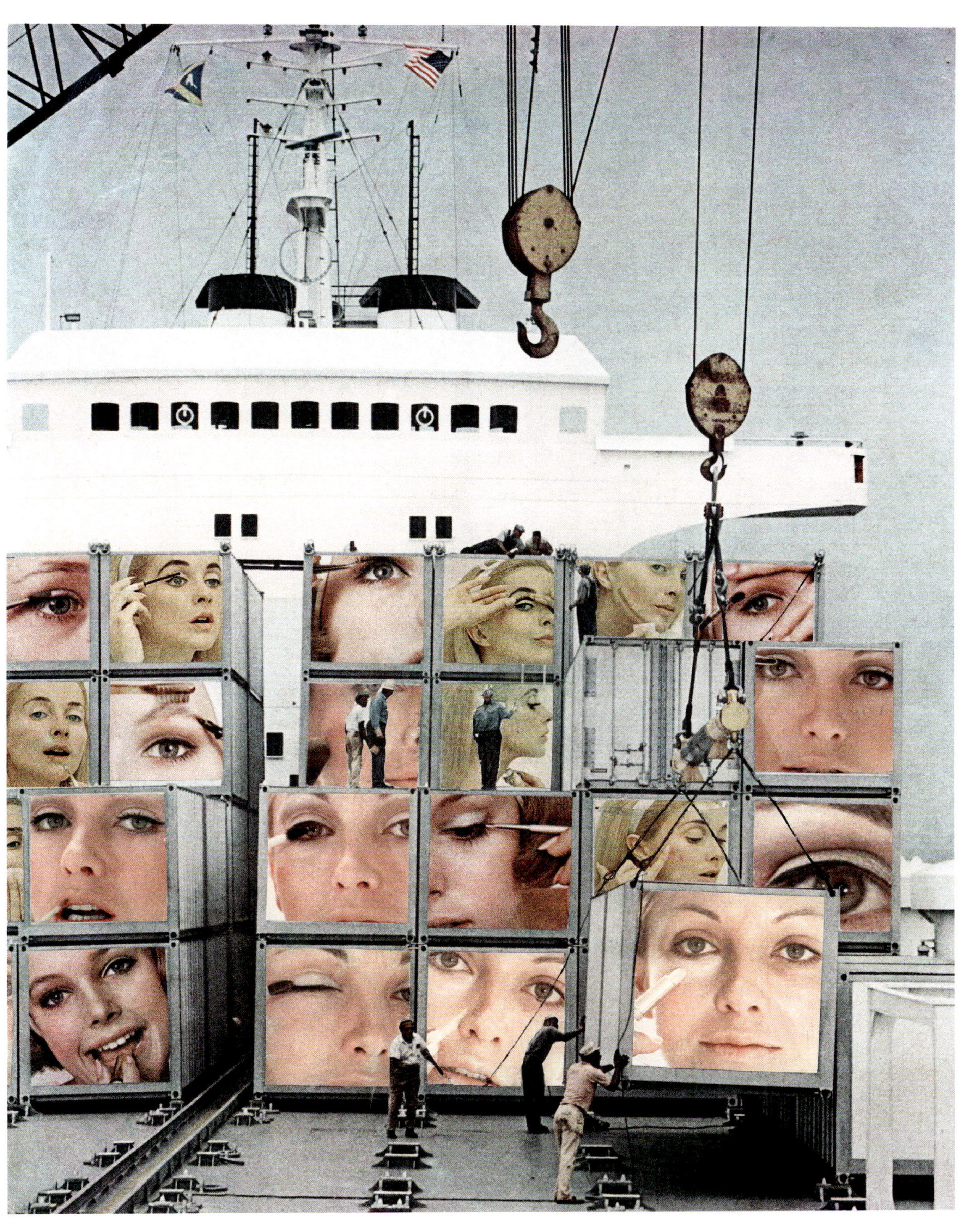

Martha Rosler,
Cargo Cult, from the
series *Body Beautiful,
or Beauty Knows No Pain*,
ca. 1966–72

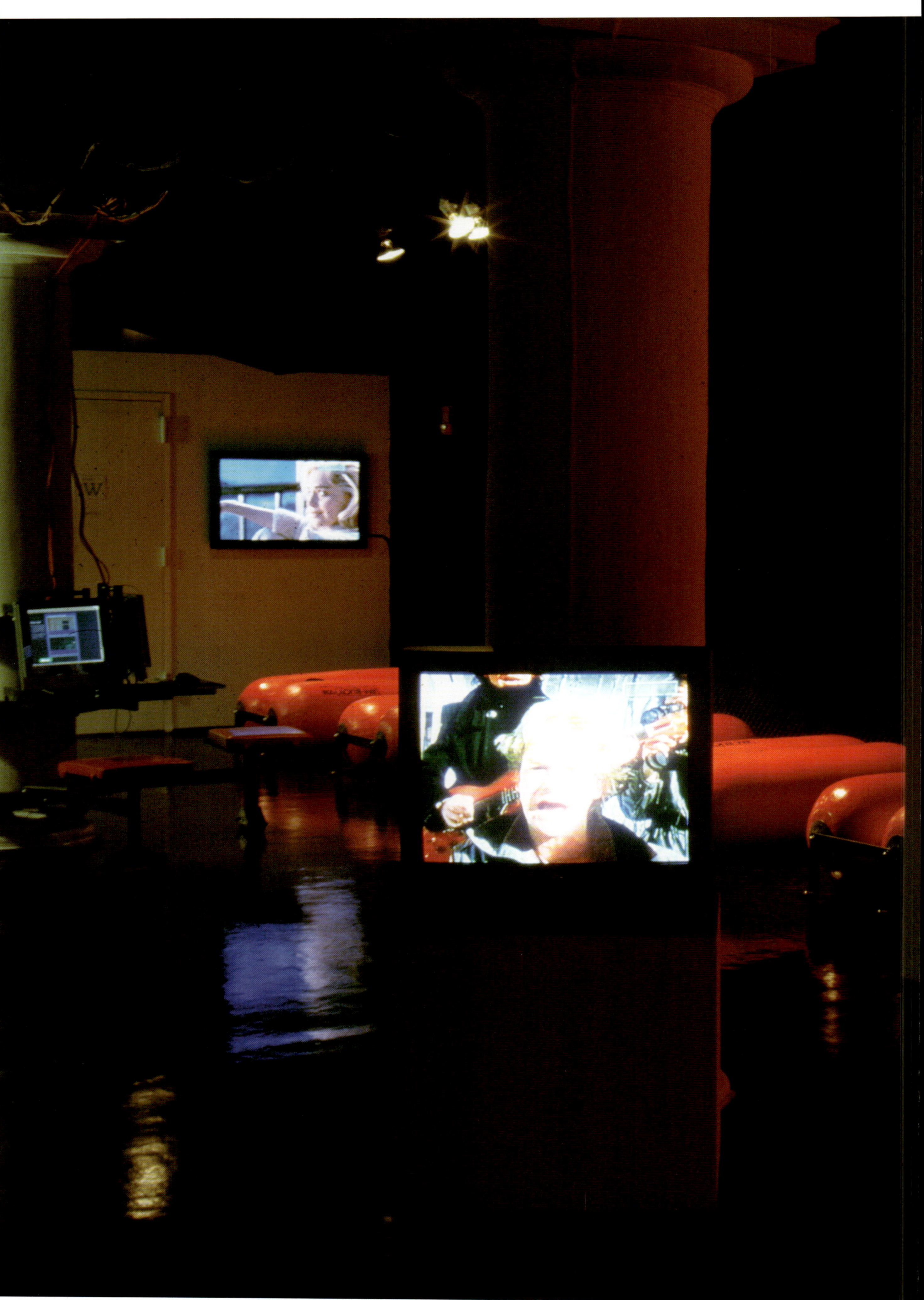

Installation view. This exhibition is one in a series of programs inaugurating the New Museum's Media Lounge, a space dedicated to the display of digital art, experimental video, and sound works

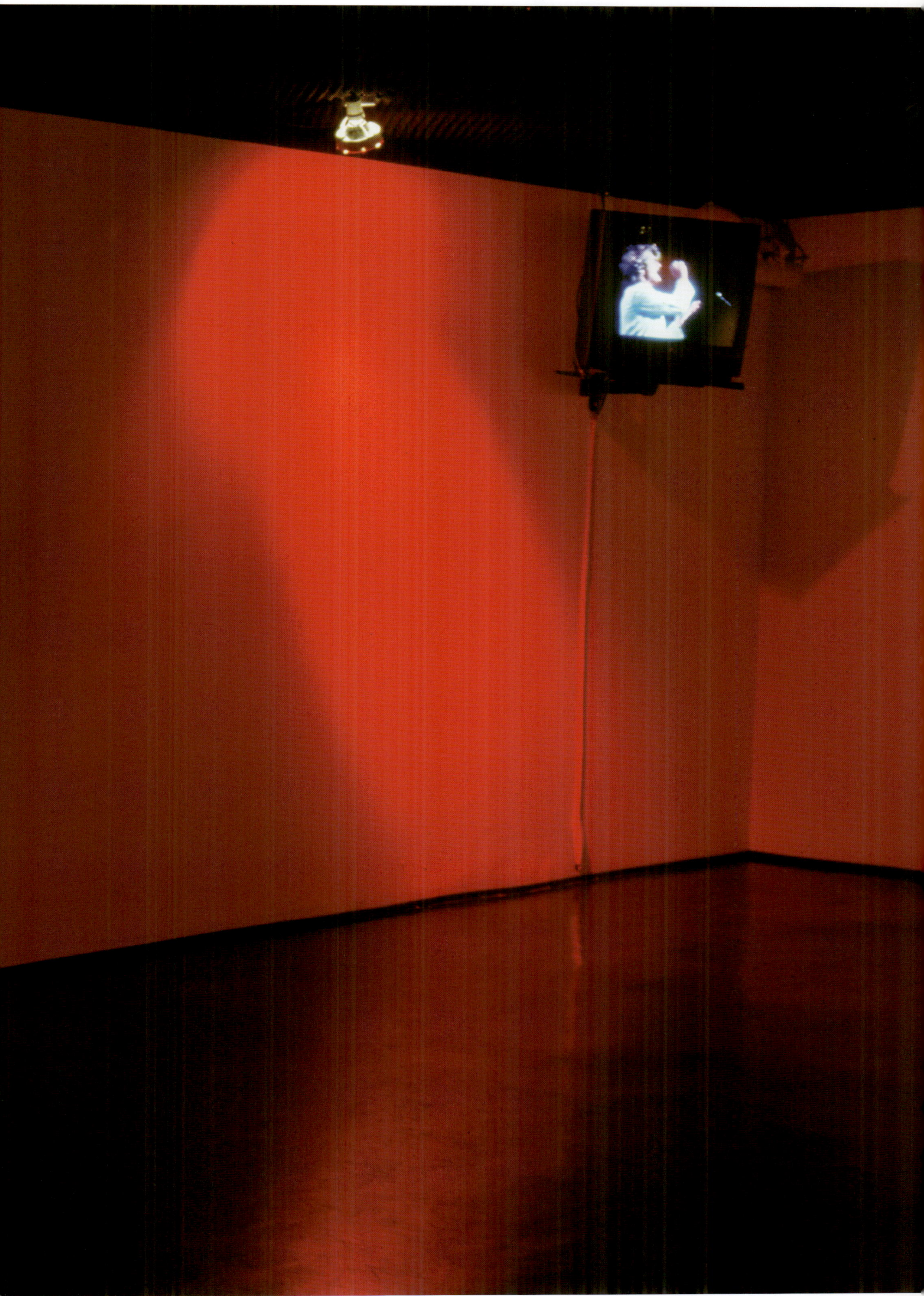

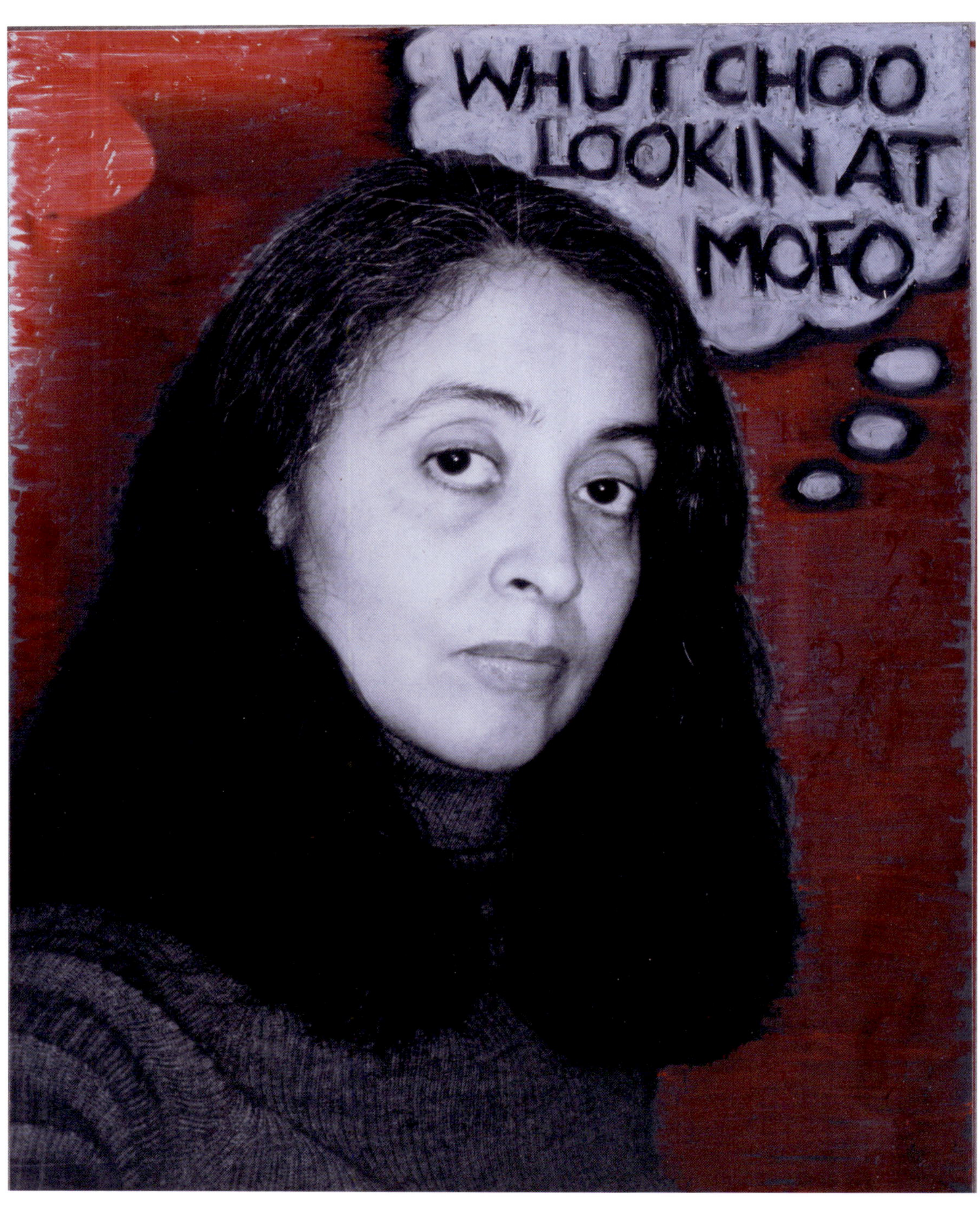

Adrian Piper,
Self Portrait as a Nice White Lady, 1995

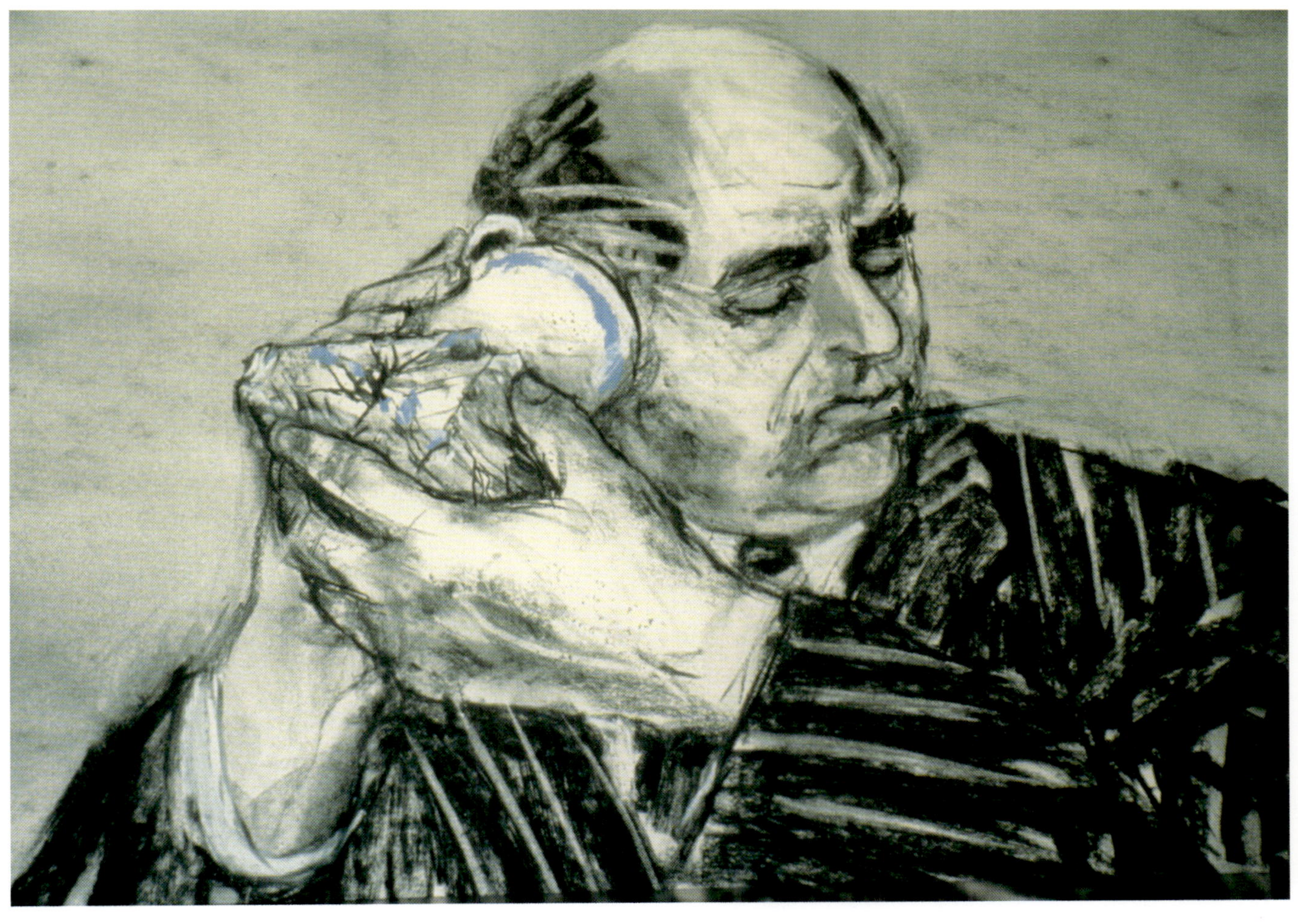

William Kentridge,
drawing for the film
WEIGHING...and WANTING, 1997

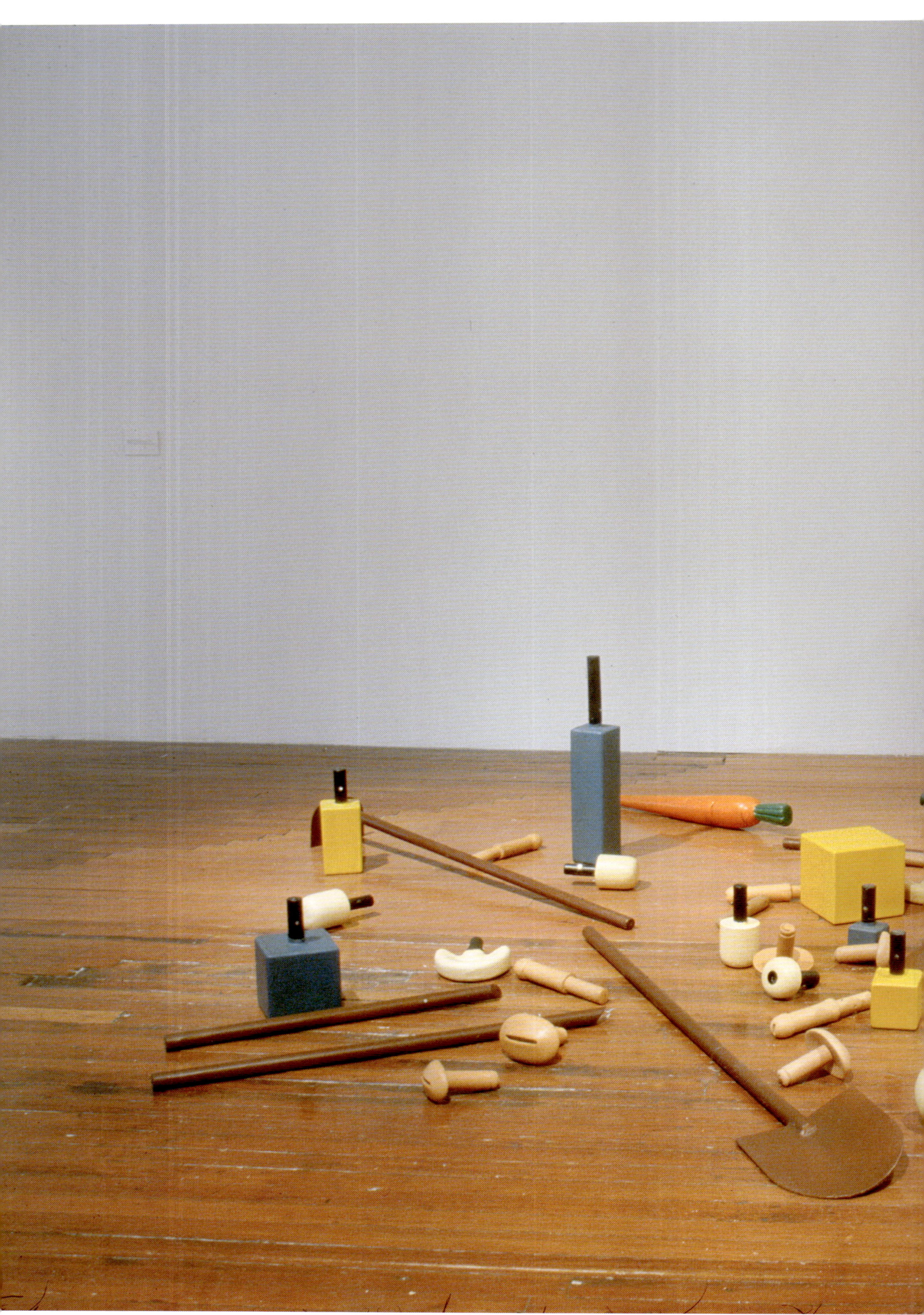

Paul McCarthy,
Tomato Head (Green), 1994

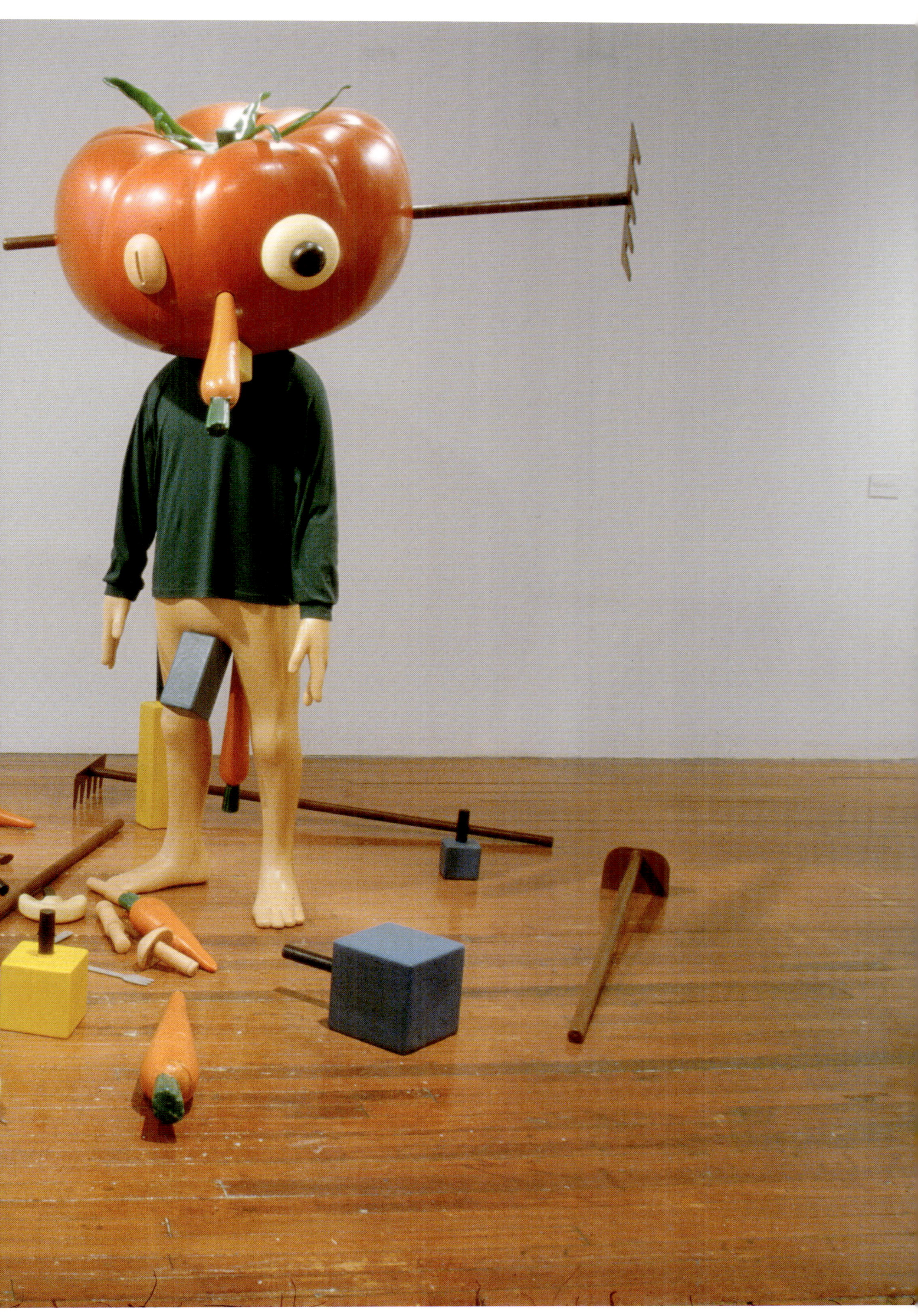

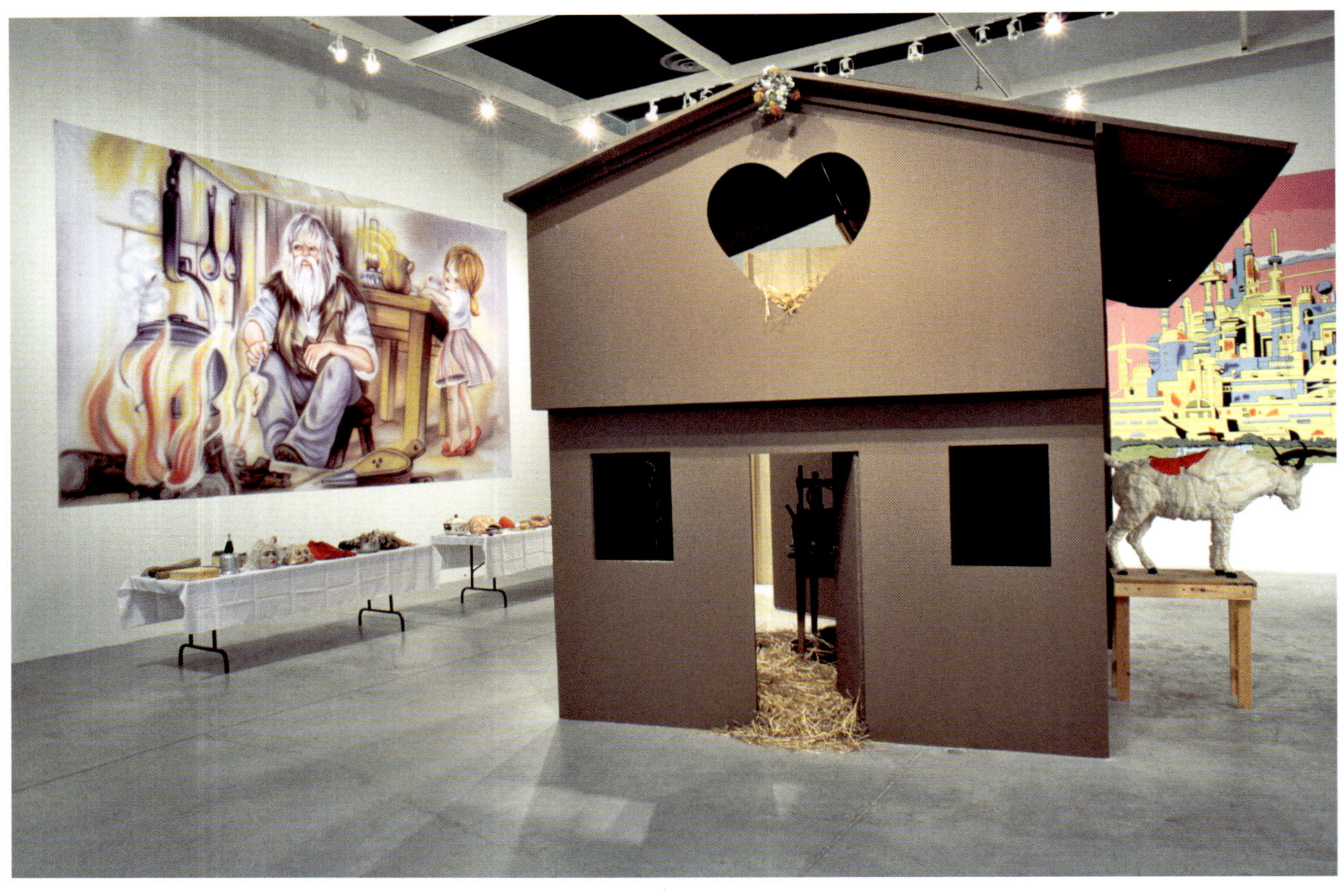

Paul McCarthy and Mike
Kelley, *Heidi, Midlife
Crisis Trauma Center and
Negative Media-Engram
Abreaction Release Zone,*
1992

The Museum as Site: Art and Activism at the New Museum

Brian Wallis

Folks strolling on Broadway in New York's SoHo neighborhood on the evening of December 8, 1984, may have been startled by the sudden apparition of an enormous padlock on the north side of the old Astor Building, its ground floor occupied at that time by the New Museum of Contemporary Art.[1] The image of a lock was a projection from an adjacent building by Krzysztof Wodiczko, a Polish-American artist and activist for the homeless. It was meant to dramatize the plight of individuals locked outside on that winter's night, like those in the full-time homeless encampment in Tompkins Square Park, near Wodiczko's East Village apartment. The projection was also meant to remind viewers that the sixteen loft floors above the Museum were empty and padlocked, warehoused for future gentrification by wealthy investors. Wodiczko's public spectacle pointed to New York City's devastating homelessness crisis—precipitated by the unrestrained redevelopment of urban housing and the city's curtailment of social services—in which over 100,000 people were without housing.

Wodiczko's activist gesture could be seen as directed at the New Museum itself for its complicity in gentrification, while also suggesting its potential as a site for oppositional discourse and action. In this respect, the lock signified the traditional role of the museum as a secure space, a protector of cultural memory, shielding what is inside from the social and political exigencies outside. The image of the locked museum raised further questions: Was there a public that the Museum was excluding?

1. Krzysztof Wodiczko was participating in a small exhibition at the New Museum—"John Hernandez, Shelley Hull, Robin Winters, Krzysztof Wodiczko" (1984)—that featured photographic documentation of his earlier work. At the last moment, he organized a simple projection for the opening night. Titled *The Astor Building Projection*, it was a guerrilla action, with no prior announcement or permit. Later in the run of the exhibition, he restaged the projection, incorporating an additional lock and chain, on the Museum's facade; the final version was named *The New Museum Projection*.

Were political ideas about culture and society being locked in or locked out? What was the social responsibility of the Museum in light of what was transpiring outside, on the street?

Wodiczko was challenging the definition of the museum as a protected elitist space and insisting that it be a forum for political debate, part of what he referred to as "an oppositional public sphere."[2] This concept, articulated by the German theorists Oskar Negt and Alexander Kluge, was conceived as a critique of the popular idea of the public sphere propounded in the 1960s by the philosopher Jürgen Habermas.[3] For Habermas, the public sphere in liberal democracies was a site of public discourse, a universal space where citizens formulate public opinion and ideas compete for recognition. In proposing an oppositional public sphere, Negt and Kluge envisioned a process rather than a place, a proletarian response in multiple local collectives to what Habermas viewed as a single ascendant agora of bourgeois liberalism. The oppositional public sphere comprised a diversity of competing communities, each responding to its own unique cultural contexts and histories. Wodiczko's outdoor projection on the New Museum addressed the interests of the homeless, but it was also part of a wider critical social practice intended to raise fundamentally political questions about public space, public discourse, and, more specifically, the museum as a site of the oppositional public sphere.

The provocative notion that the museum could be more than an idealistic and politically disengaged space for

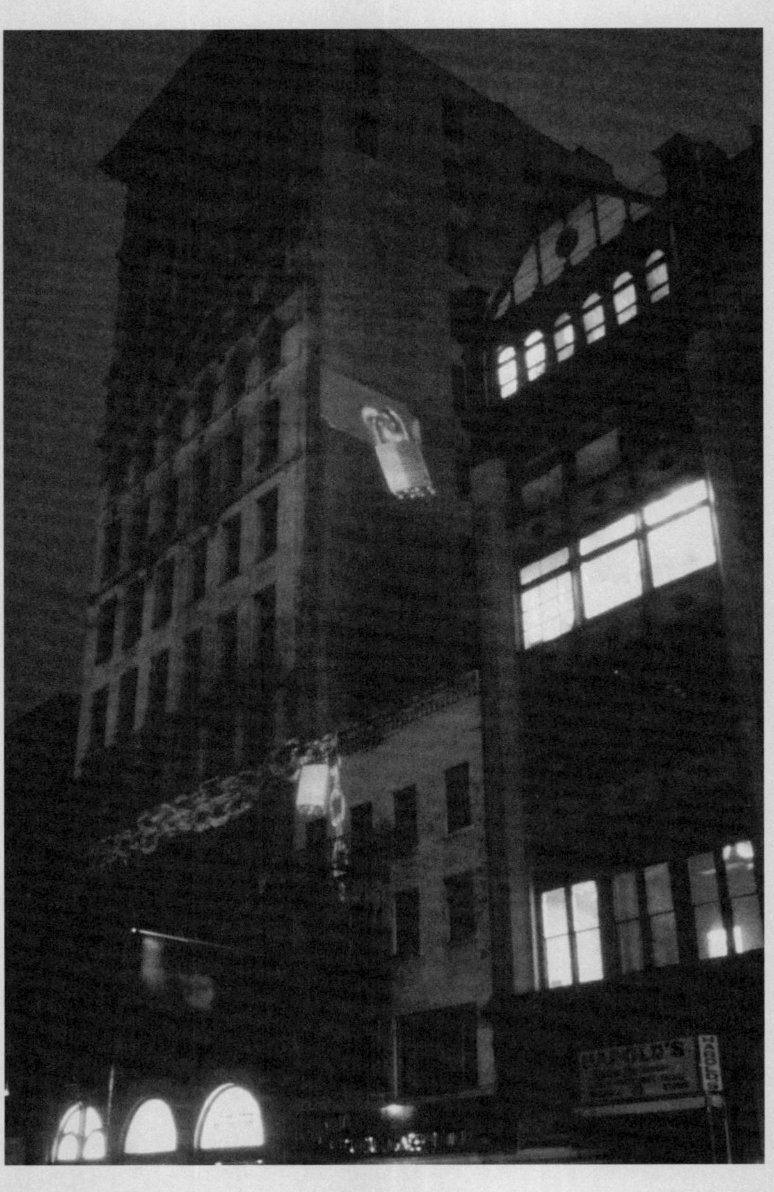

Krzysztof Wodiczko,
*The New Museum
Projection*, 1984

leisure and aesthetic contemplation and could be an active
forum for debate about public issues and everyday life was
in many ways the defining ethos of the New Museum.
Founded in 1977, by former Whitney Museum of American
Art curator Marcia Tucker, the New Museum was fundamentally an alternative space, but it pointedly retained
the word "museum" in its name precisely to challenge the
definition of that word. For Tucker, the New Museum was
an evolving political statement, a social microcosm, and an
experimental laboratory where both art and the practices
of the institution itself were always in question. To what
extent could the museum articulate the social meanings of
art and political activism? Tucker aimed to bring everyday
activities into the museum and to extend the critical analyses and dialogues inherent in cultural production to the
social sphere outside the museum.

This mission, foregrounded by the New Museum in the
1980s, elicited radical positions and strategies that
differed substantially from standard museum practices
and previous forms of political art. The new approaches
went beyond protests and propaganda. The critic Lucy
R. Lippard, in a catalogue for the 1984 New Museum
exhibition "Art & Ideology," defined activist art as a
practice in which "some element of the art takes place
in the 'outside world,' including some teaching and media
practice as well as community and labor organizing,
public political work, and organizing within the artist's
community."[4] For Lippard, activist art existed mainly
outside the museum, in public spaces and in direct
confrontation with political power. But for other thinkers,
activism was more critical and theoretical, and the
museum was a crucial platform for it. And for others still,
it was precisely inside the museum that the machina-
tions of power could best be exposed and examined.

2.   Krzysztof Wodiczko, quoted in Douglas Crimp, Rosalyn Deutsche, and Ewa Lajer-
      Burcharth, "A Conversation with Krzysztof Wodiczko," *October* (Autumn 1986): 32.

3.   See Jürgen Habermas, *The Structural Transformation of the Public Sphere: An Inquiry
      into a Category of Bourgeois Society* (1962), trans. Thomas Burger (Cambridge, MA:
      MIT Press, 1989); and Oskar Negt and Alexander Kluge, *Public Sphere and Experience:
      Toward an Analysis of the Bourgeois and Proletarian Public Sphere* (1972), trans.
      Peter Labanyi, Jamie Owen Daniel, and Assenka Oksiloff (Minneapolis: University of
      Minnesota Press, 1993).

4.   Lucy R. Lippard, "Give and Take: Ideology in the Art of Suzanne Lacy and Jerry Kearns,"
      in *Art & Ideology* (New York: New Museum, 1984), 29.

During the 1980s, the New Museum set forth an unprece-dented model of the museum as a catalyst for social transformation, a partner in activist undertakings that might take place within the galleries or beyond, and a forum for discussions of issues that could involve funda-mental challenges to the museum itself. As a curator at the New Museum from 1982 to 1987, I was directly involved in some of the exhibitions and activities mentioned here; I was an avid witness to the others. Today, when activist art, widespread protest, and guerrilla manifestations of the oppositional public sphere are increasingly urgent, it seems worthwhile to revisit that decade's innovative works and strategies, which have become precedents and models for critical thought and action now.

I want to consider three areas of investigation that the New Museum supported and which have had enduring influence: museums and institutional critique, criticism and theory in public space, and the role of collectives in socially engaged art. All three strategies center on redefining artistic practice in relation to shifting notions of democracy, free expression, collective action, and public space. It's not simply that the activities of the New Museum reflected artists' interest in these issues, but that Tucker's radical reconceptualization of the role and function of the museum made this work possible.

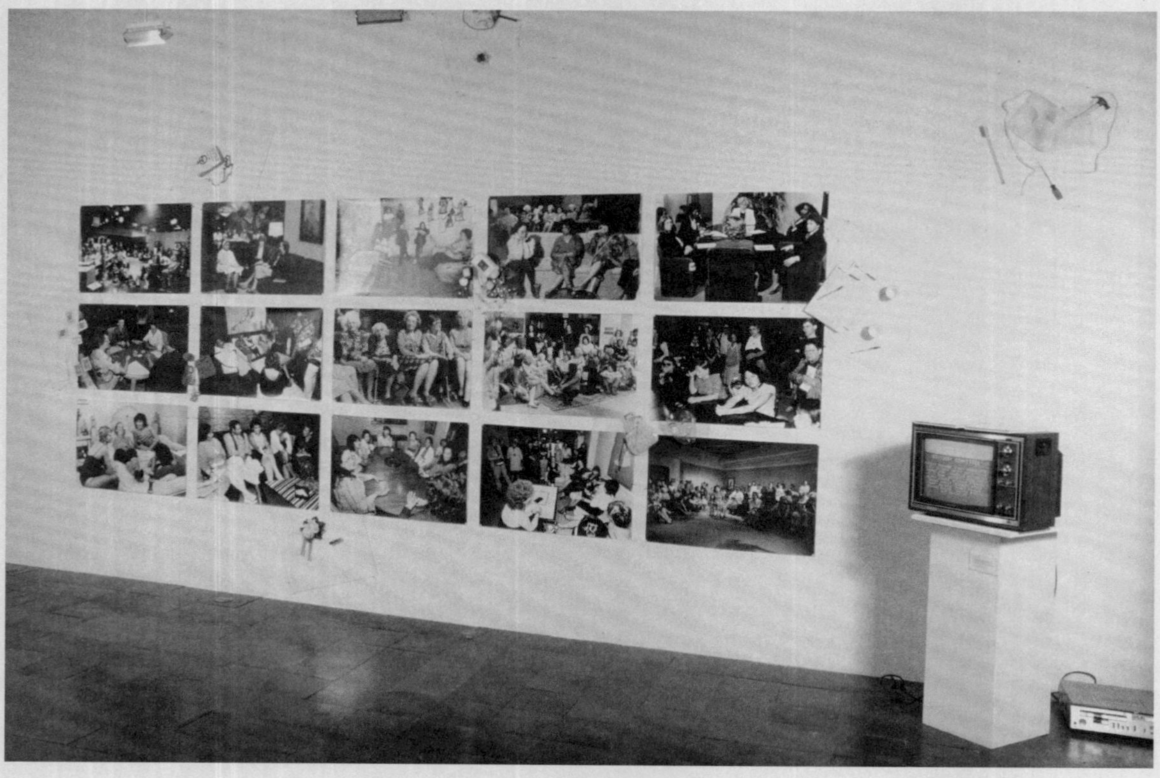

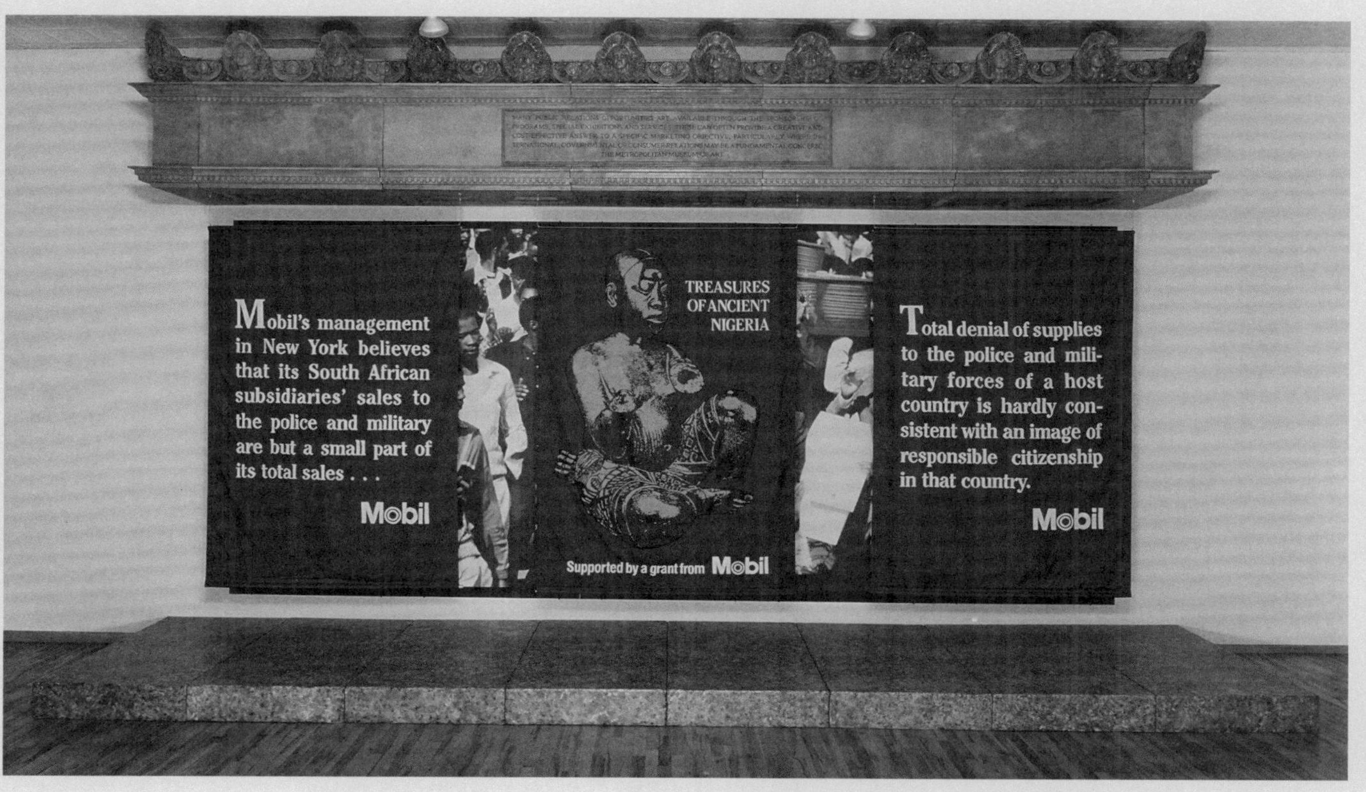

Engaging in rigorous and reflexive research into cultural institutions and their patrons and audiences, artists who practiced institutional critique regarded the museum as a social system that uses aesthetics to mask and legitimate the exercise of political and economic power and to shape ideologies. In a 1983 talk, Hans Haacke memorably referred to museums as "managers of consciousness"; many of the works in his New Museum survey, "Hans Haacke: Unfinished Business" (1986), exposed the underlying motives of the multinational corporations that sponsored art exhibitions.[5] Haacke's *MetroMobiltan* (1985) is a large-scale fiberglass mock-up of the Metropolitan Museum's upper facade that displays a promotional banner for that museum's 1980 exhibition "Treasures of Ancient Nigeria"—a show sponsored by the Mobil Corporation—flanked by Haacke's own banners, which quote a Mobil statement that justified the company's continuing supply of Nigerian oil to the sanctioned apartheid government of South Africa. Support for a glamorous exhibition of treasures from Nigeria's past was exposed as an attempt to paper over an immoral corporate policy in the present. Like Wodiczko's New Museum projection, Haacke's work targets a museum facade, rejecting the

5. A slightly altered version of the talk delivered by Hans Haacke in 1983 in Canberra, Australia, appears as the essay "Museums, Managers of Consciousness," in *Hans Haacke: Unfinished Business*, ed. Brian Wallis (New York: New Museum; Cambridge, MA, and London: MIT Press, 1986), 60–72.

museum's ostensible disengagement from politics by pointing to the power wielded behind its operations.

A younger generation of artists engaged in institutional critique in order not only to map the political and economic entanglements of museum patronage, but also to reveal the ways that the seemingly neutral space of the museum harbored coded references which shape the experiences—and even the behavior—of visitors. Andrea Fraser launched what would become a series of performances of guided tours at the New Museum in 1986. Assuming the persona of one Jane Castleton, a fictional and very prim museum docent, Fraser led viewers through the exhibition "Damaged Goods: Desire and the Economy of the Object," in which she was one of the ten participating artists.[6] In this biting parody of museum education, Fraser offered rich information on aspects of the art museum not usually discussed, such as the architecture, security systems, and board of directors. She explored the implicit psychological desires—the admiration of wealth and breeding and status—to which museums appeal as they produce an ideal consumer, a process that was replicated in the ways the viewers of her satiric performance embodied the etiquette expected of proper museum spectators.

Artists who engaged in institutional critique were often criticized for participating in the very system they purported to challenge.[7] Yet, their rigorous methodologies for researching and dramatically staging interventions in museum spaces yielded some of the most politically astute and influential artworks, ones that connected to and resonated with other activist artists and collectives. Moreover, institutional critique contributed to a nuanced understanding of the role of representation in popular culture and public space. And criticism itself became a tool of activist response. Artists became writers, and writers rallied coalitions, redefining the oppositional public sphere as an exchange, a discourse. The New Museum was unique among cultural institutions in fostering the free expression of a multidisciplinary and multicultural range of critical voices through regular stagings of performance art; screenings of alternative and political video programs; public dialogues about art and community, art and politics, and corporate support for art; education programs for at-risk high school students; a recurring forum called the Minorities Dialogues; publications of critical theory and artists' writings; and collaborations with other nonprofit organizations, including Fashion Moda, Taller Boricua, and En Foco.

These engaged, critical voices compelled viewers to think differently about their social situations and the conditions that shaped them. In her performance video *Cornered* (1988), shown in the New Museum's large window fronting on the busy Broadway sidewalk, Adrian Piper addressed the public directly, challenging each viewer to acknowledge her experience as a light-skinned black woman who is routinely taken for white. "I'm black," she says. "The problem is not just my personal one, about my racial identity. It's also your problem, if you have a tendency to behave in a derogatory or insensitive manner toward blacks when you see none present."[8] More than an exposure of racial biases in a city that prides itself on its professed tolerance, Piper's work also made an important statement about identity, visibility, and silence.

In what came to be called the culture wars of the 1980s, the mounting political awareness and outspokenness of artists during the presidency of Ronald Reagan drew virulent public opposition from right-wing politicians who chafed at the unabridged right to free speech and opposed the public display of certain controversial depictions of sexuality, religion, and patriotism. One of their favorite targets was the artist, writer, and AIDS activist David Wojnarowicz, whose works combined brutally candid expressions of sexuality and mortality (AIDS was decimating the community around him) and rare political acuity. Wojnarowicz overtly challenged the US government

6. "Damaged Goods: Desire and the Economy of the Object," which I curated, included work by Judith Barry, Gretchen Bender, Barbara Bloom, Andrea Fraser, Jeff Koons, Justen Ladda, Louise Lawler, Ken Lum, Allan McCollum, and Haim Steinbach.

7. Ten years after her New Museum performance, Andrea Fraser maintained the continued relevance of strategies of institutional critique. See Andrea Fraser, "From the Critique of Institutions to an Institution of Critique," *Artforum* (September 2005): 278–83, 332.

8. Adrian Piper, "Cornered: A Video Installation Project," in *Theory in Contemporary Art Since 1985*, ed. Zoya Kocur and Simon Leung (New York: Wiley-Blackwell, 2004), 182–86.

for its inaction in addressing the AIDS epidemic and sued a prominent conservative group that misappropriated his work. Excerpts from his early autobiographical writings, in which he reminisced about his life as a teenage gay hustler, were included in *Blasted Allegories: An Anthology of Writings by Contemporary Artists* (1987), which I edited for the New Museum, and Wojnarowicz's elaborate and politically acerbic installation *America: Heads of Family, Heads of State* (1989–90) was a centerpiece of the 1990 exhibition "The Decade Show: Frameworks of Identity in the 1980s," jointly organized by

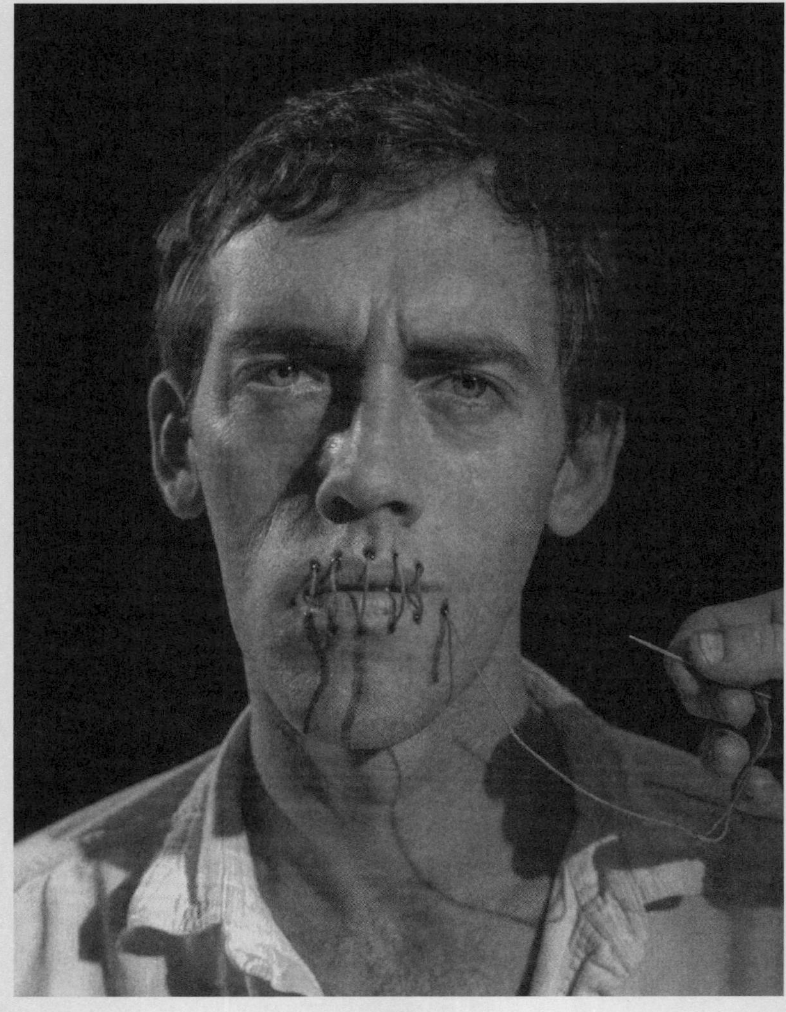

the Museum of Contemporary Hispanic Art, the New Museum, and the Studio Museum in Harlem.[9] Seven years after his death from AIDS-related illness, his engaged and influential work was the subject of "Fever: The Art of David Wojnarowicz" (1999), a survey organized by Dan Cameron at the New Museum.

Central to the new definition of political art, and to its increasing visibility in the 1980s, was the widespread readiness of artists to work together in collectives. Group Material advocated for mass culture and the free circulation of ideas in the face of the commodifying forces of the commercial art world. Expanding the notion of the oppositional public sphere, they published a politically themed advertising supplement in the *New York Times* (this 1988 project, called *Inserts*, was supported by the Public Art Fund), distributed mass-produced pamphlets, and wheatpasted disused urban walls with printouts of news and opinion pieces that emulated the Chinese dazibao, or "big character," political posters. With its changing roster of participating artists, Group Material pioneered the presentation of a collaborative thematic museum exhibition as a strategy for activist intervention. By choosing political issues (AIDS, education, national identity, democracy, and cultural participation) as themes for their shows, they appropriated the role of the museum curator and expanded the range of topics that museums were willing to address. Group Material's innovative exhibition designs combined striking graphics and displays, including meticulously researched timelines and a range of unexpectedly juxtaposed artworks, mass-produced images, and historical artifacts. For *MASS* (1985), an installation at the New Museum, Group Material invited 172 artists to submit a work of their choice in a twelve-inch-square format (then the standard size of a record album cover); the squares were assembled to spell out "mass," a word rife with social, political, and religious connotations whose very ambiguity amounted to a provocation, especially in the context of a museum.

Prominent in the ranks of AIDS activism, gay and lesbian collectives began to use public artworks and posters to challenge the US government's willful inaction in response to the crisis. The best known of the AIDS activist images

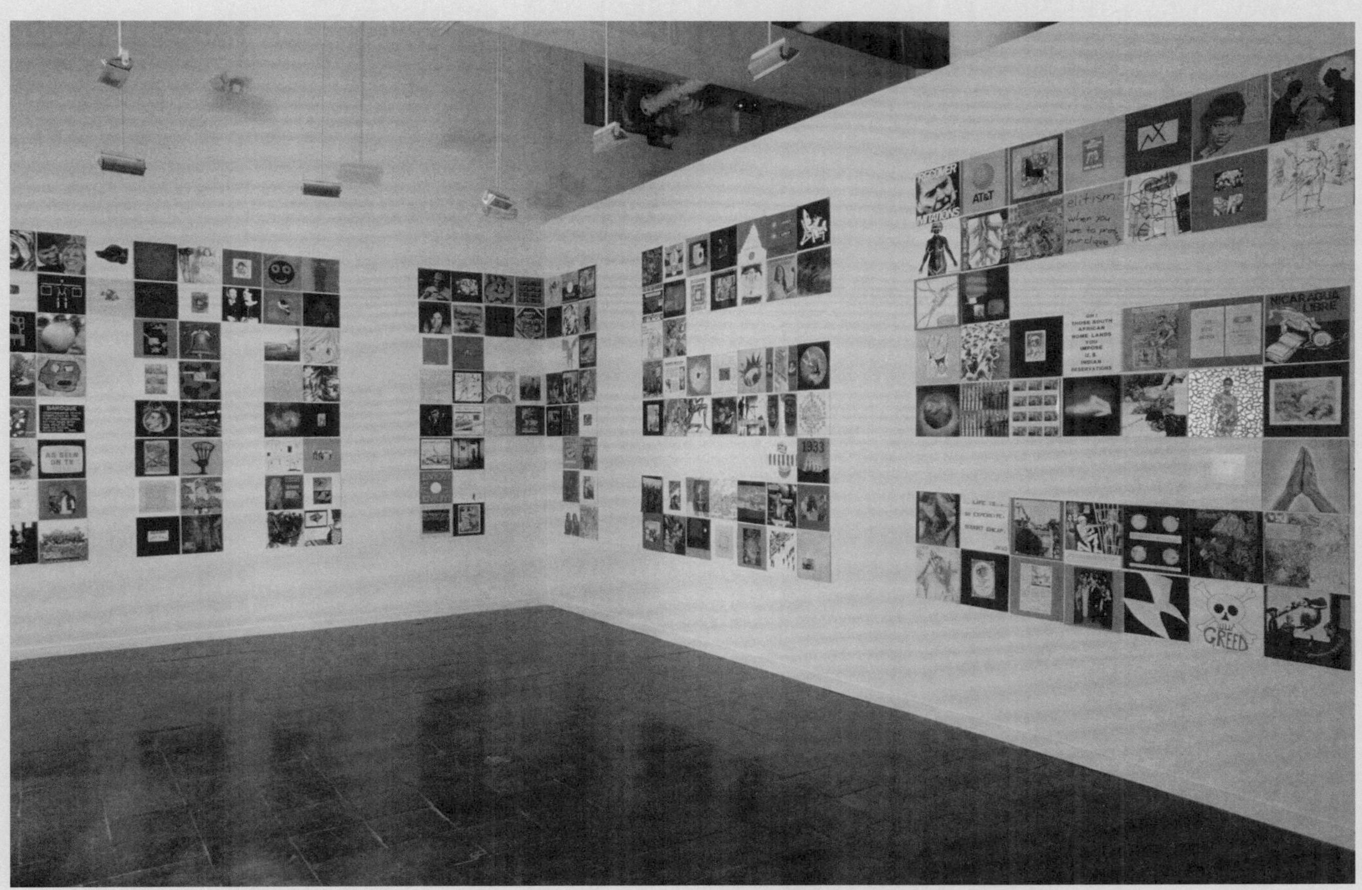

9.   David Wojnarowicz, "Sounds in the Distance," in *Blasted Allegories: An Anthology of Writings by Contemporary Artists*, ed. Brian Wallis (New York: New Museum; Cambridge, MA: MIT Press, 1987), 61–67.

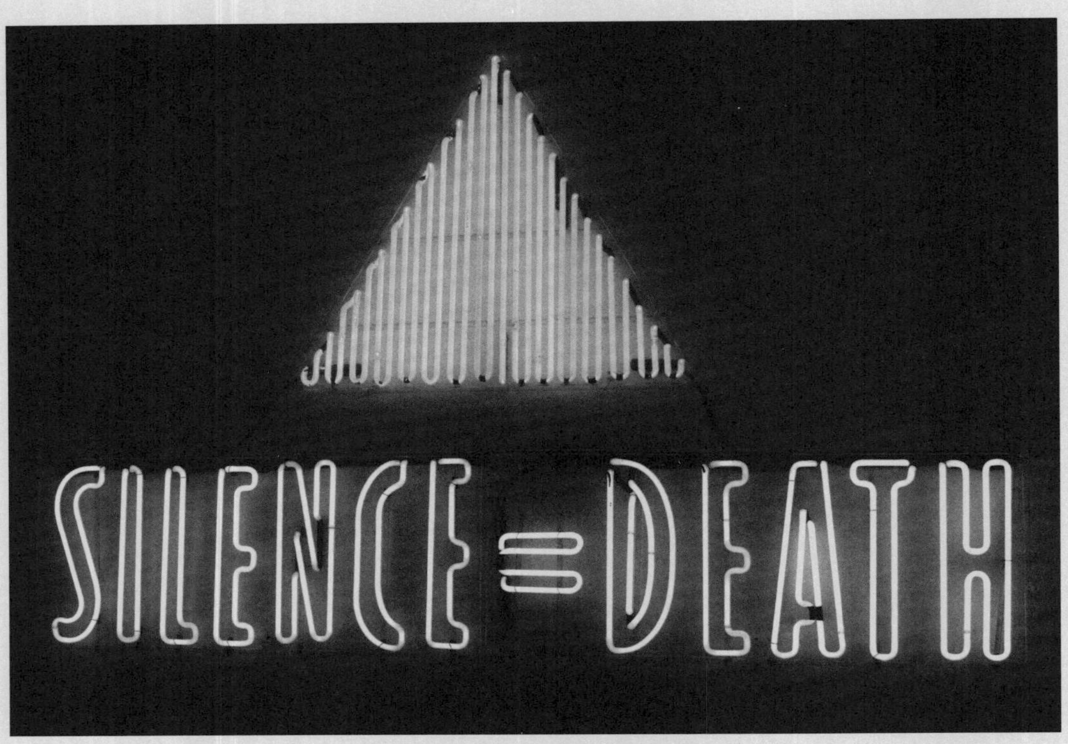

was the "Silence=Death" poster, which features simply those words and a pink triangle, the identifying badge for homosexuals imposed in Nazi Germany. The poster was created in 1987 by a small group of artists called the Silence=Death Project and debuted that year in a demonstration by the newly formed group ACT UP (AIDS Coalition to Unleash Power). Shortly thereafter, New Museum curator William Olander approached ACT UP to create an installation in the Broadway window as part of the 1987 exhibition "Let the Record Show…." Their project featured a neon version of the "Silence=Death" graphic, as well as photographs of vocal anti-gay politicians, with samples of their statements, against a photomural backdrop showing the 1945–46 Nuremberg trials of Nazi war criminals.

Speaking about political art in advance of the exhibition, Olander had emphasized the urgency of such activist projects, especially the need to present work that is "meaningful now" and the goal of devising "new strategies that will somehow initiate some kind of response from people who are frustrated, dissatisfied, repressed, oppressed."[10] The installation in the New Museum window provided a new and strategic intervention in public space, one that both engaged and incited viewers. In a review of "Let the Record Show…" critic Christian Leigh wrote, "At all hours of the day and night, spectators were seen gathered in front of the window, in small groups and alone. Their reactions and facial expressions were assorted: shock, rage, disappointment, shame, curiosity, frustration, misunderstanding, anger, disgust, and hope."[11]

In 2013, thirty years after his first projection on the New Museum, Krzysztof Wodiczko devised another, this time for the facade of the institution's new building on the Bowery, inaugurated in 2007. He proposed projecting an image of the nearby Bowery Mission, a charitable refuge for the homeless since 1897, onto the building. With this visual displacement, Wodiczko was once again addressing redevelopment, gentrification, and homelessness. His work was to have been part of an ambitious four-day international meeting exploring art, urban reconstruction, and the public sphere called Ideas City. Ironically, the projection was canceled, along with those of several other artists, when permits were denied because of recent city laws banning text in exterior projections (ostensibly to curb anything that might be construed as advertising).[12]

Wodiczko's intention to reprise his earlier activist projection should be understood as part of the recent resurgence of progressive political protests internationally, in public spaces and within museums. Massive demonstrations and movements such as the Women's March on Washington, Occupy Wall Street, Black Lives Matter, and the Standing Rock protests are echoed in new collective action networks within the art world, like Liberate Tate, the Gulf Labor Artist Coalition, and Occupy Museums. These political movements, operating both in and beyond the art world, have drawn renewed attention to the relationship between art and activism.[13] In the view of artist and curator Peter Weibel,

10. William Olander, interview by Jamey Gambrell, C. Carr, and Lynne Tillman, "What is Political Art... Now?," *Village Voice*, October 15, 1985, 79.

11. Christian Leigh, "Let the Record Show...," *Artforum* (January 1988): 138.

12. Among the other artists who, like Wodiczko, had proposed projections for the "Change of State" program of Ideas City 2013 were Cecil Balmond, Agathe de Bailliencourt, Diller Scofidio + Renfro, Nicolás Guagnini, E Roon Kang and Ahrong Han, Virginia Overton and Motoko Fukuyama, Sarah Peoples, Jeff Preiss, Martha Rosler, Nicolas Sassoon, and Ben Wolf. For a recent view of Wodiczko's take on public art and the role of the public, see Krzysztof Wodiczko, "The Inner Public," *Field: A Journal of Socially Engaged Art Criticism*, no. 1 (Spring 2015), http://field-journal.com/issue-1/wodiczko.

"Global activism as a twenty-first century movement
is providing the first examples of how mass culture
can become critical instead of affirming mass consum-
erism.... Global activism [may be] the first new art form
of the twenty-first century."[14] The fact that Wodiczko's
projection was part of Ideas City, an expansive program
of urban research launched by the New Museum, is
a reminder that the Museum has been a platform for
dissident expression and activist art for four decades.
The mission remains in force: we must continue to
develop methodologies and strategies that foster
cultural production and cultivate the ideas and actions
that can effect real social change.

Brian Wallis is a photography historian, writer, and curator living in New York. From 1982
to 1988, he was a curator at the New Museum, where he edited *Art After Modernism:
Rethinking Representation* (1985) and *Blasted Allegories: An Anthology of Writings
by Contemporary Artists* (1987). He was Chief Curator and Deputy Director of the
International Center of Photography in New York from 2000 to 2015, and is currently
Curator at the Walther Collection in New York and Ulm, Germany.

13. For an extensive treatment of recent socially engaged art, see Gregory Sholette,
     Delirium and Resistance after the Social Turn: Activist Art and the Rise of Capitalism
     (New York: Pluto Press, 2017).

14. Peter Weibel, "People, Politics, and Power," in *Global Activism: Art and Conflict in the
     21st Century*, ed. Peter Weibel (Cambridge, MA, and London: MIT Press, 2015), 60, 61.

An Ever-Expanding Field: The New Museum and Cross-Disciplinary Practices

Johanna Burton

"Cross-disciplinary," "multidisciplinary," "interdisci-plinary": these are continuously evolving terms meant to account for art practices that question the boundaries of art in one way or another. From the outset, the New Museum was revolutionary in anticipating the rise of artists working in this vein, providing them with early and unprecedented support even as—or, perhaps more accurately, precisely because—they were continually disrupting and expanding existing artistic parameters. Indeed, as founder Marcia Tucker noted in her biography, the question most often asked of such risk-taking art in her own day (and perhaps still?) was whether and how these efforts could even be considered art at all.[1]

Over the last four decades, the New Museum has remained dedicated to underlining what is at stake in this very question, devoting many of its efforts—and thereby establishing a model for other contemporary institutions —to forms such as live performance, interactive and participatory practice, collaborative production, multi-media installation, and other hybrid modalities. Without discounting the power of "art for art's sake," such cross-disciplinary endeavors have frequently emphasized the ways and means by which they are made and, in so doing, ask audiences to do the same. It is no coincidence, then, that in the history of cross-disciplinary endeavors at the Museum, one finds a history of art engaged in activism, social justice, politics, and pedagogy.

Just as the New Museum has asked what is art and what can art do, so, too, has it plumbed the definition of the

---

1. See Marcia Tucker, *A Short Life of Trouble: Forty Years in the New York Art World*, ed. Liza Lou (Berkeley: University of California Press, 2008). Here and elsewhere, Tucker repeatedly returns to art's role as an agent to "make you pay attention to things that you might otherwise take for granted" (114) and also highlights how that effect often leads to outrage or dismissal.

149

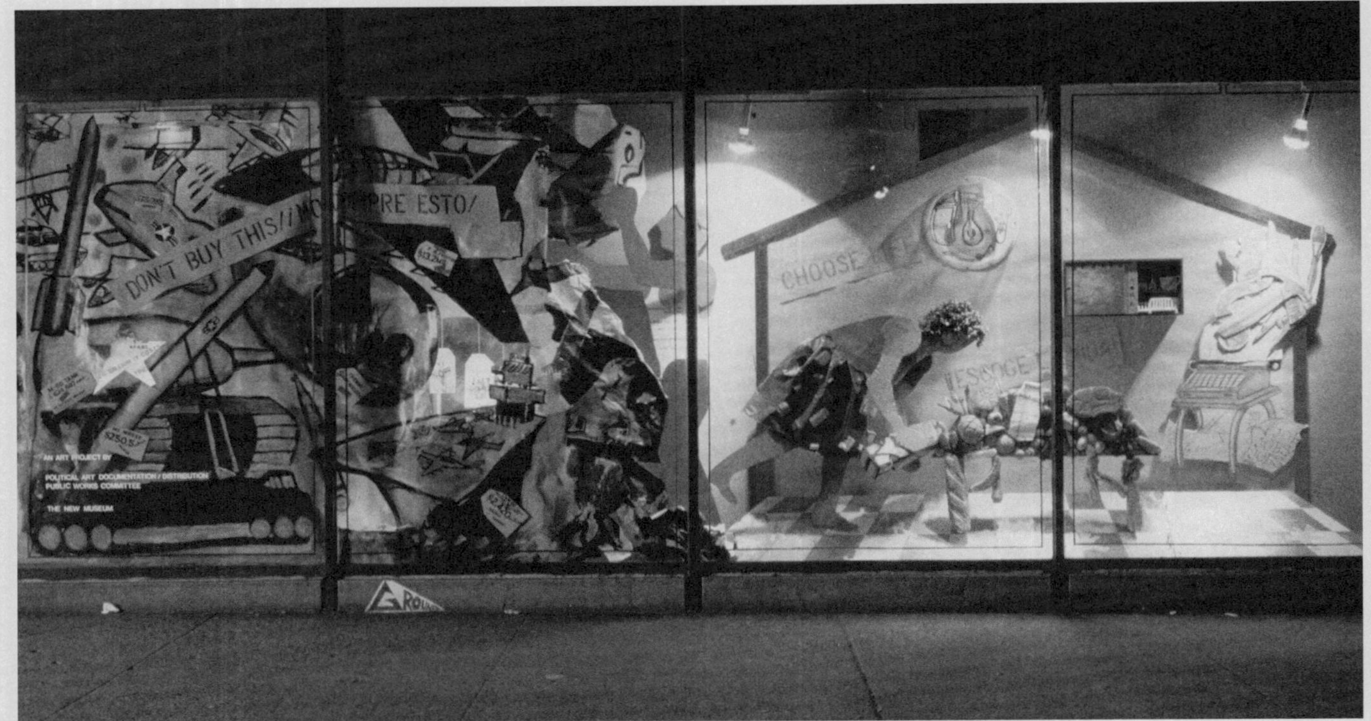

The Window: "Political Art Documentation/ Distribution, Public Works Committee: Don't Buy This/No Compre Esto," 1982

museum's role with respect to culture and community. Even as Tucker decisively named her new institution a "museum," her creation didn't really resemble one—at least not at first. Her platform for "new" art was itself a work in progress, one that was built in dialogue with and in reaction to the very efforts it would come to house. Before settling into its first permanent home at 583 Broadway in 1983, the nascent Museum found temporary exhibition space at the New School, where, in 1979, the "Window" series was inaugurated on Fourteenth Street. Capitalizing on the unusual porosity of the storefront "showcase" format, artists whose work was exhibited there could play on the space's public nature, sparking dialogues not only within the Museum but also on the street.

Notably, a number of the Museum's most stridently political projects were mounted in the window. In 1982, the collective Political Art Documentation/Distribution (PAD/D) presented an installation in the window that aimed, as the group noted, "to provide artists with an organized relationship to society, to demonstrate the political effectiveness of image making, and to encourage the development of new social and activist art forms."[2] Their project, titled *Don't Buy This/No Compre Esto*, took aim at increasing military costs and decreasing government support for health care by featuring two contrasting social realist–type vignettes: the first a scene of everyday life, including a woman laboring over a table of food, and

the second a vast arsenal of military equipment and vehi-
cles. In 1987, ACT UP (AIDS Coalition to Unleash Power)
was invited to take over the window, where they installed
what came to be the famous "Silence=Death" insignia,
rendered in neon, as well as cutouts of political and civic
leaders and an LED sign detailing facts and statistics
pertinent to AIDS. The group sought not only to heighten
awareness of the epidemic, but also to call attention to
the ways public figures were responding, which, more
often than not, was by ignoring or pathologizing the crisis.
William Olander, the exhibition's curator, who died of
AIDS less than two years later, explained that the title "Let
the Record Show..." emphasized how "actions or inactions
will soon be a matter of historical record."[3]

While these projects took on big topics, their impact and
success relied on the rather intimate nature of their
viewing. Whether a passerby sought out the Museum as
her destination or happened upon the window by chance,
the striking effect of seeing art at the threshold of everyday life should not be underestimated. Such proximity
came to mark a number of early performance-based
projects at the Museum from the early 1980s forward.
In 1984, for instance, Linda Montano began a seven-
year project whose very essence was investigating the
personal aspects of exchange. "Based on the seven
energy centers in the body," as Montano put it, *Seven
Years of Living Art* (1984–91) took place across several
activities performed by the artist, not all of which were
made visible to museum visitors or, in fact, to anyone at
all. In Montano's accounts of the features of the project,
she lists private, "inner" daily actions, such as "listen to
one pitch (minimum seven hours)"—an experience impossible for anybody but the artist to track, since it could be
neither represented nor documented. More tangible is the
"outer" component: "Once a month for seven years I will

2.   The Window: "Political Art Documentation/Distribution, Public Works Committee:
     Don't Buy This/No Compre Esto," exhibition brochure (New York: New Museum,
     1982), 2, https://archive.newmuseum.org/print-ephemera/6439.

3.   "Window on Broadway by Act Up," exhibition brochure (New York: New Museum,
     1987), 1, https://archive.newmuseum.org/print-ephemera/7910. The members
     of ACT UP responsible for "Let the Record Show..." went on to form Gran Fury, an
     activist art collective. In 1991, Gran Fury returned to the New Museum with another
     collective, Prostitutes of New York (PONY), to present a window exhibition aimed
     at debunking myths around sex work and the transmission of HIV called "Love for
     Sale... Free Condoms Inside."

sit in a window installation at The New Museum and talk about art/life with individuals who join me."[4]

The conversations Montano had over those seven years are not, to return to Olander's title, part of the public record, though the fact of their having happened is. Montano's New Museum project—significant within the scope of her life's work—is preserved only by way of a few press releases, exhibition records, photographs, and the memories of those who took part in or saw the actions. Such ephemerality, and interiority, was the very focus of "Choices: Making an Art of Everyday Life," a major exhibition curated by Tucker in 1986. Along with Montano, Tucker included Marina Abramović and Ulay, Spalding Gray, Tehching Hsieh, and several others. She described the show as presenting "twelve artists—eight individuals and two collaborative pairs—who designate their lives as art, and for whom objects, artifacts, performances, or documentation are only the ghost, or residue, of their real work."[5] Such a claim was, and still might be, a radical one, if not for its overt anti-commercialism (we know now that even ephemera has a market) then for its implications for what a museum can and cannot capture or control. It made critics uncomfortable for this reason, too. (A writer for the *New York Times* pointed to the paradox that "a show about art based on art as life and life as art has to be presented largely through objects and documents.[6]) Notwithstanding its debatable successes and failures, "Choices" heralded a position the New Museum would uphold, of refusing to draw neat boundaries between artworks, the people who made them, and those who encountered them.

Indeed, such exploration was taken to the next level in a project by the artist Laurie Parsons, who was included in New Museum Curator Laura Trippi's 1992 exhibition "The Spatial Drive." The show was an attempt to activate objects, to allow them to operate not as stable things but as configurable, responsive entities. Parsons took this idea even further, proposing that her contribution to the show be a collaboration between curatorial, education, security, and other departments in the Museum. Rather than present art objects of her own, Parsons's *Security and Admissions Project* would entail regular conversations

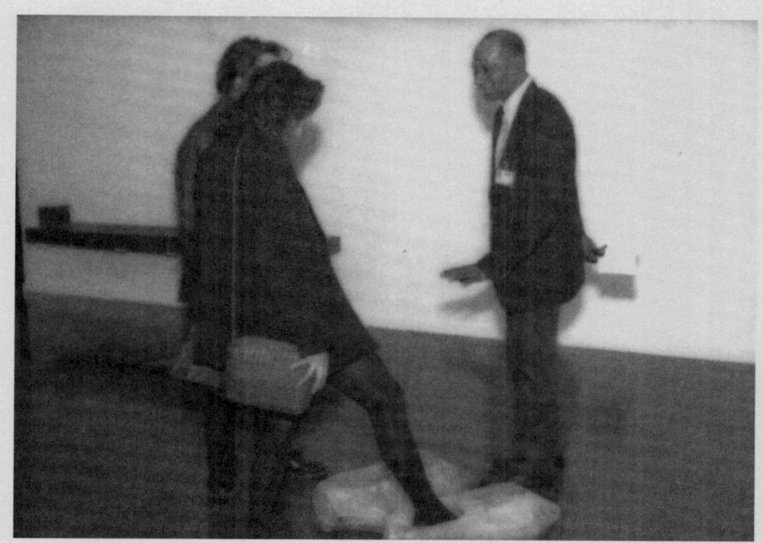

with Trippi, Susan Cahan (then the Museum's Curator of Education), and other Museum staff, notably the security guards. Working directly with the other artists in the show during the year preceding its opening, the guards learned about each work and the artist's intention for it. Rather than being presented with labels and wall texts in the galleries, visitors to "The Spatial Drive" would be engaged in conversations by the guards. Quoted in the press release, longtime guard Kimball Augustus noted that the show formalized what had long been an informal practice: "The guards are the ones who have an energized, on-going relationship with the art works. They grow on us six hours a day, five days a week."[7]

Endurance, if of another order, also formed the spine of a project the following year at the Museum. Bob Flanagan (in collaboration with Sheree Rose) presented *Visiting Hours*, a surreal hospital room/fetish dungeon in which the terminally ill artist was available to discuss death, extreme sexual pleasure, and anything in between or beyond. While it built on traditions of body and performance art, Flanagan's work nevertheless was distinct in its unusually generous tenor. Giving himself over as a kind of willing specimen and "witness," the artist rendered the discussions—medical, existential, and erotic (he detailed his cystic fibrosis as well as his embrace of masochism)—

4. Linda Montano, quoted in Marcia Tucker, *Choices: Making an Art of Everyday Life* (New York: New Museum, 1986), 108.

5. Marcia Tucker, "Preface and Acknowledgments," in *Choices*, 12. The exhibition's complete roster included Marina Abramović and Ulay, James Lee Byars, Spalding Gray, Alex Grey, Tehching Hsieh, Linda Montano, Morgan O'Hara, Michael Osterhout, United Art Contractors, and Ian Wilson.

6. Michael Brenson, "'Choices' Presents an Esthetic of Daily Life," *New York Times*, March 7, 1986, http://www.nytimes.com/1986/03/07/arts/art-choices-presents-an-esthetic-of-daily-life.html?pagewanted=all.

7. New Museum, "The Spatial Drive: Security and Admissions Project," press release, 1992, https://archive.newmuseum.org/print-ephemera/9617. Along with Laurie Parsons, the exhibition featured Marina Abramović, Lewis deSoto, Gretchen Faust, Fred Holland, Sonia Labouriau, John Lindell, Rei Naito, Marylene Negro, Fiona Templeton, and the X-Art Foundation.

nearly casual. Anne Ellegood, who would become a curator at the New Museum in 1998, gives this account of her visit to the Museum as a graduate student and her unexpected encounter with Flanagan: "I remember thinking to myself, 'You can do this in a museum?' Not because the content was sexual, or bodily, or alarming —indeed, an awareness of humanity permeated the space far more than any feeling of unease or titillation because of the imagery—but primarily because it felt so vulnerable."[8]

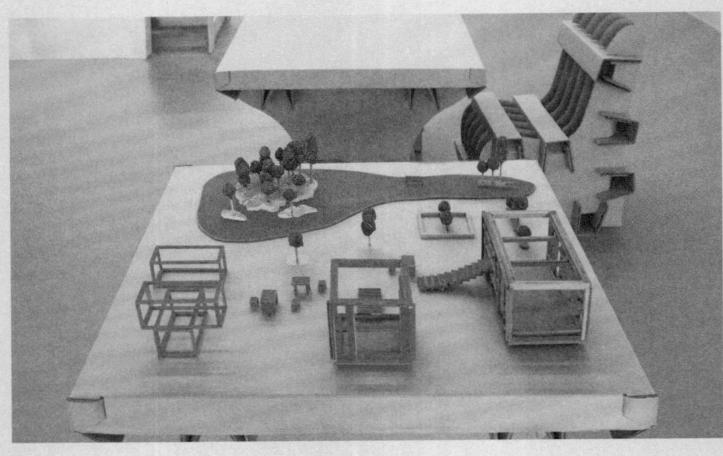

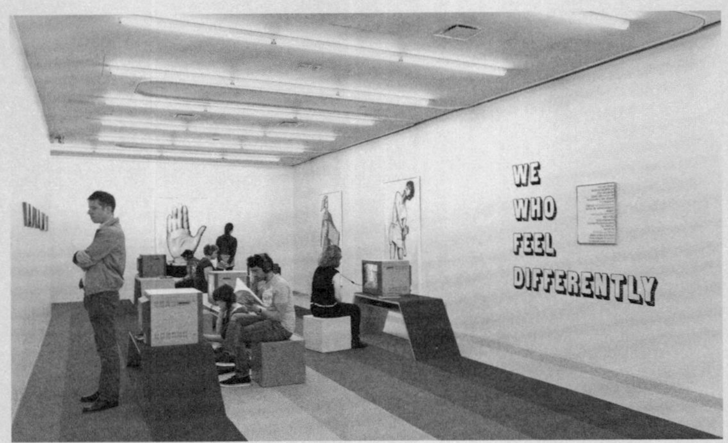

The appointment of Lisa Phillips as Director in 1999 assured the Museum's continued commitment to risk-taking endeavors and new forms of art that could only be categorized as uncategorizable. In 2007, when the *new* New Museum opened its doors at 235 Bowery, the program called Museum as Hub—a major platform for conceiving site-specific, process-based projects—was launched as well. The Hub was conceived by the Museum (and soon led by Eungie Joo, then the Director of Education and Public Programs) with institutional partners Insa Art Space (Seoul), Museo Tamayo (Mexico City), Townhouse Gallery (Cairo), and Van Abbemuseum (Eindhoven). The exhibition/education/publishing hybrid, which remained active for seven years, developed and produced such long-term undertakings as Night School (2008–09), a project by the artist Anton Vidokle that took the form of monthly seminars and workshops that examined the limits of artistic agency and institutional infrastructure, and the evolving exhibition "In and Out of Context" (2009), which fostered discussions about national identity and the international system of art production and exhibition.

The new building was equipped with a dedicated theater space, and for the first time staff could conceive artistic and discursive programs with this environment in mind.

During these first ten years on the Bowery, the Museum has staged countless and varied cross-disciplinary events, among them "Funny Girls to the Front" (2011), an evening of performances devoted to feminism and humor featuring Adira Amram, Carolyn Castiglia, Bridget Everett, Erin Markey, Larissa Velez-Jackson, and Becky Yamamoto; the research group Public Movement's "SALONS: Birthright Palestine?," a series of public debates staged at the Museum and other locations throughout Manhattan as part of the Museum's 2012 Triennial; and "NEA 4 in Residence" (2013), a project curated by Travis Chamberlain that considered the past, present, and future of funding for performance and featured four artists—Karen Finley, John Fleck, Holly Hughes, and Tim Miller—whose National Endowment for the Arts funding had been withdrawn during the culture wars of the early 1990s.

When I joined the Museum in 2013 as the Keith Haring Director and Curator of Education and Public Engagement, I understood (and was both inspired and somewhat daunted by) the legacy I was inheriting. Building on the Museum's existing commitment to supporting emerging or under-recognized artists, I structured the education department around seasonal residencies. Over the course of several months, artists conceive and execute projects in the fifth floor Education Gallery, in the New Museum Theater, and sometimes well beyond 235 Bowery. Working with staff throughout the Museum and with our teen and

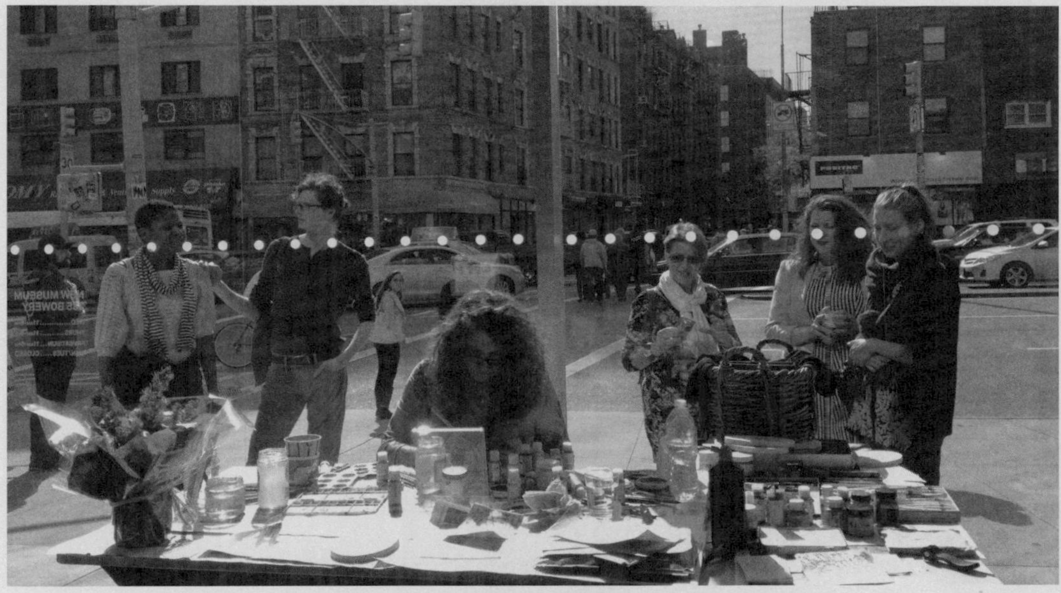

8.   Anne Ellegood, "Anne Ellegood, Senior Curator at the Hammer Museum in L.A., on Bob Flanagan's 'Visiting Hours' (1994)," *Spike Art* magazine, spring 2017, http://www.spikeartmagazine.com/en/articles/curators-key-12.

community partners, artists in
residence often push the limits of
even "cross-disciplinarity" as such.
During the last five years, we have
worked with dozens of artists and
collectives to produce all manner
of projects. My first endeavor at
the Museum, in 2013, was "XFR
STN," a collaboration between New
Museum staff and members of the
historic alternative art collective Colab. "XFR STN" was
a digital preservation lab for use by the public (equipped
with a range of equipment and trained attendants), and
it was packed every day, not only for the conservation
it offered but also for the intergenerational dialogues it
generated. Other projects of note include "P.O.L.E.
(People, Objects, Language, Exchange)," a project
executed by the duo Brennan Gerard and Ryan Kelly in
2014, which interrogated the material conditions of dance
in museums; "Simone Leigh: The Waiting Room" (2016),
a project comprising an installation, workshops, healing
treatments, and classes, all dedicated to the health,
history, and subjectivities of black women; and the 2016
return of the collective My Barbarian to the Museum with
"The Audience is Always Right," their final iteration of
PoLAAT (Post-Living Ante-Action Theater), which spanned
the pre- and post-election cycle.

Even as we find ourselves regularly looking for new terms
to describe what we are doing at the Museum—"cross-
disciplinarity" alone does not fully account for today's
political, discursive, and activist impulses—it's clear that
the seeds for this creative freedom were sown here forty
years ago. In the history of genre-challenging art, the
New Museum plays no small part. And I can't imagine that
it will cease to establish new, as yet uncharted, ground
anytime soon.

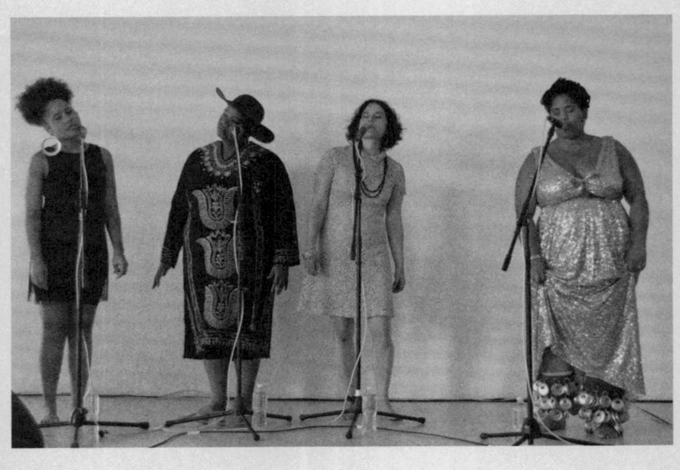

Rashida Bumbray
(right) performs her
*Motherless Child
Set* as part of the
exhibition "Simone
Leigh: The Waiting
Room," June 23, 2016

Johanna Burton is *Keith Haring Director and Curator of Education and Public
Engagement* at the New Museum and the series editor for the Museum's Critical
Anthologies in Art and Culture. At the New Museum, she has curated solo shows of
work by Wynne Greenwood (2015), Cheryl Donegan (2016), Simone Leigh (2016), and
A.K. Burns (2017), as well as the group show "XFR STN" (2013) and the major exhibition
"Trigger: Gender as a Tool and a Weapon" (2017).

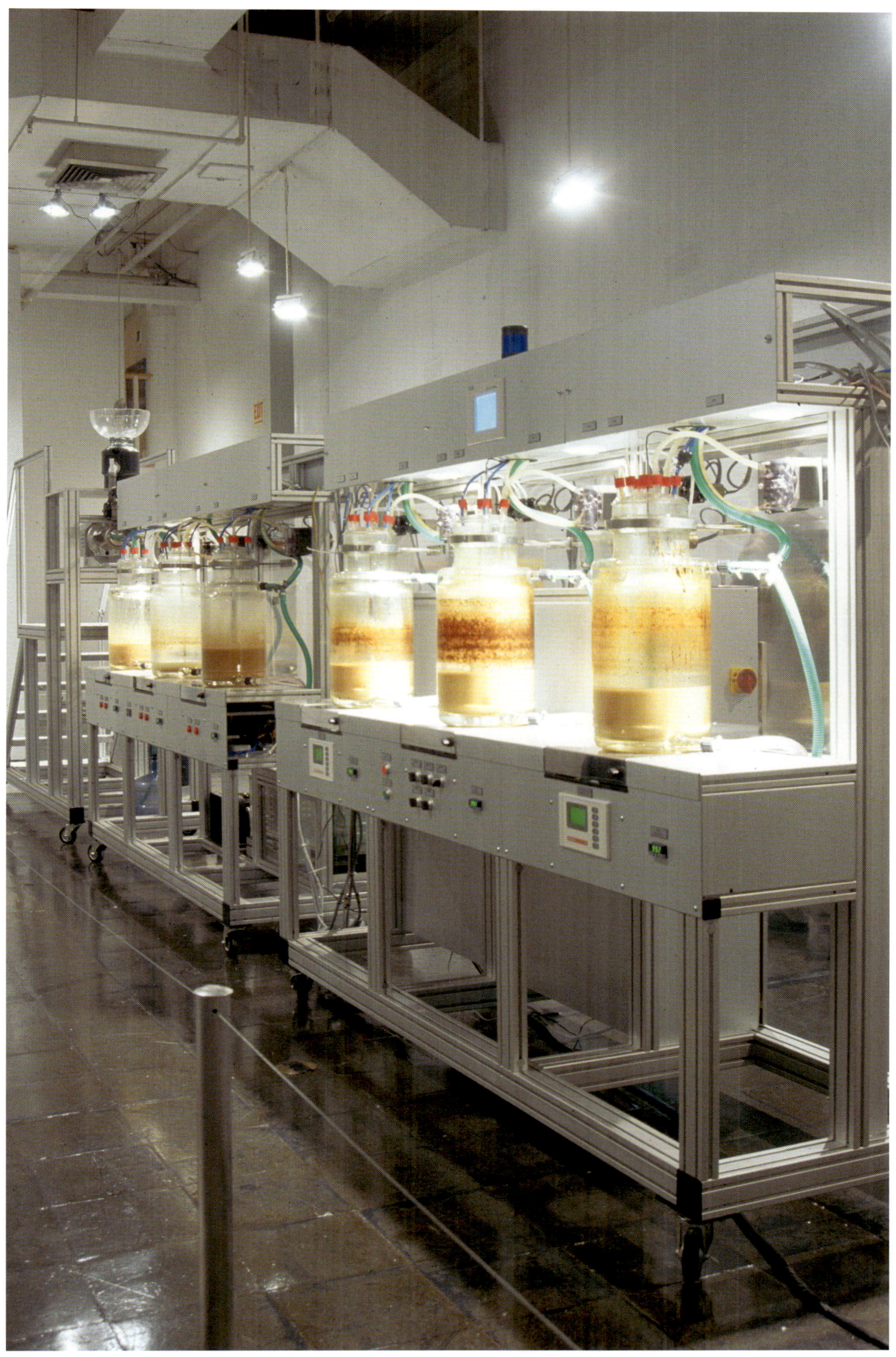

Installation view

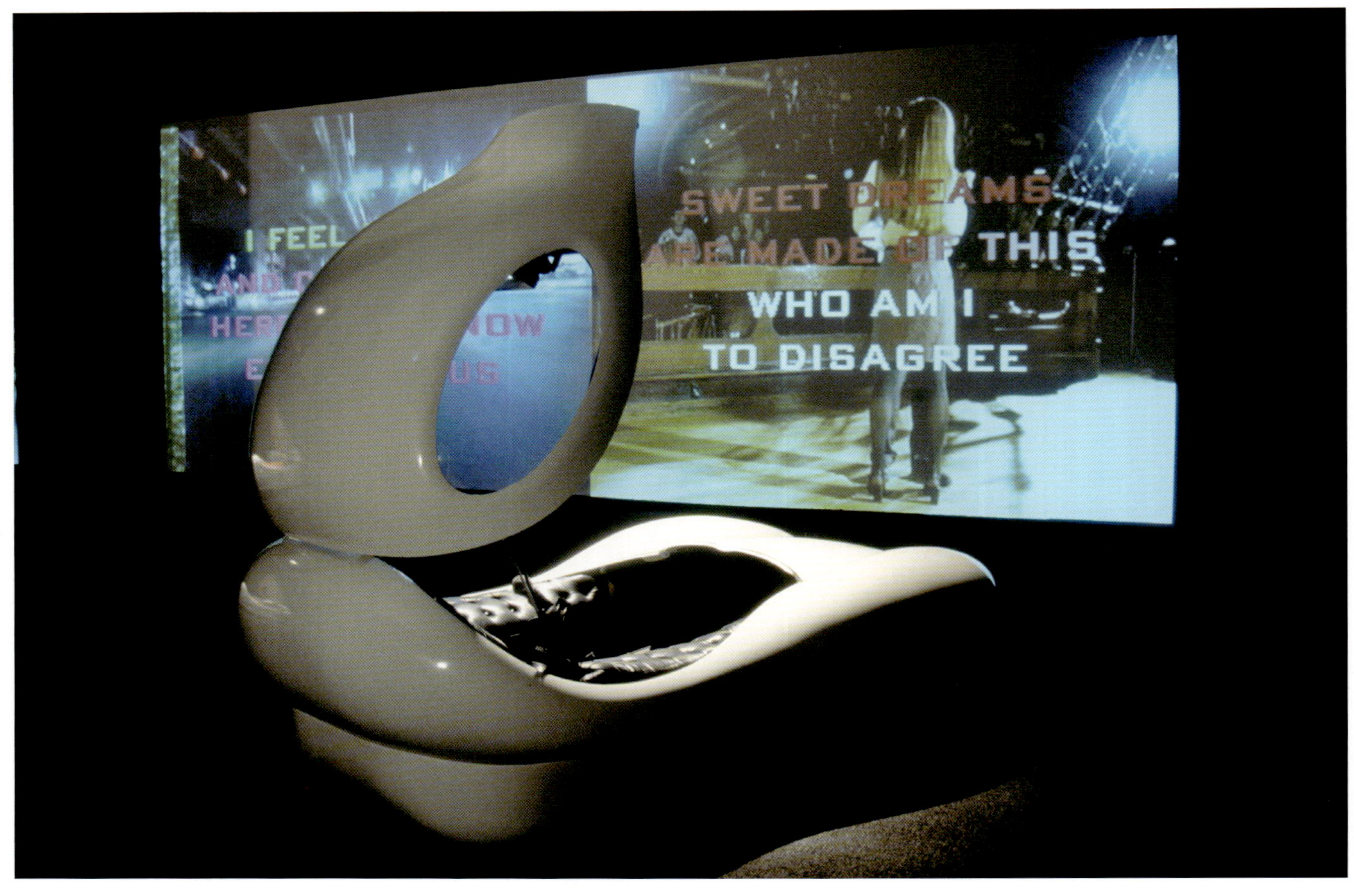

Lee Bul,
Live Forever I, 2001

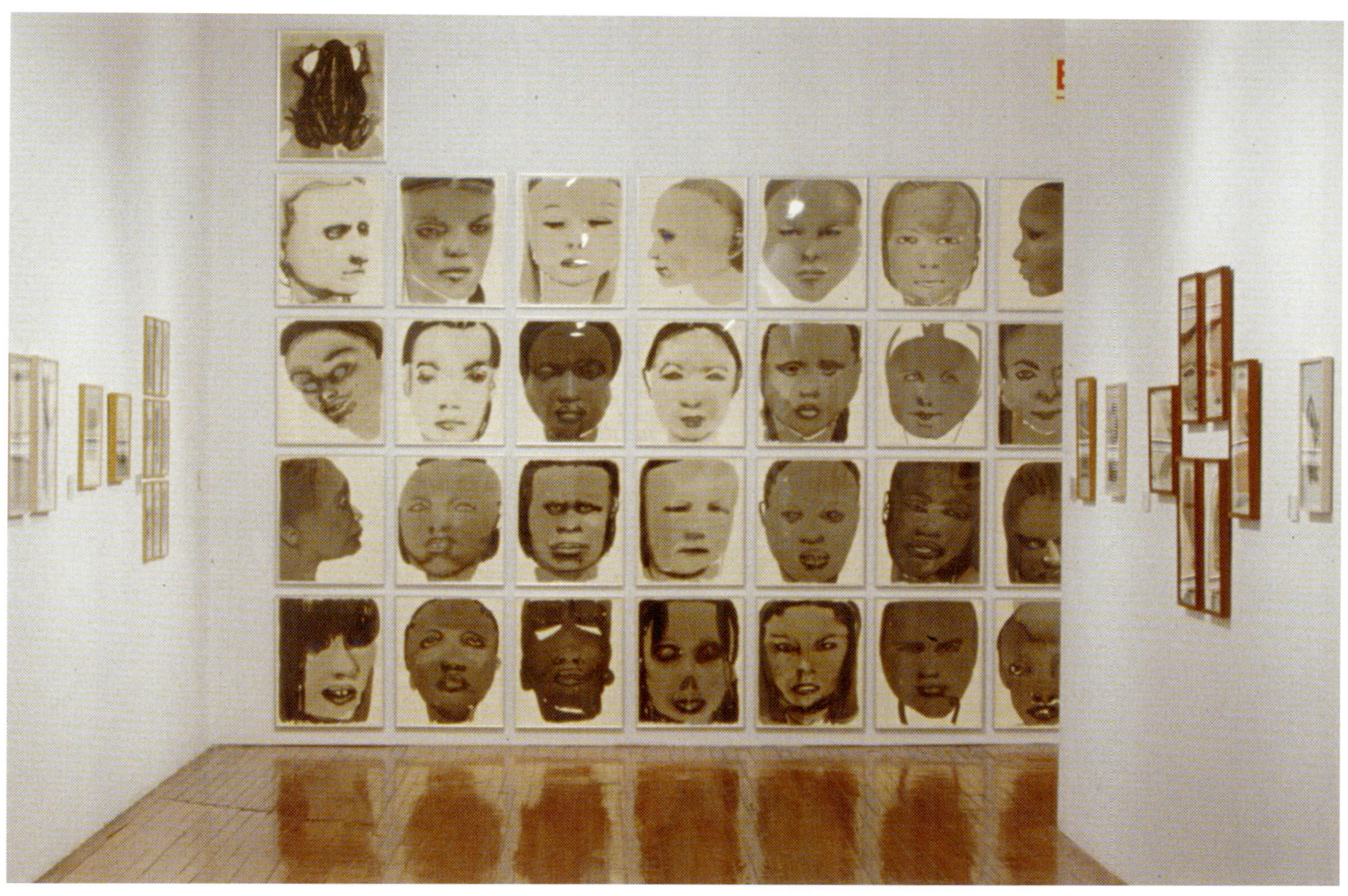

Installation view

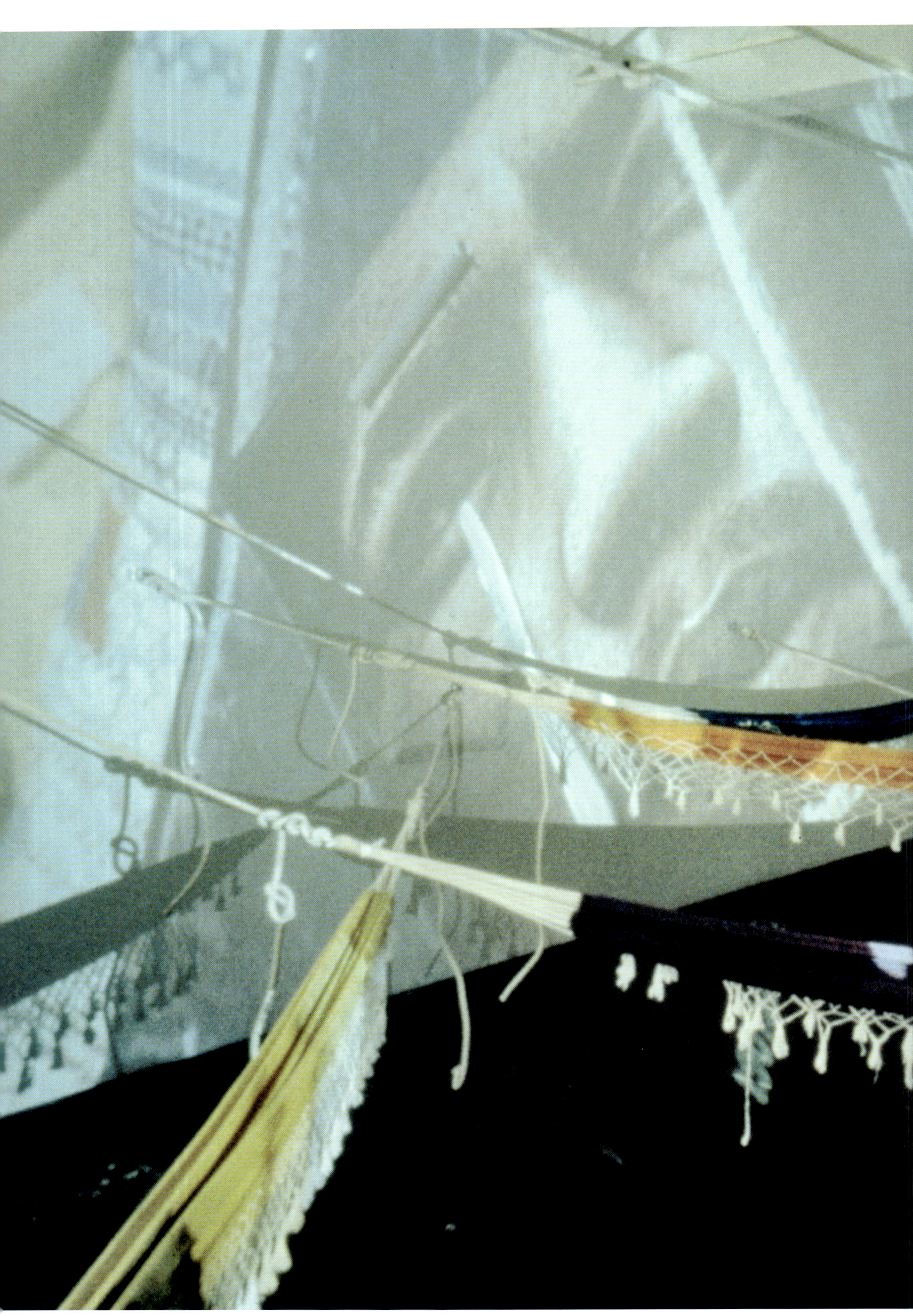

Hélio Oiticica and
Neville D'Almeida,
CC5 Hendrix-War, 1973

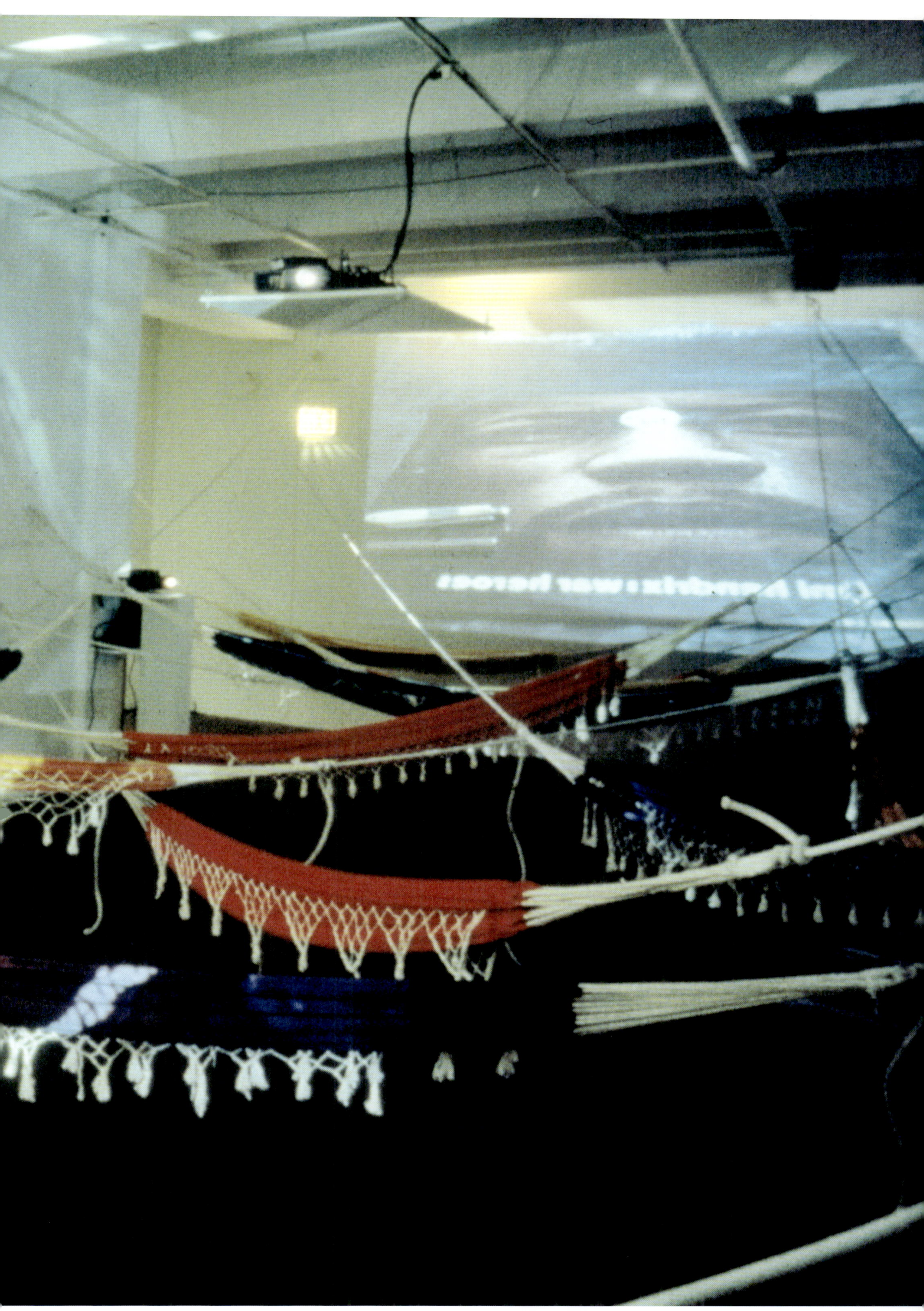

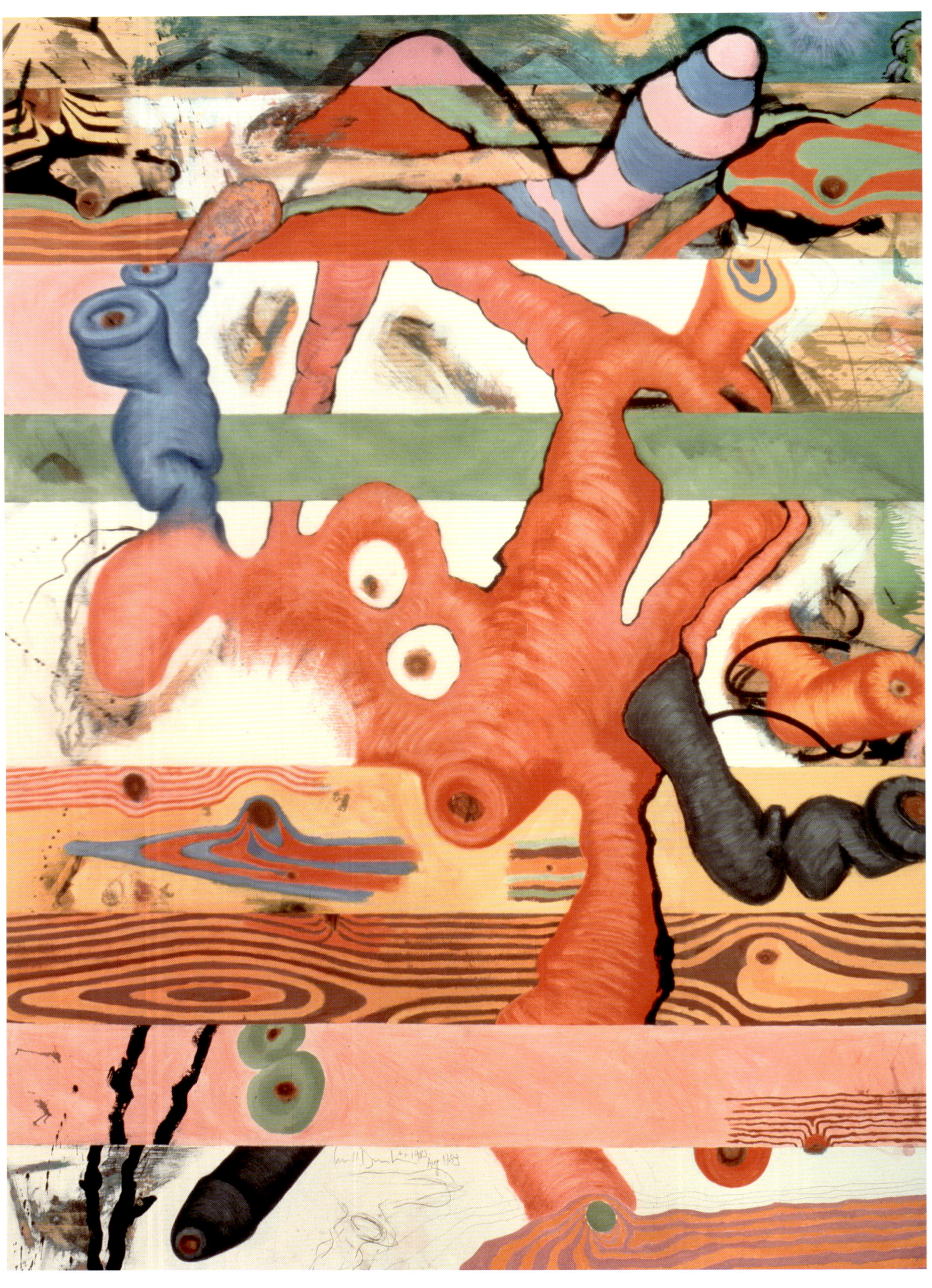

Carroll Dunham,
Fourth Pine, 1982–84

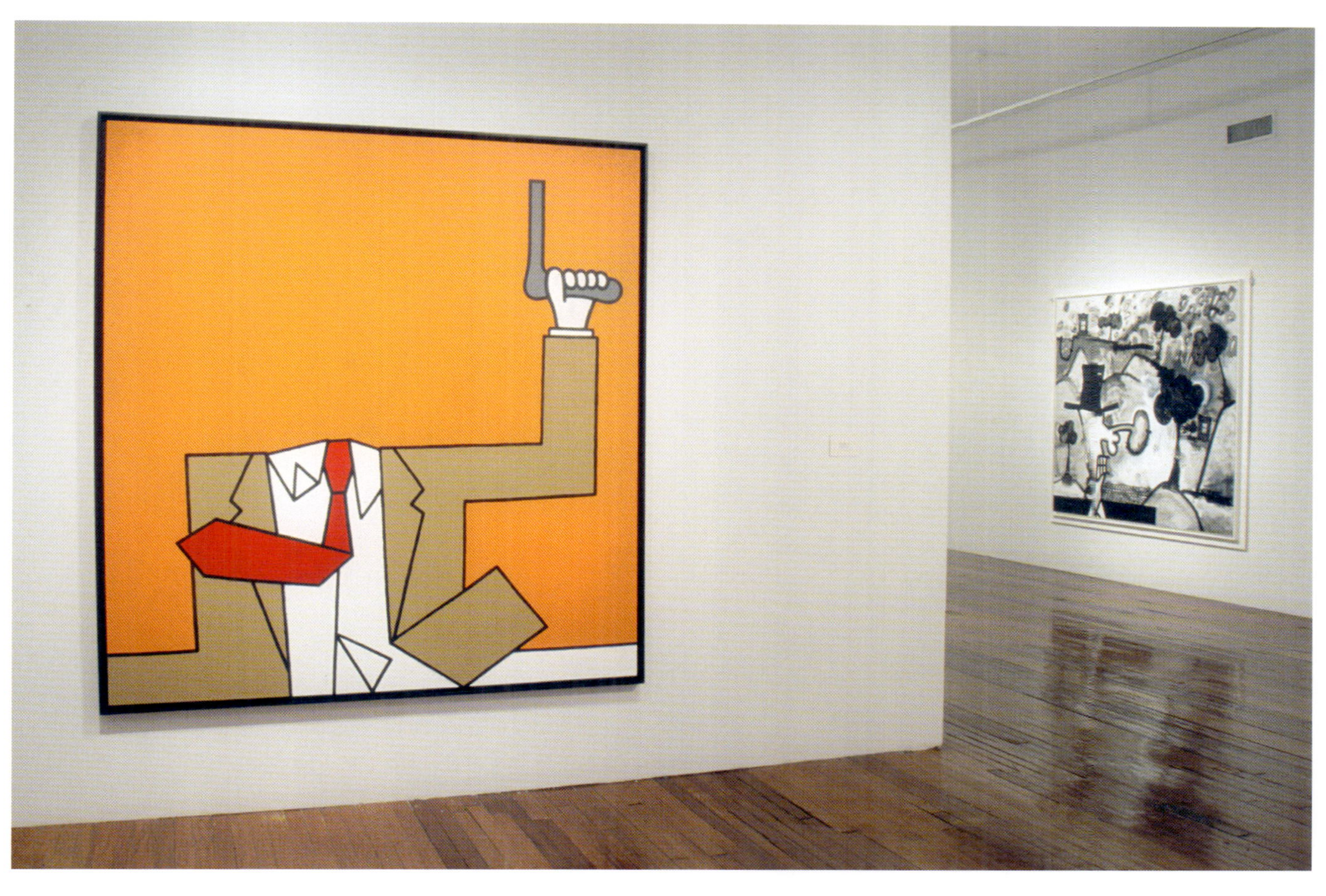

Left to right: Carroll
Dunham, *Shade*, 2002, and
Meso-Kingdom Two, 2001

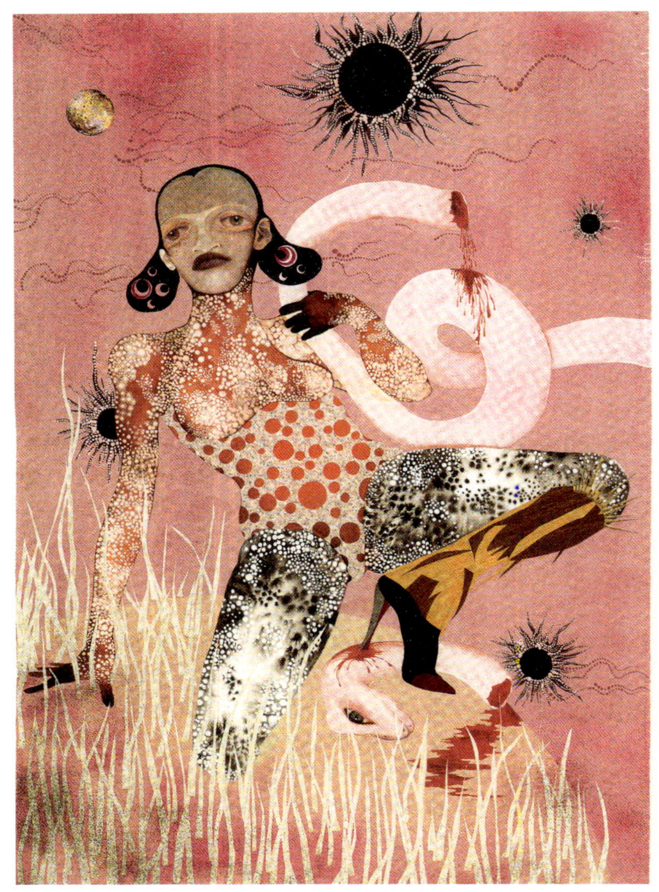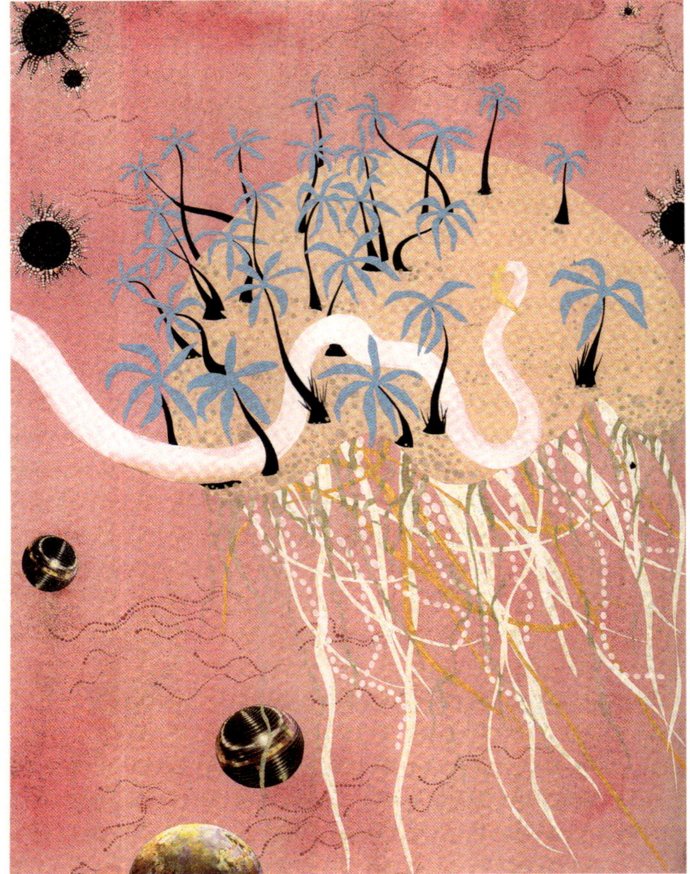

Wangechi Mutu,
Yo Mama, 2002–03

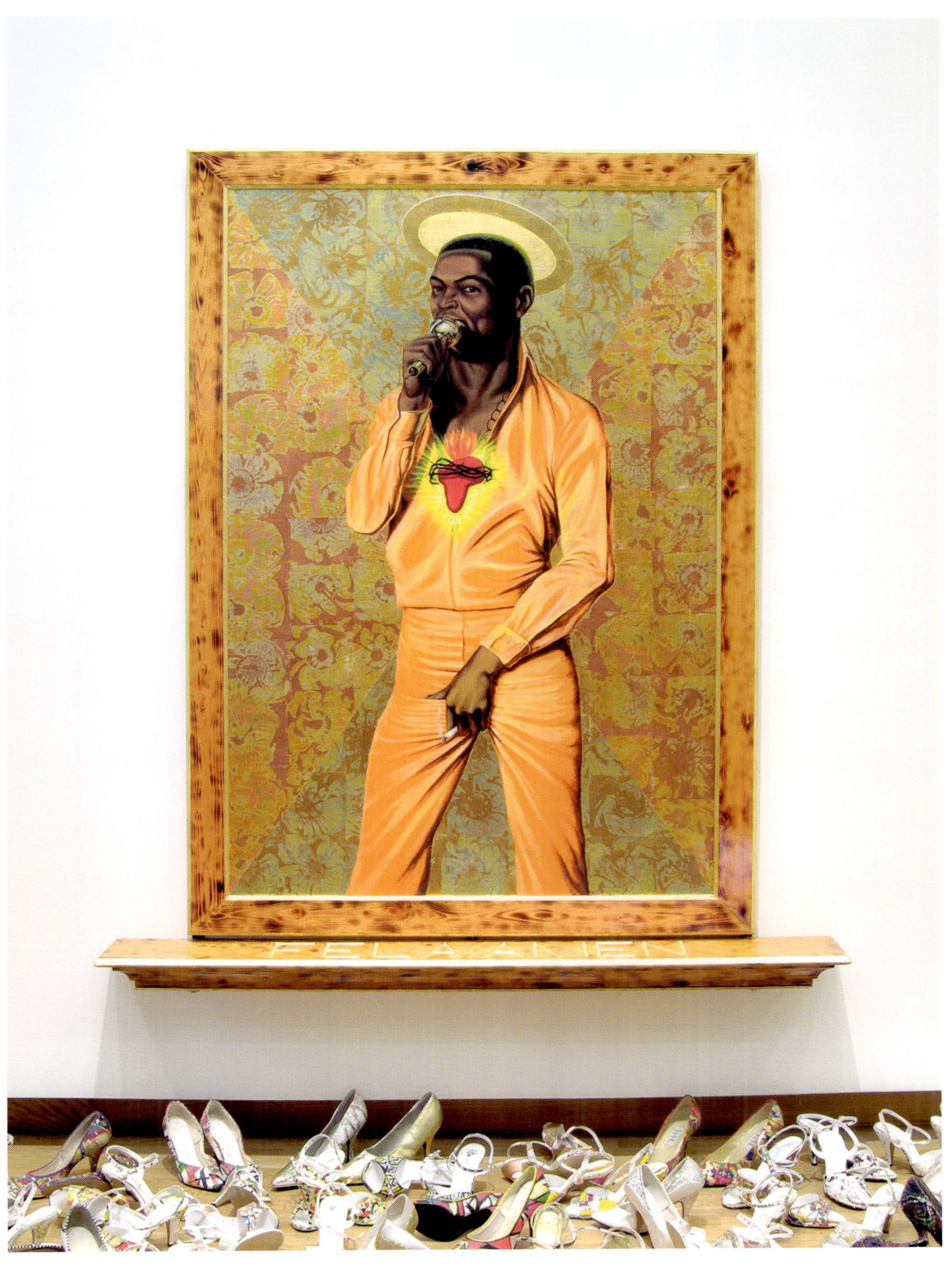

Barkley L. Hendricks,
Fela: Amen, Amen, Amen,
Amen ......, 2002

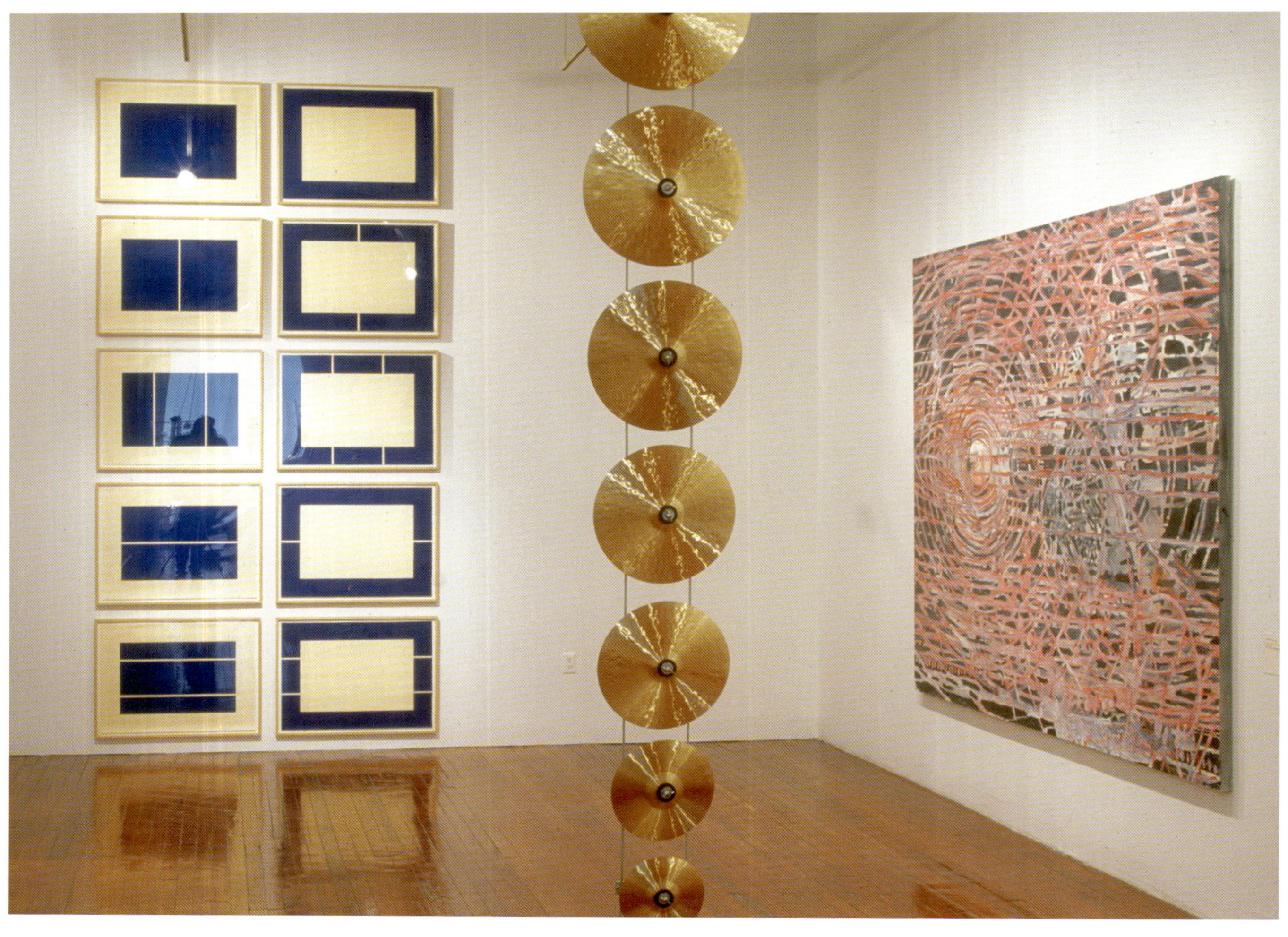

Left to right: works
by Donald Judd and
Terry Winters

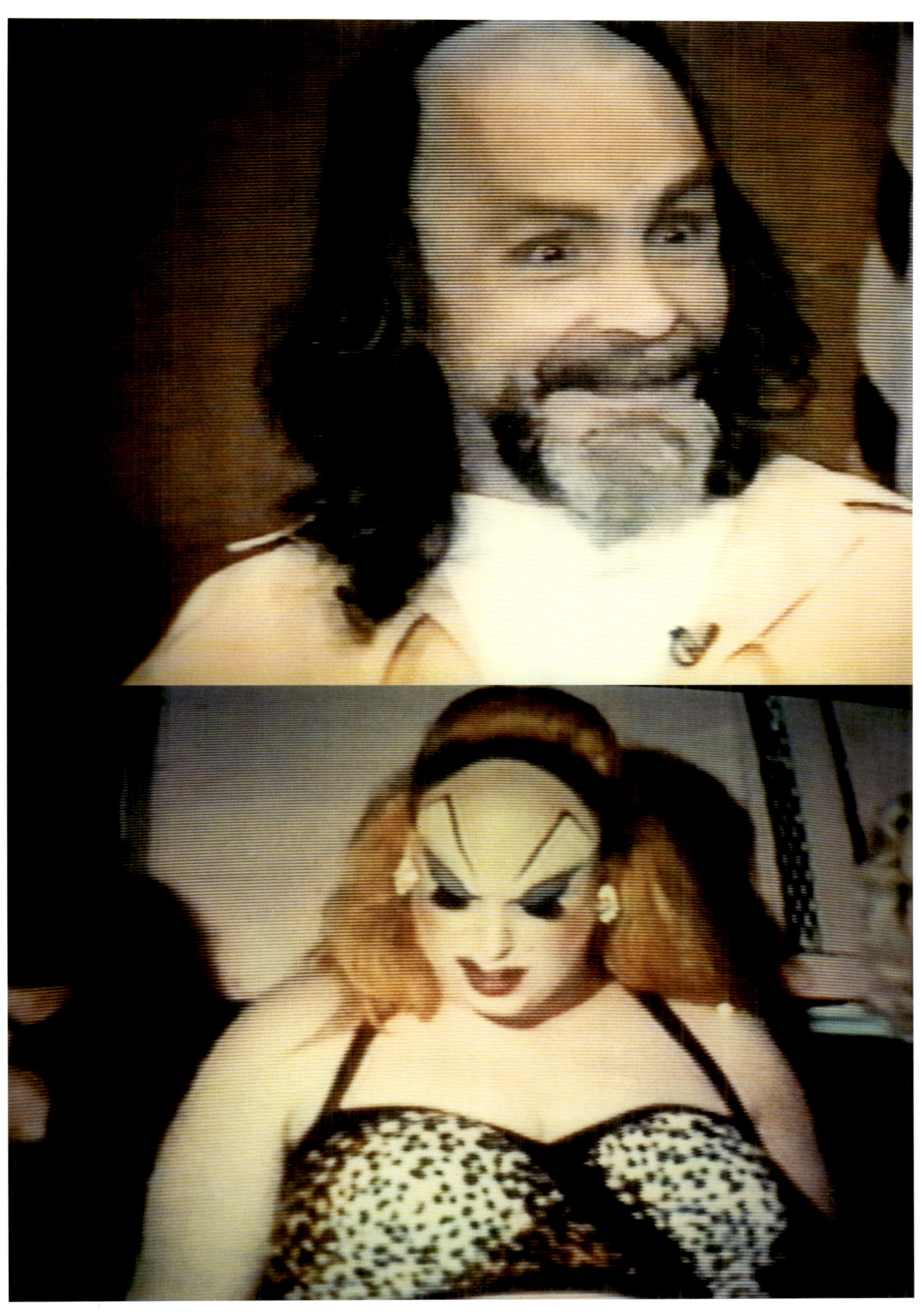

John Waters,
*Manson Copies Divine's
Hairdo*, 1993

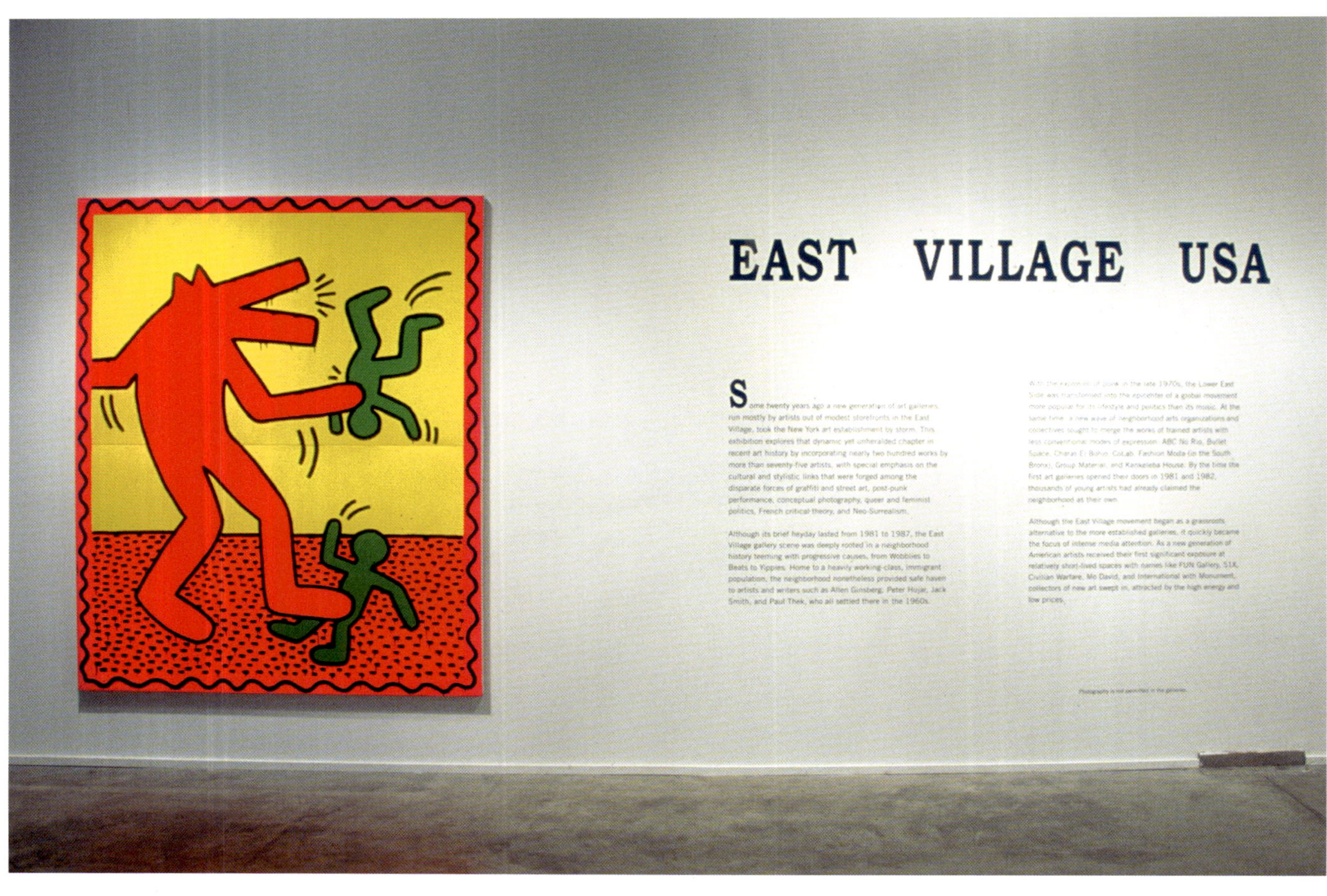

Keith Haring,
Untitled, 1982

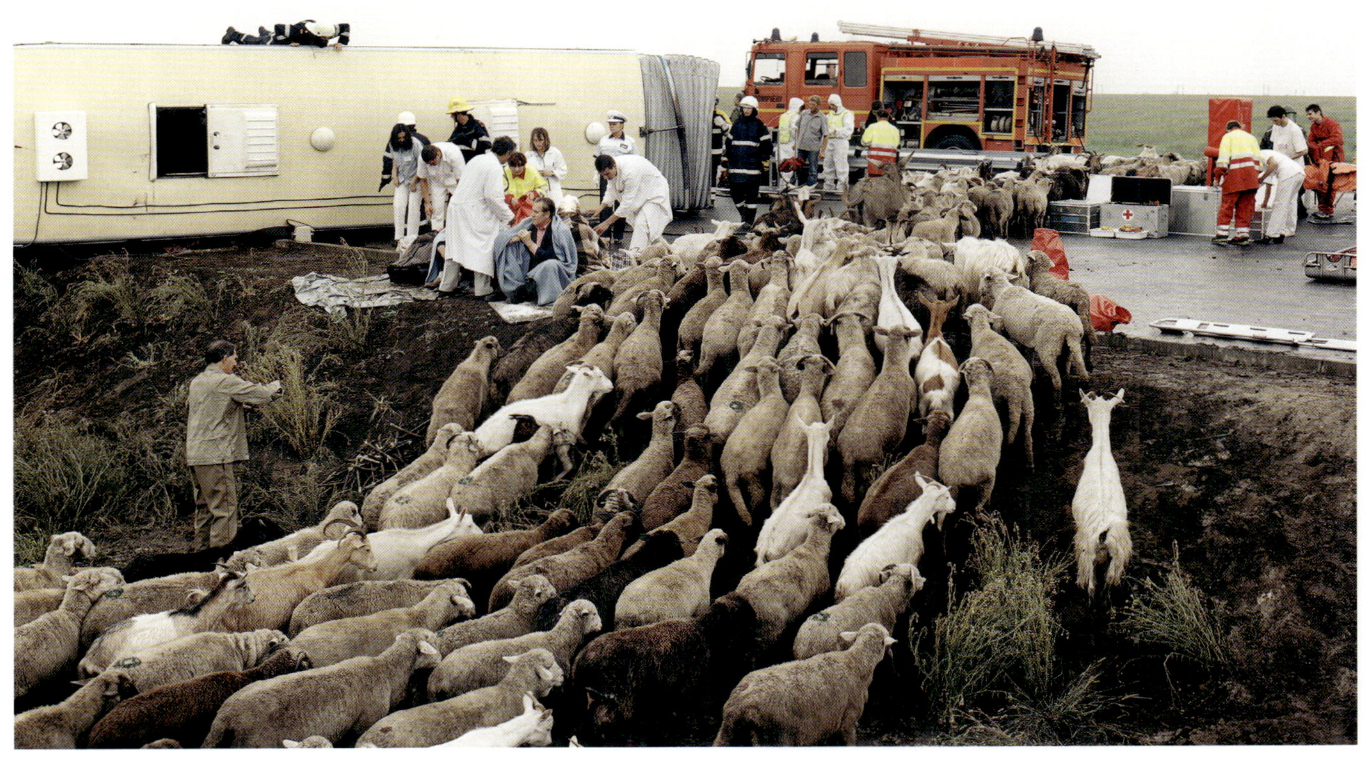

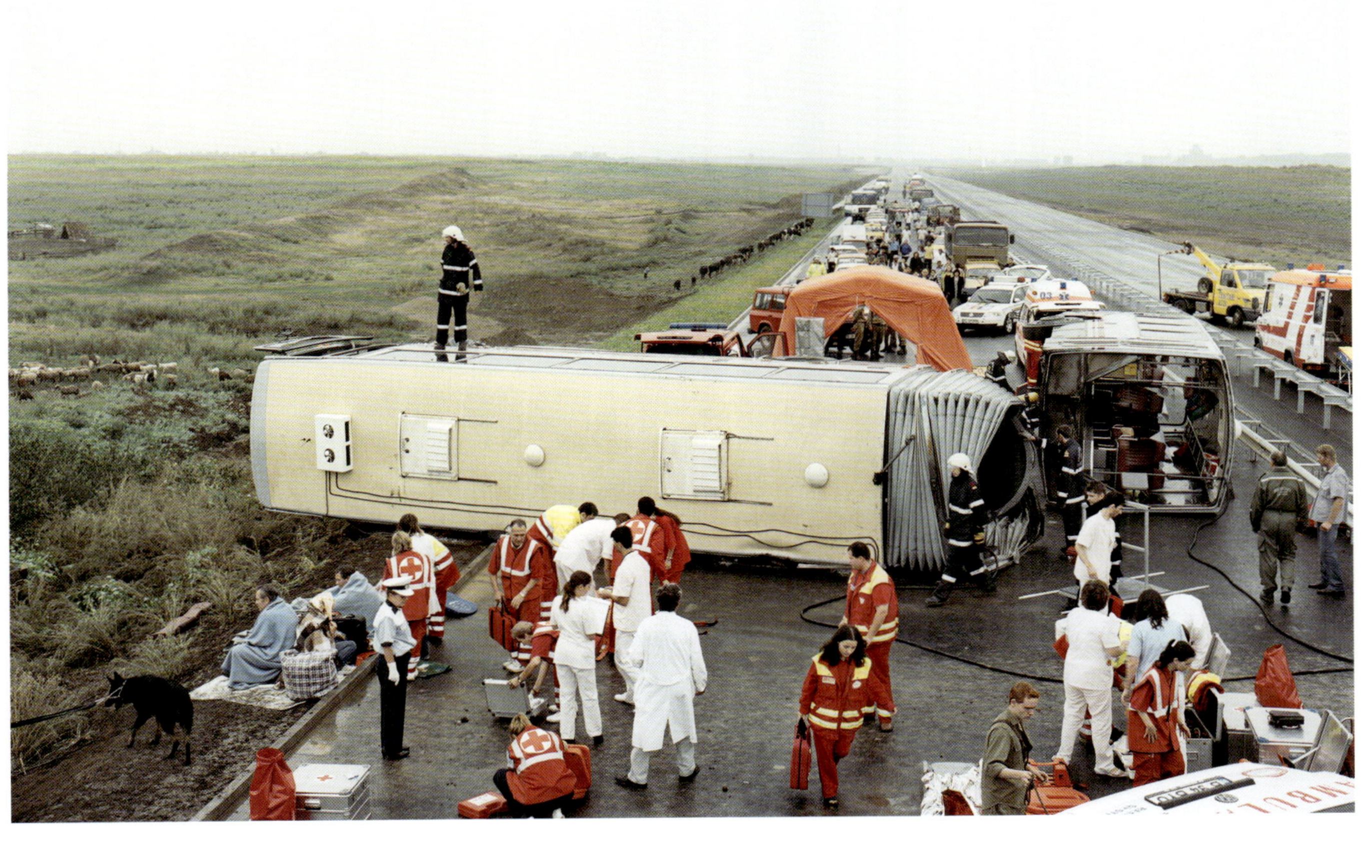

Aernout Mik,
Refraction, 2004
(stills)

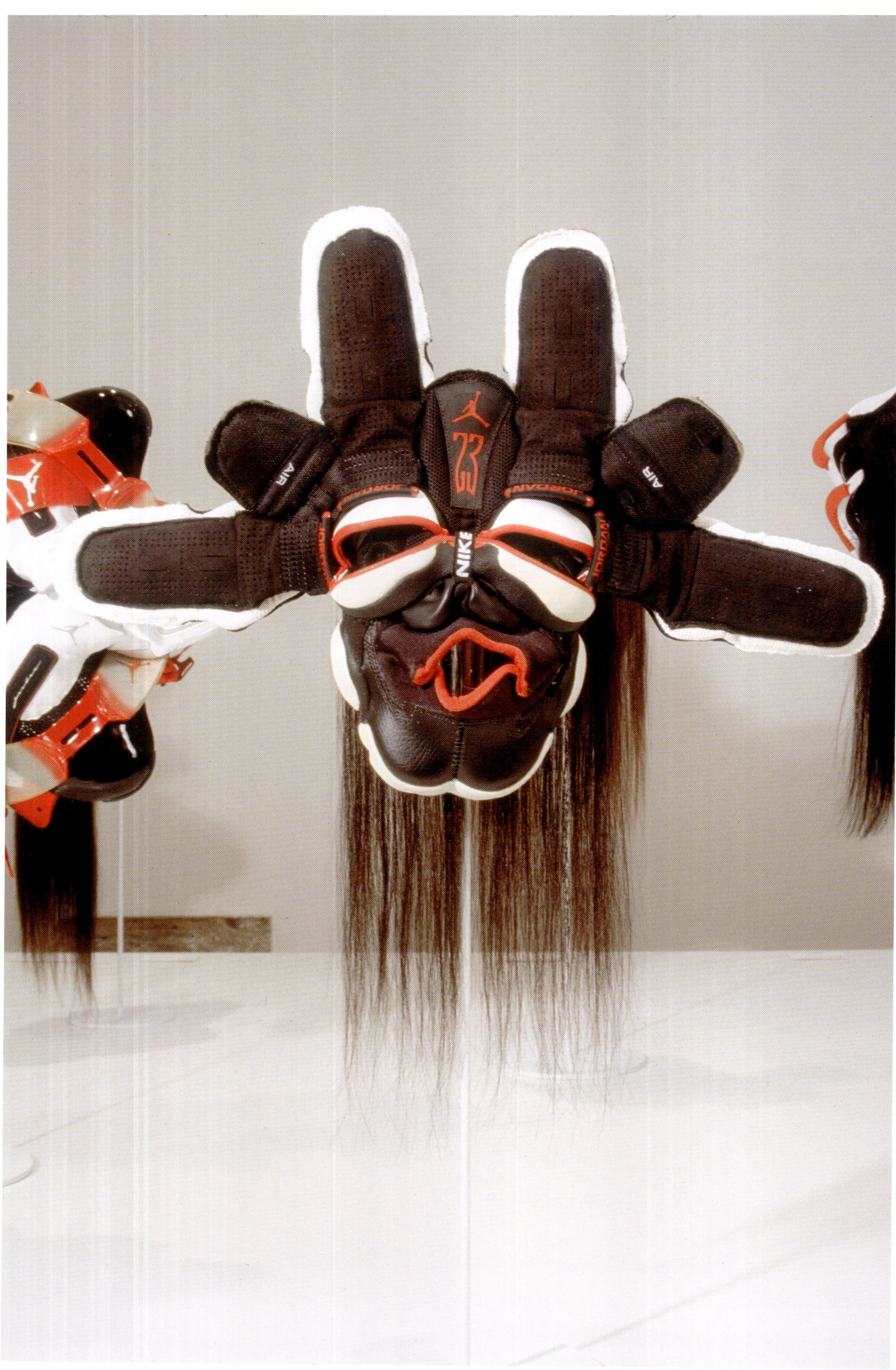

Brian Jungen,
*Prototype for New
Understanding #5*, 1999

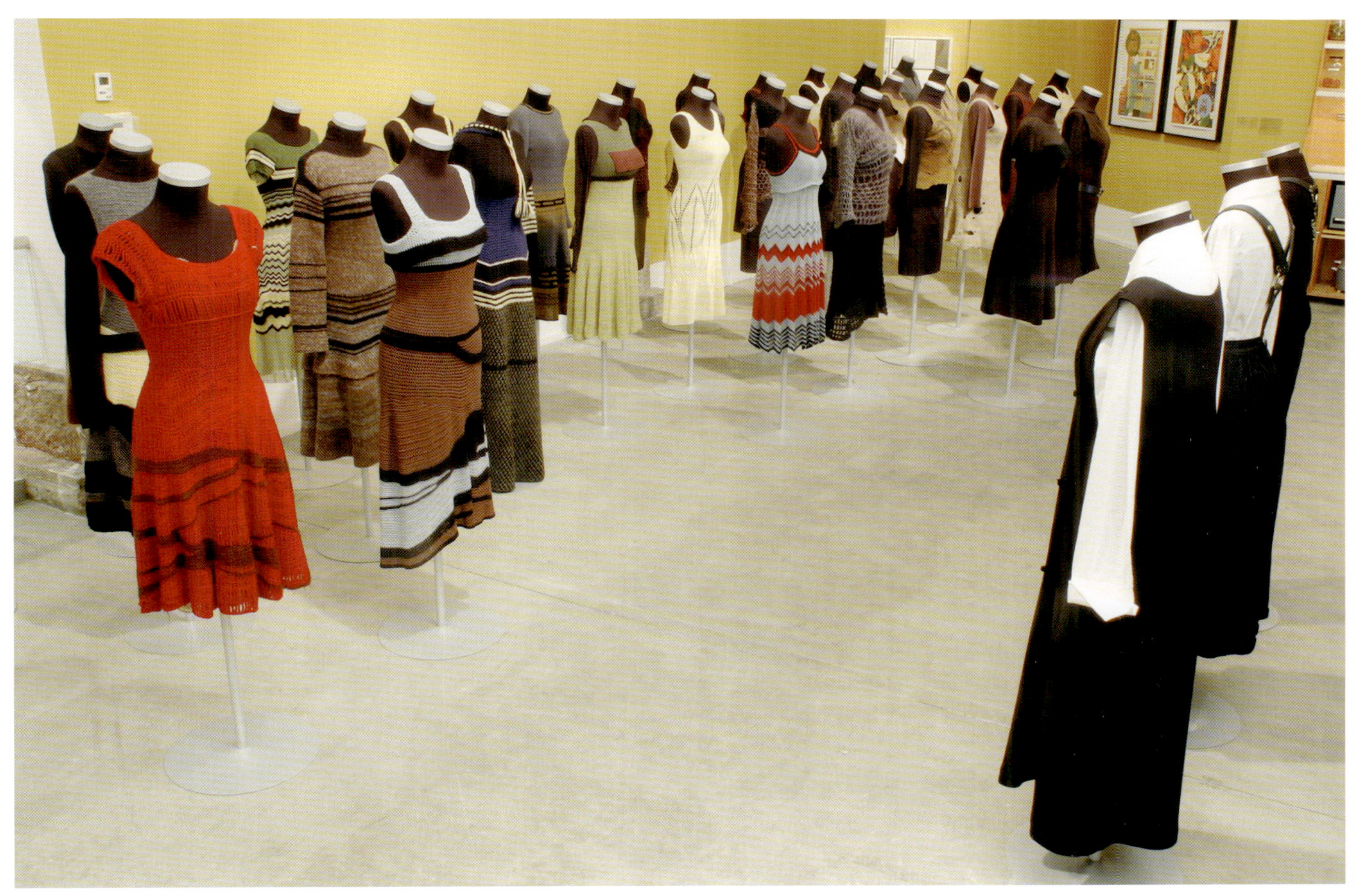

Andrea Zittel,
A–Z Personal Uniforms,
1991–2006

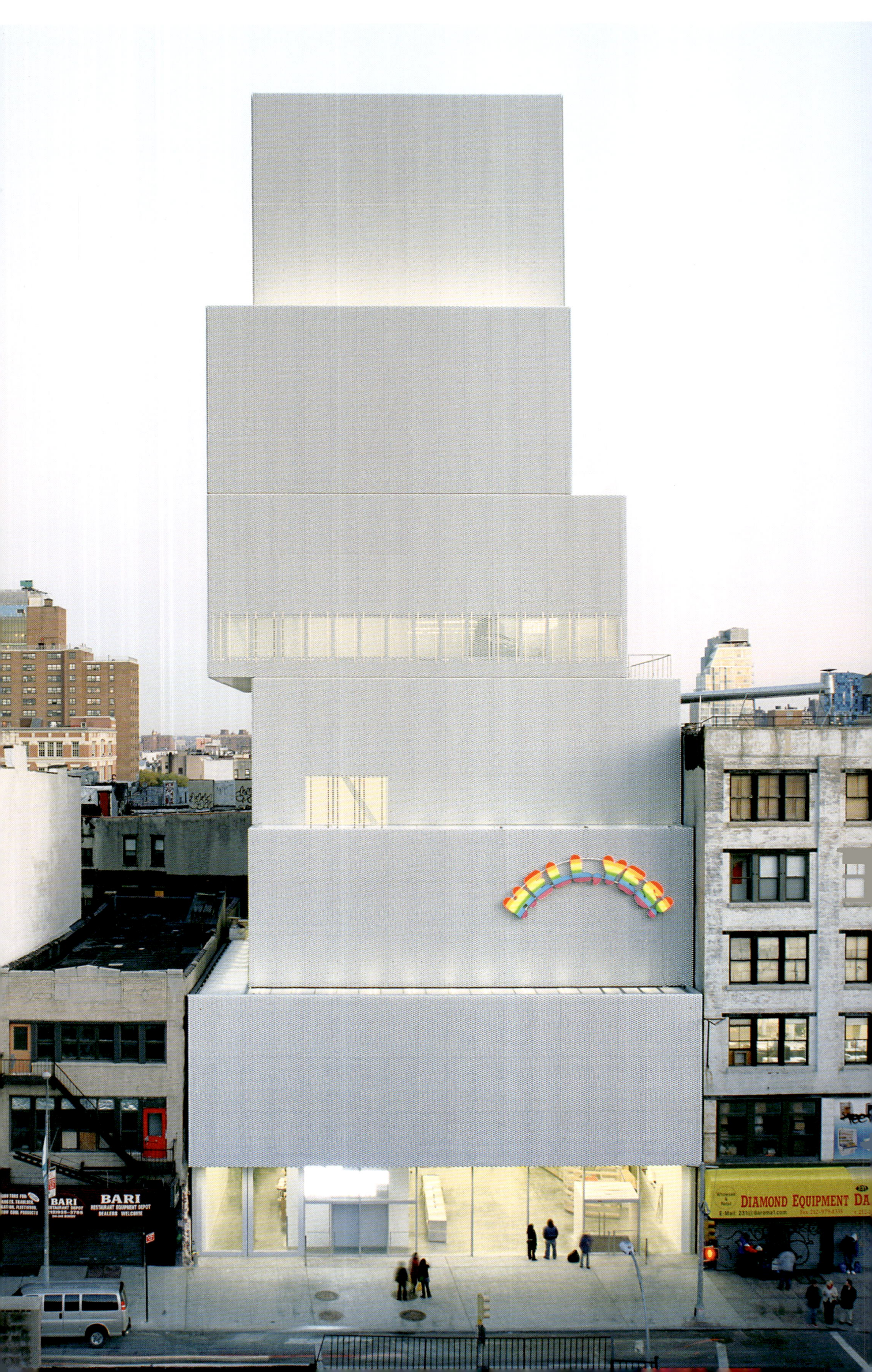

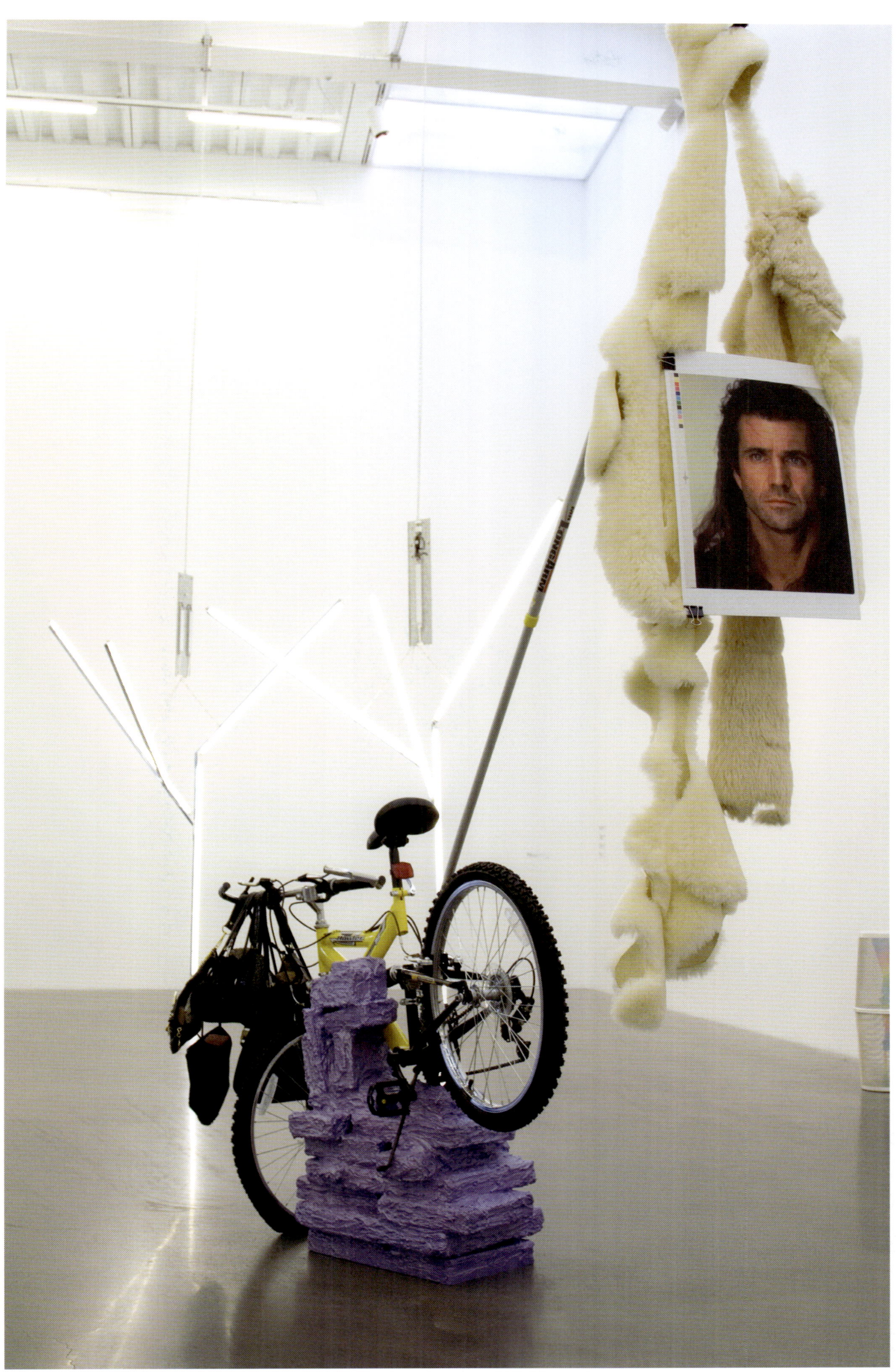

(left) The New Museum building at 235 Bowery is designed by Tokyo-based architects Kazuyo Sejima and Ryue Nishizawa of SANAA, 2007. Its opening on December 1, 2007 coincides with the institution's thirtieth anniversary season. Ugo Rondinone's *Hell, Yes!*, 2001, is installed on the building's facade, 2007–10

(above) Rachel Harrison, *Huffy Howler*, 2004

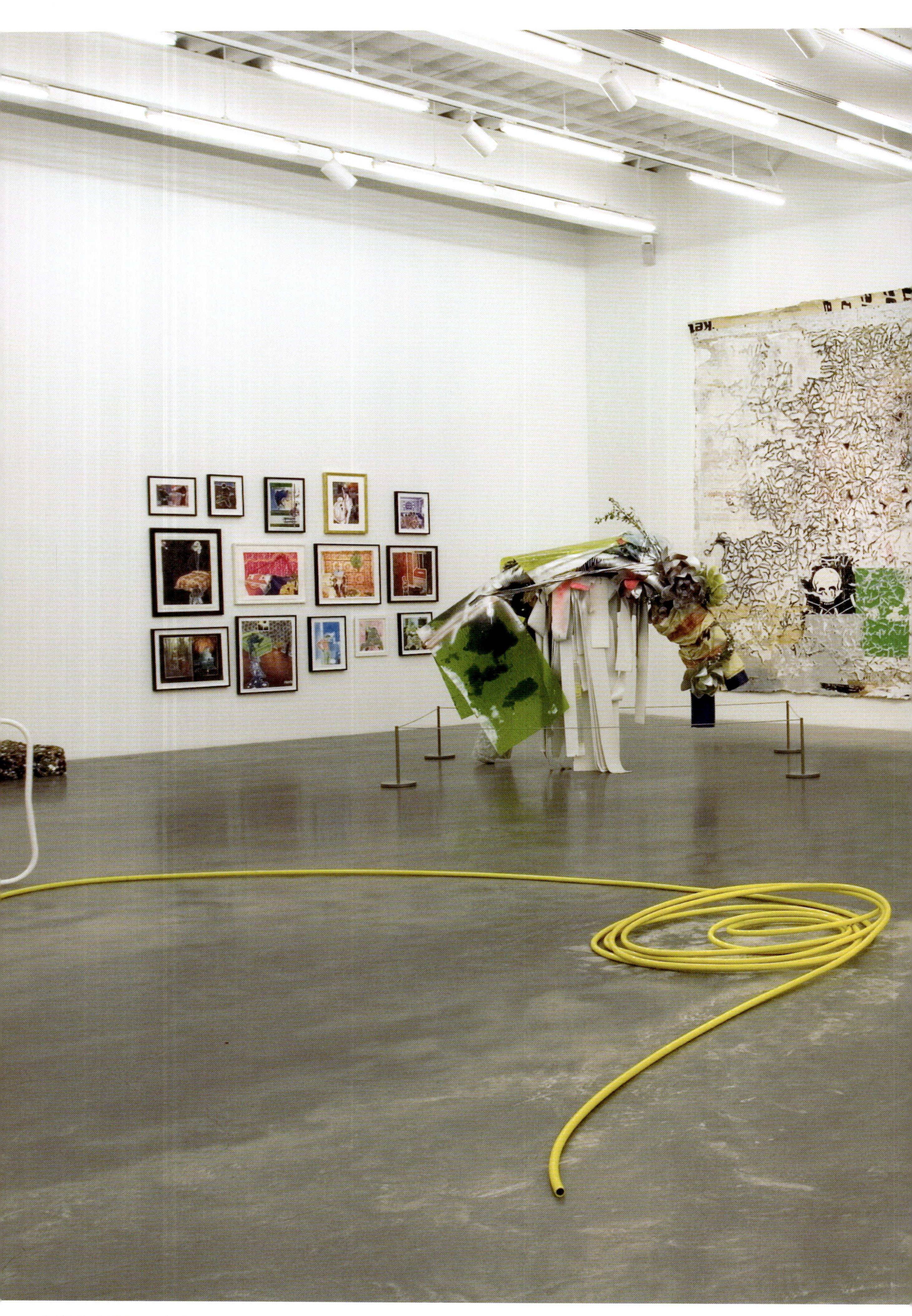

Left to right: works by
Christian Holstad, Isa
Genzken, Mark Bradford,
Martin Boyce, Tom Burr,
and Anselm Reyle

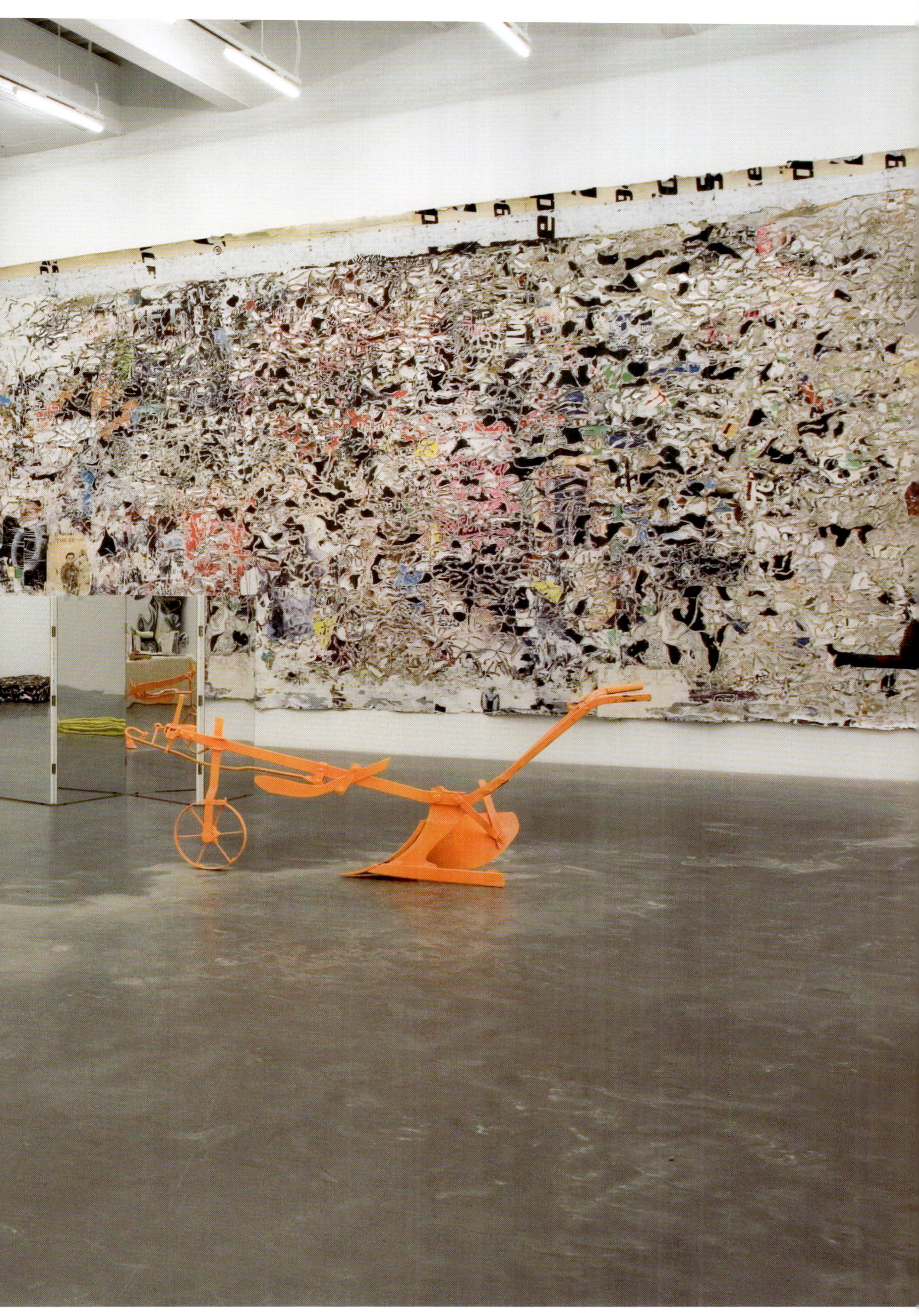

*Sharon Hayes: I march in the parade of liberty, but as long as I love you
I'm not free*

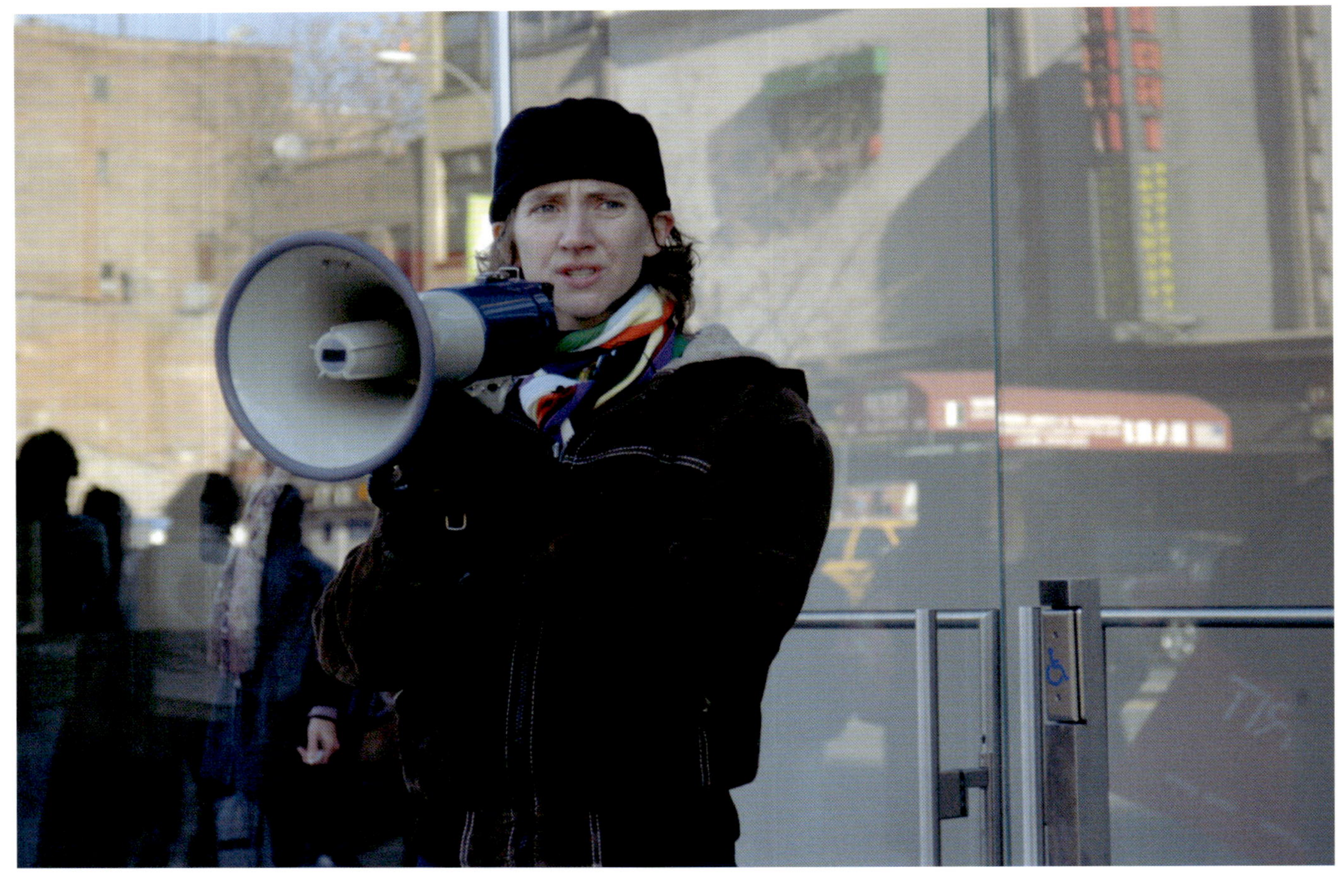

Sharon Hayes,
*I march in the parade of
liberty, but as long as
I love you I'm not free,*
2007-08. Performance: New
Museum, December 2007

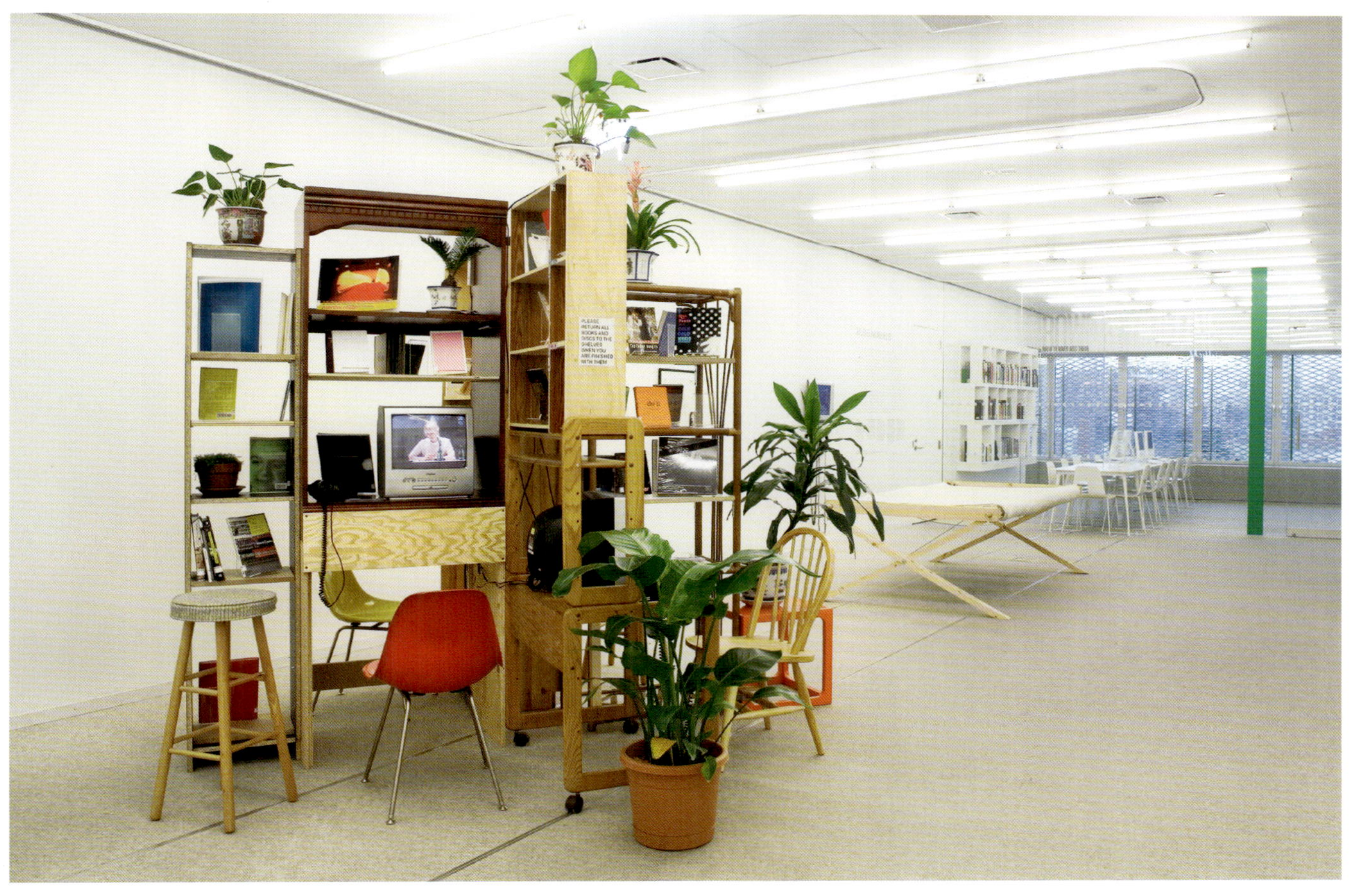

Left to right: works by
Anton Vidokle and Ginger
Brooks Takahashi

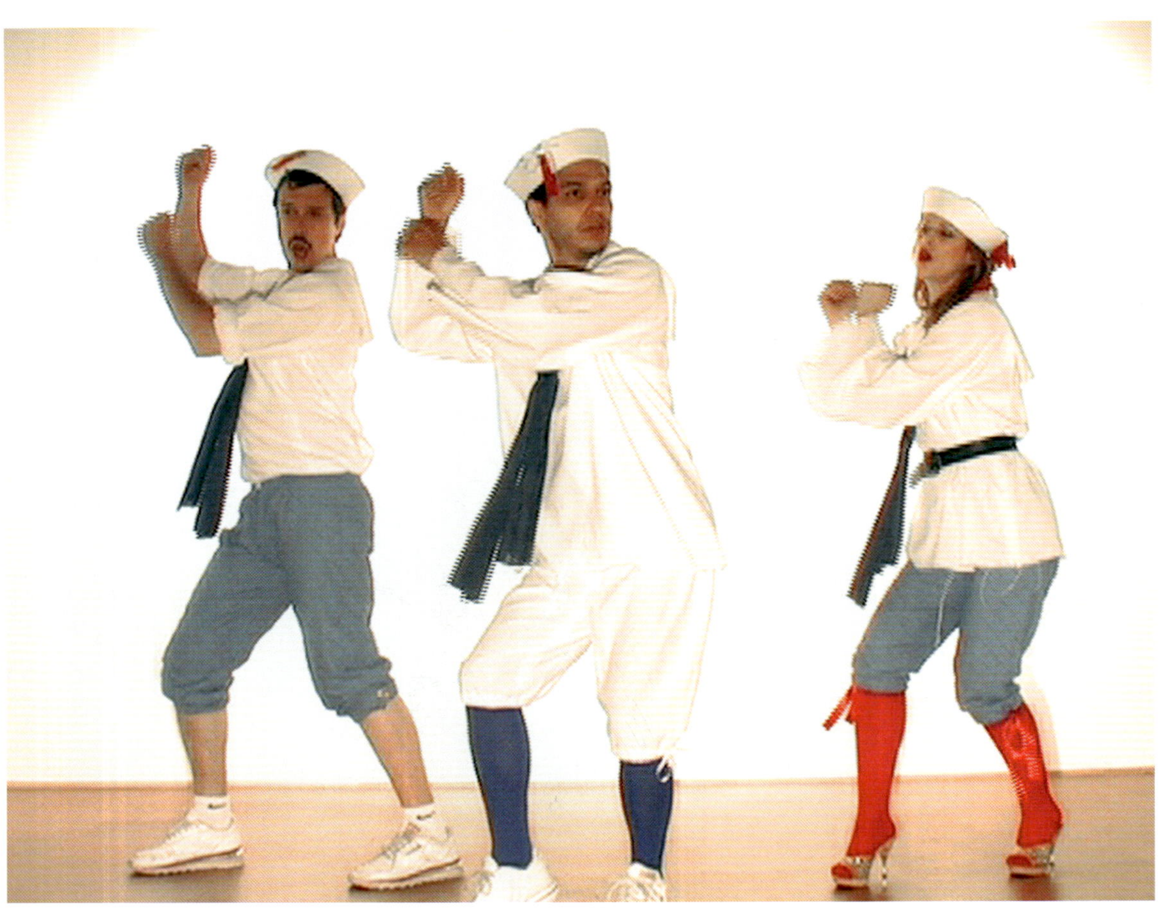

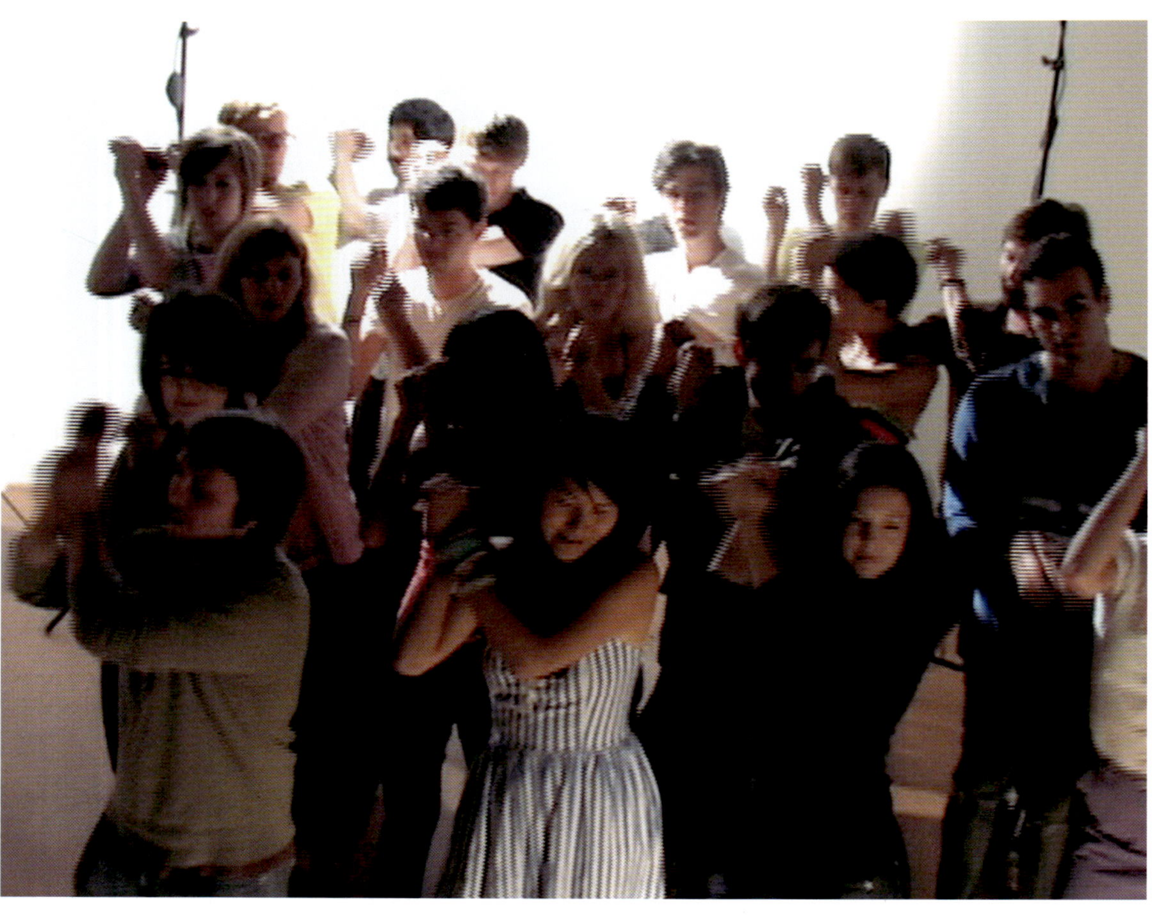

My Barbarian,
The Golden Age, 2007
(stills)

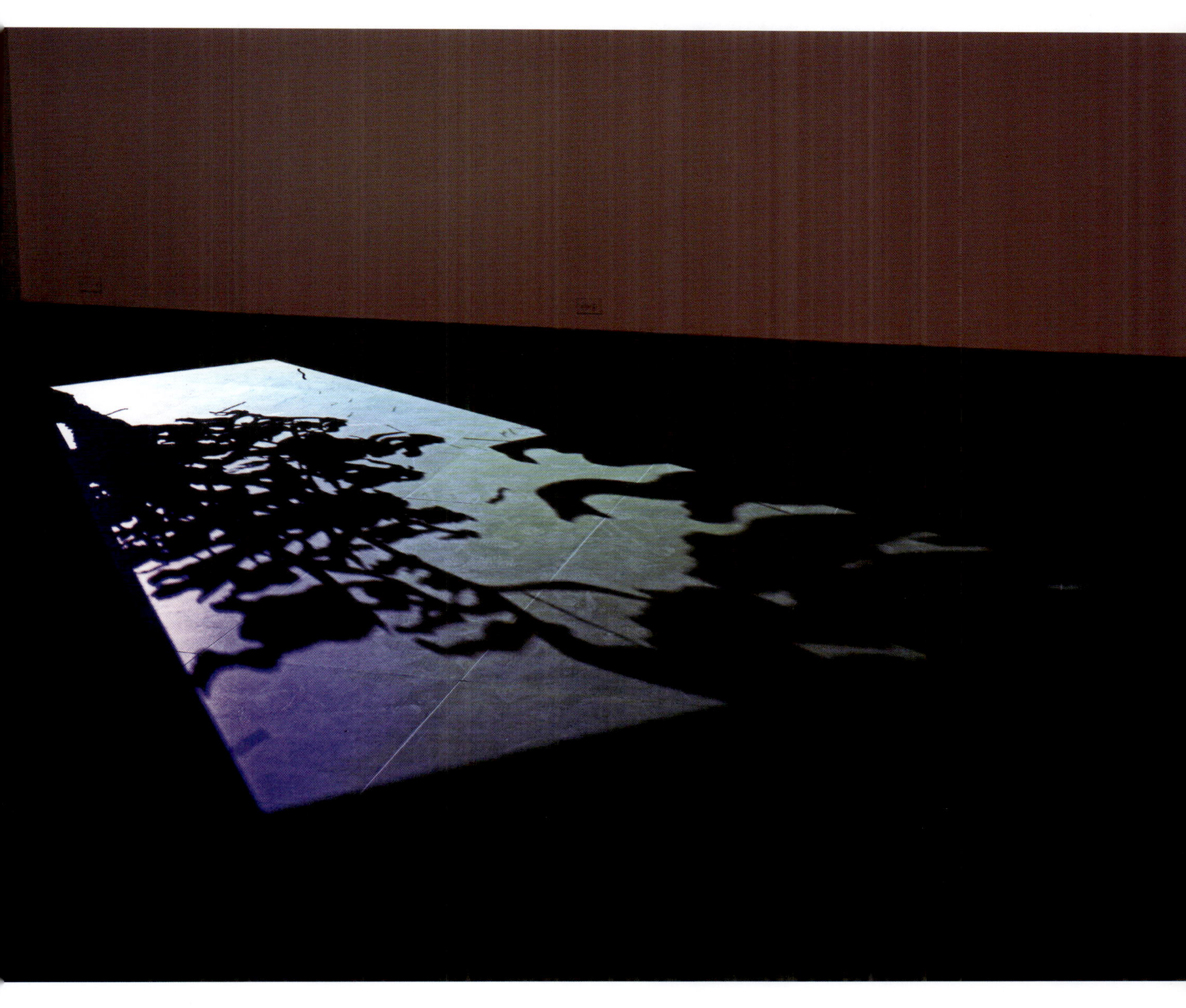

Paul Chan,
2nd Light, 2006

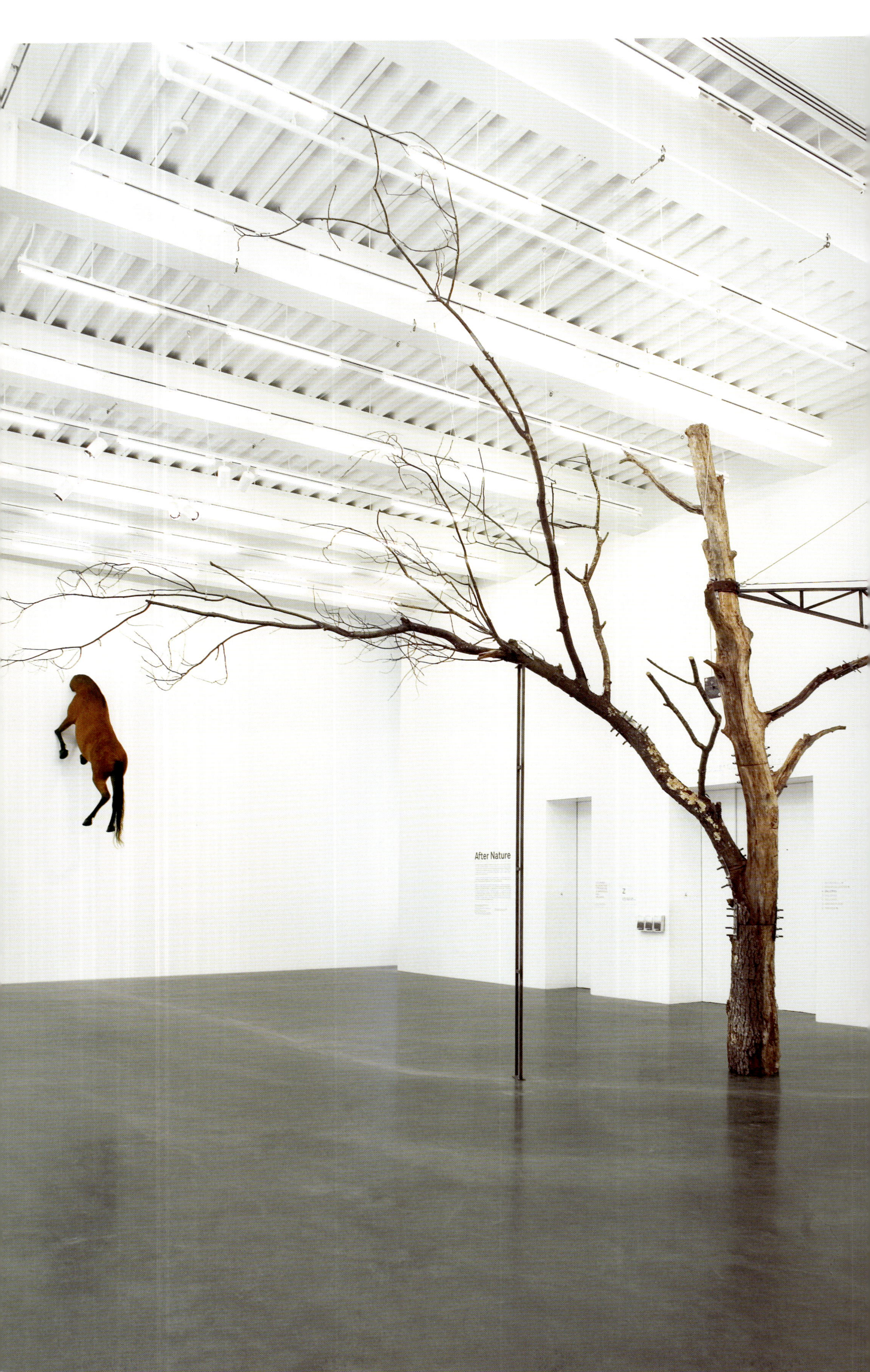

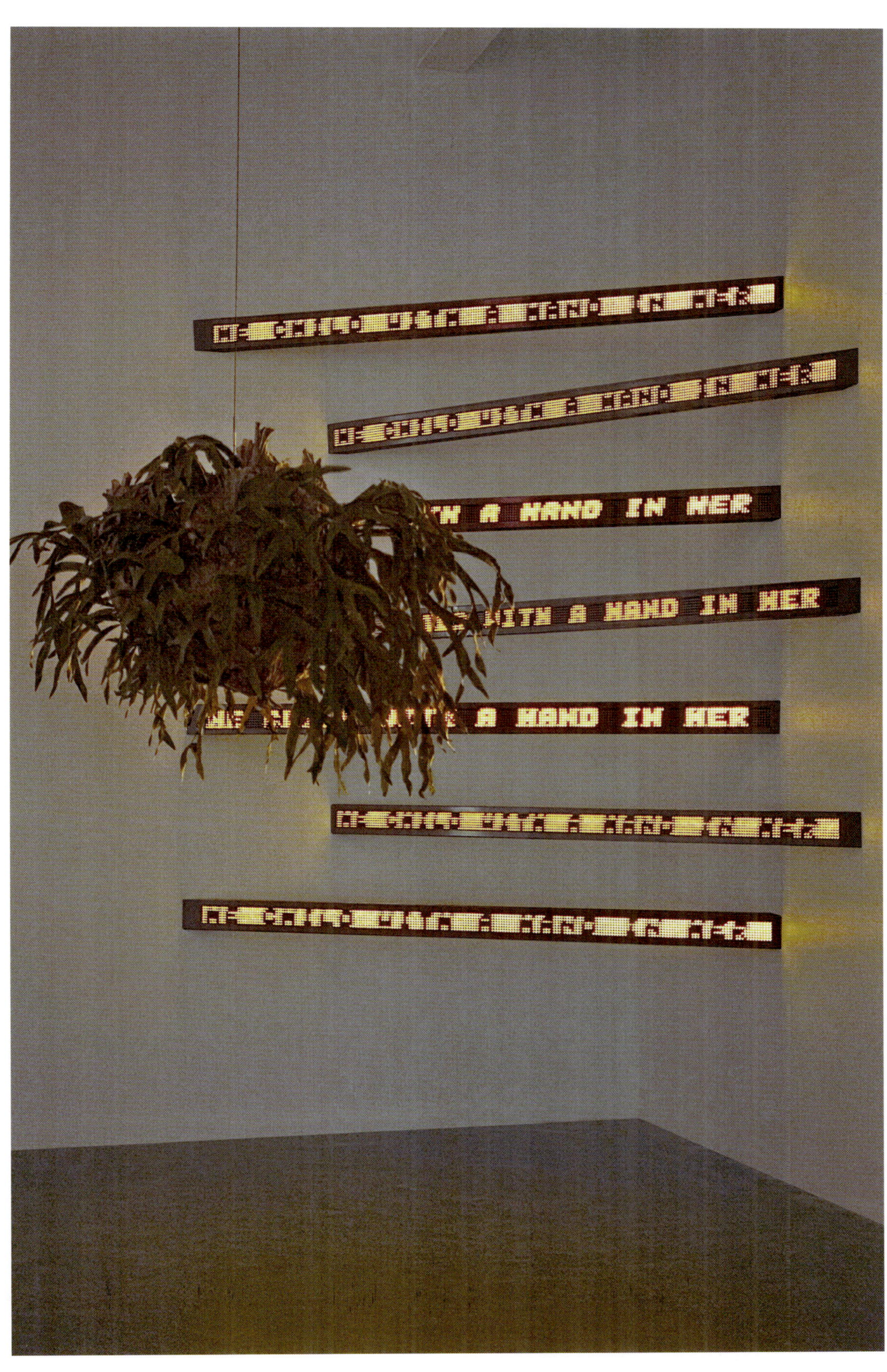

(left) Left to right: works by Maurizio Cattelan and Zoe Leonard

(above) Left to right: works by Allora and Calzadilla, and Jenny Holzer

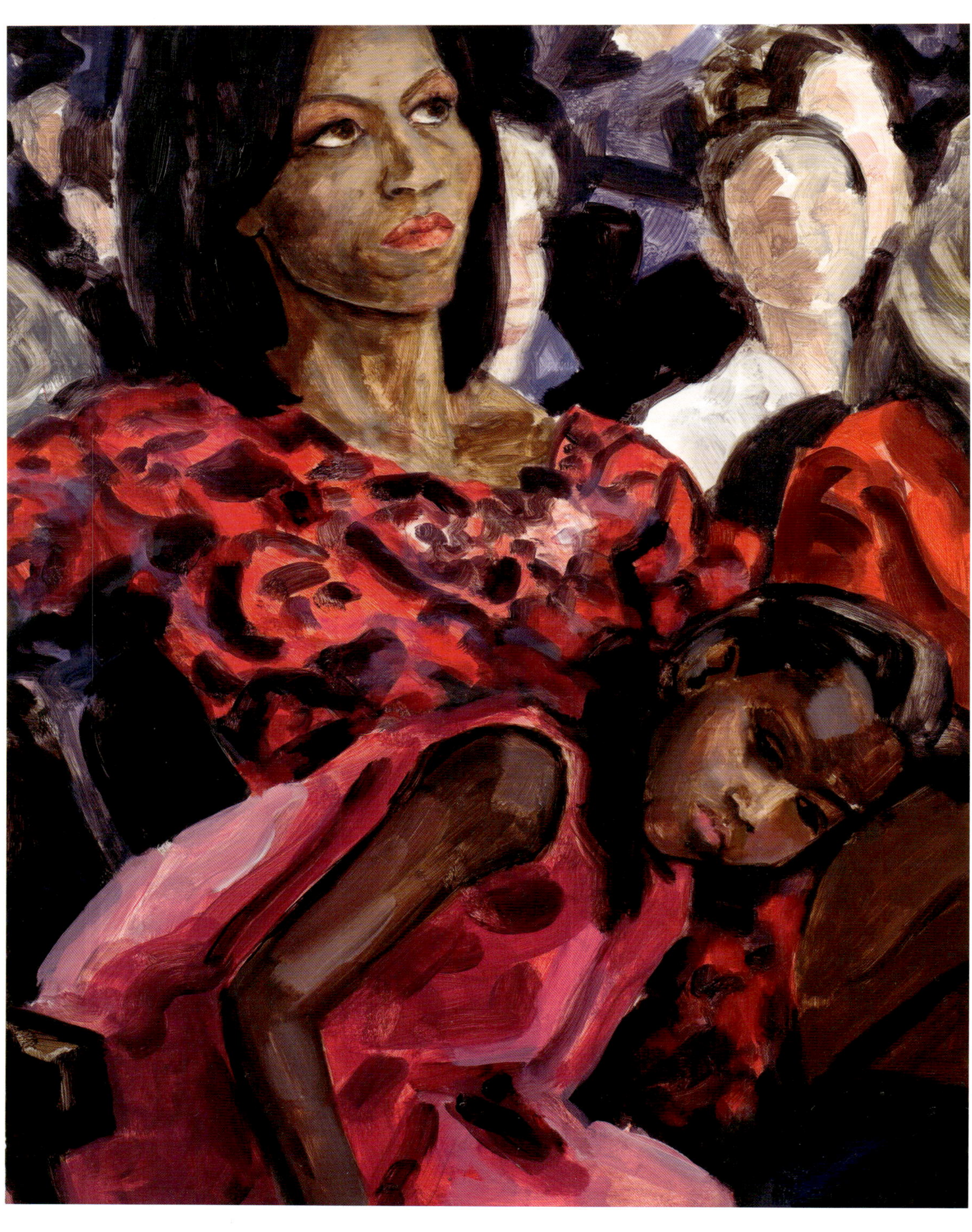

Elizabeth Peyton,
Michelle and Sasha Obama
Listening to Barack
Obama at the Democratic
National Convention
August 2008, 2008

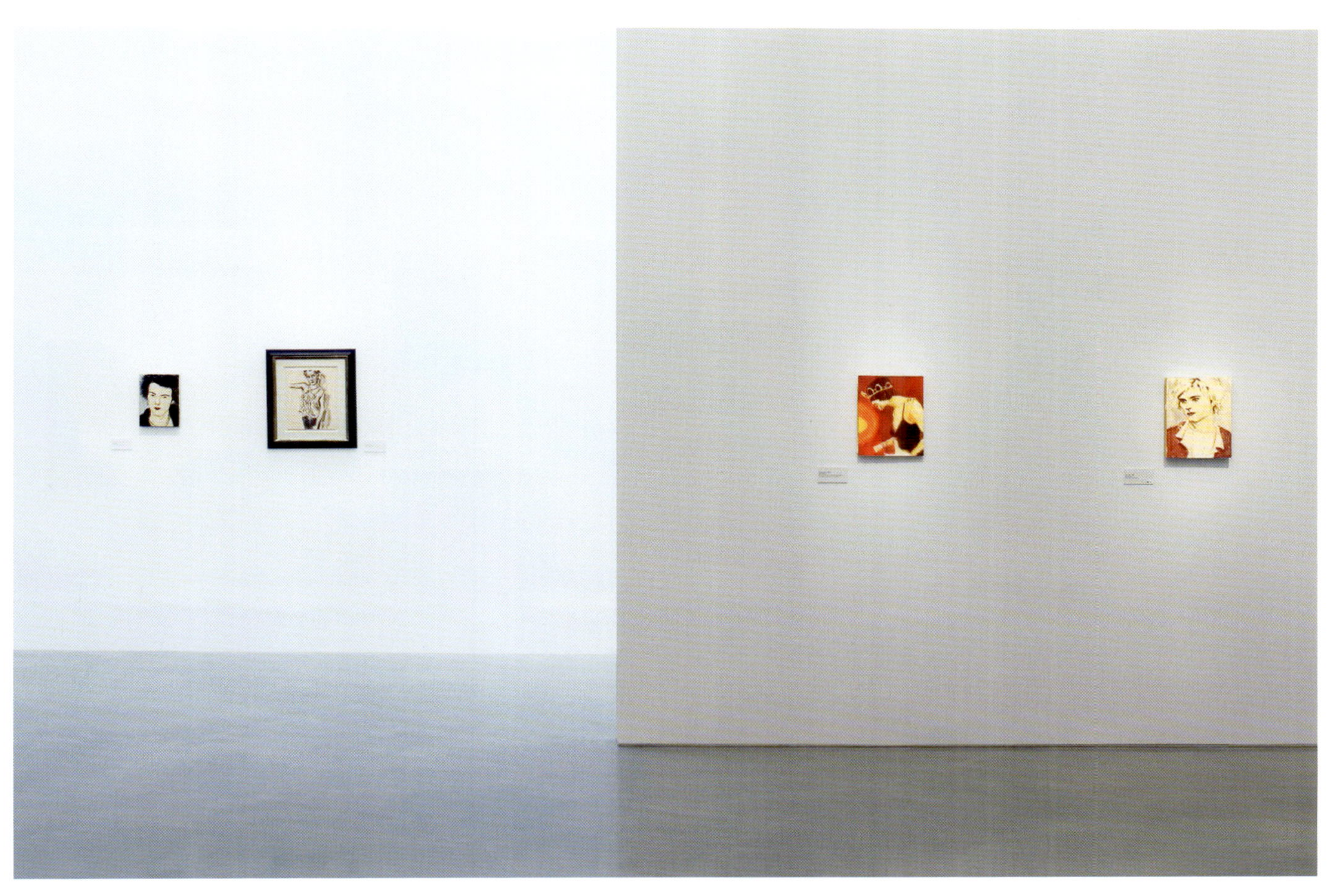

Installation view

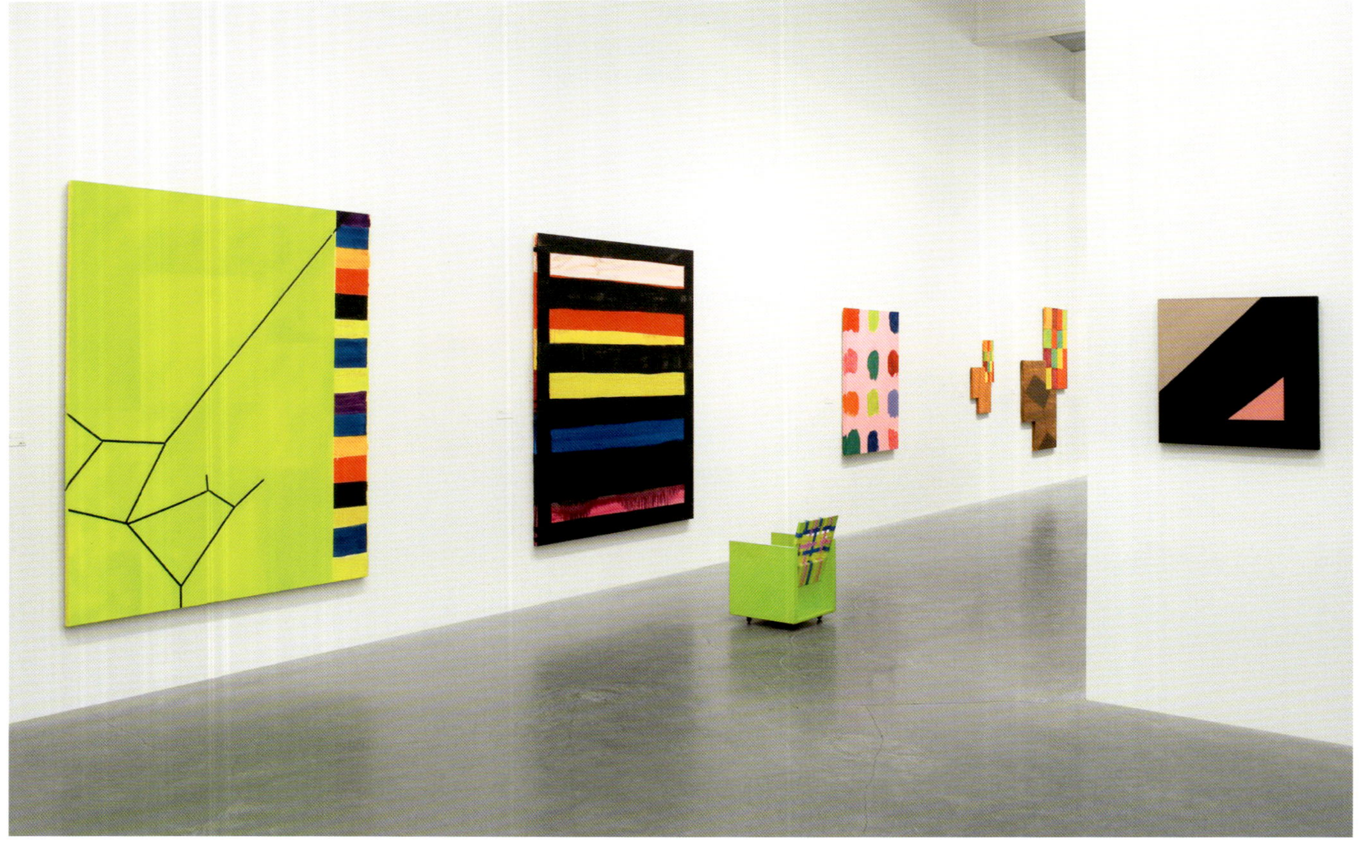

(above and right)
Installation views

(following spread)
Jeremy Deller, *It Is What
It Is: Conversations About
Iraq*, 2009

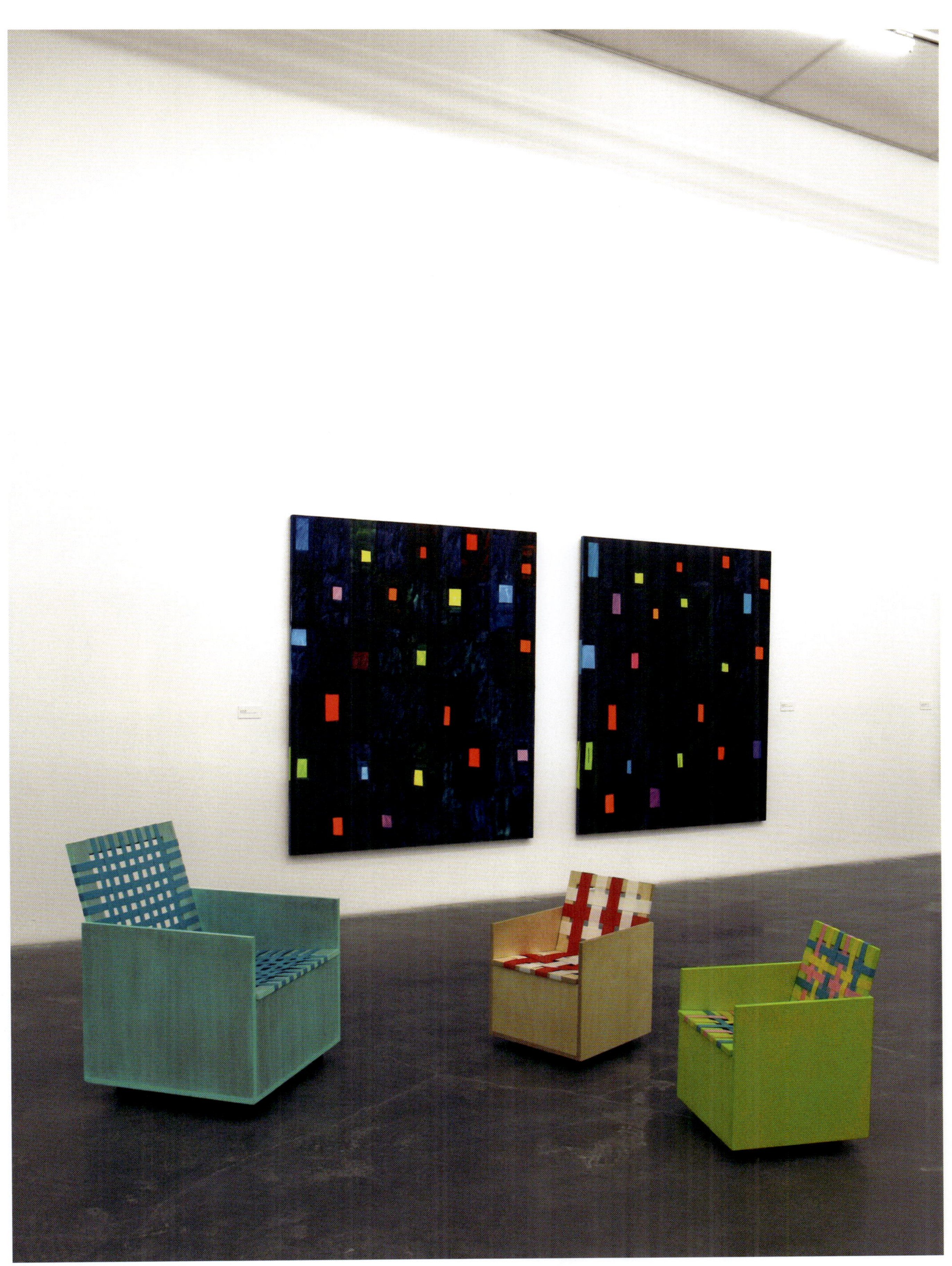

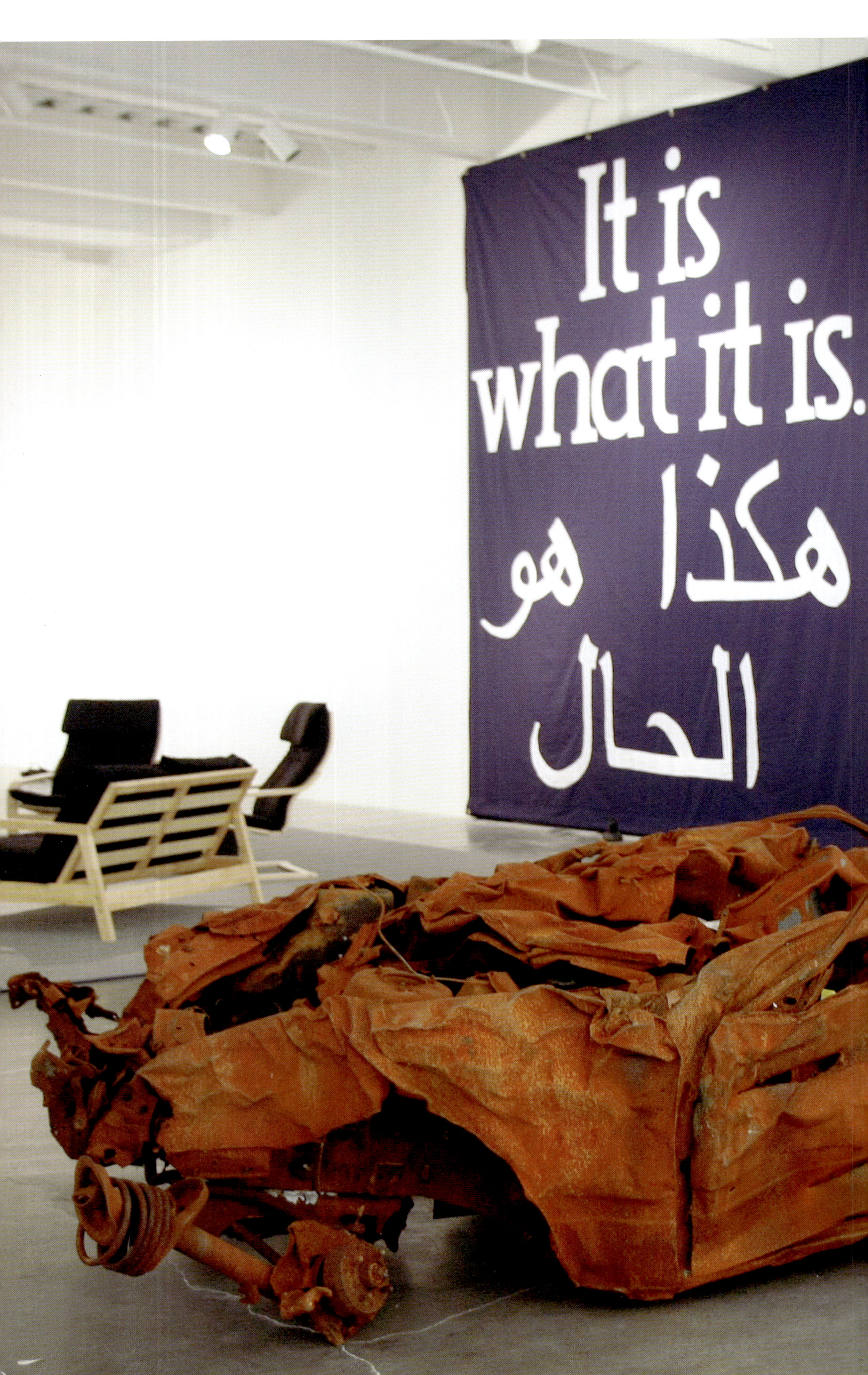
It is
what it is.
هكذا هو
الحال

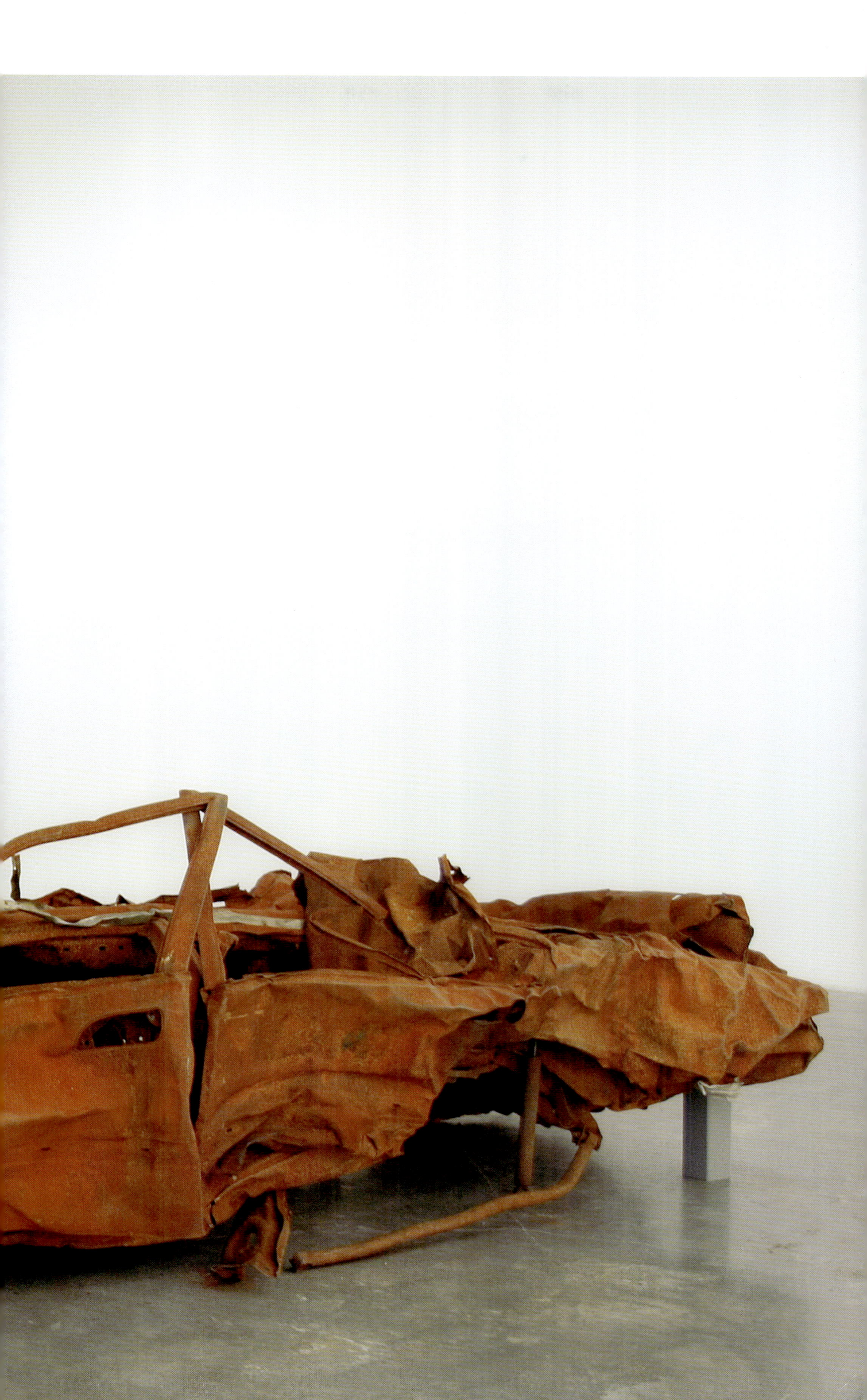

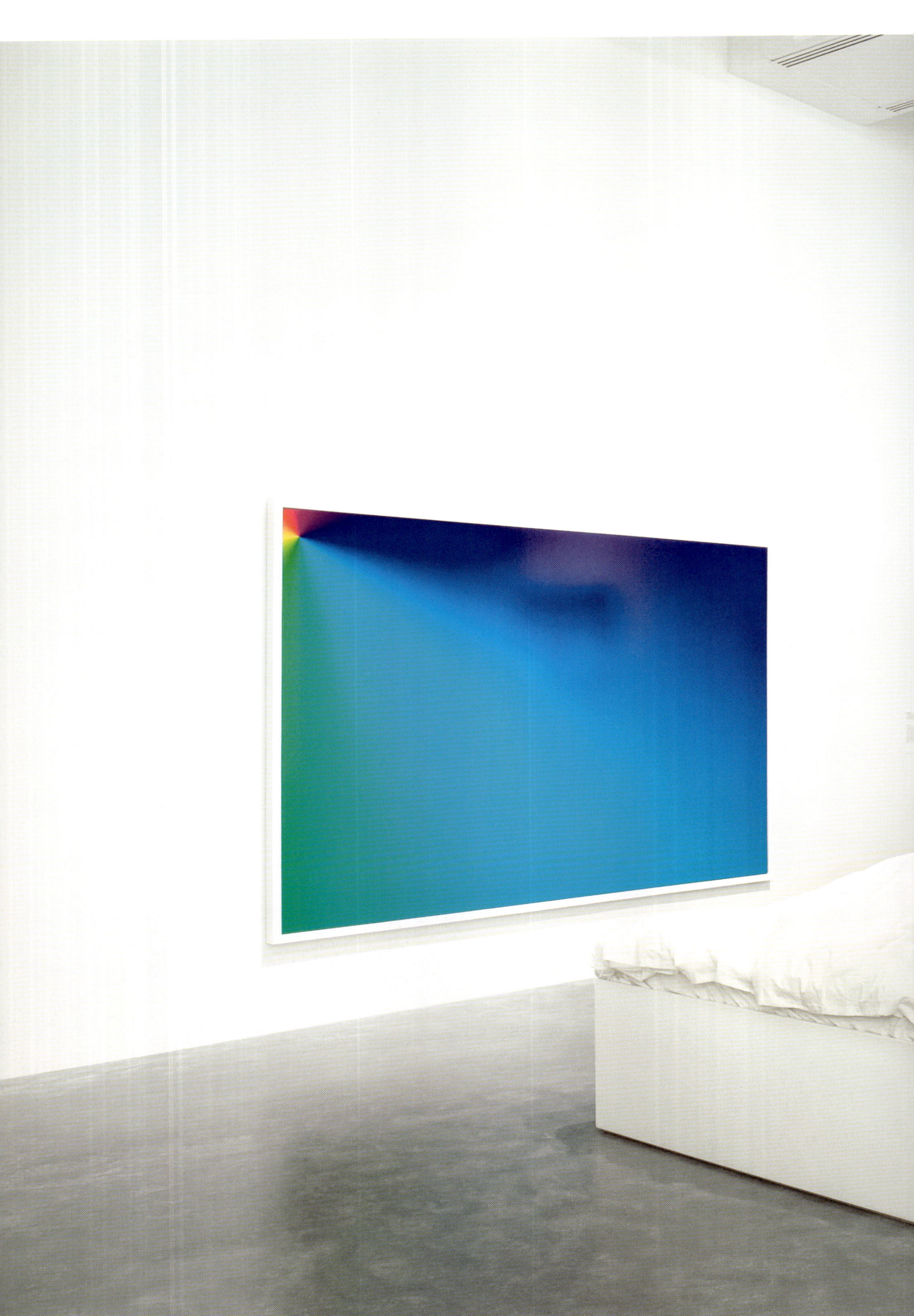

Left to right: works by
Cory Arcangel, Chu Yun,
and Tauba Auerbach

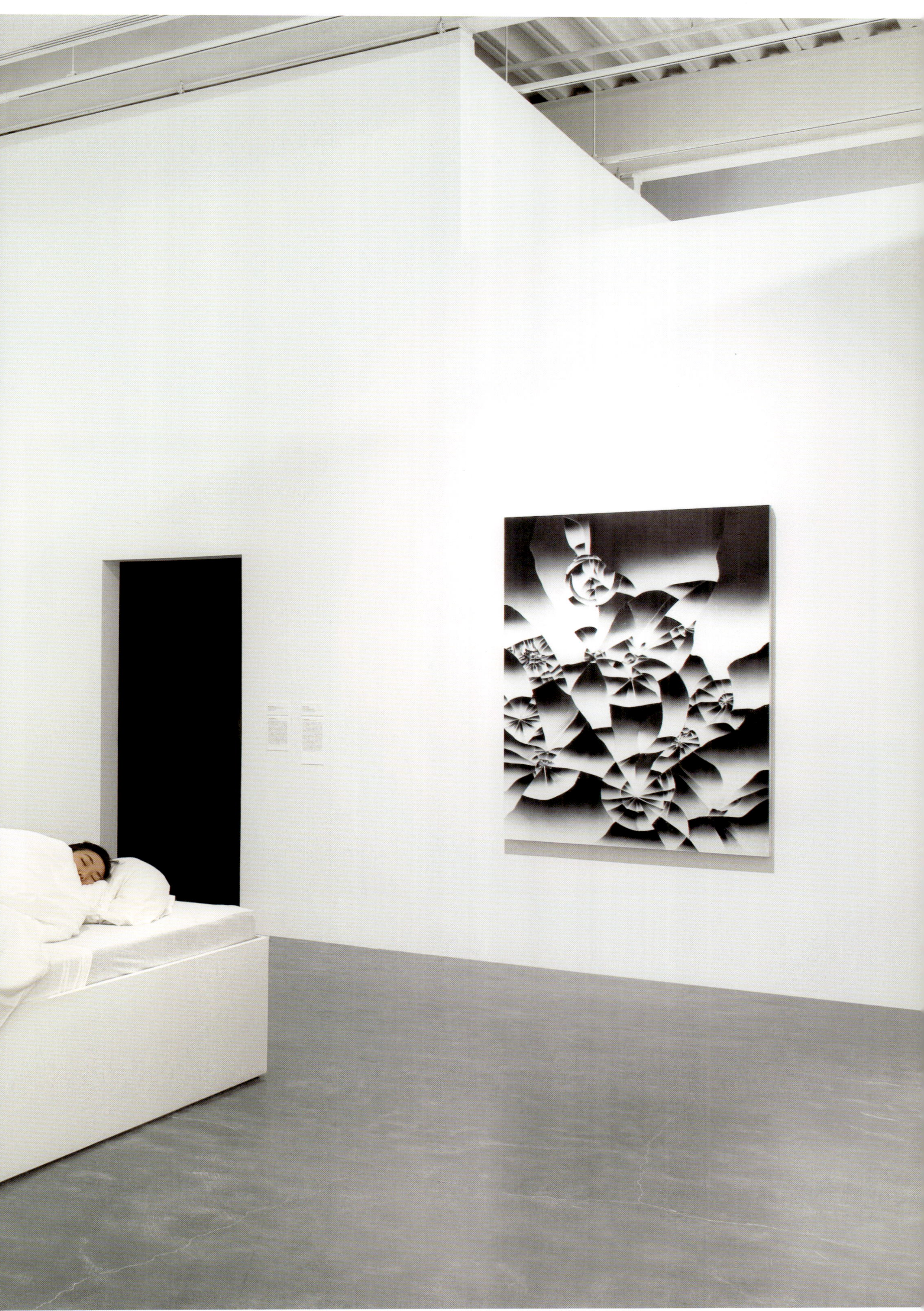

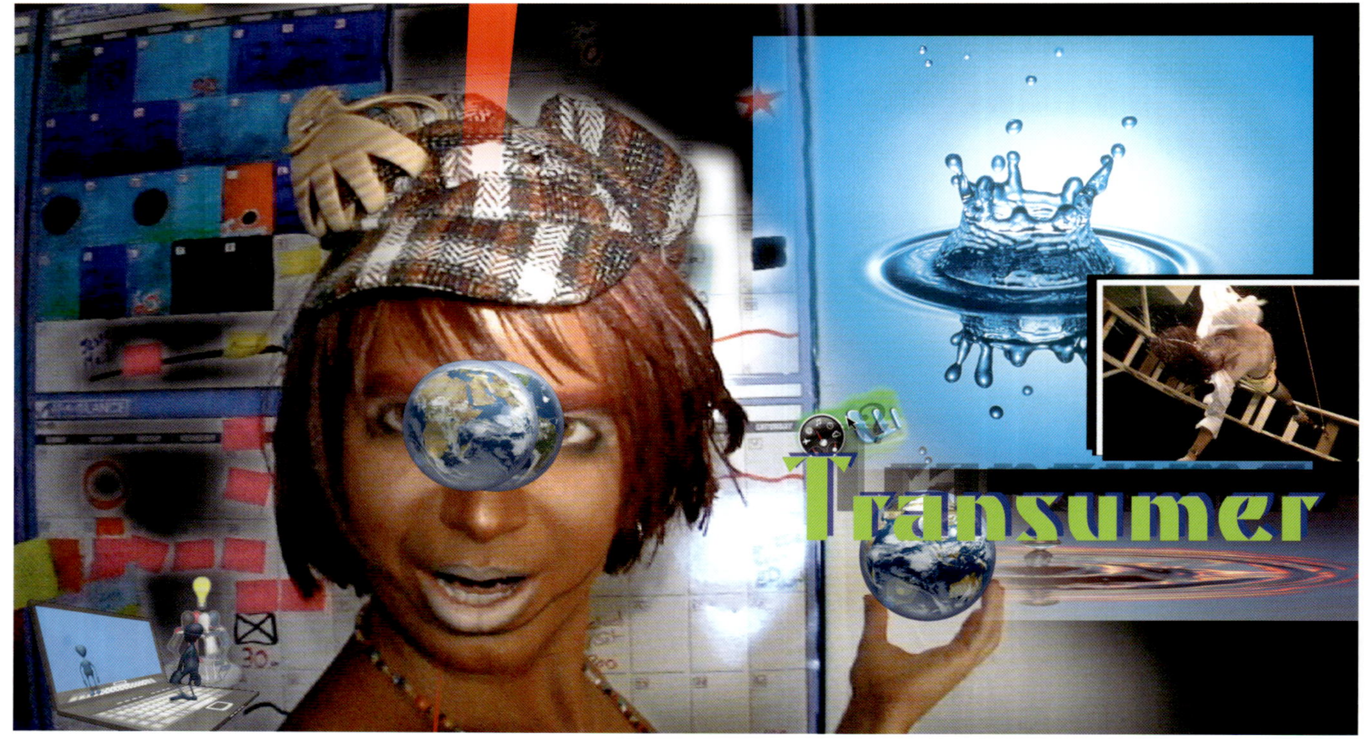

Ryan Trecartin,
P.opular S.ky
(section ish), 2008
(production still)

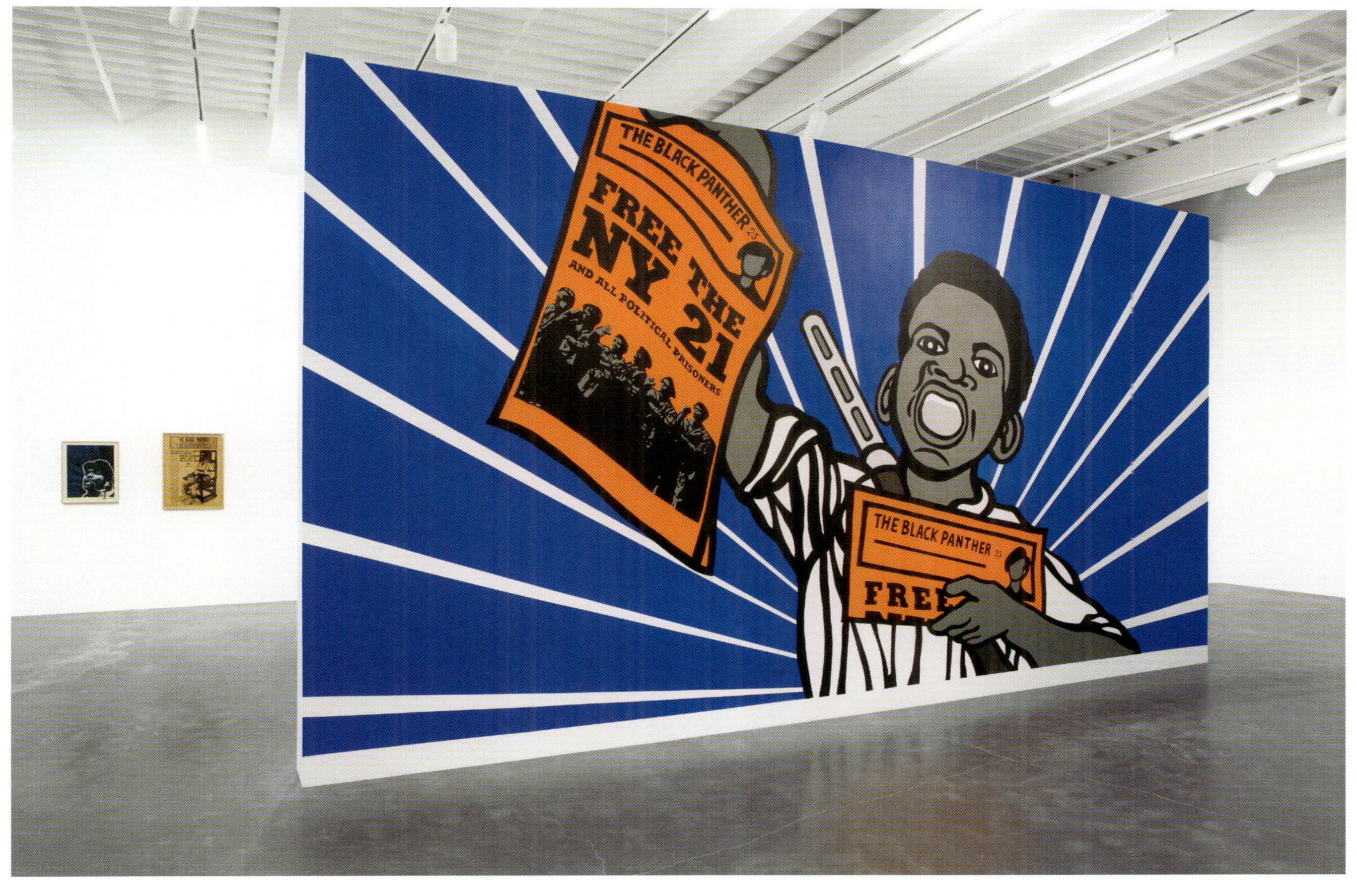

Rigo 23 mural based on
Emory Douglas posters
from *The Black Panther*,
1969

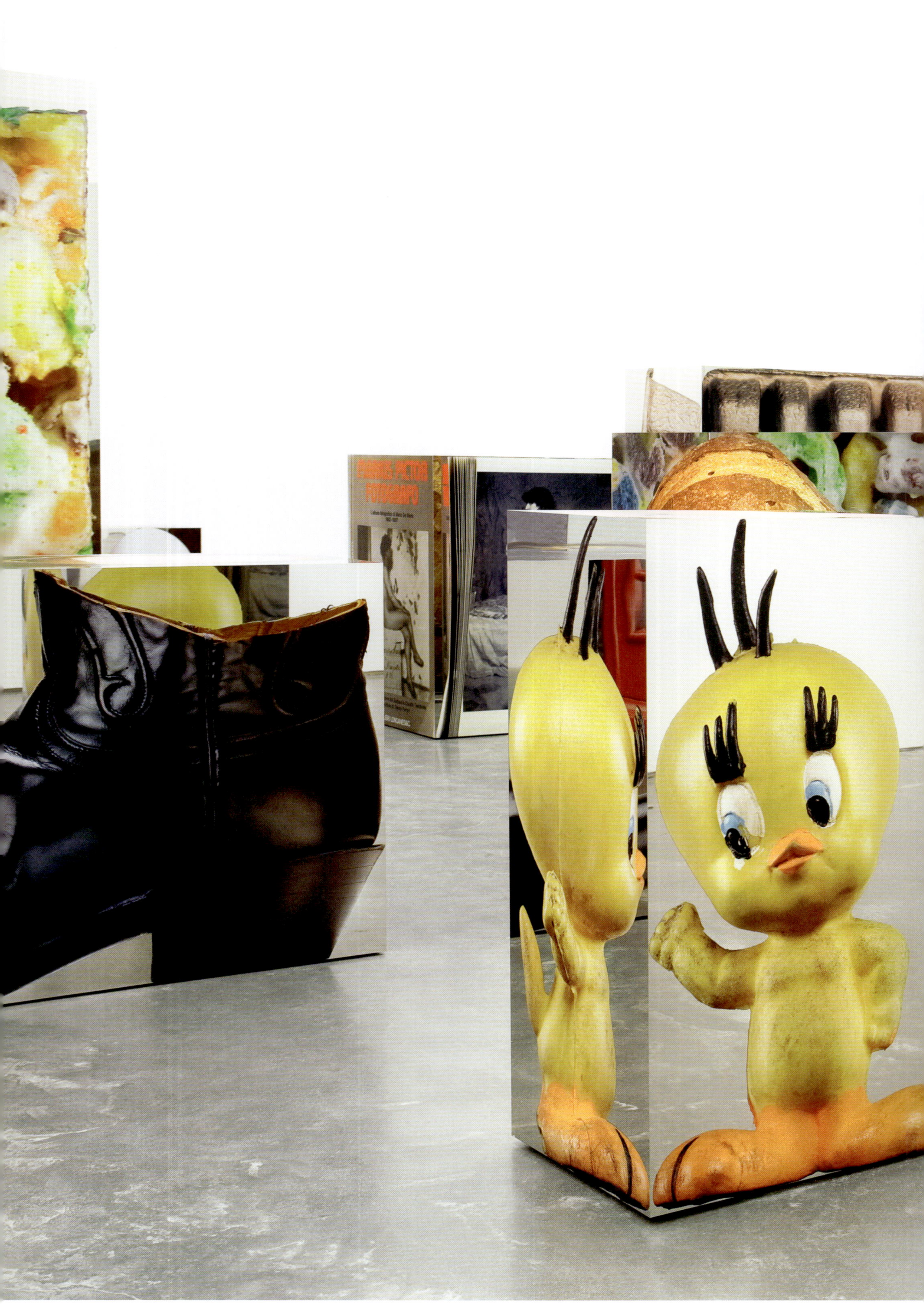

Urs Fischer,
Service à la française,
2009

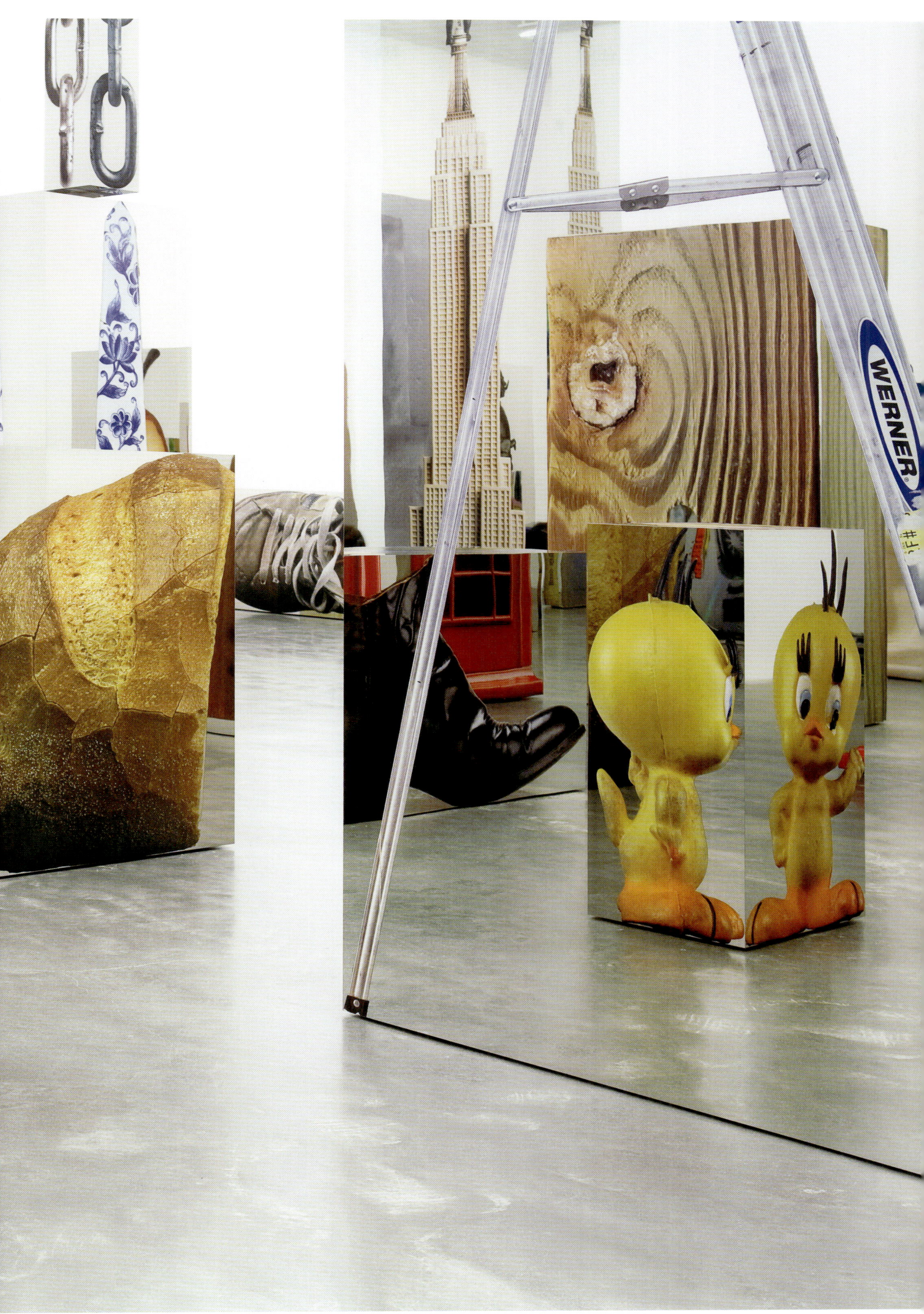

WERNER

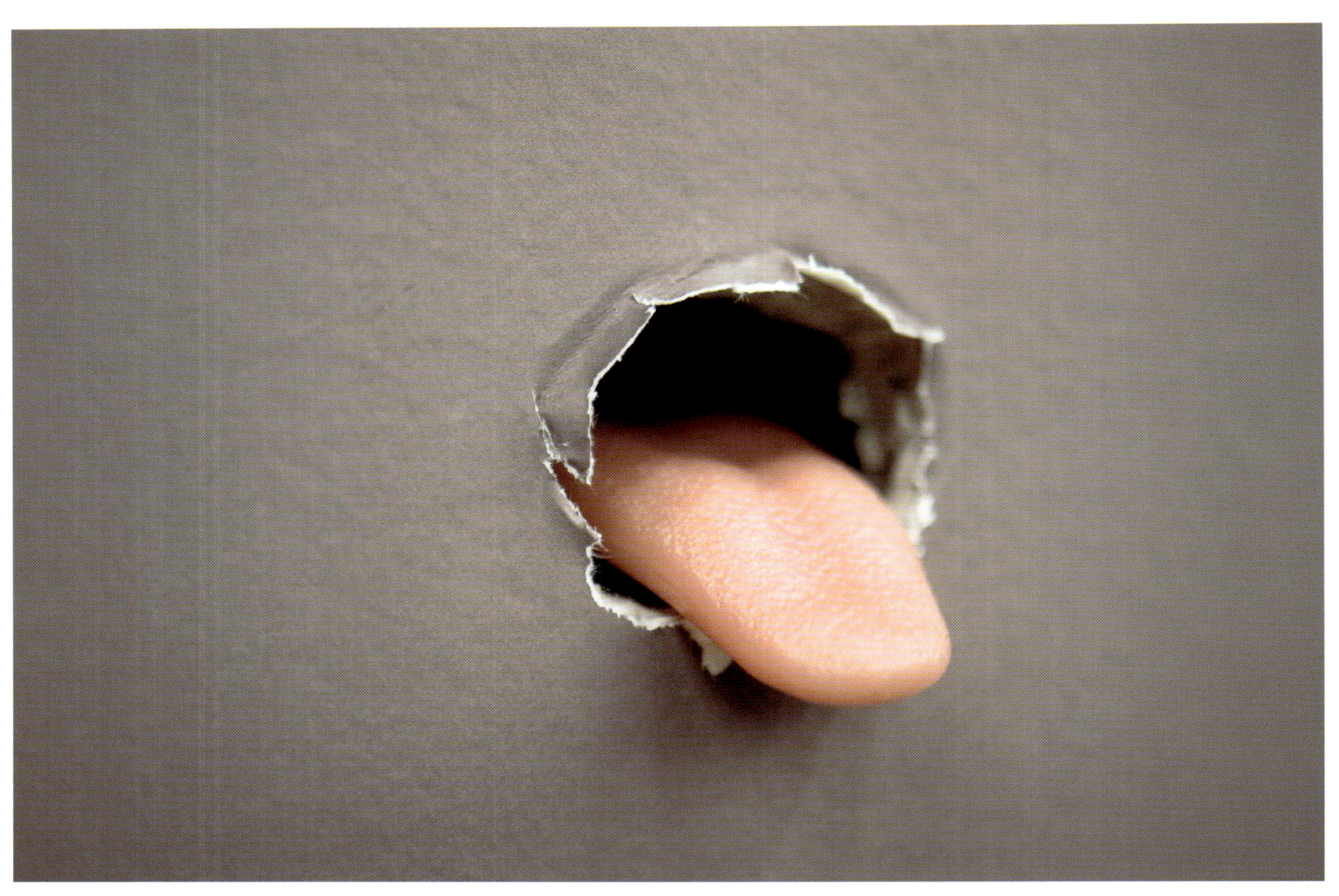

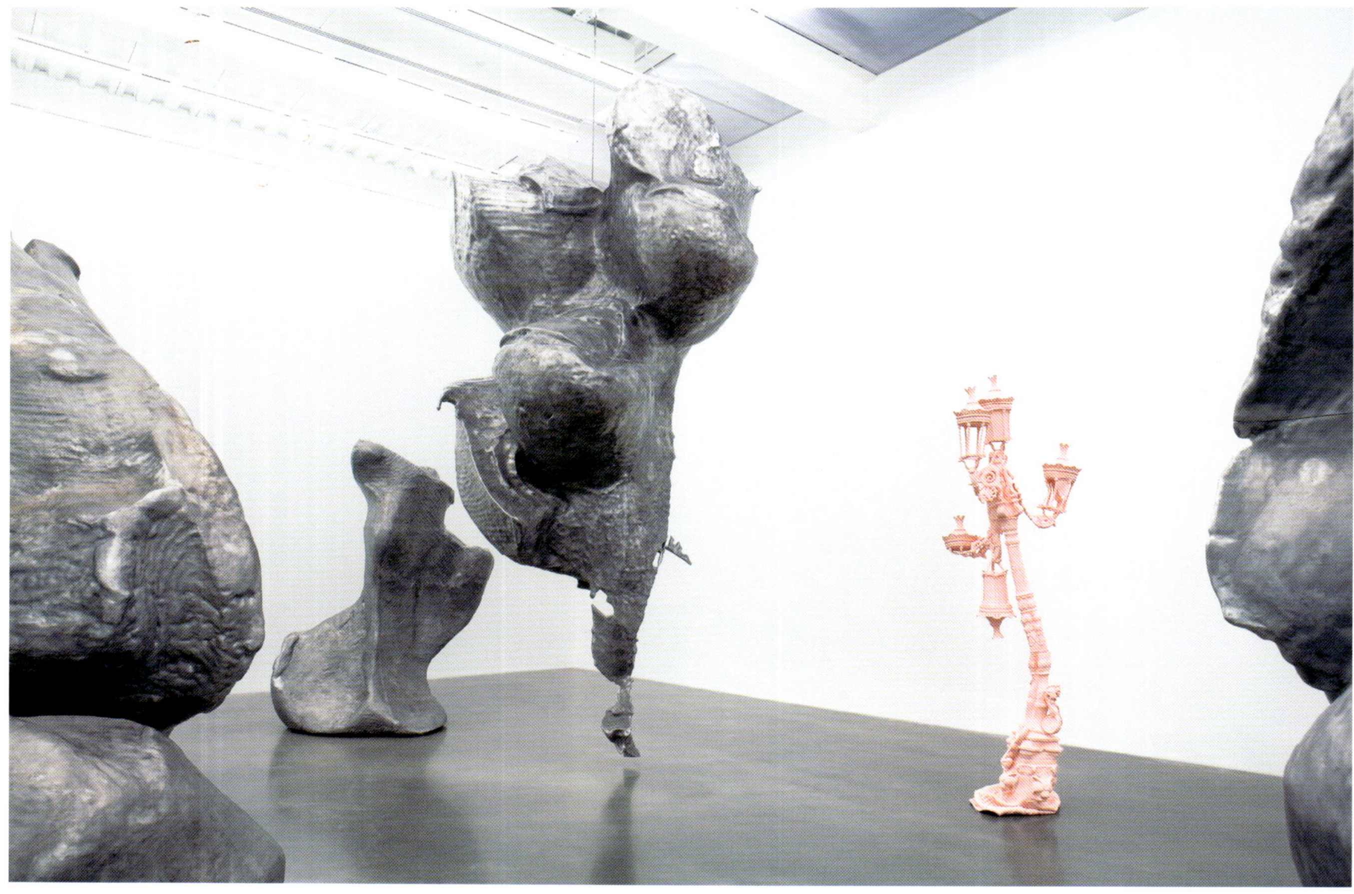

(top) Urs Fischer,
Noisette, 2009

(bottom) Urs Fischer,
works including *Miss
Satin*, 2006–08; *Ix*,
2006–08; *David, the
Proprietor*, 2008–09; and
Frozen Pioneer, 2009

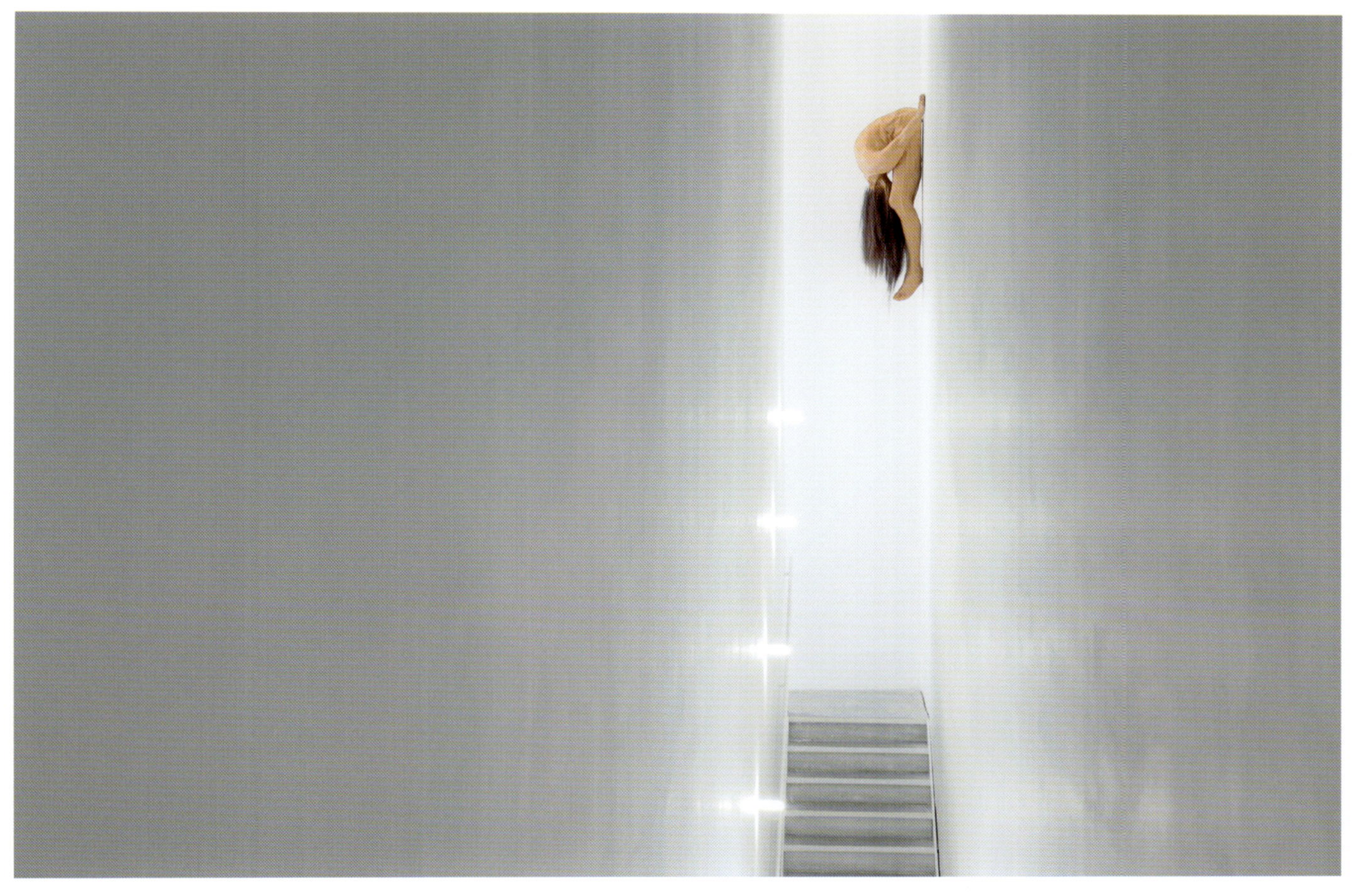

Kiki Smith,
Untitled (Bowed Woman),
1995

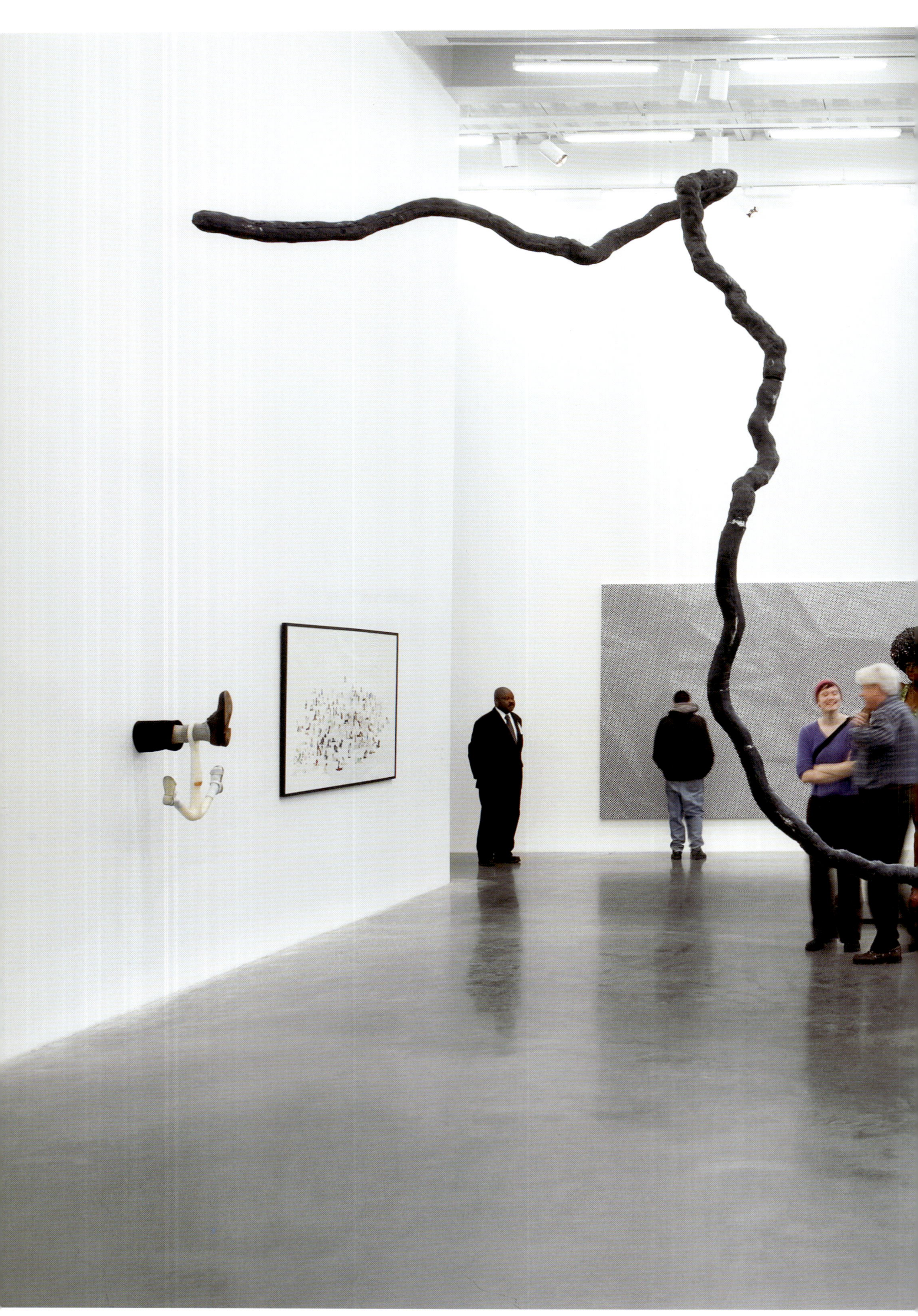

Foreground: work by Urs
Fischer. Left to right:
works by Robert Gober,
Paul Chan, Tauba Auerbach,
Liza Lou, David Altmejd,
and Charles Ray

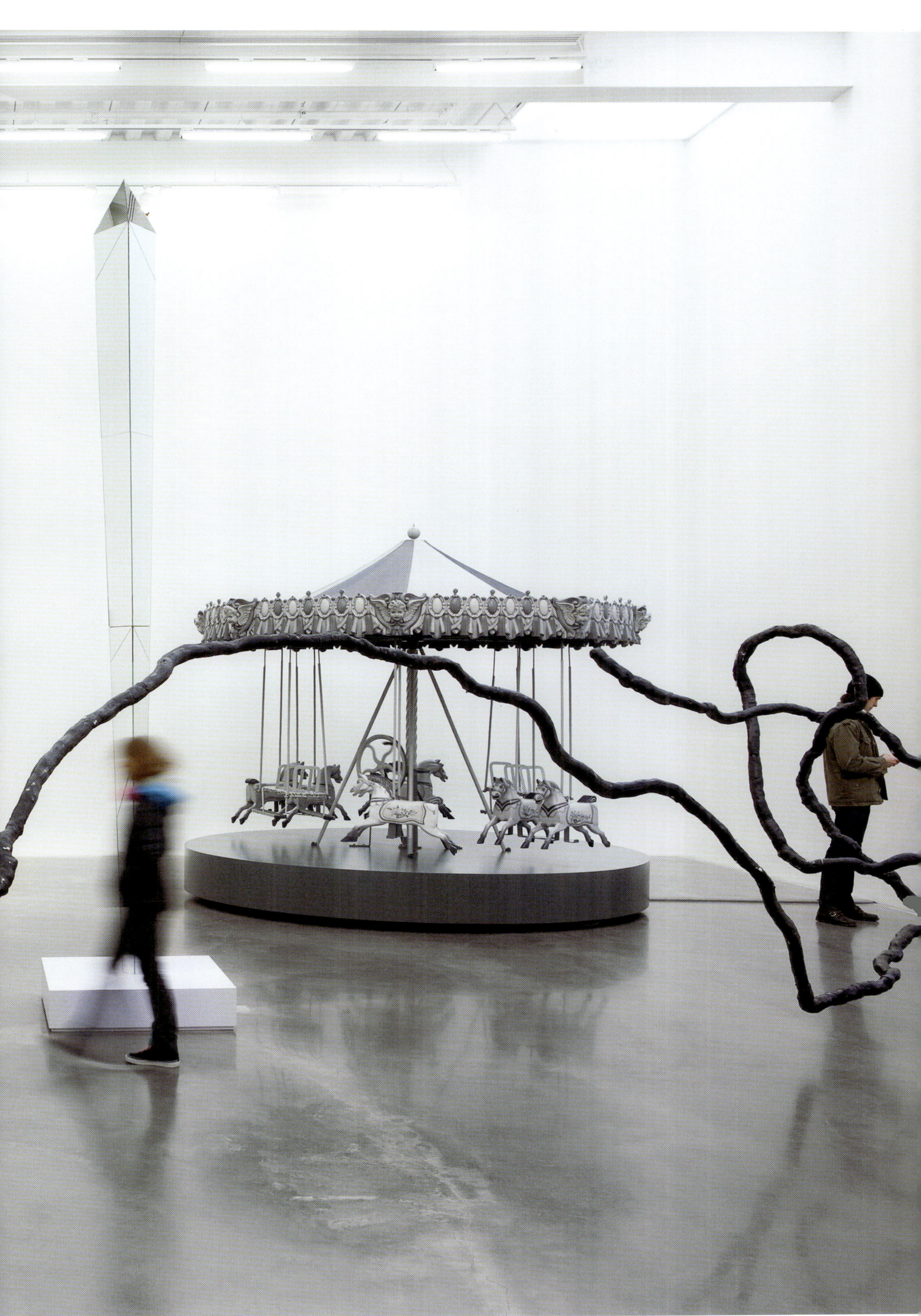

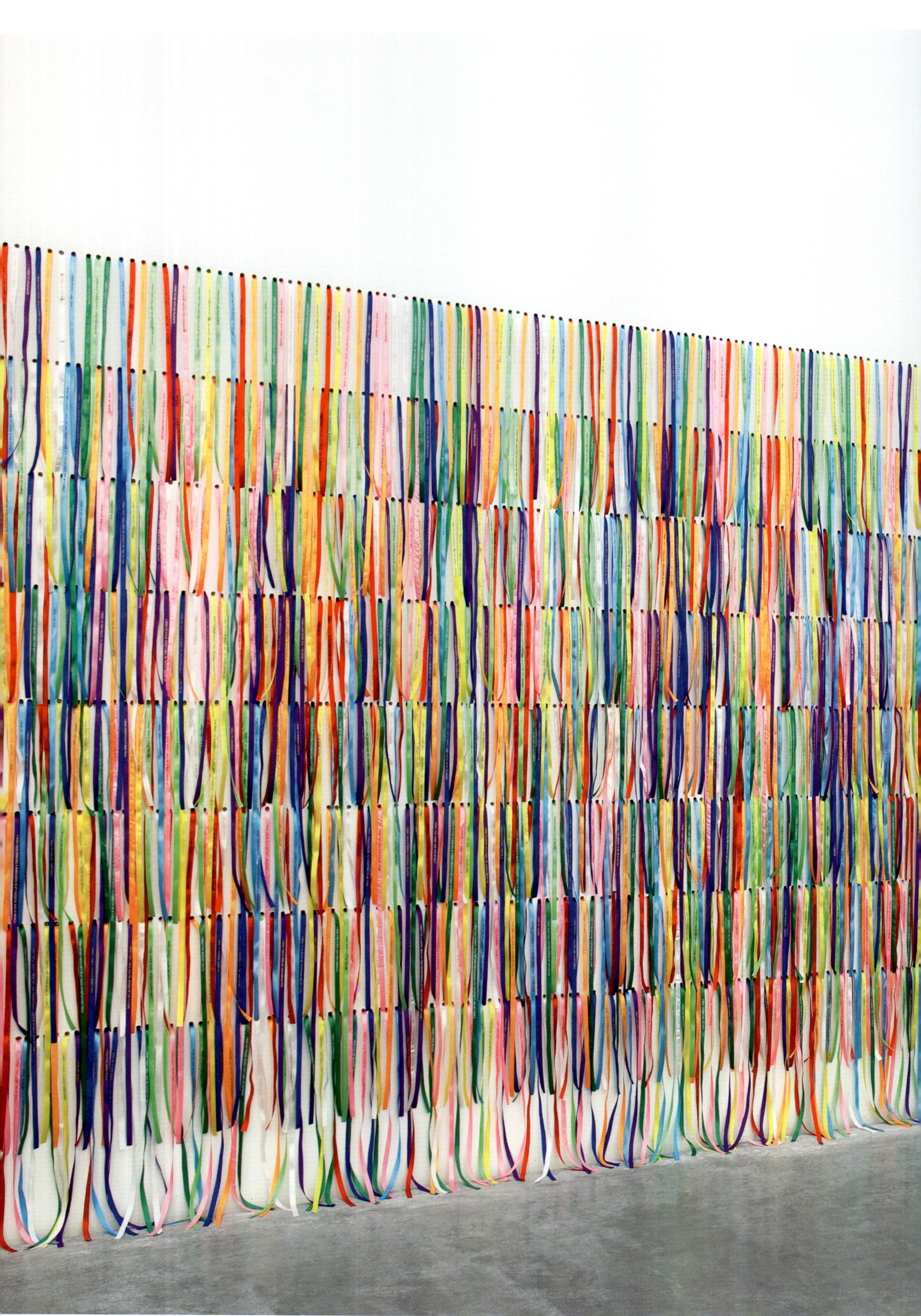

Rivane Neuenschwander,
Eu desejo o seu desejo
[I Wish Your Wish], 2003

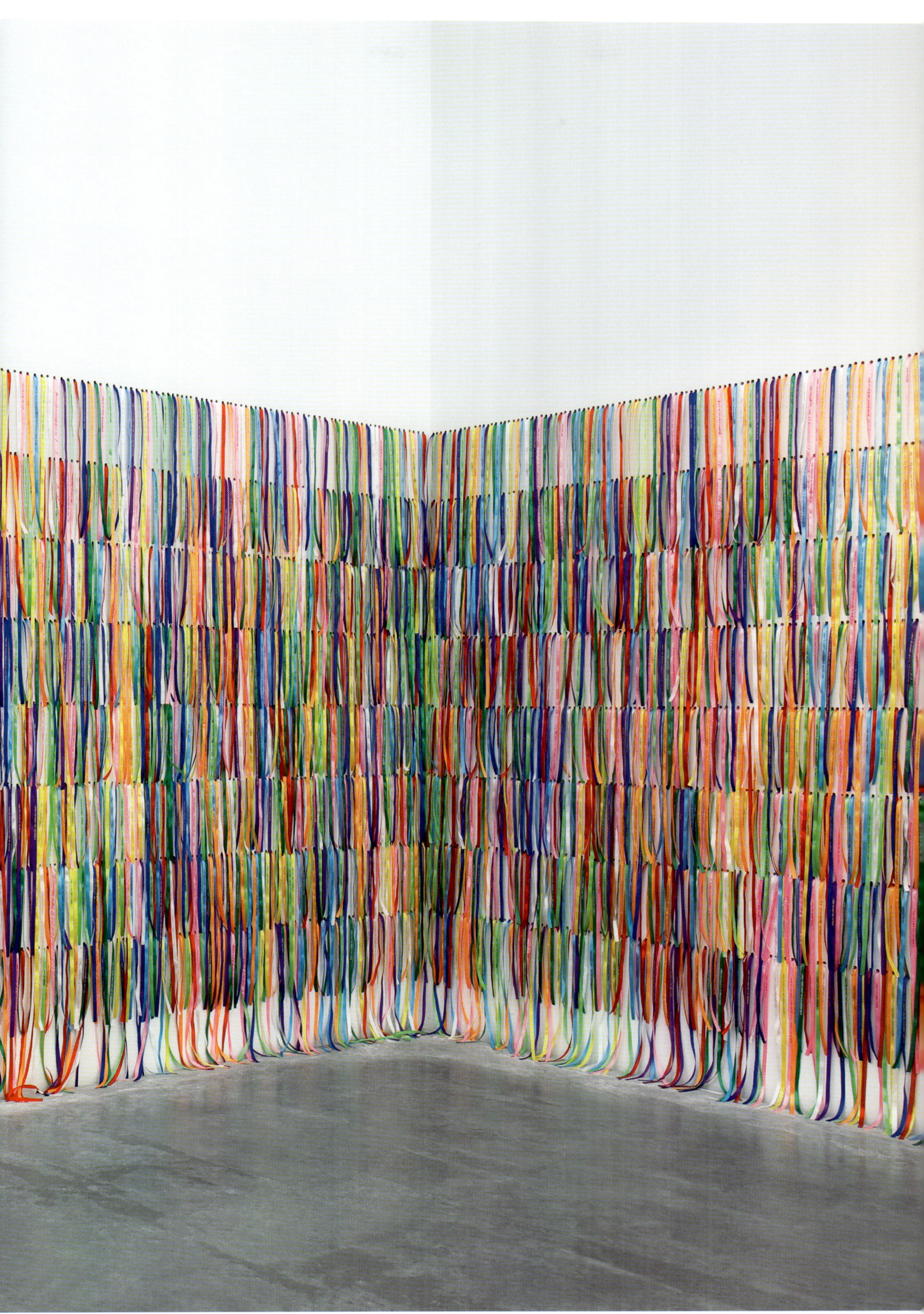

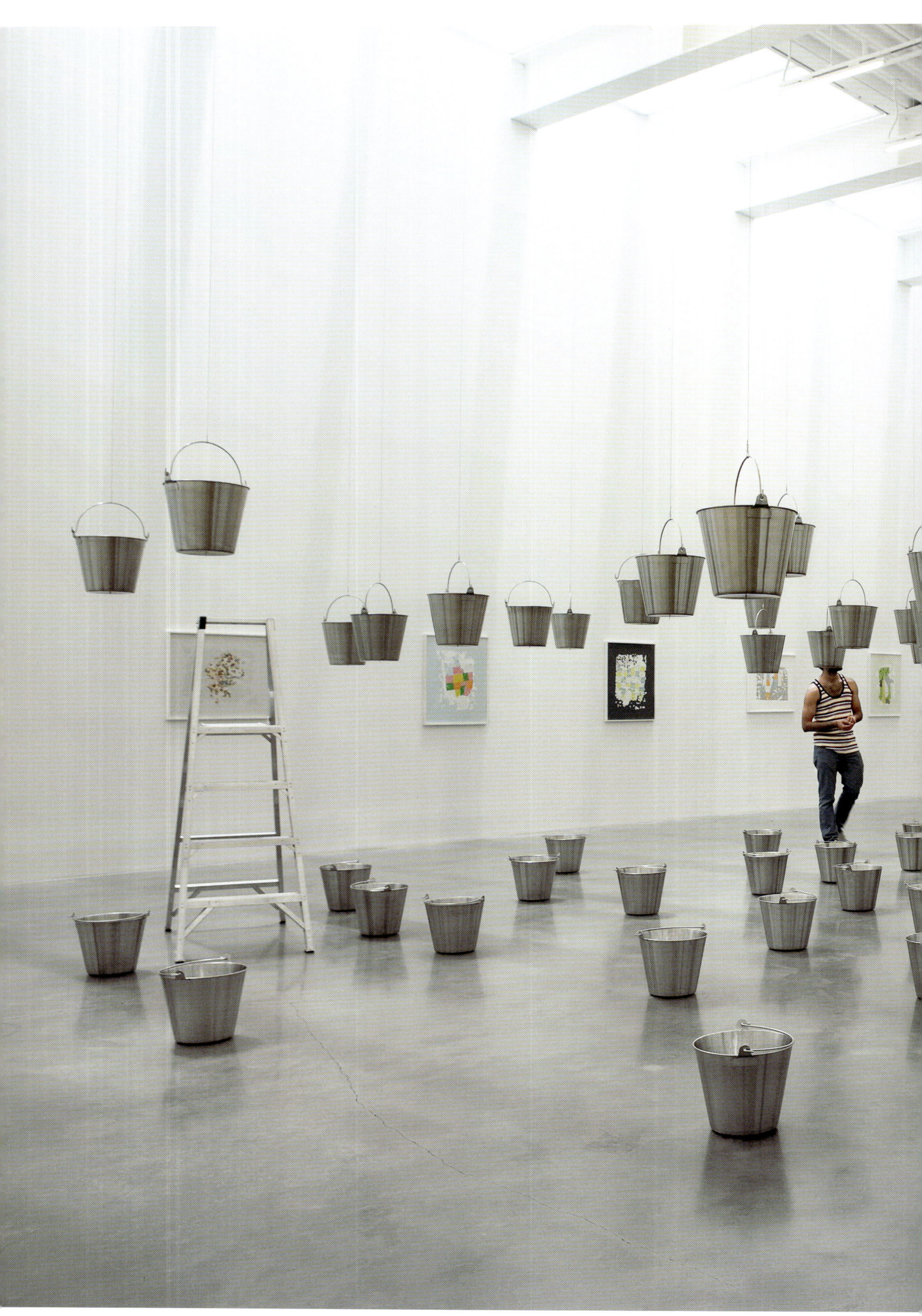

Rivane Neuenschwander,
Chove chuva [Rain Rains],
2002

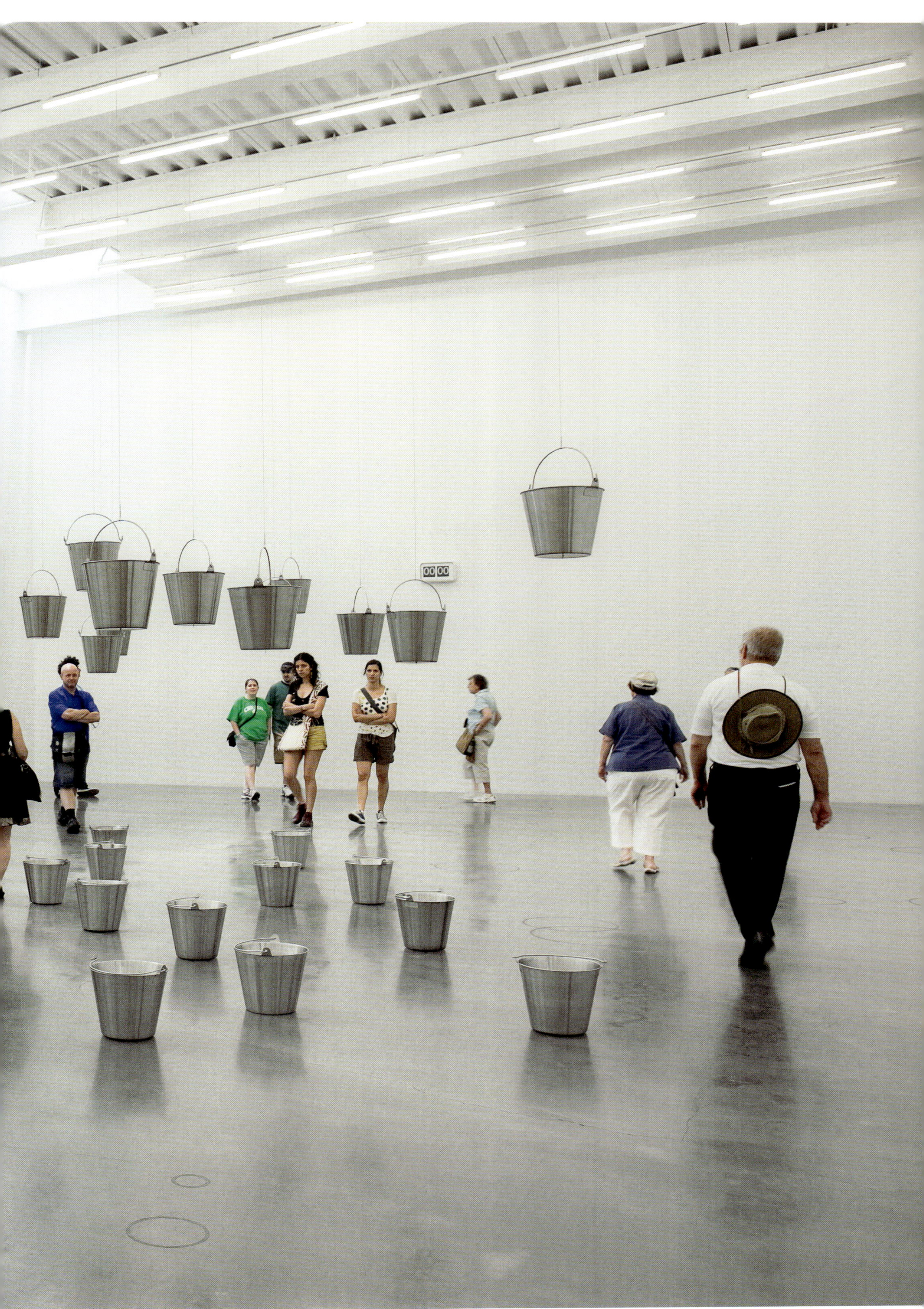

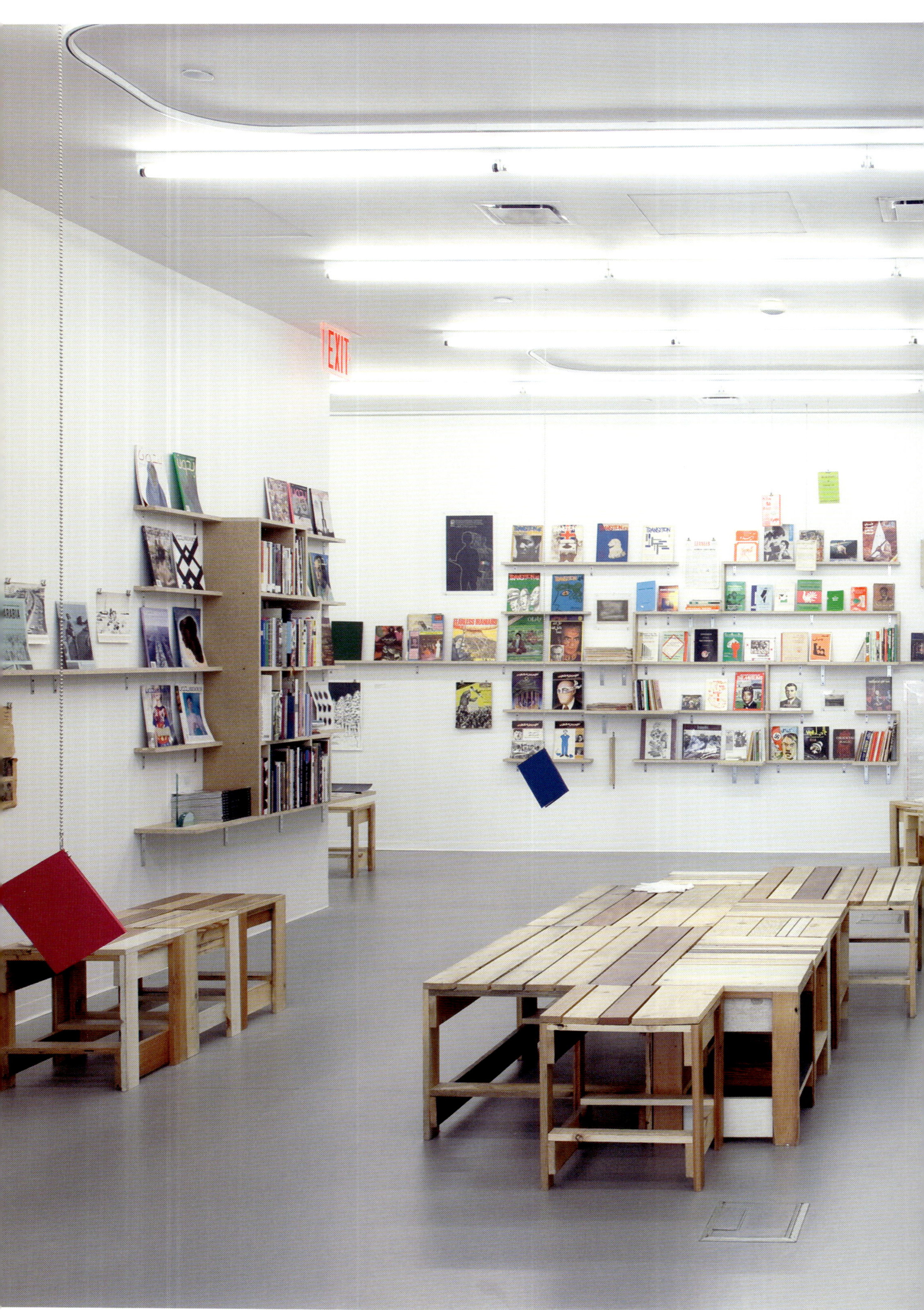

Installation view

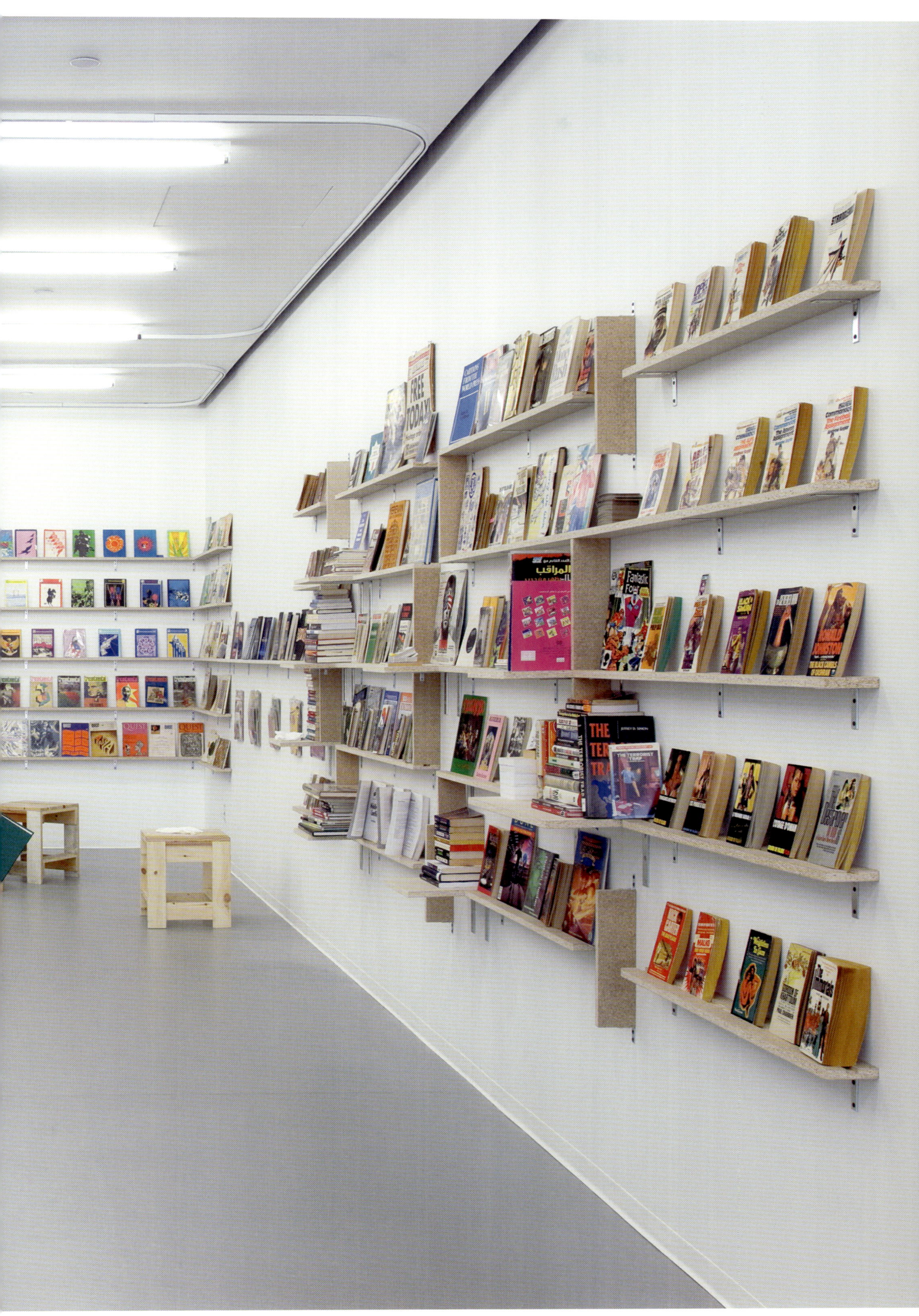

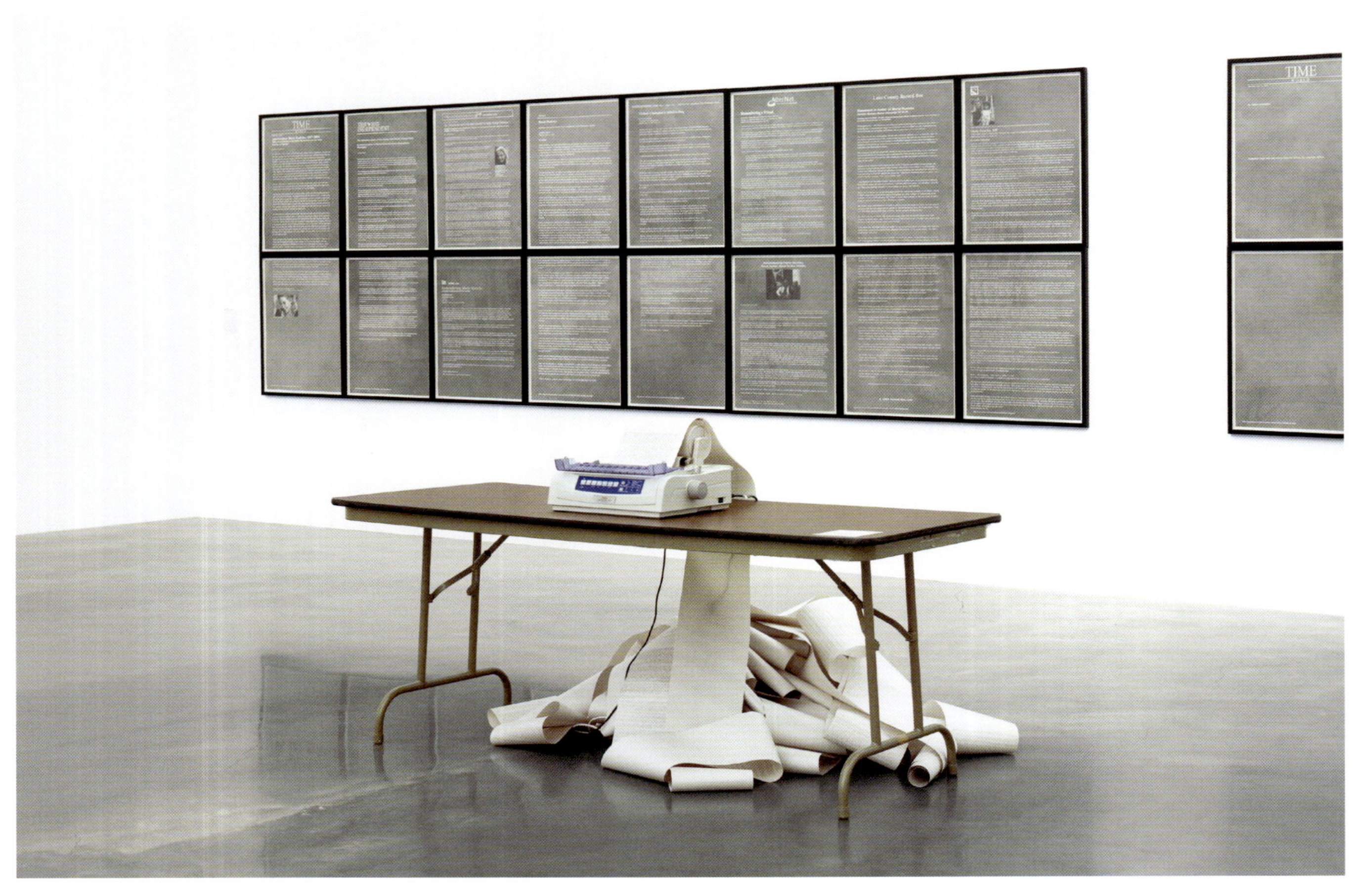

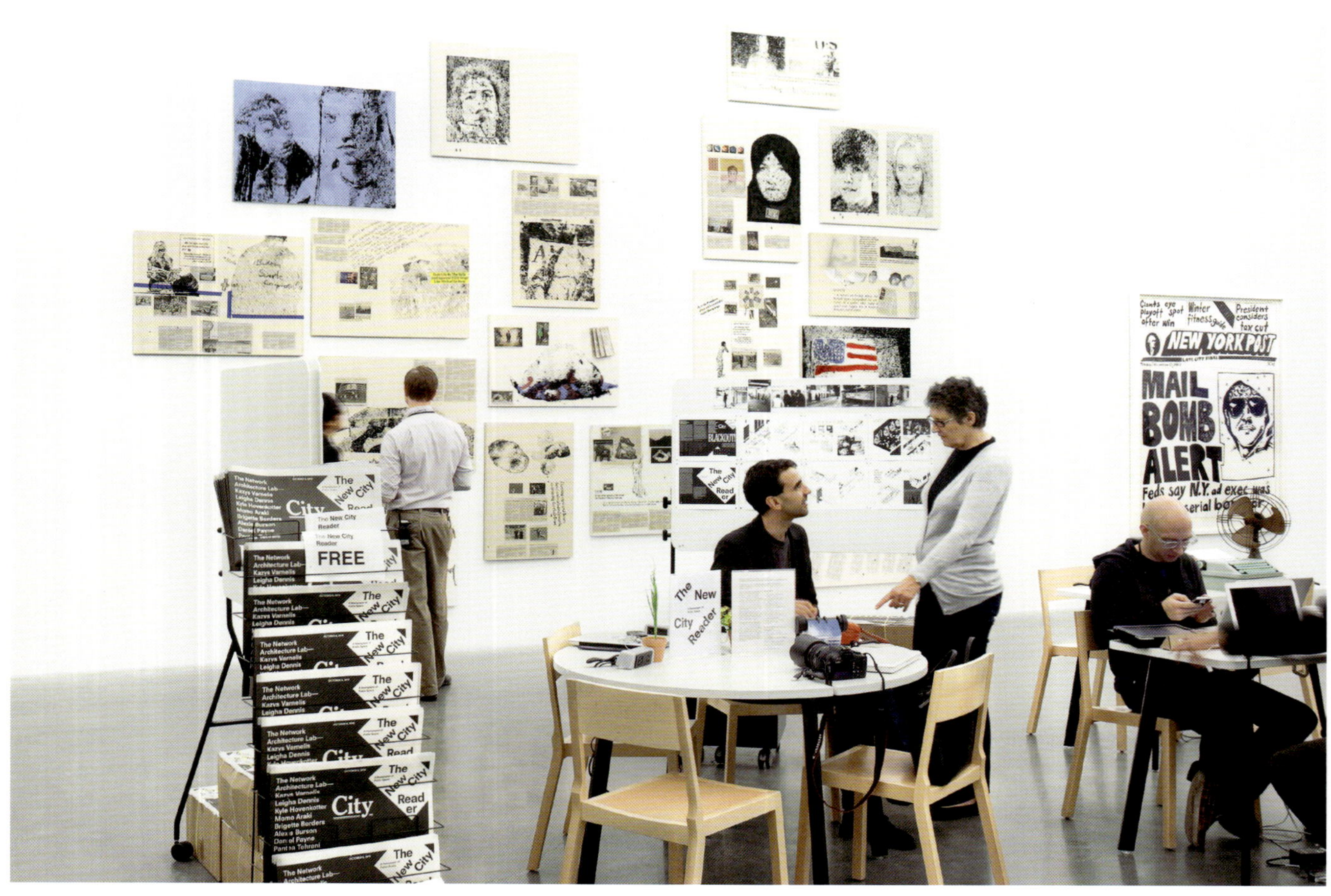

(top) Foreground: work by Hans Haacke. Background: work by Andrea Bowers

(bottom) Temporary offices of partner organizations including the Center for Urban Pedagogy; Latitudes; StoryCorps; Joseph Grima and Kazys Varnelis/ Network Architecture Lab; Jeffrey Inaba/C-Lab; Blu Dot; and the Slought Foundation

I Dont Want No Retrospective*— Monographic Exhibitions, Total Installations, and Introspectives at the New Museum

Massimiliano Gioni

Over the last forty years, the New Museum has presented an impressive series of solo exhibitions, specializing in particular in organizing the New York museum debuts of contemporary, often international, artists, many of whom were still under-recognized by the local public at the time. A partial list includes major shows early in the Museum's history by Ree Morton (1980) and John Baldessari (1981), followed by exhibitions at the Museum's Broadway venue by Leon Golub (1984), Hans Haacke (1986), Christian Boltanski (1988), Félix González-Torres (1988), Robert Colescott (1989), Nancy Spero (1989), Huang Yong Ping (1994), Chen Zhen (1994), Carolee Schneemann (1996), Mona Hatoum (1997), Doris Salcedo (1998), Xu Bing (1998), Martin Wong (1998), Cildo Meireles (1999), David Wojnarowicz (1999), Adrian Piper (2000), Martha Rosler (2000), Paul McCarthy (2001), William Kentridge (2001), Carroll Dunham (2002), Marlene Dumas (2002), and Andrea Zittel (2006).[1] And that's not to mention the exhibitions at the Museum's new Bowery building, which this essay will examine in greater detail.

Since 2007, at the New Museum's home on the Bowery, a new model of solo show has taken shape, one which I like to call an "introspective." An introspective could be described as a survey exhibition in which the choreography of the exhibition and its content are thought of in close dialogue and are constructed as a total environment. The idea of an introspective is partly indebted to the title of Richard Hamilton's 2003 exhibition ("Introspective")

---

*   The title of this essay is borrowed from Ed Ruscha's 1979 pastel, which perfectly captures artists' perennial ambivalence toward survey exhibitions.

1.   This list does not mention any of the now legendary window projects, which included interventions by Gran Fury, David Hammons, Jeff Koons, Linda Montano, Bruce Nauman, Richard Prince, and many others.

at Barcelona's Museu d'Art Contemporani. Widely regarded as one of the most important postwar artists, Hamilton also counts among the most original exhibition designers of the second half of the twentieth century —a reputation first built on such shows as "Growth and Form" (1951); "Man, Machine and Motion" (1955); and the collaboratively developed exhibitions "This is Tomorrow" (1956) and "an Exhibit" (1957). Hamilton was also a master of restagings and remakes, and is celebrated for his studies and various reconstructions of pieces by Marcel Duchamp, including *The Green Book* (1960), Hamilton's "typographical version" of *The Green Box*, as well as the 1965–66 version of Duchamp's *The Bride Stripped Bare by Her Bachelors, Even (The Large Glass)* (1915–23) that resides at the Tate in London.

This approach to history—which not only recounts past events, but revisits and recreates physical objects, artworks, and entire exhibitions—has informed many recent shows at the New Museum.[2] For every solo and group exhibition, New Museum curators study previous installation shots and other exhibition documentation, searching for display methods that are unique to the exhibiting artists and that can be either fully reconstructed or partially evoked in their presentations at the Museum.

Notwithstanding his aptitude for historical reconstructions, Hamilton also held the view that the only exhibitions that would be remembered were those that invented a new display feature.[3] A similar ethos has been at the heart of many of the New Museum's exhibitions in recent years. The effort to think about exhibitions, particularly solo exhibitions, in a new way often yields an experience in which the presentation of the artist's works offers a spatial analogue of the artist's creative universe. In other words, the New Museum's introspectives strive to layer content and form at the macroscopic and microscopic level: thinking of the individual works not only as links in a chronological, stylistic, or morphological chain, but also as agglutinations, physical parts of a dramatic structure— characters, even. In the New Museum's introspectives, the exhibition is not conceived simply as a series of discrete objects ranked on the walls and paraded before the viewer; instead, the show takes place *around* visitors as well, enveloping them, turning them into key agents and actors in a choreography that unfolds throughout the exhibition.

Of course, this approach has precedents. It belongs to a tradition dating back at least to the 1960s (but also including the visionary exhibitions of the early twentieth century organized by the Dadaists, the Surrealists, and the Constructivists) that rejected the supposed neutrality of the gallery space and used the exhibition itself as a medium and as a critical form.[4] The history of the New Museum offers many examples of shows conceived not as mere sequences of works, but as choreographed environments and critical spaces. In 1970, for instance, Pat Steir painted a self-portrait directly onto the Museum's walls, essentially equating her skin with the skin of the building. For his two-person show with Chen Zhen in 1994, Huang Yong Ping turned the Museum space into a car wash, while Xu Bing transformed his 1998 exhibition into a functioning calligraphy school. For her 2000 survey, Martha Rosler organized a yard sale (which MoMA recreated twelve years later), while in 1986 Hans Haacke discreetly altered the Museum's architecture by painting its columns with a faux marble pattern, lending a stately monumentality to his indictment of political authority.

2.   Richard Hamilton's exhibition "Man, Machine and Motion" was the subject of a prolonged study at the New Museum that led to the near complete reconstruction of the original exhibition, first under the artist's supervision and then—after his death—under that of his estate. Presented at the New Museum in 2012 as part of "Ghosts in the Machine," the reconstruction of "Man, Machine and Motion" was later exhibited at the Institute of Contemporary Arts in London on the occasion of Hamilton's retrospective at Tate Modern, and then at Museo Nacional Centro de Arte Reina Sofía in Madrid, the collection that now holds it. "Ghosts in the Machine" also presented additional reconstructions of works and exhibitions, including Stan VanDerBeek's *Movie-Drome* (1963–66), Gianni Colombo's *Ambiente Elastico* (1967–68), and various sections of the exhibitions "Arte Programmata" (1962), "The Responsive Eye" (1965), and "The Bachelor Machines" (1975). Other recent New Museum shows in which the history of exhibition-making was consciously integrated into the various strategies of display include "Ostalgia" (2011), "NYC 1993: Experimental Jet Set, Trash and No Star" (2013), and "The Keeper" (2016).

3.   Hans Ulrich Obrist, *Ways of Curating* (London: Allen Lane/Penguin, 2014), 8. Hamilton discussed his ideas about exhibition-making at length in Obrist, "Interview with Richard Hamilton," in *Hans Ulrich Obrist: Interviews, Vol. 2*, ed. Charles Arsène-Henry, Shumon Basar, and Karen Marta (Milan: Charta, 2010), 154–67. Also illuminating are *Richard Hamilton, Collected Words, 1953–1982* (London: Thames and Hudson, 1982), and Isabelle Moffat, "Richard Hamilton and Victor Pasmore, an Exhibit, 1957," in *The Artist as Curator*, ed. Elena Filipovic (Milan: Mousse, 2017), 17–32.

4.   The literature on these themes is vast. For a recent source, see James Voorhies, *Beyond Objecthood: The Exhibition as a Critical Form* (Cambridge, MA, and London: MIT Press, 2017).

These projects and those presented since the Museum's
move to the Bowery share an approach to exhibition-
making that is akin to what the artist Ilya Kabakov has
termed a "total installation." Kabakov—who made his
New York museum debut at the New Museum in the
group show "Rhetorical Image" (1990), curated by Milena
Kalinovska—has described his total installations as
spaces where the visitor is both viewer and interpreter,
detective and "victim." In Kabakov's environments, the
viewer is "overcome by the intense atmosphere of
total illusion" that results from experiencing objects,
artworks, and texts as part of a complex but carefully
crafted whole.[5]

In Kabakov's vision, the viewer's role in a total installation
also resembles that of a reader who surrenders to the
fiction of a novel and is "submerged in its depth," but
remains perfectly conscious of being in the presence of
a fabrication. Even when readers willfully embrace the
illusion of literature, they remain capable of admiring
the tools used to craft it—recognizing an author's style
compared to that of other writers, for example, or staying
alert to a narrator's distinctive voice. In both literature
and Kabakov's notion of the total installation, the reader
or viewer is granted the bifold experience of "the illusion
and simultaneously the introspection on it." According to
Kabakov, fitting analogies for his total installations can
be found in theater as well as in fiction: installation is a
form of "halted action," in which a drama unfolds not in
time, but in space. It is, in other words, a *theatricalization*
of the experience of art, punctuated by fractures and
moments of disorientation that break through the fiction
and awaken a sense of critical remove in the viewer.[6]

Departing from similar considerations, Judith Barry, an
artist responsible for some of the most original displays
at the New Museum in the 1980s, used the expression
"dissenting spaces" to describe the alternation of illusion,
disorientation, and critical perspective that she engi-
neered in her exhibition designs.[7] In these installations,
and particularly in the seductive geometries she staged
in "Damaged Goods: Desire and the Economy of the
Object" (1986), curated by Brian Wallis, Barry conflated
the strategies of "theatrical, ideological, and consumer

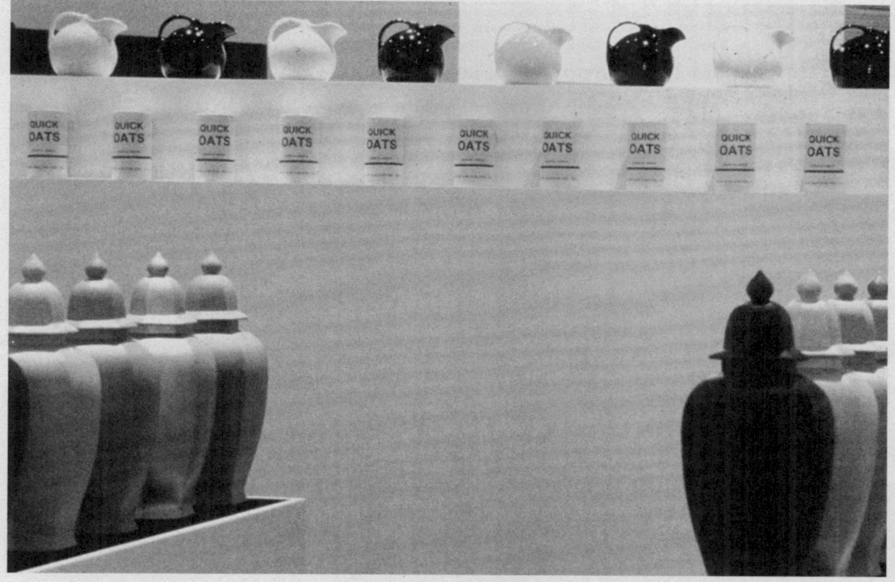

displays," to borrow the artist's description of, respectively, the dioramas in natural history museums, the installations of the Constructivist avant-garde, and the layout of retail stores.[8] Engaging these schematics of display and their effects on the viewer, Barry conceived of the exhibition space as a hall of mirrors in which the viewer's desires are reflected, performed, and critically analyzed.

Mirrors and desires also played a key role in "Urs Fischer: Marguerite de Ponty" (2009), the first solo exhibition to use all three main gallery floors of the New Museum's Bowery building.[9] While "introspective" qualities do not

5. Kabakov's remarkable lectures on exhibition-making are collected in Ilya Kabakov, *On the "Total" Installation*, English trans. Cindy Martin, German trans. Gabriele Leupold (Ostfildern: Hatje Cantz, 1995). Quotes from Kabakov in this essay are found on pages 245 and 246.

6. In the United States, the debates around art and theatricality inevitably lead back to the 1967 publication of Michael Fried's "Art and Objecthood" in *Artforum*. For a summary of these debates see Voorhies, *Beyond Objecthood*. Kabakov, in contrast, finds his references in literary theory. When reading Kabakov's writings, one cannot help but think of the concepts of "defamiliarization" and "estrangement" in the work of Viktor Shklovsky and Bertolt Brecht, respectively.

7. In particular, in the group shows "Damaged Goods: Desire and the Economy of the Object" (1986) and "From Receiver to Remote Control: The Television Set" (1990), Judith Barry took approaches to exhibition design that channeled a range of display and design vernaculars.

8. See Judith Barry, "Dissenting Spaces," in *Damaged Goods: Desire and the Economy of the Object*, ed. Brian Wallis (New York: New Museum, 1986), 46–48. Quite interestingly, the exhibition "Damaged Goods: Desire and the Economy of the Object" followed the show "Sots Art" (1986), curated by Margarita Tupitsyn. While examining completely different art movements (the 1970s and 1980s Russian avant-garde in the case of "Sots Art," and the artists loosely grouped within the Neo-Geo movement in the case of "Damaged Goods"), the exhibitions shared similar design strategies adopted from both the history of modernism and the display of merchandise.

9. Unless otherwise noted, all the exhibitions discussed in this essay were curated by the author, often in collaboration with the New Museum curatorial team and in particular with Gary Carrion-Murayari ("Carsten Höller: Experience," "Ghosts in the Machine,"

necessarily depend on scale, Fischer's show exemplified how entrusting all of a museum's principal exhibition space to a single artist can allow an exhibition to become a full-fledged organism. For the duration of the exhibition, the identity of the Museum and the identity of the artist seemed to merge, and in turn, both artist and exhibition came to shape the nature of the institution. The design of the New Museum's building (by the Tokyo-based firm SANAA), with its relatively modest dimensions and windowless, enclosed spaces, is also particularly well suited to exhibitions in which the viewer is enveloped in an artist's installations and forced into an intense proximity to the works.[10] This quality of self-enclosure contributes to the dreamlike, or even hallucinatory, effect of disorientation that more than a few artists have deliberately played with in their exhibitions at the new New Museum, exploiting the visitor's impression of repeated, near-identical gallery spaces, and amplifying the effects of an architecture that seems to willingly turn its back to the outside world. By the same token, in keeping with the "introspective" approach, when invited to exhibit their work at the New Museum, artists are also encouraged to think of their exhibitions as tours of their own minds and creative universes—as journeys into parallel worlds from which reality has been temporarily banished.

Fischer is one of the most original exhibition designers to have emerged in recent years, and his exceptionally dramatic projects include holes excavated in gallery floors or museum walls. At the New Museum, he chose to construct his show as three environments stacked atop each other in a neo-baroque dramaturgy of contrasting forms and spaces that both heightened and obfuscated perceptions. In the towering spaces of the Museum's fourth floor, Fischer installed a series of suspended sculptures that resembled giant rock formations, or a forest of stalactites and stalagmites, while on the third floor he left the gallery almost completely empty, achieving an absurd tour de force of pictorial illusionism and trompe l'oeil by covering the walls and ceiling in photographic reproductions of the same architecture, perfectly reconstructed and lowered by just under a foot. The second floor housed a grid of mirrored chrome steel boxes silkscreened with images of knickknacks and cheap consumer items in various states of abandonment and deterioration, all monumentally enlarged to adorn these bastardized Minimalist sculptures. The fusion of Pop vividness, geometric rigidity, and decaying beauty intensified this hall of mirrors; the exhibition space appeared crammed with oversize, imposing everyday things, but each was rendered weightless, almost to the point of disappearance by its own succession of mirror images. The reflective surfaces of the works caught the visitors' bodies, seeming to literally make visible the very process of theatricalization that art critic Michael Fried had criticized in Minimalist art of the 1960s. In Fischer's hands, however, theatricality was taken to new levels of spectacularization, simultaneously dissected and analyzed in a play of mirrors in which viewers saw their own reflections within an extraordinary concentration of bodies, objects, and images—a conflation of the real and its facsimiles.[11]

The relationships between embodiment, representation, and desire; between vision and consumption; and, by extension, between entertainment and the space of the museum have been central to some of the solo shows that the New Museum has organized in the last few years, and have been a recurring theme in the exhibitions of many other artists from the generation that began to emerge in the 1990s.[12] Among recent introspectives at the New Museum, Carsten Höller's programmatically titled 2011 exhibition "Experience" addressed these relation-

"Paweł Althamer: The Neighbors," "Here and Elsewhere," "Chris Ofili: Night and Day," "Jim Shaw: The End is Here," and "Raymond Pettibon: A Pen of All Work"), Margot Norton ("Roberto Cuoghi: Šuillakku Corral," "Ragnar Kjartansson: Me, My Mother, My Father, and I," "Here and Elsewhere," "Chris Ofili: Night and Day," "Anri Sala: Answer Me," "The Keeper," and "Pipilotti Rist: Pixel Forest"), Natalie Bell ("Here and Elsewhere," "Anri Sala: Answer Me," and "The Keeper"), and Helga Christoffersen ("Here and Elsewhere," "The Keeper," and "Pipilotti Rist: Pixel Forest").

10. Ilya Kabakov described the absence of windows and apertures to the exterior as one of the defining characteristics of "total installations," which allows the exhibition to be perceived as a self-contained world. See Kabakov, *On the "Total" Installation*, 256.

11. I am indebted here to Michelle Kuo's observation that in Fischer's sculptures "things and views, the real and the represented, are compacted with extraordinary stress." See Michelle Kuo, "Taste Tests: The Art of Urs Fischer," *Artforum* (November 2009): 172.

12. In the 1980s, the New Museum's use of a shop window as an exhibition space already seemed to invite reflection on the increasing similarity between the museum experience and the shopping experience. The fact that one of the first window installations was designed by Jeff Koons in 1980 perfectly foretokens decades of debate about the power of display and the relationship between art and the market.

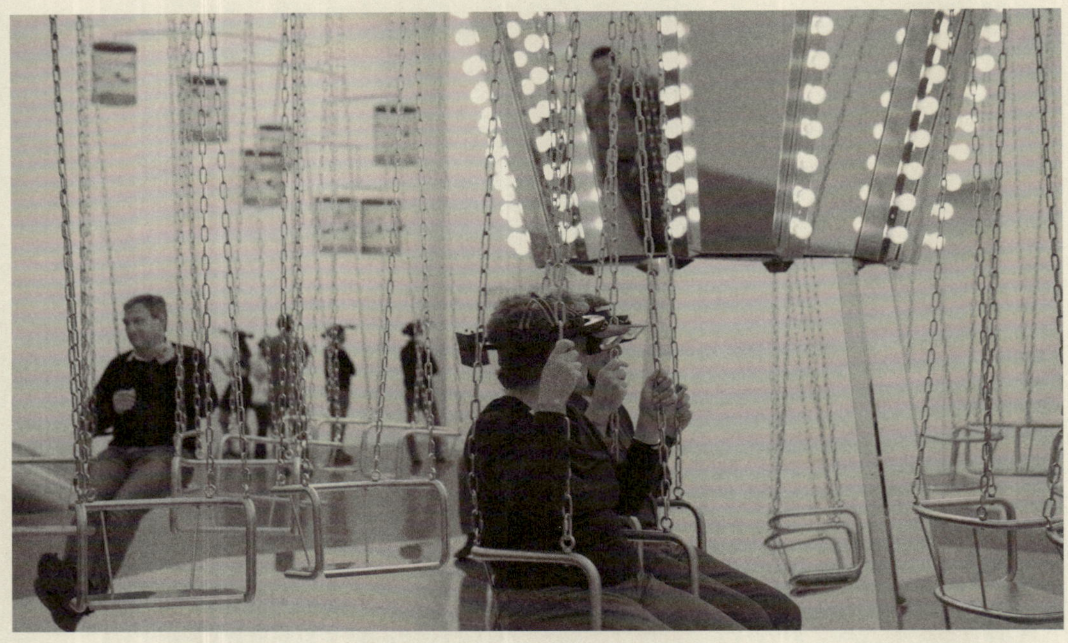

ships in the most explicit and provocative way. Höller set out to transform the Museum into a test site, where he could try out a temporary disruption of the normal functioning of an institution. Although Höller—due perhaps to his background as an entomologist—often turns to the world of science and technology for terms and metaphors with which to describe his work, it is actually folklore, fantasy, and literature that offer the most apt analogies for his practice. In particular, the concept of the carnivalesque—famously described by Russian literary critic Mikhail Bakhtin as a "feast of becoming, change, and renewal"—may be best suited to describing the suspension of conventional rules and expectations that Höller seeks in his work, for it thrives on subversion and the excitement of vertigo and play that the para-Surrealist writer Roger Caillois described as "voluptuous panic."[13]

Höller's show at the New Museum included one of his trademark slides, which, for the first time, was built into the building's architecture. A spiraling vertical chute more than one hundred feet long, with a drop of over thirty feet, ran through holes bored through two of the Museum's concrete floors: functioning as both a sculpture and an entertainment device, Höller's slide also became an actual means of circulation within the Museum. In addition, "Experience" included a life-size model of a carousel, its speed slowed to an extra-leisurely one revolution per five minutes; a sensory deprivation chamber, where visitors could float weightlessly in a body-temperature potion of water and Epsom salt; and various devices that physically and psychologically destabilized the viewer, including rooms with shifting walls, goggles fitted with prisms for upside-down vision, a selection of drugs and placebos freely distributed to viewers, and strobe-light installations.

Although Höller's work is conventionally interpreted in the context of relational aesthetics—the artistic current in which he got his start in European exhibitions of the 1990s—in "Experience" these relations manifested in harsher and more aggressive terms, radicalizing the exchange between artworks and viewers and between viewers and the institution. Visitors, for example, were asked to sign a series of forms alerting them to the potential dangers presented by the slide and other artworks on view—a measure that acted not only as a legal precaution in a litigious city like New York, but also as another mode of manipulating the viewer's state of mind, much like the liability release forms that visitors had to sign before viewing Walter De Maria's *Bed of Spikes* (1968–69). Mounting this exhibition had also entailed an extraordinary organizational effort on the part of the Museum, which remained wholly committed to realizing the artist's vision, even when that vision aimed to undermine the institution itself. Indeed, Höller's work might best be described as suspending the established order of a museum: for his show, an entire spectrum of behaviors not normally allowed in that setting was not only encouraged, but taken to a fever pitch.

Laughing, cheering, clapping, and shouting were just some of the reactions frequently heard throughout the duration of the show, but more unusual actions like getting undressed in public, or even just freely touching artworks, radically transformed the museumgoing experience for visitors. As Dorothea von Hantelmann observes in the exhibition catalogue, contrary to the conception of the museum as "a machine for education, civilization, and rationalization," Höller proposes ecstasy and euphoria as desirable outcomes, and "against the self-reflexive and

13. On these subjects see Gary Carrion-Murayari and Massimiliano Gioni, ed., *Carsten Höller: Experience* (New York: New Museum and Skira/Rizzoli, 2011). On Höller's work in relation to the writings of Mikhail Bakhtin and Roger Caillois, see Mark Windsor, "Art of Interaction: A Theoretical Examination of Carsten Höller's Test Site," *Tate Papers*, no. 15, Spring 2011, http://www.tate.org.uk/research/publications/tate-papers/15/art-of-interaction-a-theoretical-examination-of-carsten-holler-test-site.

self-controlled visitor," he imagines a viewer who literally loses control, reviving aspects of the self that the museum typically excludes.[14] In this respect, perhaps the most unusual response that Höller encouraged in his viewers was boredom: sitting on the carousel as it turned at an excruciatingly slow pace, viewers were invited to become bored, to experience the time spent in the museum not just as a series of surprising events, but also as time wasted, time taken away from any sort of productive activity.

While Fischer and Höller subjected the Museum to extreme forms of pressure and tension—physical and institutional—recent history also offers examples of solo shows that likewise questioned accepted notions and hierarchies but explored the definitions of art and exhibitions in gentler ways. A remarkable example of this approach was Rosemarie Trockel's subtle but radical 2012 exhibition "A Cosmos," curated by Lynne Cooke. Trockel and Cooke discreetly rejected the usual trappings of a monographic exhibition: the celebration of the artist's brand and style; the narcissistic pleasure of seeing a systematic overview of a life and career rewritten with the benefit of hindsight; and the crafting of a narrative exclusively focused on a single artist so as to edit out any dialogue across generations, histories, and disciplines, as well as any deviation from a supposedly unified guiding vision or coherent project. By contrast, Trockel and Cooke deliberately left out many of Trockel's more famous

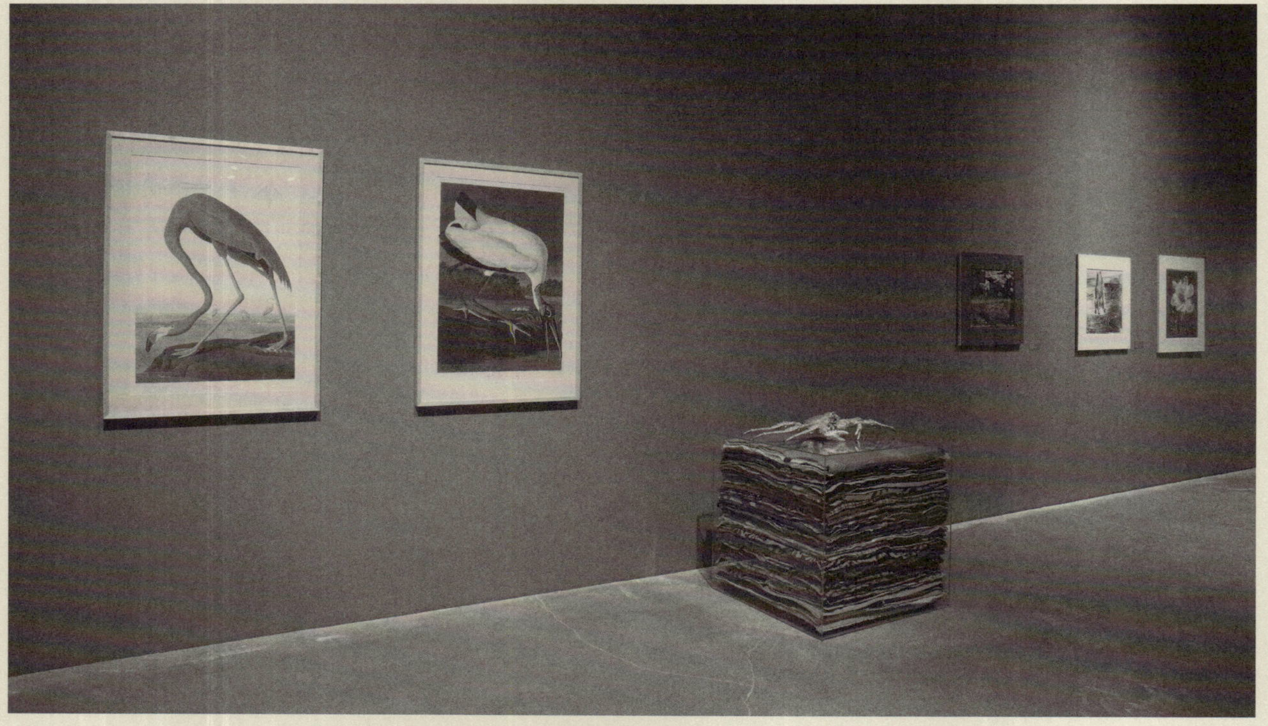

pieces and complicated the presentation with works by other artists, found objects, archival materials, and historical documents. These ranged from nature illustrations by Maria Sibylla Merian to scientific glass models by the Blaschka family; to the dolls, cutouts, and transitional objects of Morton Bartlett, James Castle, and Judith Scott; all the way to a series of canvases painted by an ape. The effect was like a wunderkammer, in which the objects are connected by free association and formal rhymes; or perhaps it would be better to say that what was on view was far from just the artist's work, but that it offered her entire creative universe—a true exercise in "introspective" research—by exposing that intricate web of influences and resemblances, partialities and elective affinities that is an essential part of the artistic process.

The comparison to a wunderkammer might seem to imply the very hierarchical system—with the artist-collector at the center—that "A Cosmos" aimed to dismantle and transform. Indeed, the radical aspect of the show was its rejection of the idea of authorship as indicative of authority and ownership. In its place, the show proposed a system of reciprocal hospitality that turned the exhibition—and with it the museum as a whole (and not just the New Museum, but the very idea of a modern and contemporary art museum)—into a set of gravitational fields and constellations that eluded the categories, taxonomies, and hierarchies according to which art history is normally organized. The fact that this hermeneutic model was presented by Cooke and Trockel, two authors who throughout their careers have often defied and criticized gendered expectations, further highlights the originality of their curatorial approach, which embodied a feminist vision of inclusiveness and multiplicity rather than foregrounding an individual ego.

A comparably polyphonic approach was followed in Jim Shaw's 2015 survey "The End is Here," which presented the artist's work and displayed his collections of thrift store paintings and pedagogical religious materials. Like many recent thematic exhibitions at the New Museum,

14. Dorothea von Hantelmann, "Experience," in Carrion-Murayari and Gioni, *Carsten Höller: Experience*, 164.

the solo shows of
Trockel and Shaw
also discarded the
canonical distinc-
tions between art and
non-art, as well as
accepted notions
of taste and the hier-
archical division
between fine art and
applied, popular,
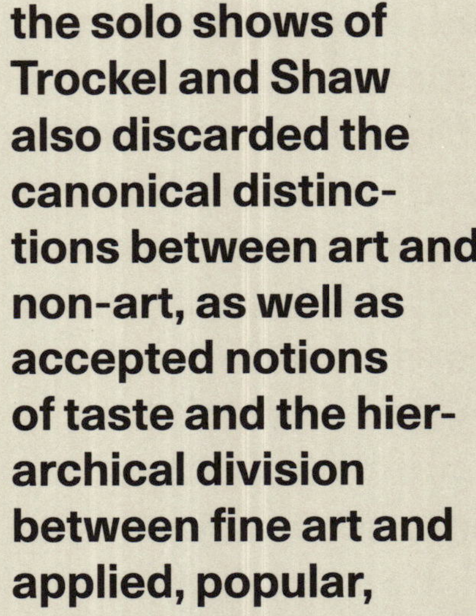
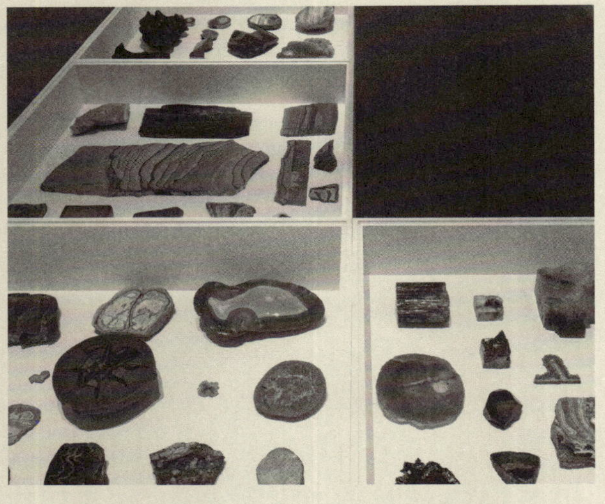

and vernacular art. Indeed, these exhibitions—and this
has been even more explicit in recent group shows,
especially "After Nature" (2008), "Ostalgia" (2011), "Ghosts
in the Machine" (2012), and "The Keeper" (2016)—were
based on an understanding of art as part of a broader
field of visual culture, presented in manifestations that
include historical artifacts, archival materials and found
objects, folk art and high art, originals, reconstructions,
and copies. In these shows, the juxtaposition of documents, artworks, and objects served both to question
the accepted value of the presumed masterpieces and
to avoid the overly obedient contemplation of individual
works, inviting instead different forms of active interpre-
tative engagement.[15]

In these exhibitions, the number of objects and works
on view took on a strategic significance: the supposed
uniqueness of the masterpiece was countered by
presenting sequences and series composed of
hundreds—in some cases even thousands—of items.
Many exhibitions at the New Museum have offered a
profusion of objects and artworks; the emphasis is not on
uniqueness or commercial value, but on abundance and
intensity, and on the capacity of these objects to capture
and describe the world they come from. This strategy of
excess also serves to transform the architecture of the
exhibition spaces. In some sense, it is an opposite yet
complementary approach to the one adopted by Fischer
and Höller, who conceived each floor of the exhibition as
a tableau or as a single artwork. By comparison, in the
exhibitions of Jim Shaw and, in 2015, Raymond Pettibon,
or with the extraordinary salon hanging in George
Condo's exhibition, curated by Laura Hoptman and Ralph

Rugoff in 2011, it was the sheer number of objects on view that yielded a sense of spatial unity, as individual paintings and drawings were combined into new installations comprising dozens, even hundreds of parts.

Chris Ofili's 2014 exhibition "Night and Day" is a further example of how the very architecture of the museum can be transformed and absorbed as an integral part of the show. Here, the exhibition shifted from a traditional layout on the second floor, where works from the 1990s were on view; to the third floor, where a chapel-like, dimly lit environment had been created to house a selection of what Ofili calls his "blue paintings" (2006–11); to a mesmerizing total installation on the fourth floor, where the artist had painted the walls to depict a tropical forest in shades of purple and blue to hold a selection of his most recent works. Ofili's painted jungle was a backdrop and a baroque decorative device, but, more critically, it was also a hallucinatory violation of the fourth wall, a ploy that simultaneously revealed and enhanced the fiction of the museum as a space for contemplation and escape, concentration and oblivion—a space of presence and remove.

The disorienting sensation of being simultaneously in the museum and elsewhere is an effect that seems to have resonated with many of the artists who have staged exhibitions at the New Museum. In some ways, Chris Burden's 2013 exhibition "Extreme Measures," curated by New Museum Director Lisa Phillips, followed Fischer's and Höller's models by presenting a series of environments laid out over three floors of the museum, treating each as an installation where individual works became part of a new sculptural ensemble. Specifically, works like *Beehive Bunker* (2006), a sculpture weighing more than eleven tons; *The Big Wheel* (1979), a functioning motorcycle that sets a giant metal wheel in motion; and *Tower of Power* (1985), made from one hundred one-kilo ingots of gold, posed a series of challenges to the physical and organizational limits of the institution that agreed to display them;

15.   Similar approaches to exhibition-making are described in Claire Bishop, *Radical Museology: Or What's "Contemporary" in Contemporary Museums of Art?* (Cologne: Walter König, 2014).

they literally threatened the museum with their weight or with their mere presence, exposing both the real and metaphorical "foundation of the museum," to paraphrase another legendary piece by Burden, for which he dug into the floor of the Los Angeles Museum of Contemporary Art in 1986. Despite their menacing presence, many of Burden's works in his New Museum show preserved the qualities of models or games, offering the rather uncanny experience of standing before objects that resembled toys built on an adult scale. In their company, one feels miniaturized—an effect only amplified by the works displayed on the exterior of the Museum, *Ghost Ship* (2005) and *Quasi-Legal Skyscrapers* (2013), which turned the entire building into a model or diorama.

In other cases, the New Museum has been used as a site for experimenting with different forms of social behavior. Beds, cushions, plush carpets, and curtains deployed by Pipilotti Rist in her 2016 exhibition "Pixel Forest" created inviting, soothing environments, extending the hypnotic qualities of her videos into three dimensions and encouraging forms of communal viewing. The entire exhibition was conceived as a digital landscape, in which images hovered below the ceiling or were rendered even less palpable by being projected onto diaphanous curtains and deconstructed into thousands of pixels floating in the darkened spaces of the galleries, activating an oneiric

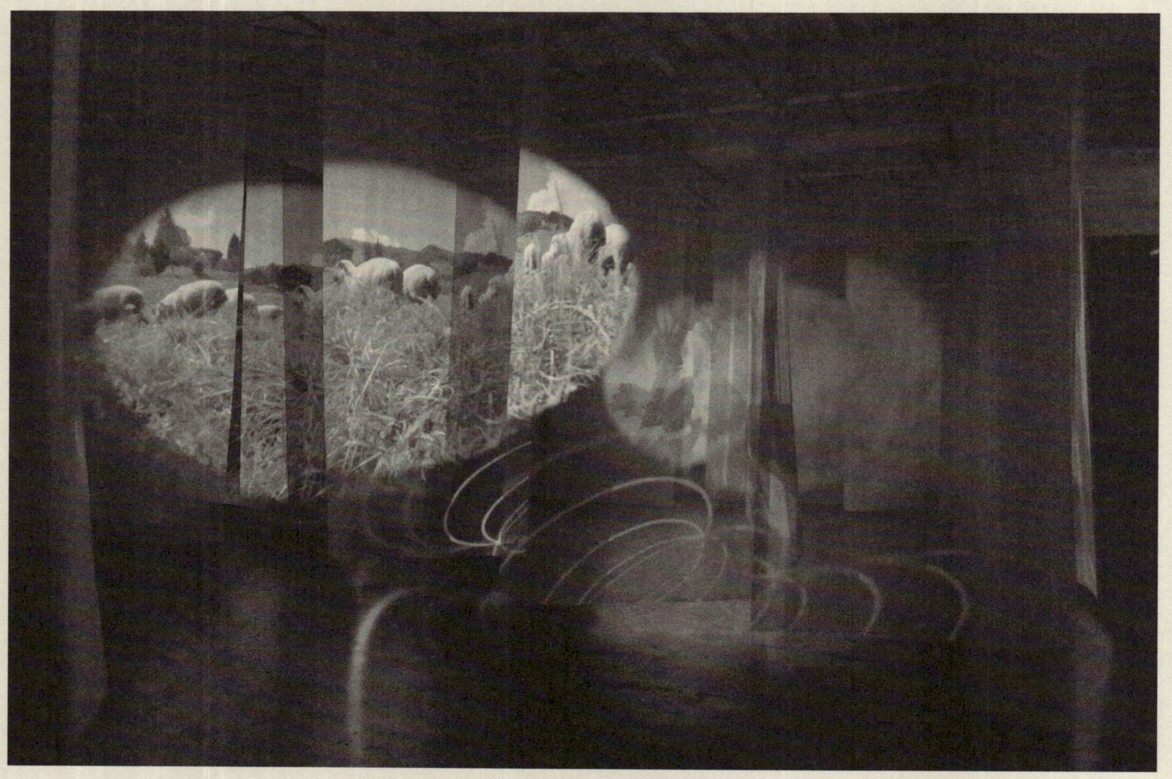

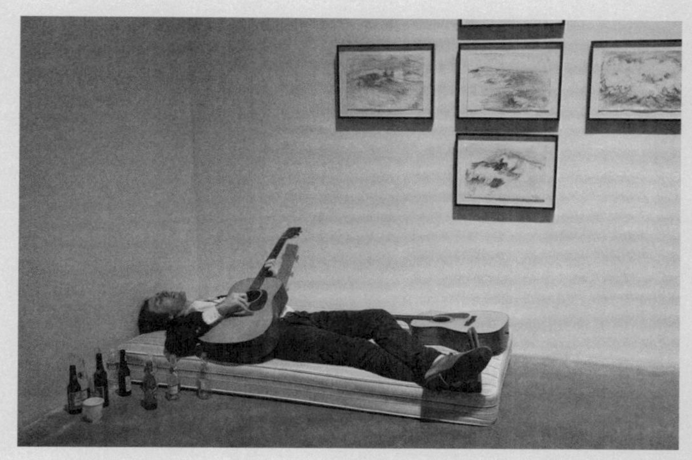

space where technology and biology seemed to overlap in a new collective body electric.

With much more basic, even rougher means, a similar space of communal gathering was created by Ragnar Kjartansson for his 2014 exhibition "Me, My Mother, My Father, and I." The artist transformed a floor of the museum into a bachelor's squat—with mattresses thrown on the floor, worn-out couches, and a fridge perennially stocked with beer—where a group of musicians hung out for the duration of the show, playing the same song over and over again. In other recent exhibitions at the Museum, the aural dimension has become as important as the visual, or even replaced it altogether, further emphasizing the "introspective" quality of these exhibitions. For example, Roberto Cuoghi presented *Šuillakku – corral version* (2008–14), a sound sculpture to be experienced in almost total darkness. For his 2016 solo show, Anri Sala conceived the alternation of his video, sound, and performance works as a musical ensemble, effectively composing the exhibition as a score and turning his installation into a temporal device as much as a spatial one.

It may be Paweł Althamer's *Draftsmen's Congress* (2012/14)—presented as part of the artist's 2014 survey "The Neighbors"—that condensed all of these strategies into a space that was physical and psychological, personal and collective. On the Museum's fourth floor, Althamer created a large cylindrical gallery—"as round as our heads," the artist explained, perhaps remembering Francis Picabia's saying that our heads are round so that our thoughts can change direction. Having covered every surface in white, Althamer invited visitors, as well as various school groups and civic associations, to contribute to an ongoing mural, a vast experiment in what Joseph Beuys, in the 1970s, would have called "social sculpture." For the entire run of the show, the fourth floor became a vast, crazed social arena that gathered and preserved the traces of everything that happened there and the memory of anyone who passed through—an

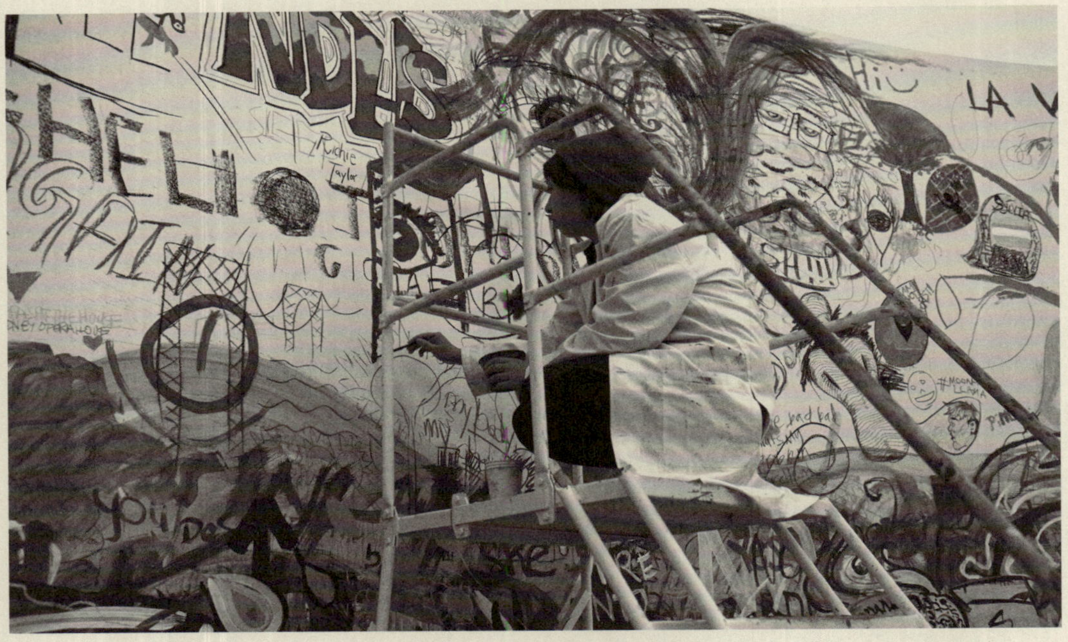

architecturally scaled palimpsest that combined the power and rage of vandalism with the more convivial possibilities of participation and community.

In spite of its openness, *Draftsmen's Congress* was not a naïve celebration of peaceful coexistence. Anyone who took part can attest that, in this project, the line separating play from violence was a thin one indeed; as soon as you saw your own drawing erased by a newcomer, you understood that Althamer's project was meant to highlight all the day-to-day social negotiations that are so habitual as to be invisible, to call fresh attention to the conflicts and alliances at work within the politics of everyday life, the thousands of microemotional decisions that mark the boundary between self and others.

By actualizing this invisible boundary, Althamer's *Draftsmen's Congress* also showed that introspectives do not imply a position of solipsism or withdrawal on the part of the artist or the viewer; the total installation, as Kabakov observed, is a model of the world that does not hide its flaws, but rather accentuates them, because art— and the museum—is the space where we learn to coexist with what we do not understand.

Massimiliano Gioni is *Edlis Neeson Artistic Director* of the New Museum, where he has curated numerous solo shows as well as the group exhibitions "After Nature" (2008), "Ostalgia" (2011), "Ghosts in the Machine" (2012), "Here and Elsewhere" (2014), and "The Keeper" (2016). He founded the New Museum Triennial in 2009 and curated the first edition, "The Generational: Younger Than Jesus." Gioni has also organized major international exhibitions, including Manifesta 5 (2004), the 6th Berlin Biennale (2006), the 8th Gwangju Biennale (2010), and the 55th Venice Biennale (2013).

Art and Technology

Lauren Cornell

Over the past forty years, the use of new media and technologies has proliferated in art, scripting new disciplines and resetting the conditions and codes of preexisting ones. Influential artists working with new technologies—among them video, sound, digital media, games, and virtual reality—had their first turns at the New Museum, and many of the institution's exhibitions were early to articulate the way art has evolved in tandem with new mediums. Starting in 2000, under the directorship of Lisa Phillips, the New Museum formalized its commitment to art engaged with technology by initiating successive groundbreaking partnerships and programs that would offer answers to the pressing turn-of-the-millennium question: *What can a twenty-first-century museum be?*

"Technology" is a distinctly elastic term encompassing rudimentary tools, pivotal inventions, and vast systems such as the internet. At the time of the New Museum's founding, "technology" in the arts referred to video and electronic art and, more broadly, to experiments with light, perception, and interactivity. For their 1979 exhibition "Dimensions Variable" at the Museum, the curatorial team of Susan Logan, Allan Schwartzman, and Kathleen Thomas framed technology as a raw material that artists could use to redefine the boundaries and operations of an artwork. "In the context of the present show," they wrote in the exhibition catalogue, "technology is neither Satan nor Messiah, but a familiar tool to be utilized imaginatively and economically."[1] This differentiation between art and material, between technology and ideology—evoked by the featured works variously utilizing light, air, water, sound, and photographic equipment—has been repeatedly debated and restated throughout the history of contemporary art.

1. Susan Logan, Allan Schwartzman, and Kathleen Thomas, "Dimensions Variable," in *Dimensions Variable*, ed. Susan Logan, Allan Schwartzman, and Kathleen Thomas (New York: New Museum,1979), 40, https://archive.newmuseum.org/print-ephemera/6419.

In the late 1980s and '90s, critical discourse in the arts around "information technologies"—meaning TV, radio, and the burgeoning web—became increasingly inflected by questions of globalization and identity. Would such media break down borders? What sway would national and local identifications have in a more connected society? And what impact would all of this have on the body, or would this most fundamental of tools become vestigial in a newly virtualized world? Questions such as these were addressed in a series of three prescient exhibitions—"Trade Routes," "The Final Frontier," and "In Transit," all staged in 1993—which set out to explore how the legacies of colonialism were at play in the processes of globalization.[2]

Laura Kurgan's *Interface: Information Overlay* (1993), an early data visualization work in "Trade Routes," involved six viewing stations sited throughout the Museum, each of which transposed live data feeds from Dow Jones onto a teleprompter. In a statement about the work, Kurgan asked: "Where do we meet these flows? How to account for what is called the interface between bodies, of things and people, and the information that codes and recodes them?"[3] Featured in "Final Frontier," the large-scale C-print *Man With Computer*, from the 1992 series *Faith,*

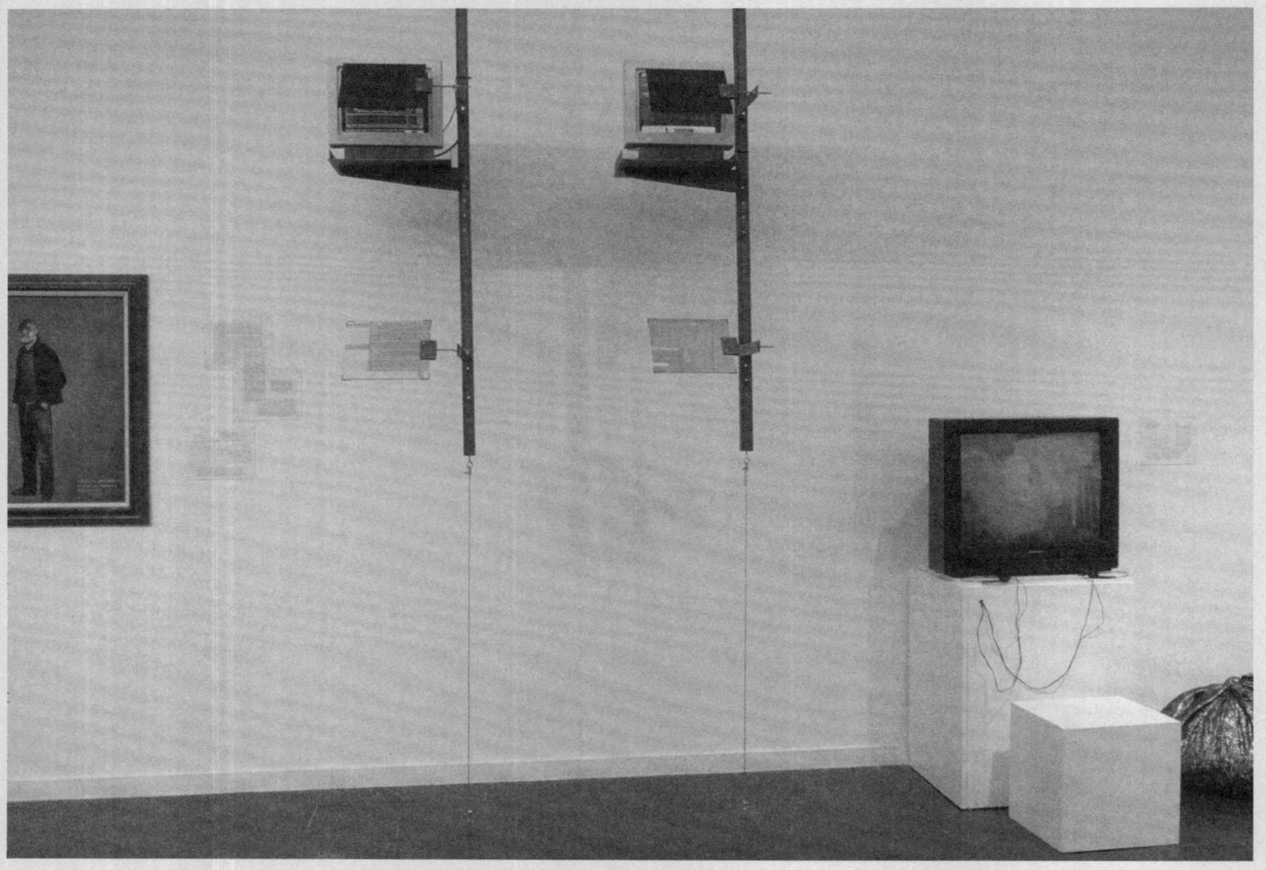

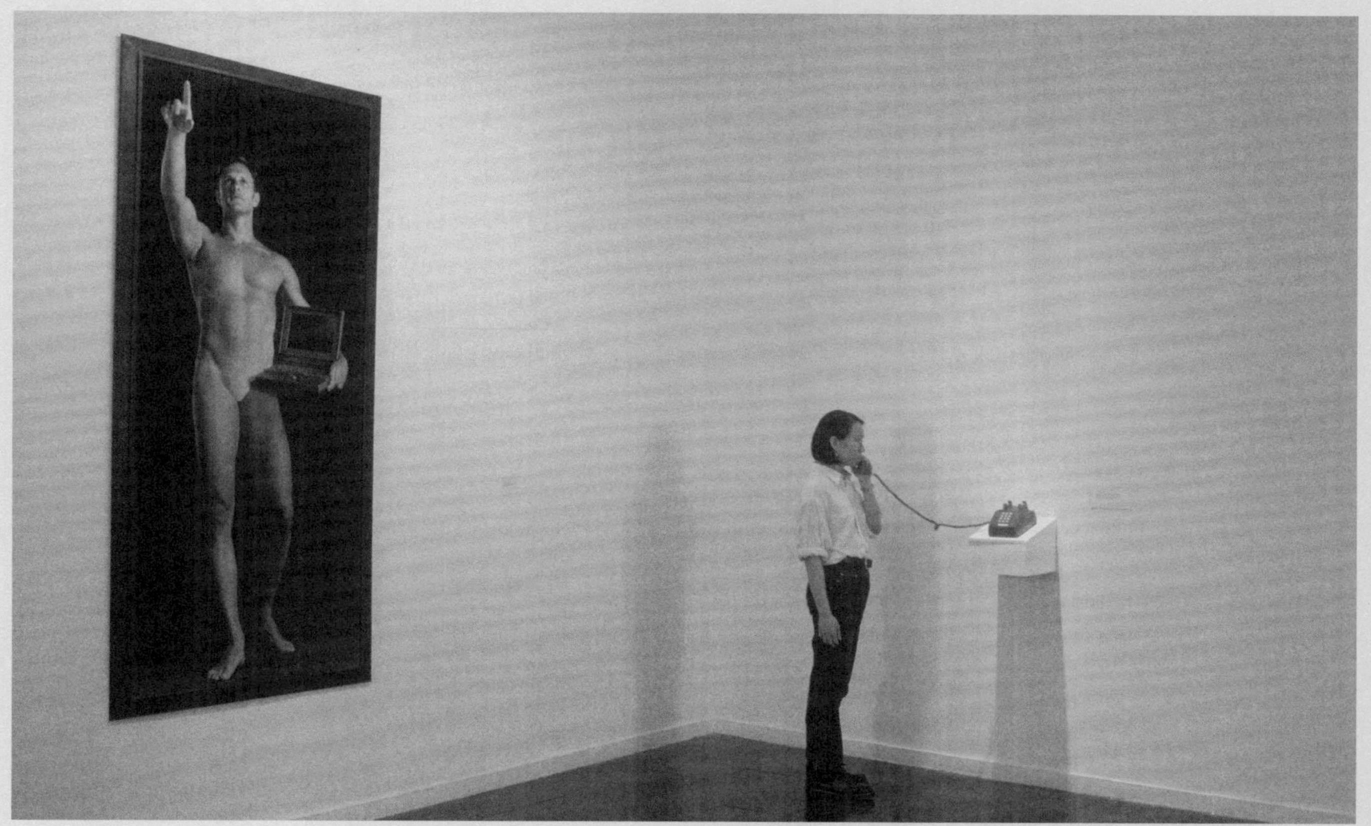

Honor and Beauty by the artist collaborative Aziz + Cucher, depicts a nude white man, his pose and athletic perfection recalling classical sculpture. One arm stretches outward and up in some combination of a point and a salute, while the other arm cradles a personal computer. The viewer's eyes are drawn to the blank patch of skin where the man's genitals would be. Embodying a cybernetic future in which sexuality has been erased—and reminiscent of some of the twentieth century's darkest currents (eugenics, Nazism)—he represents a frighteningly exclusionary future ideal.

In 2000, the New Museum inaugurated the Media Lounge, the first museum space in New York dedicated exclusively to new media exhibitions. The curatorial program of the Media Lounge built on the Museum's previous explorations of technology as both an artistic material and a vector of globalism, society, and identity. Designed by the architectural studio LOT-EK, the Media Lounge, which would

2. Senior Curator France Morin organized "In Transit" with anthropologist Kostas Gounis and political economist John Jeffries. Assistant Curator Alice Yang organized "The Final Frontier" with media and technology scholar Lisa Cartwright and mass media and popular culture critic Celeste Olalquiaga. Curator Laura Trippi organized "Trade Routes" with cultural critic and feminist scholar Gina Dent and sociologist Saskia Sassen.

3. Laura Kurgan, "Interface: information overlay," artist statement, 1993, https://archive. newmuseum.org/print-ephemera/8860.

present more than twenty exhibitions during its four-year run, is an example of the Museum's propensity to reach beyond the convention of the white cube gallery to test-drive new modes of display for emergent art forms. It also reflects a broader discursive shift toward new media art, which has contested and sometimes blurry boundaries. Mark Tribe and Reena Jana offered the following succinct definition of the field in their book *New Media Art*, echoing the curatorial description of the exhibition "Dimensions Variable" almost thirty years later:

> Deciding what counts as media technology is a difficult task. The Internet, which is central to many New Media art projects, is itself composed of a heterogeneous and constantly changing assortment of computer hardware and software—servers, routers, personal computers, database applications, scripts, and files—all governed by arcane protocols, such as HTTP, TCP/IP, and DNS. Other technologies that play a significant role in New Media art include video and computer games, surveillance cameras, wireless phones, hand-held computers, and Global Positioning System (GPS) devices. But New Media art is not defined by the technologies discussed here; on the contrary, by deploying these technologies for critical or experimental purposes, New Media artists redefine them as art media.[4]

Overseen by curators Anne Barlow and Anne Ellegood, the program of the Media Lounge launched with "Candice Breitz: Babel Series," a presentation of the Berlin-based artist's 1999 video and sound installation, which evoked global pop culture with English as its emergent lingua franca. The exhibition "Trust Me," also in 2000, explored how much private information people were willing to disclose on their personal computers. "If the computer becomes our 'confidante,'" the show's description asked, "how much will we reveal and what kind of intimacy does this create?"[5] Successive Media Lounge exhibitions explored the effects of networked platforms on geography ("Location/ Dislocation," 2001); on entertainment ("Kristin Lucas and Joe McKay: The Electric Donut," 2001); and on cultural memory ("Leah Gilliam: Agenda for a Landscape," 2002). The concerns of

224

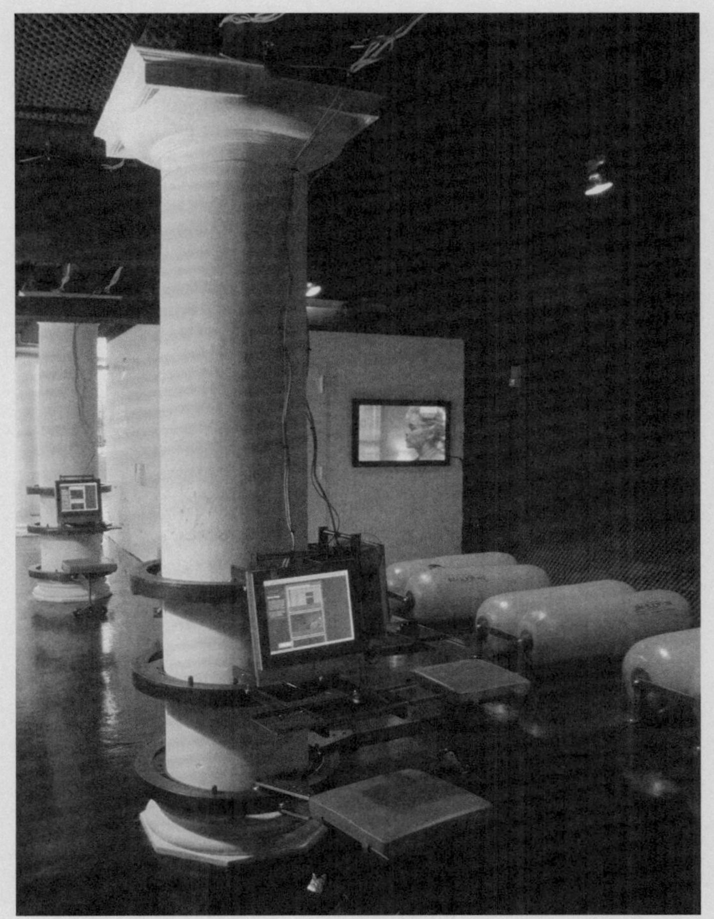

many of these presentations remain relevant, as do those of concurrent projects and performances staged outside the Media Lounge. In *GenTerra*, a pseudo-science lab created by the collective Critical Art Ensemble (CAE) and Beatriz da Costa and staged in the Media Lounge in 2002, participants "manipulated transgenic bacteria in an effort to develop a more nuanced understanding of risk assessment regarding the uses of recombinant DNA."[6] Exemplifying their controversial practice—between 2004 and 2008, two of CAE's members battled federal charges of bioterrorism and mail fraud[7]—*GenTerra* can be seen in hindsight to correspond with scientific developments like the genome-editing technology CRISPR.

Concurrent with the new media work shown in the Media Lounge was a swell of internet art made online during the '90s and '00s. Internet art is distinguished from a broader rubric of new media work by its use of browsers, code, internet protocols, and files native to the web (e.g., GIFs, Flash, SWF). Prominent among the organizations that had sprung up in the '90s to support this nascent field was Rhizome. An experimental and highly active artist community founded by Tribe in 1996, Rhizome also commissioned, collected, and supported writing about internet art. In the wake of the 2001 dot-com bust and the contemporaneous withdrawal of broader institutional support (mainly grants) from the nascent field, Rhizome

4.   Mark Tribe and Reena Jana, *New Media Art*, ed. Uta Grosenick (Cologne: Taschen, 2009), 7.

5.   *Media Lounge Calendar, Nov.00–Mar.01* (New York: New Museum, 2000), https:// archive.newmuseum.org/print-ephemera/8696.

6.   A full account of *GenTerra* (2001–03) is available on the website of Critical Art Ensemble. See "GenTerra 2001–03. Critical Art Ensemble and Beatriz da Costa," Critical Art Ensemble, accessed August 1, 2017, http://critical-art.net/?p=86.

7.   Gary Younge, "Art Becomes the Next Suspect in 9/11 Paranoia," *Guardian*, June 11, 2004, https://www.theguardian.com/world/2004/jun/11/arts.usa.

found itself financially struggling, and Tribe sought a
way to stabilize the organization. He found a partner in
Phillips, who saw the potential in Rhizome's early embrace
of the internet as a new artistic medium. Since 2002,
Rhizome has been an organization in residence, with
offices, event space, and administrative support provided
by the Museum, an advantageous arrangement that has
helped Rhizome to grow and thrive, doubling its budget
size many times over. Reciprocally, Rhizome's directors
and staff have played a significant curatorial role at
the New Museum. Rachel Greene, Rhizome's Executive
Director from 2002 to 2005, organized exhibitions at
the Museum's temporary space in Chelsea, including
"Rules of Crime: Kayle Brandon and Heath Bunting"
(2004), which explored hacking as a political tool, and
"Contagious Media" (2005), which looked at how and
why culture spreads online. The latter show included a
presentation of mid-'00s memes like the Dancing Baby
and Hot or Not websites, which are silly, crass, and
decidedly not fine art, but whose popularity prefigured
the texture and humor of an online pop culture yet to
fully manifest.

When Greene stepped down in 2005, I became Rhizome's
Executive Director, a position I would hold until 2012.[8] One
of my first tasks was to finish organizing a show Greene
had only begun to shape, "Rhizome ArtBase 101," which
would survey salient themes in internet art through a
presentation of over forty works from Rhizome's archive.
Online culture and art move quickly, and the challenge

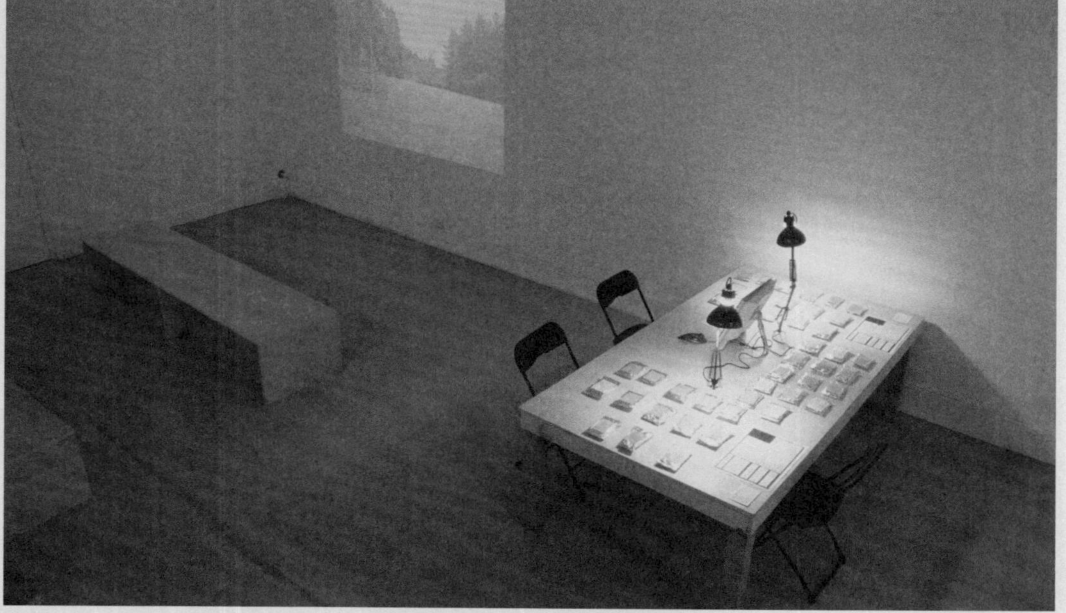

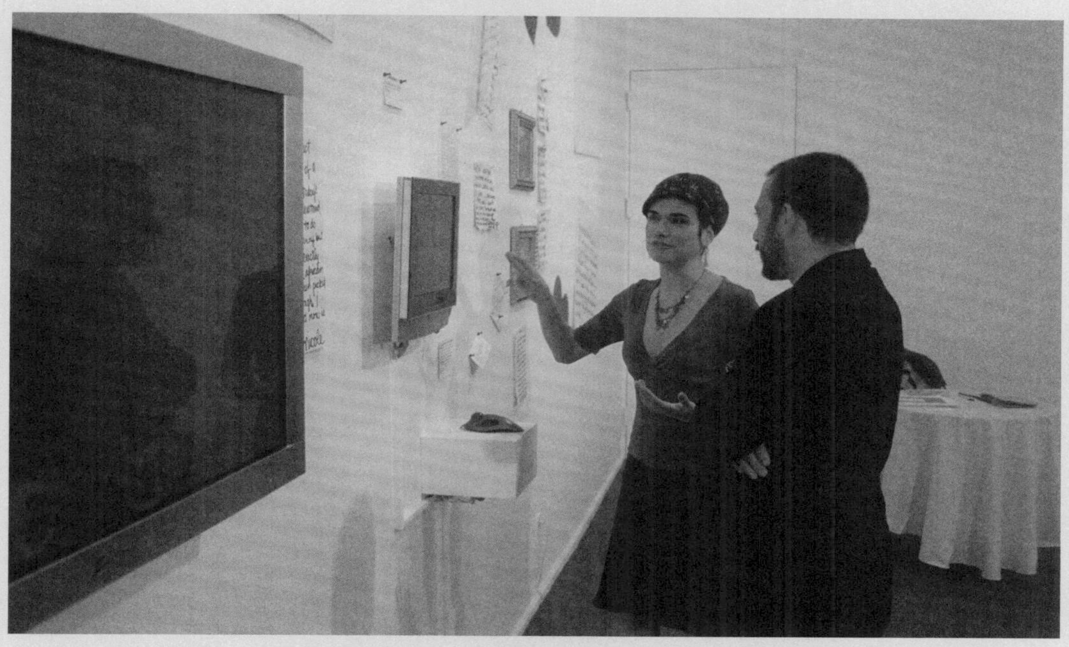

was to evaluate and demonstrate how the field of internet art had changed in the course of a decade—a period in which the web had transformed from a landscape littered with 404 signs and nascent social networking sites into a sprawling commons for billions of people. Internet art was now no longer a new medium, but a mass medium that was, through its participatory nature and global reach, redefining popular culture, community, and public speech. In the years to come, artists would become preoccupied with new forms of creativity enabled by social media, with more fluid expressions of identity available online, with vast user-made virtual worlds, with new systems of mapping the globe, with viral culture and hashtag-based activism, with the rise of widespread tracking and surveillance, and with changes in consciousness and daily life wrought by 24/7 connectivity. This period (aspects of which continue to define our present moment) is the focus of the anthology *Mass Effect: Art and the Internet in the Twenty-First Century*, jointly published by the New Museum and MIT Press in 2015, which I coedited with curator and writer Ed Halter.

During the time covered by *Mass Effect*, a new generation of artists emerged, one different from those who had discovered the internet in the '90s and turned away from mediums like painting and sculpture. This so-called second generation of internet artists had grown up with

8.   I was succeeded by Heather Corcoran (2012–15). Rhizome's current Executive Director is Zachary Kaplan.

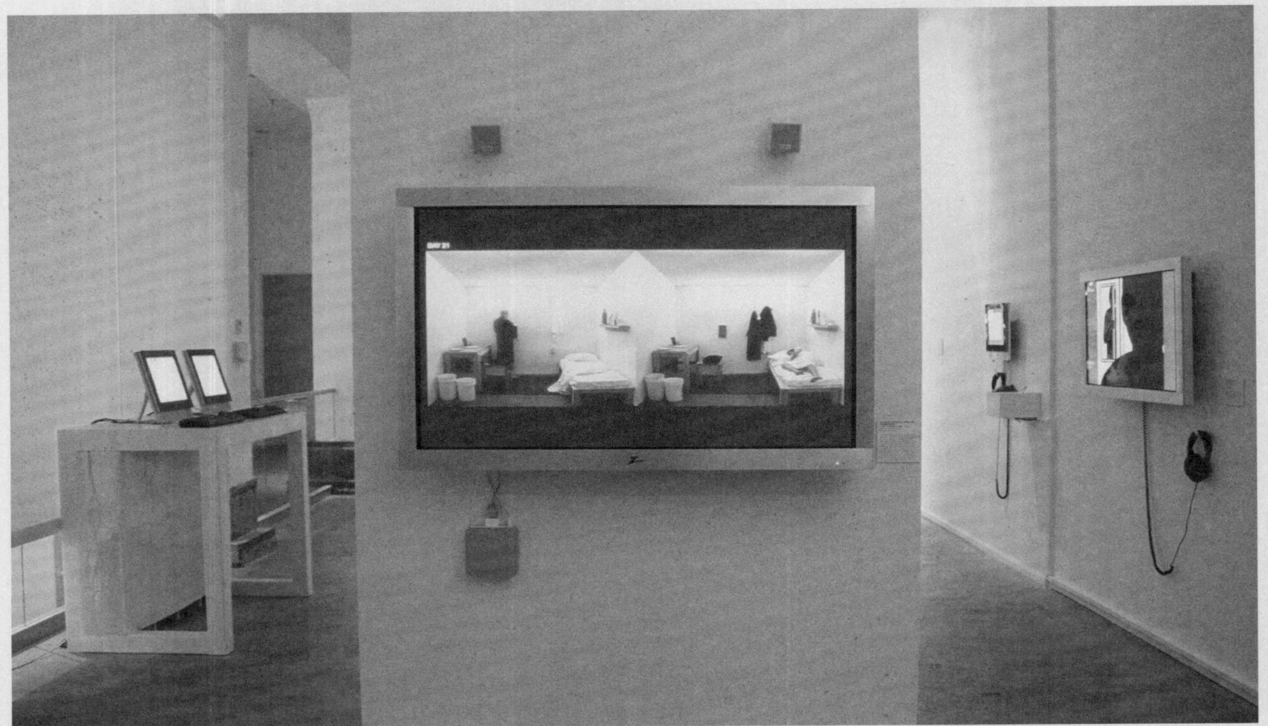

the web, and their perspective on it was more embedded: they were nostalgic for, even celebratory of, digital culture, but, at the same time, they were clear-eyed about its limitations and threats. More consistently than any other museum in the US, the New Museum captured and presented the activities of this emerging cohort, thanks in part to its affiliation with Rhizome. The first New Museum Triennial, "Younger Than Jesus" (2009), organized by Massimiliano Gioni, Laura Hoptman, and me, was aimed at assessing if there was anything cohesive among "millennial" artists—those who were born after 1978 and have been awkwardly characterized as "digital natives," among other generation-specific terms, by journalists, sociologists, and the media more broadly. The show featured many artists who were exploring how culture was being redefined due to the internet, including AIDS-3D, Cory Arcangel, Kerstin Brätsch, Cao Fei, Ida Ekblad (then known as Computer Princess), Guthrie Lonergan, James Richards, and Ryan Trecartin. For many of these artists, it was their first institutional show in the US.

Six years later, the third Triennial, "Surround Audience," curated by Trecartin and me, examined questions of identity and technology, and mobilized digitally enabled formats for art. The Museum commissioned the artist collective K-HOLE to create the exhibition's digital and print ad campaign, *Extended Release* (2015), which debuted before the Triennial opened in February 2015.

We supported an online TV show, Casey Jane Ellison's *Touching the Art* (2014–16), and presented a virtual reality–based work, Daniel Steegmann Mangrané's *Phantom* (2015), which relied on an Oculus Rift VR development kit. Josh Kline's *Freedom* (2015)—a searing look at rising inequity during the Obama years and the contemporaneous invasion of personal spaces like Facebook by commercial interests—channeled some of the political and economic forces that contributed to the outcome of the 2016 American presidential election.

Other thematic shows at the New Museum during the 2010s foregrounded key artistic and cultural concerns of the present moment and the recent past. "Free" (2010), which I organized, explored the ways in which the nature of information was changing with the growth of new collective, public spaces of social media. The exhibition introduced the artists Aleksandra Domanović, Jon Rafman, and Trevor Paglen to a wider audience. "Ghosts in the Machine" (2012), organized by Gary Carrion-Murayari and Massimiliano Gioni, was a dynamic survey of artists working with technology in the 1950s and '60s. It memorably included a re-creation of Stan VanDerBeek's enveloping *Movie-Drome* (1963–66), a dome illuminated within by moving images, which anticipated the fully immersive visual experiences of VR and our contemporary digital environment.

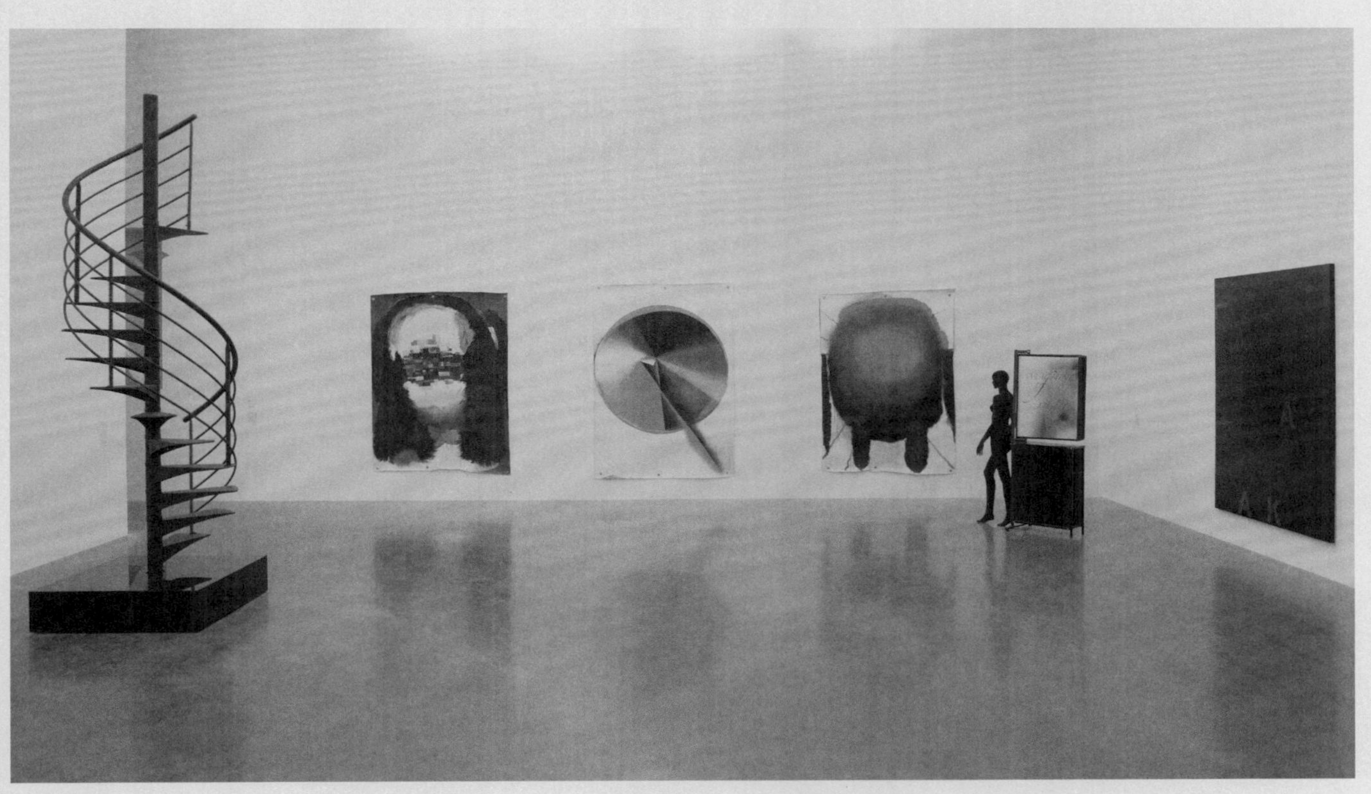

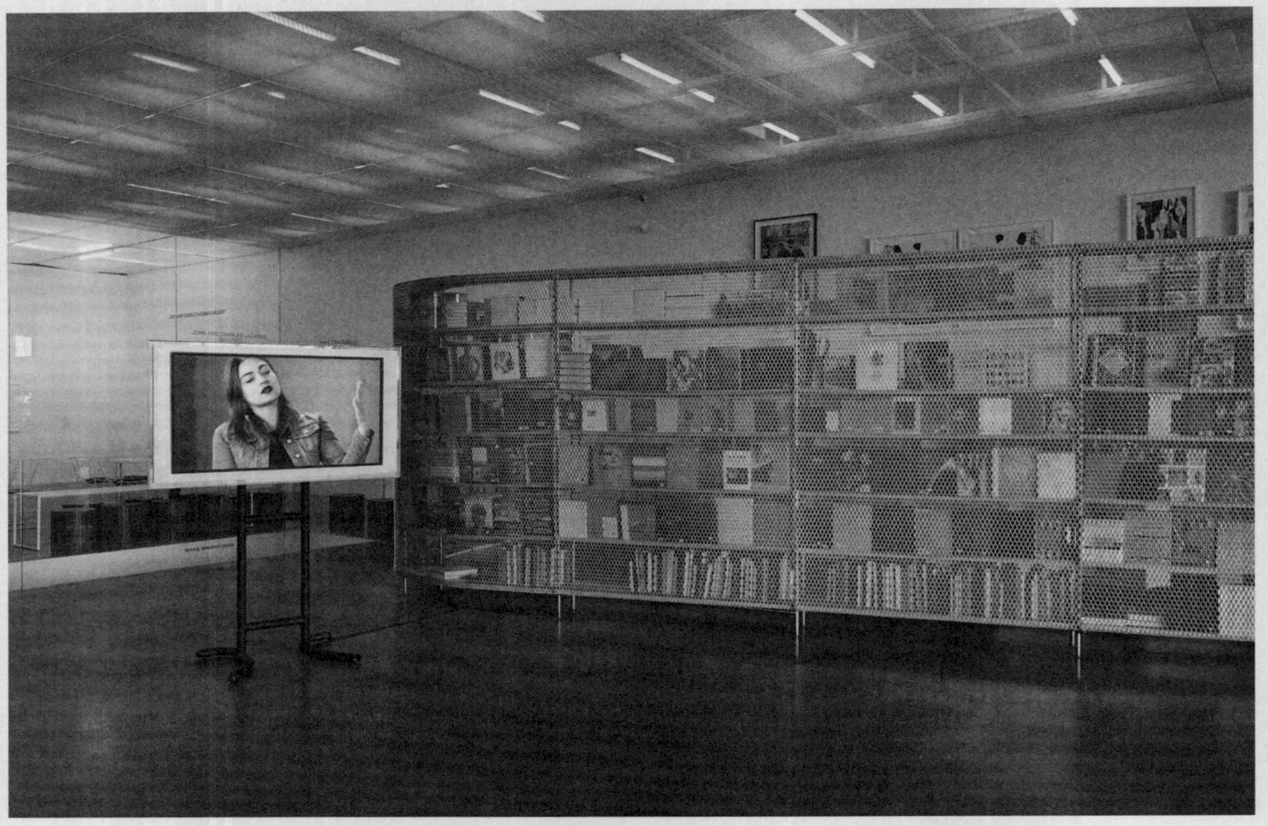

In the 2010s, the New Museum increasingly assumed the role of a producer, supporting artists in residence and commissioning new works across departments. The vast empty floors of 231 Bowery, the building adjacent to and owned by the Museum, were given over to artists participating in Triennials, preparing for solo exhibitions, and fulfilling residencies organized by the Department of Education and Public Engagement. First Look, a program for commissioning digital and mobile VR works, was launched in 2012 and has presented some seventy works in thirty-eight exhibitions to date. Its debut commission was *Image Atlas* (2012), a custom search engine developed by Taryn Simon and the late programmer and activist Aaron Swartz that juxtaposes top image search results from local search engines around the world. The range of responses to terms such as "love," "war," "religion," and "freedom" reveals differences in cultural norms and values, as well as the role of governments in determining what constitutes available information. *Image Atlas* was facilitated by Rhizome's annual Seven on Seven conference, launched in 2010, which pairs leading artists and technologists and provides the opportunity for them to create something new.

In 2014, Phillips and Deputy Director Karen Wong cofounded NEW INC, the first museum-led cultural incubator dedicated to supporting "innovation, collaboration, and entrepreneurship," with Julia Kaganskiy as its first Director.[9] Occupying eight thousand square feet at 231 Bowery and comprised of artists, technologists, and designers, the NEW INC community is often working at the forefront of technological innovations, such as 3-D printing, biometrics, augmented reality, and VR. NEW INC's support of VR has been particularly noteworthy, with many in-house projects illustrating the artistic potential of this new platform, whose commercial and popular development is largely focused on gaming. Developed by NEW INC members Milica Zec and Winslow Turner Porter III, *Giant* (2016), which premiered at Sundance New Frontiers, employed VR to tell the story of a young family during a bombing raid. That same year, Kaganskiy founded Versions—an annual conference dedicated to exploring VR as an emerging medium and to considering the hype and true potential of consumer VR—in collaboration with Jamin Warren, the founder of the video game company Kill Screen.

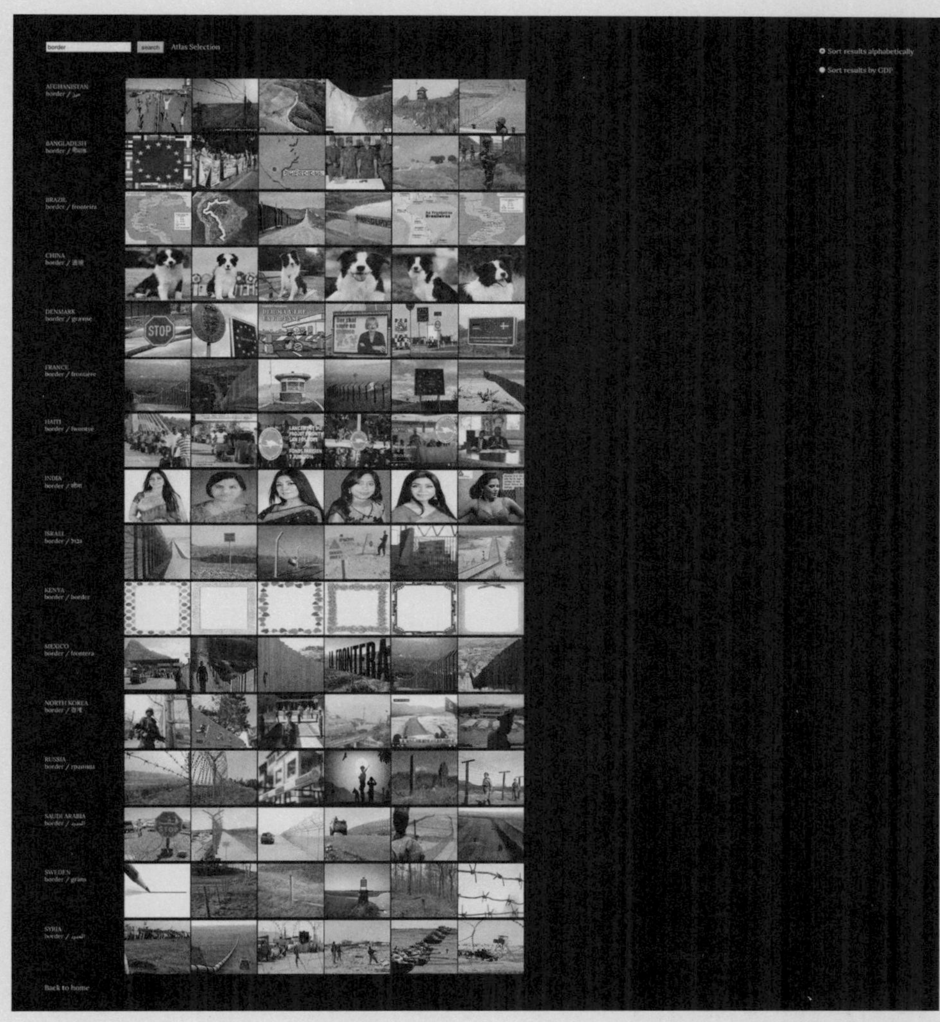

9.   "Our Mission," NEW INC, accessed July 31, 2017, http://www.newinc.org/about/.

NEW INC's exploration of VR encapsulates the New Museum's commitment to art engaged with new technology: the commitment was early and has remained steadfast. From experiments with light, sound, and video to the Media Lounge; to web-, mobile-, and browser-based exhibition platforms; to an incubator for art that defies categorization; the institution has tacked its exhibition strategies in tandem with advances in art. Starting at the New Museum twelve years ago, I encountered a cohort of colleagues deep in conversation, returning repeatedly to questions around how technology was transforming culture and society, and what this might mean for art. As the Museum enters its fifth decade, this probing spirit—radically open to risk—still fills the building. Now, with an active partnership with Rhizome, vibrant activity from NEW INC, and a singular record of nimble and prescient responses to new tools and forms, the Museum has become not just a site of presentation, but a preeminent center for art and technology, ready to embrace developments to come.

Lauren Cornell is Director of the Graduate Program at the Center for Curatorial Studies and Chief Curator of the Hessel Museum at Bard College, Annandale-on-Hudson, NY. She was Curator at the New Museum and, from 2015 to 2017, its Associate Director, Technology Initiatives. From 2005 to 2012, she served as Executive Director of Rhizome, the Museum's affiliate. At the Museum, Cornell organized several exhibitions, including the "New Museum Triennial: Surround Audience" (2015); produced over eighty performances, screenings, and conversations in the New Museum Theater; and founded Rhizome's annual Seven on Seven conference.

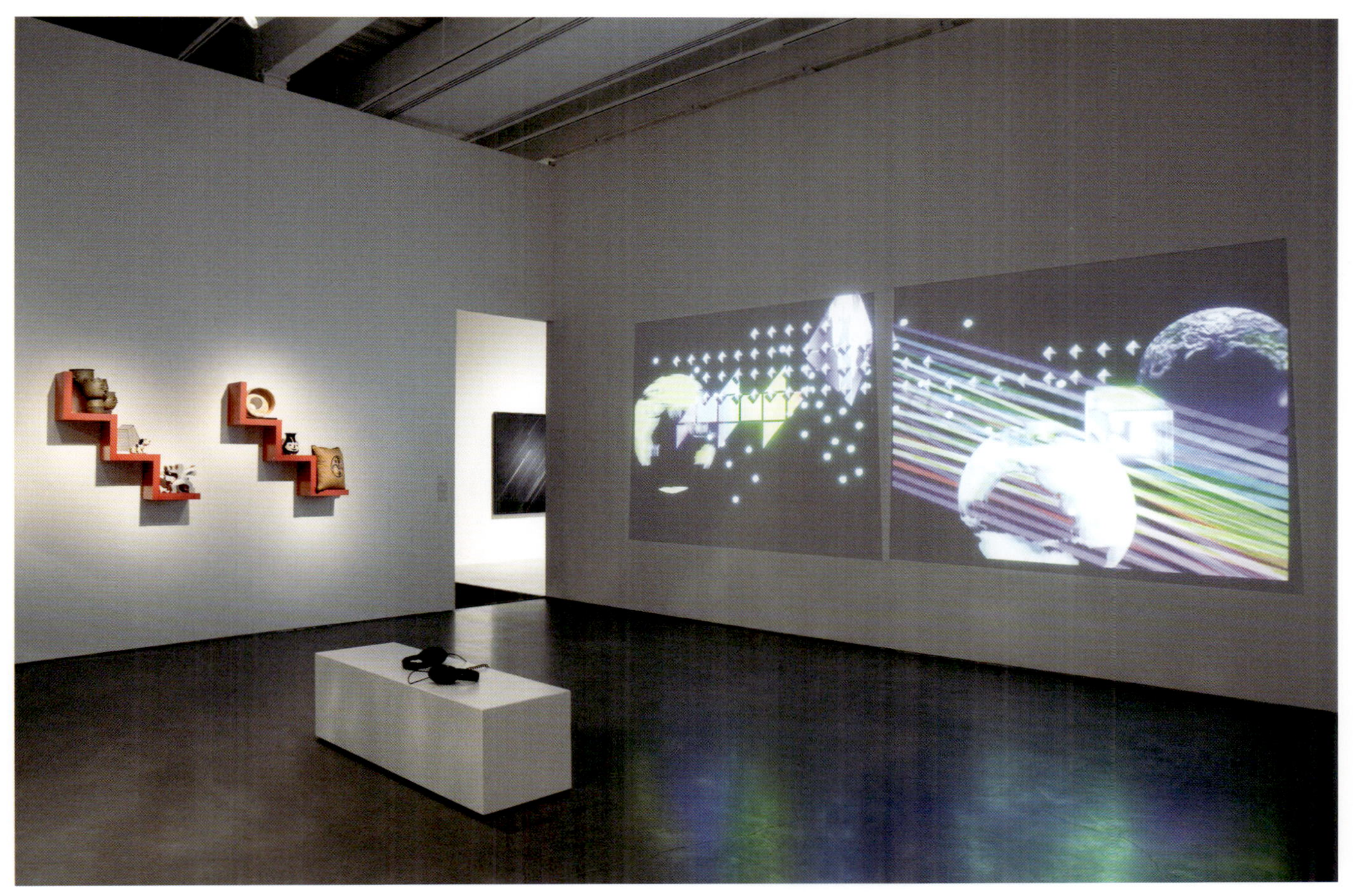

Left to right: works
by Hanne Mugaas and
Aleksandra Domanović

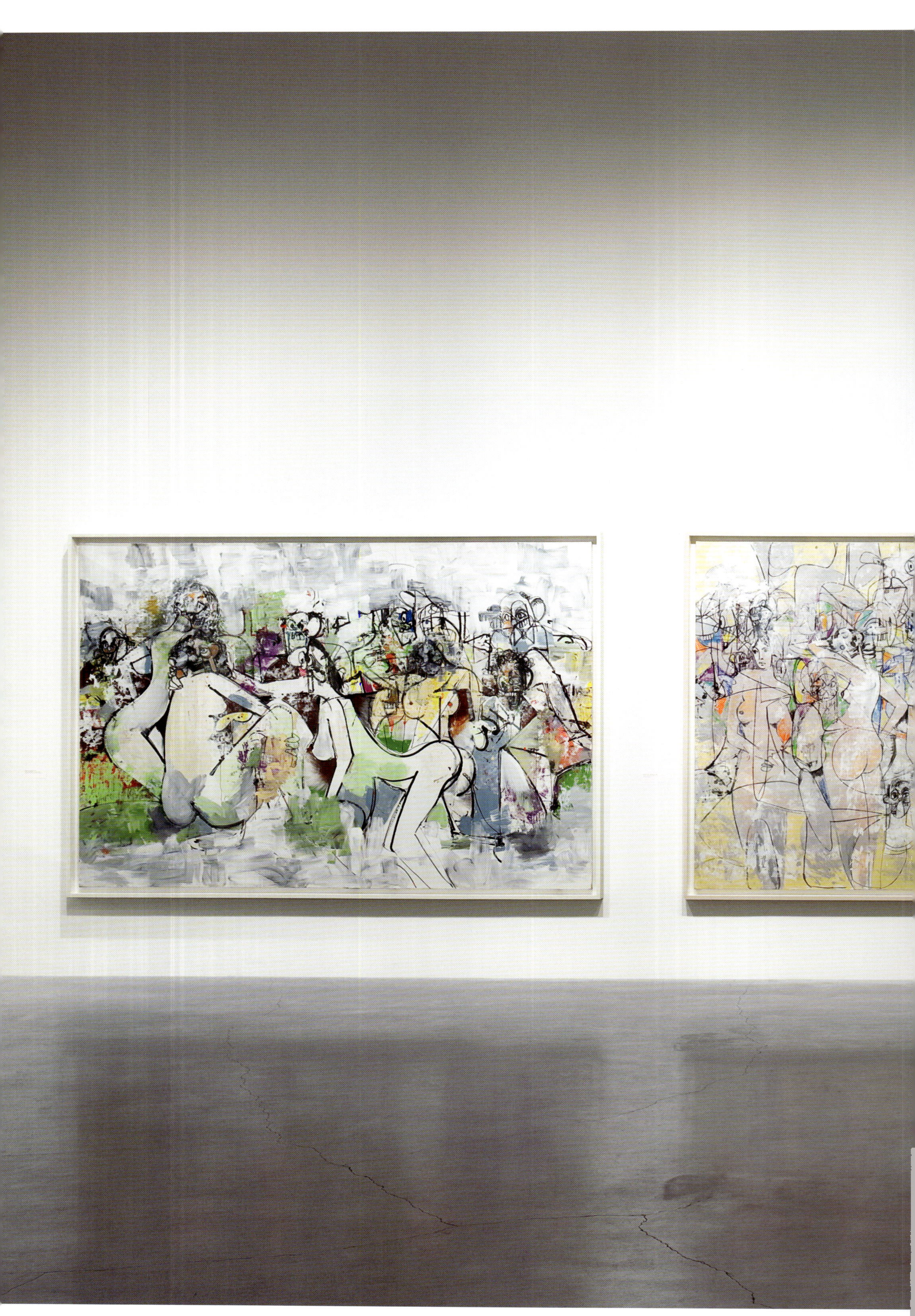

Left to right: George
Condo, *Figures in a
Garden*, 2010; *Female
Figure Composition*, 2009;
and *Spatial Figures*, 2010

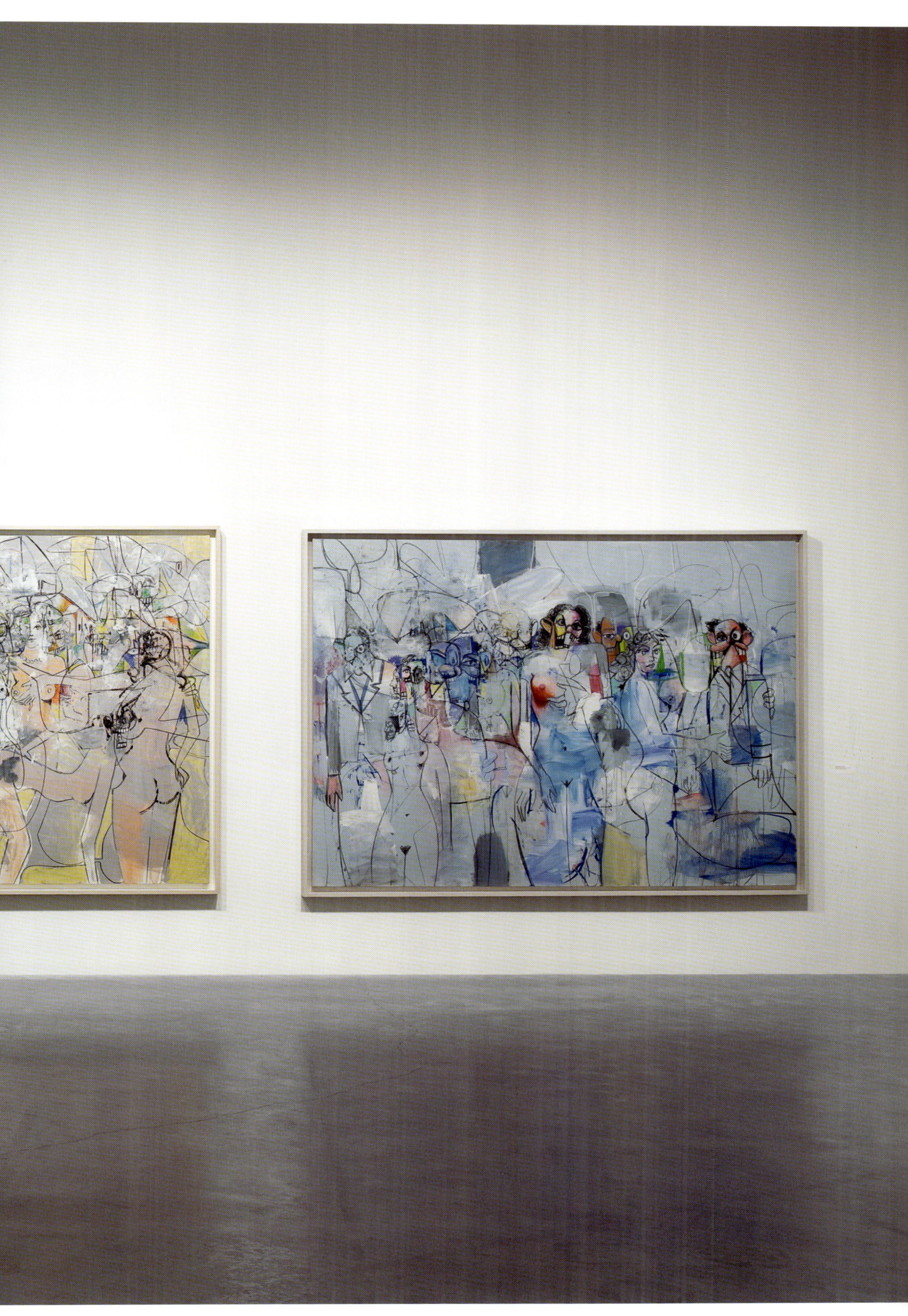

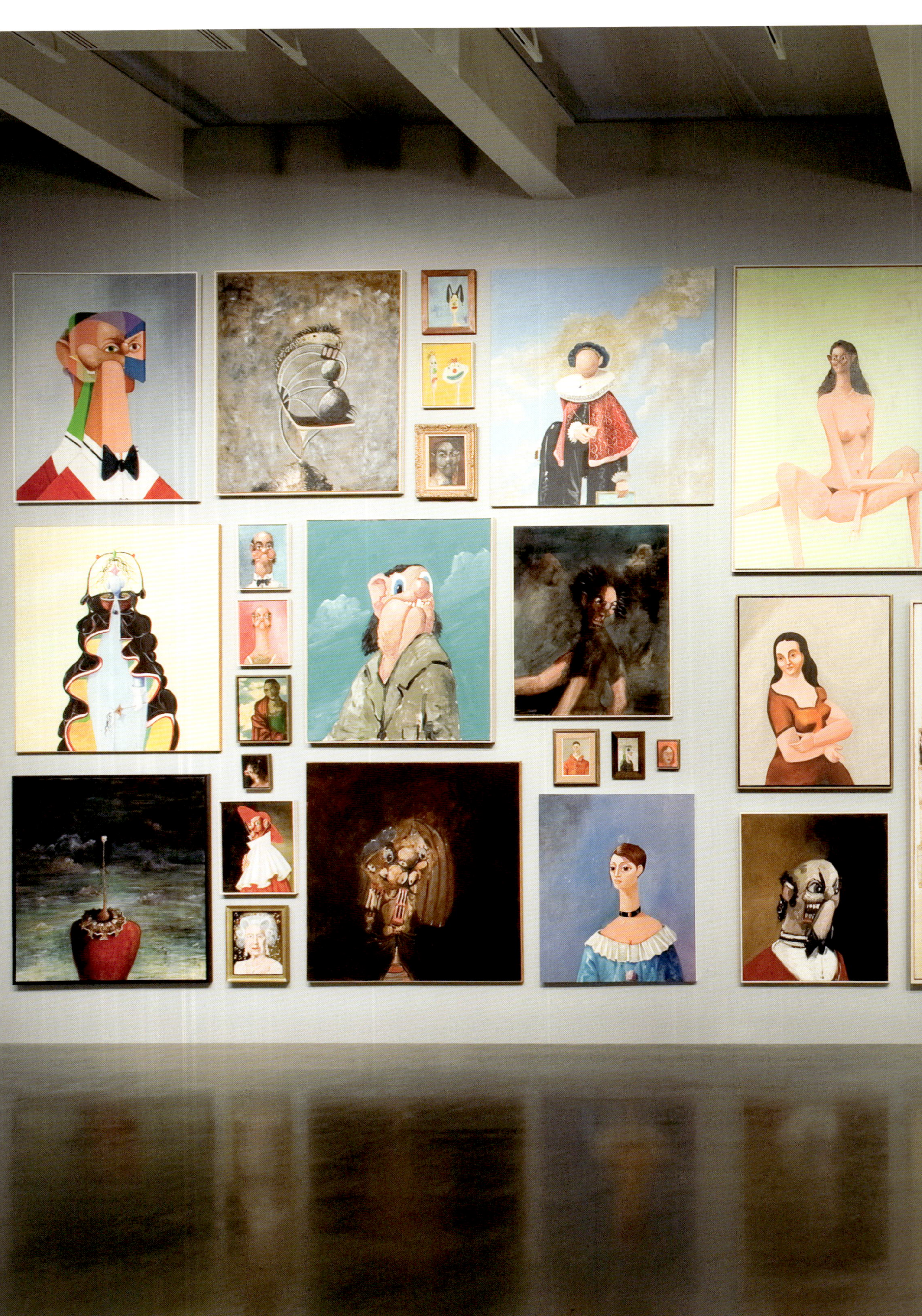

Installation view

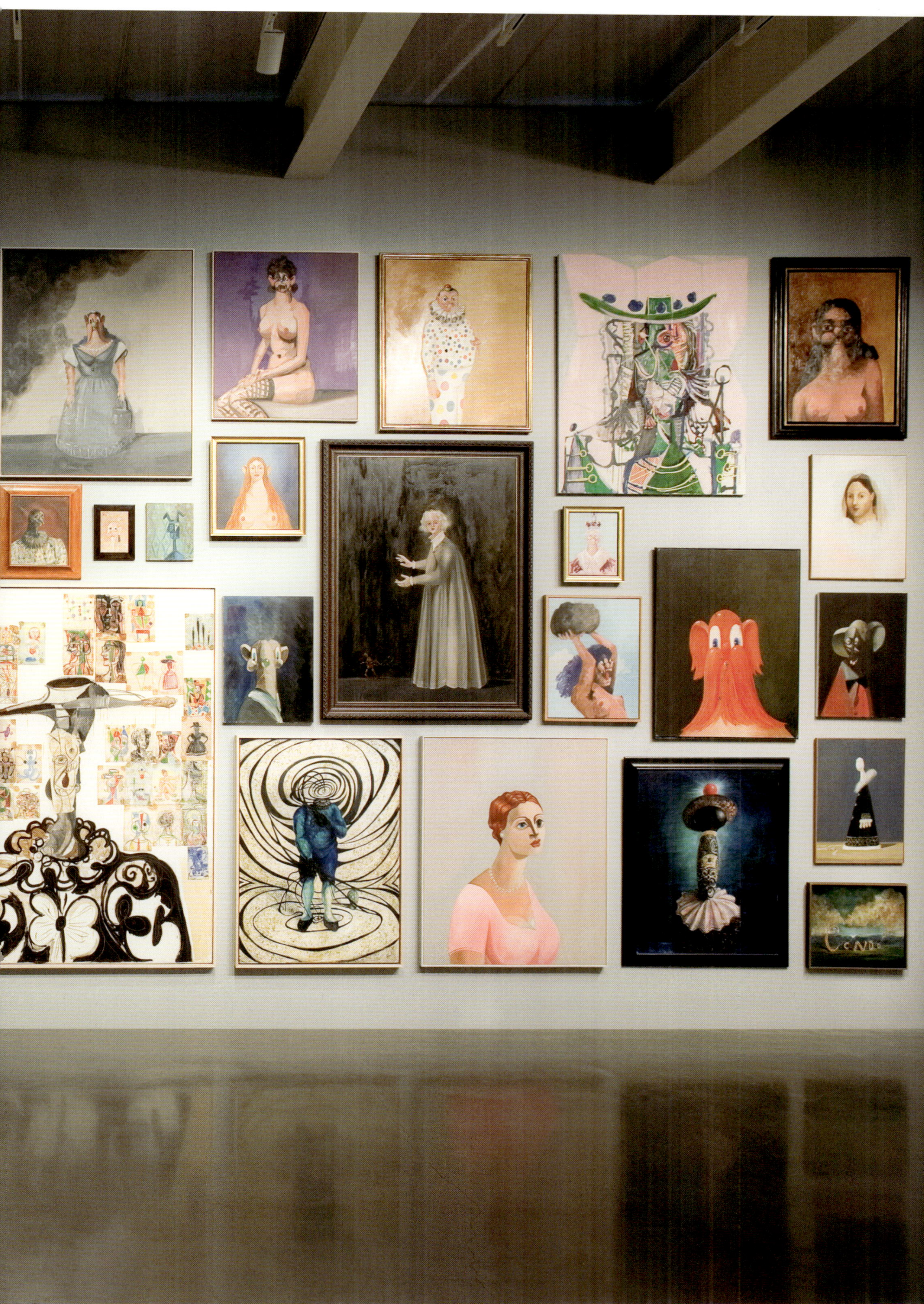

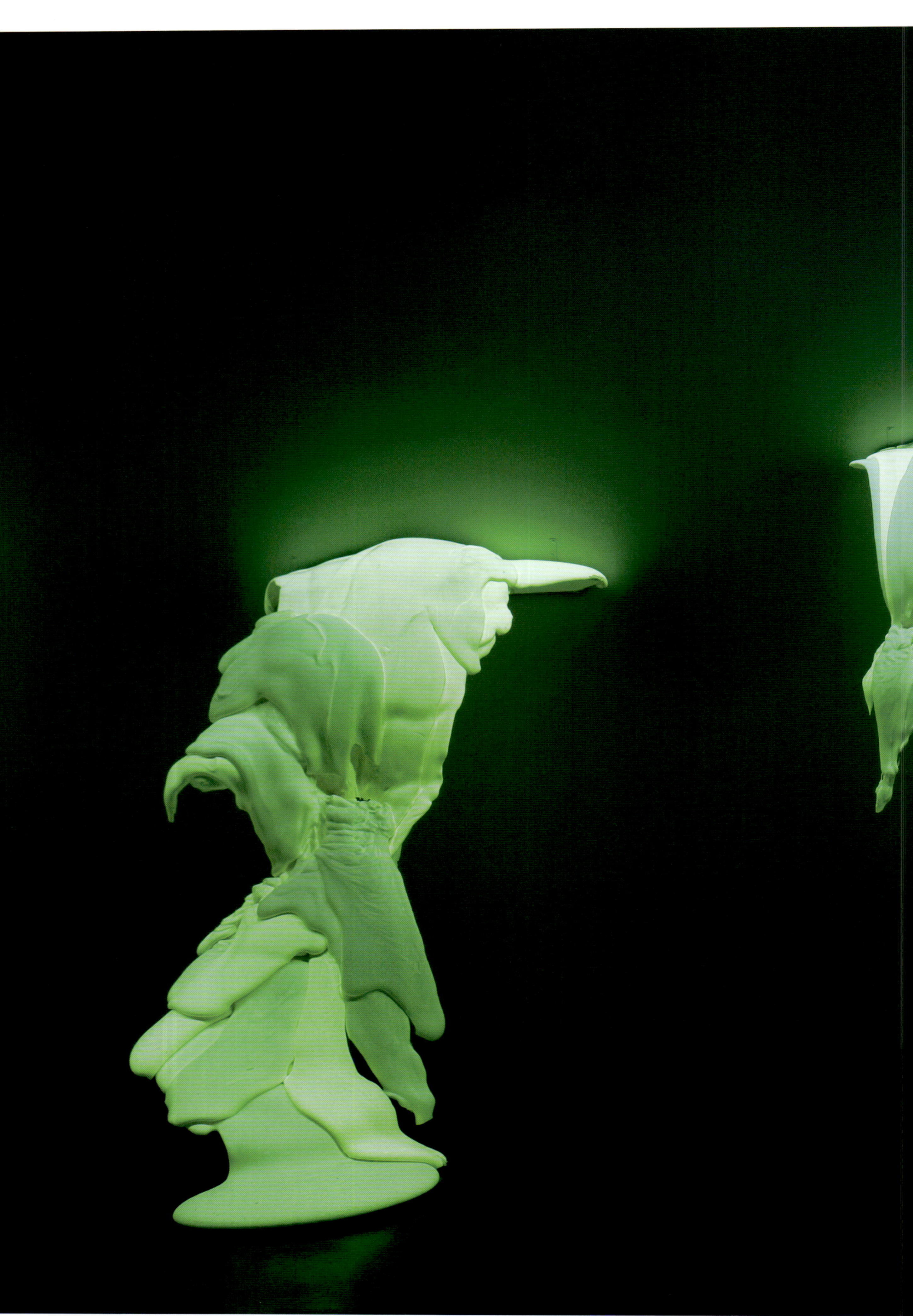

Lynda Benglis,
Phantom, 1971 (detail)

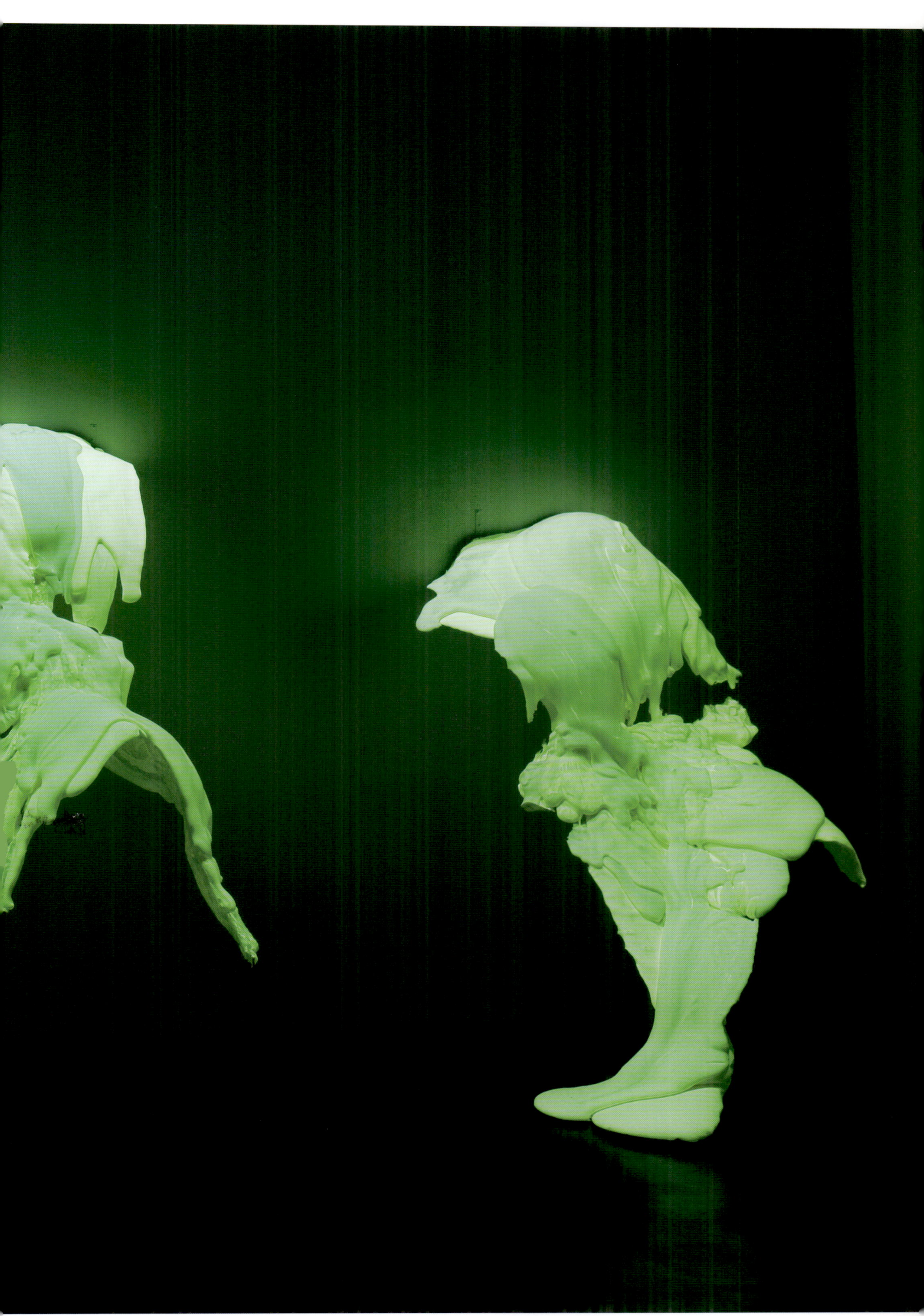

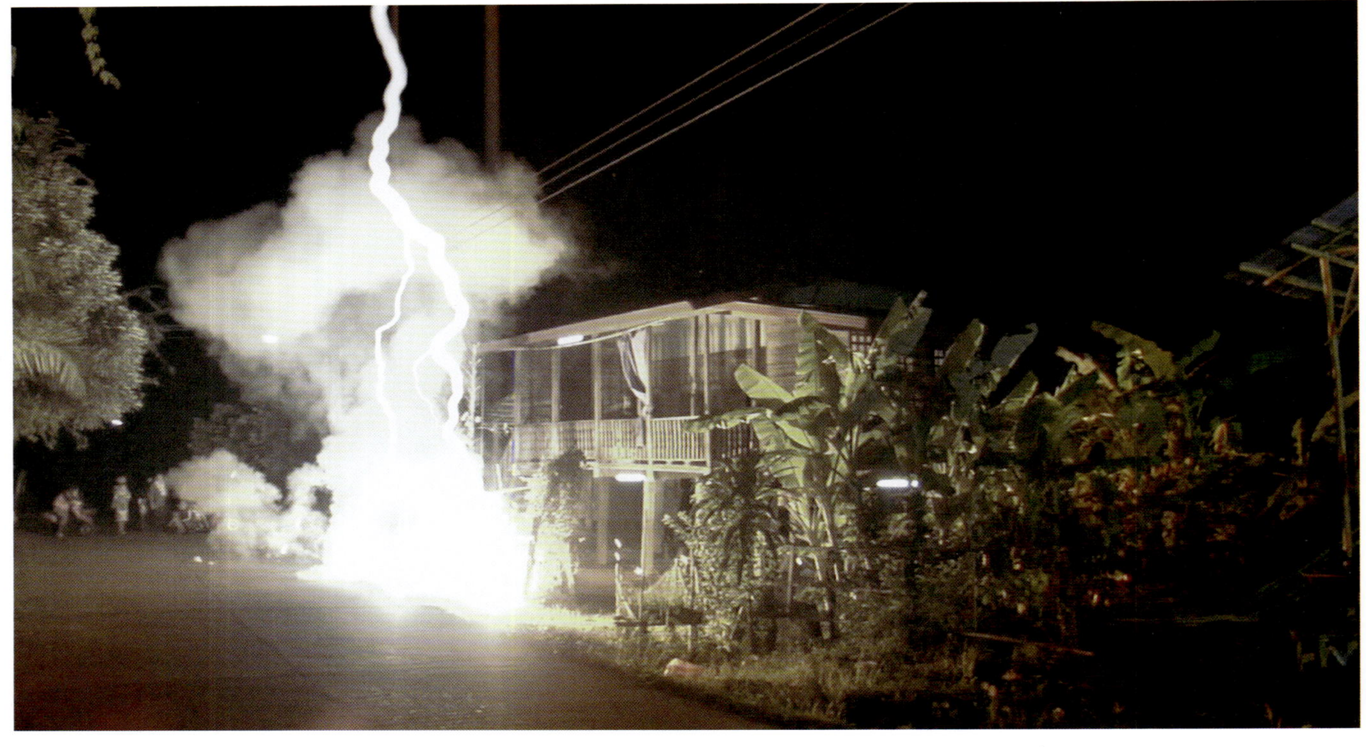

Apichatpong Weerasethakul,
Nabua, 2009 (still)

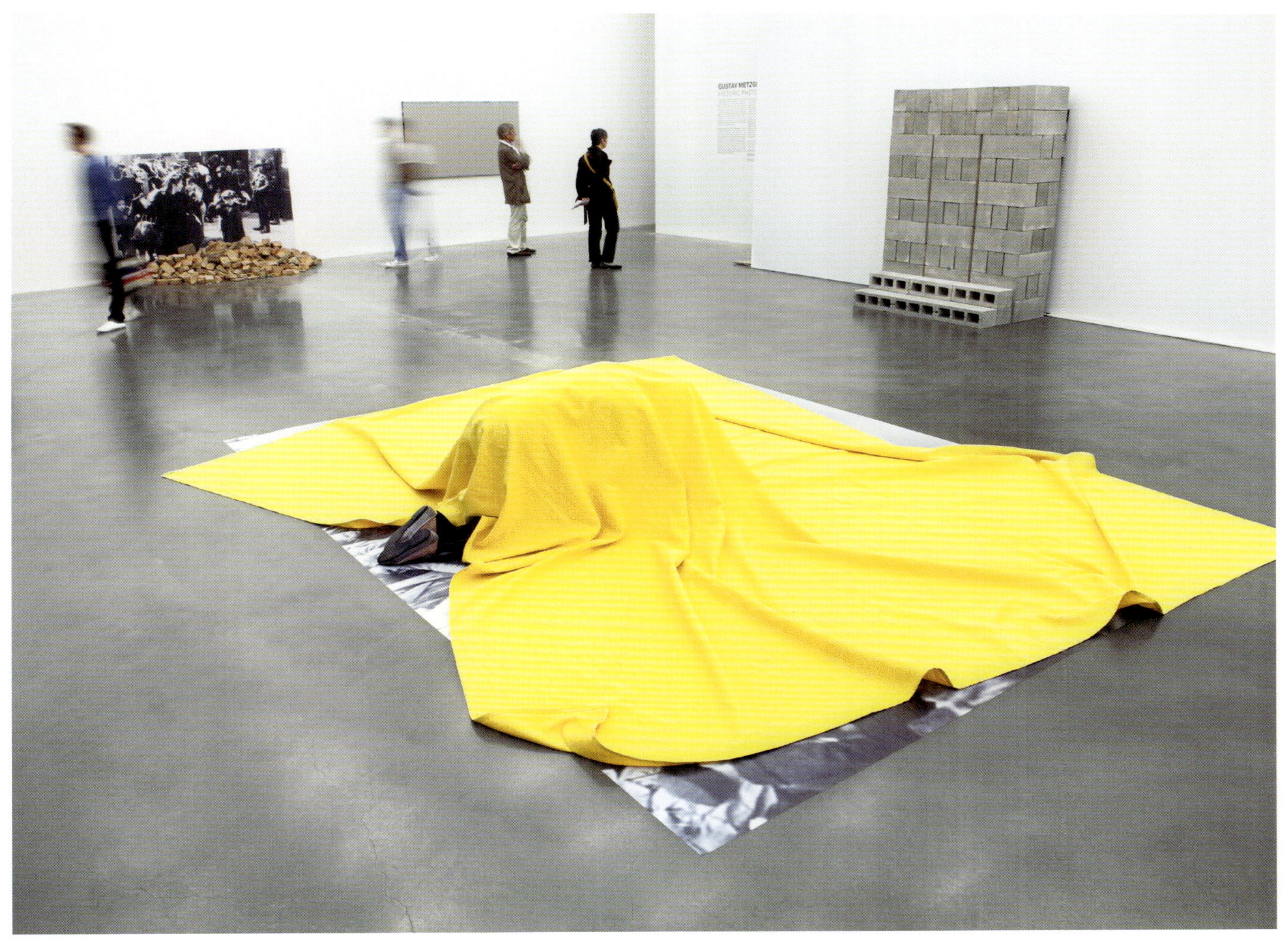

Foreground: Gustav
Metzger, *Historic
Photographs: To Crawl
Into–Anschluss, Vienna,
March 1938*, 1996/2011

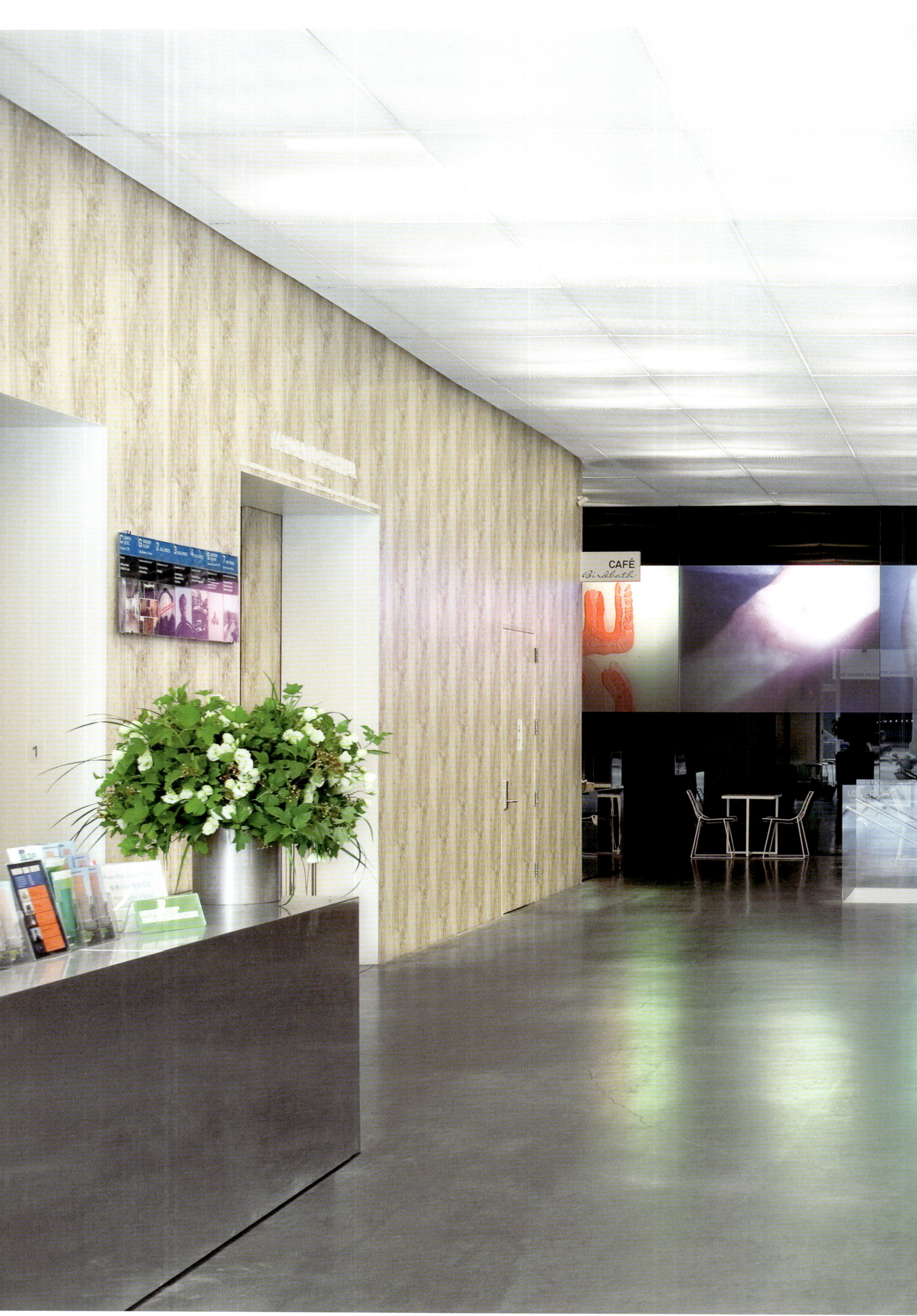

Installation view through
Museum lobby

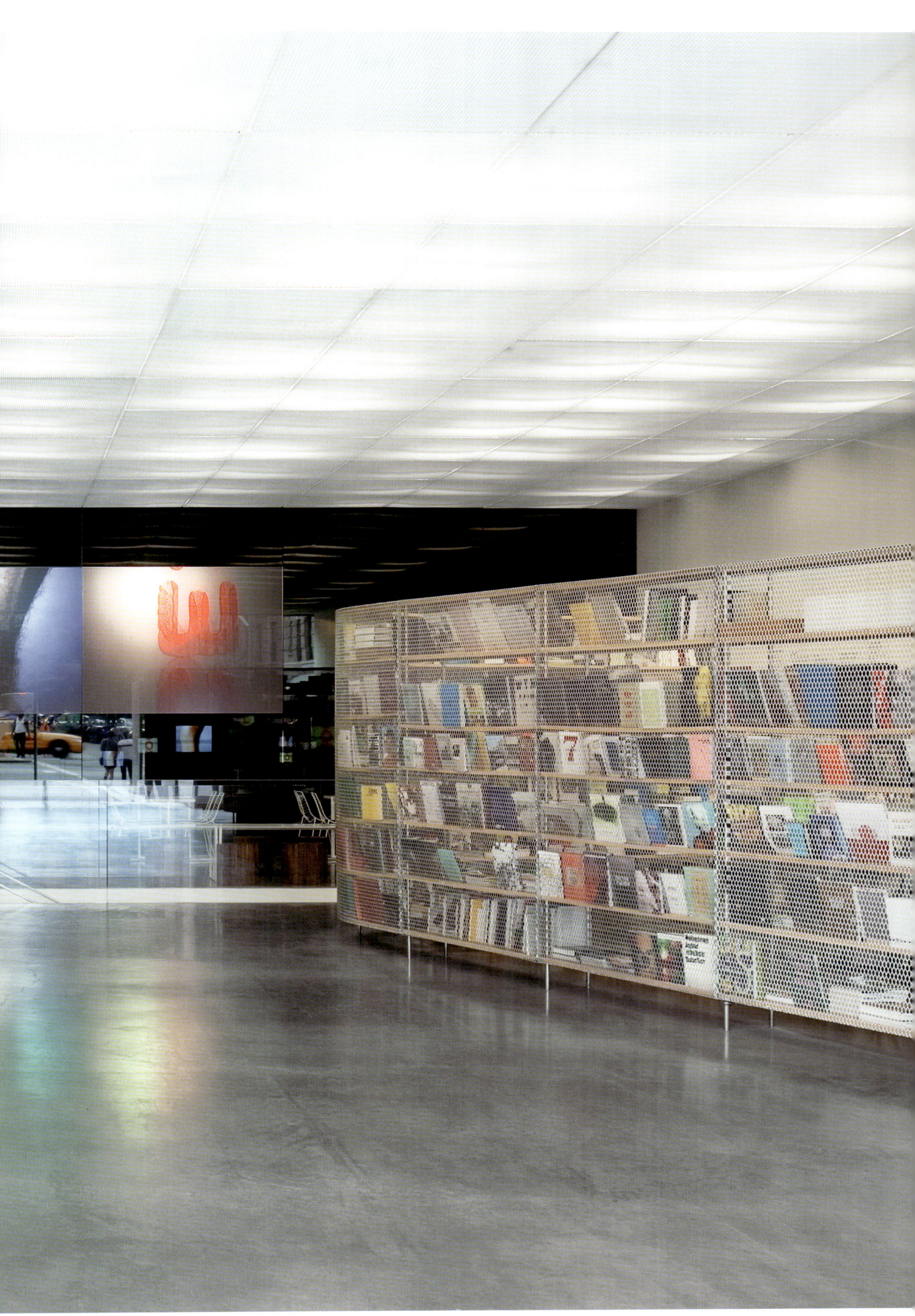

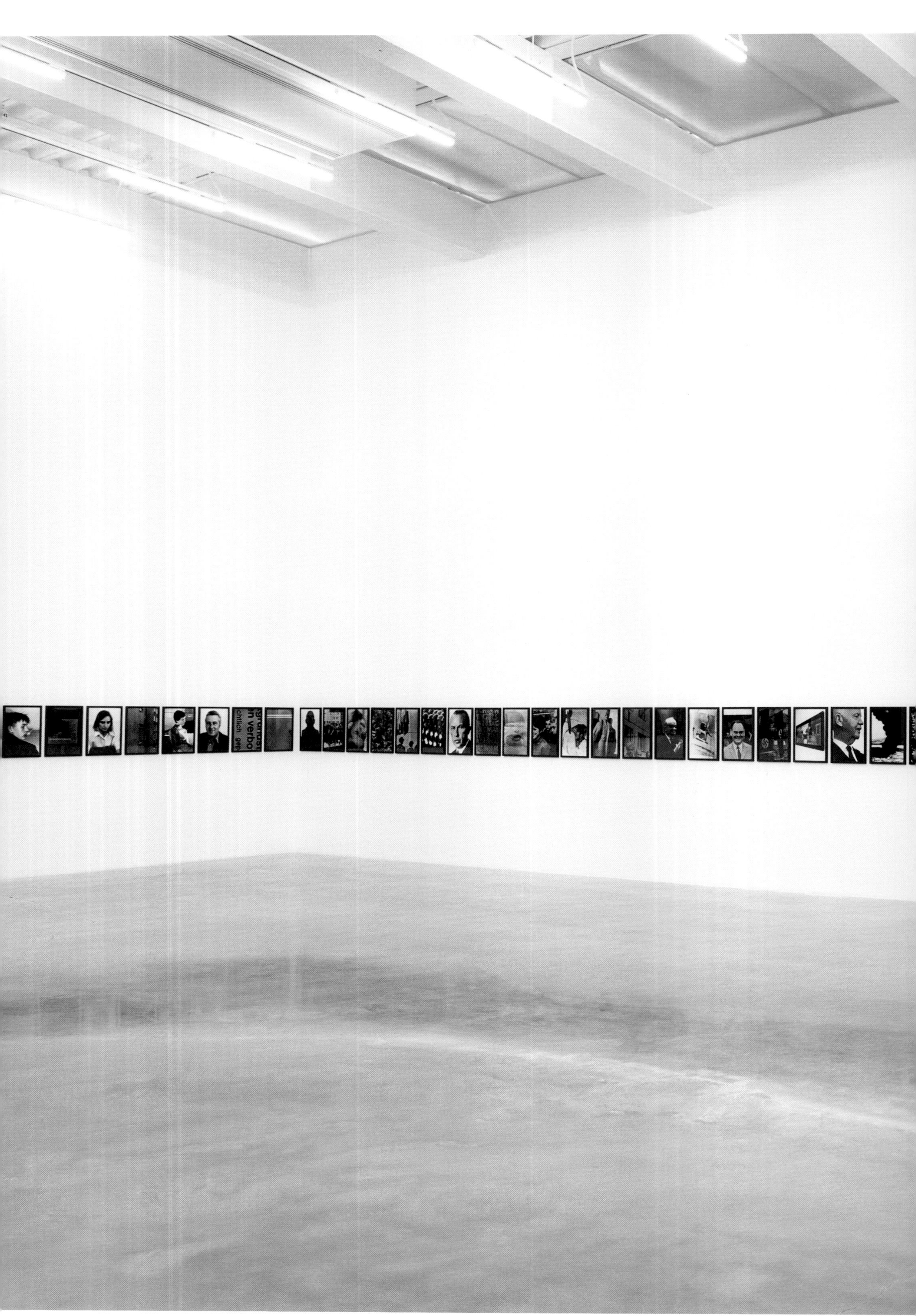

Foreground: work
by Thomas Schütte.
Background: work by
Michael Schmidt

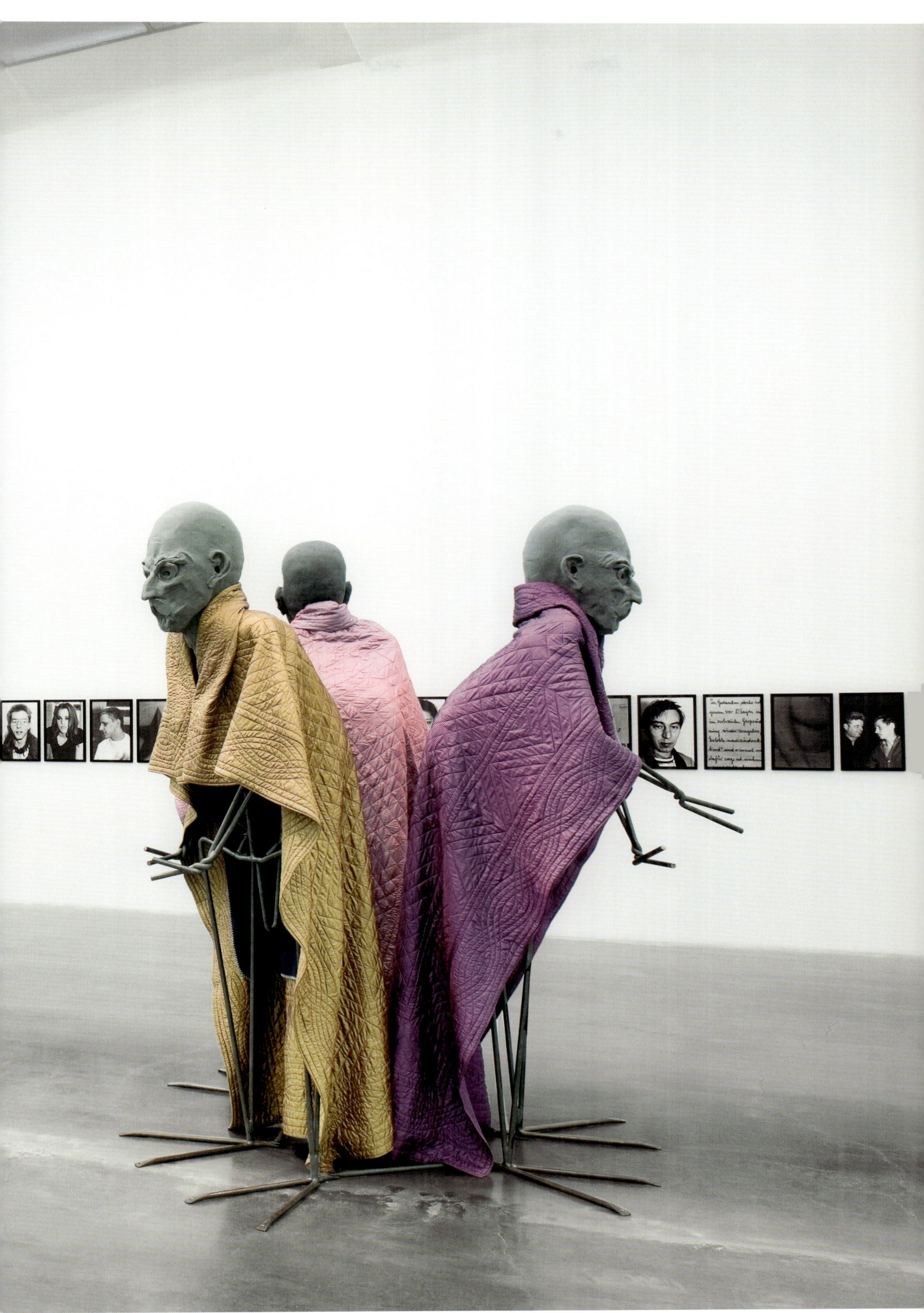

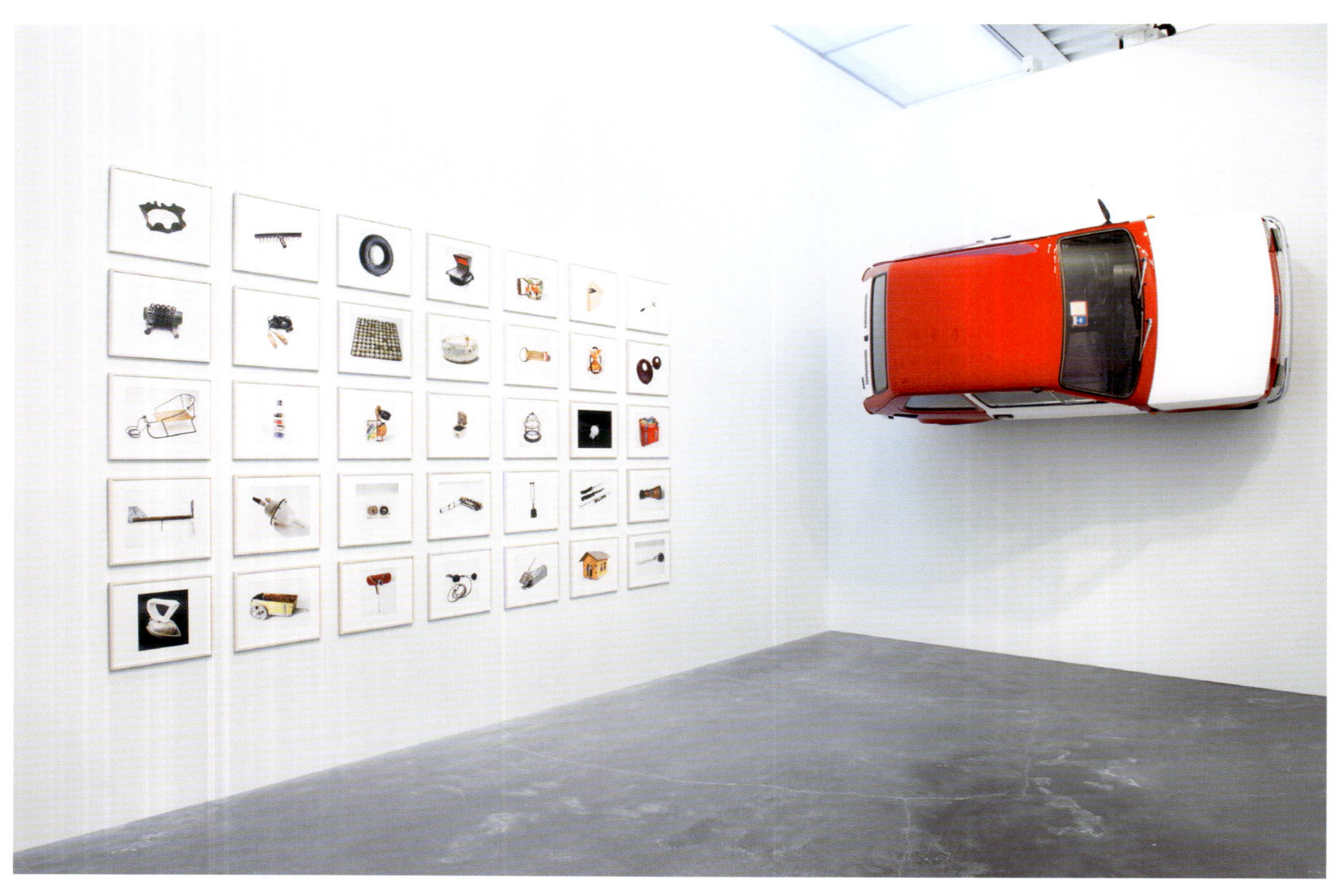

Left to right: works by
Vladimir Arkhipov and
Simon Starling

Museum as Hub: *Steffani Jemison and Jamal Cyrus: Alpha's Bet Is Not Over Yet!*

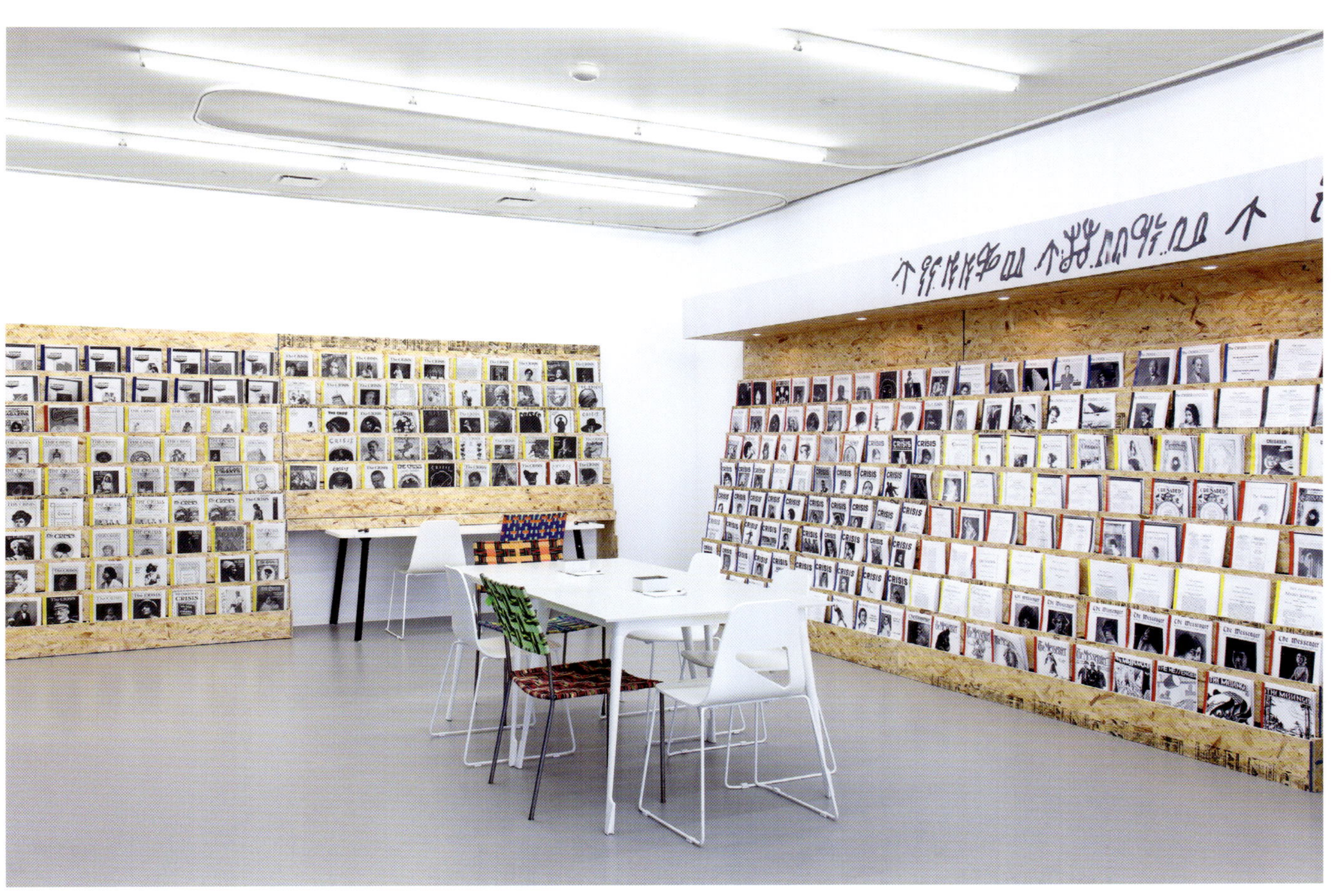

Installation view

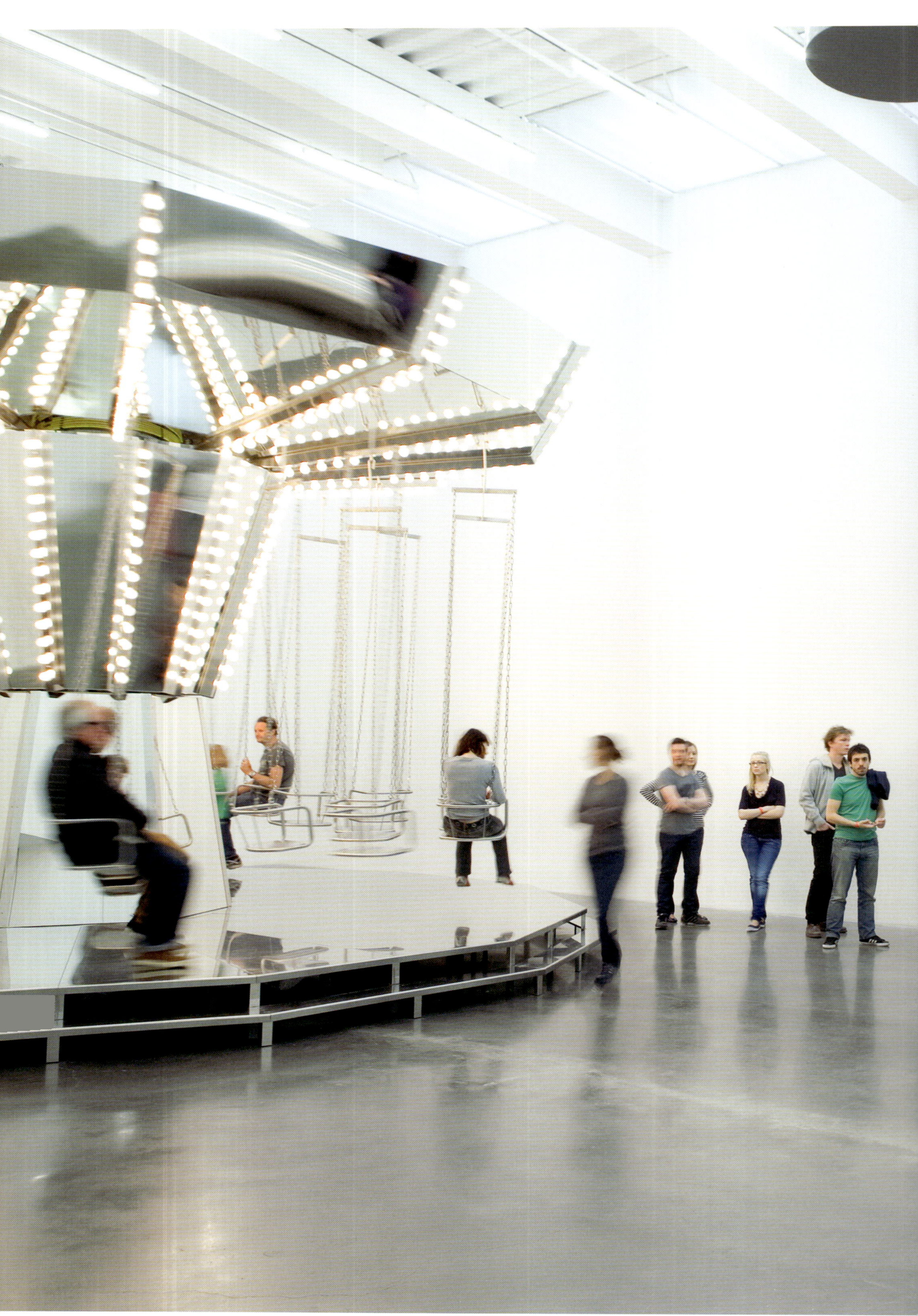

Left to right: Carsten
Höller, *Mirror Carousel*,
2005; *Singing Canaries
Mobile*, 2009; and
Untitled (Slide), 2011

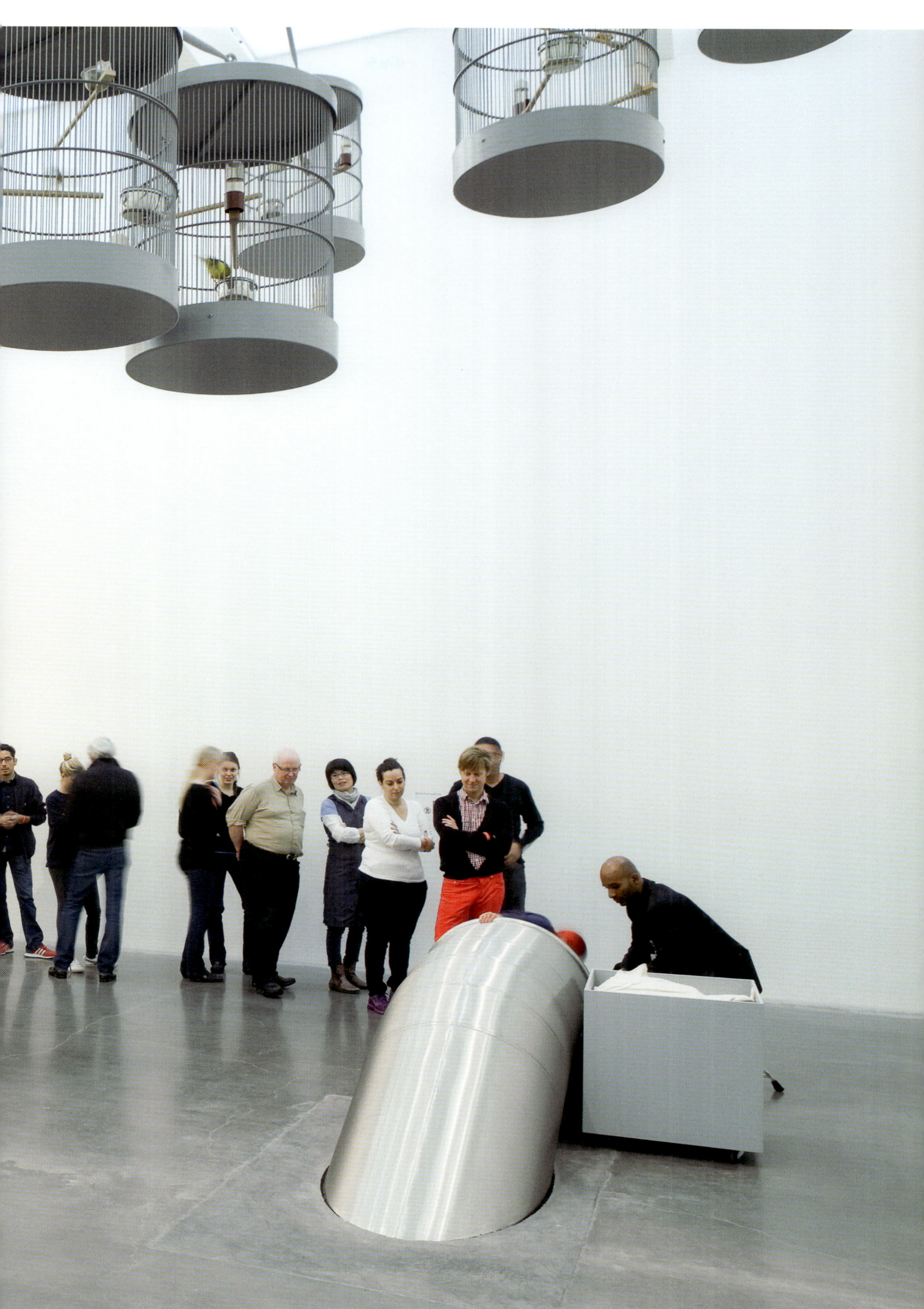

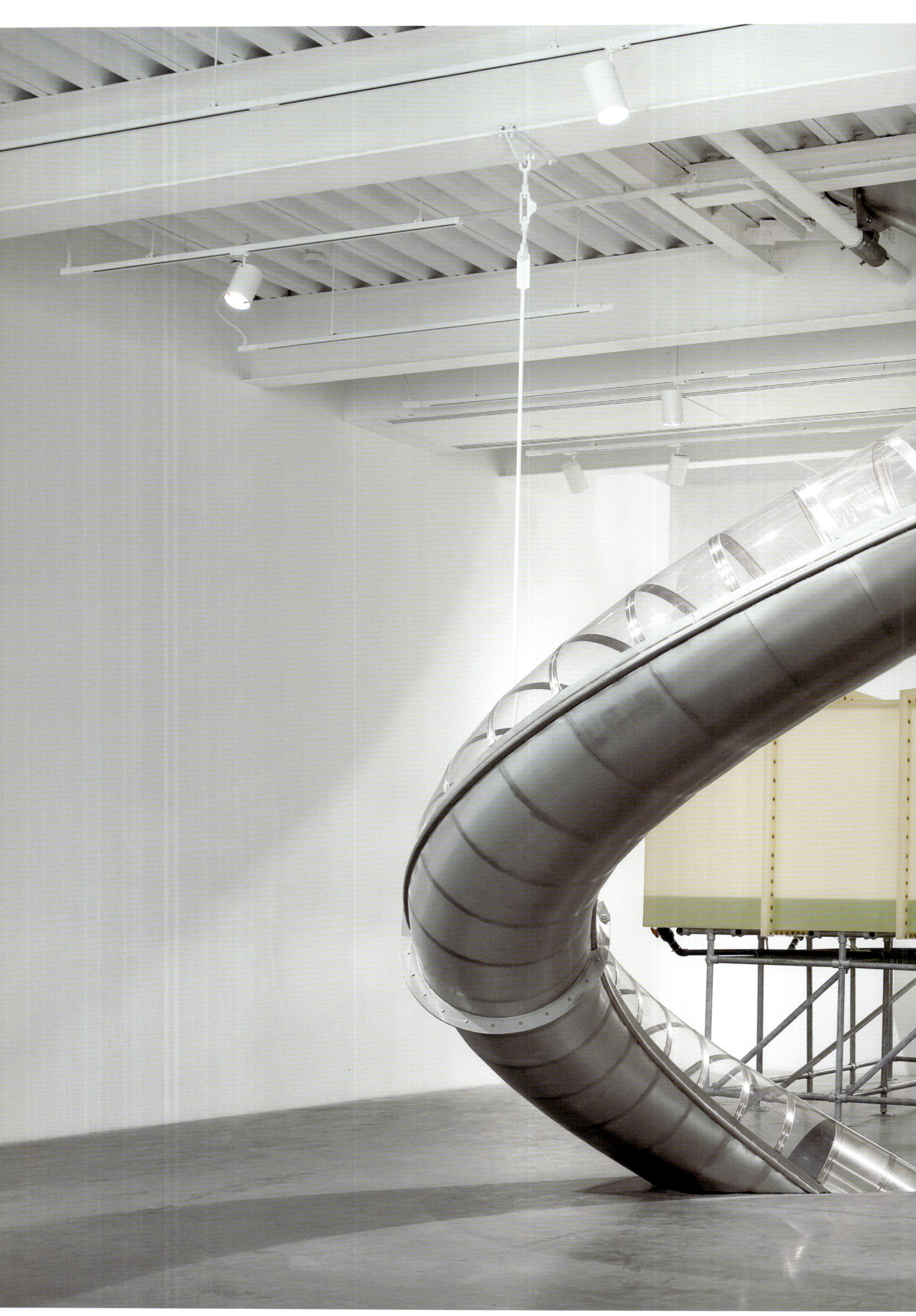

Left to right: Carsten
Höller, *Untitled (Slide)*,
2011, and *Giant Psycho
Tank*, 1999

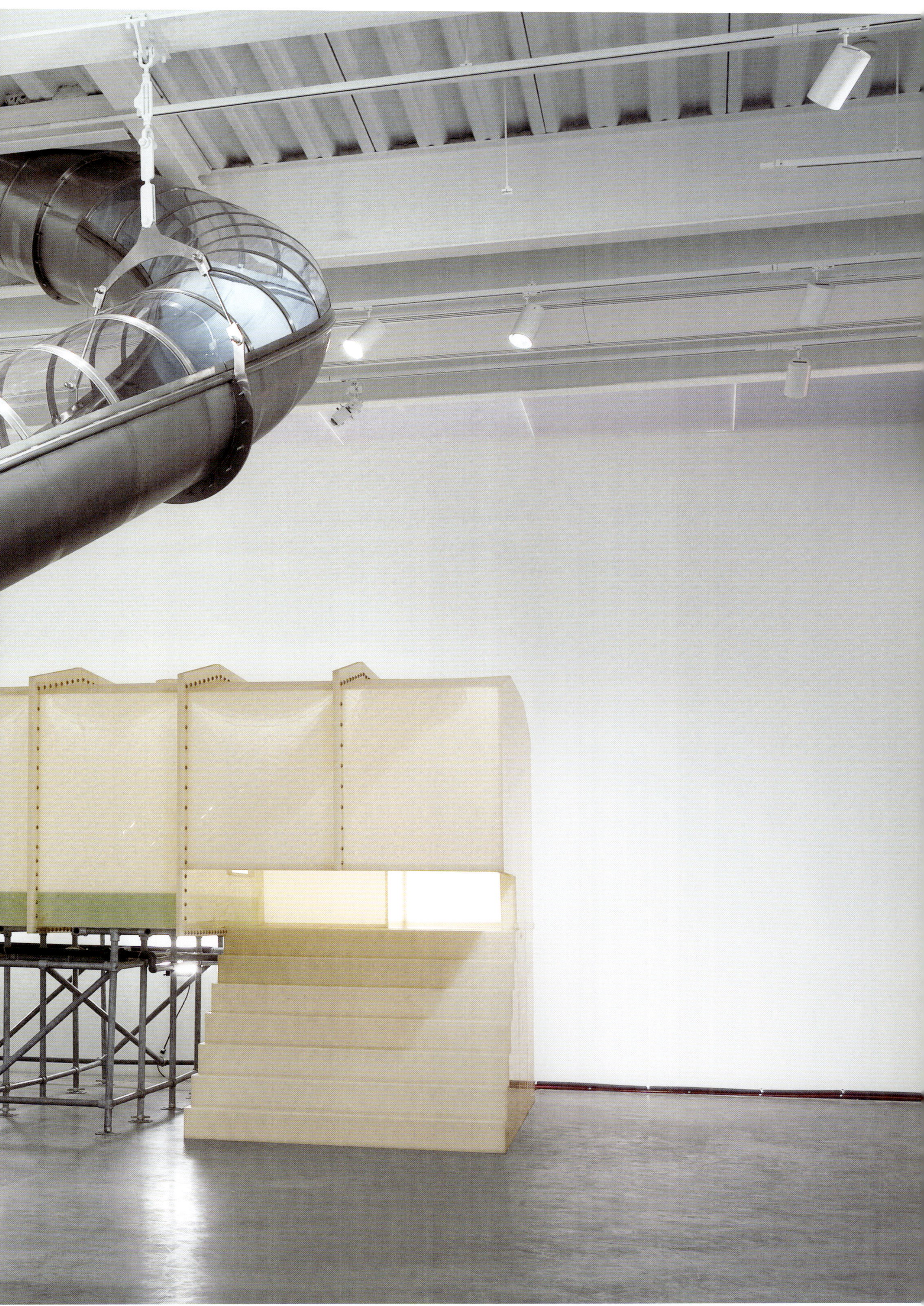

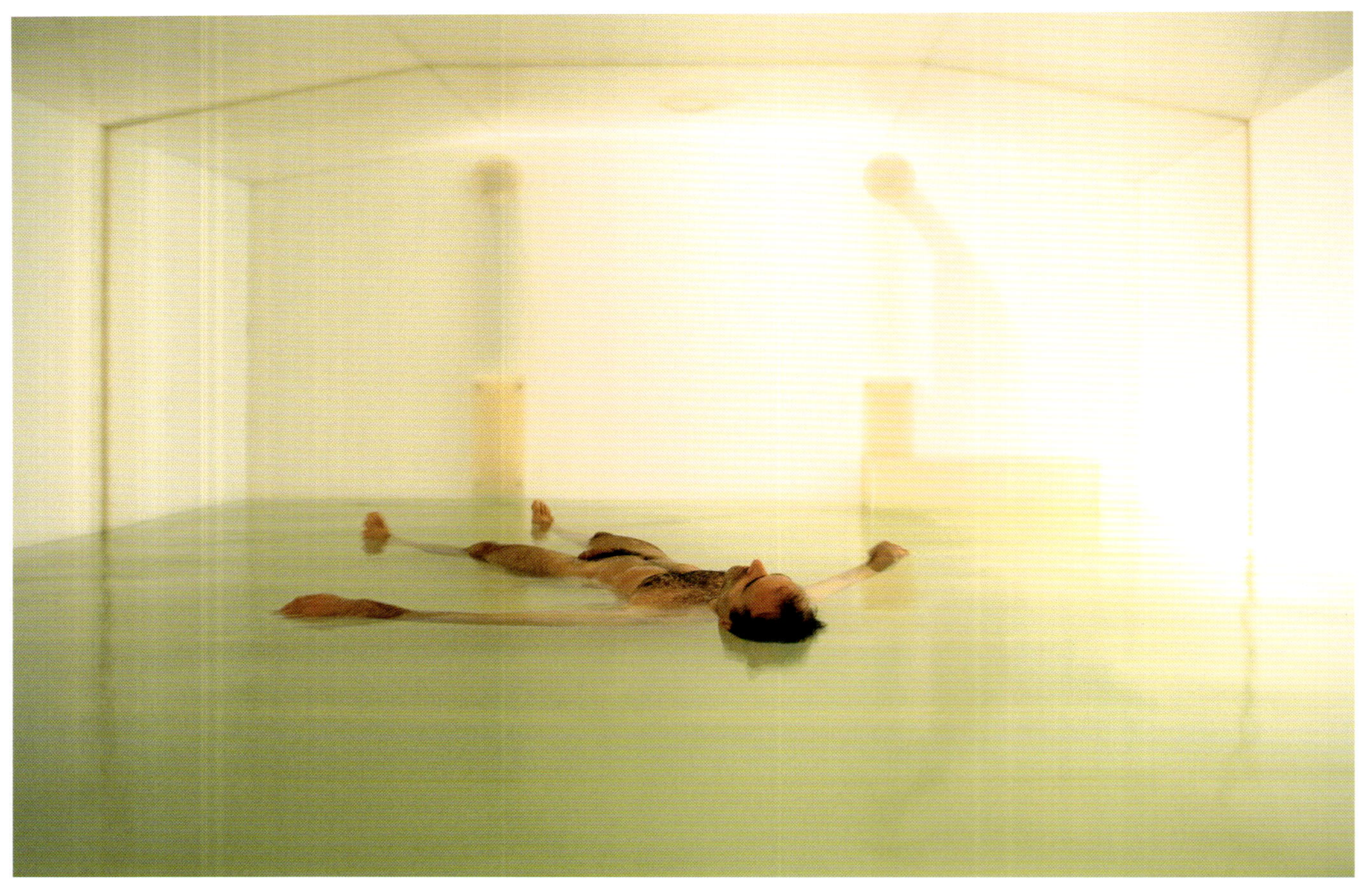

Carsten Höller,
Giant Psycho Tank, 1999
(interior)

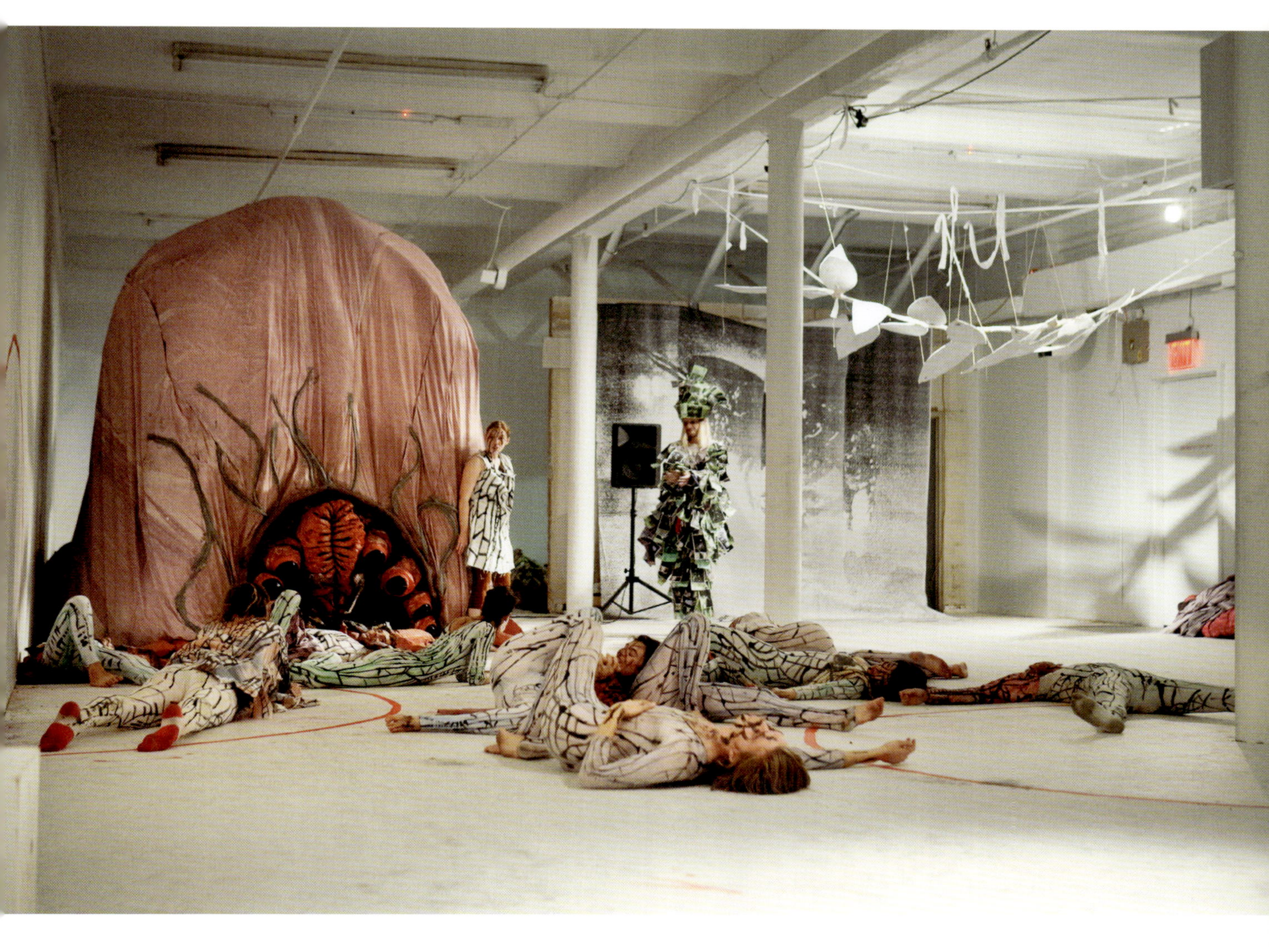

Installation view

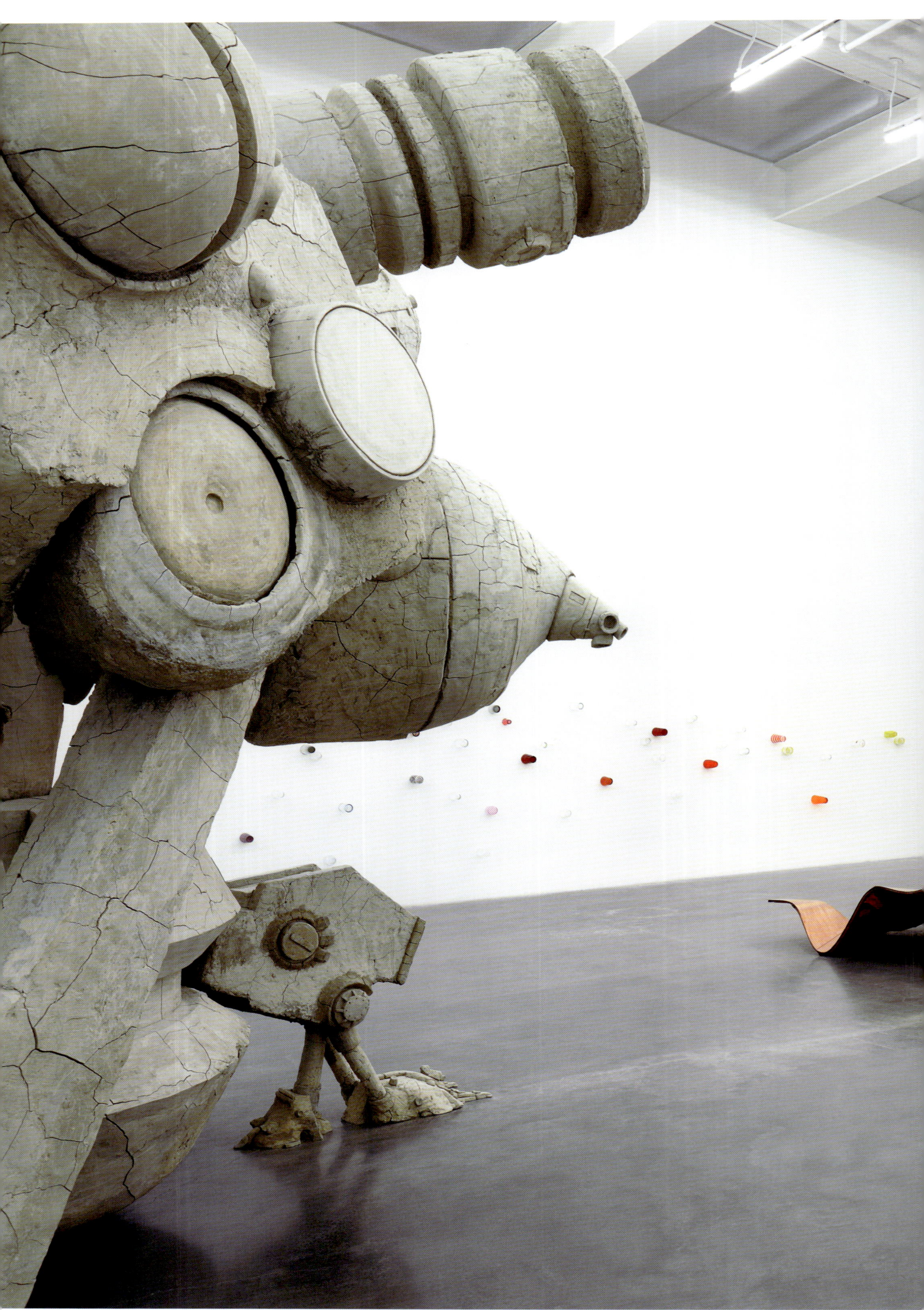

Left to right: works by
Adrián Villar Rojas,
Amalia Pica, and Danh Võ

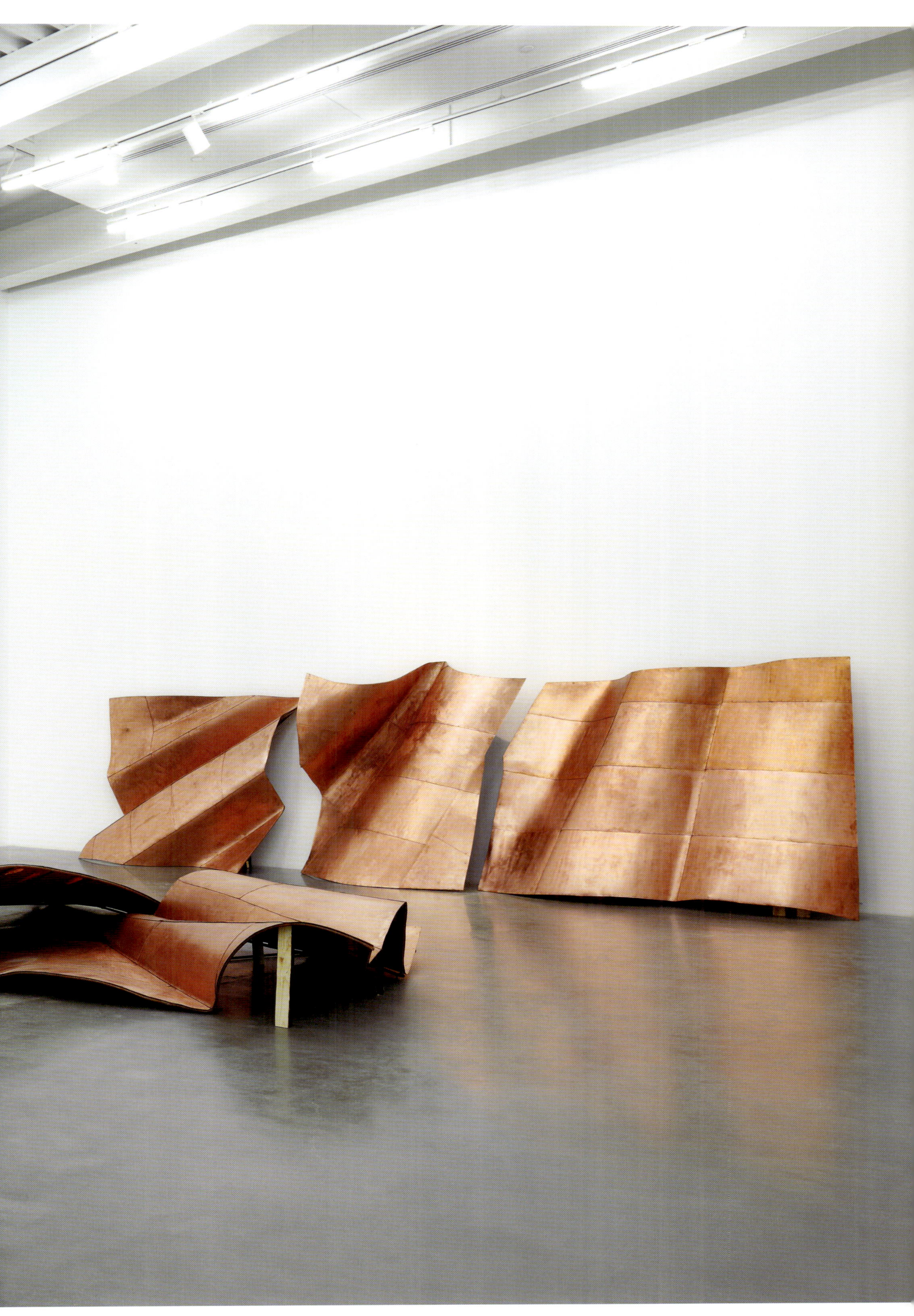

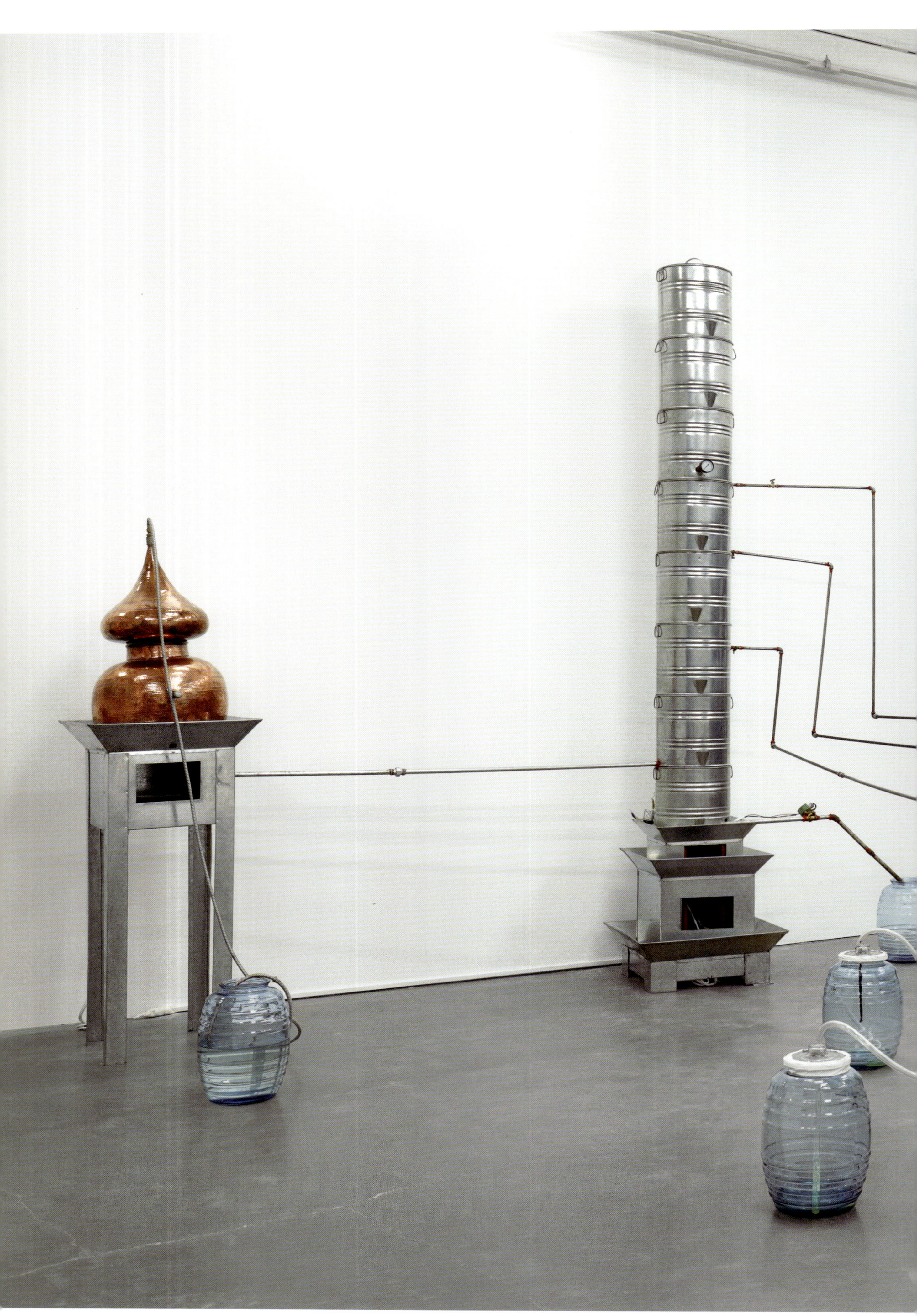

Left to right: works
by José Antonio Vega
Macotela and Kemang Wa
Lehulere

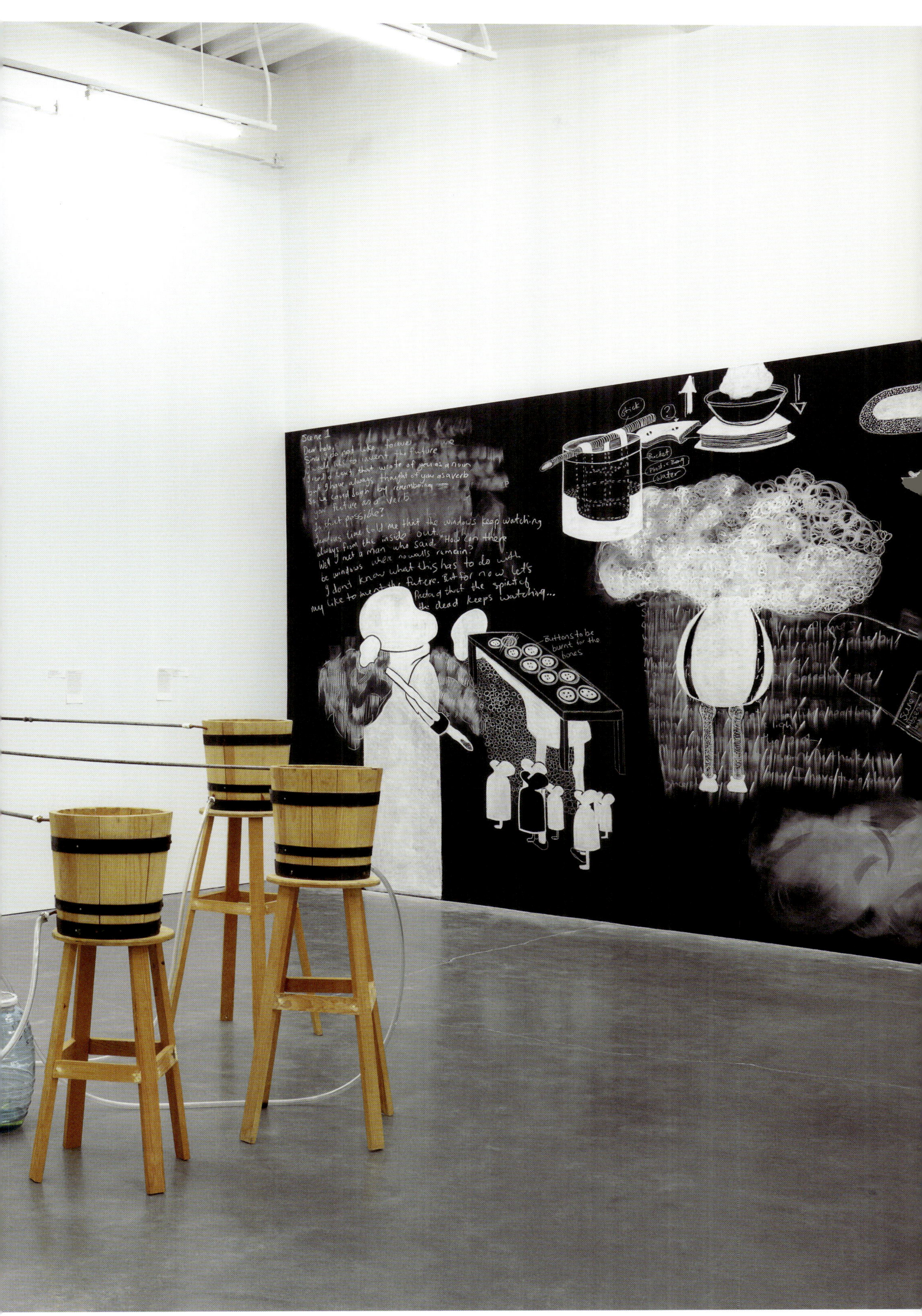

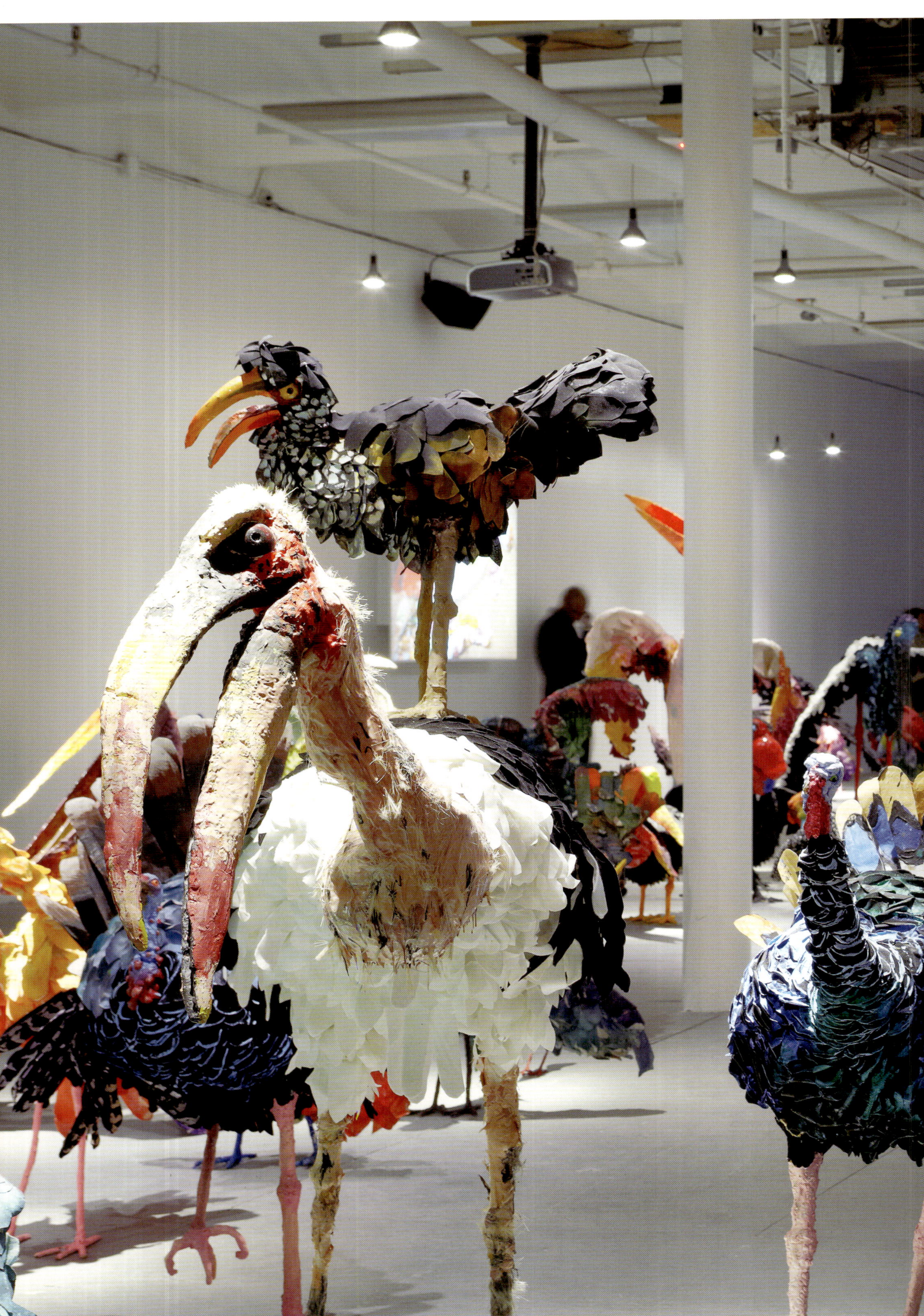

Installation view

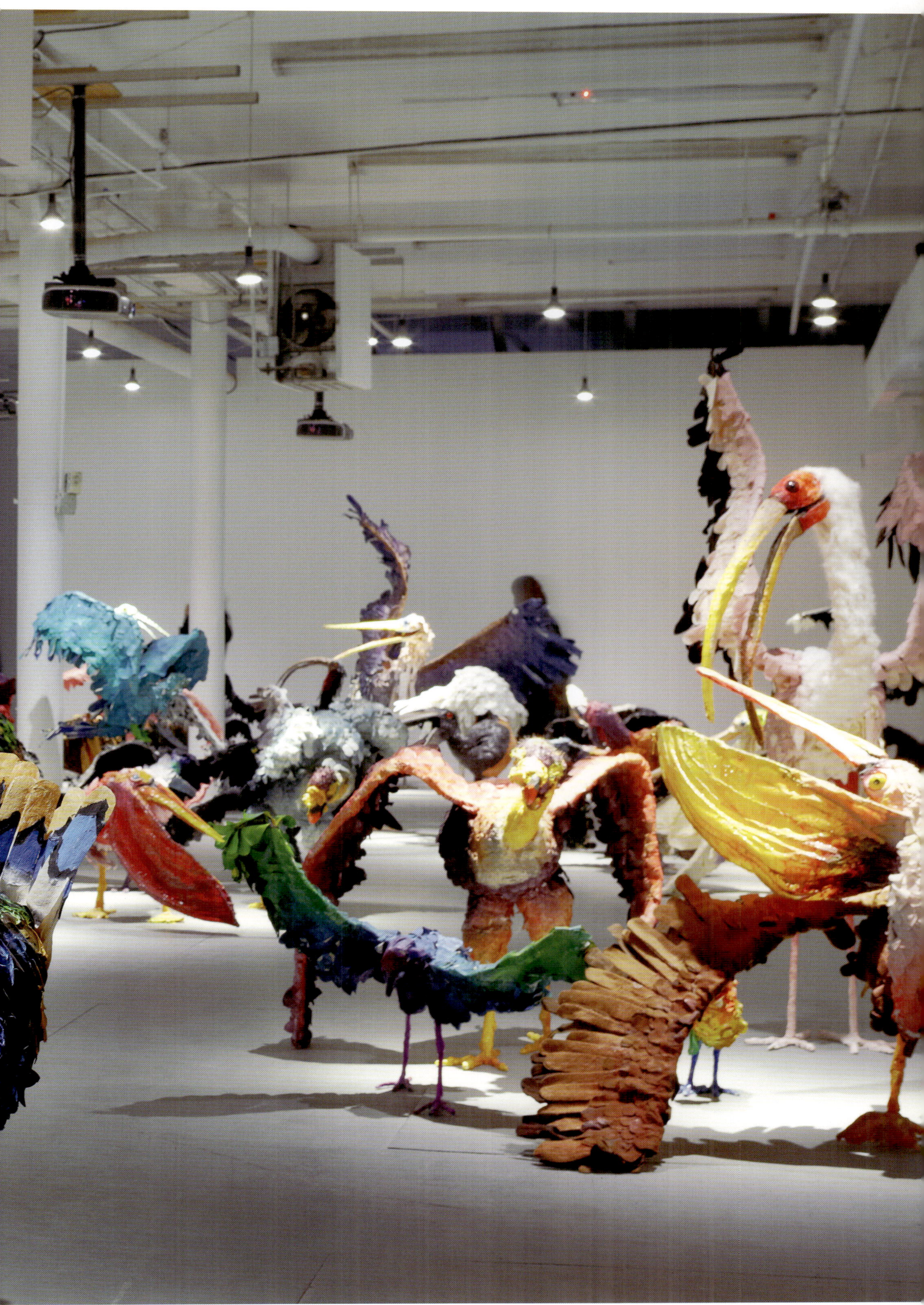

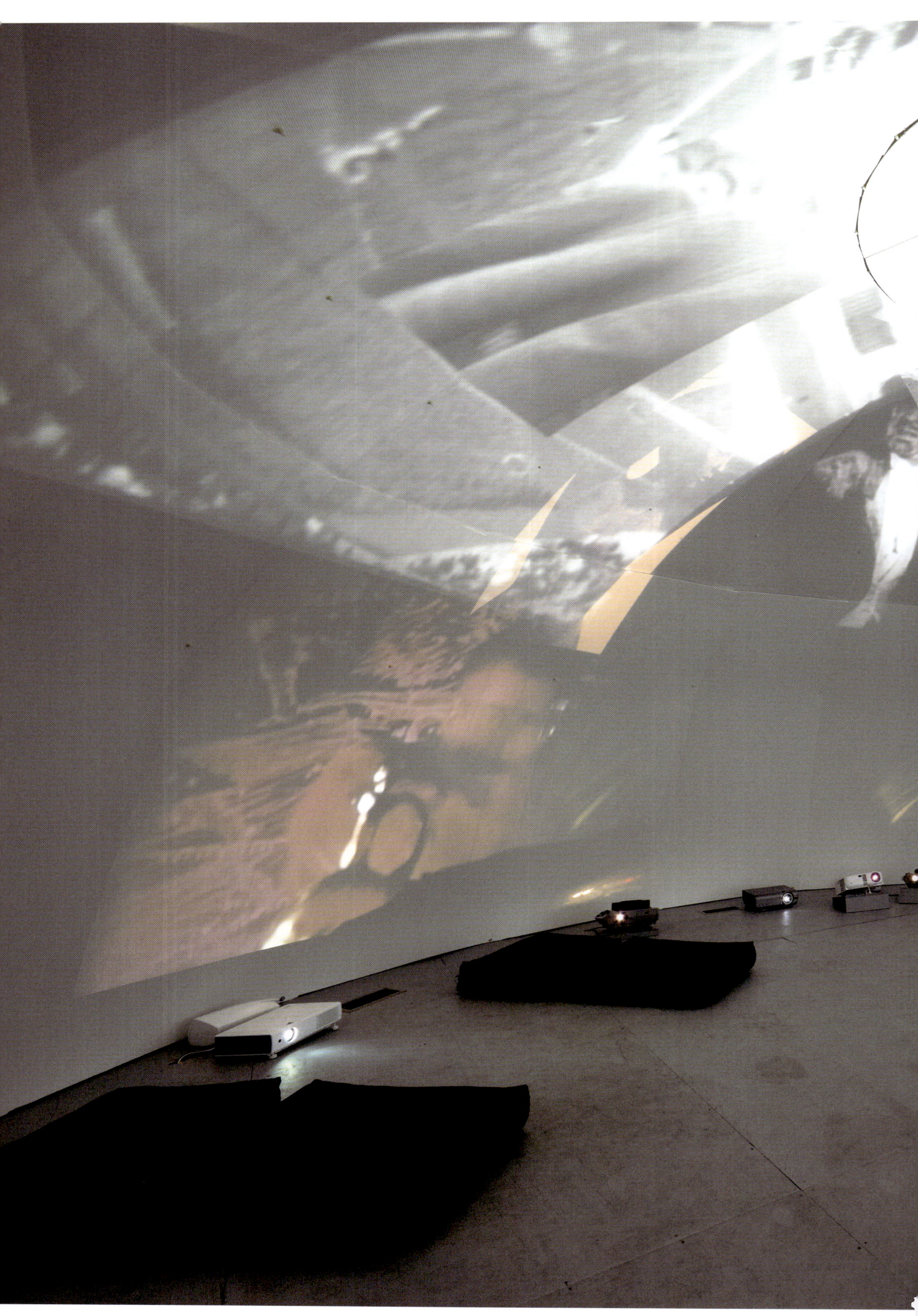

Stan VanDerBeek,
Movie-Drome, 1963–66/2012
(interior)

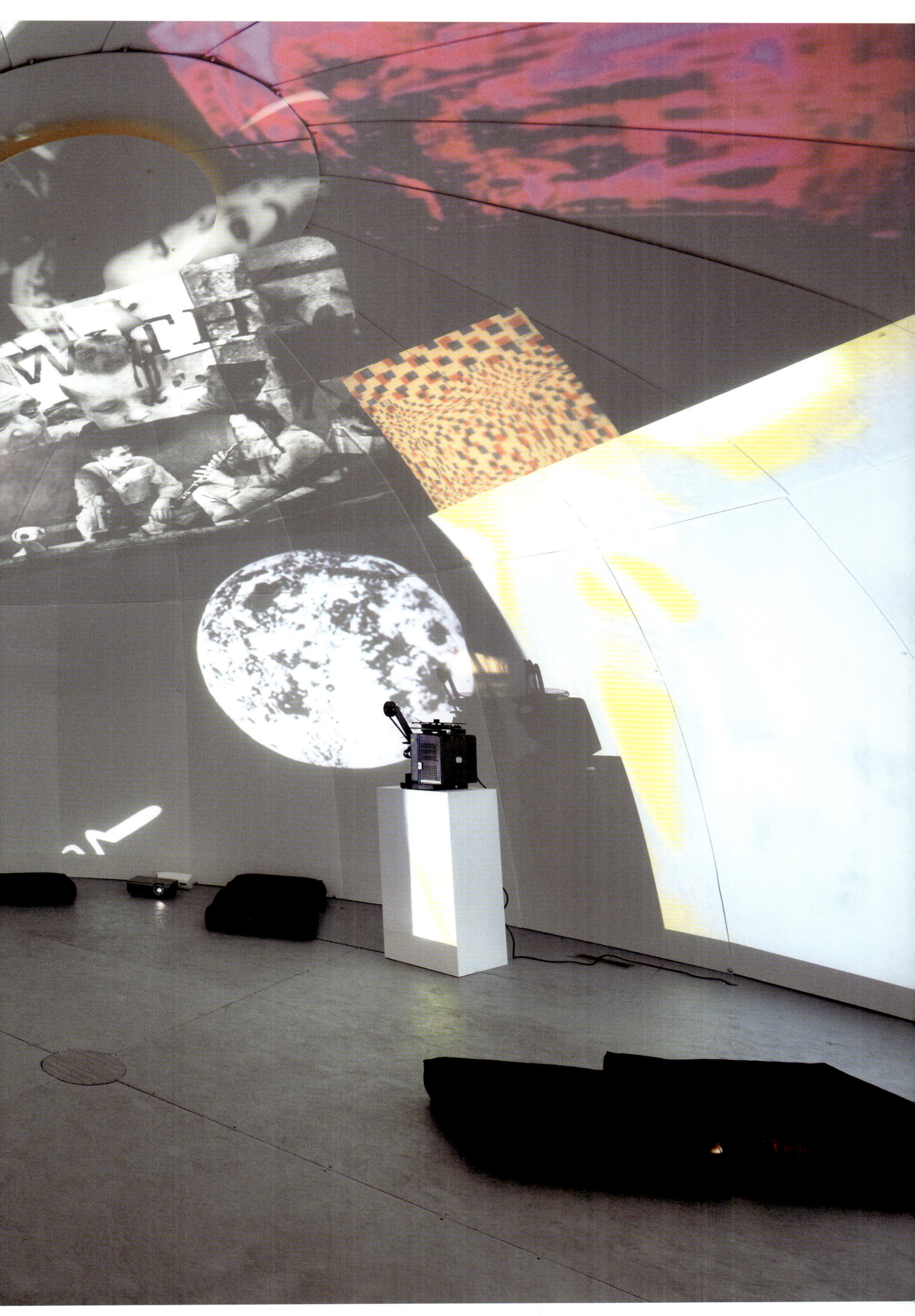

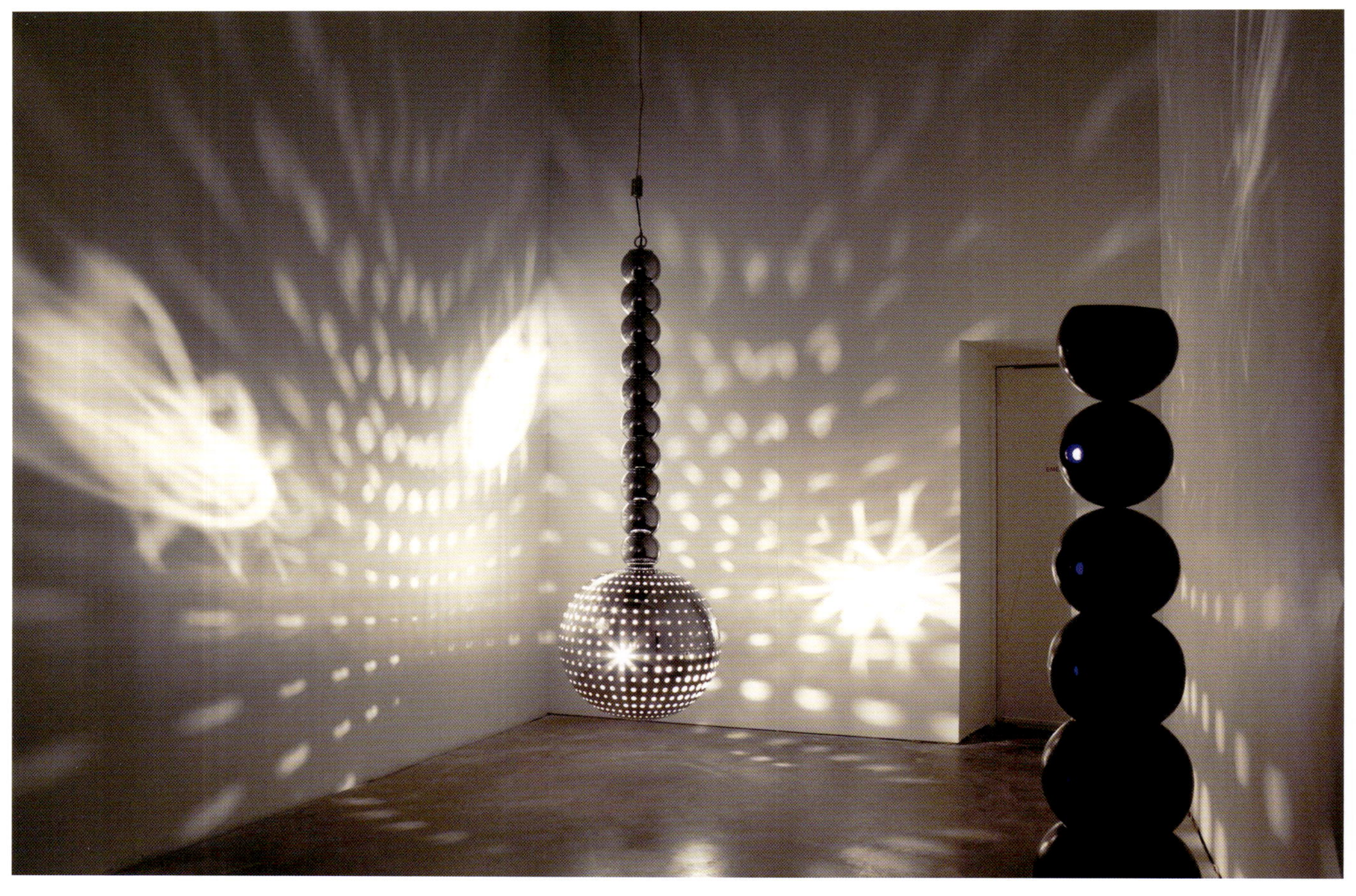

Left to right: Otto Piene,
Hängende Lichtkugel, 1972,
and *Electric Anaconda*,
1965

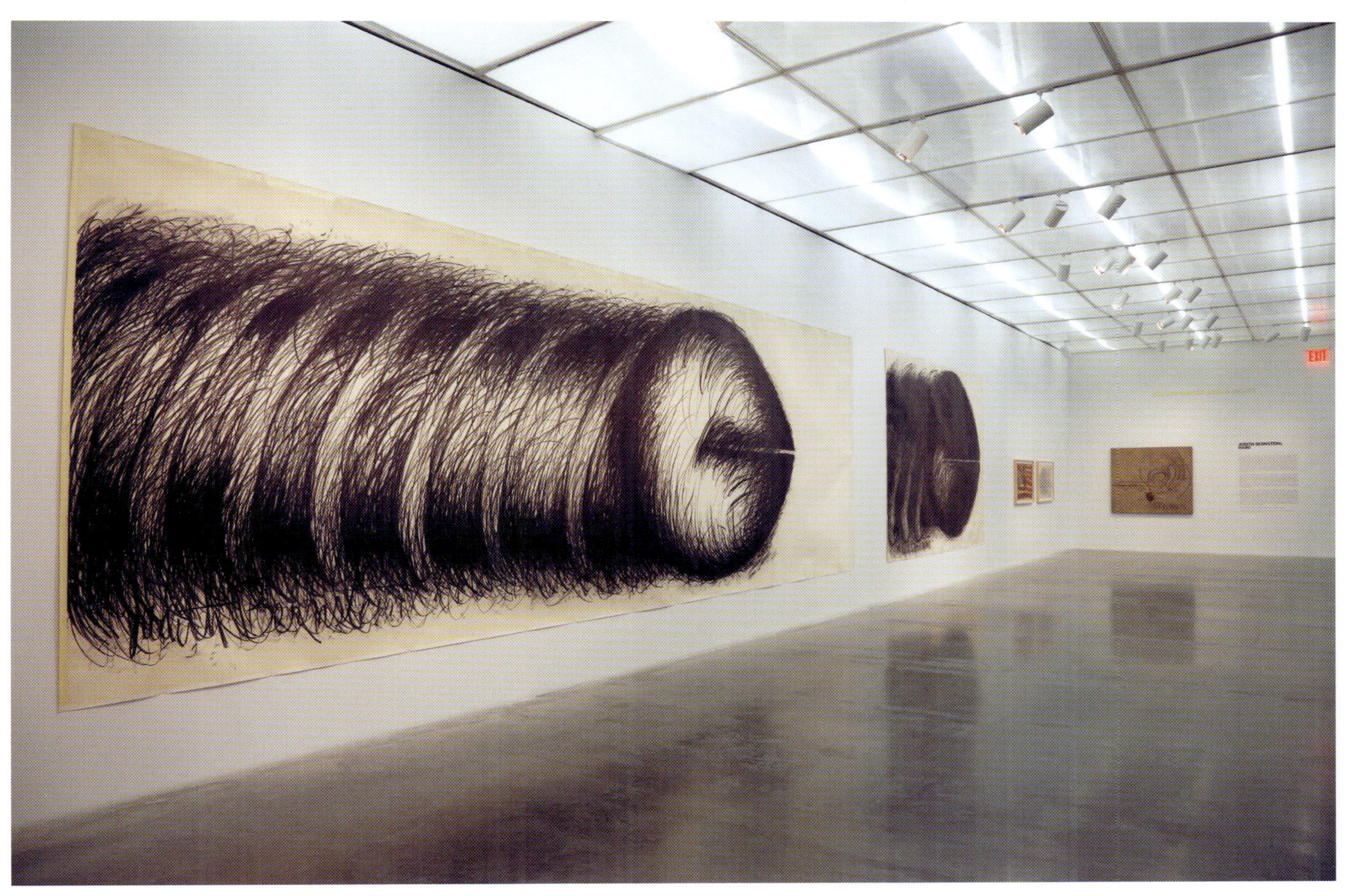

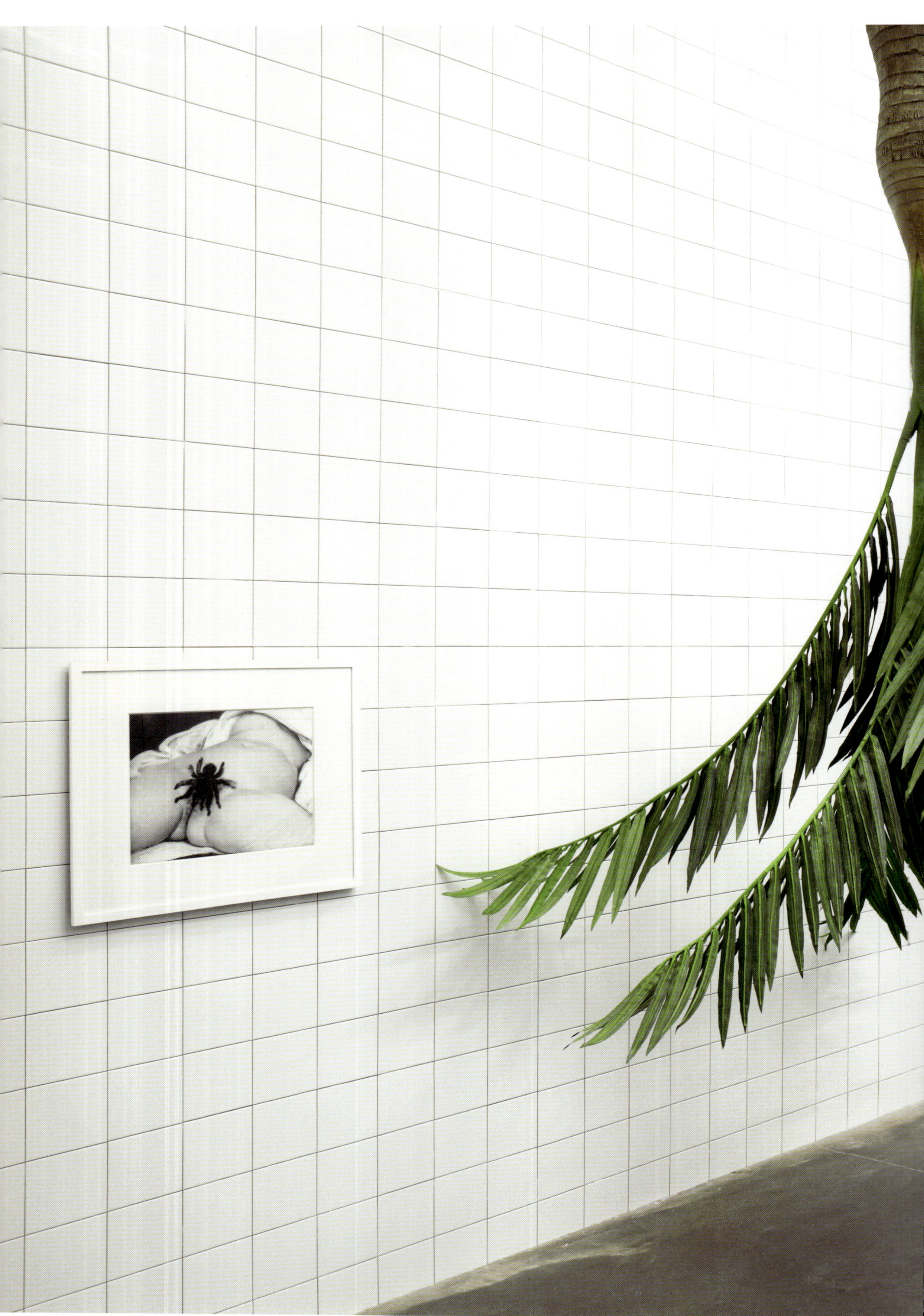

Left to right: Rosemarie
Trockel, *Replace Me*, 2011;
Untitled, 2012; and *Made
in China*, 2012, installed
in *Ceramic Room*, 2012

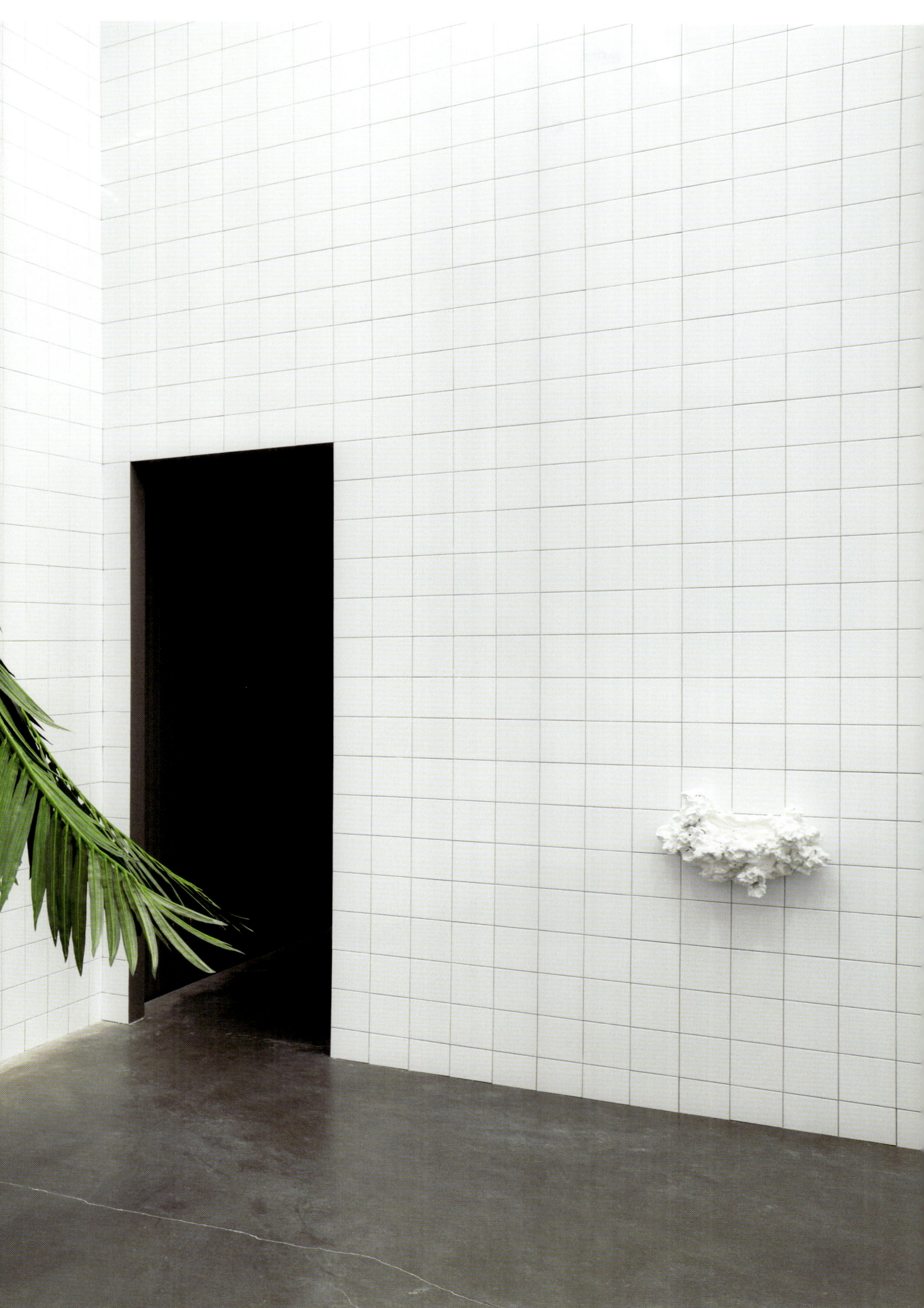

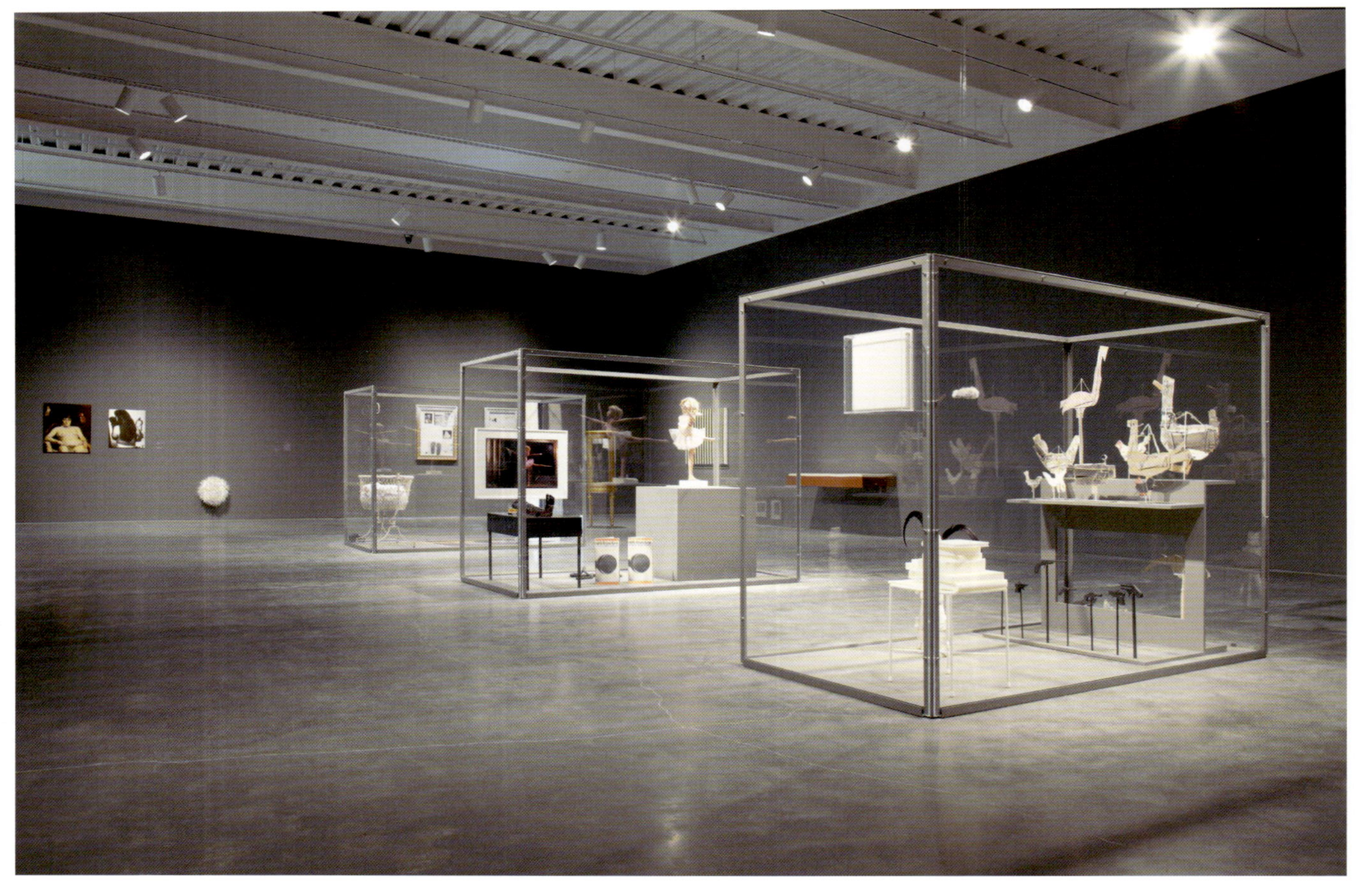

Installation view

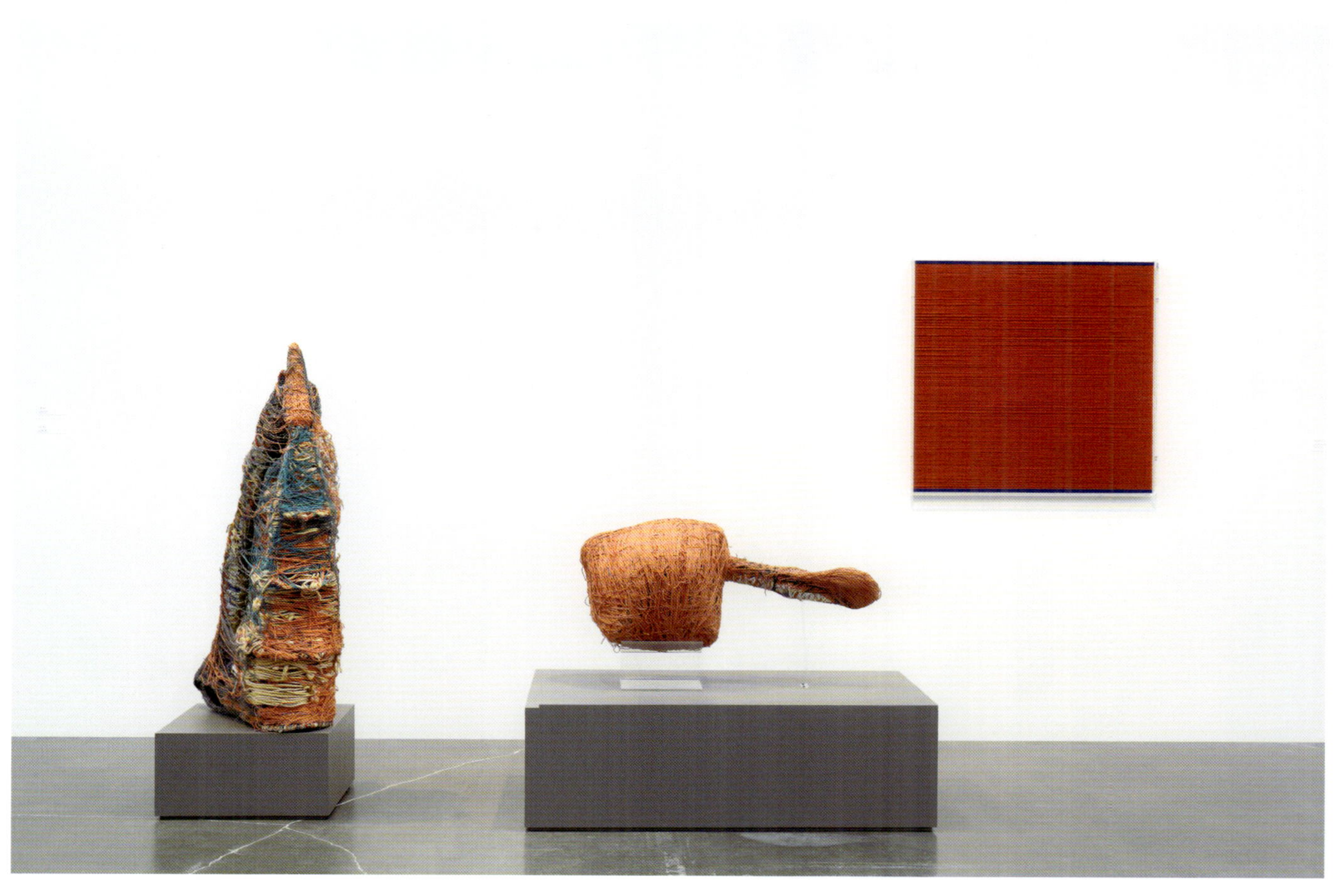

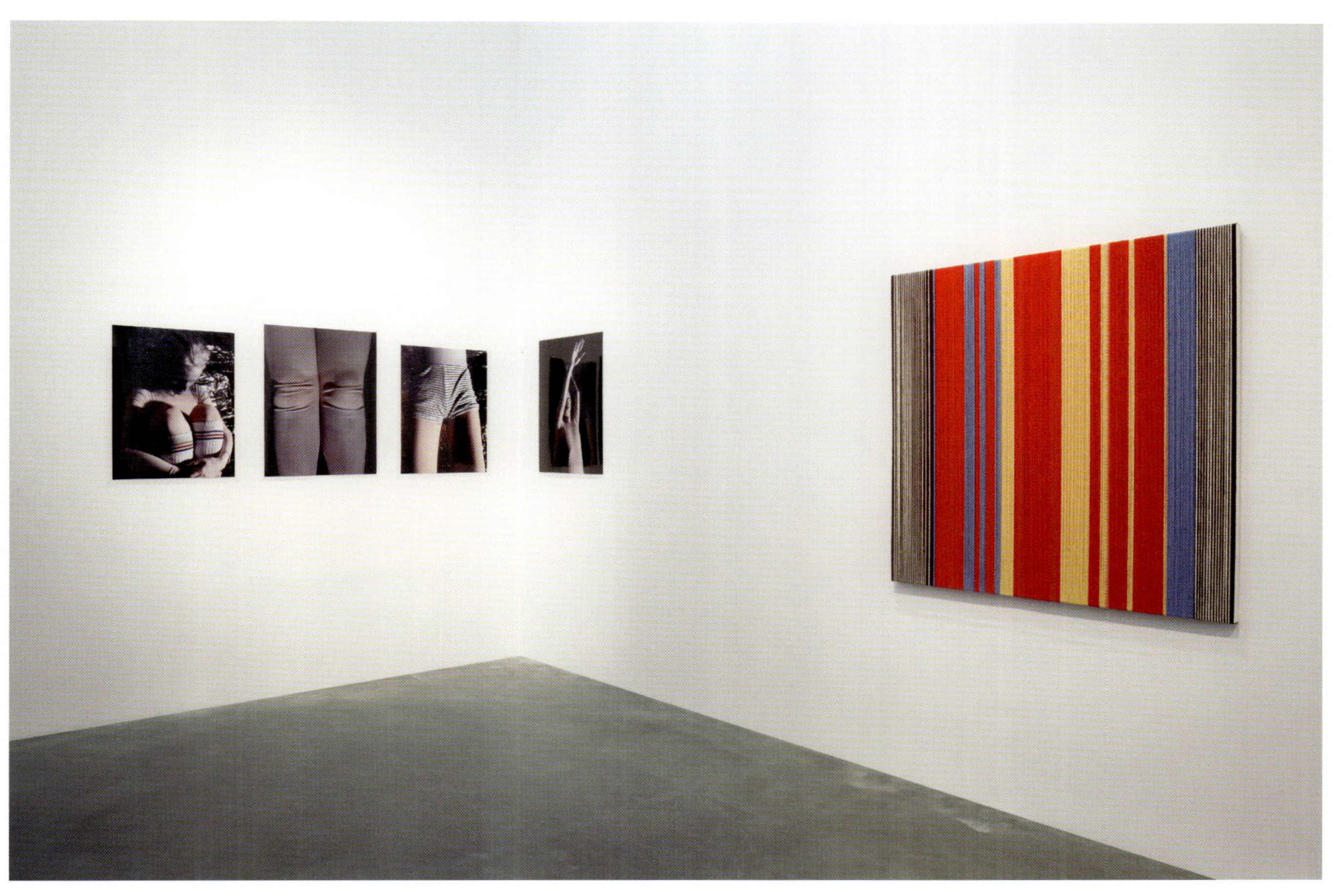

(top) Left to right: works by Judith Scott and Rosemarie Trockel

(bottom) Left to right: Rosemarie Trockel, *From a French Magazine*, 2005, and *Dress – Stage 2*, 2012

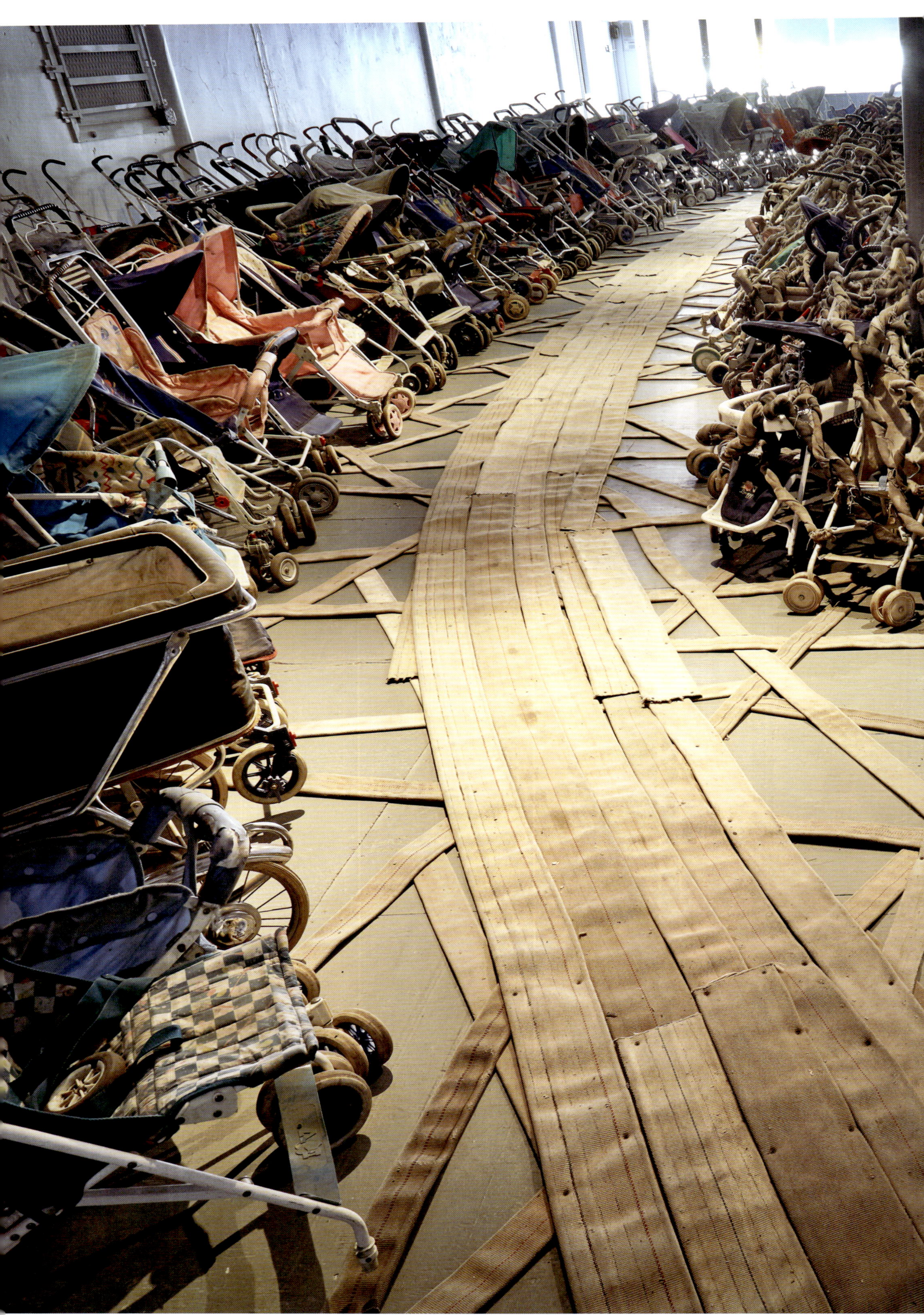

Nari Ward,
Amazing Grace, 1993

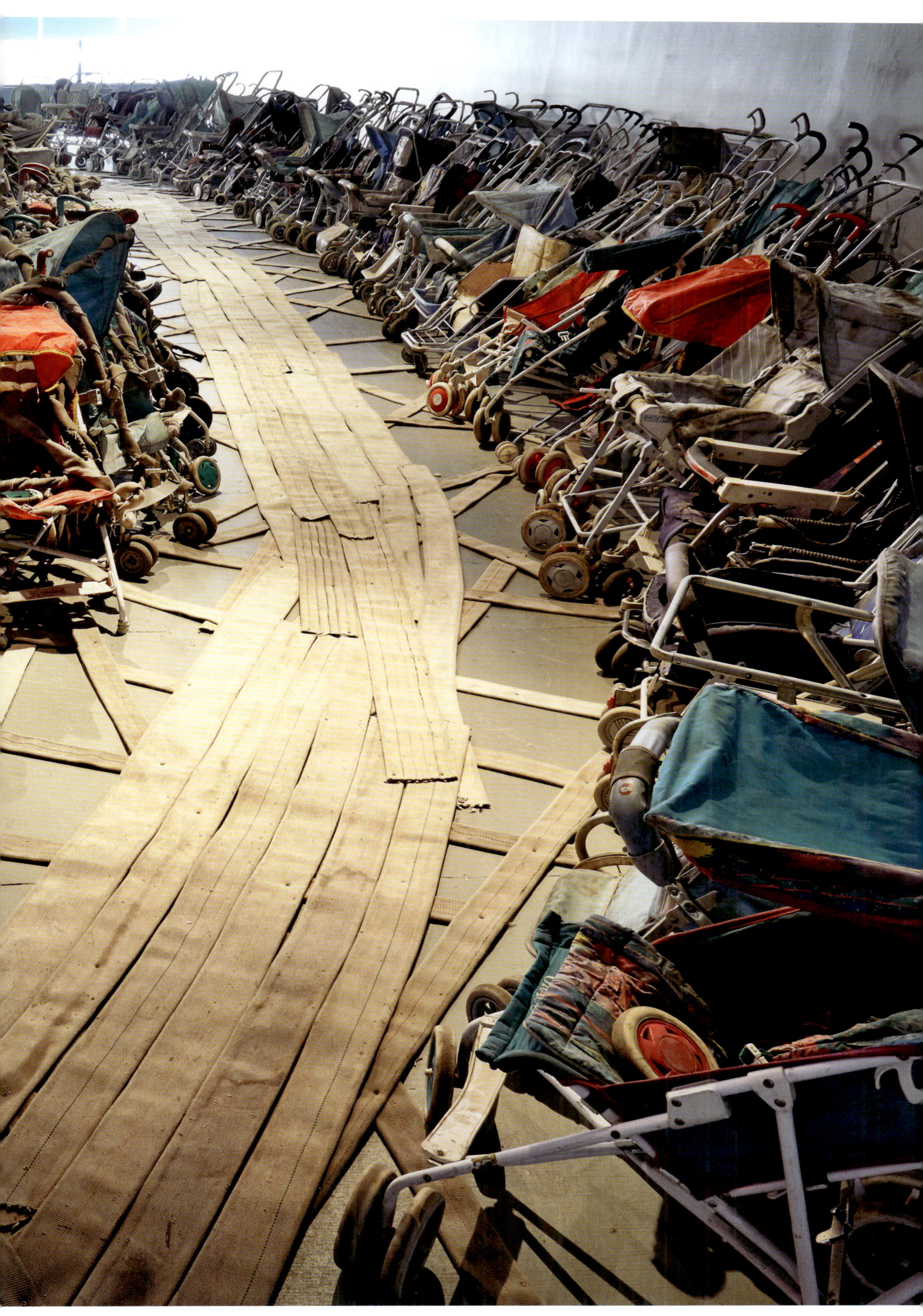

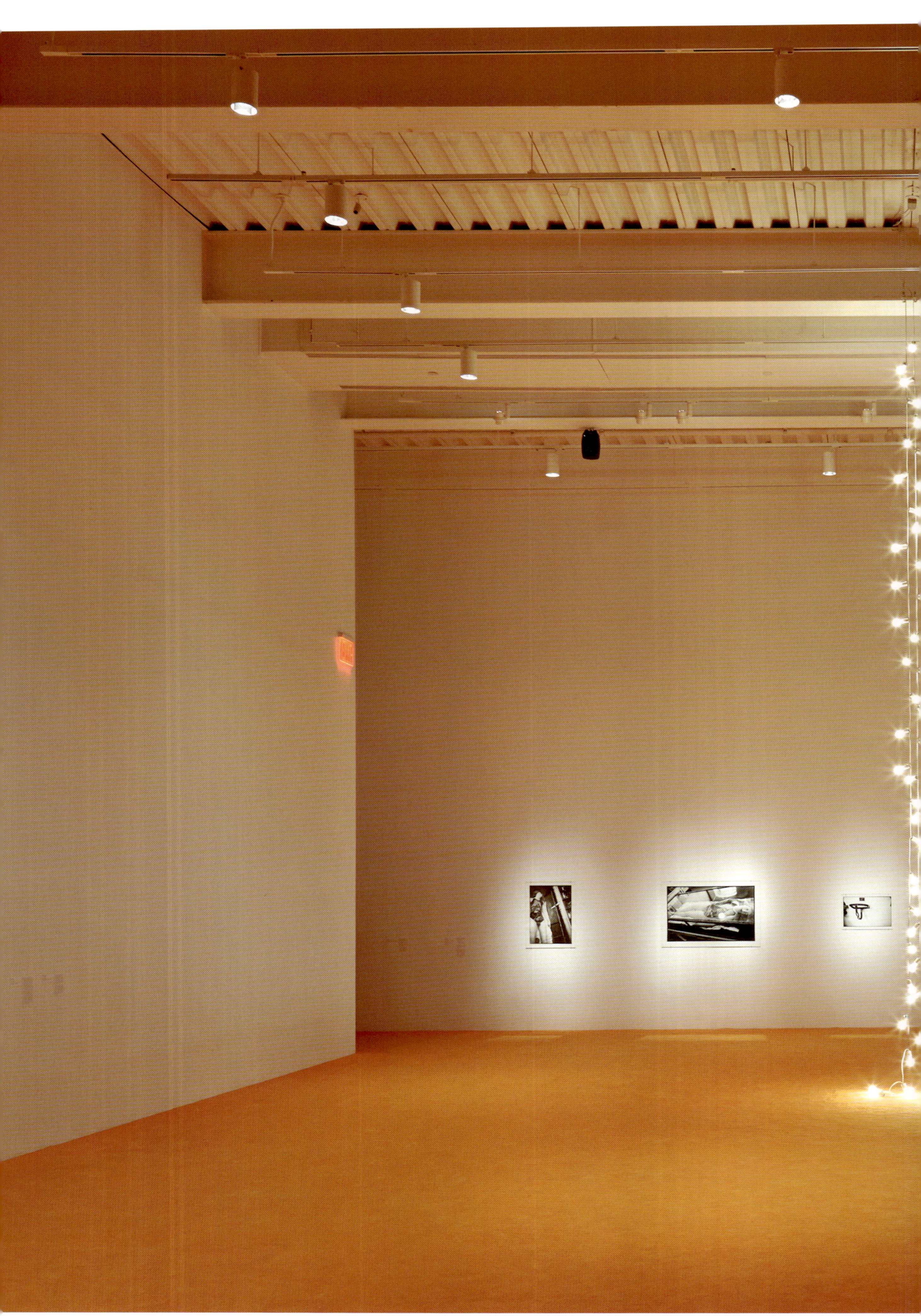

Foreground to
background: works by
Rudolf Stingel (carpet),
Félix González-Torres,
and Zoe Leonard

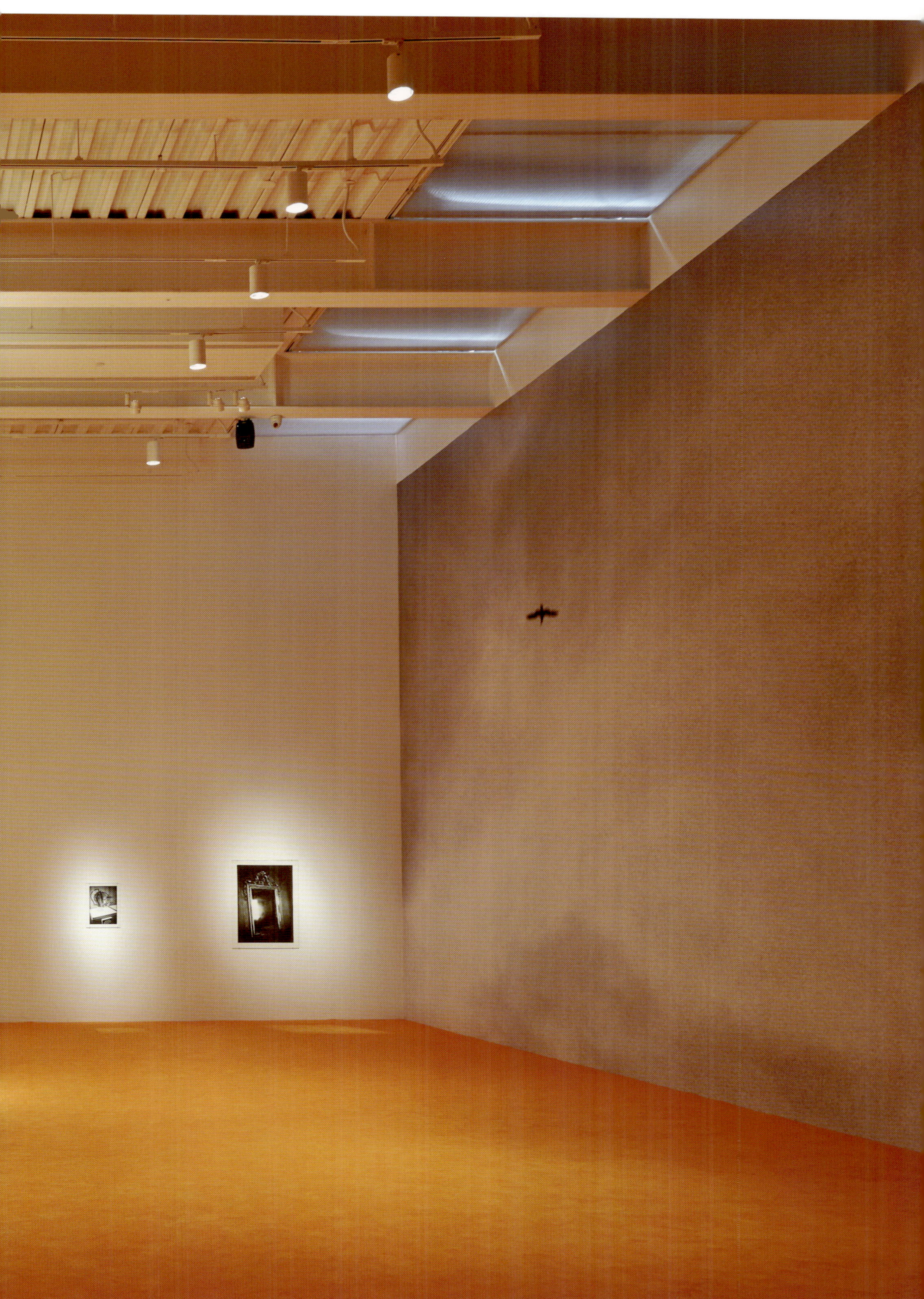

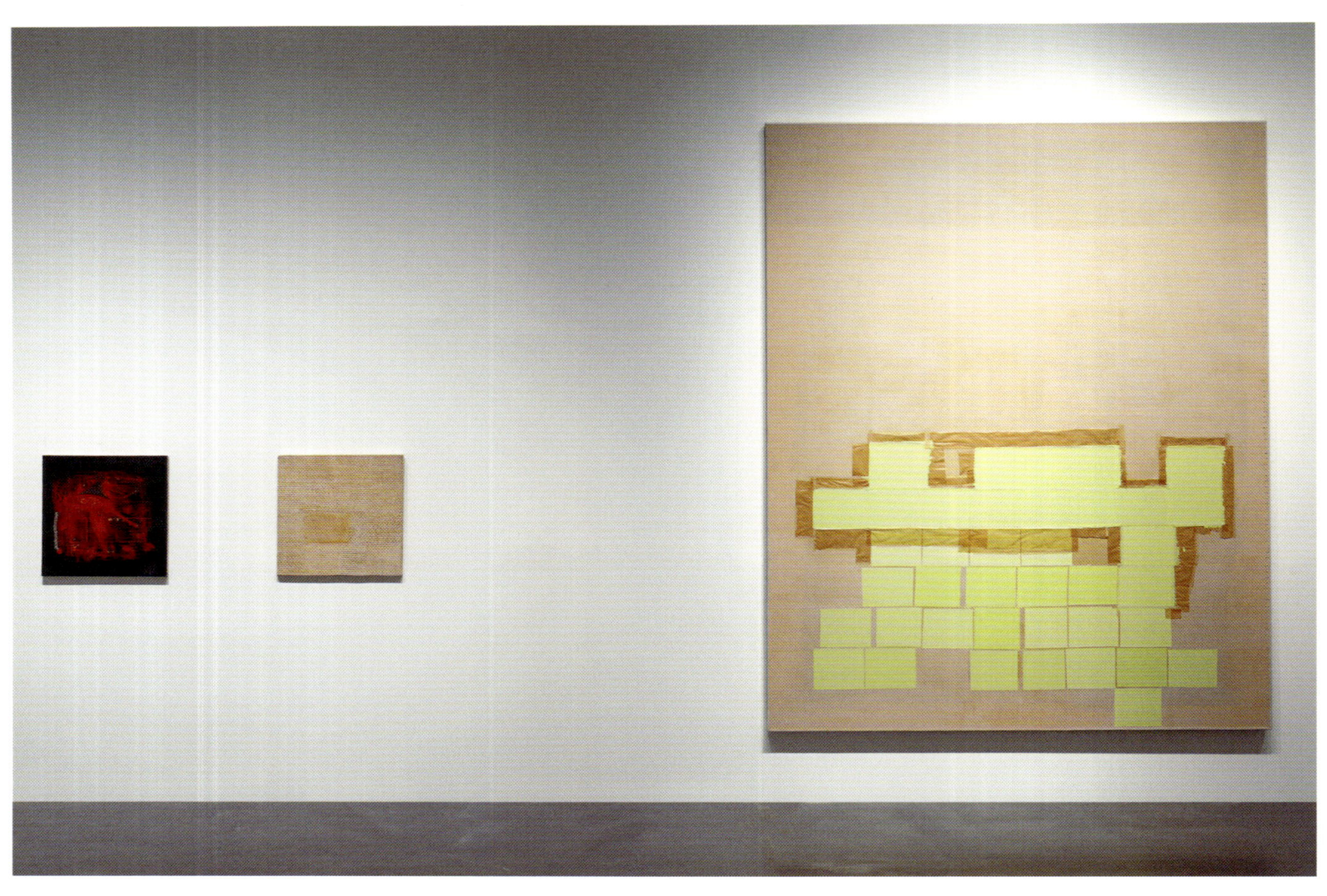

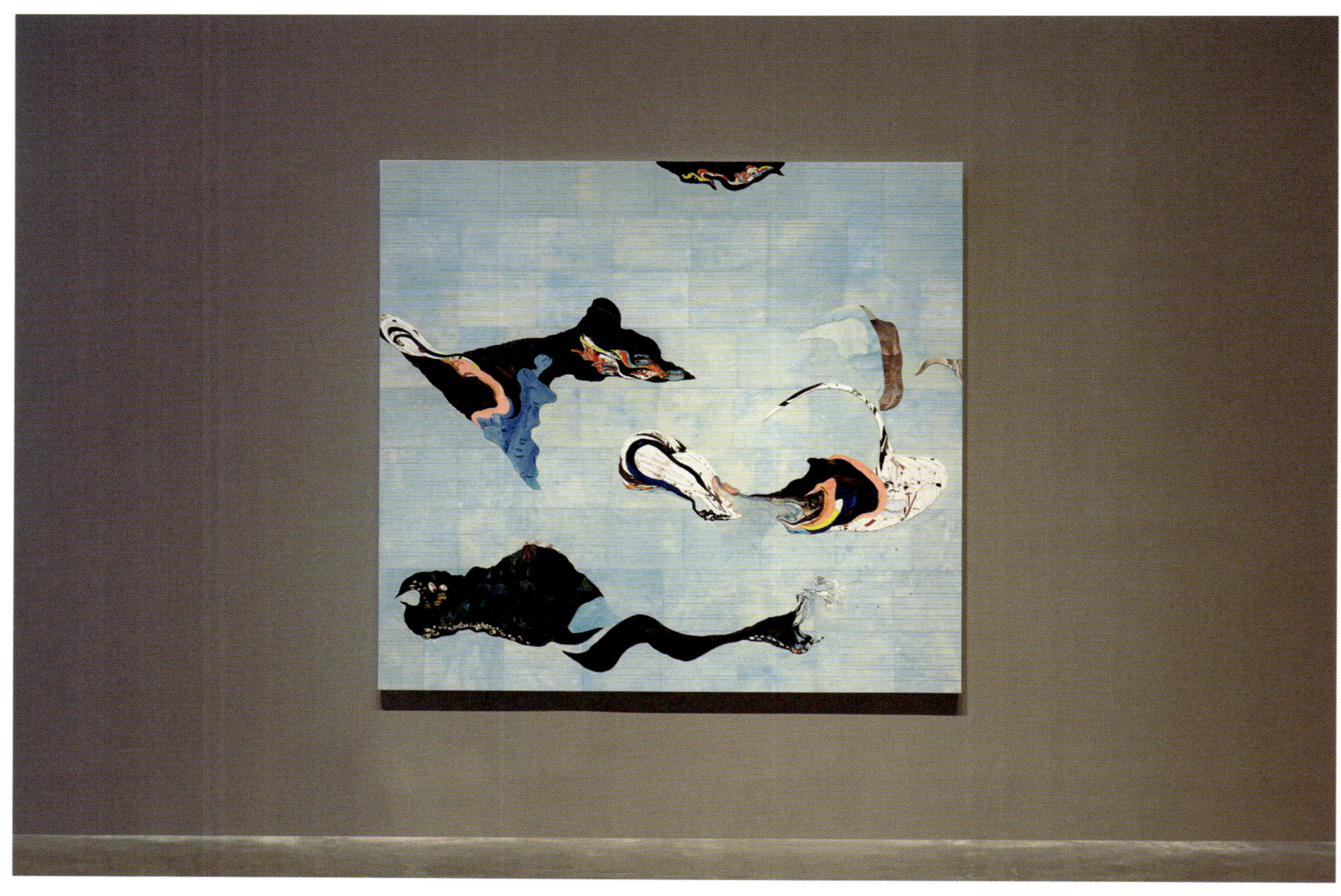

(top) Left to right:
Ellen Gallagher, *Recipe for Butter*, 1994;
Untitled, 1995;
and *Fronts*, 1997

(bottom) Ellen Gallagher,
Untitled, 2013

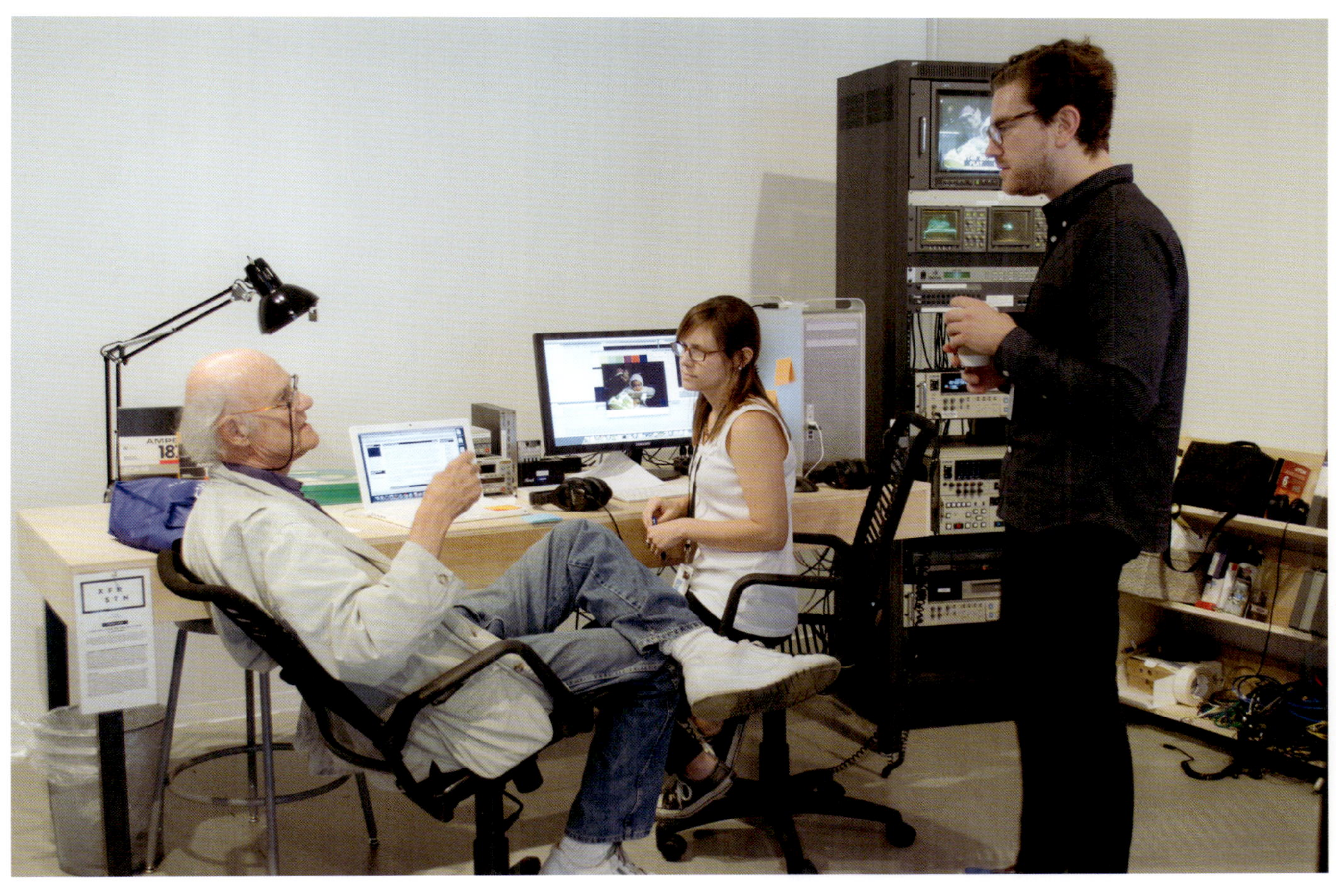

"XFR STN," an open-door,
artist-centered media
archiving project by
Alan W. Moore with Taylor
Moore, Alexis Bhagat,
and the artists of
Collaborative Projects

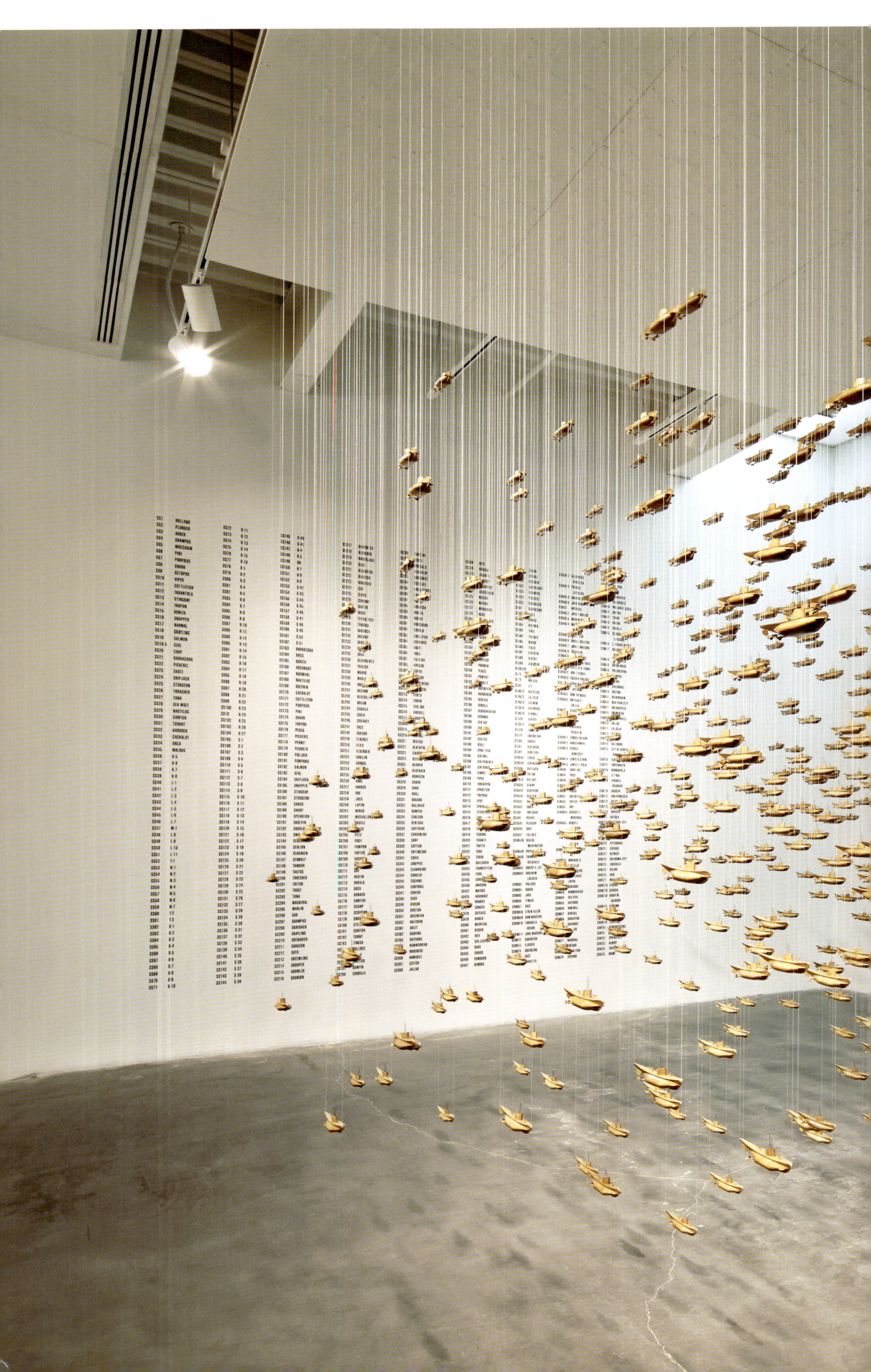

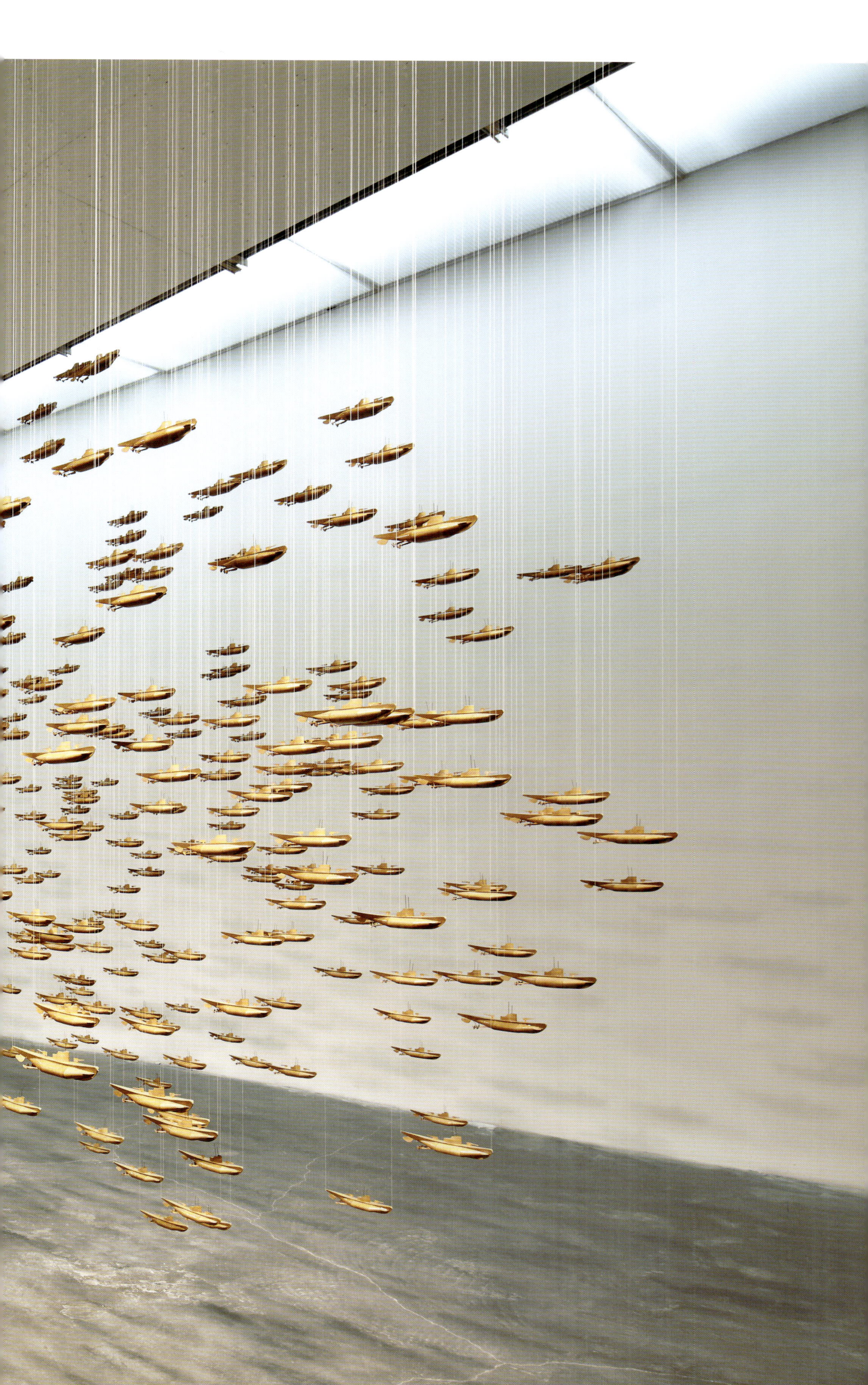

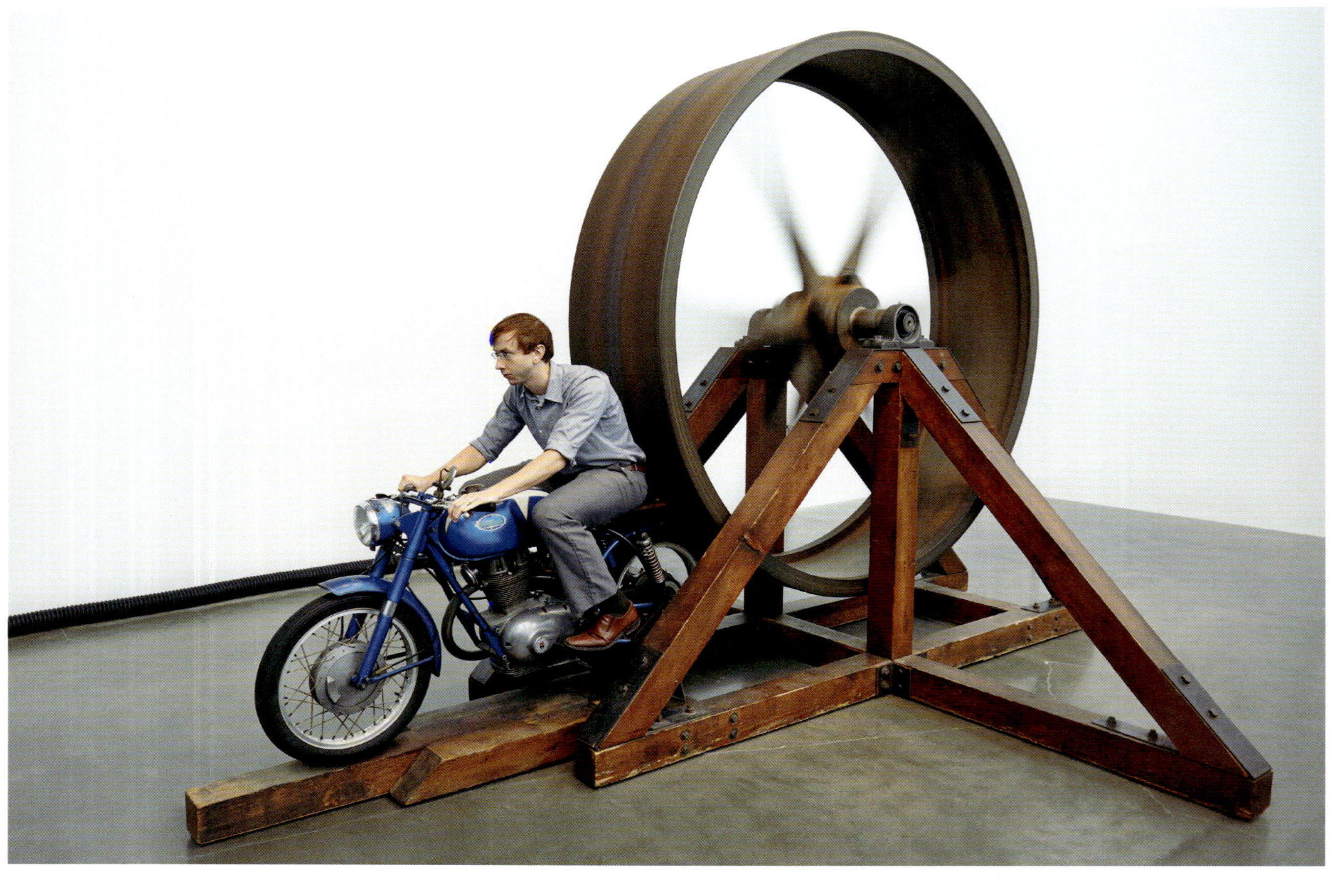

(previous spread)
Chris Burden, *All the Submarines of the United States of America*, 1987

(above) Chris Burden, *Big Wheel*, 1979

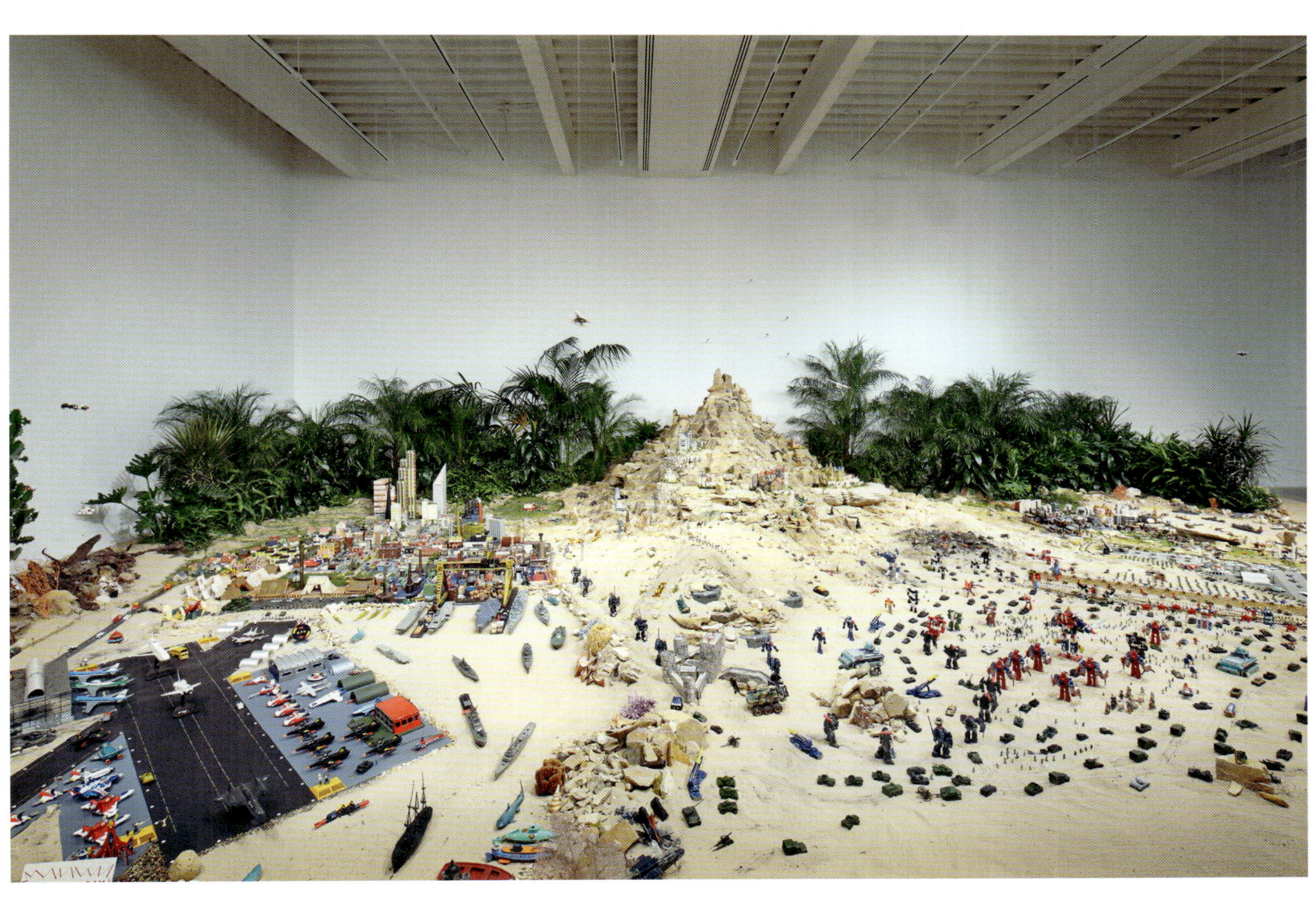

Chris Burden,
A Tale of Two Cities, 1981

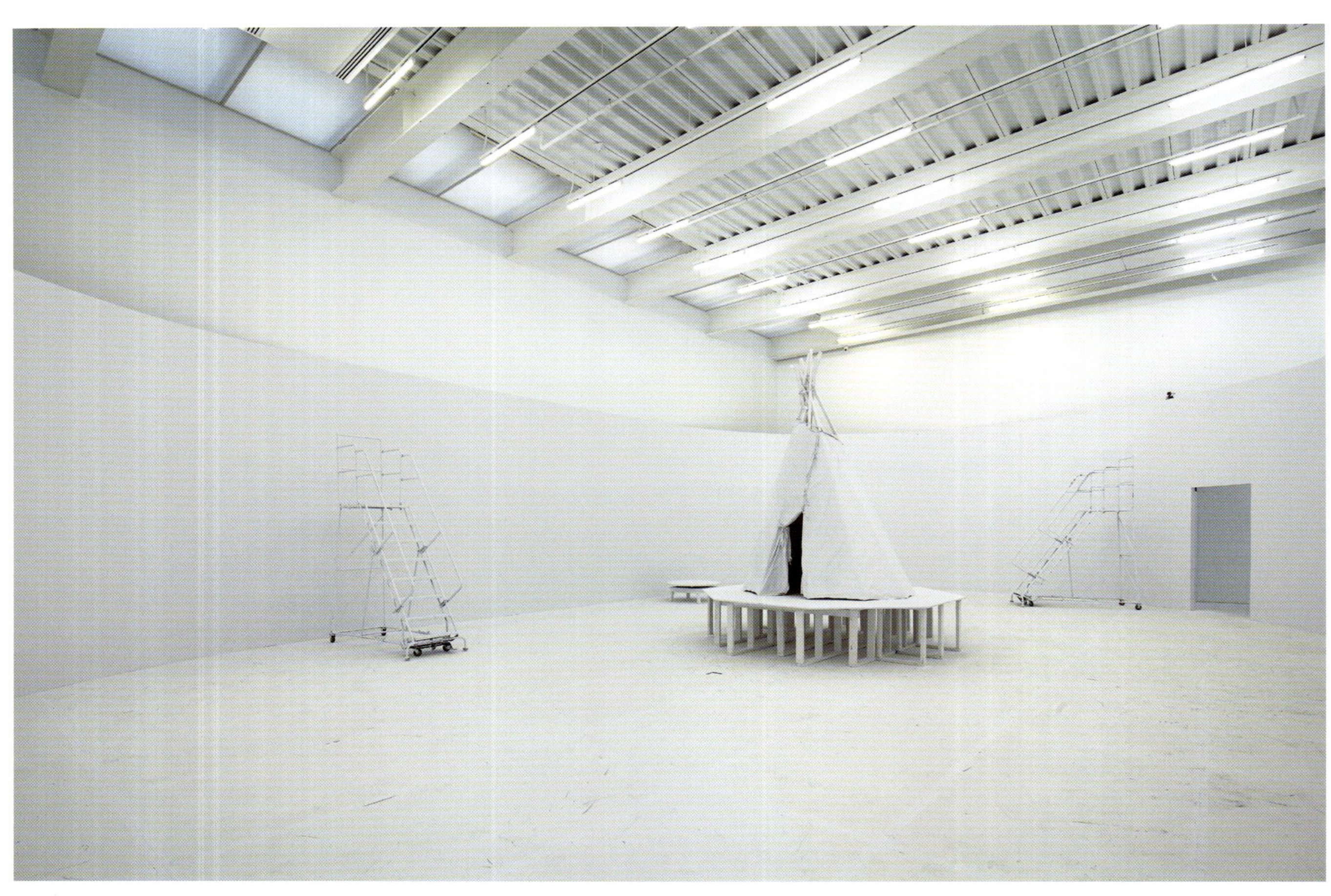

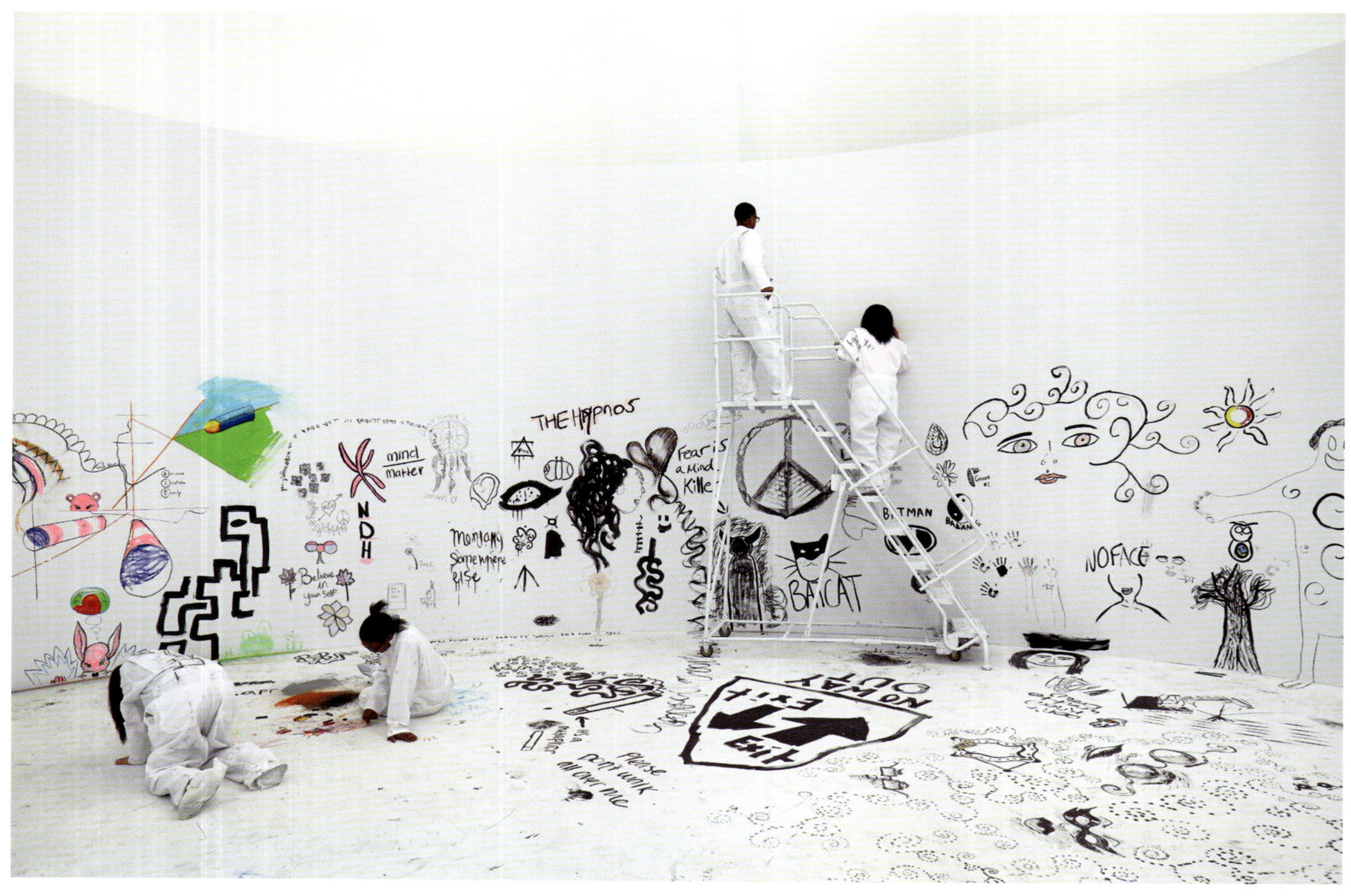

Paweł Althamer,
Draftsmen's Congress,
2012/2014 (four views in
progress)

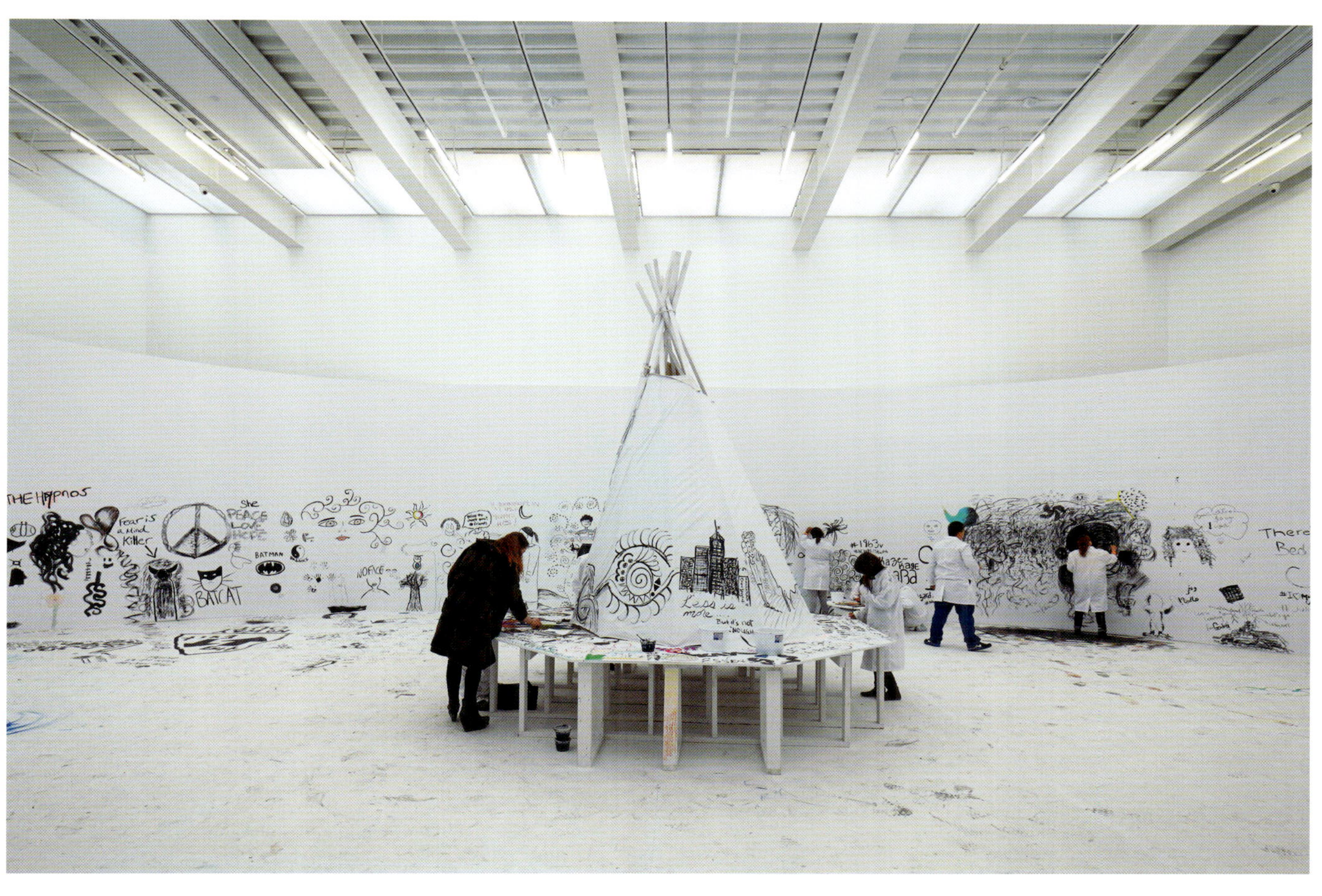

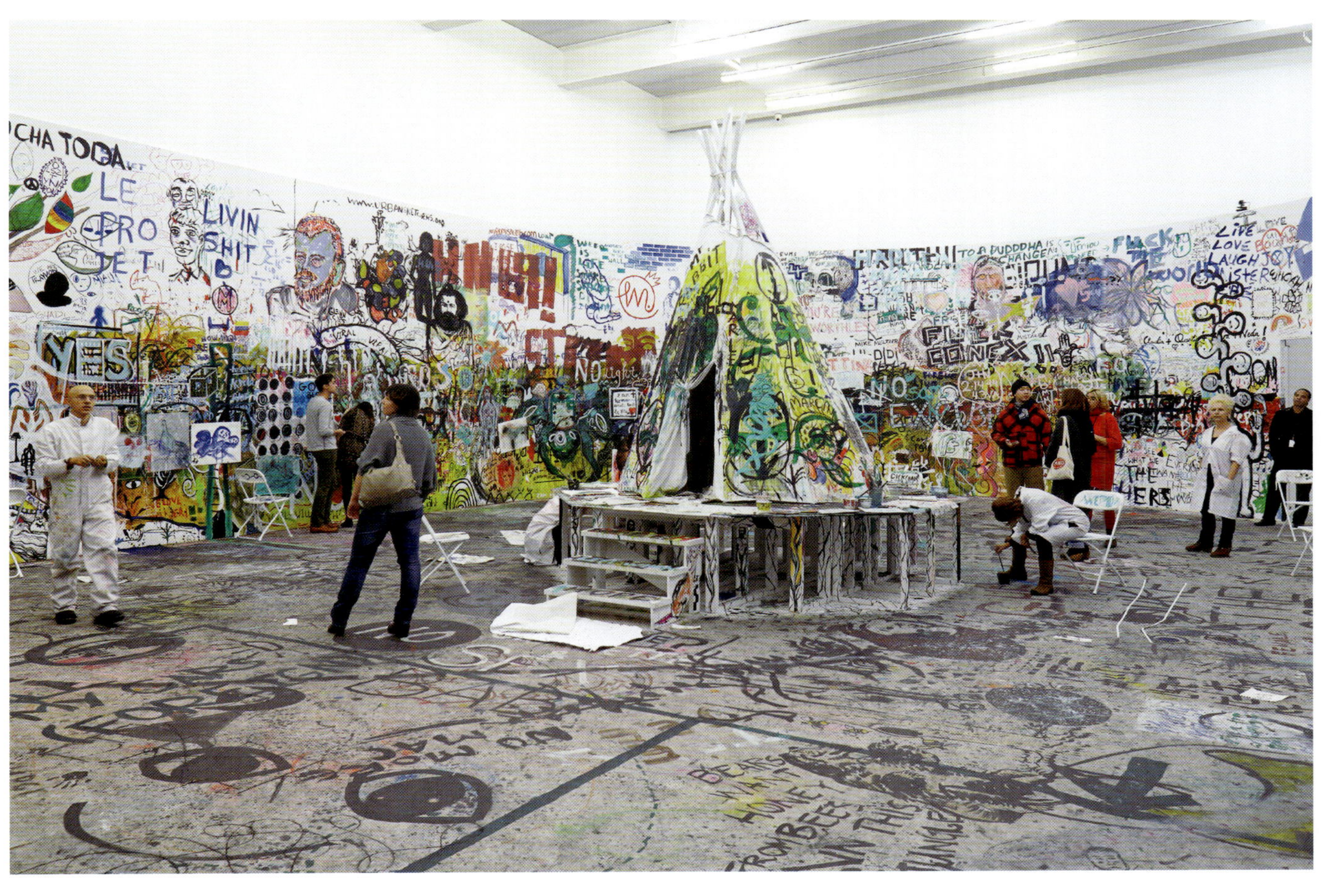

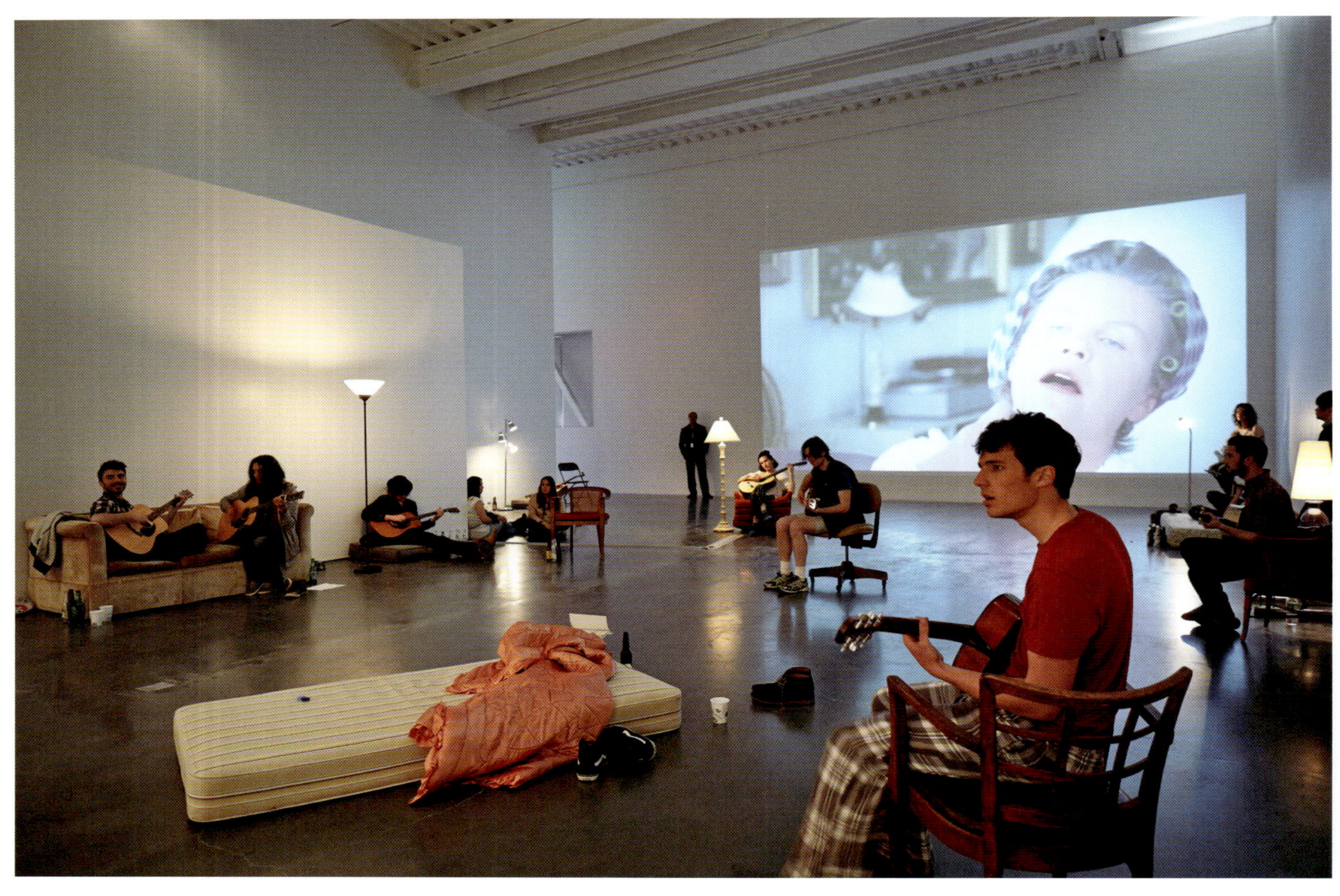

Ragnar Kjartansson,
*Take Me Here by the
Dishwasher: Memorial for
a Marriage*, 2011/2014

Innovation and Entrepreneurship: Breaking the Mold in Museums and Contemporary Culture

Julia Kaganskiy

Traditionally, the terms "innovation" and "entrepreneurship" were applied to industry and business—to new inventions, products, and ventures. In 2017, one could argue, these words have transcended their original context to permeate contemporary culture at large, having grown exponentially in prominence and influence since the 1960s. Given the perpetually accelerating pace of technological development and the start-up craze of the past twenty years, it's little wonder that innovation and entrepreneurship have infiltrated even the most unlikely corners of the economy and culture. The rise of the freelance workforce and the so-called gig economy have made de facto entrepreneurs out of nearly half the working population, and projections estimate that free-lancers will account for more than 40 percent of the US workforce by 2020.[1] Digital technology is the basis for cheaper means of production, a distributed and decen-tralized workforce, and a global distribution platform via the internet that provides creative producers with a direct line to audiences and consumers. These developments have eliminated many of the historic barriers to entry and presented individuals, not just corporations, with the opportunity to explore new methods, introduce new ideas, and develop innovative services and products.

What have been the implications for creative producers? One might assume that twenty-first-century creatives were experiencing more agency and autonomy in their professional lives than ever before. Yet, the vast majority of them were feeling ill-prepared for this brave new world: 88 percent of the arts and design graduates surveyed by

1.   Intuit, *Intuit 2020 Report: Twenty Trends That Will Shape the Next Decade* (October 2010), 21, https://http-download.intuit.com/http.intuit/CMO/intuit/ futureofsmallbusiness/intuit_2020_report.pdf.

the Center for an Urban Future in 2012 felt that they had
not received sufficient hands-on business and entrepreneurship training.[2] This was becoming a critical oversight
in an era when artists with large Instagram followings
might be contacted by collectors or potential sponsors
via direct message; Kickstarter and similar crowdfunding
platforms were introducing new forms of fundraising; and
creatives working with cutting-edge commercial software or hardware—a game engine or a virtual reality
headset, for instance—might find themselves collaborating with industry partners. The worlds of commerce
and culture were becoming ever more tightly intertwined,
and creatives were increasingly managing their own
careers—in part by choice, in part out of necessity.

It was becoming obvious that a new framework of
support was required to cultivate, nurture, and provide a
platform for the activities of creative entrepreneurs—
artists, designers, filmmakers, technologists, and other
cultural producers whose ventures were too entrepreneurial for a typical artist residency but not sufficiently
entrepreneurial for a traditional business incubator or
accelerator. Many digital-born creatives whose materials
of choice included code, software, and hacked hardware
applications were working in ways that operated outside
of the traditional art market. Some sought commercial
applications for their ideas, taking on client-based work
or developing product or service offerings in an effort to
subsidize their more artistic pursuits. Others developed

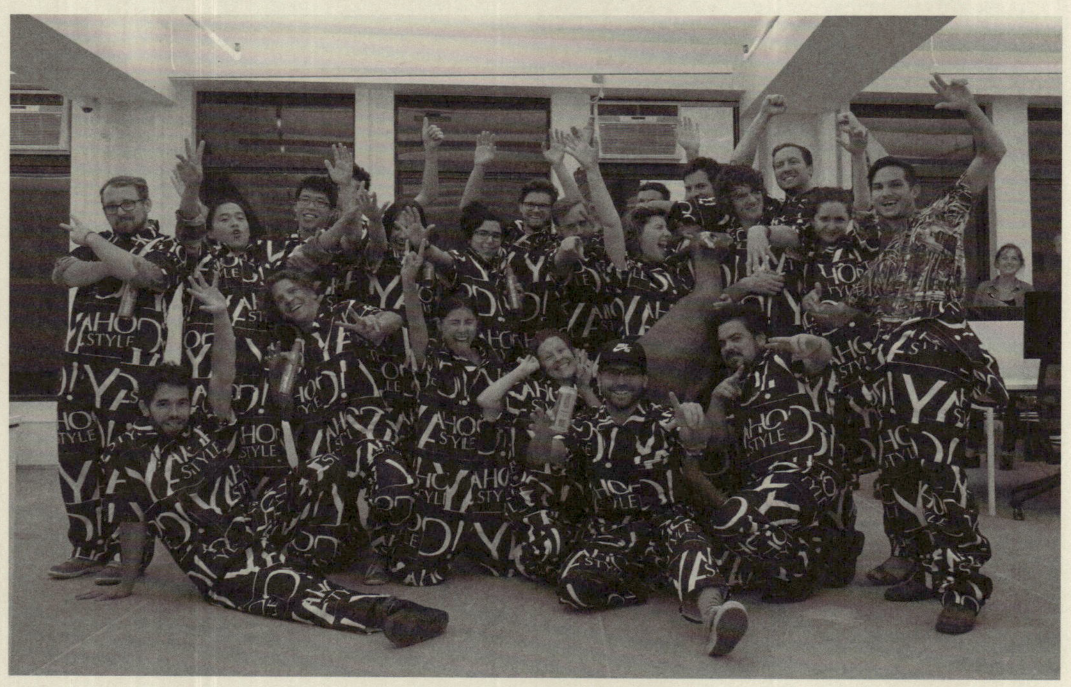

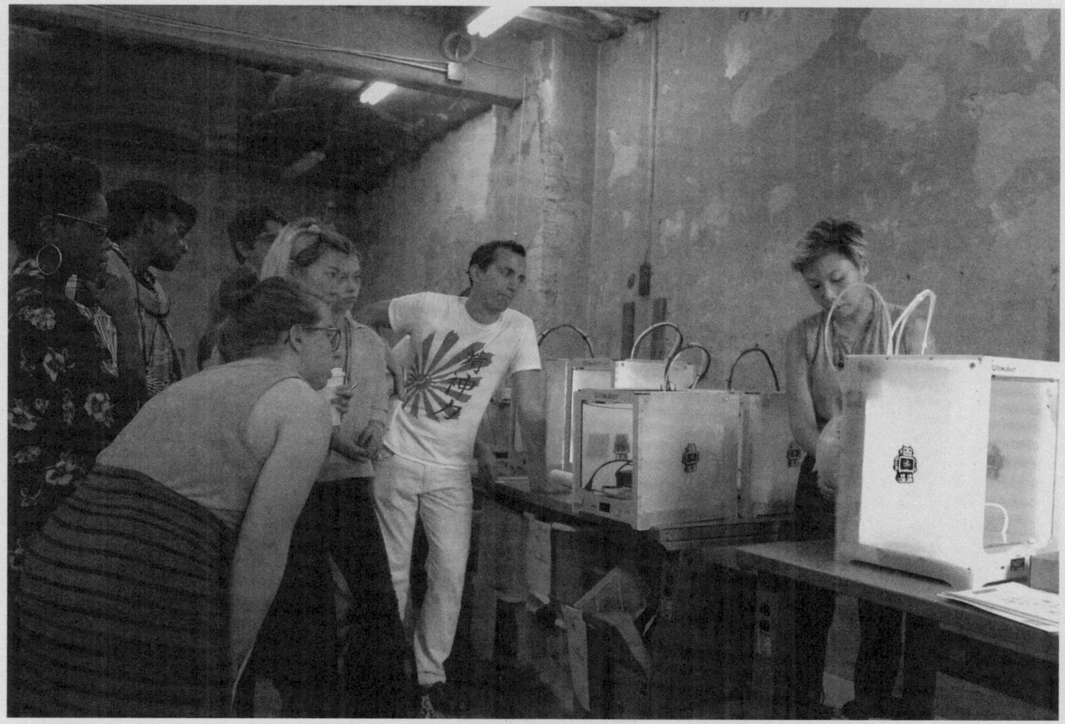

hybrid forms of cultural production—working fluidly between industries and combining seemingly disparate disciplines like fashion and 3-D printing, or design and artificial intelligence—but found that the market had yet to catch up with their visionary ideas. Still others sought to build new cultural institutions—alternative exhibition venues, publications, creative platforms, and education programs—that would articulate a new approach to the creation, presentation, and discourse of contemporary culture, much as Marcia Tucker had intended by founding the New Museum in 1977.

The New Museum has been exceptionally well-positioned to understand and respond to these challenges and concerns. Its 2002 affiliation with Rhizome, a digital art and culture organization, gave it a front row seat to the rapid cultural changes being wrought by digital technology and to the emerging forms of creative practice being embraced by digital artists. In 2011, Ideas City, now a roving international platform, was inaugurated in New York by the Museum with scores of collaborating organizations to investigate the role of culture in shaping the future of cities. Conceived in the wake of the 2008 reces-

2. "In our survey of New York design professionals, only 12 percent of respondents said that the schools provided significant opportunities to develop these sorts of business and entrepreneurial skills; 43 percent said the schools provide some opportunities; and 44 percent said it was not a major focus." Center for an Urban Future, *Designing New York's Future* (March 2012), 8–9, https://nycfuture.org/pdf/Designing_New_Yorks_Future.pdf.

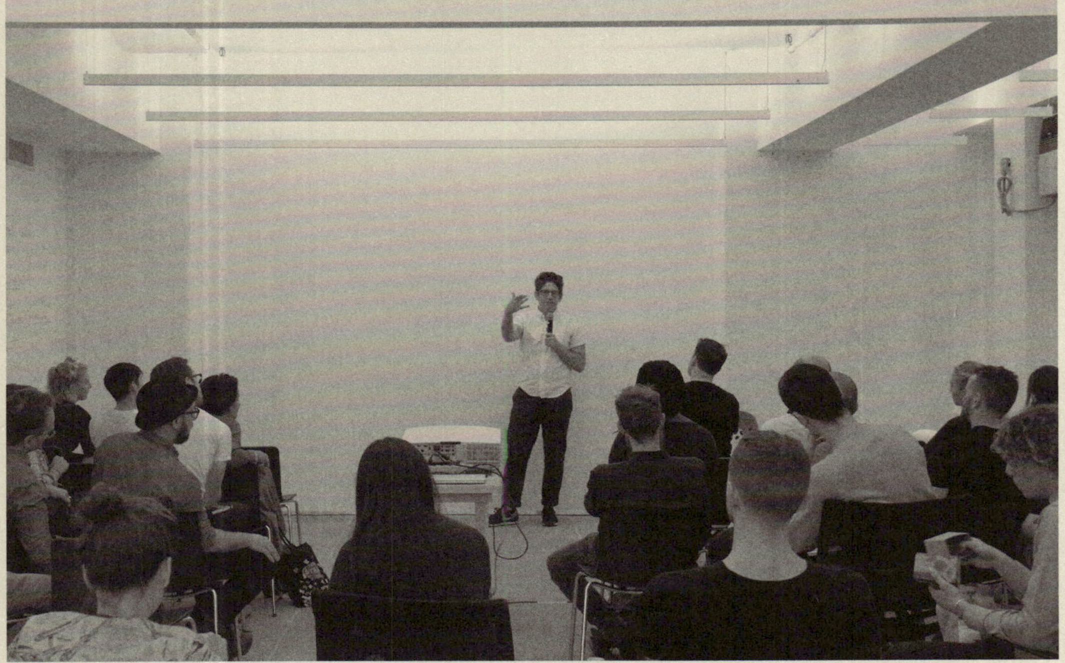

sion, Ideas City has examined, among other issues, how the changing natures of work and creative production are physically altering the urban fabric, made visible through the rampant spread of coworking spaces, the decline in the number of affordable artist studios, and the displacement of local craftsmen and fabricators. When the Museum purchased the adjacent building at 231 Bowery, Lisa Phillips and Karen Wong, the Director and the Deputy Director, were determined to commit the space to bringing creative practice back to the Bowery and to addressing some of the urgent issues faced by the entrepreneurial community today.

The result was NEW INC, the first museum-led incubator dedicated to supporting new ideas and creative enterprises at the intersection of art, design, and technology. NEW INC opened its doors in September 2014 and welcomed its first cohort of sixty members—a carefully selected, interdisciplinary group of artists, creative technologists, architects, product designers, animators, fashion designers, and filmmakers. For a modest monthly fee, incubator members received access to an eight-thousand-square-foot coworking space, mentorship opportunities, and professional development programs that would help them learn to navigate business challenges such as fundraising, contract negotiation, and marketing and promoting their work. The goal was to provide a safe space in which they could develop concepts and ideas, test their feasibility, find collaborators, and build out a strategy for the successful launch and eventual sustainability of new creative endeavors.

The program was very much an experiment and functioned as a bit of a hybrid itself—borrowing elements from traditional artist residencies, incubator and accelerator programs, and even "anti-disciplinary" innovation labs like the MIT Media Lab. The underlying quest was for fresh models to facilitate every facet of cultural production: tools, techniques, forms, processes, business structures. Unlike other incubators, at NEW INC scale and profit margins didn't necessarily define success. Creative excellence, cultural impact, and thought leadership did.

Despite its experimental nature, NEW INC found traction fairly quickly. The first cohort's bold new ventures included Monegraph, developed by artist Kevin McCoy. A media licensing tool built on the blockchain technology used by cryptocurrencies like Bitcoin, Monegraph was originally born from a collaboration at Rhizome's 2014 Seven on Seven conference, where McCoy worked with technologist Anil Dash to create a prototype for tracking and authenticating transactions of digital media goods such as GIFs. McCoy, who together with his partner and collaborator Jennifer McCoy had been working as a new media artist for almost twenty years, wanted to create an easier way for people to collect digital media and believed that the blockchain—a digital ledger in which transactions made in Bitcoin or another cryptocurrency are recorded chronologically and publicly—could provide a solution.

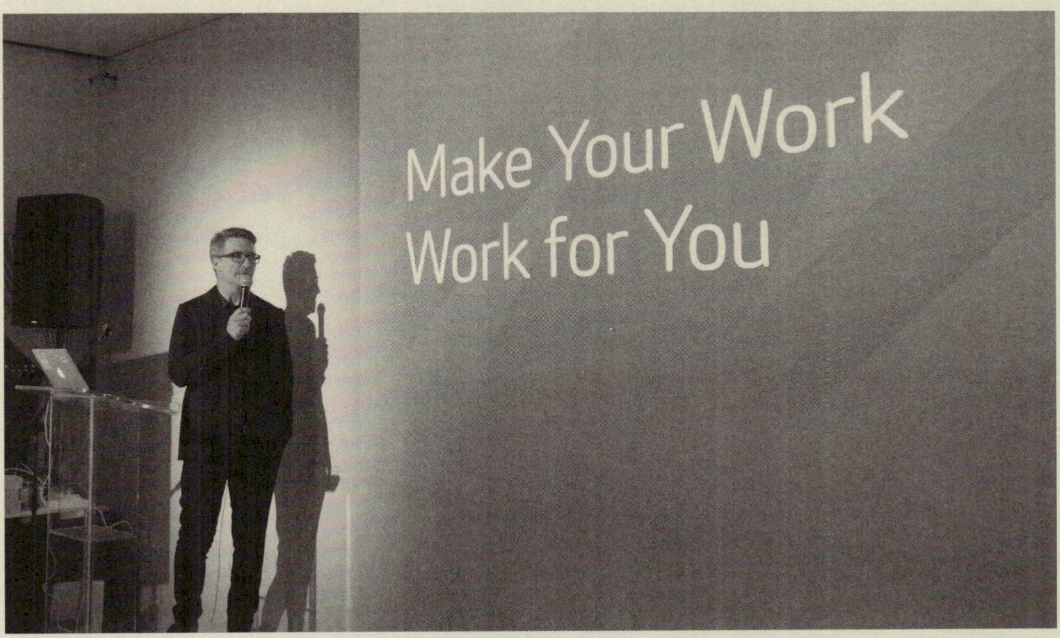

At NEW INC, Monegraph quickly grew from an idea into
a business. Within his first year at NEW INC, McCoy
attracted over $1.5 million in angel investment and grew
his team to six full-time employees.

Other early successes at NEW INC included artist-led
technological inventions that arose from the artists' own
creative practices, including Carlo van de Roer's high-
speed light-imaging technology, Satellite Labs, and the
DepthKit volumetric filmmaking software developed by
James George and Alexander Porter of Scatter. Cutting-
edge designers and creative technologists launched
studios that specialize in interactive media and spatial
sound design (Dave and Gabe), web and mobile design
(4REAL), architecture and product design (The Principals),
and virtual and augmented reality (Odd Division). Also
developed at the incubator were online platforms that
fostered creativity, such as Print All Over Me, a brother-
and-sister-founded fashion start-up that lets users create
custom-designed clothing and accessories by uploading
their own imagery, and New Hive, a no-coding-necessary
digital art platform that combines the robust features of
Adobe Suite with the social and networked capabilities of
Tumblr or YouTube.

Over the past three years, during which I've served as the
Director of NEW INC, we've continued to experiment and
adapt, refining NEW INC as a professional development
program and community. Each year's cohort is different
and requires tailored forms of mentorship and support,
and each year's application pool reflects emerging trends
in the cultural and technological spheres, demanding
that NEW INC remain nimble and responsive. It already
has distinguished itself as a home for cutting-edge
virtual reality creators, with the 2017 Sundance and
Tribeca film festivals showcasing work from NEW INC
members and alumni like Milica Zec and Winslow Turner
Porter III, Scatter, Rachel Rossin, and Hyphen-Labs.
Other emergent trends include a focus on alternative
education and social impact initiatives that dovetail with
the flourishing of social practice within the art world.
During the 2016–17 cycle, NEW INC was home to several
museum projects—a somewhat meta but wholly apropos
twist on the notion of "museum incubator." The trend led

to the development of a new program track that will focus on technological innovation in the museum field, aiming in particular to support audience engagement at small and midsize museums.

In a way, NEW INC seems to have brought the New Museum back full circle to its origins. The museum field isn't particularly known for innovation and entrepreneurship—our domain is one dedicated to scholarship, preservation, and the presentation of historically and culturally significant material. To those moving at the speed of technological advancement, it may seem as if museums serve to make time stand still. In 1977, Marcia Tucker set out to update and reimagine the museum to meet the shifting needs, concerns, forms, and tastes of contemporary artists and audiences, to not merely embrace change, but to lead and propel it. Tucker's determination to introduce audiences to emerging topics of cultural discourse could be seen in exhibitions devoted to then-provocative subjects—"Extended Sensibilities: Homosexual Presence in Contemporary Art" (1982) and "Girls Night Out (Femininity as Masquerade)" (1988)—and in her advocacy for outsider art forms like tattoo art.[3] Tucker constantly questioned how we define "good" art and the role of a museum, and she applied that testing of limits to the design of the museum itself, experimenting with unconventional fundraising, collecting, and even management strategies. Early on, she introduced the Semi-Permanent Collection, which would acquire and hold works for approximately a decade, a collection policy that would be as fluid and dynamic as contemporary art itself.[4] Other early experiments included establishing a horizontal management structure that would do away with administrative hierarchies, offering equal pay for all employees, and implementing consensus-based decision-making. Although the personnel experiments rarely proved effective, Tucker's willingness to put new practices

3.   See Marcia Tucker, "Tattoo: the State of the Art," *Artforum* (May 1981): 42–47.

4.   "Culture is living and changing, not static," Marcia Tucker wrote in her autobiography. "The resources taken up by the collection expand at the expense of contemporary, experimental programs and exhibitions…. The collection at the New Museum was premised on the acknowledgment that artistic value is not absolute." See Marcia Tucker, *A Short Life of Trouble: Forty Years in the New York Art World*, ed. Liza Lou (Berkeley: University of California Press, 2008), 134.

to the test helped position the New Museum as an important proving ground for innovative approaches to art, curation, and museum administration.

Today, even as the New Museum has become a global leader in shaping the discourse around contemporary art, it maintains a firm commitment to programs like NEW INC, which supports the "outsider" work that is just taking shape on the fringes of creative practice and contemporary culture at large. While much of the work that emerges from NEW INC is not necessarily destined for a gallery space and sits outside the routine purview of a contemporary art institution, the activity that takes place within the incubator—the creative and technological innovation, the probing of the potential of new media, and the experimentation with new organizational structures, business models, systems of connoisseurship, and community organizing—is in alignment with Marcia Tucker's boundary-breaking legacy. NEW INC provides a home for the visionary thinking that will allow creative producers and cultural institutions to change, to innovate, and to thrive.

Julia Kaganskiy is the founding Director of NEW INC. She joined the New Museum in 2014 to help shape and define the incubator program as a hub for creative experimentation and cultural innovation. A seasoned cultural producer, she has served as an editor, an independent curator, and a community organizer.

Ideas City: The Museum as a Platform for Civic Action

Joseph Grima

Market-based economies such as the interconnected, transnational one we operate within are well known for their oscillations between growth and stagnation. Yet, when the global markets came close to collapse in 2008, the magnitude of the distress that swept across much of the Western world had never been seen before, and this struck fear into the hearts of financiers, politicians, and academics alike. Unlike financial crises that had preceded it, the significance of this one was not merely visible in the landscape—it was impossible to miss. Entire neighborhoods in foreclosure, increasing numbers of homeless people, small businesses closing, and buildings set on fire to claim insurance became the norm in many cities. Each year brought higher levels of tragedy. This was no "adjustment of the markets." These were uncharted waters in the history of the capitalist experiment, and there was a genuine sense that the point of failure, the point of no return, was imminent.

The crisis, or "Great Recession" as it later came to be known, was abstract and obscure in its origins and mechanics. Machiavellian financial transactions involving the packaging and reselling of derivatives of subprime mortgages cloaked an entirely unscrupulous exploitation of both the investors and the homeowners; yet, the Great Recession's effects could hardly have been more tangible in terms of their impact on the social fabric of American cities. Even in well-established and gentrifying enclaves of Manhattan, there was a sense that the financial crisis was exposing what had been simmering just beneath the surface for much longer: a creeping polarization of society, legible in urban space, that was producing an increasingly insurmountable gap between those (relatively few) who benefited from the mechanisms of financialization and the commodification of the landscape, and those whose jobs, security, and future were threatened by them.

Ideas City was launched in this context in 2011, arguably
the moment of deepest despair. Cofounded by Director
Lisa Phillips and Deputy Director Karen Wong, with
Richard Flood, Director of Special Projects, providing
critical program development, the initiative was a
direct response to the distress just outside the walls of
the New Museum. The Museum had opened its doors
on the Bowery in December 2007, and the arrival of a
glamorous space for contemporary art in the neighborhood—historically a safe haven for diverse populations
but already the target of real estate developers—was
inevitably a significant turning point in the histories of
both the institution and the street. The Museum was
faced with a paradox: having chosen to relocate to one
of the sites in New York most beloved by artists, it might,
by virtue of its very presence, contribute to making the
neighborhood inaccessible to those it was there to serve.
Furthermore, the knock-on effects of a change in the
market's perception of the neighborhood risked dis-
placing not just the artists, but also the other nonprofits,
organizations, and entire communities that had made
Lower Manhattan an epicenter of creativity and leadership in the arts.

The first Ideas City Festival was a response to this
paradox. A cross-institutional collaboration led by the

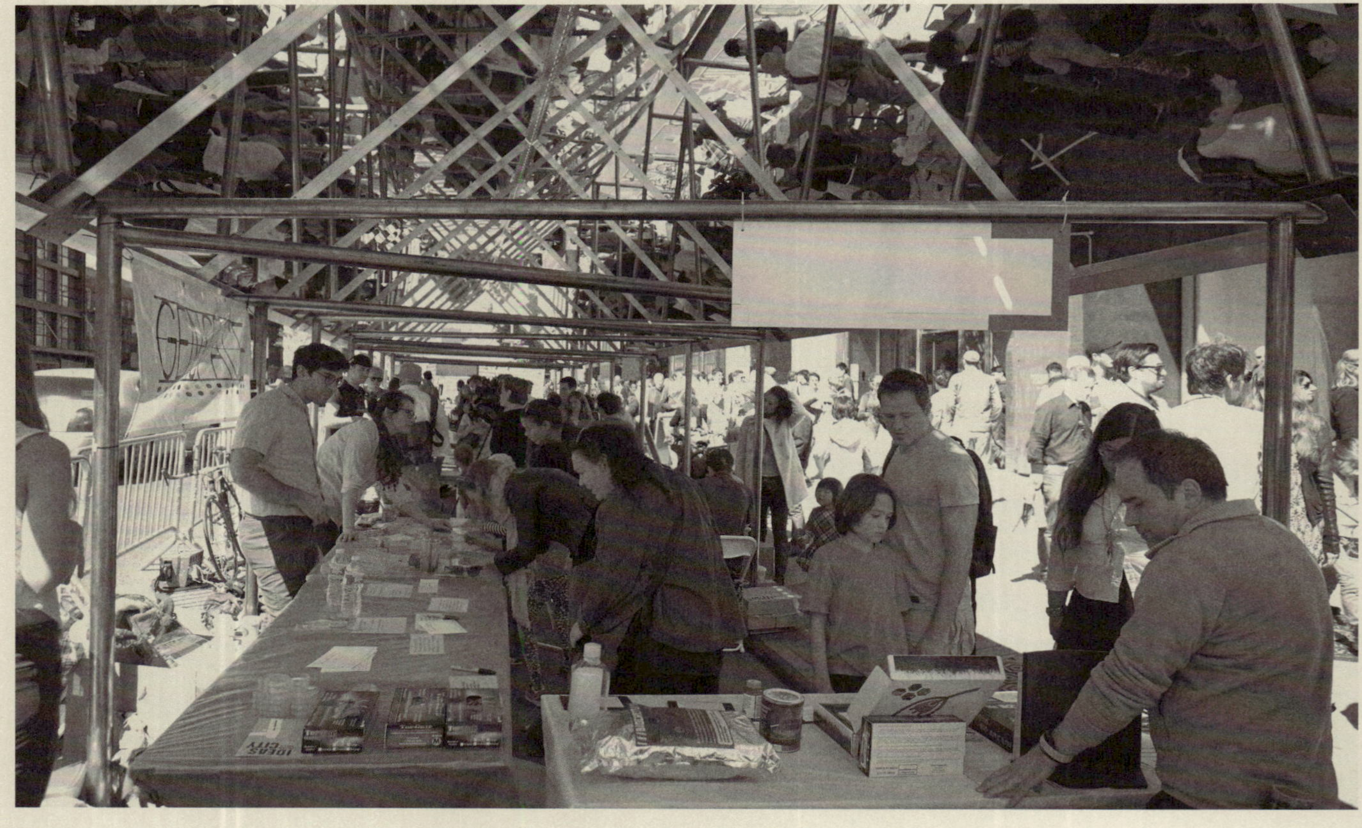

New Museum and involving over one hundred nonprofits, cultural organizations, citizen associations, and artist groups, Ideas City took over the streets surrounding the Museum for a full weekend in May 2011. This collective "occupation" of the area brought organizations together, giving them a sense of shared purpose and support in their efforts to keep the local tradition of art and culture alive. Ideas City also gave participants local and international visibility, and it was a crucial opportunity for the New Museum—an institution clearly at home within an elite global network of art organizations—to publicly affirm its commitment to its own neighborhood and community. The event was radically open, and it built on New York's long tradition of street festivals, using that familiar structure to make conventional museum-based formats, such as conferences, more welcoming to a broad audience.

The convergence of nonprofits, artists, activists, citizens, and policymakers in New York brought like-minded individuals and organizations together, and new initiatives were born. Ideas City's greatest contribution would prove to be its role as a catalyst for the creation of new networks. Some of its key features, such as the Mayoral Panel, brought politicians into contact with artists, progressive designers, thinkers, and activists who were addressing shared community challenges. It soon became evident that this formula of "urban therapy" through a convening of stakeholders around a table—spearheaded by a neutral and respected organization such as the New Museum—had international potential and could be applied to other situations. Ideas City Istanbul (2012) and Ideas City São Paulo (2013) were the first experiments in scaling up the initiative for an international audience and proved the resilience of Ideas City as a network; in particular, they demonstrated the willingness of participants and partner organizations to become long-term, recurring collaborators of the program rather than one-off interlocutors, as is often the case with international conferences.

As a platform within the New Museum, Ideas City has emerged as the preeminent model for how a cultural institution can play a meaningful role in promoting civic action. Sustaining every initiative is the conviction that there is more to the process of shaping cities than laying out roads and zoning maps, and that there is a need for a point of encounter between the disciplinary practice of urbanism and those individuals—such as the artists who participate in the Museum's programs—whose work investigates the more subtle, ephemeral forces at the basis of urban life. Beyond considering well-known subjects of current debate, such as gentrification and inequality, participants introduced singularly probing analyses of topics, with Trevor Paglen examining the politics of surveillance and architect Bjarke Ingels, in conversation with science fiction writer Kim Stanley Robinson, discussing the transformative power of technology. Ideas City was born from the observation that, despite the exponential growth in the number of schools, research bodies, government agencies, and professional associations dedicated to advocating the creation of better cities through design, the result of their endeavors almost universally ignores the fact that design alone— or the "invisible hand" of the market that led to the near implosion of the economy in 2008—is insufficient to produce a genuinely vital and vibrant urban space. The rhetoric of "livable cities by design" tends to ignore the subtleties of what it actually takes to produce better urban environments, and while good design plays a critical part in this process, it cannot by itself account for

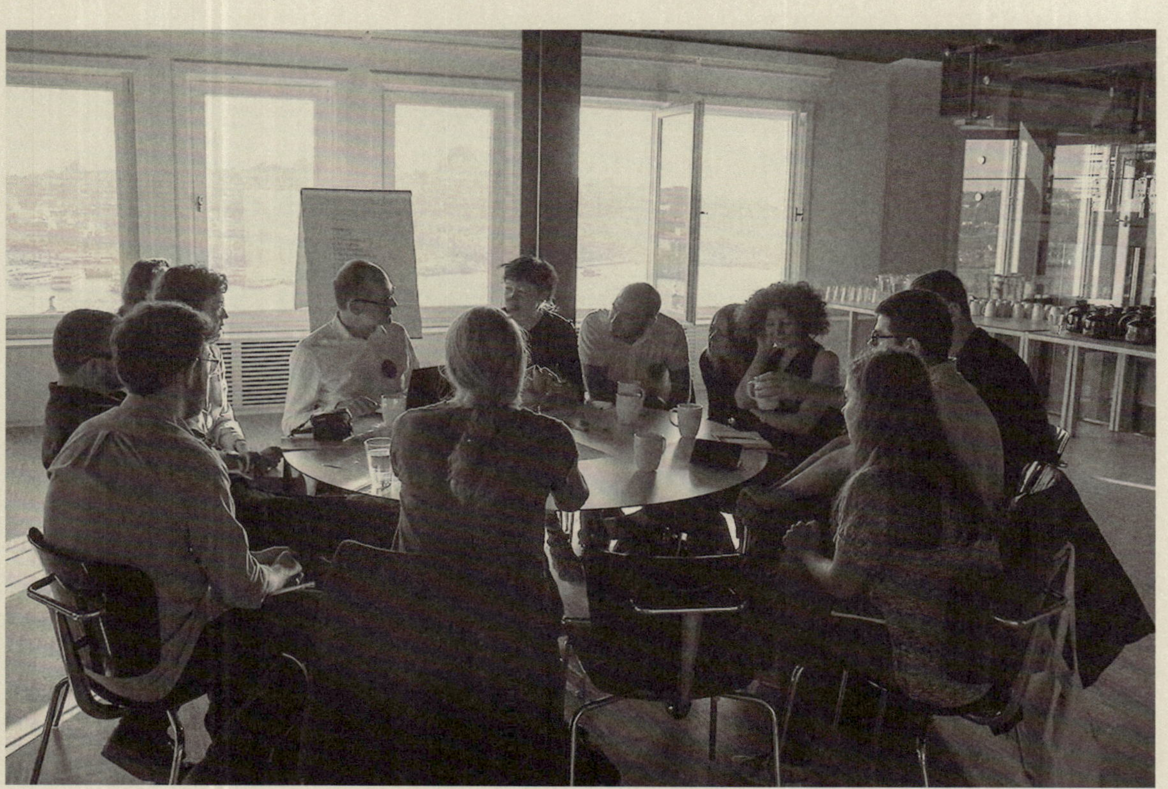

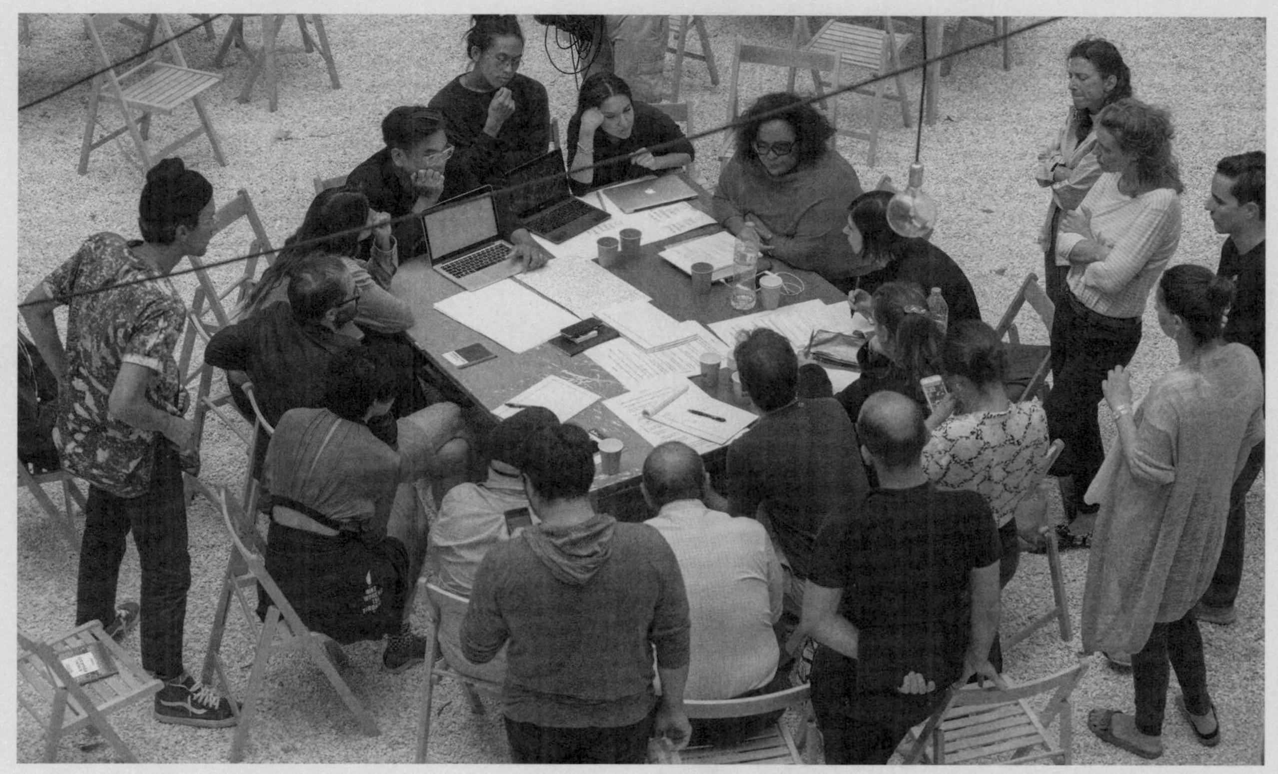

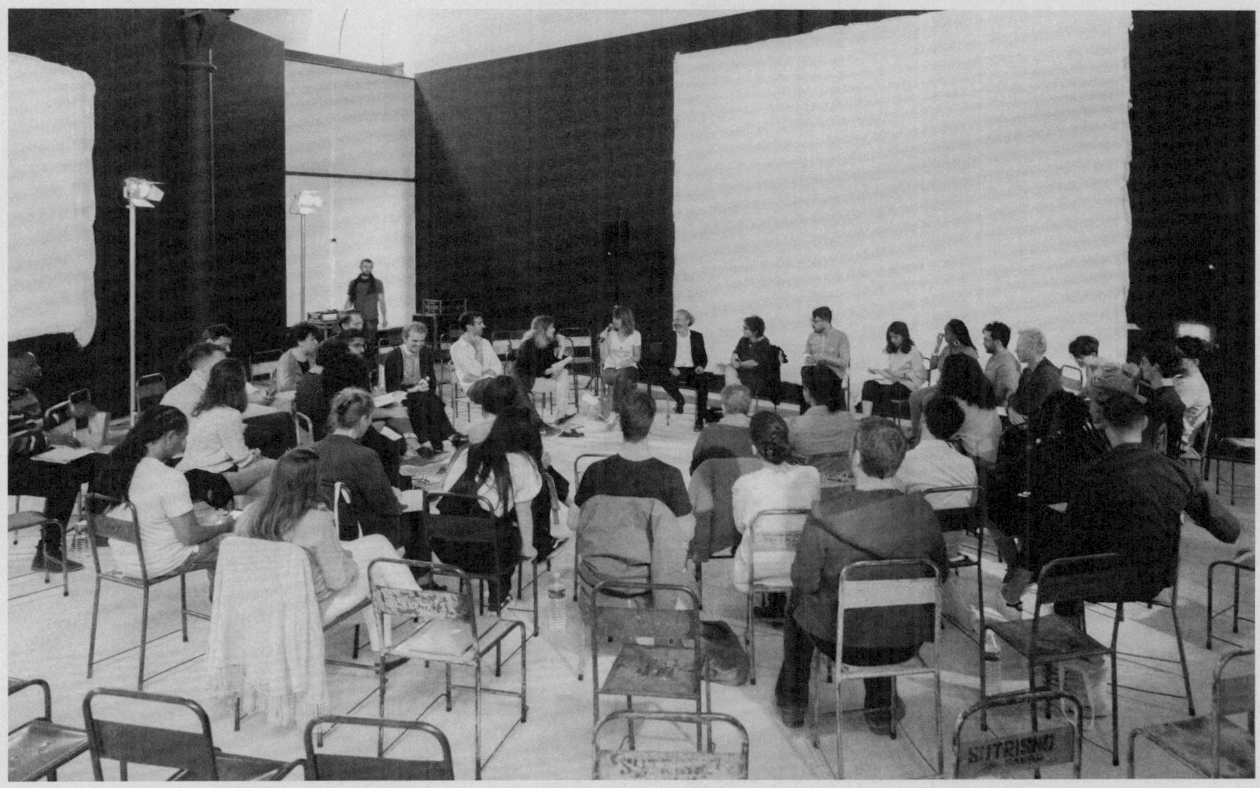

or accommodate the extraordinary complexity and delicacy of the ingredients that make healthy and livable cities the fundamental building blocks of a thriving society.

These insights led to a transformation of the structure of Ideas City that would allow the platform to dig deeper into the culture, context, and social fabric of destinations beyond New York. The new format sought to move beyond the problematic yet all too common practice of parachuting into a location for a twenty-four- or forty-eight-hour

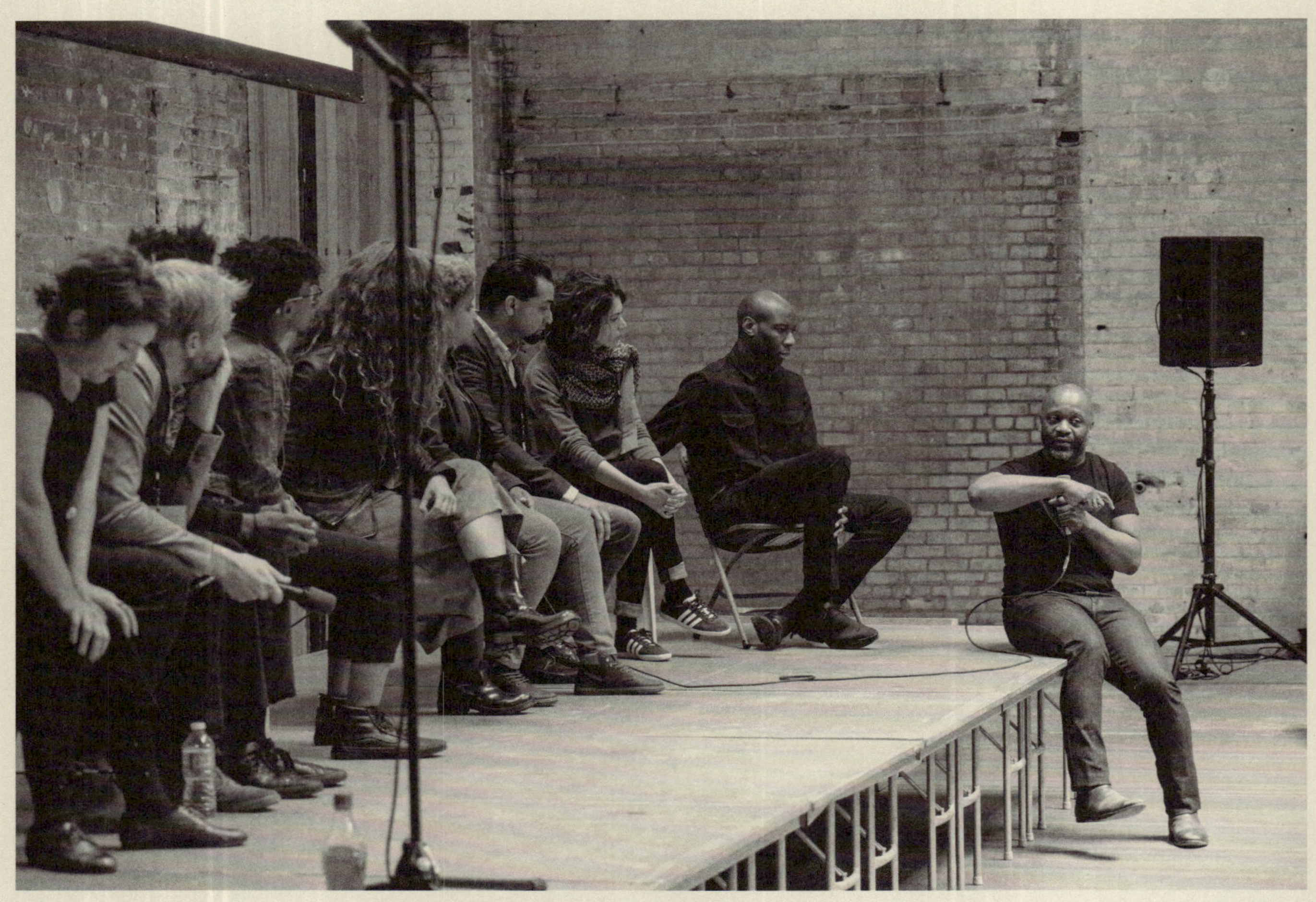

conference, and to permit participants to not just present preexisting work, but also generate new strategies and ideas in response to their observations on-site. During editions held in Detroit and Athens in 2016 and in Arles in 2017, Ideas City evolved into a residency program, in which forty Fellows chosen by the New Museum (with one third from the city, one third from the host country, and one third from international locations in order to create a diverse and balanced group) work and live together under one roof for a period of five days, operating in teams of five members to produce critical and creative responses to the conditions they encounter on the ground. In many ways this model represents a new operational structure for the design office, one in which highly qualified individuals from diverse disciplinary and cultural backgrounds join forces to develop unconventional and notably original strategies for the future city.

Although it may be counterintuitive for a contemporary art institution such as the New Museum to take a leadership role in addressing some of the urban problematics it can be seen as compounding, such as gentrification, Ideas City puts forward the argument that the fundamental dynamics of urban life today—the commitment to art and culture, the struggle for social justice, and the resistance to the commodification and privatization of public space—can be advanced only through a convergence of cross-disciplinary approaches that involves bringing mayors, citizens, designers, activists, and artists to the same table. Ideas City proposes a new way of making the work of an arts-based institution relevant to the reality of a rapidly urbanizing world. As a platform for interdisciplinary action, it counters the perception that art and culture are superfluous luxuries with the assertion that bridging the spheres of design, policy, and administration with the critical practice of art is essential to civic life.

Over the past four decades, the Lower Manhattan neighborhoods in which the New Museum was born and flourished have functioned both as laboratories for some of the most extreme developments in market capitalism's transformation of the cityscape and as incubators for radical thought on the part of artists, architects, and activists engaged in a critical analysis of those unfolding developments. Ideas City was first introduced as a bridge between the institutional space within the New Museum and the communities around its new home on the Bowery. It responded to the paradoxical institutional practice of scheduling indoor programs to address the theme of public space by initiating a temporary takeover of the streets that invited all to participate.

From its earliest street festivals to its most recent iterations as an itinerant global residency program, Ideas City has aimed to serve as a platform through which to research the state of the urban realm, viewed from the perspective of art and cultural practice and with the ambition of bringing together multidisciplinary networks of collaboration that span geographical boundaries. Ideas City is an experiment in the creation of a new kind of artistic and design agency that has been liberated from the reigning imperative to engage with the city solely as a value-generating mechanism. To achieve this, everyone must be involved.

On the occasion of an exhibition of his work in Genoa in 2015, the Italian architect and urbanist Giancarlo De Carlo

stated, "architecture is too important to be left to architects." Likewise, in our time, cities are too important to be
left to city planners. In order to realize the potential of
cities to improve the lives of the world's rapidly growing
population, we need to pioneer new models of civic life in
which culture and art are not extraneous luxuries but
inalienable ingredients.

Joseph Grima has been Director of Ideas City since 2015. Trained as an architect, he is
also the founder of the Genoa-based design research studio Space Caviar and Creative
Director of Eindhoven Design Academy. He was previously Editor in Chief of *Domus*
magazine and Director of Storefront for Art and Architecture, New York.

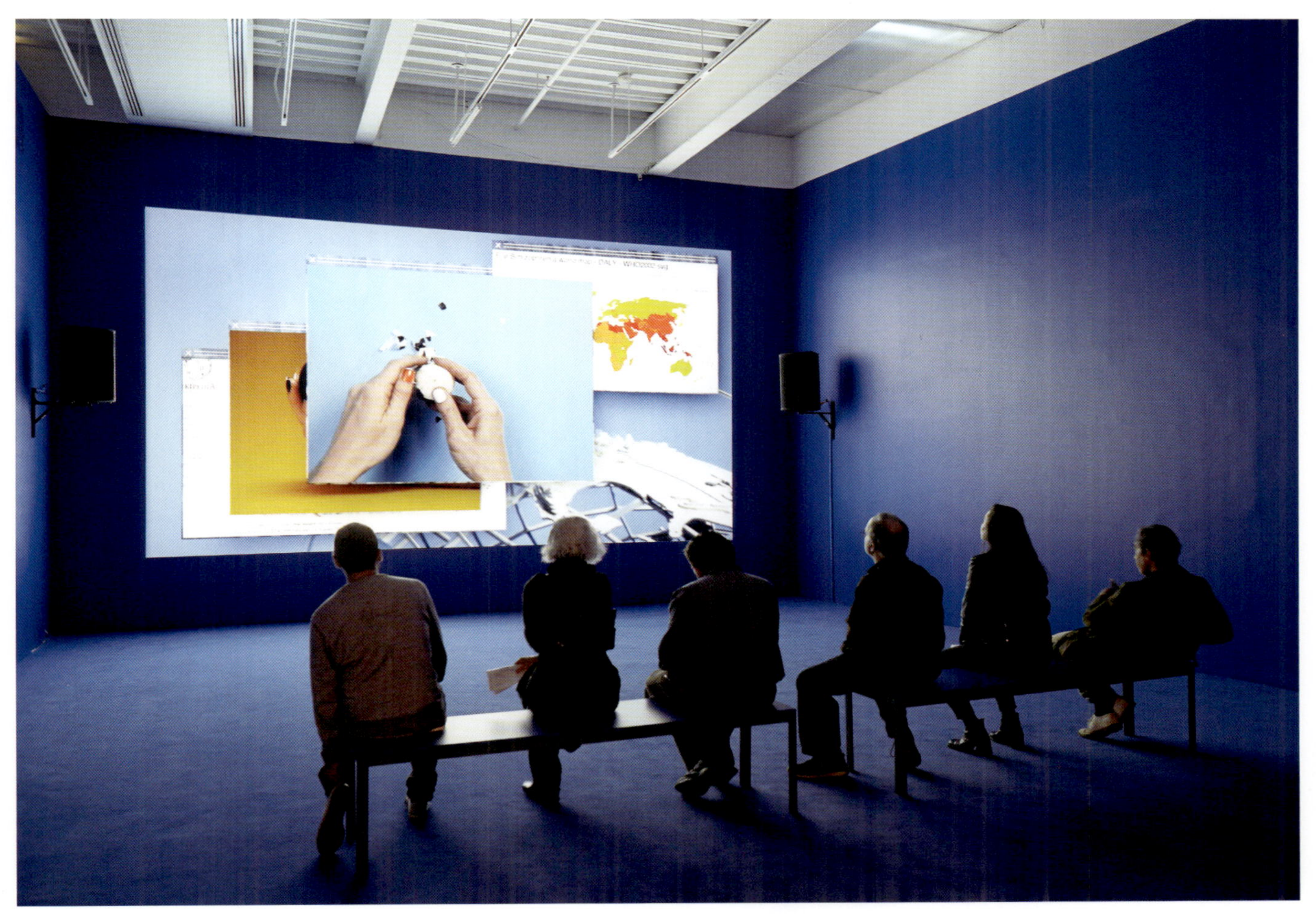

Camille Henrot,
Grosse Fatigue, 2003

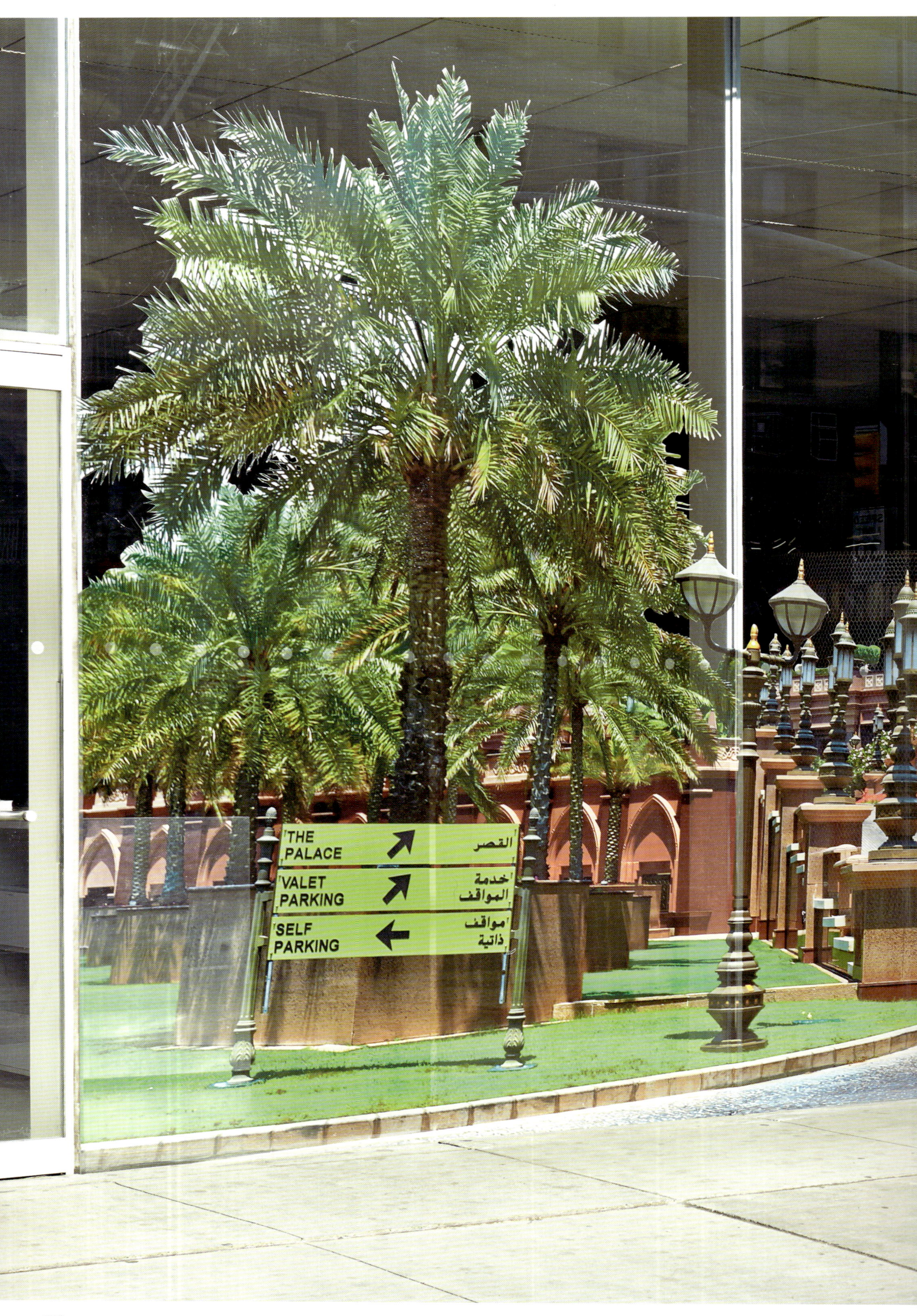

GCC,
*The One and Only Madinat
New Museum Royal Mirage,*
2014 (detail)

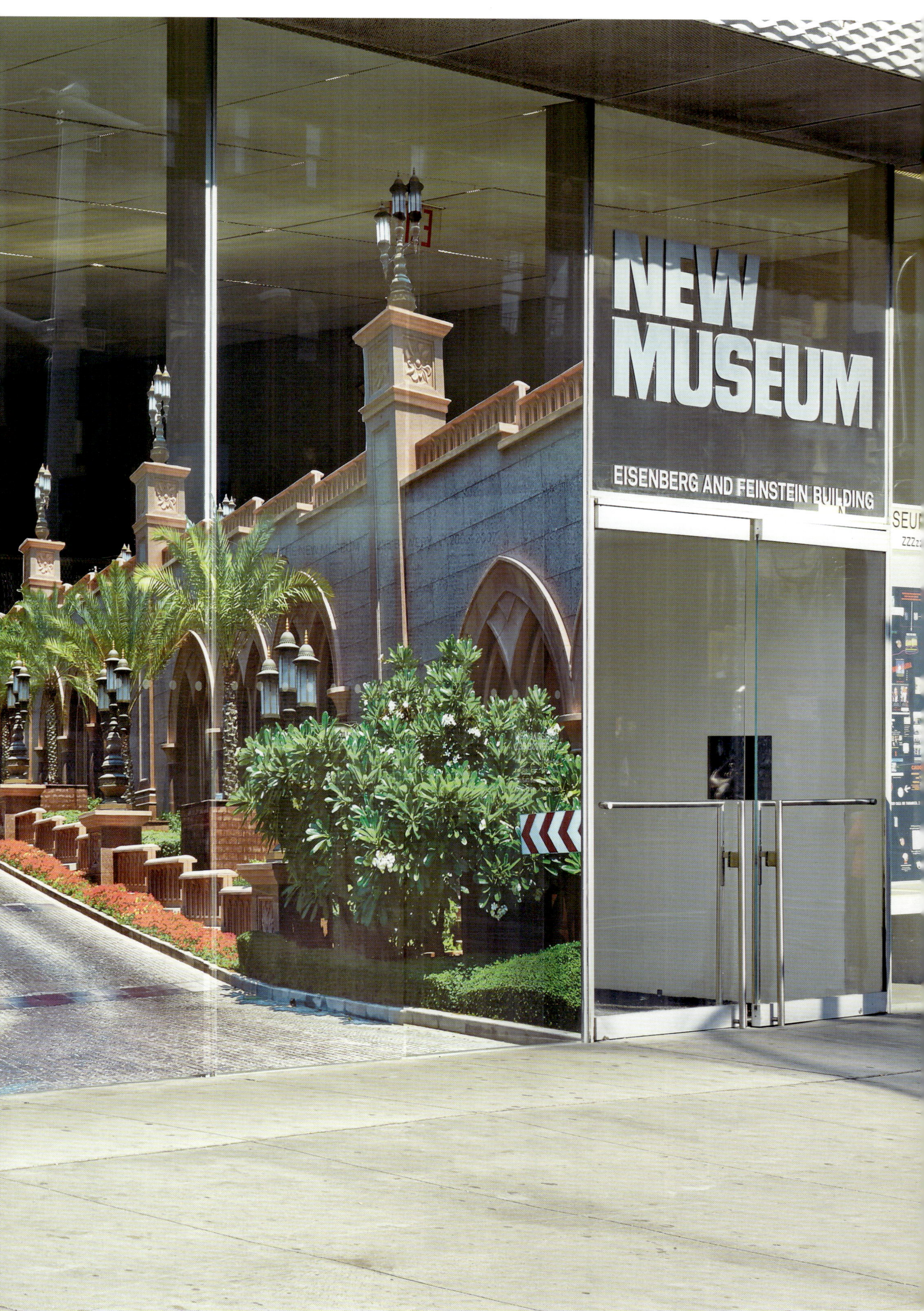

NEW
MUSEUM
EISENBERG AND FEINSTEIN BUILDING

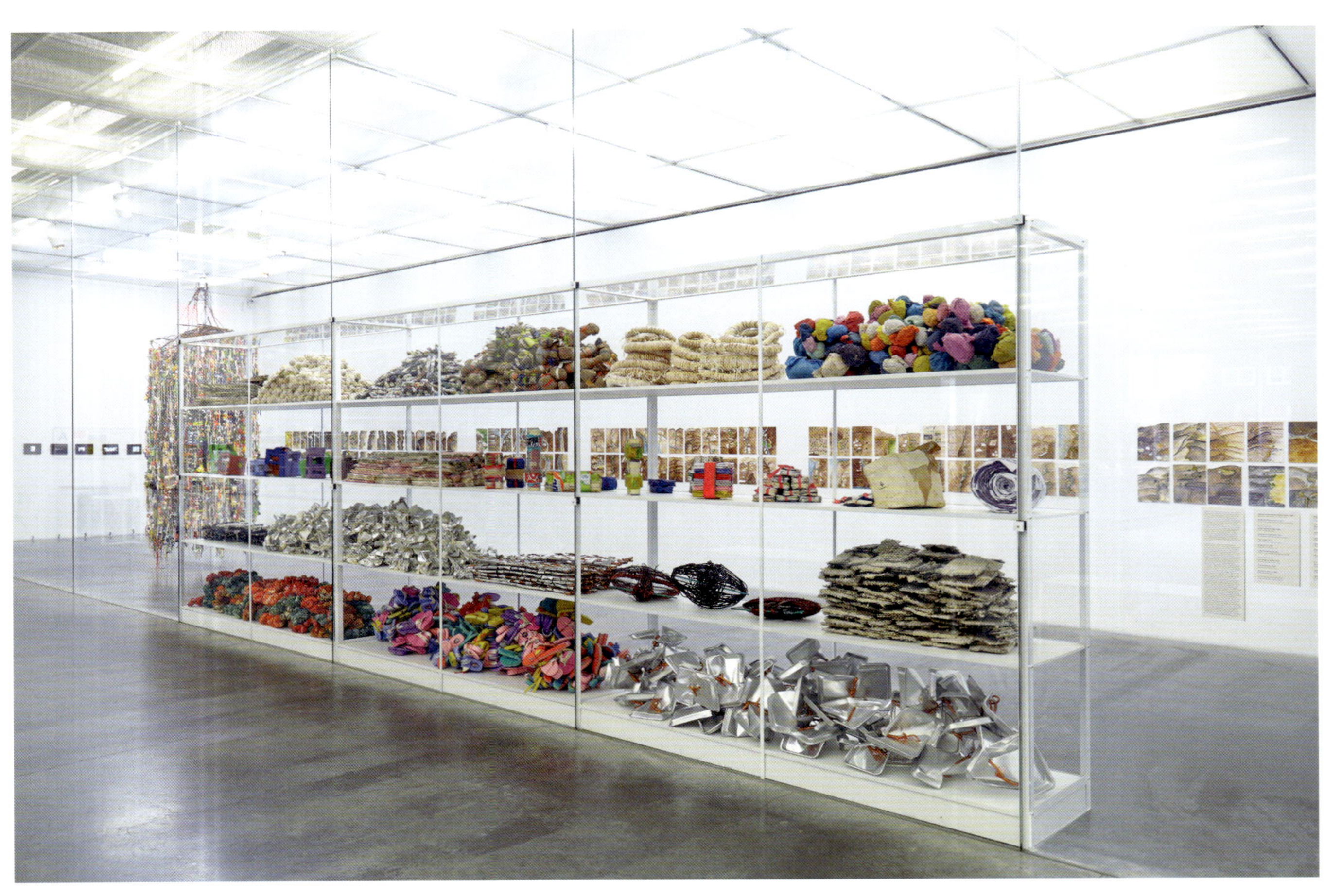

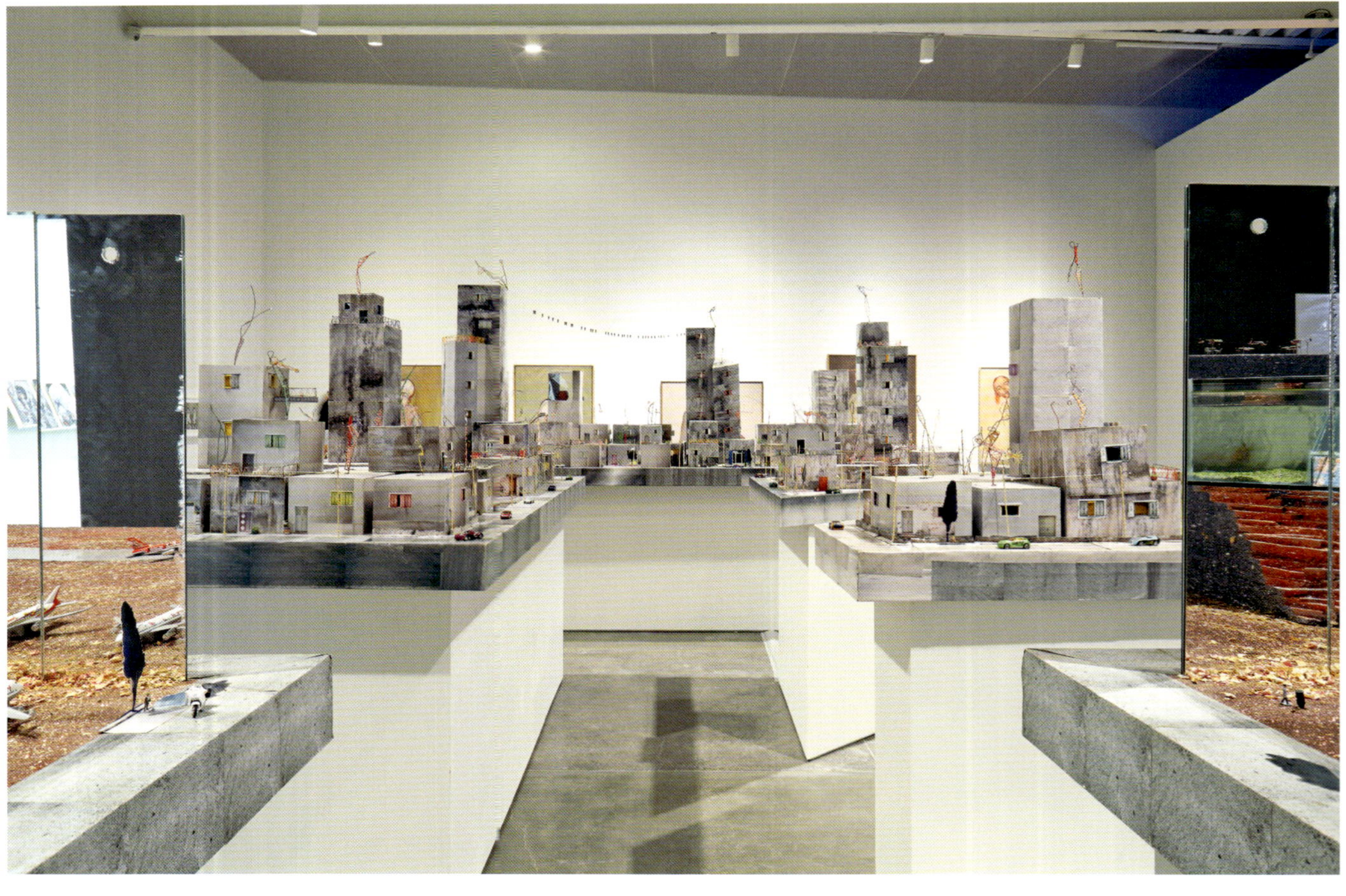

(top) Foreground: work
by Hassan Shariff.
Background: work by
Abdullah Al Saadi

(bottom) Foreground:
work by Wafa Hourani

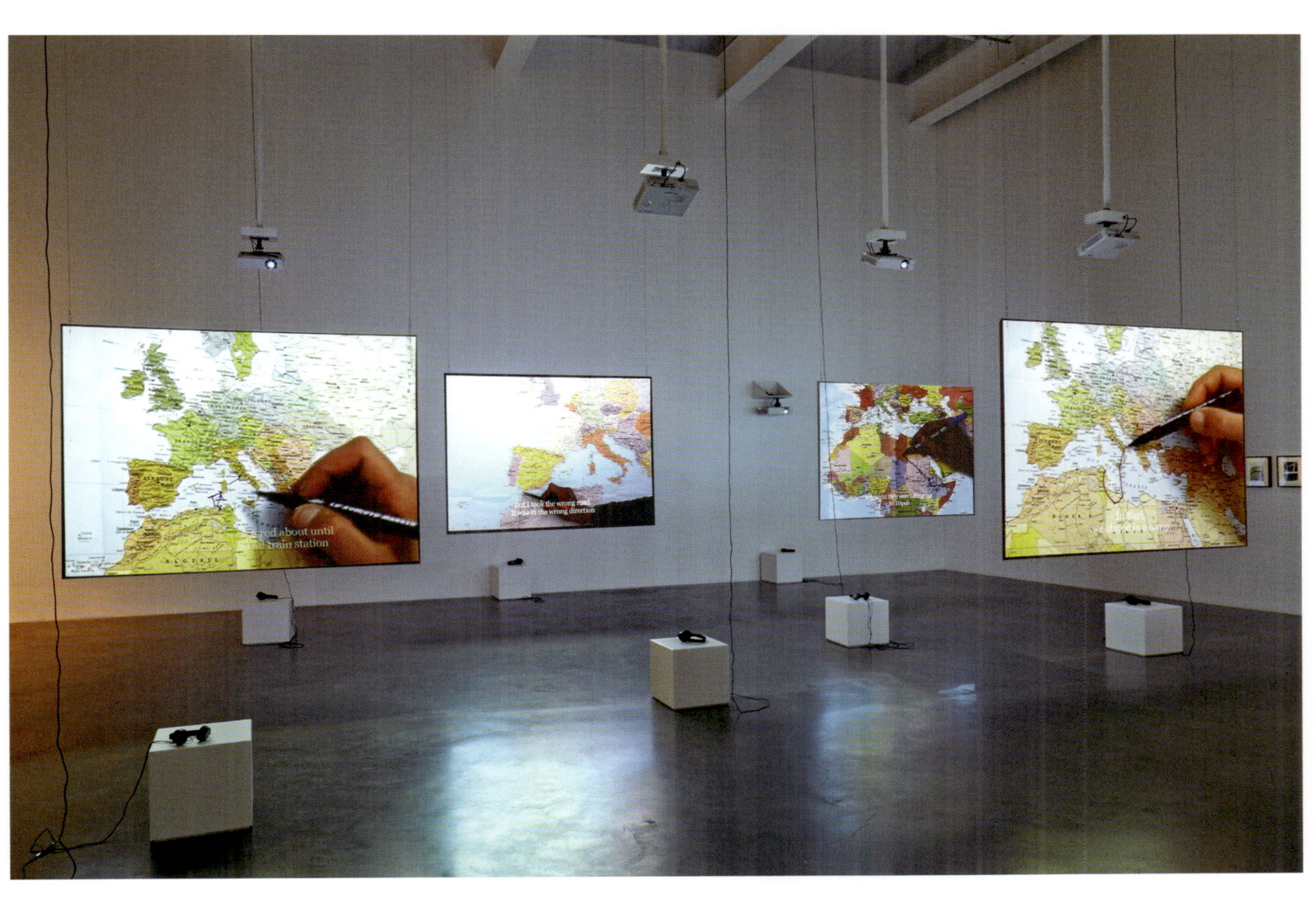

Bouchra Khalili,
*The Mapping Journey
Project*, 2008–11

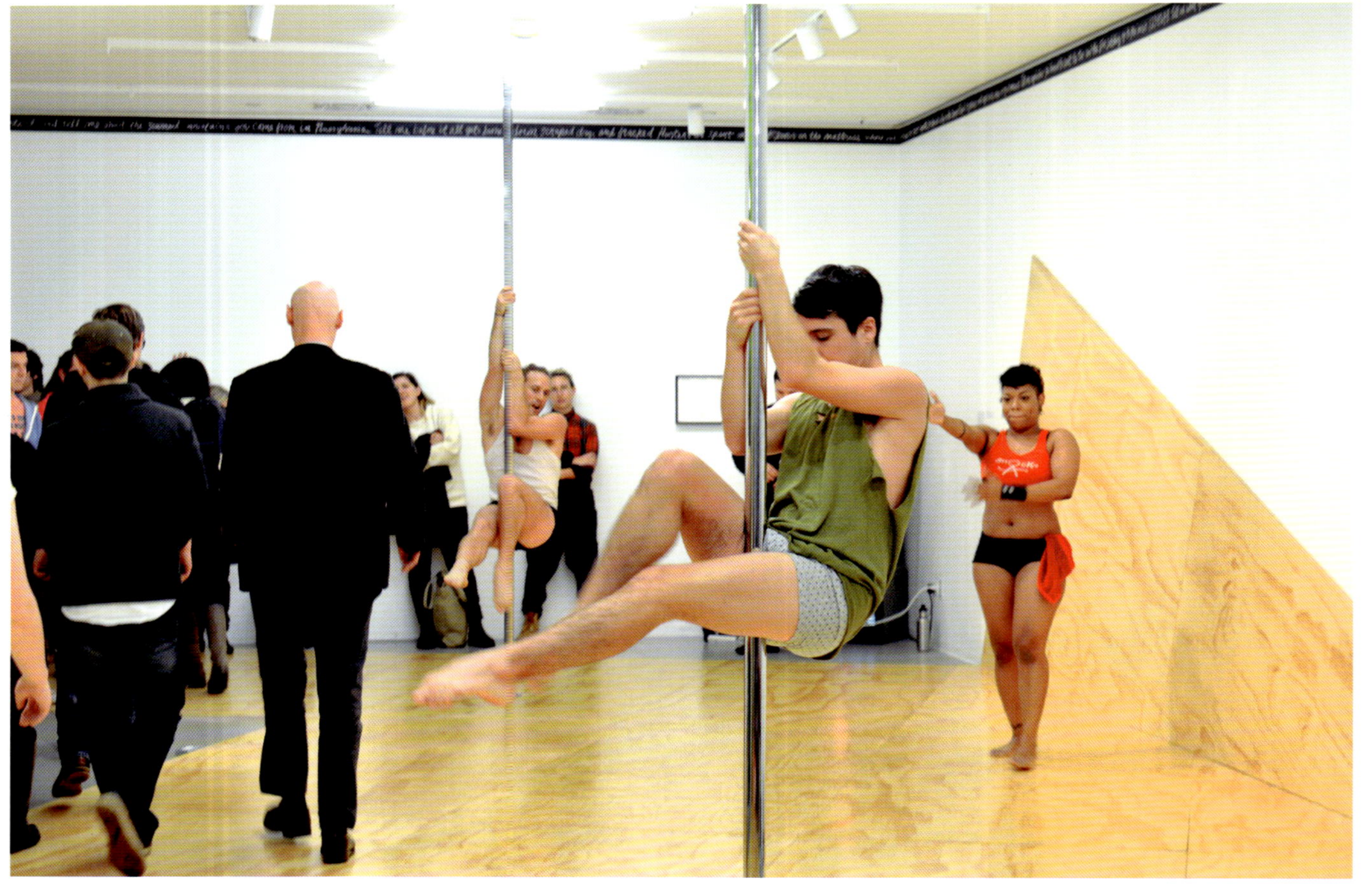

"Open Pole" session,
part of "Gerard &
Kelly: P.O.L.E. (People,
Objects, Language,
Exchange)," 2014.

Left to right:
Ryan Kelly, devynn emory,
and Keisha Franklin

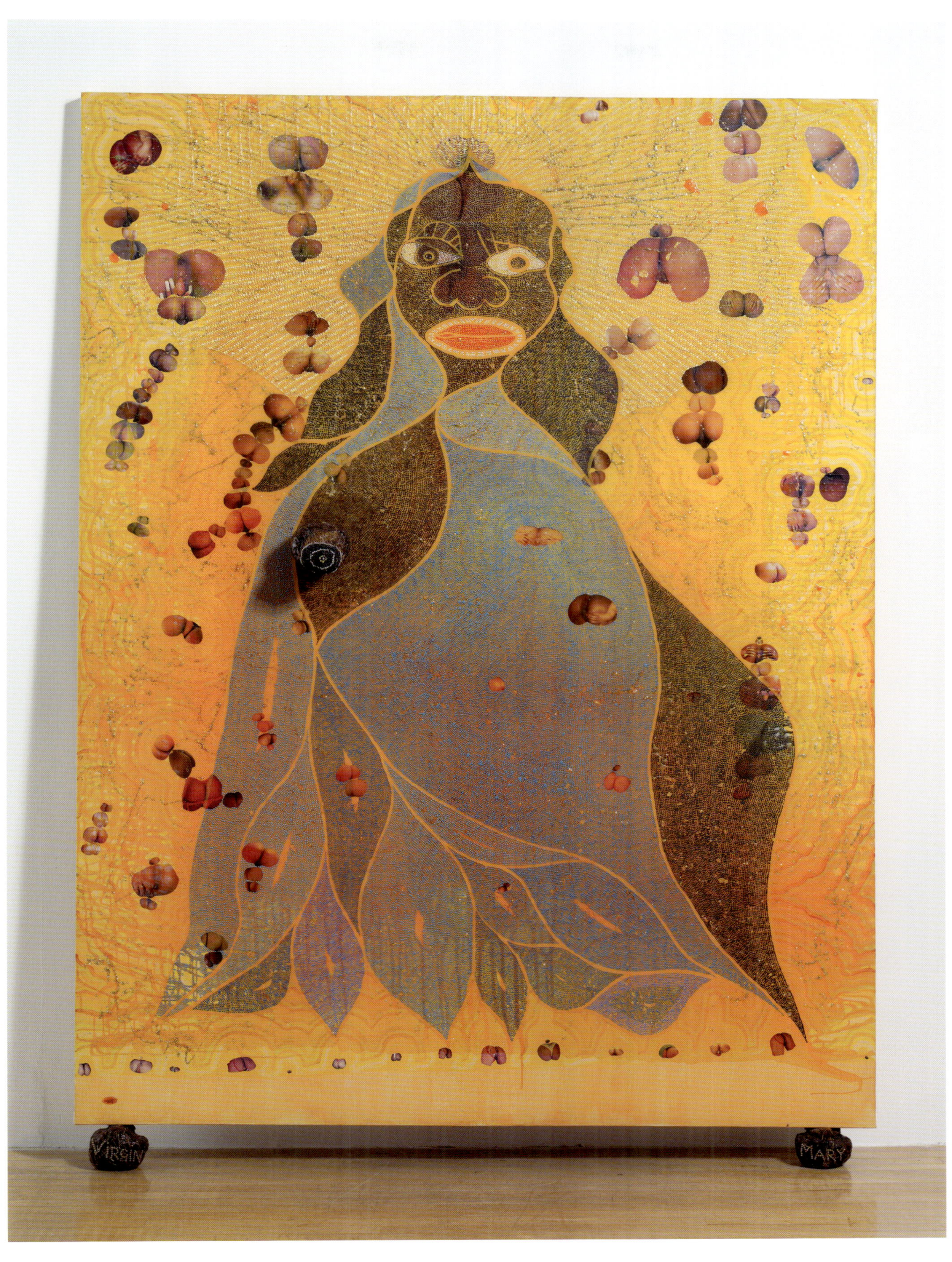

Chris Ofili,
The Holy Virgin Mary, 1996

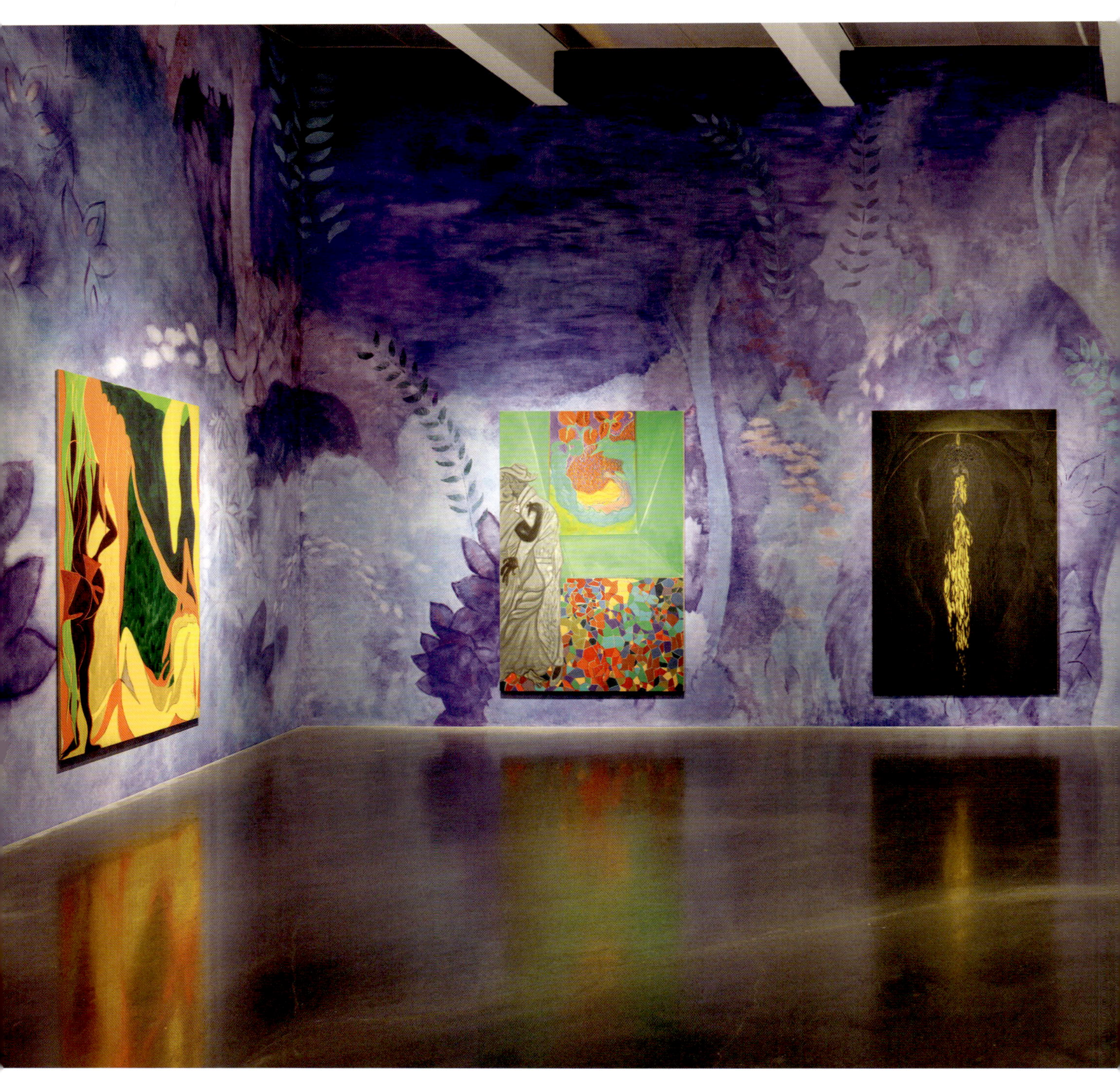

Left to right: Chris Ofili, *The Raising of Lazarus*, 2007; *Ovid-Destiny*, 2011–12; *The Healer*, 2008; *Ovid-Desire*, 2011–12; *Ovid-Actaeon*, 2011–12; and *Lime Bar*, 2014

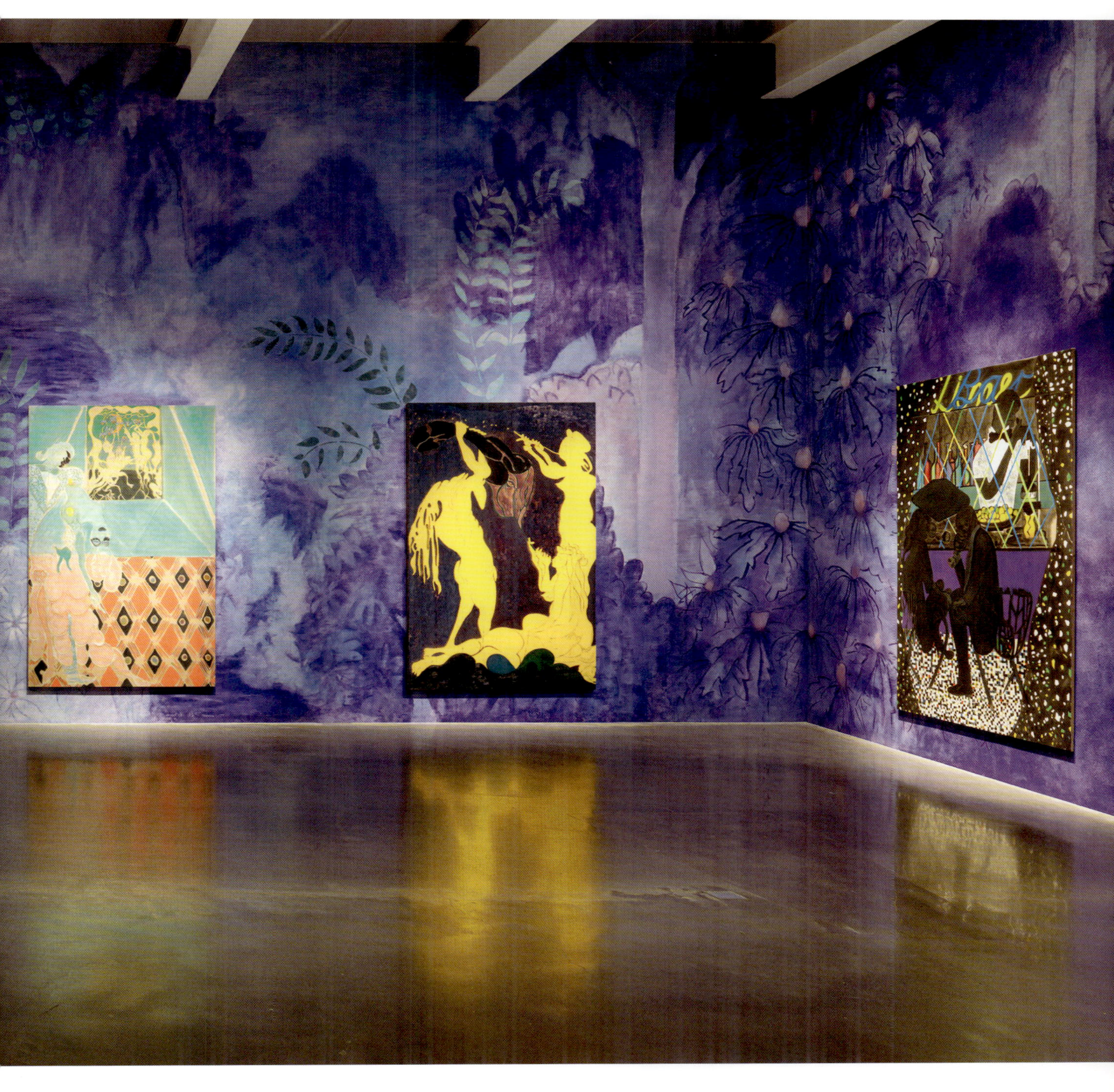

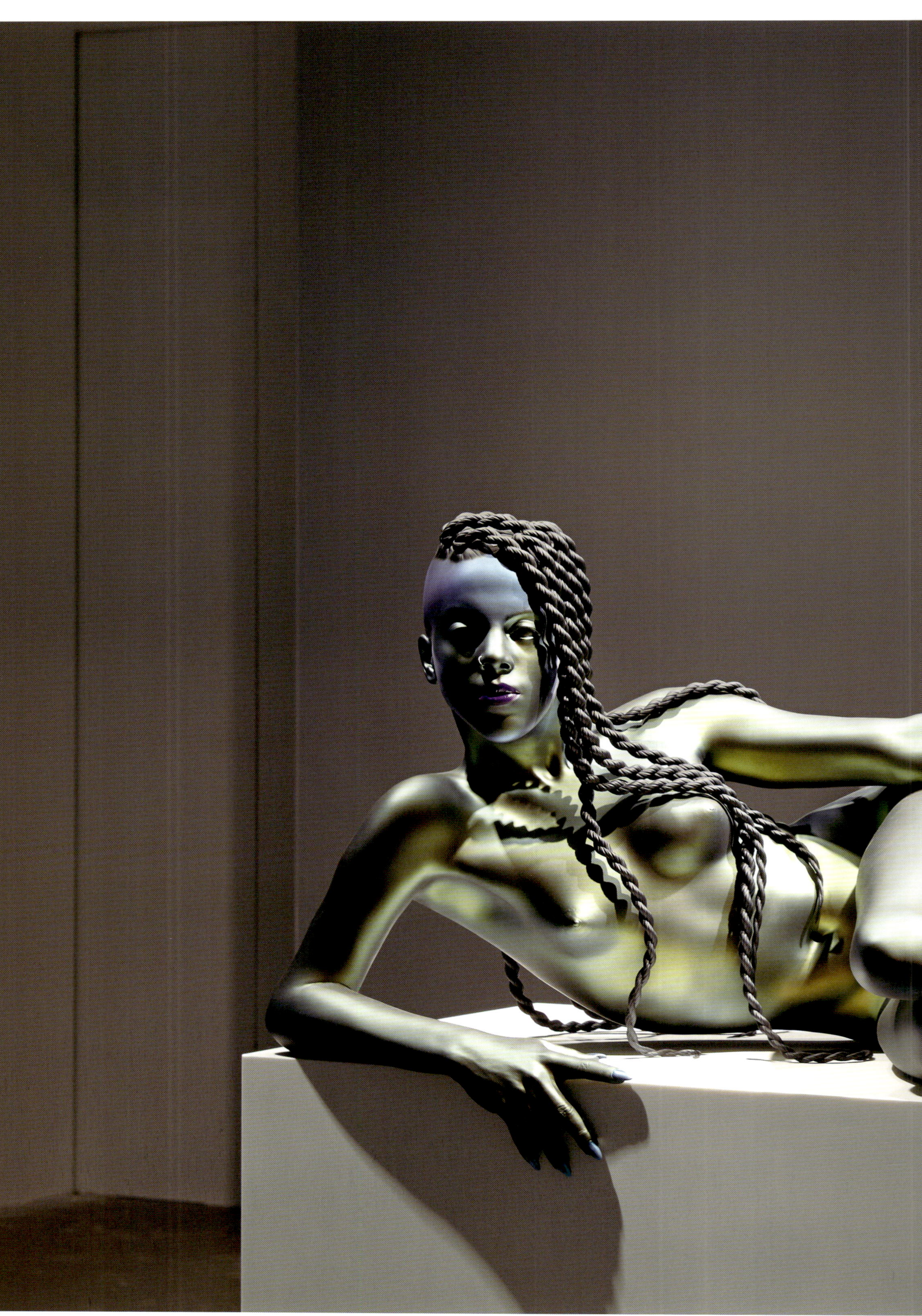

Frank Benson,
Juliana, 2015

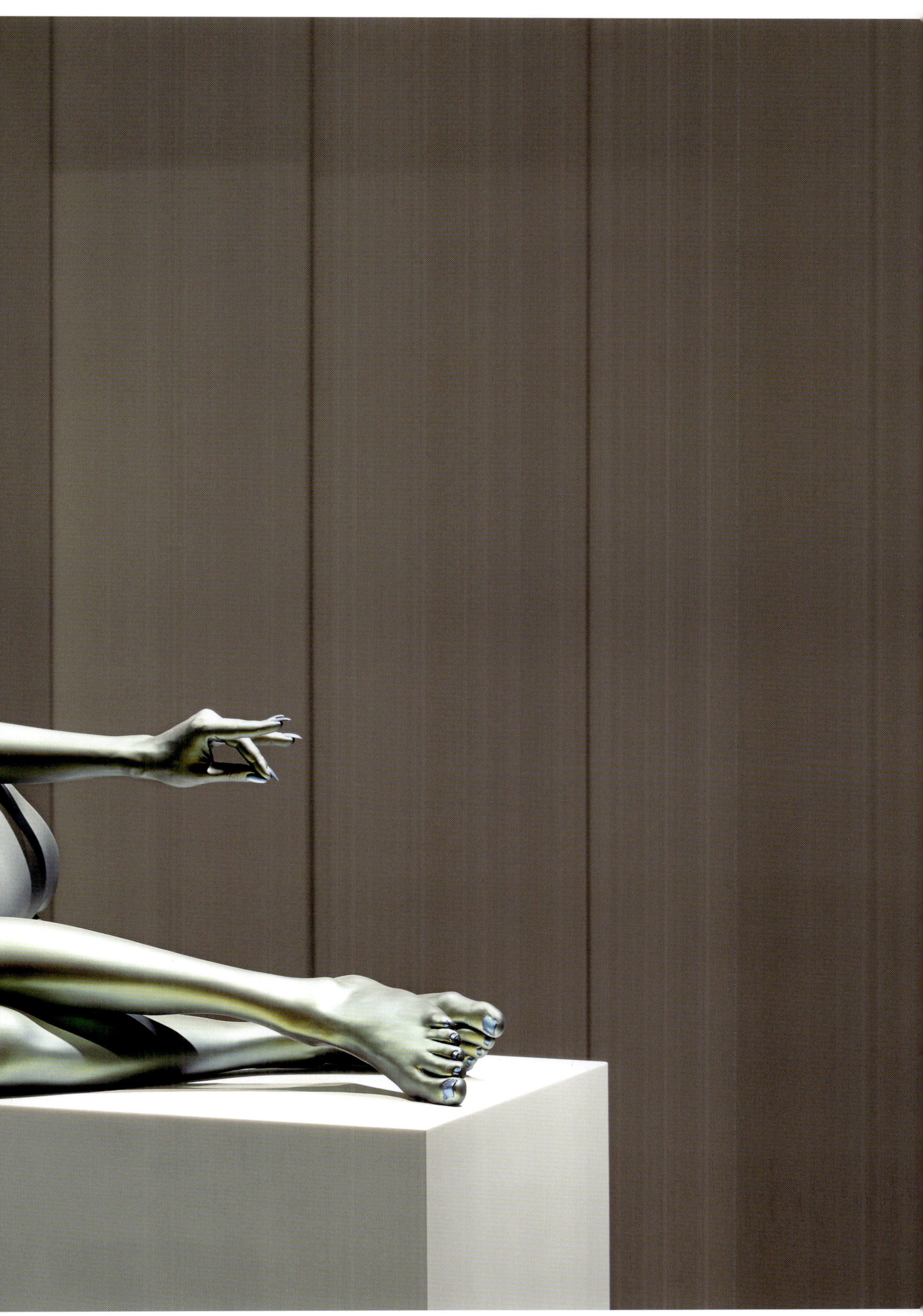

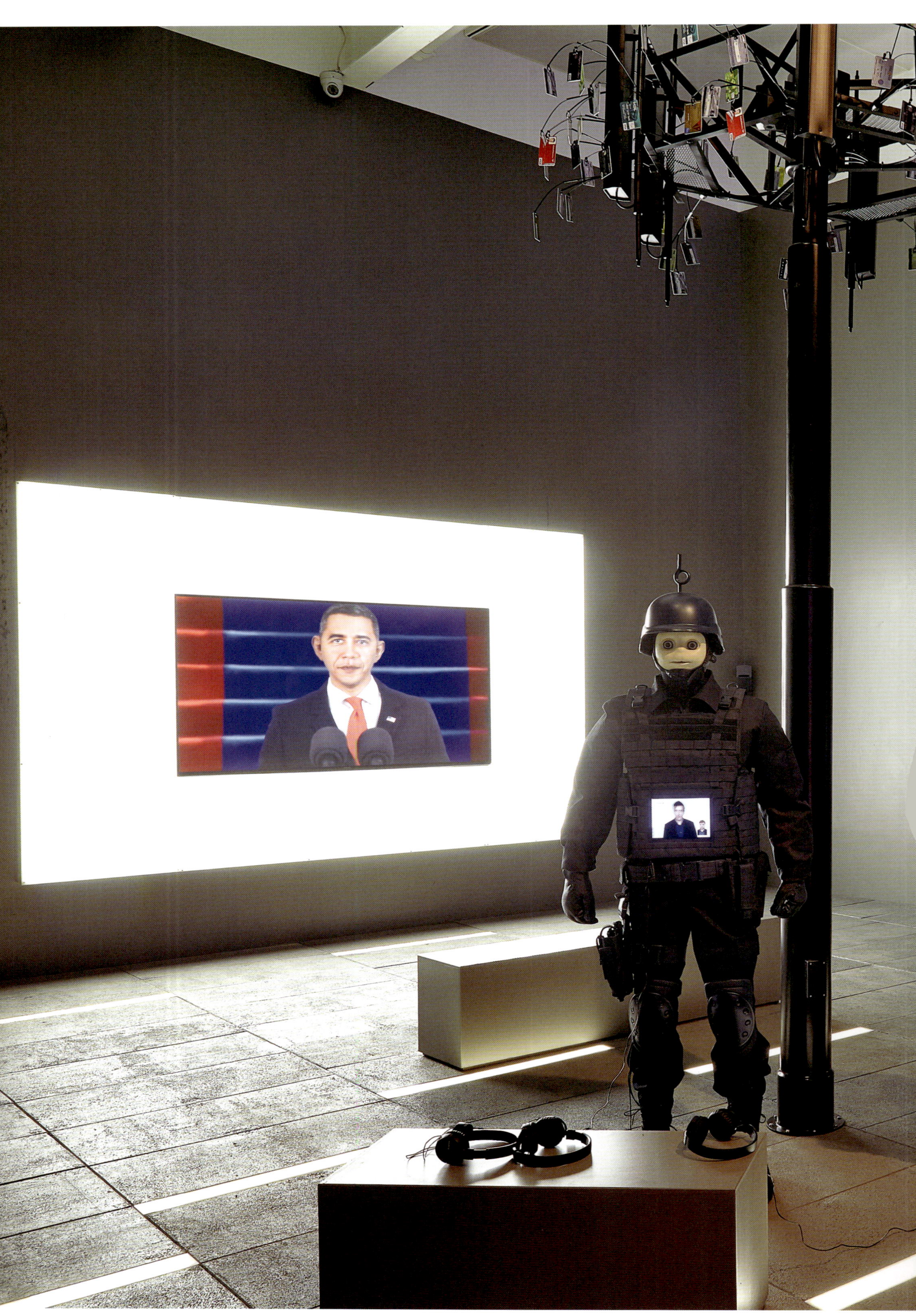

Josh Kline,
Freedom, 2015

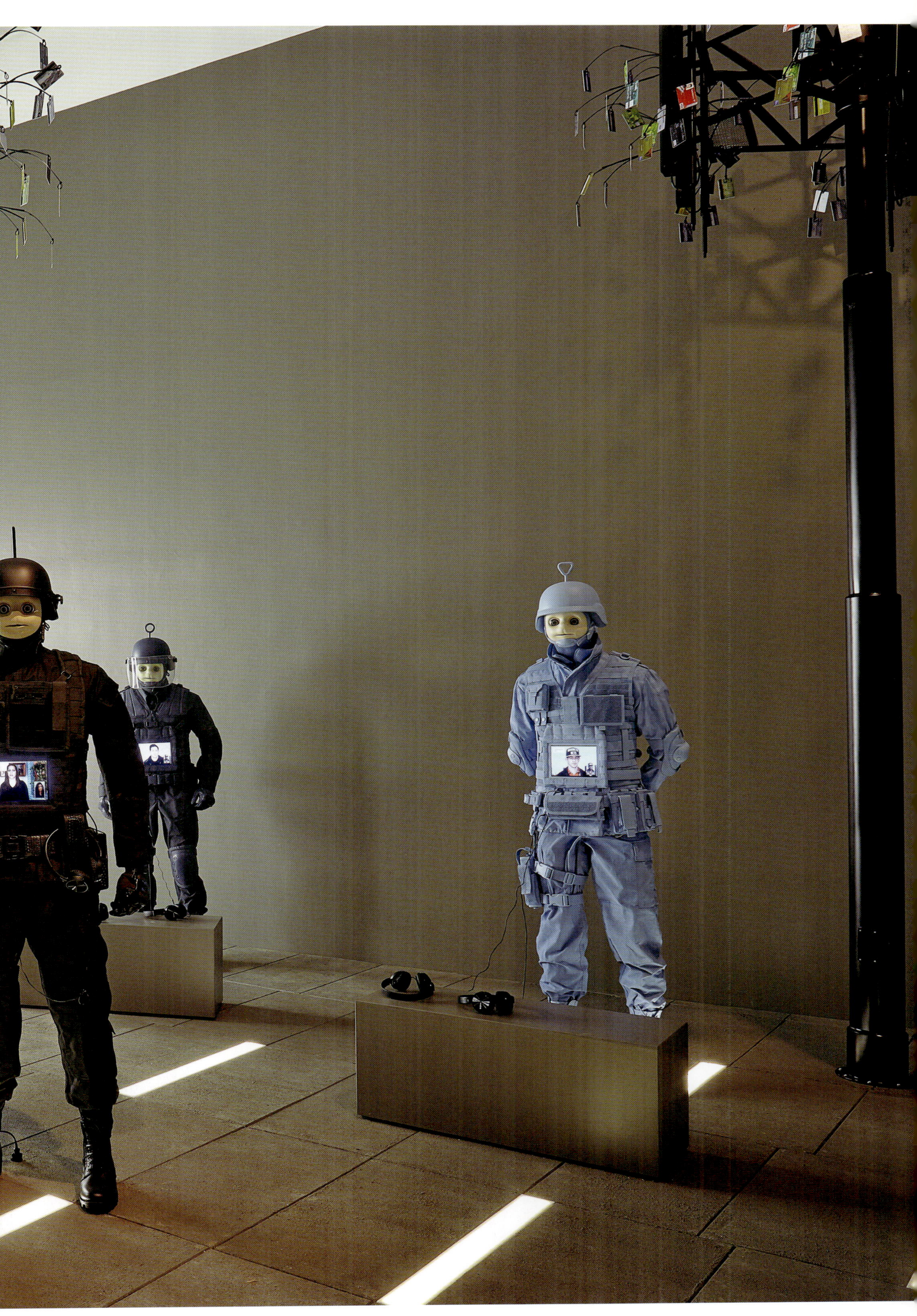

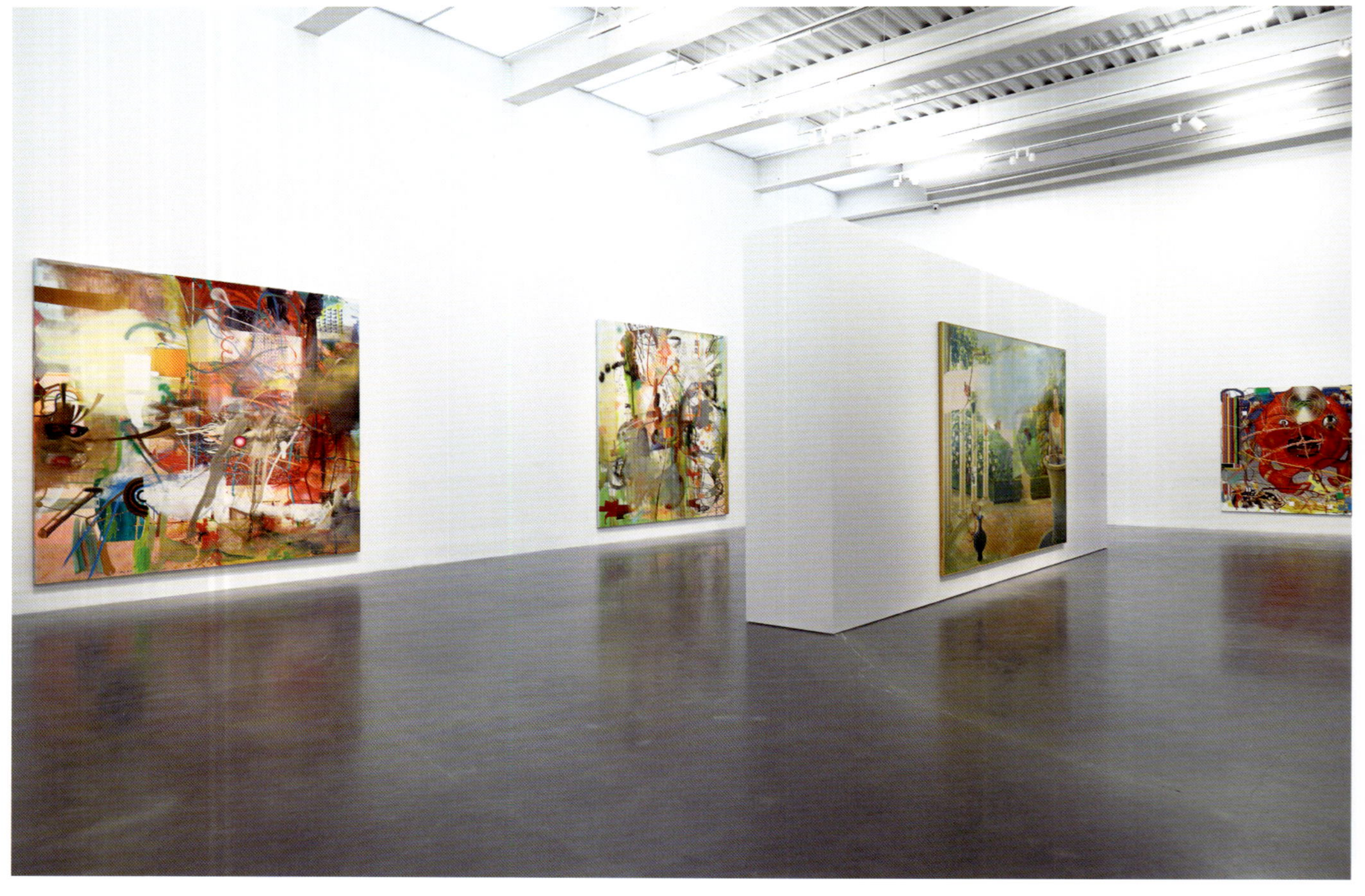

Left to right: Albert Oehlen, *Born to be late*, 2001; *More Fire and Ice*, 2001; *Selbst als Frühling* [Self-portrait as Spring], 2006; and *Captain Jack*, 1997

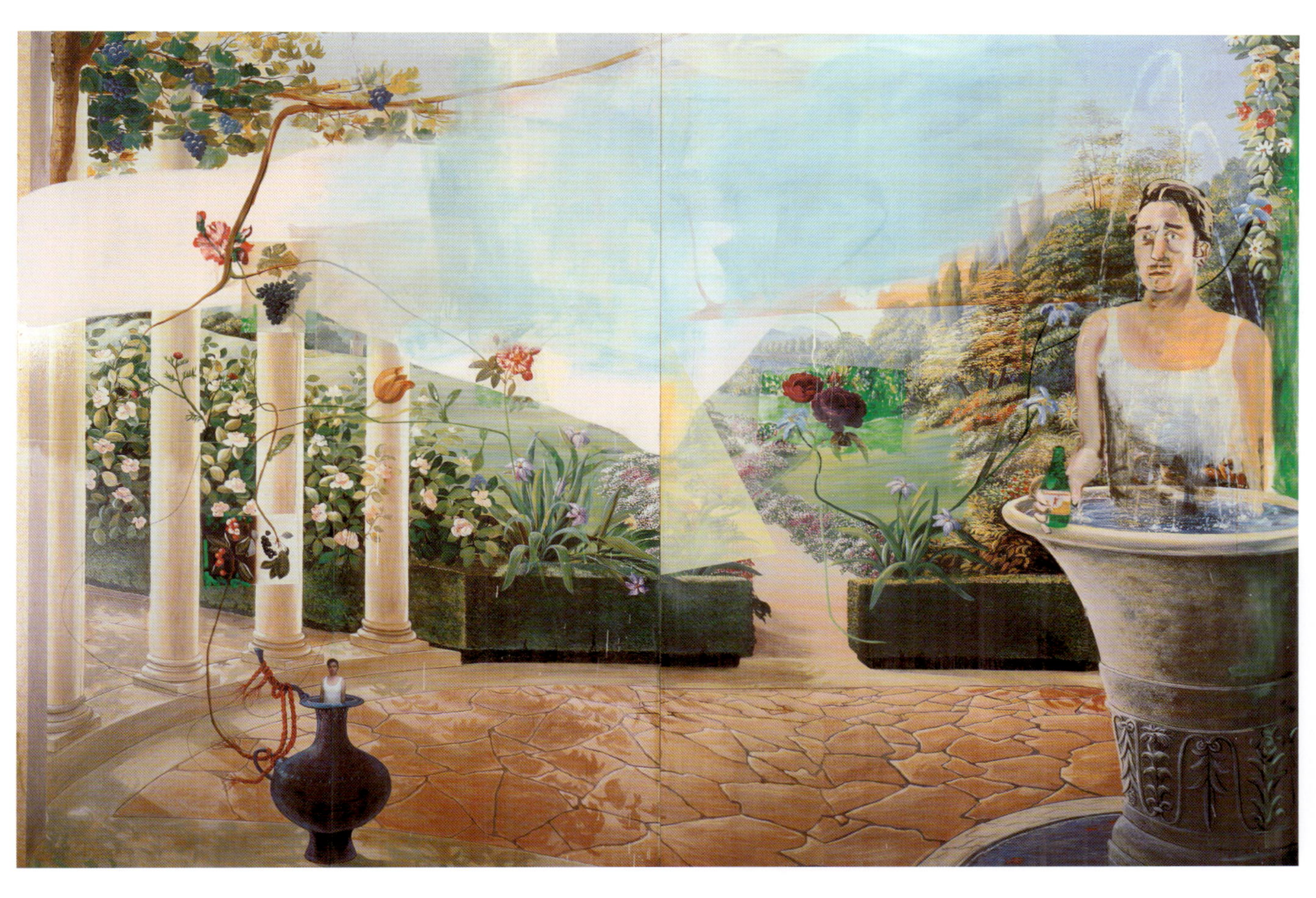

Albert Oehlen,
Selbst als Frühling [Self-
portrait as Spring], 2006

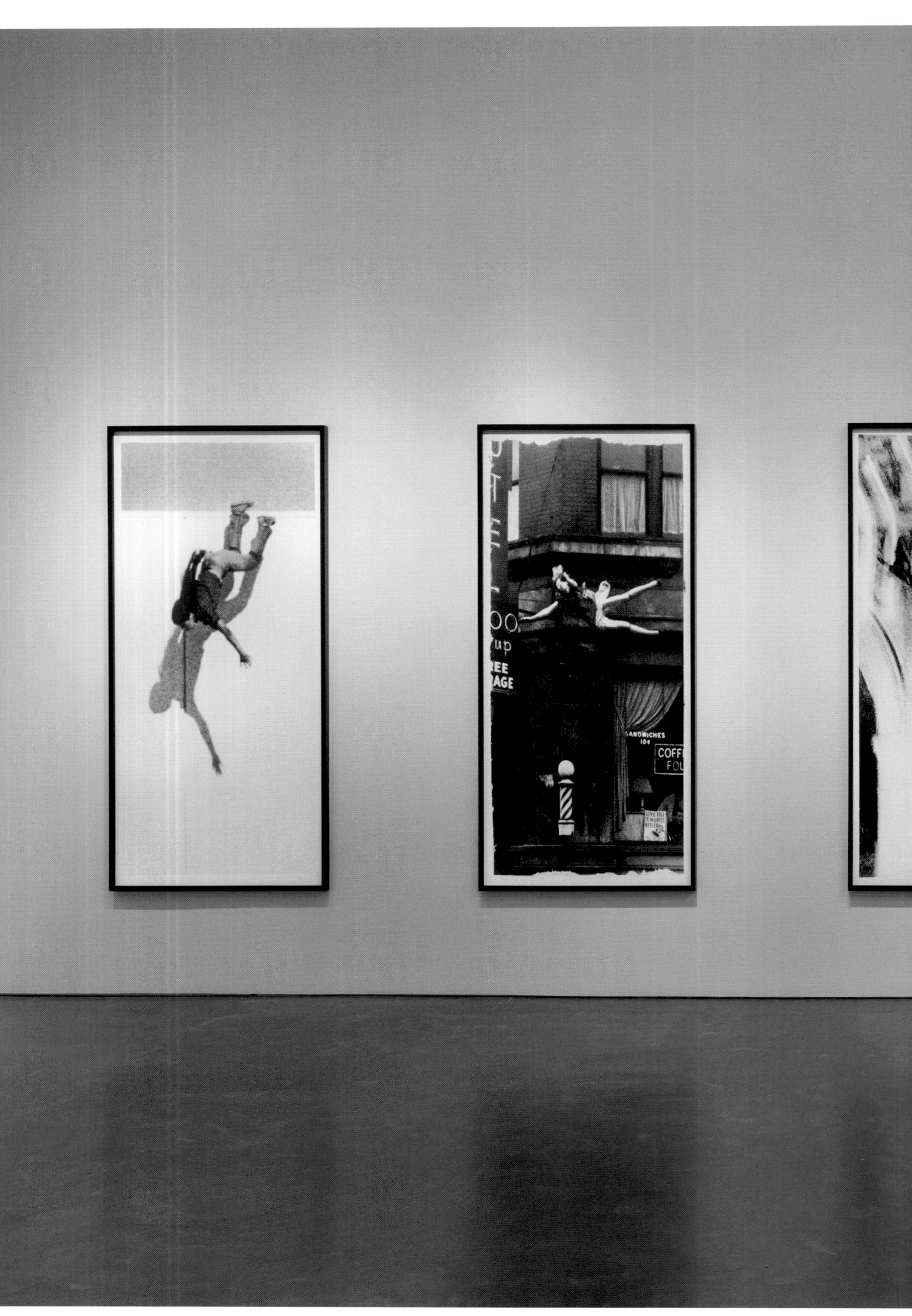

Sarah Charlesworth,
Stills, 1980, printed in
2012 (detail)

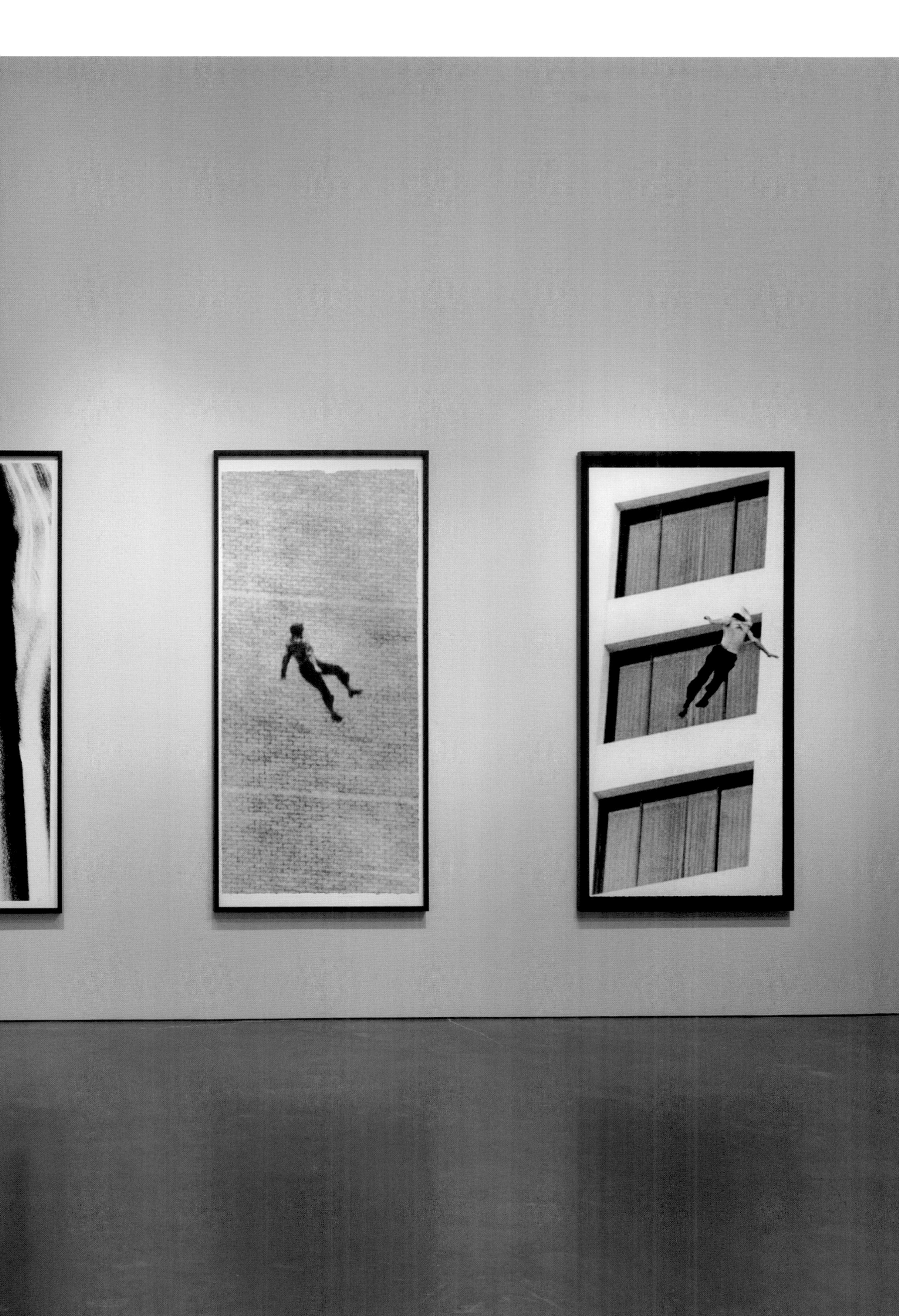

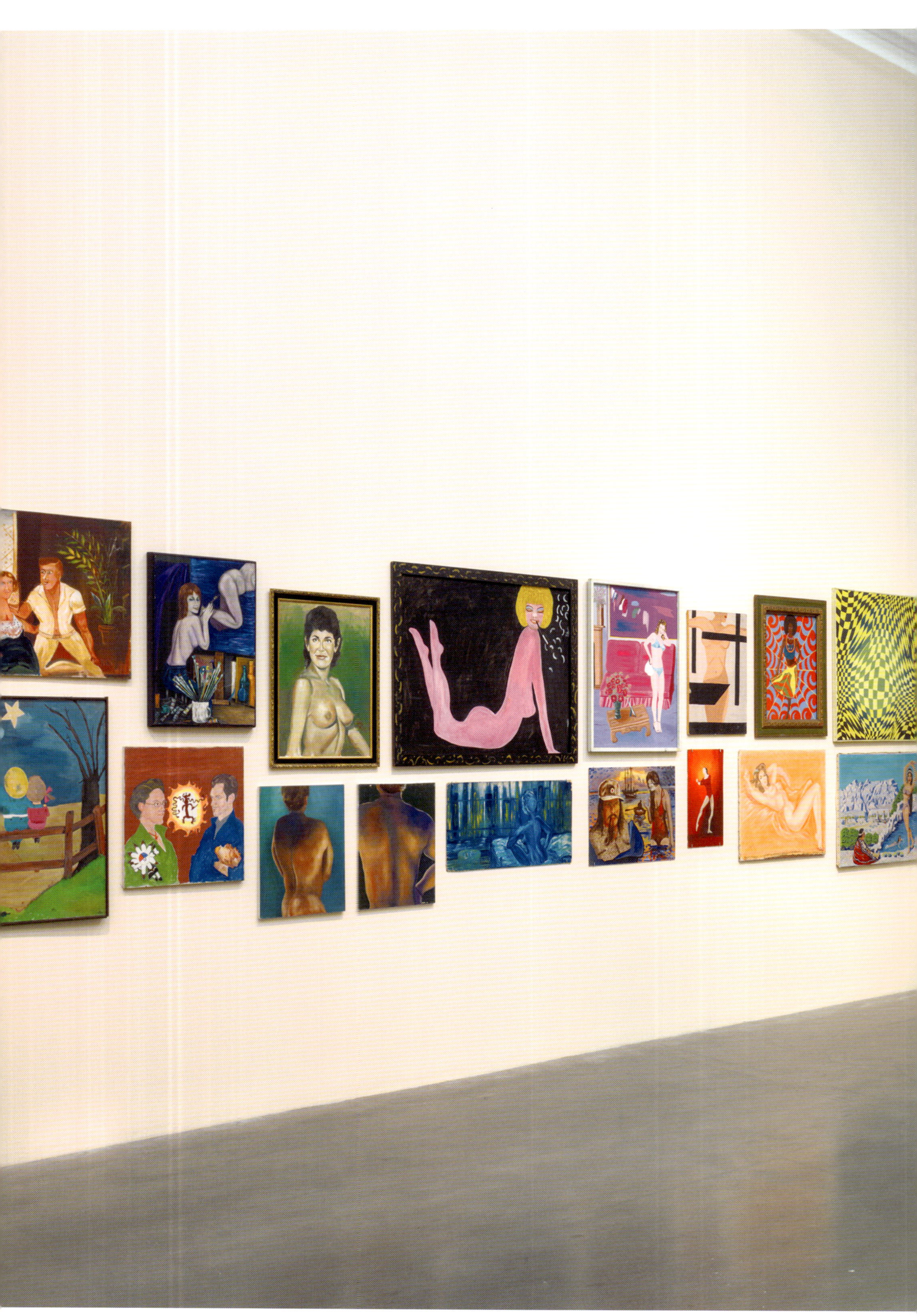

Jim Shaw,
Thrift Store Paintings,
n.d. (detail)

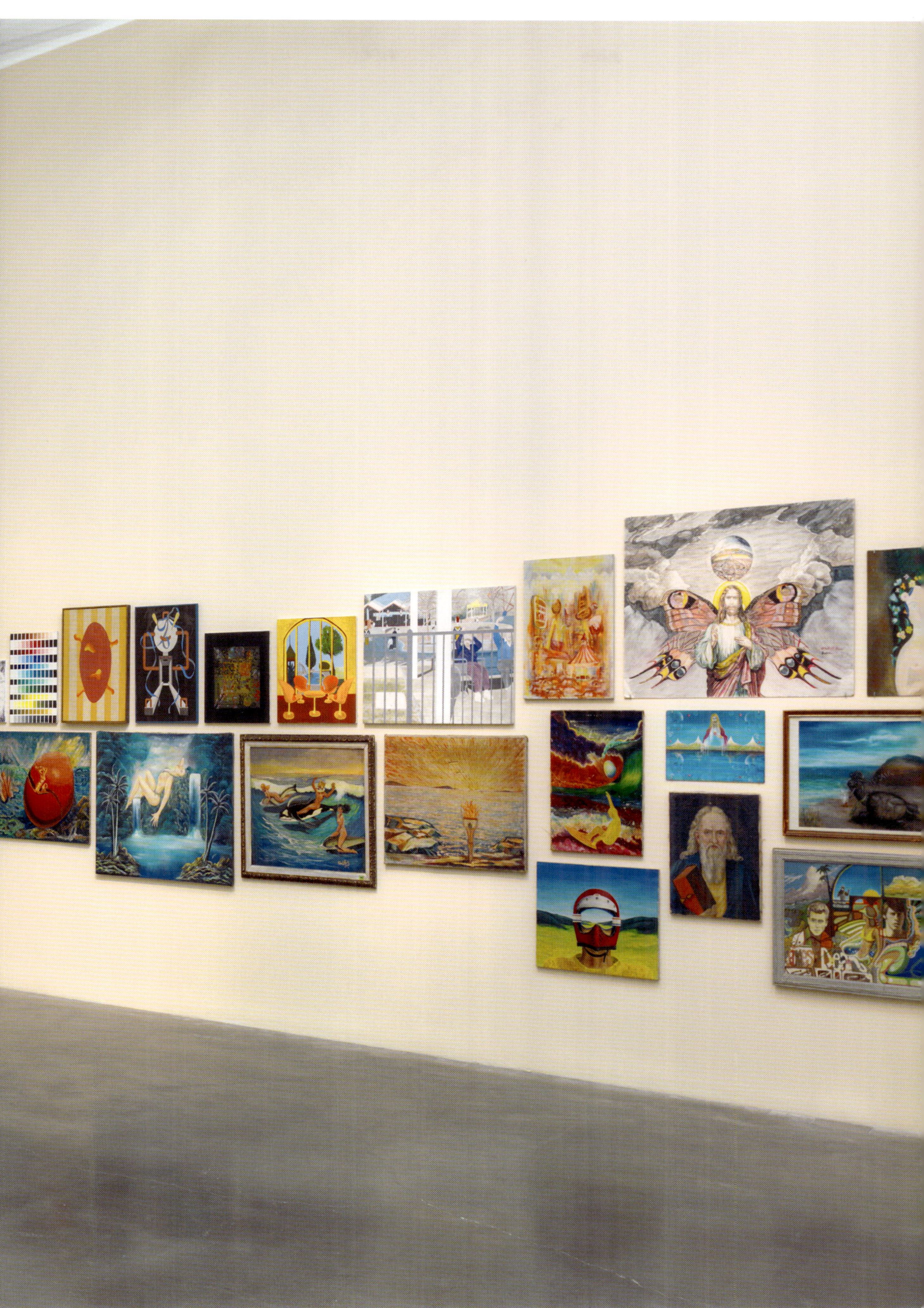

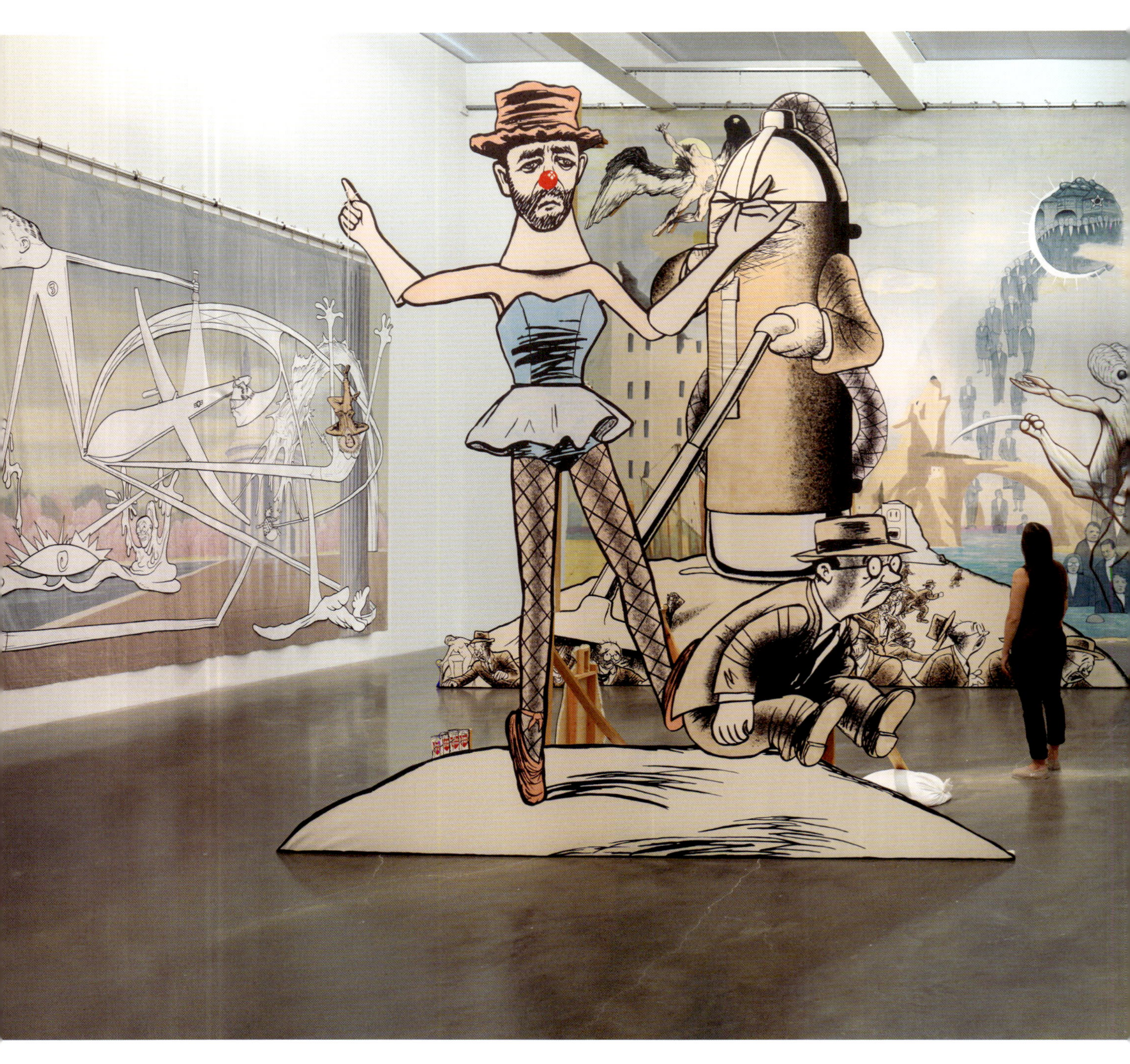

Jim Shaw,
*Labyrinth: I Dreamt I
was Taller than Jonathan
Borofsky*, 2009

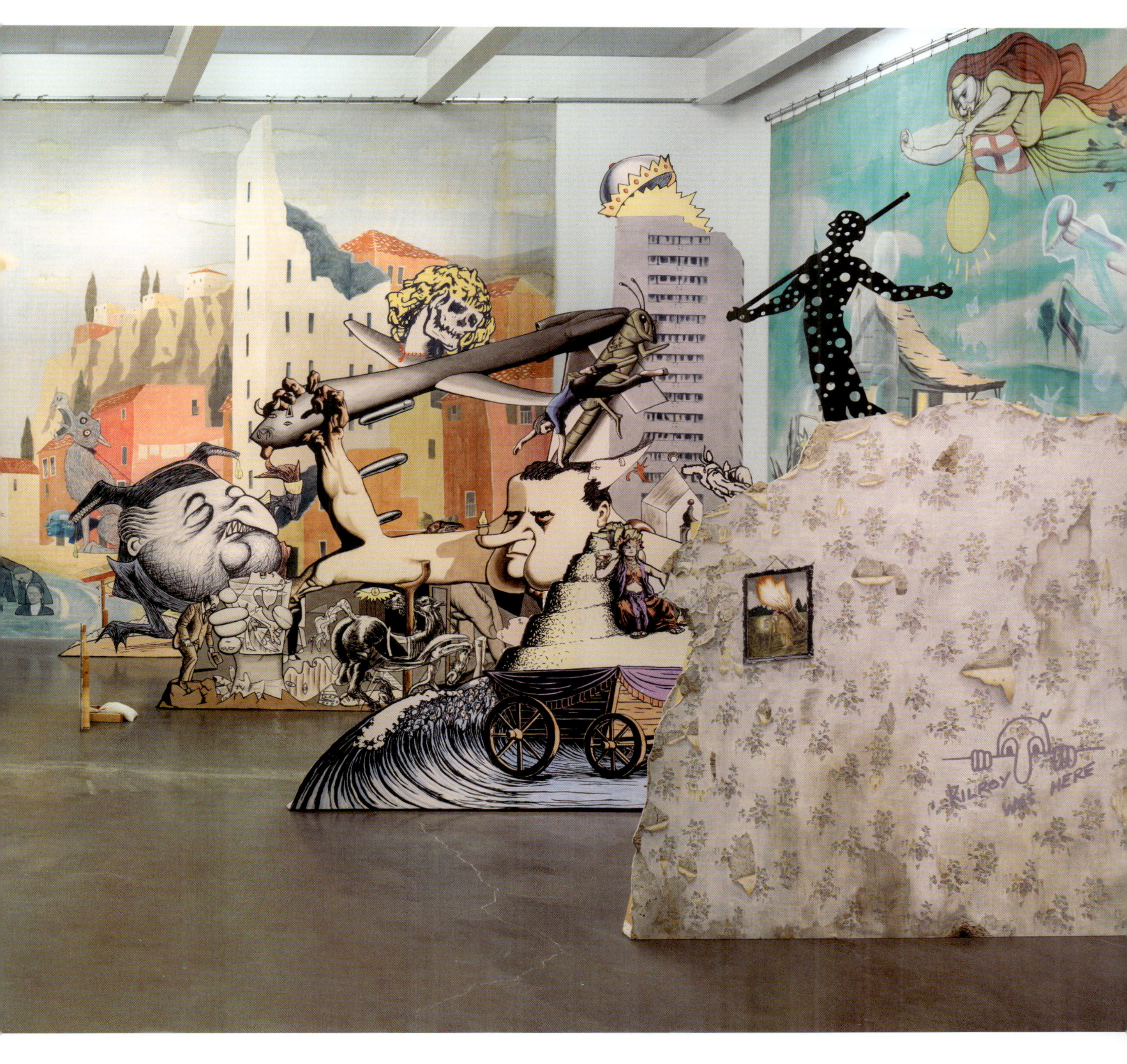

KILROY
WAS HERE

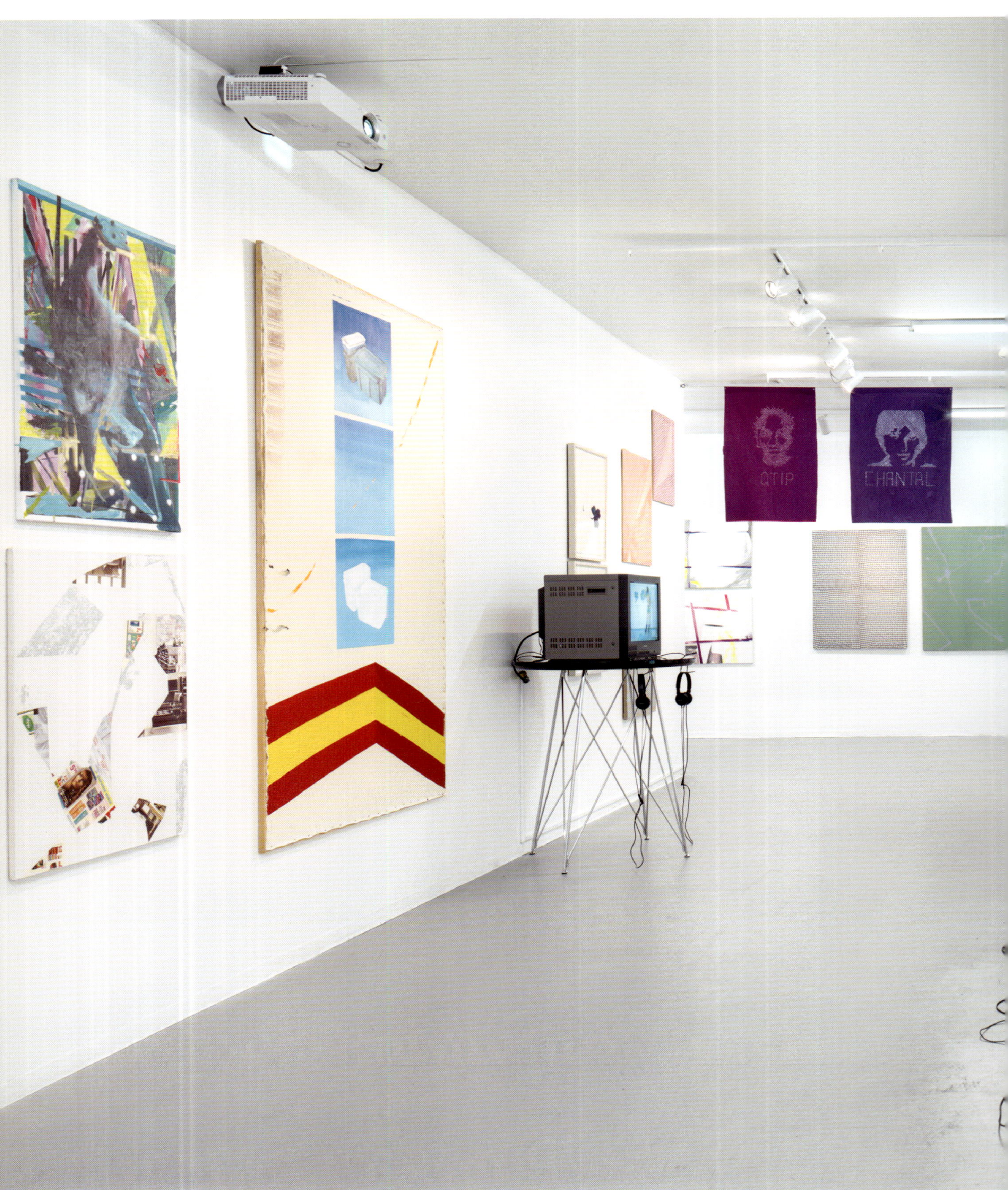

Installation view

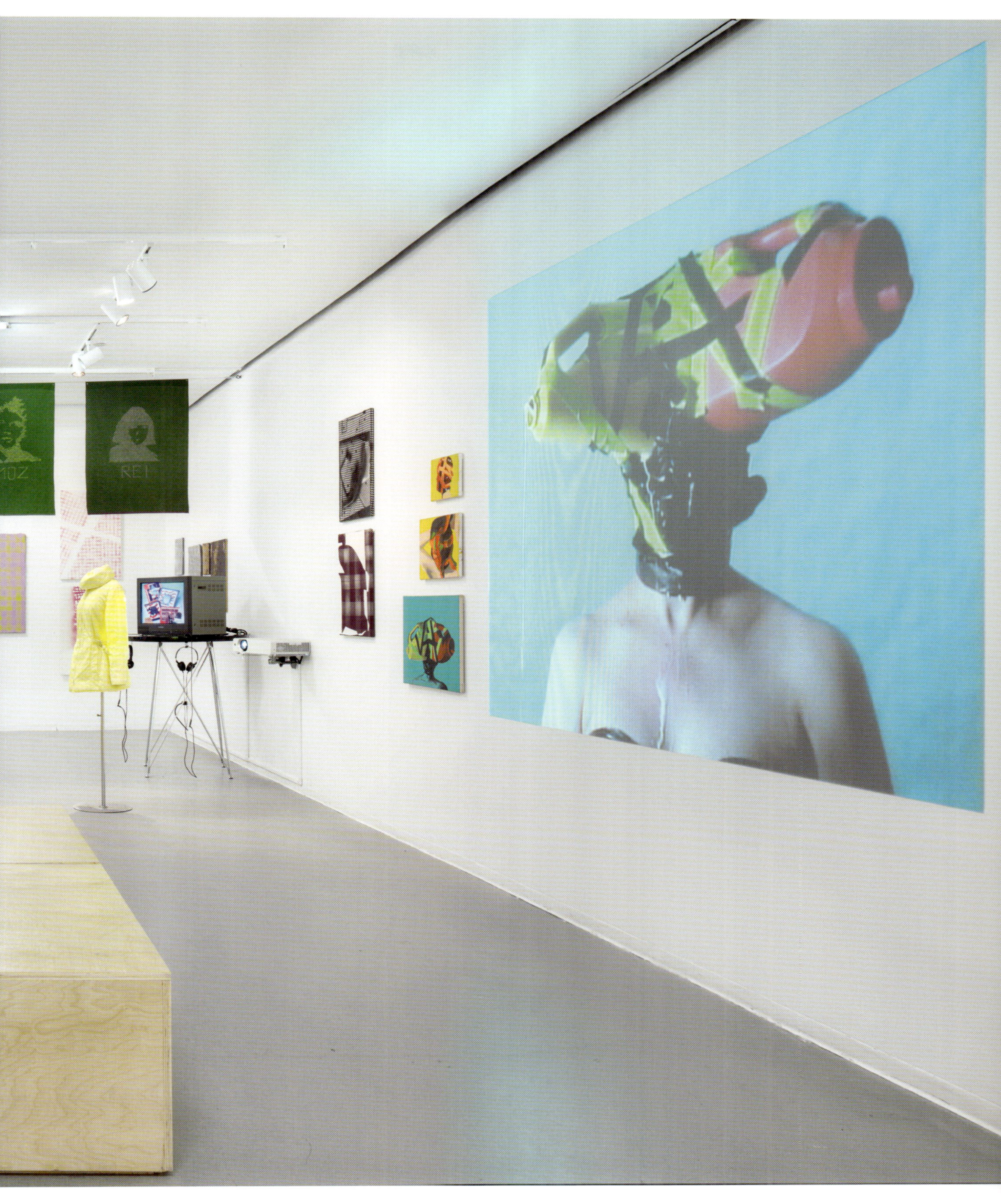

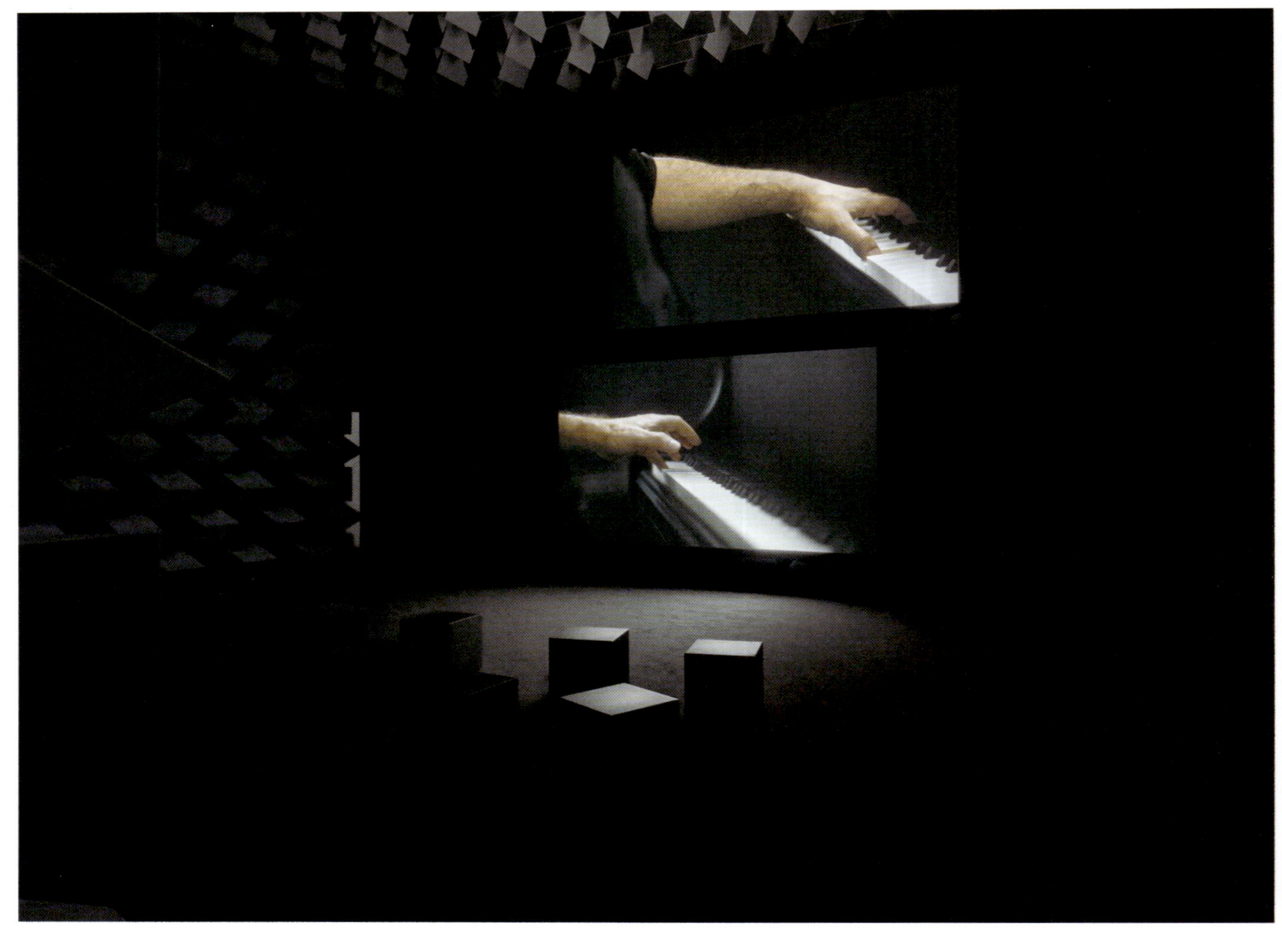

Anri Sala,
Ravel Ravel, 2013

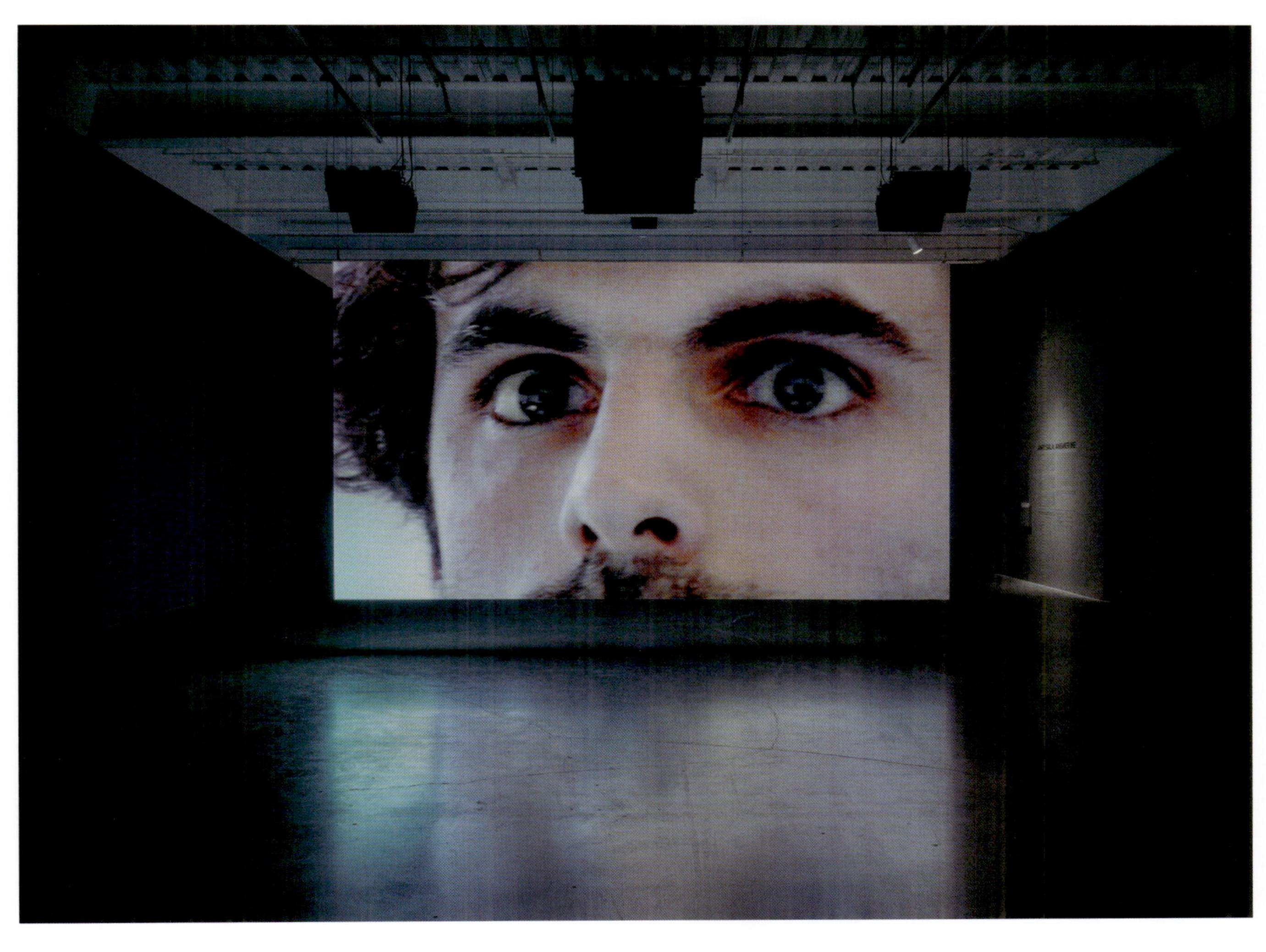

Anri Sala,
Answer Me, 2008

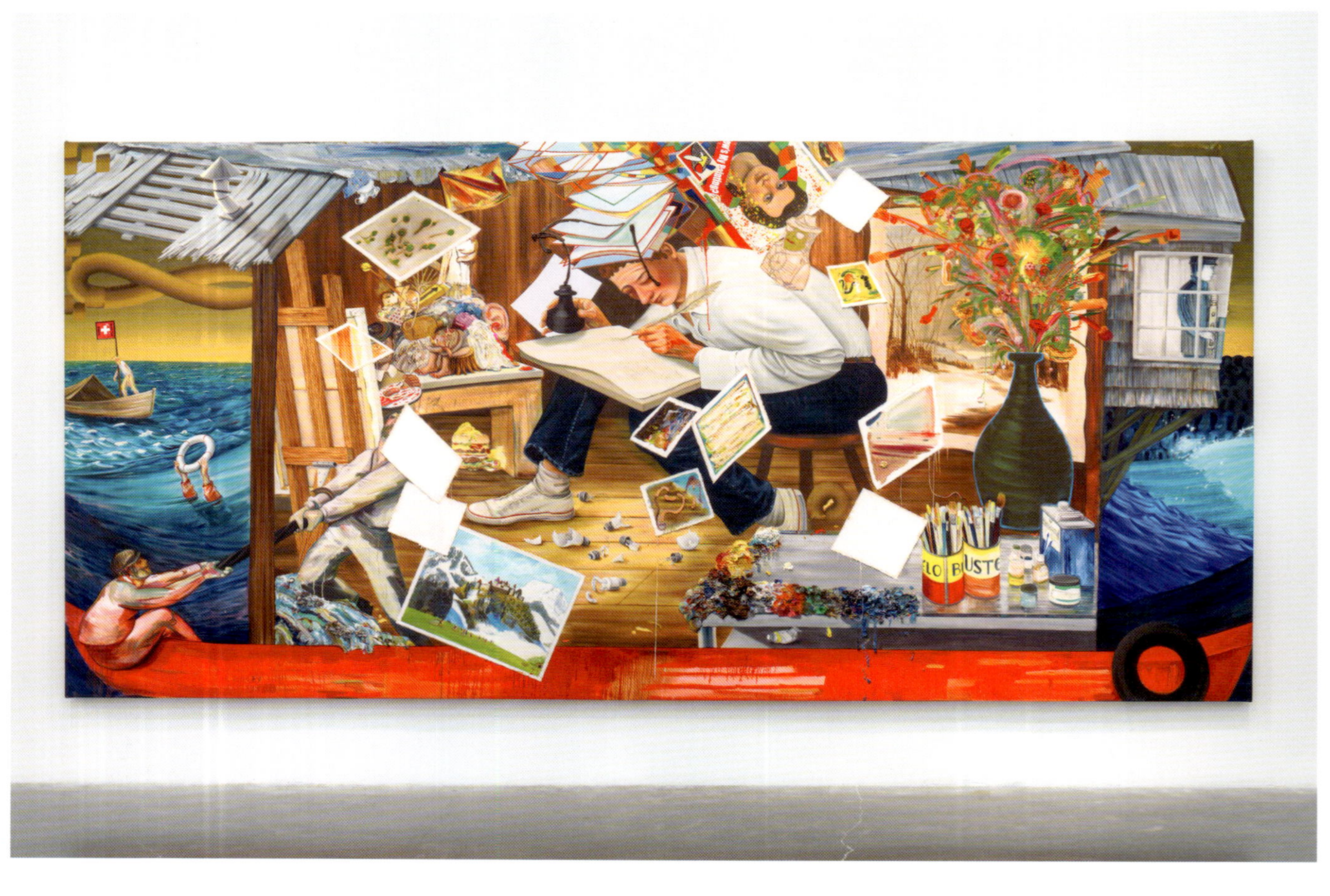

Nicole Eisenman,
*Progress: Real and
Imagined*, 2006

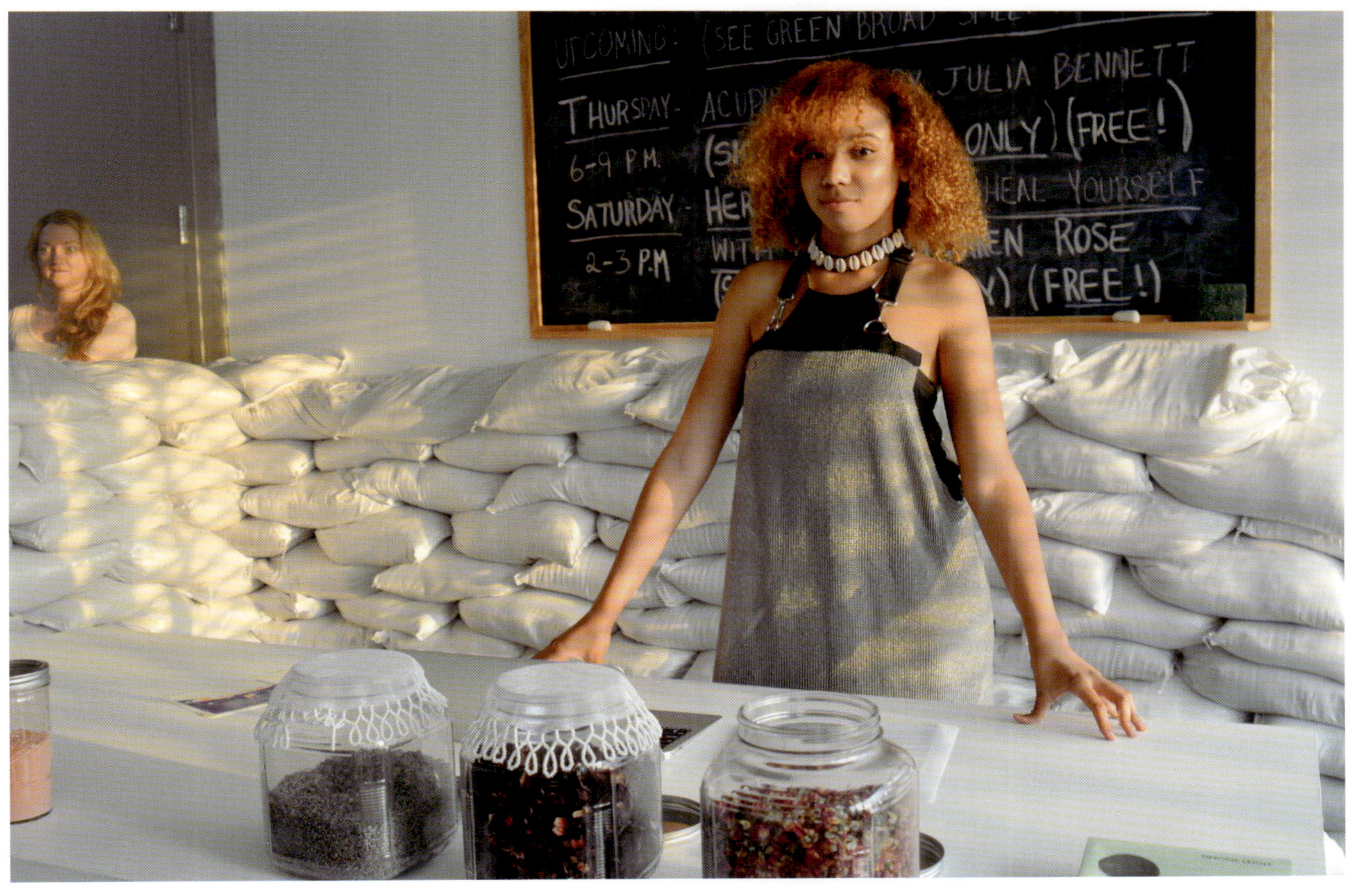

"Simone Leigh:
The Waiting Room"
Teen Apprentice in
the Apothecary

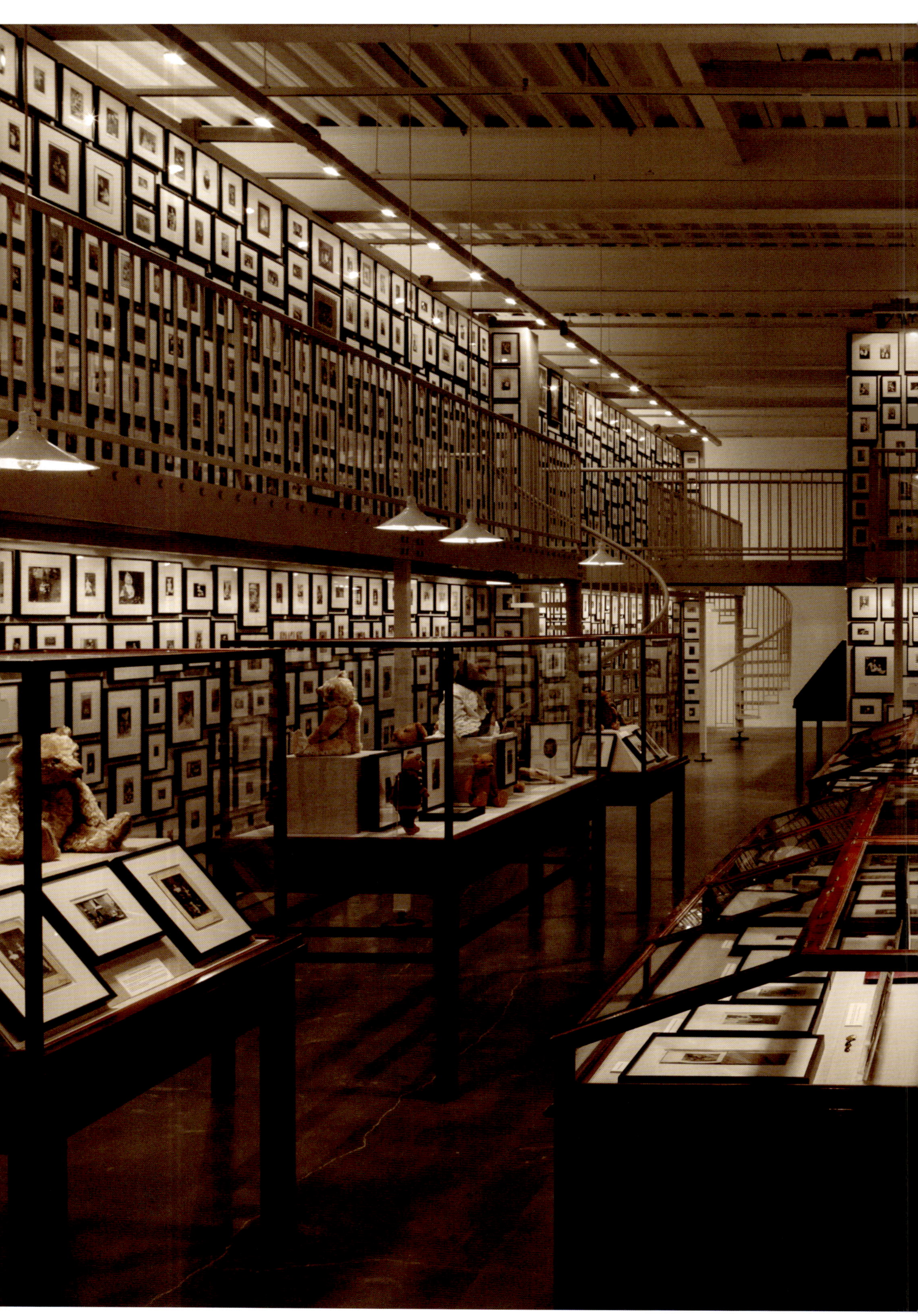

Ydessa Hendeles,
Partners (The Teddy Bear
Project), 2002 (detail)

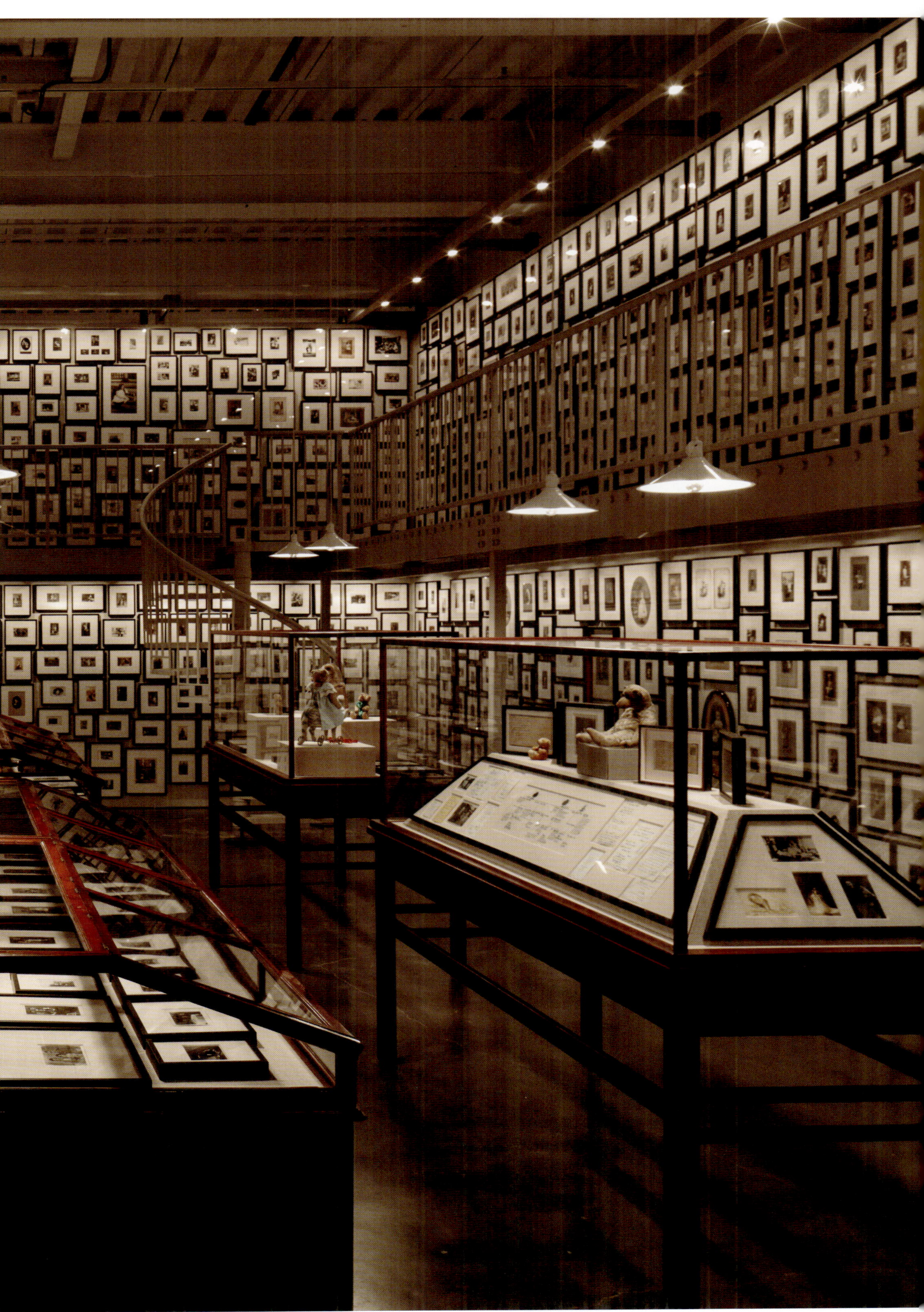

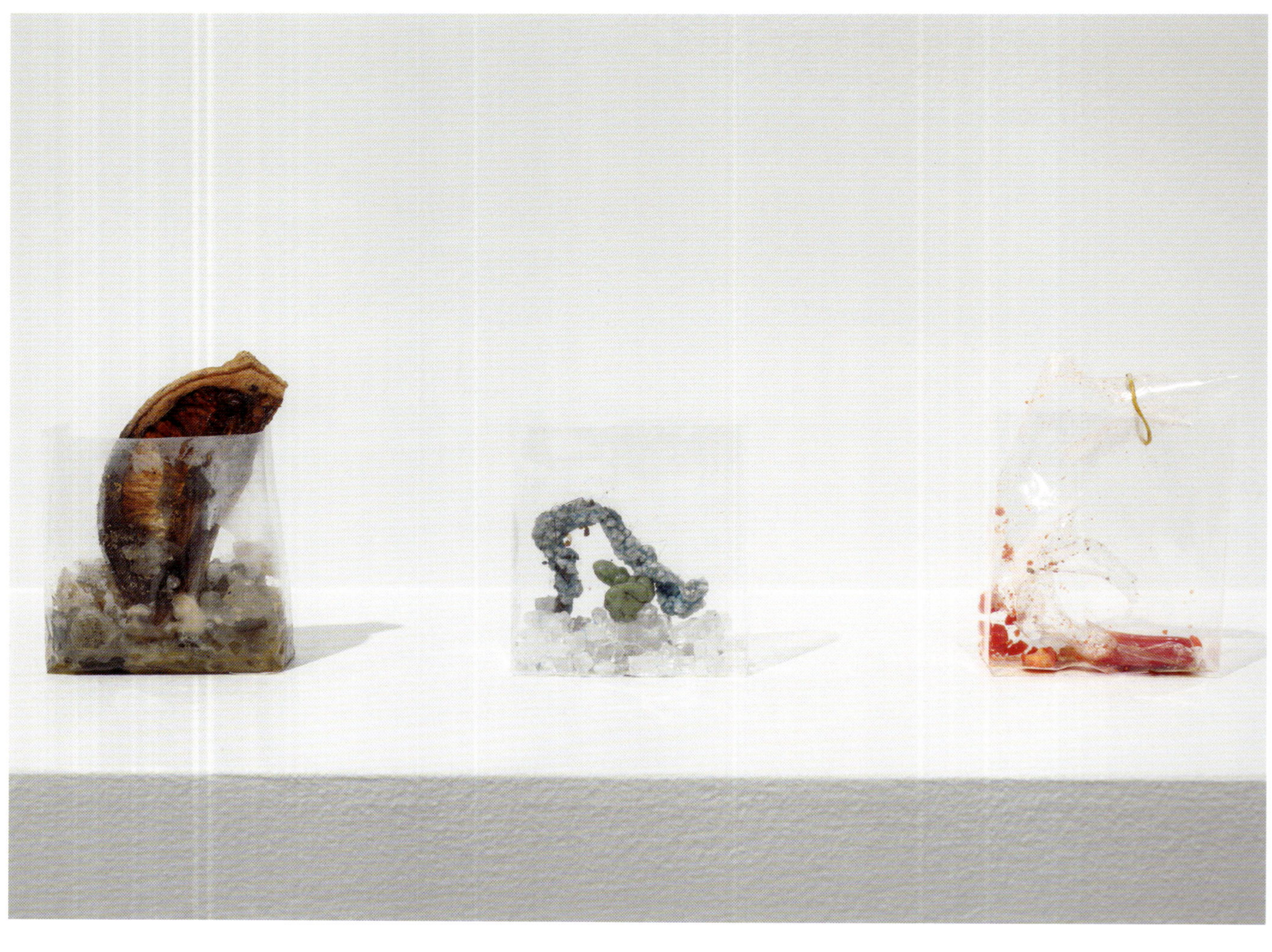

Yuji Agematsu,
*01-01-2014–12-31-2014
(01-01-14–02-29-14)*, 2014

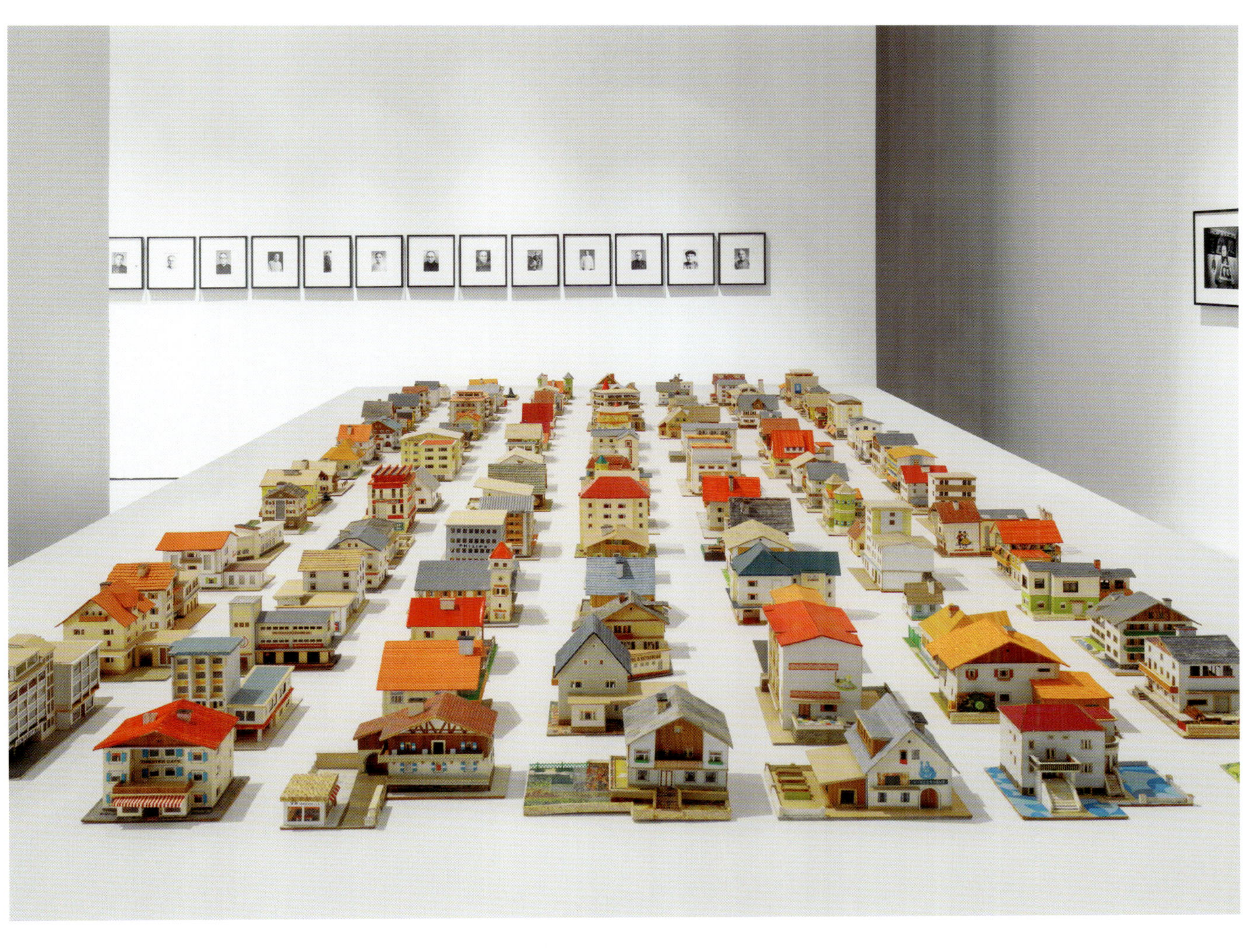

Foreground: *The 387 Houses of Peter Fritz (1916–1992), Insurance Clerk from Vienna, 1993–2008*, preserved by Oliver Croy and Oliver Elser

Background: *A Sixty-Three-Year Photo-Biography of Ye Jinglu*, discovered by Tong Bingxue, 1901/1907–68

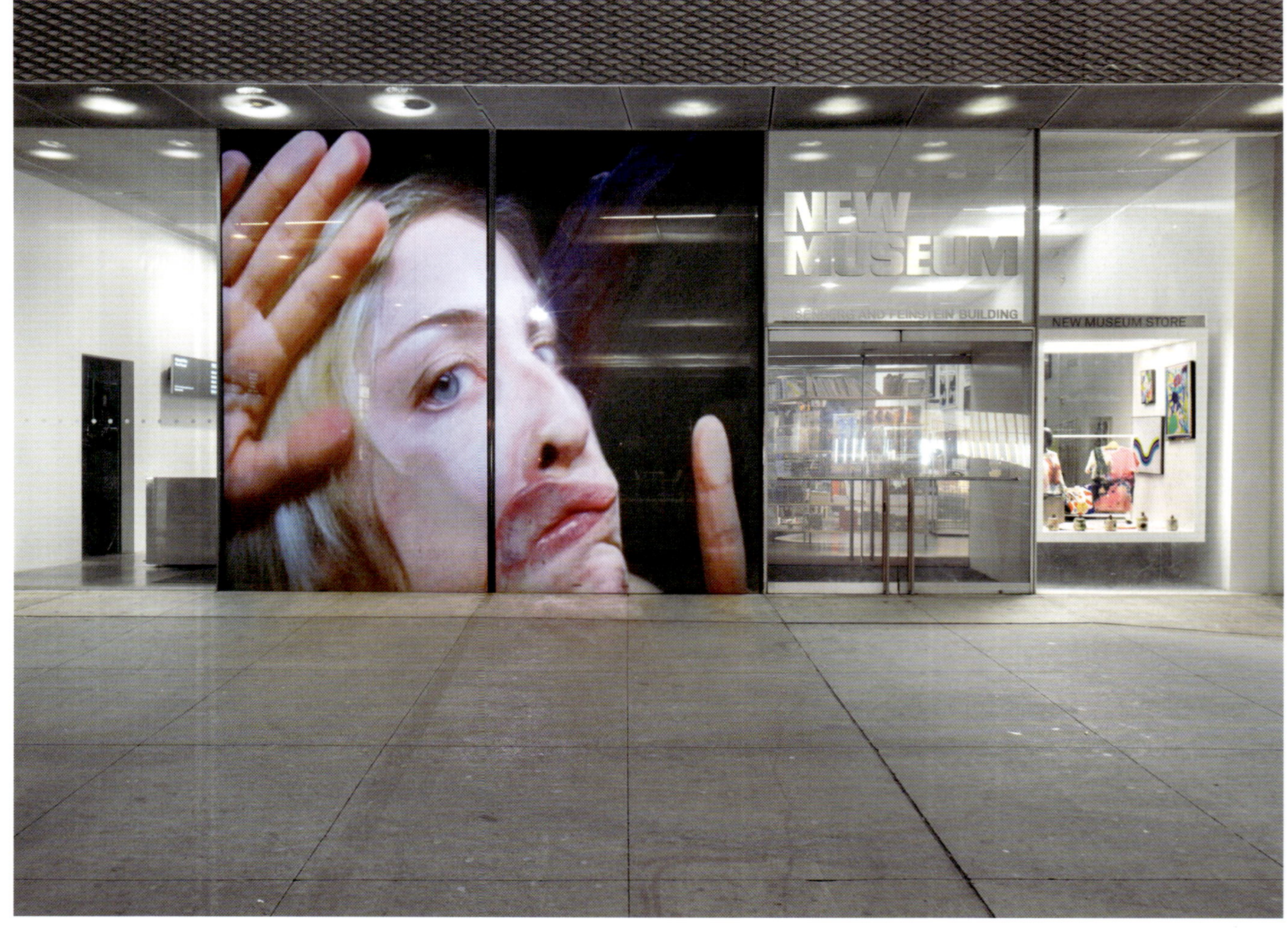

Pipilotti Rist,
Open My Glade (Flatten),
2000

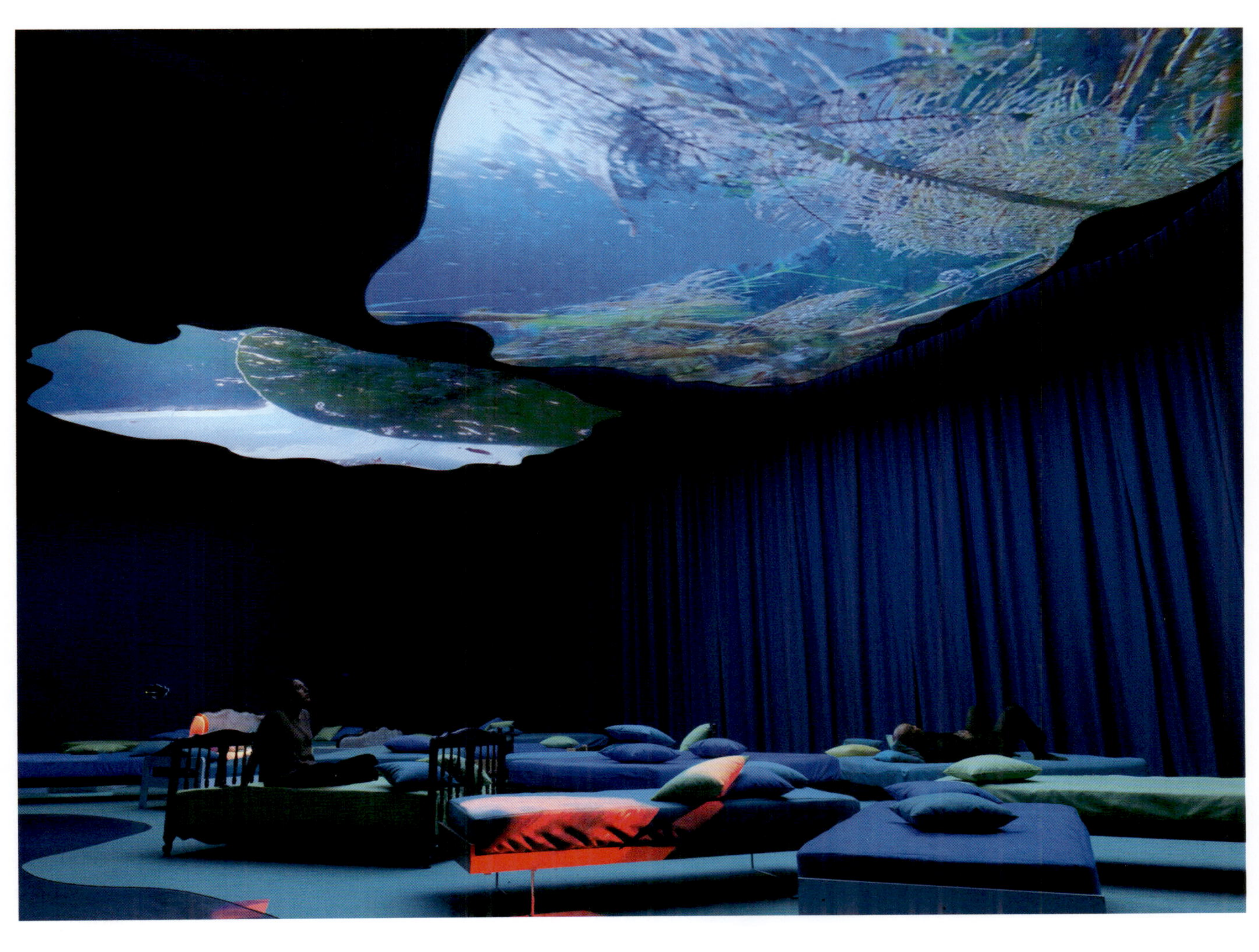

Pipilotti Rist,
4th Floor To Mildness,
2016

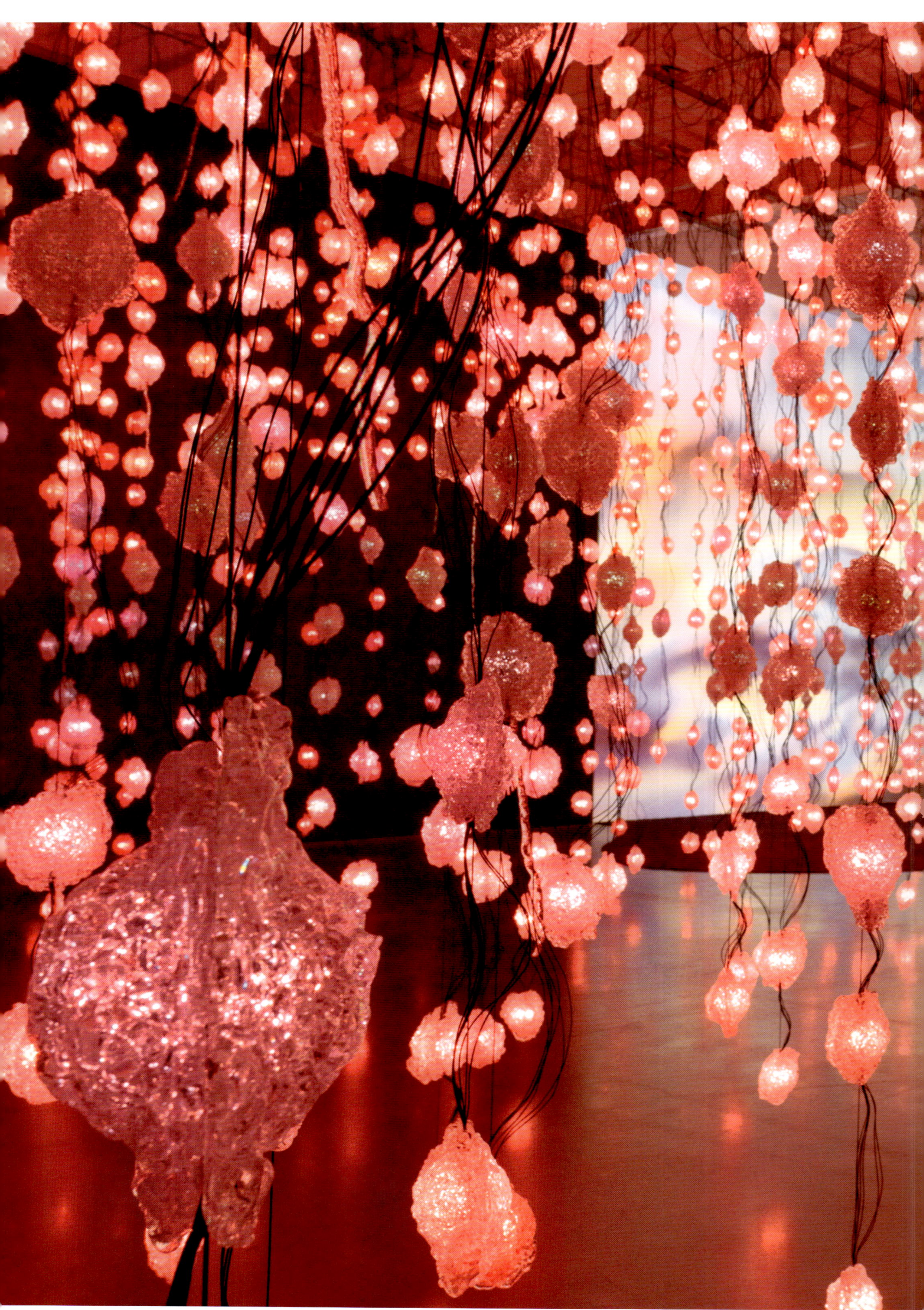

Pipilotti Rist,
Pixelwald [Pixel Forest],
2016

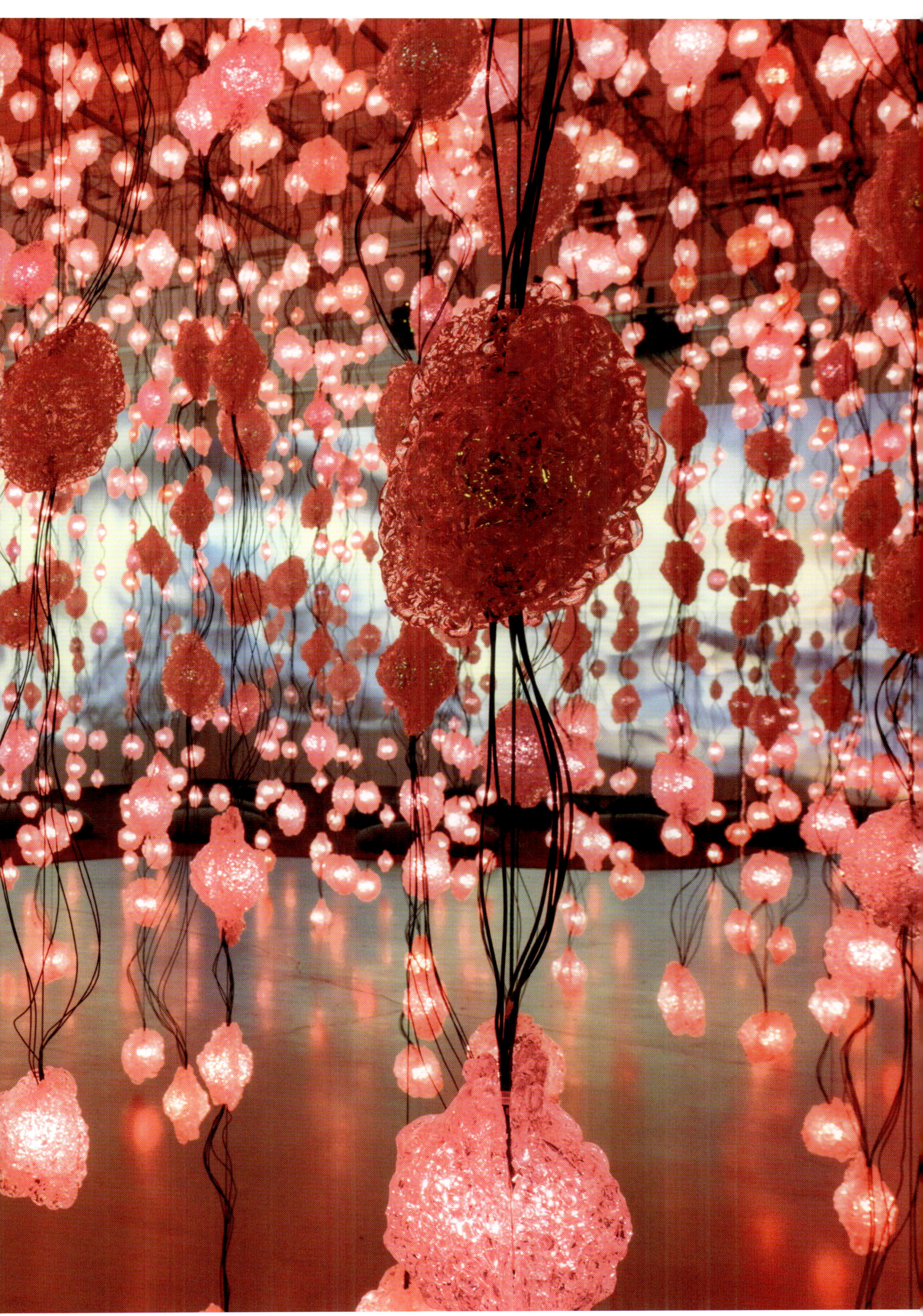

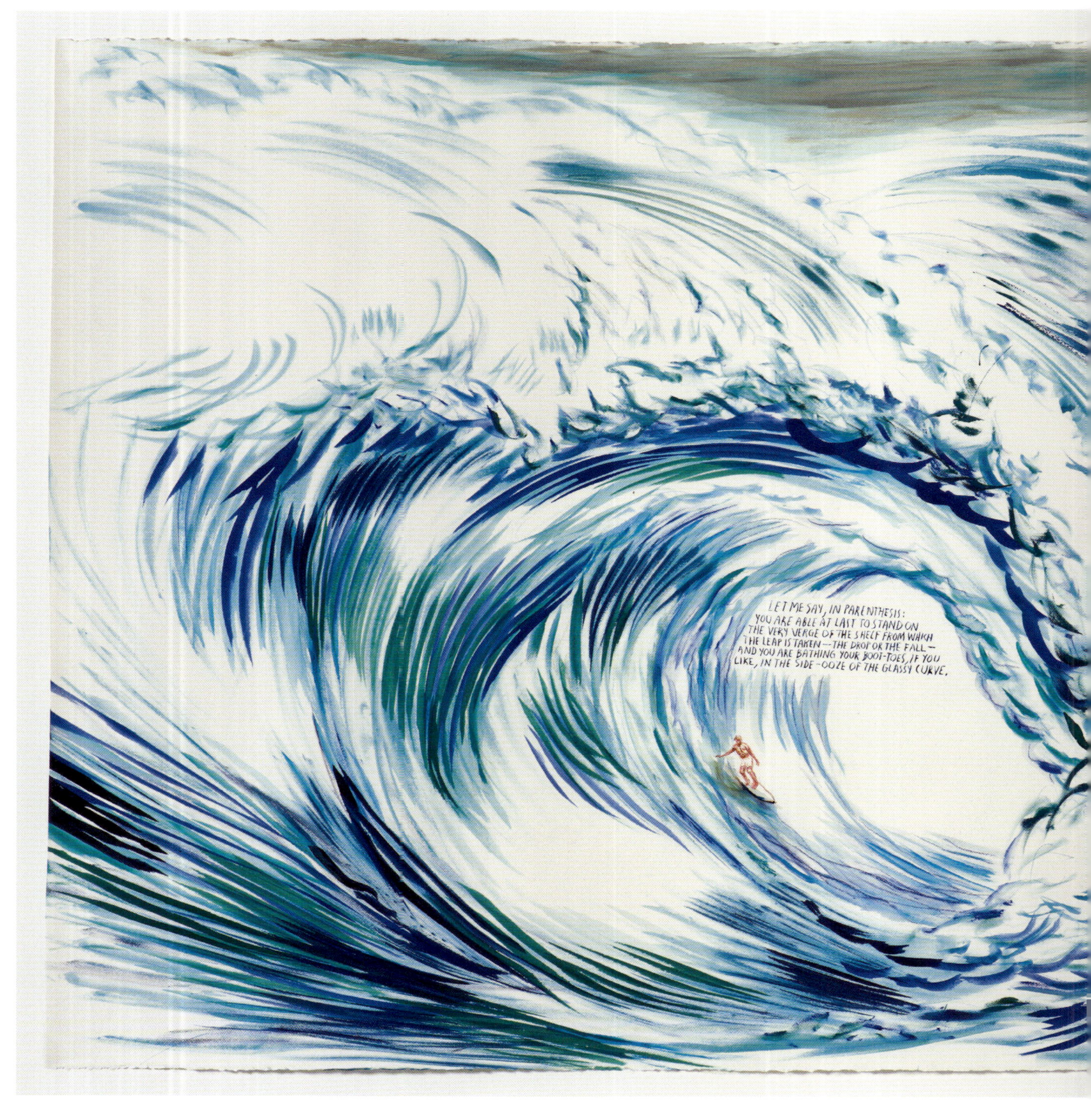

Raymond Pettibon,
No Title (Let me say,),
2012

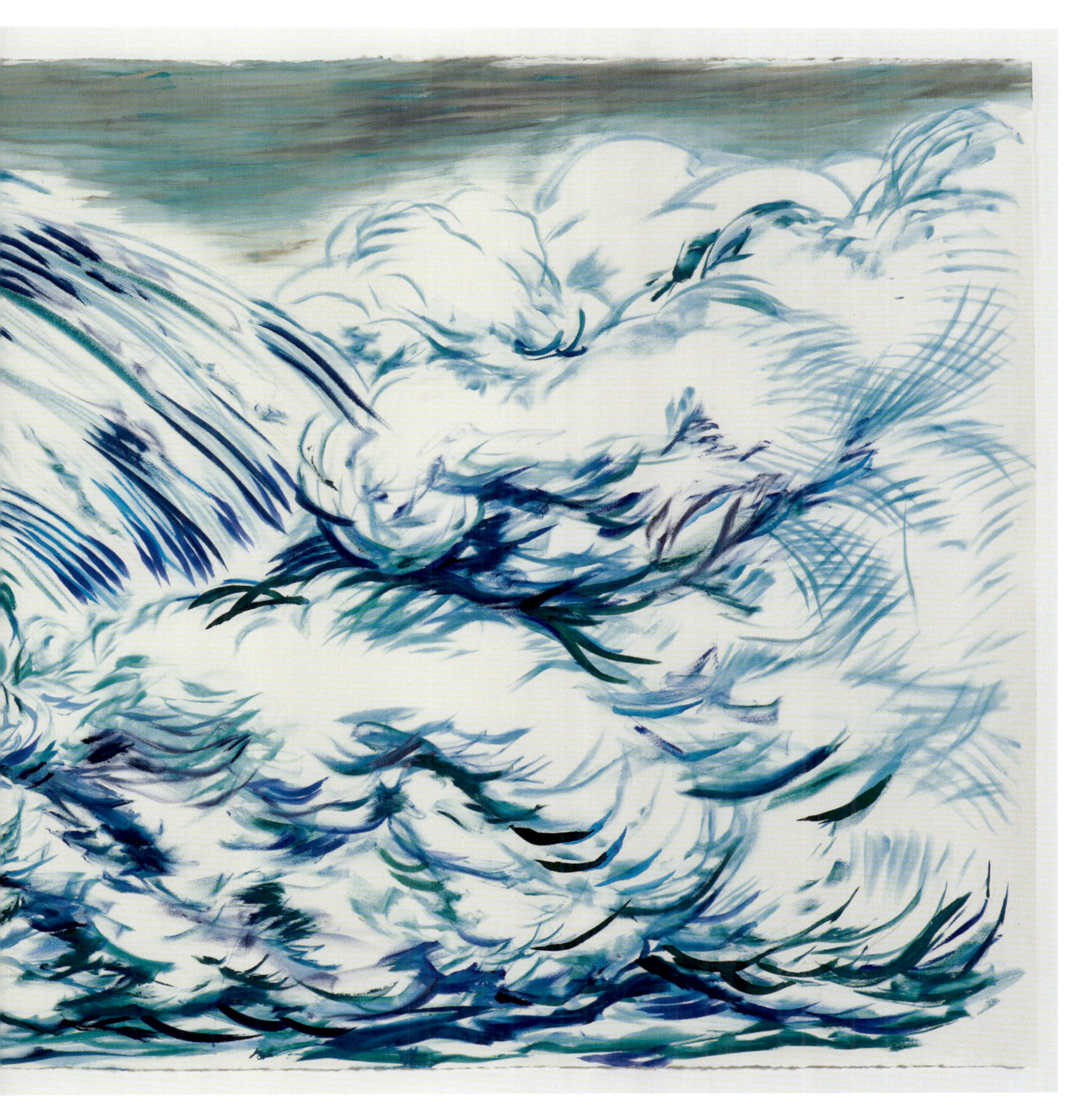

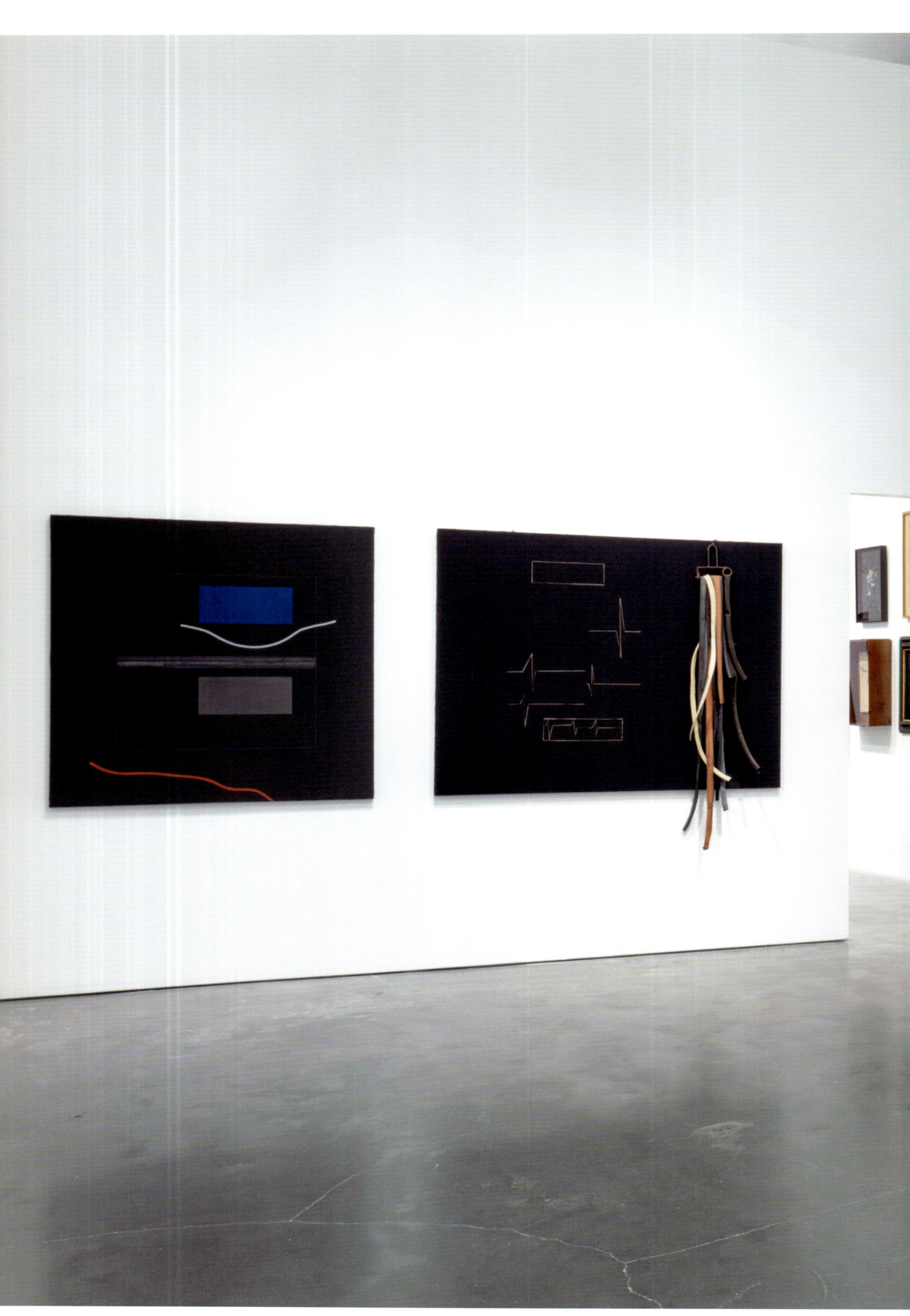

Front room, left to right:
Carol Rama, *Luogo e segni*
[Place and Signs], 1975;
Presagi di Birnam [Omens
of Birnam], 1979–95;
Ecologia [Ecology], 1971;
and *Spazio anche più che
tempo* [Even More Space
Than Time], 1971

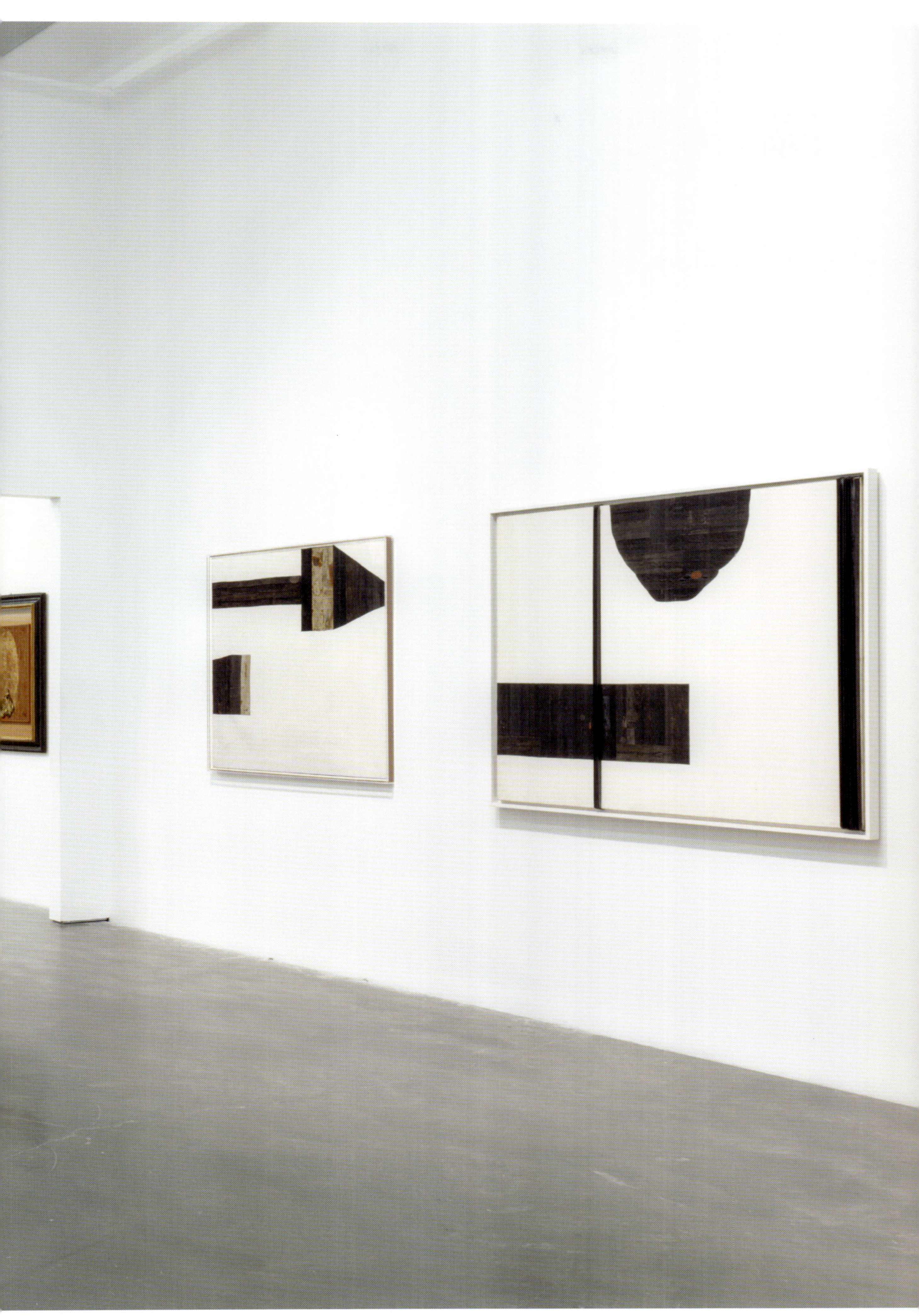

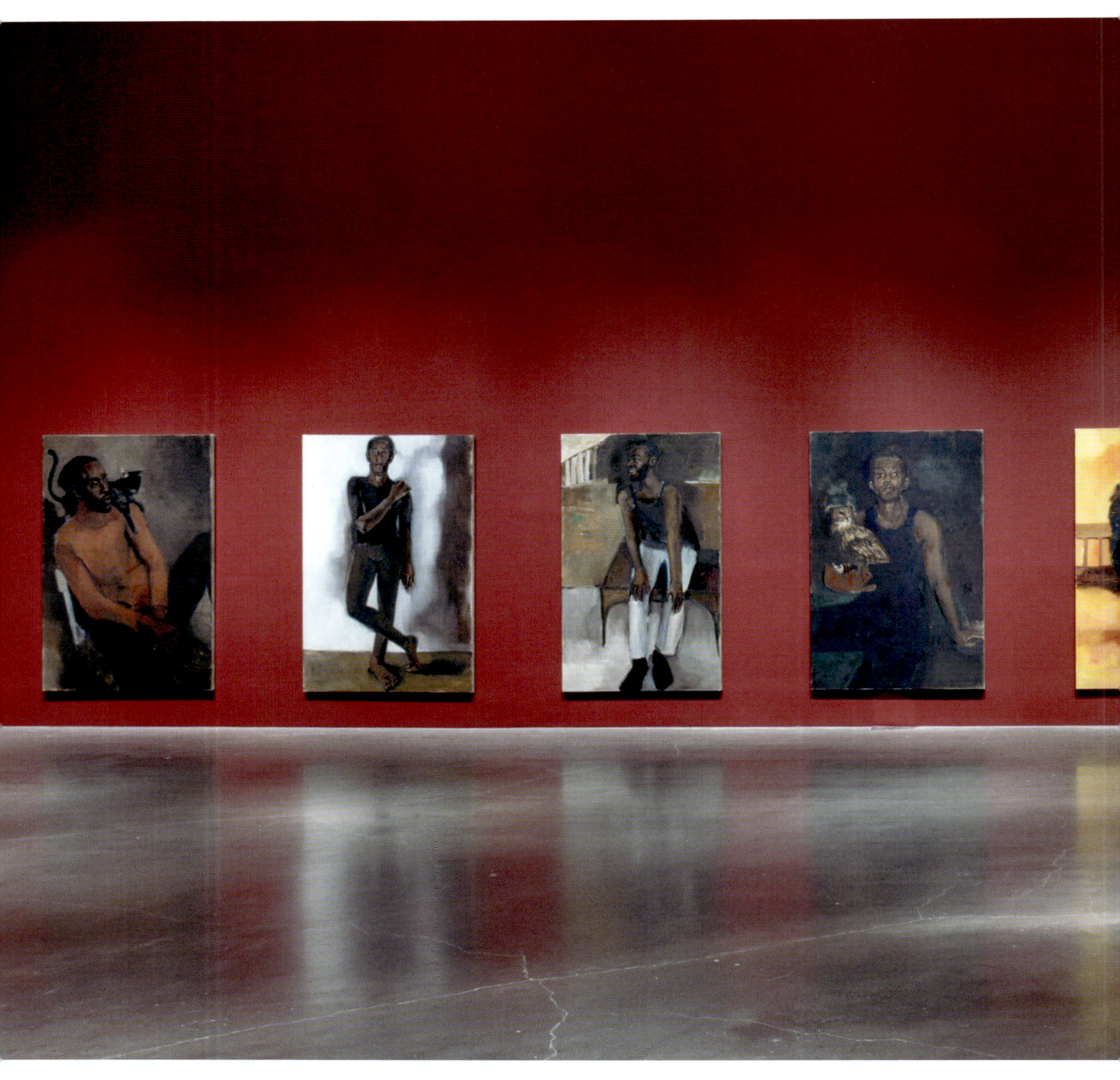

Left to right: Lynette Yiadom-Boakye, *In Lieu of Keen Virtue*, 2017; *Ropes For A Clairvoyant*, 2017; *A Cage For The Love*, 2017; *The Matters*, 2017; *Mercy Over Matter*, 2017; *Medicine At Playtime* 2017; *The Much-Vaunted Air*, 2017; *Repose III*, 2017; and *Light Of The Lit Wick*, 2017

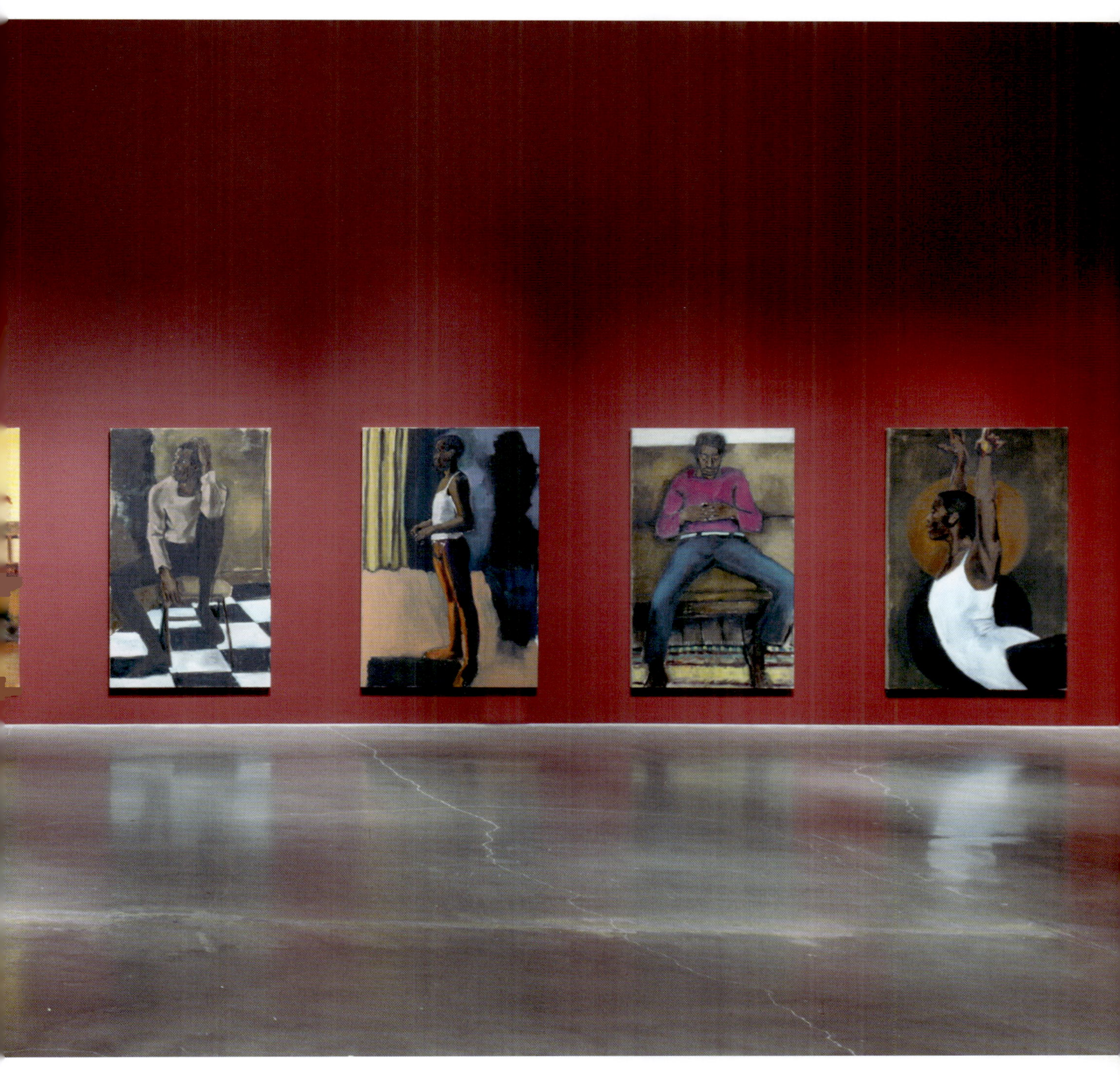

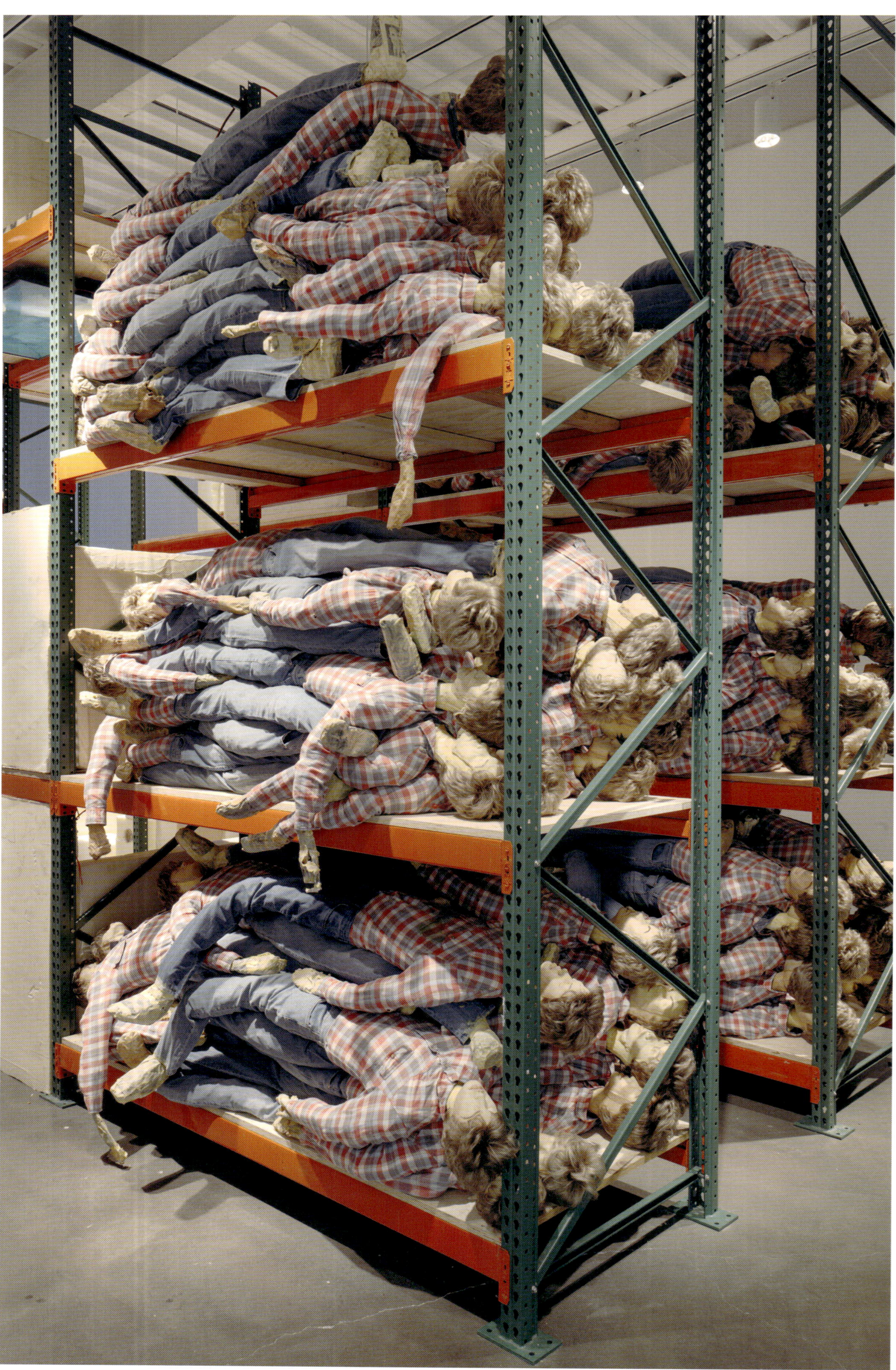

Kaari Upson,
Hers, 2017

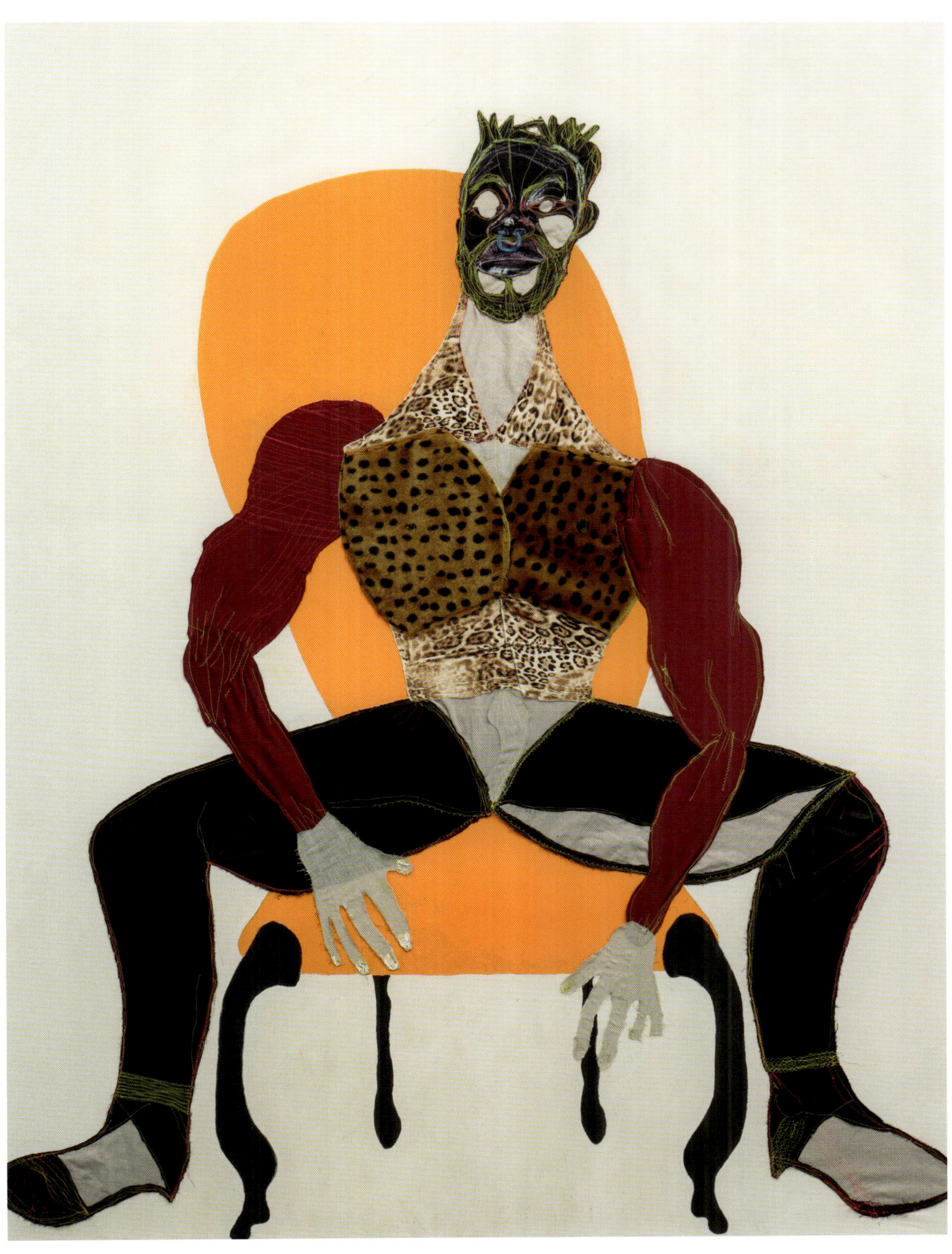

Tschabalala Self,
Mane, 2016

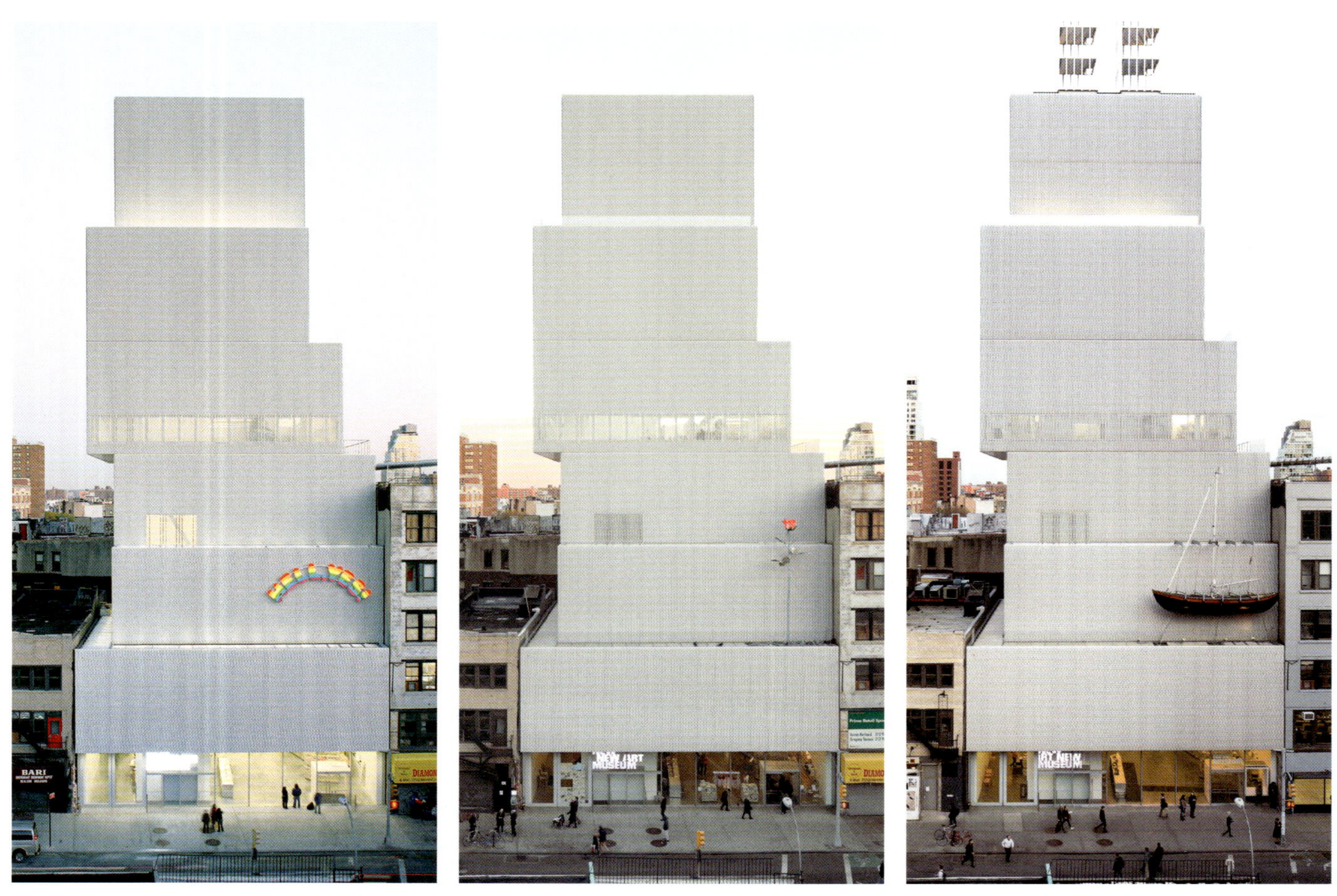

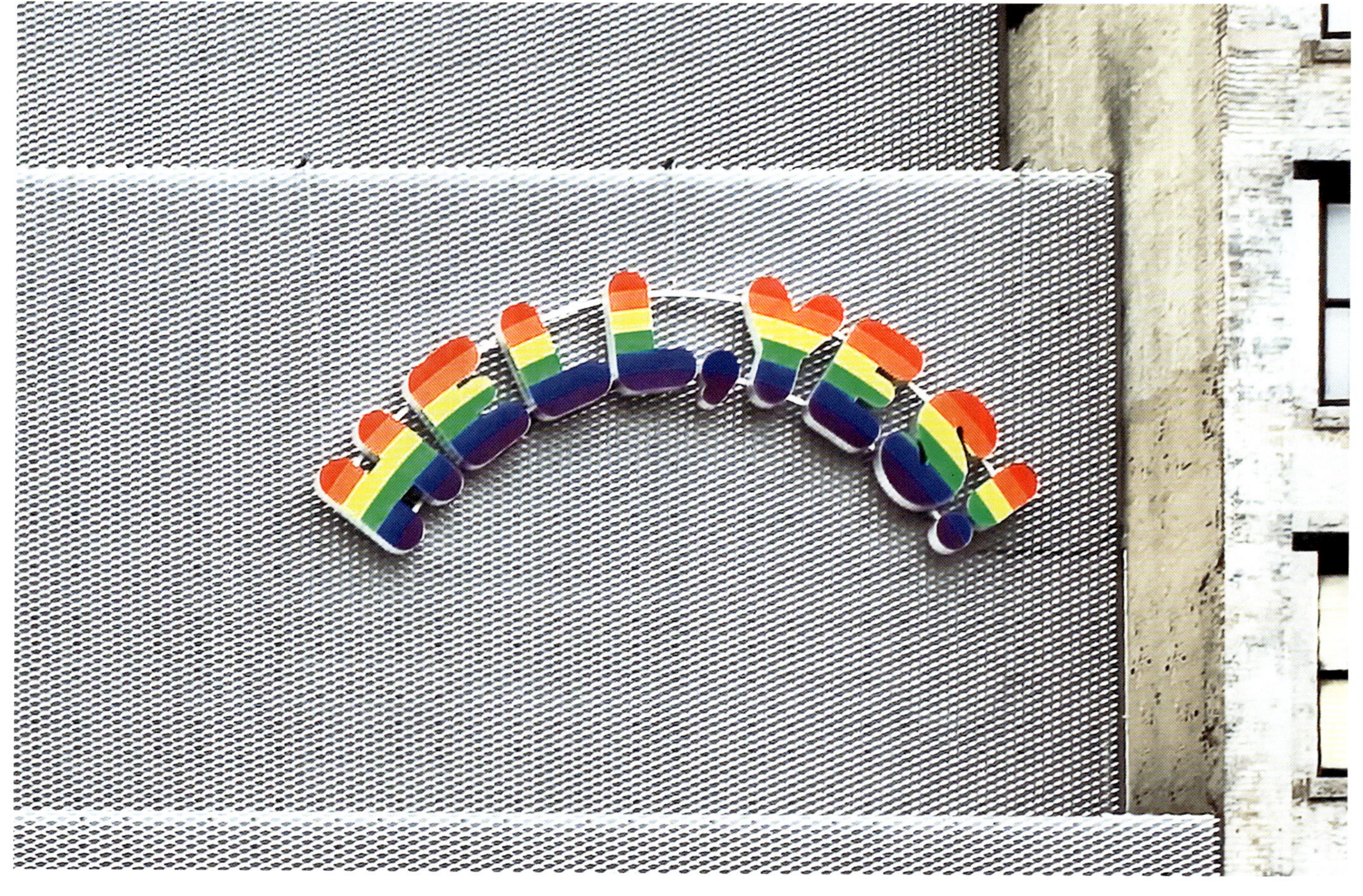

(top, left to right)
Works installed on the
New Museum facade: Ugo
Rondinone, *Hell, Yes!*,
2001; Isa Genzken, *Rose
II*, 2007; and Chris Burden,
Ghost Ship, 2005

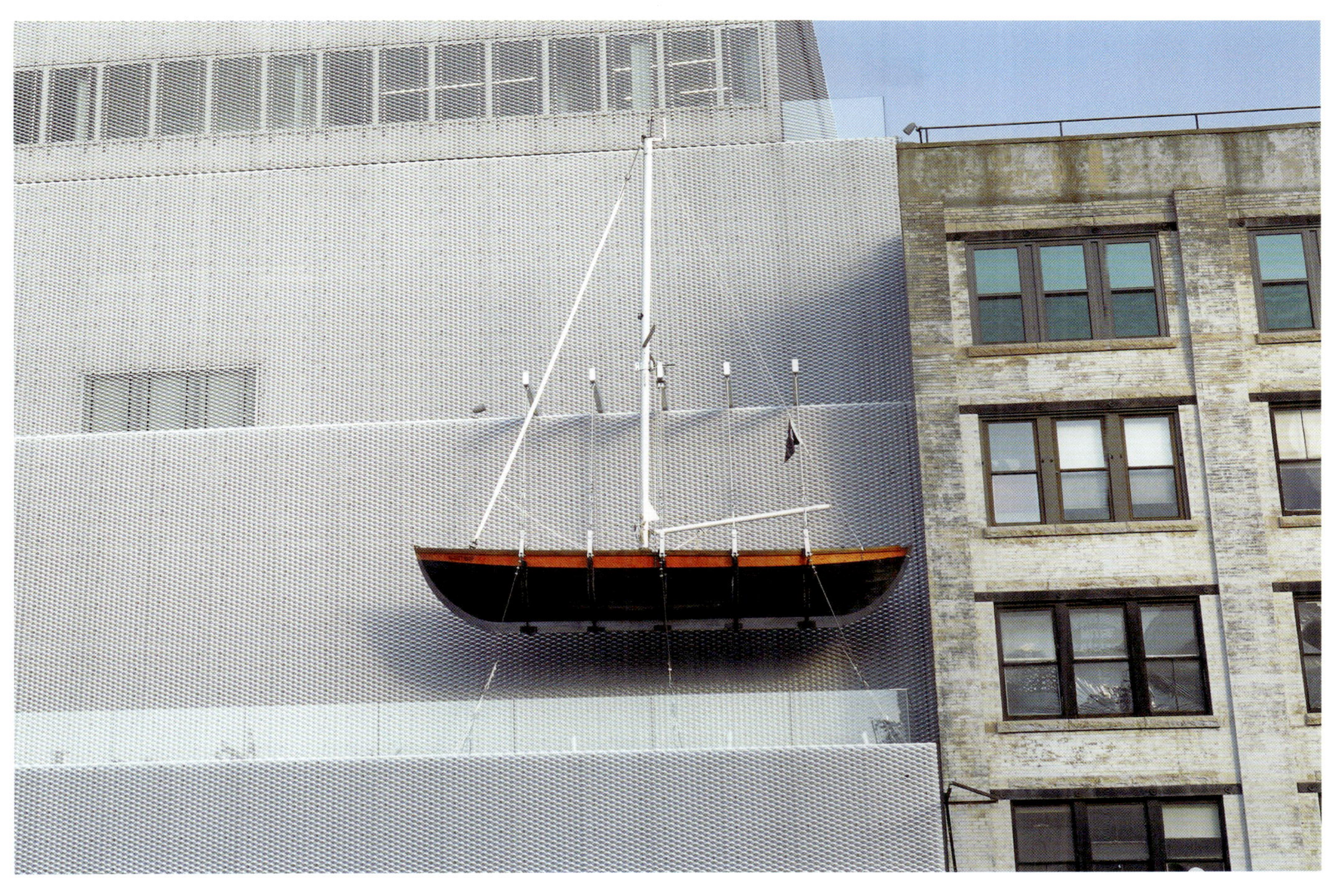

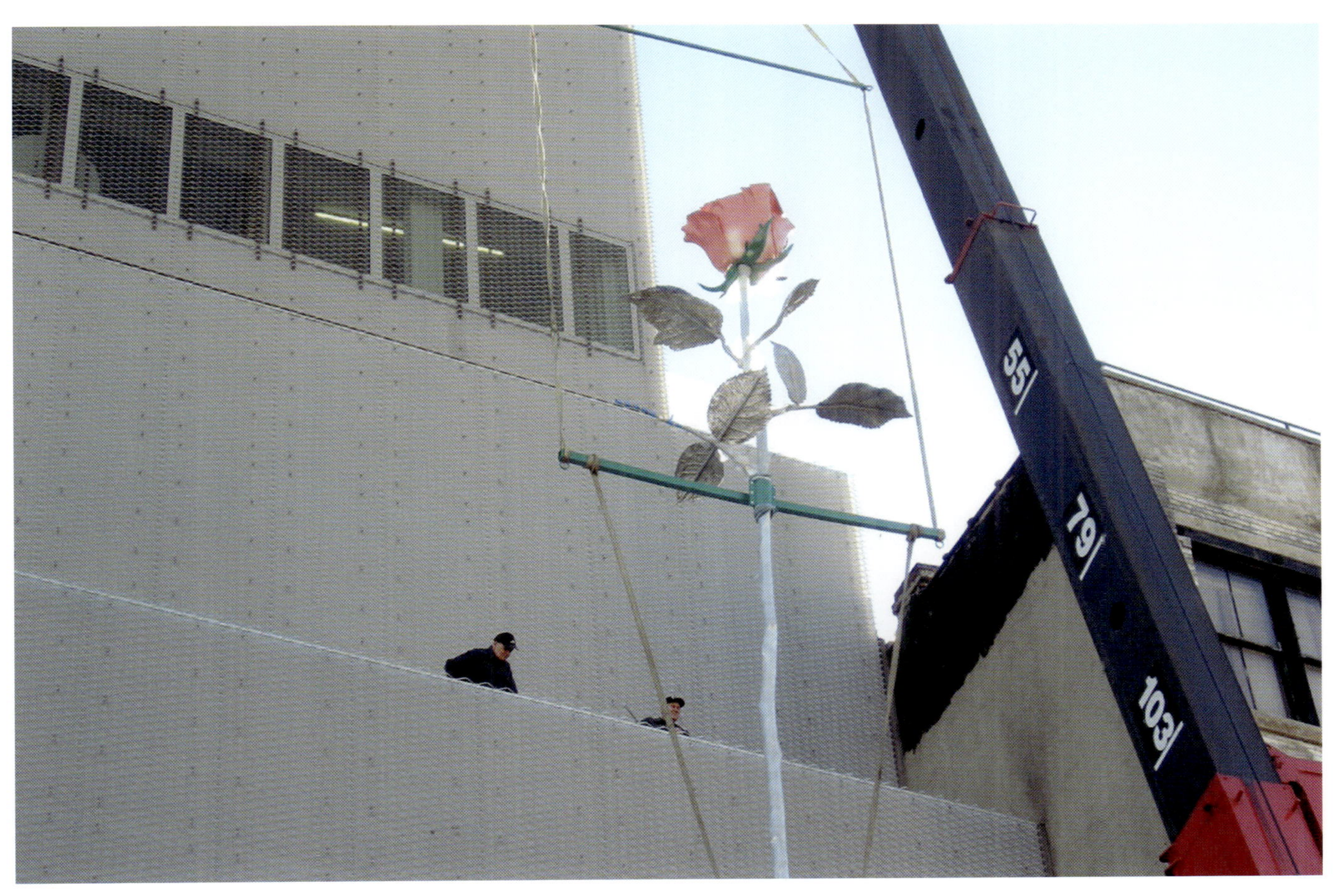

55|
79|
103|

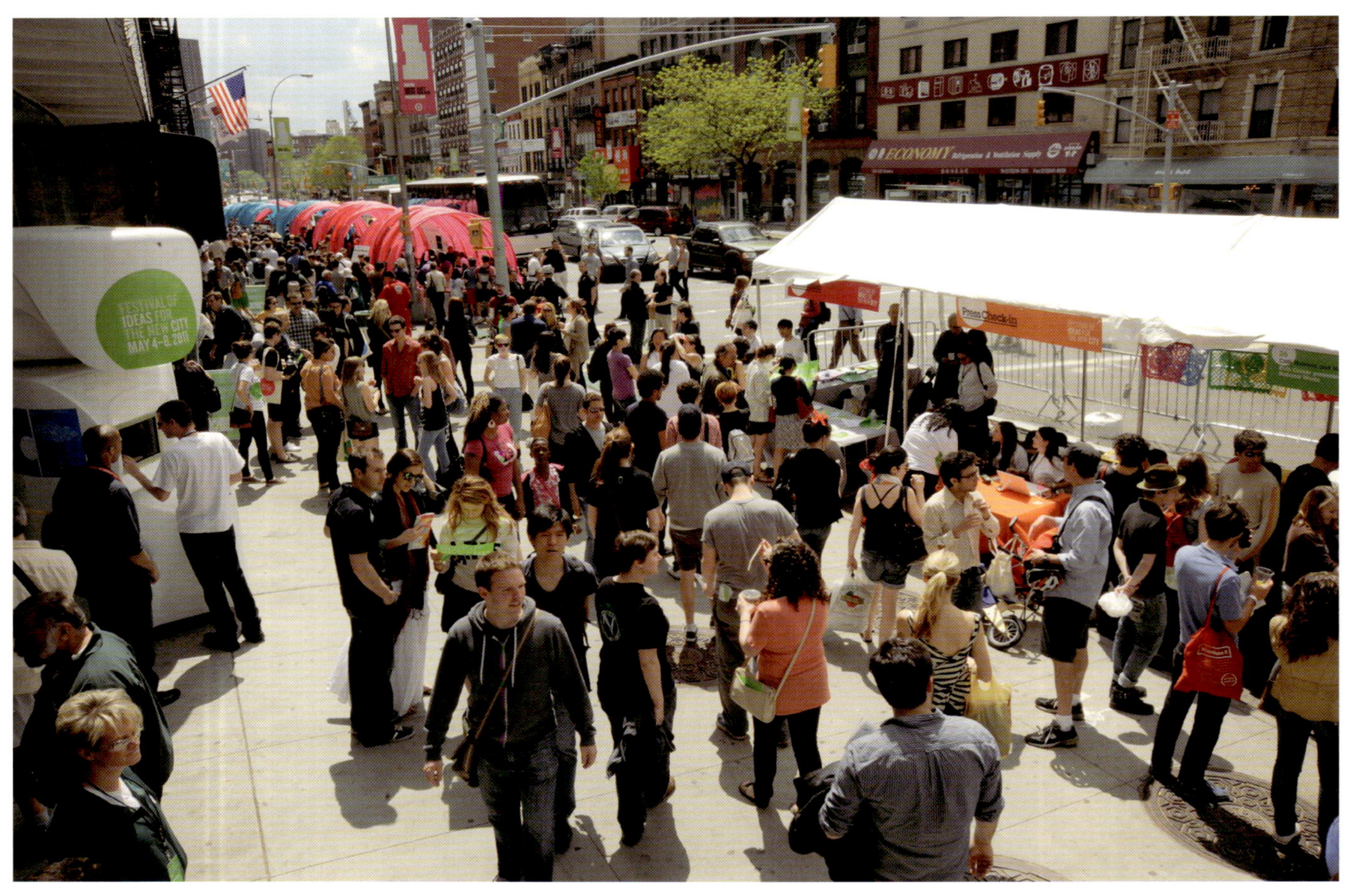

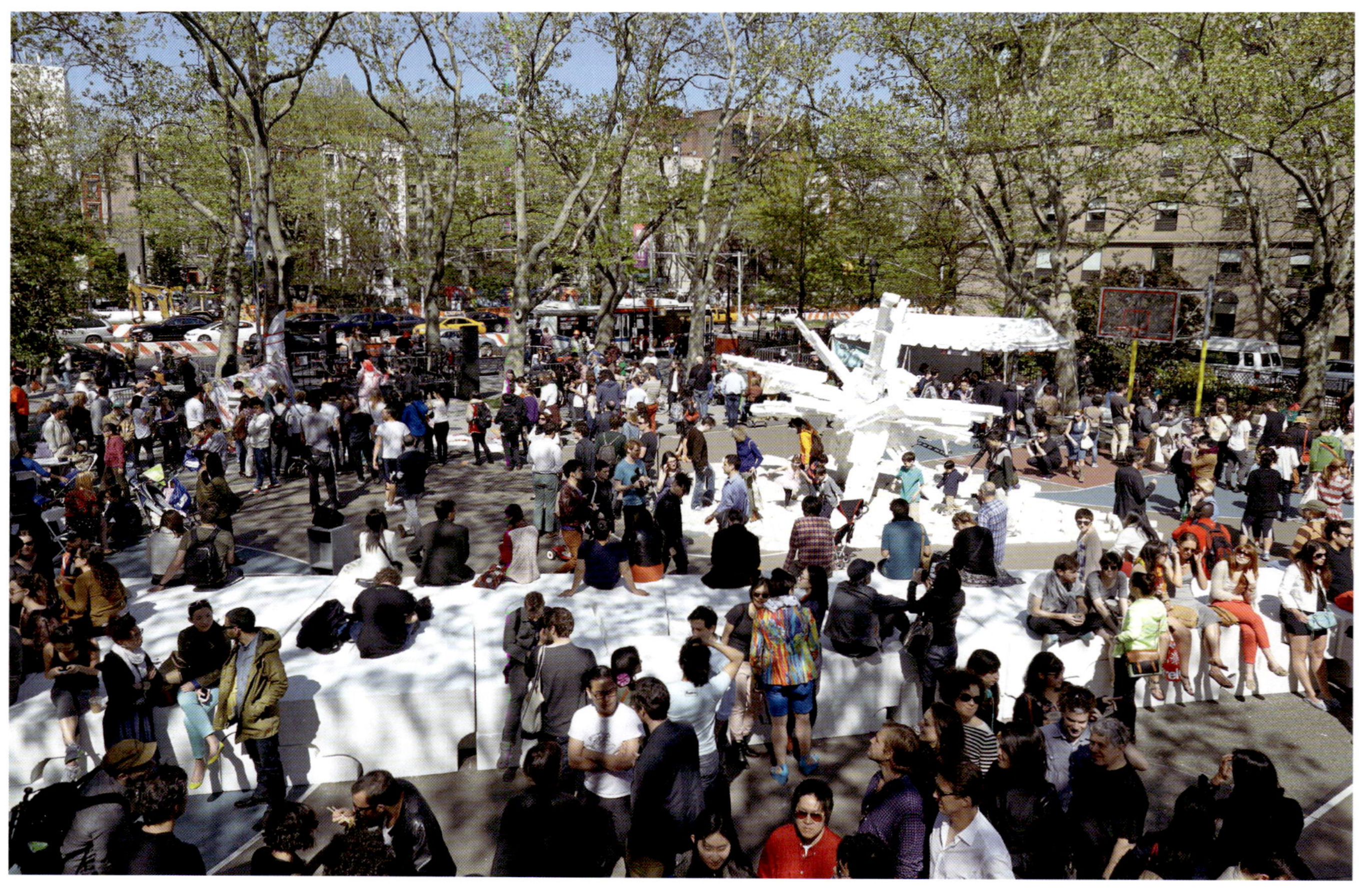

(top) The Street
Festival along the
Bowery at the inaugural
Ideas City, May 2011

(bottom) The
Speechbuster, an
urban mobile table
commissioned by
Storefront for Art
and Architecture

at Sarah D. Roosevelt
Park, Ideas City
New York, May 2013

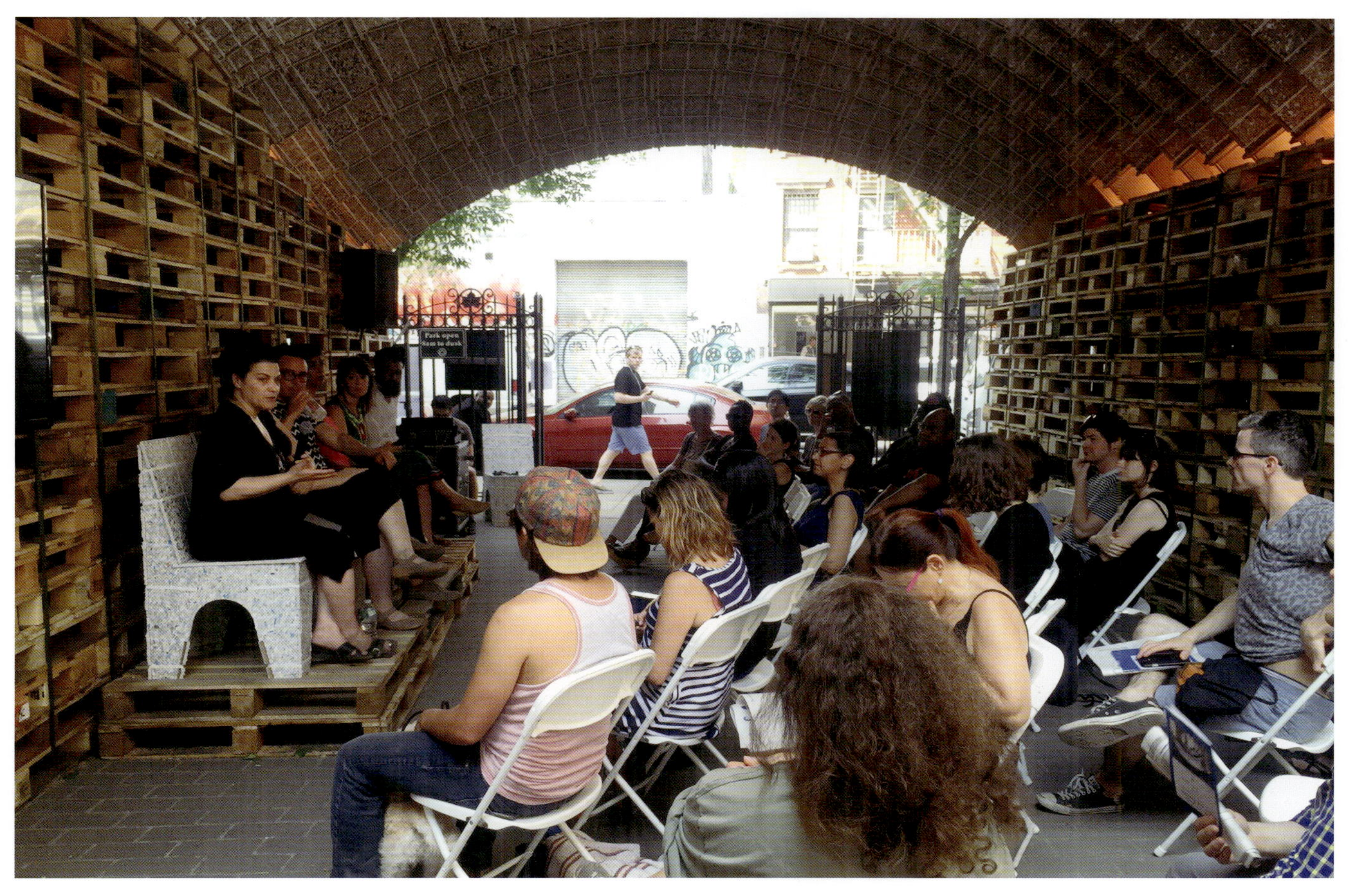

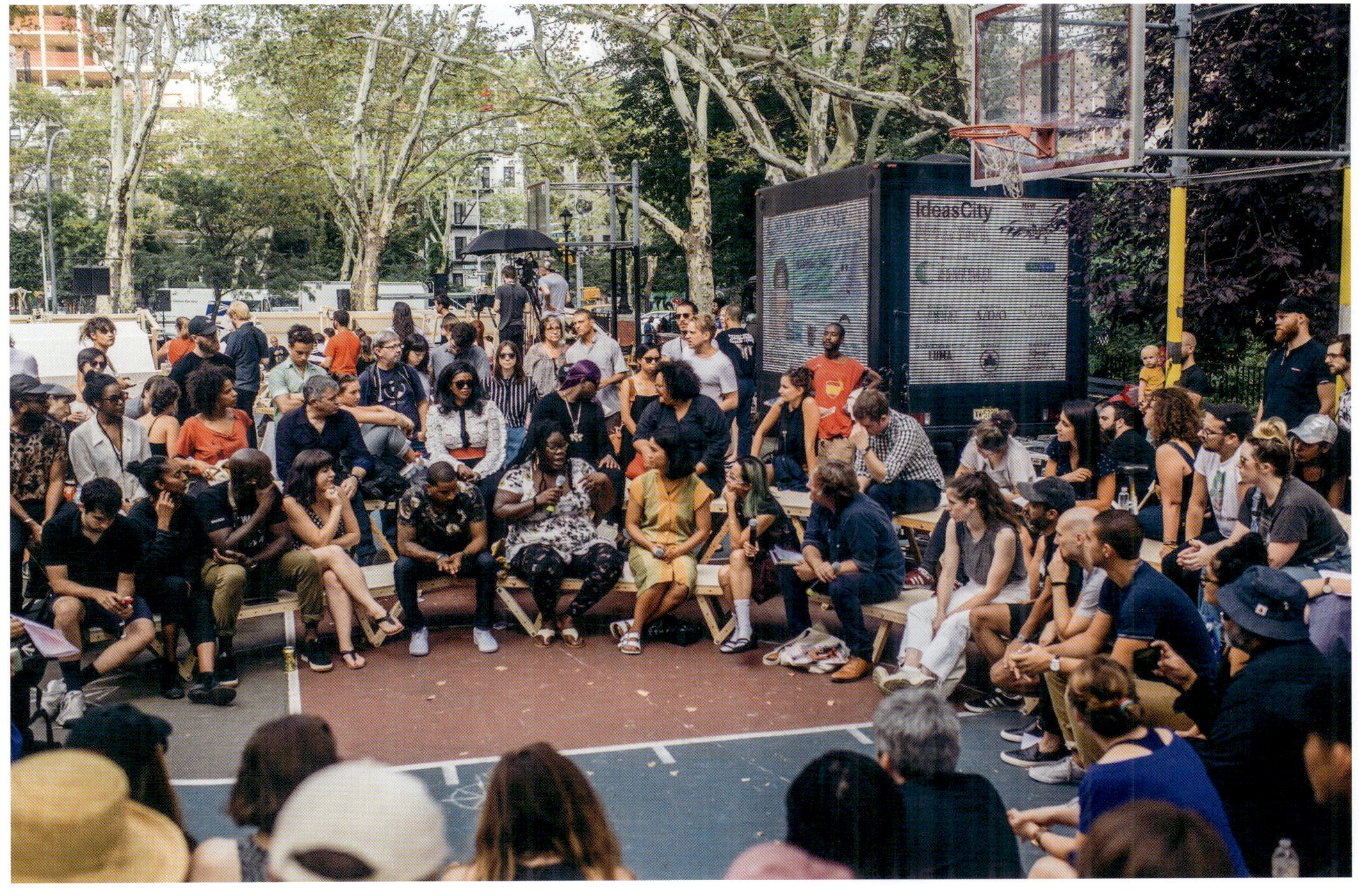

(top) ETH Zurich Future
Garden and Pavilion, a
special project at First
Street Garden, Ideas City
New York, May 2015

(bottom) "Setting the
Table for Tomorrow,"
a panel discussion
organized by Ghetto
Gastro at Ideas City
New York, September 2017

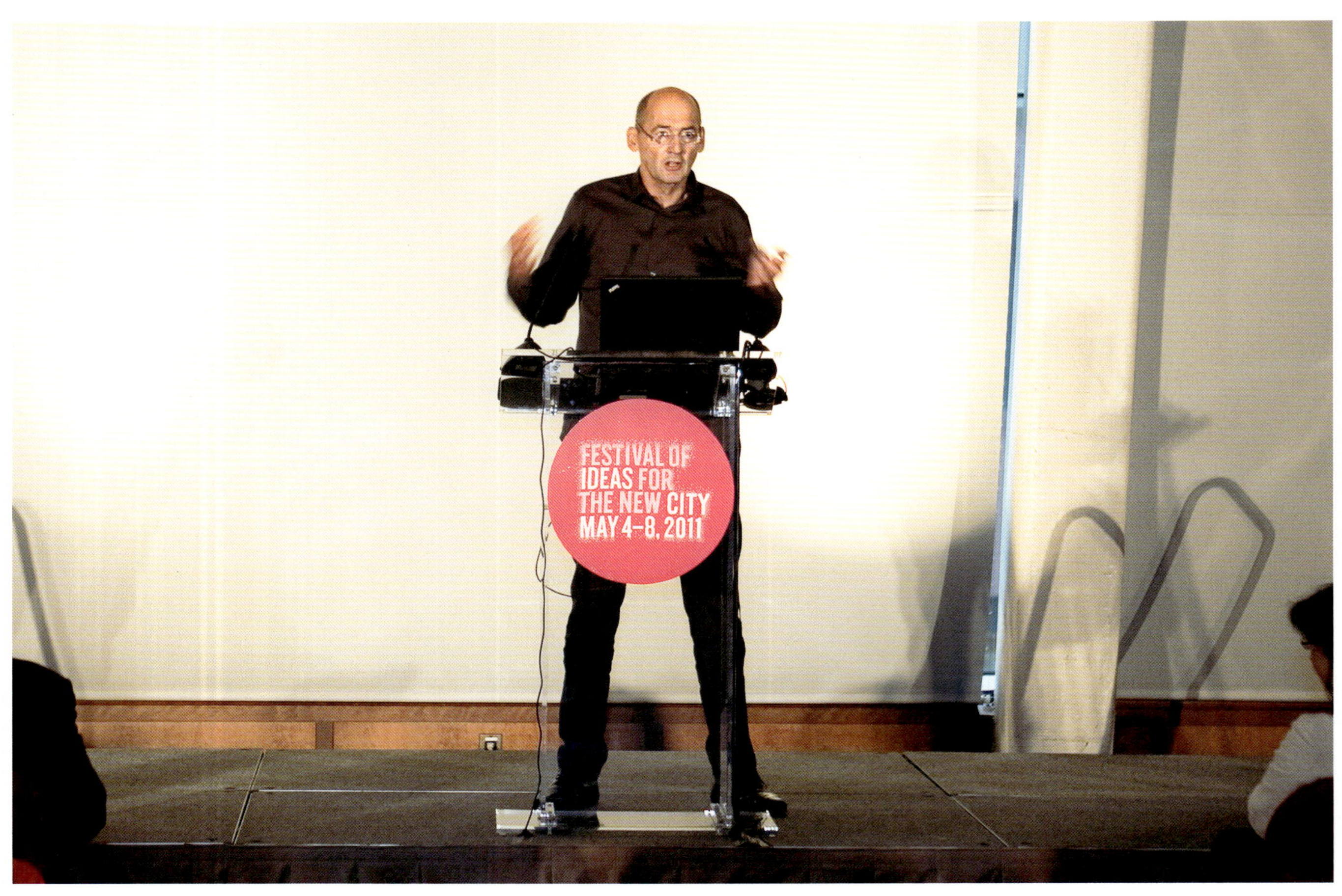

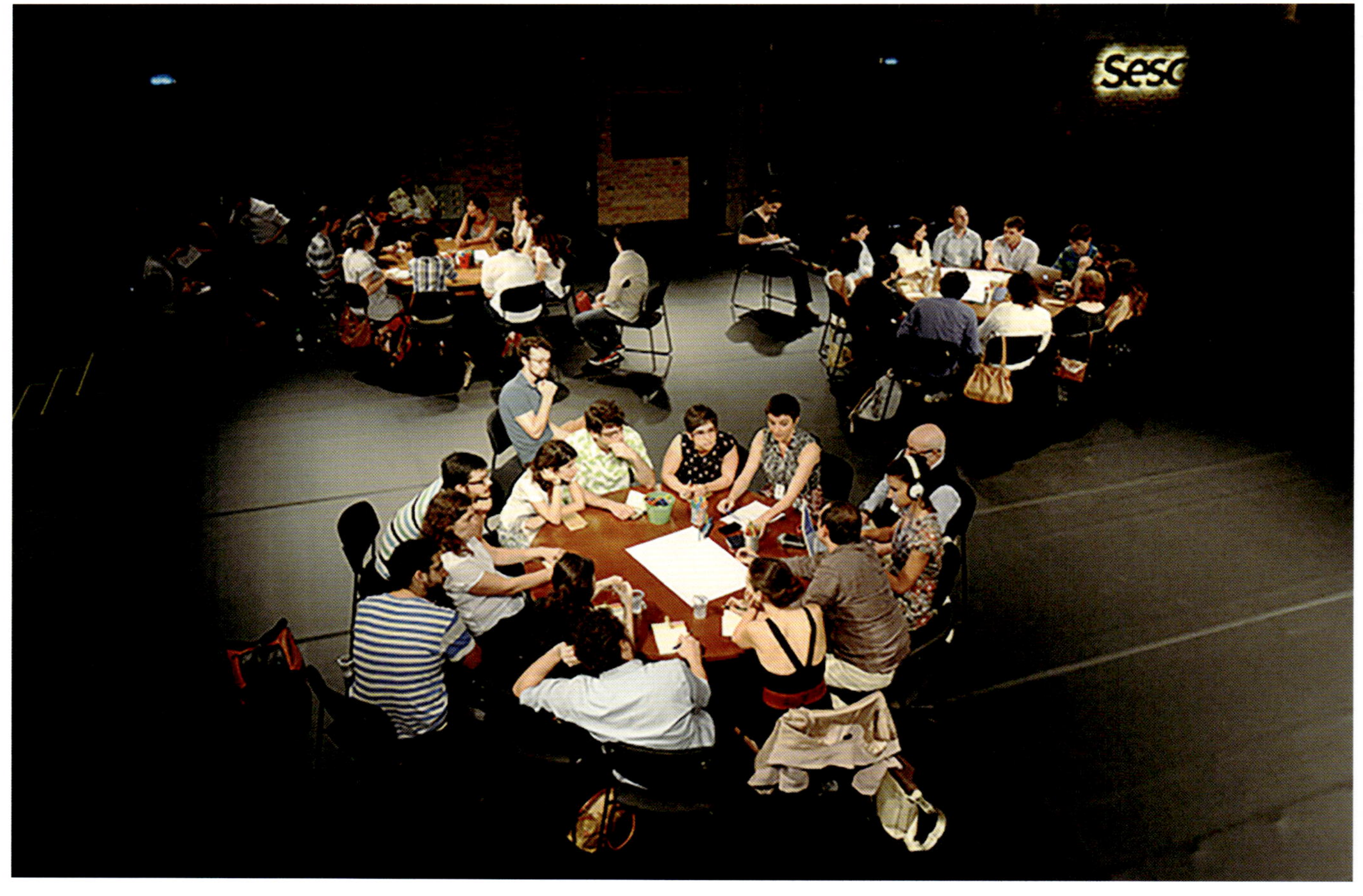

(top) Keynote Address
by Rem Koolhaas, at
the inaugural Ideas City,
May 2011

(bottom) Ideas City's
World Café Workshops
exploring the theme of
untapped capital at
SESC in São Paulo,
October 2013

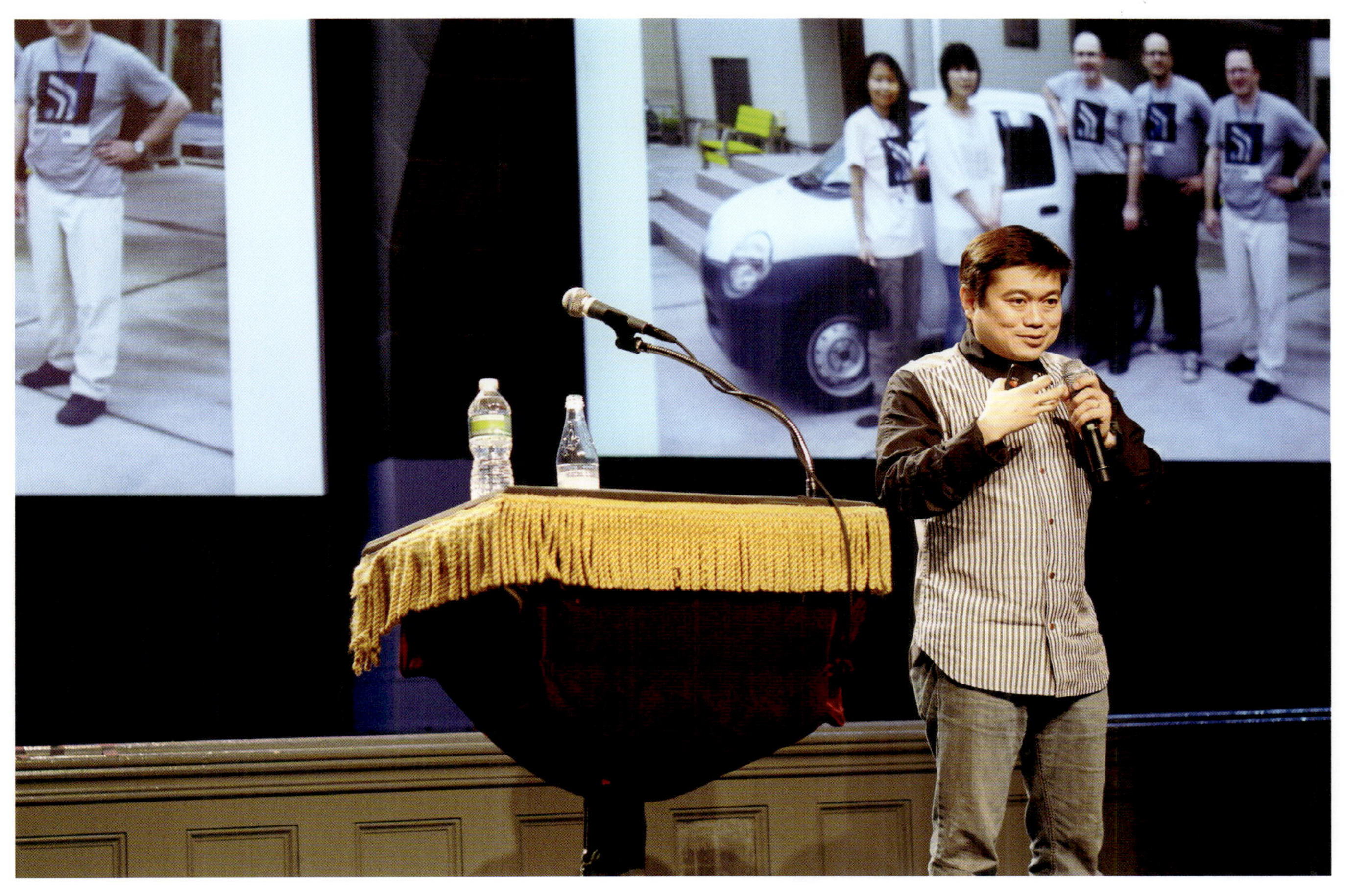

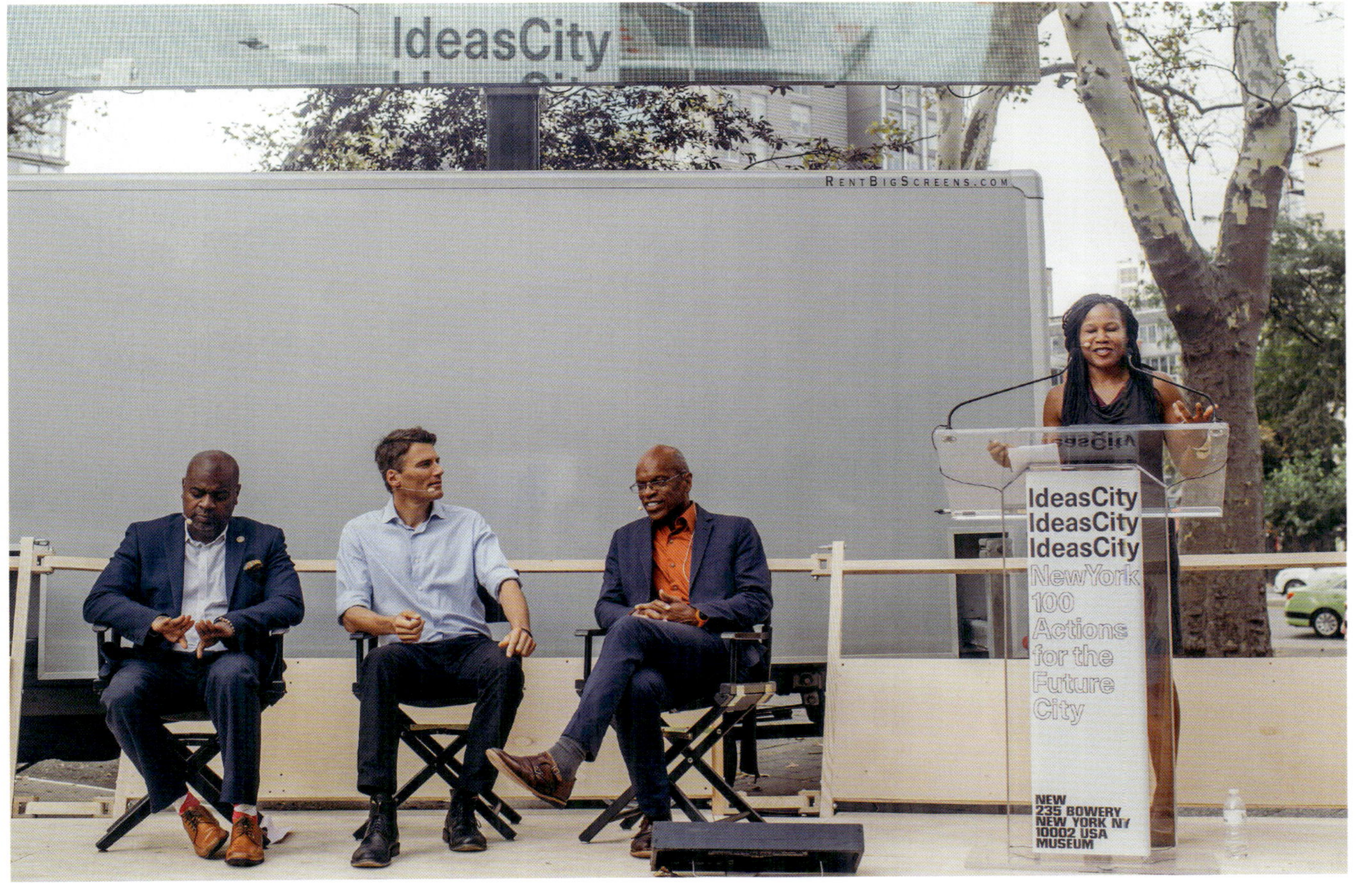

(top) Keynote Address by
Joi Ito, Director of MIT
Media Lab, Ideas City
New York, May 2013

(bottom) Mayoral Panel
moderated by Majora
Carter with Ras Baraka,
Gregor Robertson, and
Maurice Cox, Ideas City
New York, September 2017

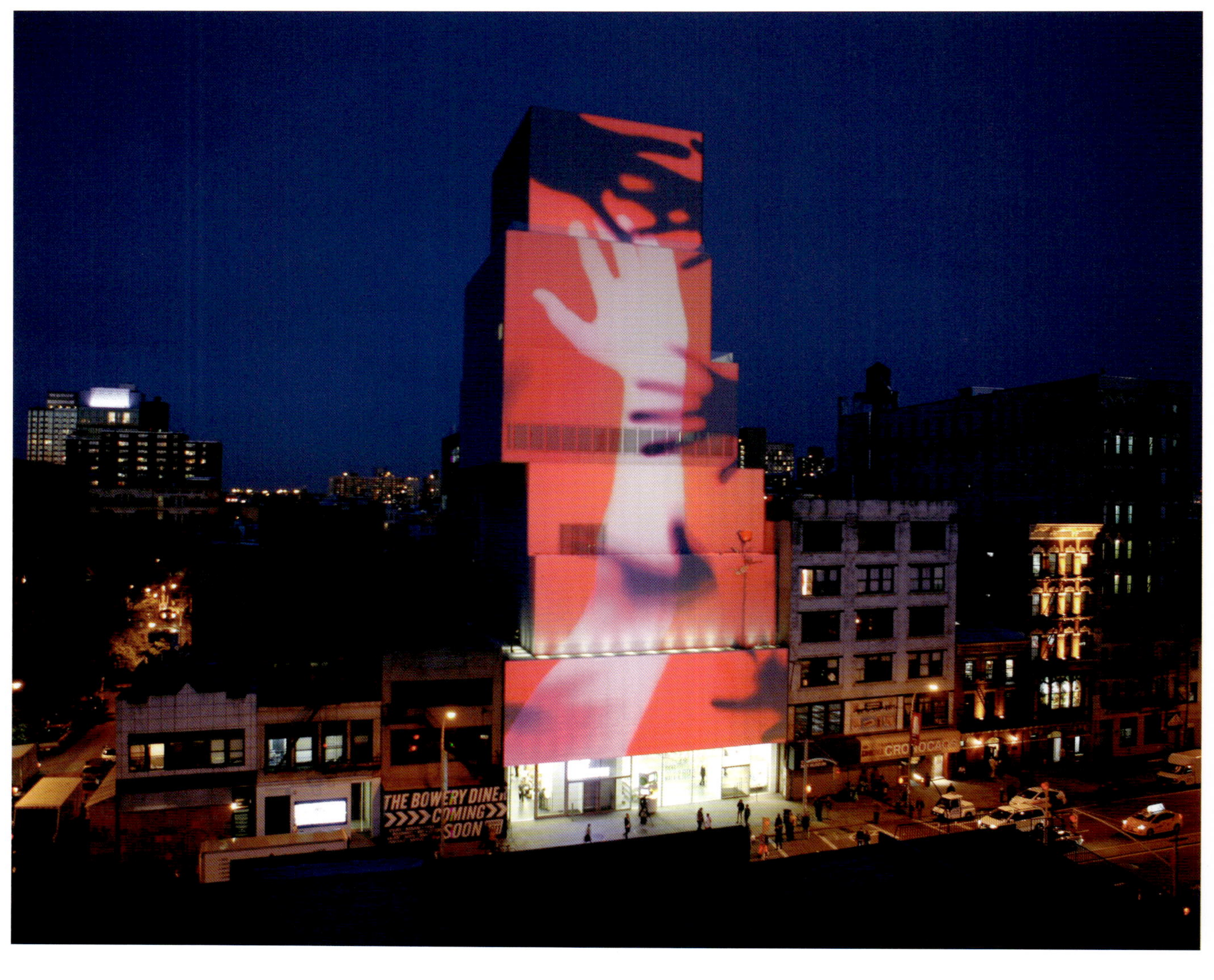

Multiple artists
transform the New Museum
building in "Flash: Light"
organized by Nuit Blanche
New York, Ideas City New
York, May 2011

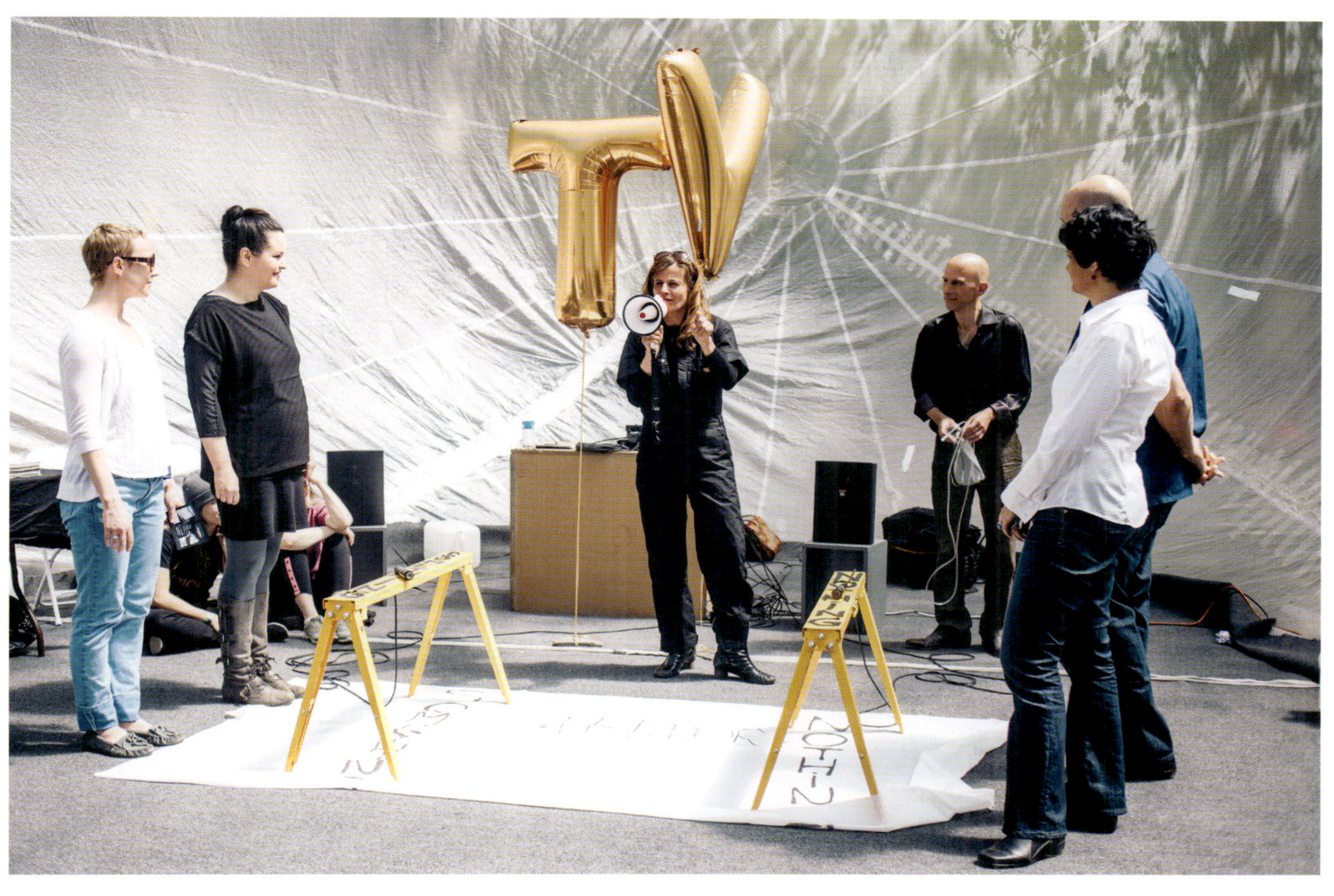

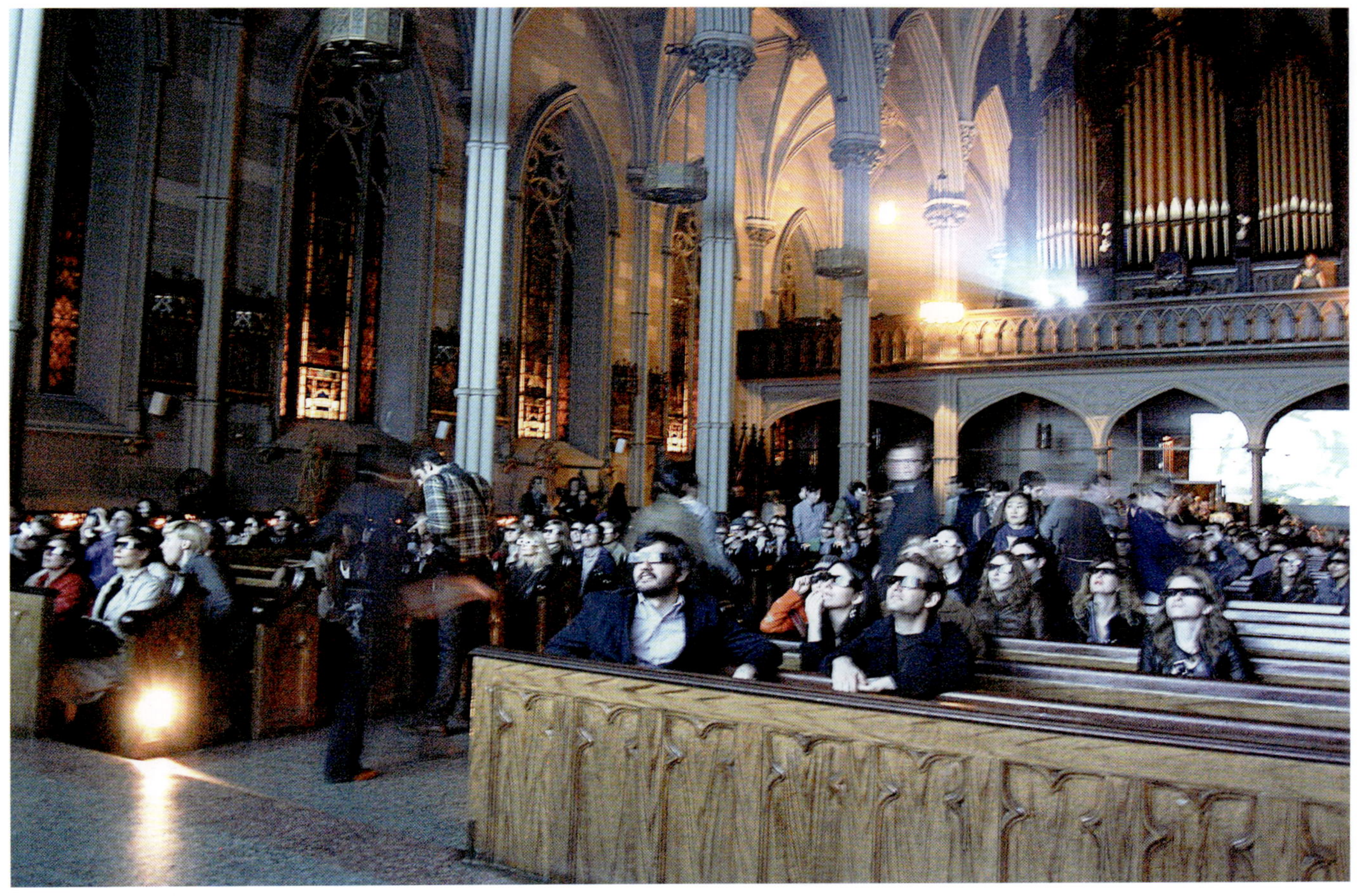

(top) The interior of the Spacebuster, an inflatable mobile structure designed by Raumlabor, commissioned by Storefront for Art and Architecture, Ideas City New York, May 2013

(bottom) Spectators watch a film by Marco Brambilla at the Basilica of St. Patrick's Old Cathedral, Ideas City New York, May 2011

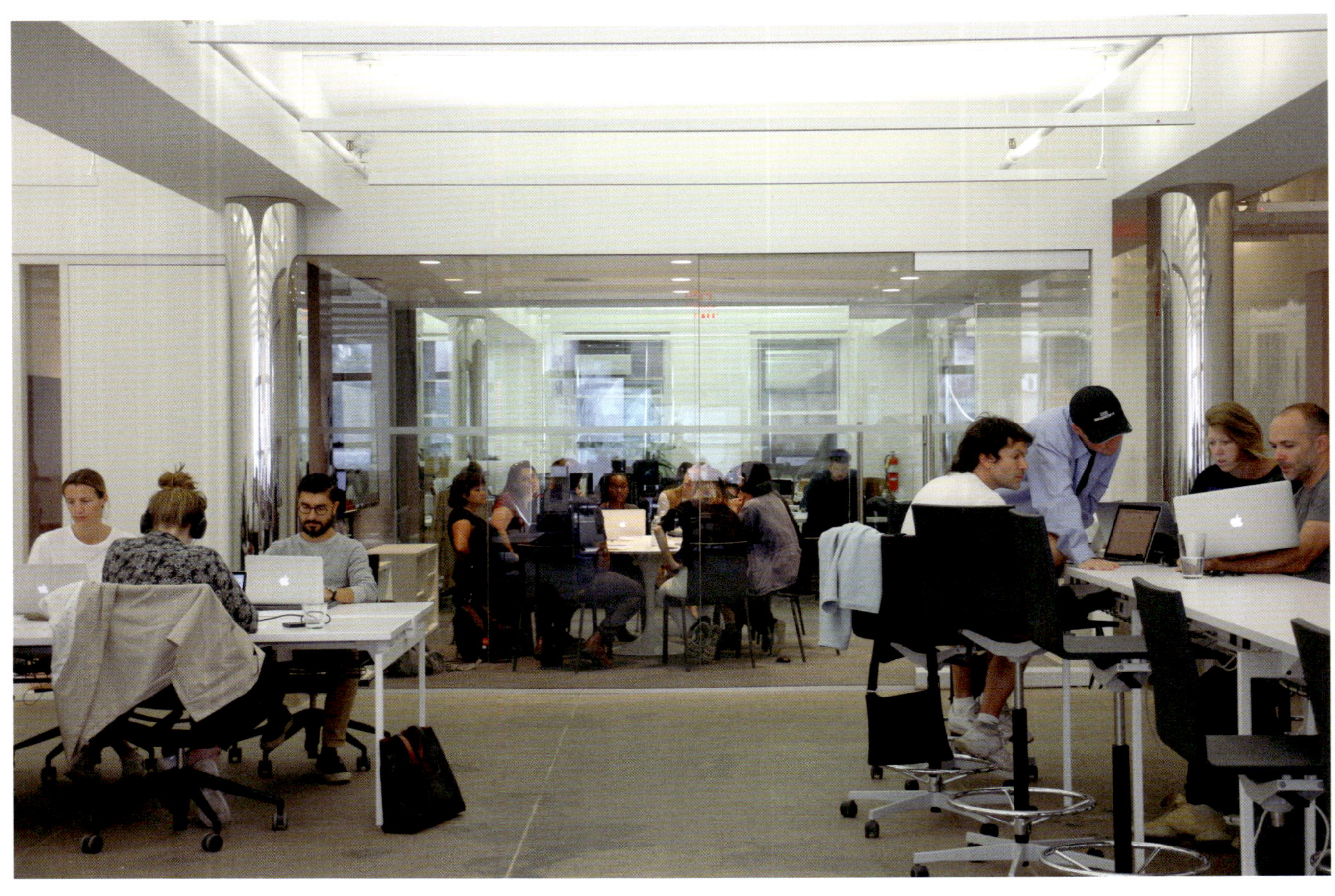

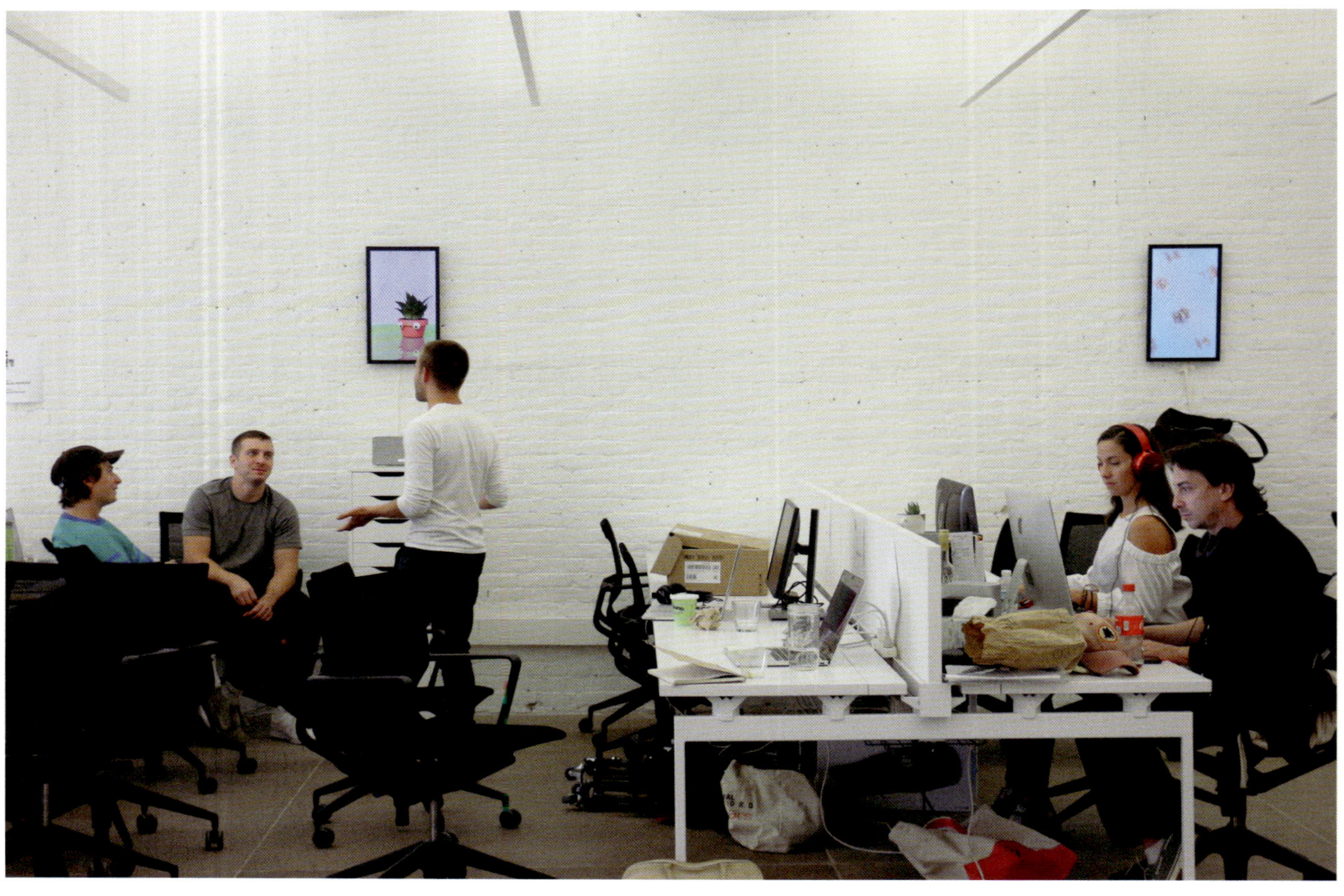

(top) A view of NEW
INC's meeting spaces
at 231 Bowery

(bottom) Workspace of
full-time NEW INC members

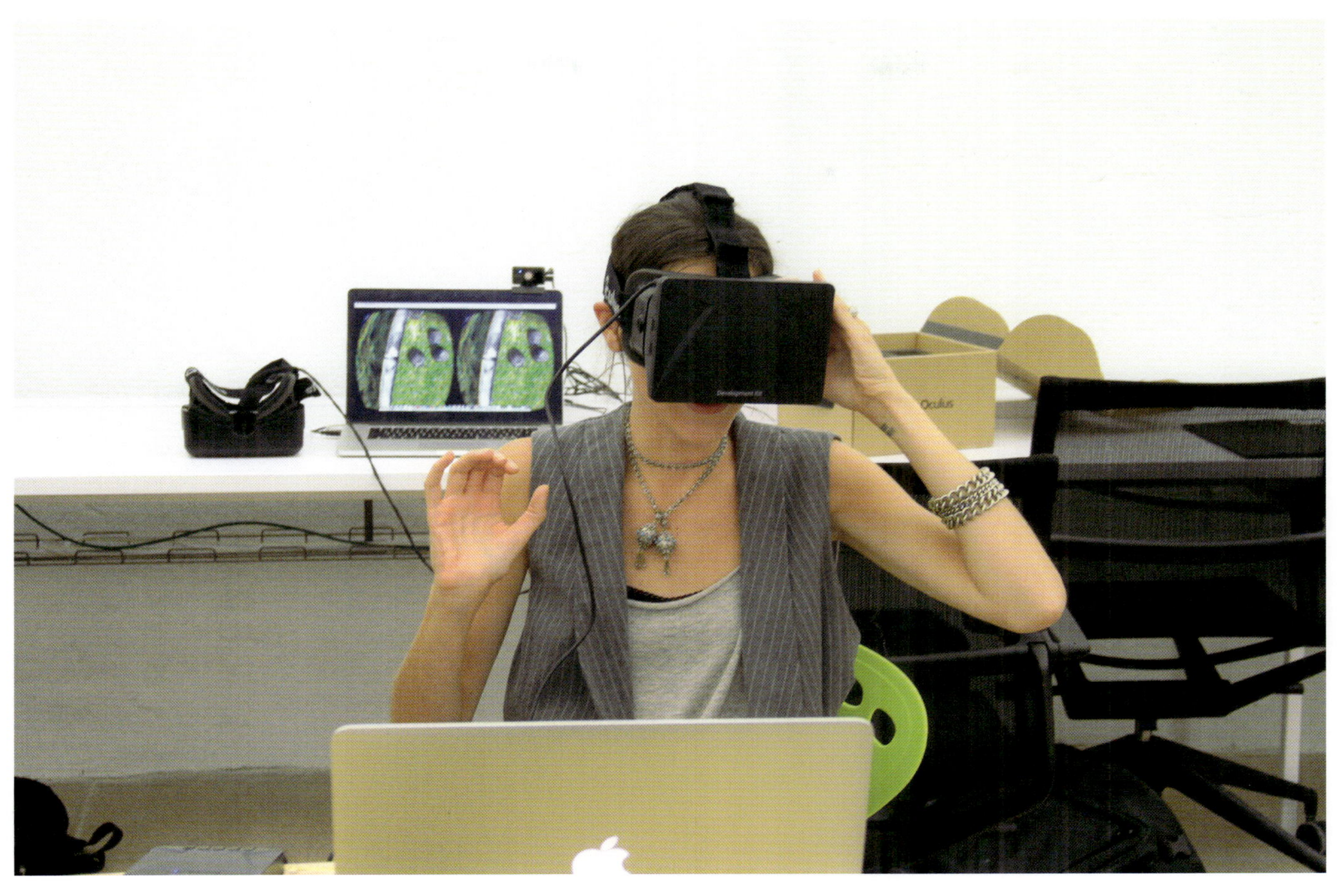

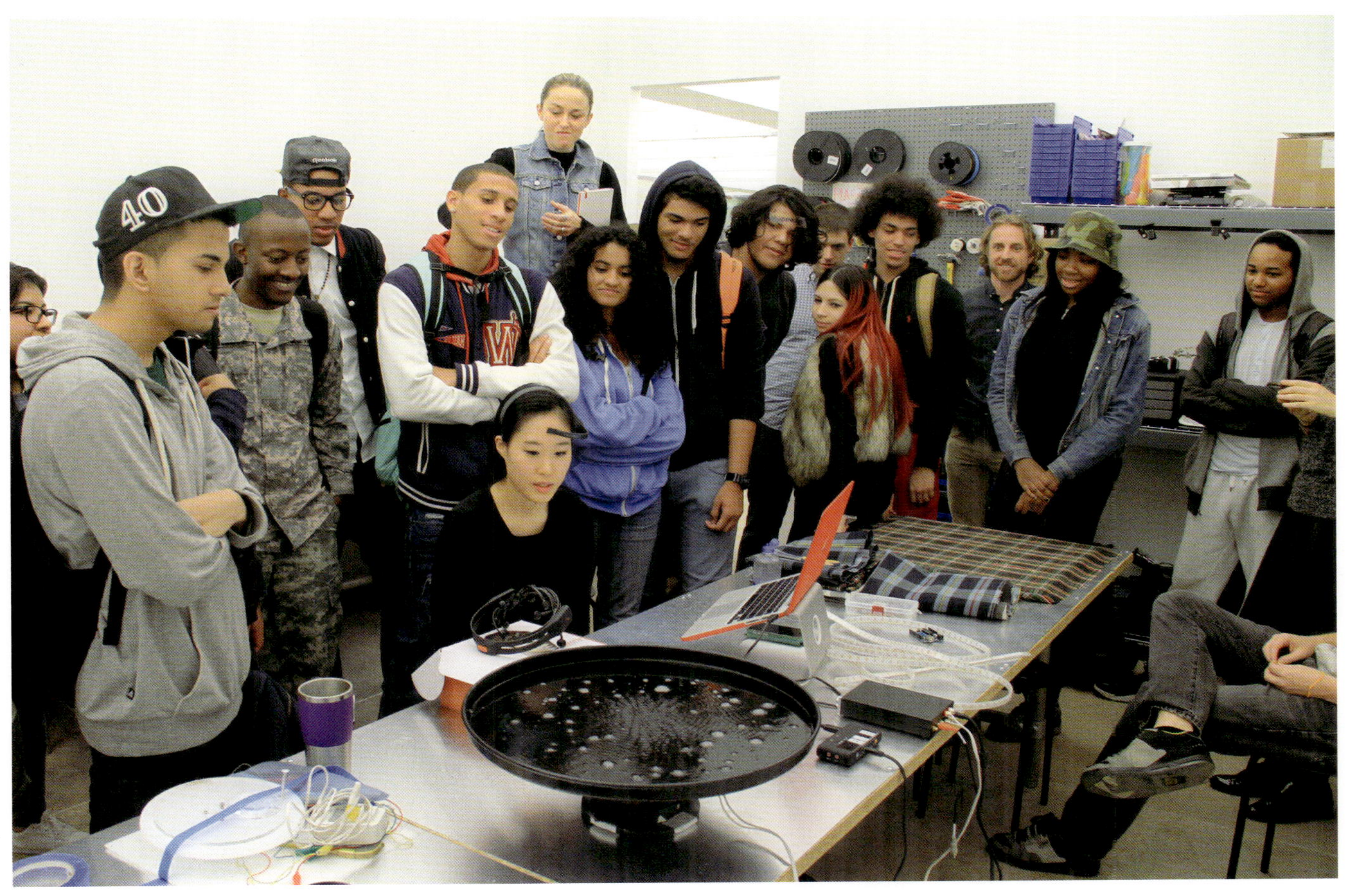

(top) A NEW INC member
tests a new headset

(bottom) NEW INC member
Lisa Park demonstrates
biometric sensors at NEW
INC's workshop space

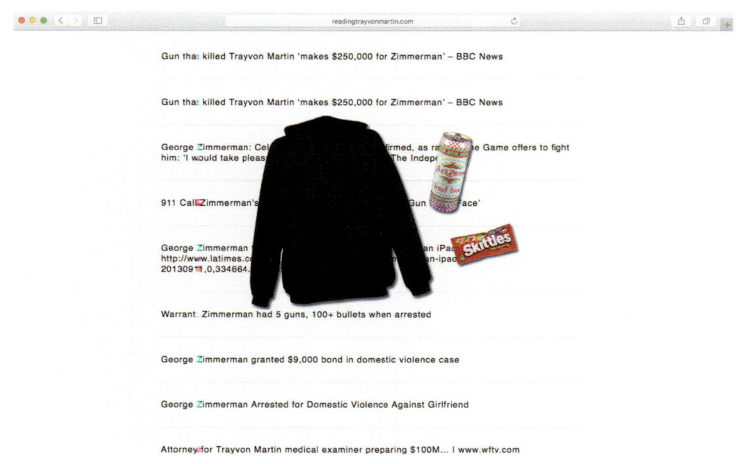

readingtrayvonmartin.com

Gun that killed Trayvon Martin 'makes $250,000 for Zimmerman' – BBC News

Gun that killed Trayvon Martin 'makes $250,000 for Zimmerman' – BBC News

George Zimmerman: Cel... ...irmed, as ra... ...e Game offers to fight him: 'I would take pleas... ...The Indep...

911 Call Zimmerman's ... ...Gun ...ace'

George Zimmerman ... ...an iPa... http://www.latimes.c... ...an-ipad 201309...,0,334664.

Warrant: Zimmerman had 5 guns, 100+ bullets when arrested

George Zimmerman granted $9,000 bond in domestic violence case

George Zimmerman Arrested for Domestic Violence Against Girlfriend

Attorney for Trayvon Martin medical examiner preparing $100M... | www.wftv.com

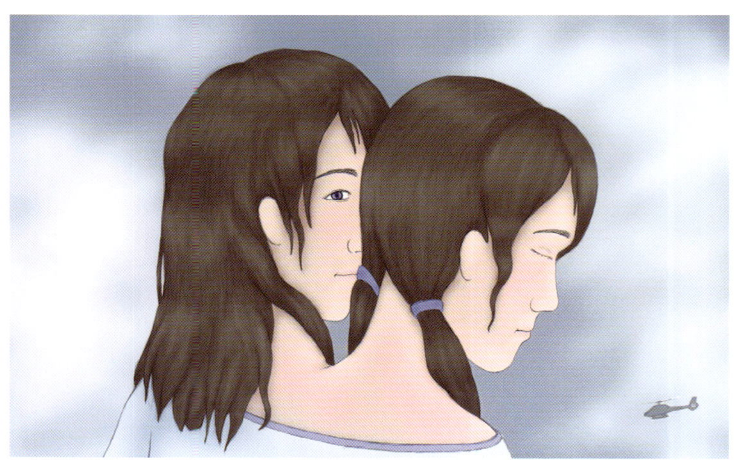

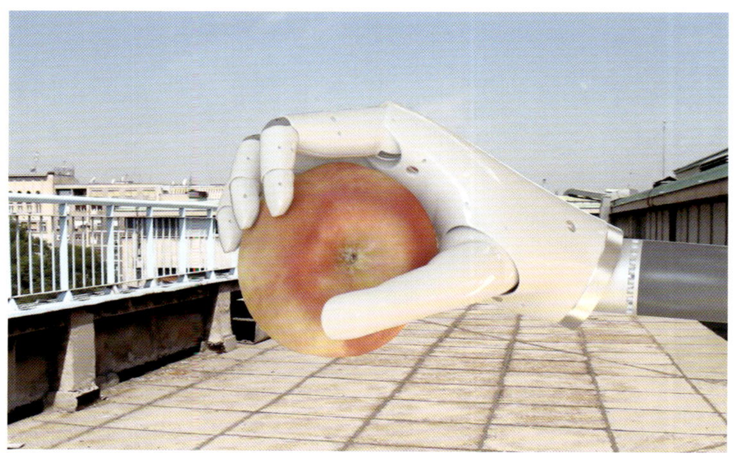

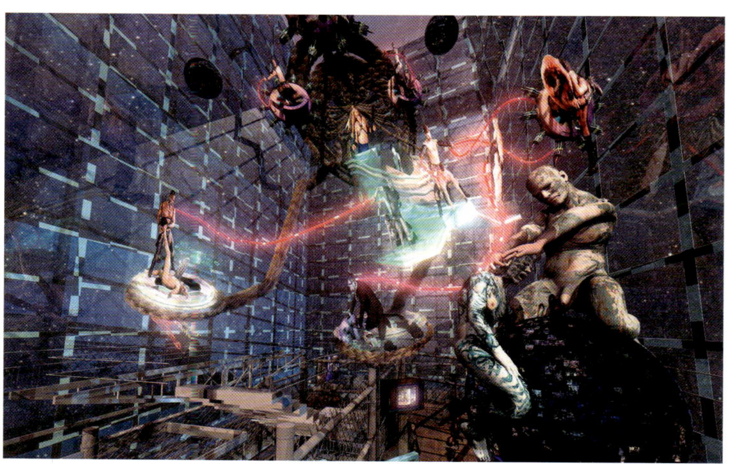

(Top to bottom) Martine Syms, *Reading Trayvon Martin*, 2012–ongoing. Included in First Look, 2014. Andrej Ujhazy, Untitled, 2015. Included in First Look: "Brushes." Porpentine Charity Heartscape and Brenda Neotenomie, *Probiotic River Therapy*, 2016. Included in First Look: "Psycho Nymph Exile." Jacolby Satterwhite, *Domestika*, 2017 (still). Included in First Look: "Artists' VR"

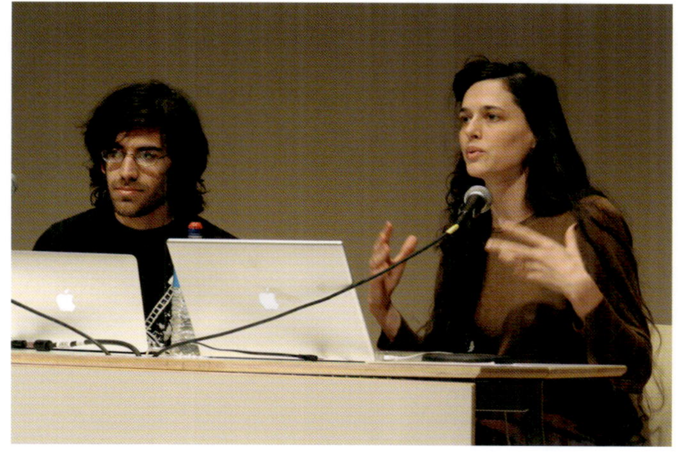

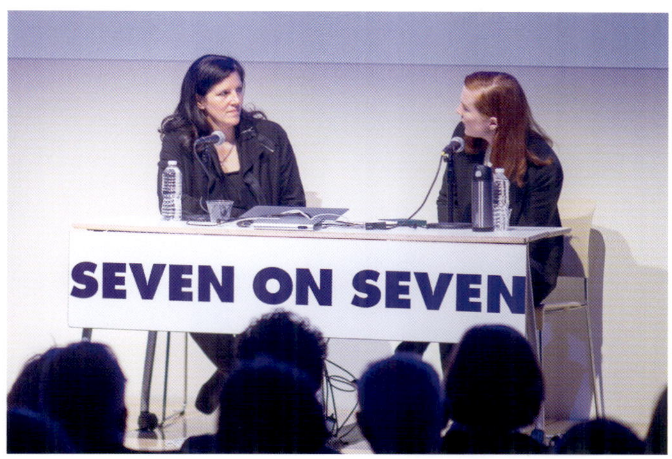

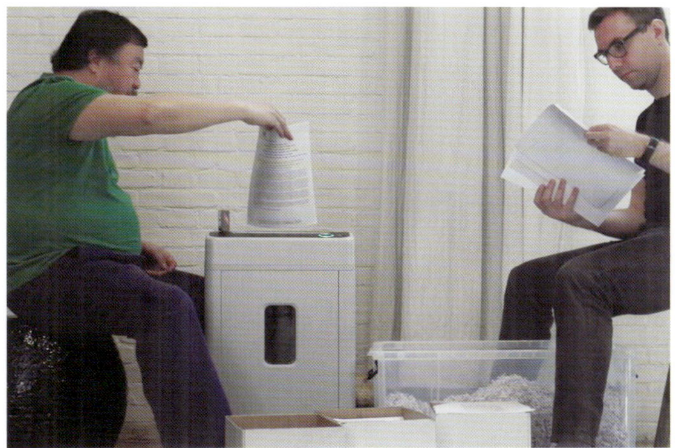

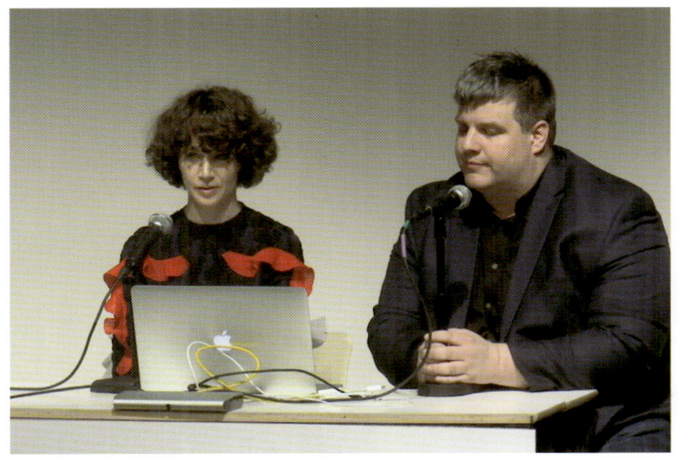

(top to bottom)
Programmer Aaron Swartz and artist Tayrn Simon present *Image Atlas*, 2012. Opening keynote address by Laura Poitras and Kate Crawford, 2015. Artist Ai Weiwei and technologist Jacob Applebaum collaborate on their project in Beijing for Rhizome's Seven on Seven. Artist Miranda July and writer and programmer Paul Ford, 2016

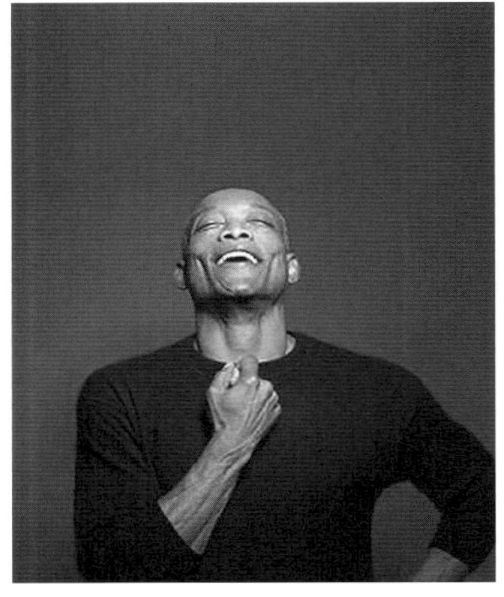

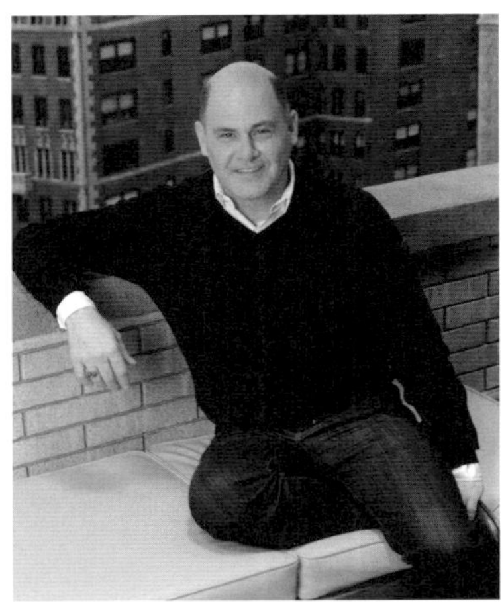

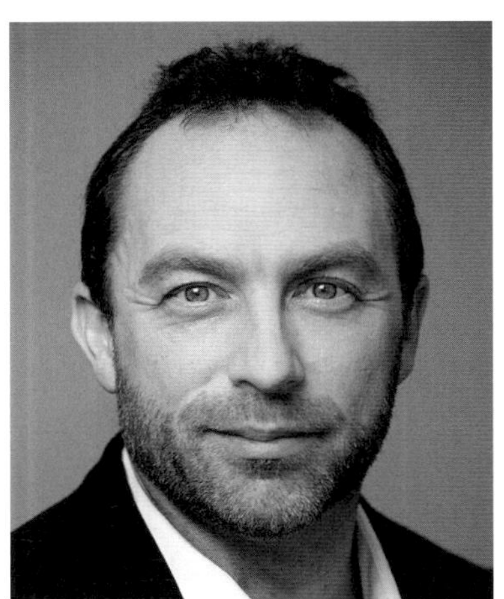

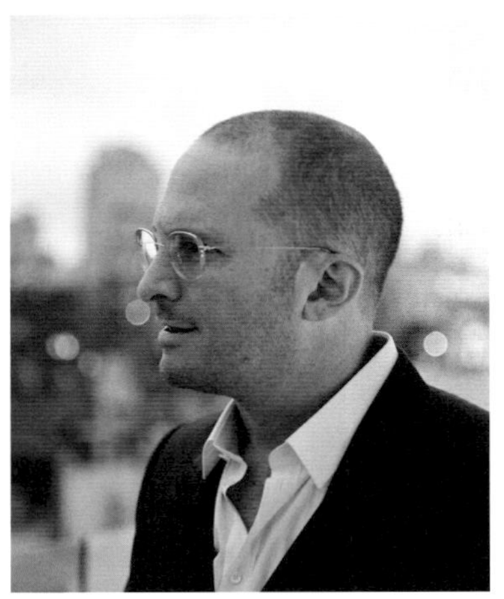

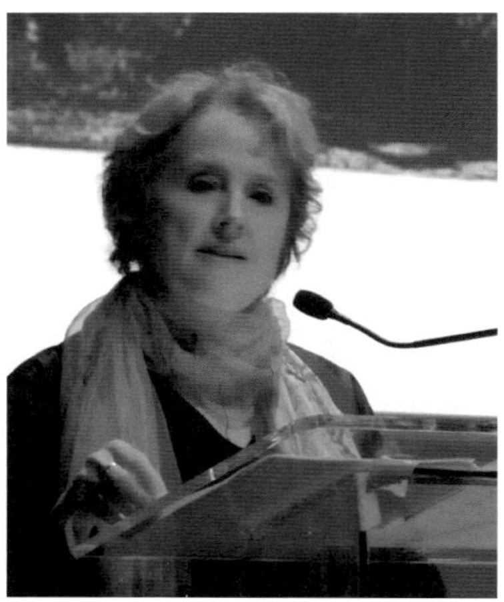

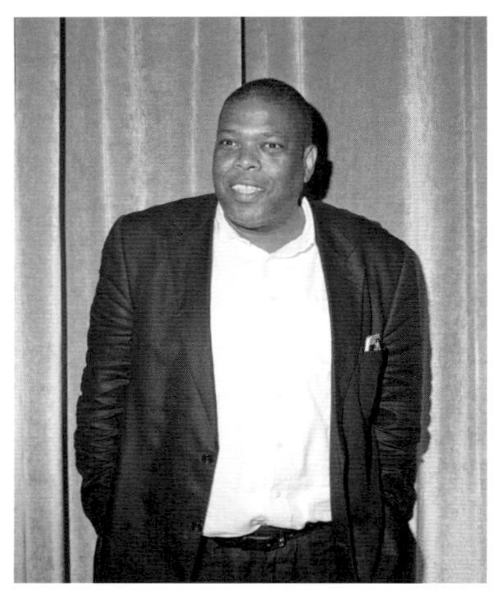

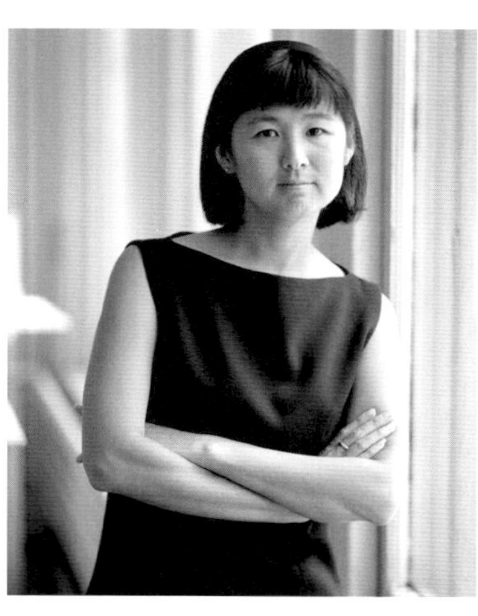

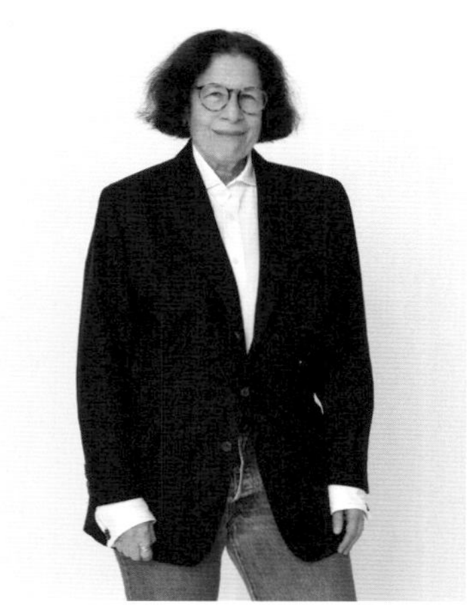

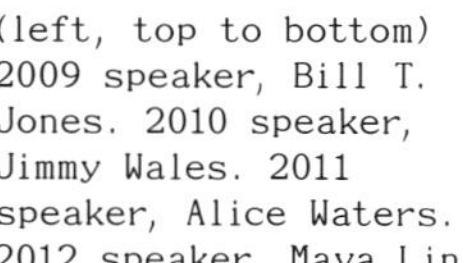

(left, top to bottom)
2009 speaker, Bill T.
Jones. 2010 speaker,
Jimmy Wales. 2011
speaker, Alice Waters.
2012 speaker, Maya Lin

(right, top to bottom)
2013 speaker, Matthew
Weiner. 2014 speaker,
Darren Aronofsky 2015
speaker, Hilton Als. 2016
speaker, Fran Lebowitz

1977

The New Museum is founded in 1977 by Marcia Tucker with support from founding Trustee Allen Goldring. Tucker and a small staff of volunteers start work at the New Museum on the first business day of 1977. The New Museum's headquarters are located in an office in the Fine Arts Building, 105 Hudson Street, in Tribeca, New York. The first staff members include A.C. Bryson, Susan Logan, Michiko Miyamoto, and Allan Schwartzman, and early exhibitions are organized at off-site locations.

"Memory"
May 10–21, 1977
Curated by Marcia Tucker and the New Museum
Presented at C Space, 81 Leonard Street, New York
Artists: Sarah Canright, Brenda Goodman, Steve Gwon, Kent Hines, Ronald Morosan, Earl Ripling, Martin Silverman, and Katherine Sokolnikoff

The New Museum is granted 501 (c)(3) status on May 17, 1977.

The New Museum secures gallery space at the Graduate Center of the New School for Social Research, 65 Fifth Avenue, New York, with the help of Trustee Vera List. Over three thousand people attend the opening of the new space and the preview of the Museum's first exhibition there on November 11, 1977.

"Early Work by Five Contemporary Artists"
November 11–December 30, 1977
Curated by Susan Logan, Allan Schwartzman, and Marcia Tucker
Artists: Ron Gorchov, Elizabeth Murray, Dennis Oppenheim, Dorothea Rockburne, and Joel Shapiro

1978

The New Museum's Semi-Permanent Collection is conceived with the intention of questioning institutional conventions of collecting.
The Museum seeks to acquire at least one work from each major exhibition to be held for approximately a decade. After that time, works would be deaccessioned to make room for new works. This concept is never fully realized, and the Semi-Permanent Collection is suspended in 2001.

"'Bad' Painting"
January 14–February 28, 1978
Curated by Marcia Tucker
Artists: James Albertson, Joan Brown, Eduardo Carrillo, James Chatelain, CPLY (William N. Copley), Charles Garabedian, Robert Chambless Hendon, Joseph Hilton, Neil Jenney, Judith Linhares, P. Walter Siler, Earl Staley, Shari Urquhart, and William Wegman

"Alfred Jensen: Paintings and Diagrams From the Years 1957–1977"
March 18–April 21, 1978
Curated by Linda L. Cathcart, the Albright-Knox Art Gallery, Buffalo, NY, and Marcia Tucker
Chosen to represent the United States at the 54th Bienal de São Paulo, prior to opening at the Albright-Knox Art Gallery and the New Museum

"New Work / New York"
May 13–July 8, 1978
Curated by Susan Logan, Allan Schwartzman, and Marcia Tucker
Artists: Susan Dallas-Swann, Lynne Elton, Steve Keister, David Middaugh, Fred Smith, and Jeff Way

"Outside New York"
September 23–November 11, 1978
Curated by Susan Logan, Allan Schwartzman, Kathleen Thomas, and Marcia Tucker
Artists: Katherine T. Carter, Tom Hatch, James Hill, Alexa Kleinbard, Janis Provisor, and Dan Rizzie

"Barry Le Va: Four Consecutive Installations & Drawings 1967–1978"
December 16, 1978–February 10, 1979
Curated by Marcia Tucker
Presented at the New Museum and the Parsons School of Design, 2 West 13th Street
The Parsons installation, comprising most of the exhibition's drawings, opened on December 21, 1978.

1979

"The Invented Landscape"
February 17–April 14, 1979
Curated by Christopher English (guest curator)
Artists: Peter De Lory, Bonnie Donohue, Victor Landweber, David Maclay, Martha Madigan, Richard Ross, Tricia Sample, Michael Siede, Carl Toth, and Gwen Widmer

"Perspectives: A New York Art Community Dialogue"

"Artists and the Community"
May 2, 1979
Panelists: Jennifer Bartlett, Gaylen C. Hansen, Claire Moore, and Salvatore Scarpitta
Moderator: Ron Gorchov

"Art Writing and Criticism"
May 9, 1979
Panelists: Nicolas Calas, Douglas Davis, Joseph Masheck, Carter Ratcliff, and Barbara Rose
Moderator: Irving Sandler

"Museums and Exhibitions of Contemporary Art"
May 16, 1979
Panelists: John I.H. Baur, Linda L. Cathcart, Linda Shearer, and Palmer Wald
Moderator: Marcia Tucker

"Galleries, Artists, and the Public"
May 23, 1979
Panelists: Leo Castelli, Betty Parsons, Julian Pretto, Holly Solomon, and Jock Truman
Moderator: Arnold Glimcher

"Collectors and the Private Patronage System"
May 30, 1979
Panelists: Richard Brown Baker, Sondra Gilman, Barbara Schwartz, Dorothy Vogel, and Herbert Vogel
Moderator: Eugene Schwartz

"Dimensions Variable"
September 29–November 29, 1979
Curated by Susan Logan, Allan Schwartzman, and Kathleen Thomas
Artists: James O. Clark, Gary Allen Justis, Ann Knutson, Cork Marcheschi, Stephen Miller, Carlton Newton, and Mike Roddy

"Art and Politics"

"Corporate Support (A Positive or Negative Influence on the Arts)"
November 3, 1979
Panelists: Jack Boulton, Gideon Chagy, Christo, Barbara Gladstone, Hans Haacke, and Robin Winters
Moderator: Mary Lanier

"Populism and Elitism: Censorship"
November 10, 1979
Panelists: Mel Edwards, Colen Fitzgibbon, Richard Goldstein, Jim Reinish, and Carrie Rickey
Moderator: Dieter Kearse

"Populism and Elitism: Aesthetic Control and Public Involvement"
November 17, 1979
Panelists: Stefan Eins, Robert Godfrey, John Halpern, Jenny Holzer, and Lucy R. Lippard
Moderator: Marcia Tucker

The Window: "Mary Lemley"
December 7, 1979–January 3, 1980
The inaugural "Window" series installation

1980

"Ree Morton: Retrospective 1971–1977"
February 16–April 17, 1980
Curated by Allan Schwartzman and Kathleen Thomas
Exhibition traveled to other museums

The New Museum Education Program is established in the spring of 1980.

The Minorities Dialogue Series is organized to address the special concerns of early-career minority artists. New Museum staff and an inclusive group of emerging artists gather for informal, bimonthly meetings, each one cohosted by a New Museum staff member and one of the artist participants. Marcia Tucker cohosts the first meeting at her home on March 13, 1980, with Linda Goode Bryant, founding

Director of Just Above Midtown. The meetings on May 7, 1980 and July 22, 1980 are held at the New Museum and hosted respectively by Howardena Pindell, artist and professor at the State University of New York at Stony Brook, and John Neely, Bronx Museum. Ed Jones, Education Director/Foundation Development at the New Museum, hosts the September 12, 1980 social gathering at his home.

The Window: "The New: Jeff Koons"
May 29–June 26, 1980

The Window: "Rented Earth: David Hammons"
July 11–September 18, 1980

The Window: "Richard Prince"
September 26–October 27, 1980

Events: "Fashion Moda"
December 13, 1980–January 8, 1981
Curated by Fashion Moda
(guest curators)
Artists: Charlie Ahearn, John Ahearn, Ali (Mark Edmunds), Jules Allen, Andrew Bascle, Marc Brasz, Leni Brown, David Butler, Stewart Carstater, Robert Colescott, Luis Colmenares, Crash (John Matos), Peter Cummings, Jane Dickson, Marianne Edwards, Stefan Eins, John Fekner, Futura (Lenny McGurr), Juan Galvez, Martin Green, Keith Haring, Candace Hill-Montgomery, Christof Kohlhöfer, Julius Kozlowski, Lady Pink (Sandra Fabara), Lee Quiñones, Joe Lewis, Michael Lokensgard, Mario, Lyle Mathews, Mitch (Mitchell Lopez), Polly Esther Nation, Willie Neal, Paulette Nenner, Valery Oisteanu, Martin Payton, Philip Pearlstein, Joe Perez, Rammellzee Mic Controller, Jim Richard, Judy Rifka, Raymond Ross, Christy Rupp, Wes Sanderson, John Scott, William Scott, Carmen Spera, Louise Stanley, Rigoberto Torres, and Zephyr (Andrew Witten)

1981

Events: "Taller Boricua"
January 17–February 5, 1981
Curated by Taller Boricua
(guest curators)
Artists: Marcos Dimas, Gilberto Hernandez, Fernando Salicrup, and Jorge Soto

Events: "Artists Invite Artists"
February 14–March 5, 1981
Curated by artist participants of the Minorities Dialogue Series: Benny Andrews, Ellsworth Ausby, Rudolf Baranik, Camille Billops, Mel Edwards, Howard Goldstein, Zarina Hashmi, Janet Henry, Jamillah Jennings, Margo Machida, Joe Overstreet, and Howardena Pindell (guest curators)
Artists: Charles Abramson, Camille Billops, Judy Blum, Sydney Blum, James A. Brown, Vivian E. Browne, Benjamin Grubler, Janet Henry, M.L.J. Johnson, Nina Kuo, Margo

Machida, Howard McCalebb, Mr. Mental, Algernon Miller, Kathleen Migliore Newton, Mary O'Neal, Adrian Piper, Jim E. Reynolds, Hayward (Bill) Rivers, Ivy Sky Rutzky, Juan Sánchez, Deborah Whitman, and Grace Williams

The Window: "Jim Holl: World Toy Company"
March 14–April 4, 1981

"John Baldessari: Work 1966–1980"
March 14–April 28, 1981
Curated by Marcia Tucker
Exhibition traveled to other museums

"Alternatives in Retrospect: An Historical Overview 1969–1975"
May 9–July 16, 1981
Curated by Jackie Apple
(guest curator)
Artists: Cecile Abish, Vito Acconci, Eleanor Antin, Billy Apple, Artwiser/Artweiser, Bill Beckley, Bill Beirne, Colette, Jaime Davidovich, Brad Davis, Douglas Davis, Peter Downsbrough, Stefan Eins, Dieter Froese, Tina Girouard, Susan Hall, Suzanne Harris, Ed Hee, Geoffrey Hendricks, Jene Highstein, Nancy Holt, Davi Det Hompson, Peter Hutchinson, Lenore Jaffee, Neil Jenney, Robert Kushner, Thomas Lanigan-Schmidt, Jeffrey Lew, Gordon Matta-Clark, Christopher McNeur, Larry Miller, Rita Myers, Robert Newman, Richard Nonas, Dennis Oppenheim, John Perreault, Virginia Piersol, Carmen Sanchez, George Schneeman, Stuart Sherman, David Troy, Jerry Vis, and Roger Welch
Alternative Spaces: 3 Mercer, 10 Bleecker Street, 98 Greene Street, 112 Greene Street Workshop, Apple, Gain Ground, and Idea Warehouse

"Stay Tuned"
July 25–September 10, 1981
Curated by Ned Rifkin
Artists: Robert Cumming, Brian Eno, Charles Frazier, Donald Lipski, Howardena Pindell, Judy Rifka, Allen Ruppersberg, and Irvin Tepper

"Persona"
September 19–November 12, 1981
Curated by Lynn Gumpert and Ned Rifkin
Artists: Eleanor Antin, Mr. Apology, Colin Campbell, Bruce Charlesworth, Colette, Redd Ekks, Lynn Hershman, James Hill, and Martial Westburg

"Not Just for Laughs: The Art of Subversion"
November 21, 1981–January 21, 1982
Curated by Marcia Tucker
Artists: Terry Allen, Glen Baxter, Robert Colescott, Steven Cortright, Steve Gianakos, Louie Grenier, J.P. Hutto, Jeff, Pamela Kelly, John Malpede, Linda Montano, Tony Oursler, Richard Ross, Erika Rothenberg, Nina Salerno, Michael Smith, Terry Sullivan, Mark Tansey, David Troy, and William Wegman

1982

"Early Work"
April 3–June 3, 1982
Curated by Lynn Gumpert, Ned Rifkin, and Marcia Tucker
Artists: Lynda Benglis, Joan Brown, Luis Jiménez, Gary Stephan, and Lawrence Weiner

The Window: "Political Art Documentation/Distribution, Public Works Committee: Don't Buy This/No Compre Esto"
June 12–July 29, 1982

"Extended Sensibilities: Homosexual Presence in Contemporary Art"
October 16–December 30, 1982
Curated by Dan Cameron
(guest curator)
Artists: Charley Brown, Scott Burton, Craig Carver, Arch Connelly, Janet Cooling, Betsy Damon, Nancy Fried, Jedd Garet, Gilbert & George, Lee Gordon, Harmony Hammond, John Henninger, Jerry Janosco, Lili Lakich, Les Petites Bonbons, Ross Paxton, Jody Pinto, Carla Tardi, and Fran Winant

---

1983

Events: "Classified: Big Pages from the Heresies Collective"
June 11–July 20, 1983
Curated by Heresies Collective members Sandra De Sando, Michele Godwin, Vanalyne Green, Sue Heinemann, Lyn Hughes, Patricia Jones, Kay Kenny, Nicky Lindeman, Lucy R. Lippard, Sabra Moore, and Holly Zox
(guest curators)

*In July 1983, with help from Trustee and Legal Counsel Herman Schwartzman, Board President Henry Luce III negotiates a donation of space in the landmark **Astor Building at 583 Broadway in SoHo, New York**, to the New Museum. Renovations begin.*

***The New Museum reopens at its new location at 583 Broadway on October 8, 1983** with a preview of the exhibition "Language, Drama, Source, & Vision." The newly renovated space occupies 22,000 square feet across three floors and comprises a lobby, a museum shop, flexible exhibition spaces, a preparation shop, storage, a space for public programs, a library, a curatorial archive and viewing room, offices, and a conference room.*

"Language, Drama, Source, & Vision"
October 8–November 27, 1983
Curated by Lynn Gumpert, Ned Rifkin, and Marcia Tucker
Artists: Vito Acconci, Nicholas Africano, John Ahearn and Rigoberto Torres, Terry Allen, Mr. Apology, Luis Jiménez Aranda,

Nancy Arlen, John Baldessari, Lynda Benglis, Dara Birnbaum, Joan Brown, Tom Butter, Bruce Charlesworth, Robert Cumming, Jaime Davidovich, Douglas Davis, Eleanor Dube, Lauren Ewing, John Fekner, Reverend Howard Finster, Vernon Fisher, Claudia Fitch, Ed Flood, Ron Gorchov, Keith Haring, Al Held, James Hill, Joseph Hilton, Alfred Jensen, Bill Jensen, Steve Keister, Barry Le Va, Donald Lipski, Brice Marden, Brad Melamed, Steve Miller, Linda Montano, Claire Moore, Ree Morton, Elizabeth Murray, Howardena Pindell, Adrian Piper, Richard Prince, David Reed, Earl Ripling, Dorothea Rockburne, Mike Roddy, Erika Rothenberg, Allen Ruppersberg, Ed Ruscha, David Saunders, Joel Shapiro, Al Souza, Pat Steir, Gary Stephan, Terry Sullivan, Jamie Summers, Mark Tansey, Irvin Tepper, Anne Turyn, William Wegman, Lawrence Weiner, William T. Wiley, and Grace Williams

"The End of the World: Contemporary Visions of the Apocalypse"
December 10, 1983–
January 22, 1984
Curated by Lynn Gumpert
Artists: Rudolf Baranik, Richard Bosman, Roger Brown, Linda Burgess, Bruce Charlesworth, Michael Cook, Robert Fichter, Reverend Howard Finster, Dana Garrett, Frank Gohlke, Louie Grenier, Donald Lipski, Melissa Miller, Robert Morris, Beverly Naidus, Helen Oji, James Poag, Katherine Porter, Craig Schlattman, Michael Smith with Alan Herman, Nancy Spero, Marianne Stikas, and Robert Younger

---

1984

The New Museum launches the Documentary Sources in Contemporary Art series with the publication of the first book, *Art After Modernism: Rethinking Representation*, edited by Brian Wallis.

The Museum's High School Art Program (HSAP) begins, offering semester-long series of museum, studio, and gallery visits, discussions with artists and critics, and writing projects with a view to building students' critical thinking and communication skills, as well as their knowledge of contemporary art in a social context. HSAP courses use the classroom instead of the museum gallery as their base and are organized in collaboration with public schools across the city.

"Art & Ideology"
February 4–March 18, 1984
Curated by Benjamin H. D. Buchloh, Donald Kuspit, Lucy R. Lippard, Nilda Peraza, and Lowery Stokes Sims (guest curators)
Artists: Ismael Frigerio, Alfredo Jaar, Jerry Kearns, Suzanne Lacy, Fred

Lonidier, Allan Sekula, Nancy Spero, Kaylynn Sullivan, Francesc Torres, and Hannah Wilke

On March 21, 1984, the New Museum's first docent class graduates after an intensive eight-week training program. Docents give gallery talks (often in Spanish) to museum visitors and occasionally give presentations in area schools.

WorkSpace: "Joan Jonas"
April 11–May 13, 1984
"Paradise Lost/Paradise Regained: American Visions of the New Decade"
June 10–September 30, 1984
Curated by Marcia Tucker, Lynn Gumpert, and Ned Rifkin
Presented at the US Pavilion, 41st Venice Biennale
Artists: Richard Bosman, Roger Brown, Louisa Chase, Janet Cooling, Peter Dean, Reverend Howard Finster, Eric Fischl, Charles Garabedian, Jedd Garet, April Gornik, George Thurman Green, Barbara Kassel, Cheryl Laemmle, Robert Levers, Judith Linhares, John Mendelsohn, Melissa Miller, Ronald Morosan, Lee N. Smith III, Earl Staley, David True, Russ Warren, Tony Wong, and Robert Yarber

"Martin Puryear"
July 28–September 9, 1984
Originated at University Gallery, the University of Massachusetts, Amherst, where it was curated by Hugh M. Davies and Helaine Posner

WorkSpace: "The Nicaragua Media Project"
September 21–November 25, 1984
Participants: Marta Noemi Bautis, James Bradley, Christopher Phillips, Mel Rosenthal, Mary Sabbatino, and Abigail Solomon-Godeau

"Golub"
September 22–November 25, 1984
Curated by Lynn Gumpert and Ned Rifkin
Artist: Leon Golub

"Seven Years of Living Art: Linda Montano"
December 8, 1984–
December 7, 1991
Curated by Marcia Tucker
For one day a month for seven years, Linda Montano occupies the Mercer Street Window of the New Museum, where she spends the afternoon discussing art and life with visitors who wish to join her.

"John Hernandez, Shelley Hull, Robin Winters, Krzysztof Wodiczko"
December 8, 1984–January 14, 1985
Curated by Brian Wallis

"Difference: On Representation and Sexuality"
December 8, 1984–
February 10, 1985
Curated by Kate Linker (guest curator) and Jane Weinstock (guest curator, film and video)
Exhibition traveled to other museums

Artists: Max Almy, Ray Barrie, Judith Barry, Raymond Bellour, Dara Birnbaum, Victor Burgin, Theresa Cha, Cecelia Condit, Jean-Luc Godard, Hans Haacke, Mary Kelly, Silvia Kolbowski, Barbara Kruger, Sherrie Levine, Yve Lomax, Stuart Marshall, Martha Rosler, Philippe Venault, Jeff Wall, and Marie Yates

> **"Sexual Identity: You Are Not Yourself"**
> **December 12, 1984**
> **Panelists:** Judith Barry, Victor Burgin, Mary Kelly, Laura Mulvey, Craig Owens, and Jane Weinstock
> **Moderator:** Kate Linker

1985

"Signs"
April 2–July 7, 1985
Curated by Ned Rifkin (guest curator)
Artists: Gary Falk, Ken Feingold, Marian Galczenski, Jenny Holzer, John Knight, MANUAL, Matt Mullican, Tad Savinar, and Al Souza

"Allen Ruppersberg: The Secret of Life and Death"
September 21–November 10, 1985
Originated at the Museum of Contemporary Art, Los Angeles, where it was curated by Julia Brown

In the fall of 1985, the SoHo Center Library is donated by Larry Aldrich, the library's founder, to the New Museum. The library continues to grow as a result of generous donations of art library collections from artists, critics, and others, eventually comprising over 48,000 volumes of artists' monographs and books, art history and theory publications, exhibition catalogues, art periodicals, and more. The free, non-lending resource center is the only library in the United States devoted exclusively to contemporary art and criticism. In 2006 the library is regifted to the New York University Libraries, where it currently resides under the name of the New Museum Library.

"The Art of Memory / The Loss of History"
November 23, 1985–
January 19, 1986
Curated by William Olander
Artists: Bruce Barber, Judith Barry, Troy Brauntuch, Sarah Charlesworth, Louise Lawler, Tina L'Hotsky, Adrian Piper, Stephen Prina, Richard Prince, Martha Rosler, René Santos, Hiroshi Sugimoto, Christopher Williams, and Reese Williams

> **"Re-Viewing History: Video Documents"**
> **November 23, 1985–January 19, 1986**
> **Artists:** Peter Adair, Nancy Buchanan, Downtown Community Television, Dan Graham, Vanalyne Green, Ulysses Jenkins, Miners Campaign Tape Project, Paper Tiger Television, Dan Reeves, David Shulman, and El Taller de Video "Timoteo Velasquez"

The Visible Knowledge Program (VKP) is launched in 1985. This signature New Museum educational and professional development program for public high schools runs for twenty-one years. The VKP pairs artist instructors with high school teachers on a semester-long basis, with the goal of integrating contemporary art with social studies, language arts, and studio art curricula. The program takes a multicultural and interdisciplinary approach, encouraging students to explore contemporary art practices in the context of broader cultural and social issues. From 2002 to 2005, the VKP focuses on the interdisciplinary study of race through art, as part of a subsidiary program known as Re-Presenting Race in the Digital Age.

1986

"Choices: Making an Art of Everyday Life"
February 1–March 30, 1986
Curated by Marcia Tucker
Artists: Marina Abramović and Ulay, James Lee Byars, Spalding Gray, Alex Grey, Tehching Hsieh, Linda Montano, Morgan O'Hara, Michael Osterhout, United Art Contractors, and Ian Wilson

> ***Nightsea Crossing***
> **February 21, 22, and 23, 1986**
> A meditation piece by Marina Abramović and Ulay

"William Copley: The Tomb of the Unknown Whore"
April 12–May 28, 1986
Curated by Marcia Tucker

"Sots Art"
April 12–June 12, 1986
Curated by Margarita Tupitsyn (guest curator)
Exhibition traveled to other museums
Artists: Erik Bulatov, Kazimir Passion Group, Vitaly Komar and Alexander Melamid, Alexander Kosolapov, Leonid Lamm, and Leonid Sokov

"MASS by Group Material"
April 12–June 12, 1986
Curated by William Olander

"Past, Present, Future"
June 21–August 10, 1986
Curated by Marcia Tucker
Artists: Daniel Faust, Amanda Means, Andres Serrano, Susan Unterberg, and Carrie Mae Weems

"Damaged Goods: Desire and the Economy of the Object"
June 21–August 10, 1986
Curated by Brian Wallis
Artists: Judith Barry, Gretchen Bender, Barbara Bloom, Andrea Fraser, Jeff Koons, Justen Ladda, Louise Lawler, Ken Lum, Allan McCollum, and Haim Steinbach

"HOMO VIDEO: Where We Are Now"
December 12, 1986–
February 15, 1987
Curated by William Olander
Artists: Peter Adair and Robert Epstein, Jerri Allyn, Lyn Blumenthal, Gregg Bordowitz, Richard Fung, John Goss, John Greyson, Heramedia, Stuart Marshall, David Merieran, Joyan Saunders, Suzie Silver, and Rick "X"

"Hans Haacke: Unfinished Business"
December 12, 1986–
February 15, 1987
Curated by Brian Wallis
Exhibition traveled to other museums

1987

The New Museum publishes the second volume in the Documentary Sources in Contemporary Art series, *Blasted Allegories: An Anthology of Writings by Contemporary Artists*, edited by Brian Wallis.

"Pat Steir: Self-Portrait: An Installation"
February 27–April 12, 1987
Curated by Marcia Tucker

"Fake: A Meditation on Authenticity"
May 7–July 12, 1987
Curated by William Olander
Artists: Dennis Balk, Nancy Burson, David Cabrera, Laurel Chiten and Cheryl Tamar, Clegg & Guttmann, Stanton Davis, Mark Dion and Jason Simon, Duvet Brothers, Tim Ebner, John Glascock, Day Gleeson/Dennis Thomas, Gorilla Tapes, Fariba Hajamadi, Reginald Hudlin, Joan Jubela and Stanton Davis, Annette Lemieux, Paul McMahon, MICA-TV, Branda Miller, Peter Nagy, David Robbins, John Scarlett-Davis, Andres Serrano, Shelly Silver, Michael Smith, and Sarah Tuft

"The Other Man: Alternative Representations of Masculinity"
May 8–July 12, 1987
Curated by Marcia Tucker
Artists: Nicholas Africano, Ken Aptekar, John Coplans, Greg Drasler, Walton Ford, Mike Glier, Lee Gordon, Pier Marton, Tony Mendoza, Manuel Pardo, and Kevin Wolff

"Bruce Nauman Drawings: 1965–1986"
September 11–November 8, 1987
Originated at Kunstmuseum Basel, where it was curated by Dieter Koepplin and Coosje van Bruggen

> Window on Broadway: "Bruce Nauman: No, No, No, No!"
> September 11–November 8, 1987

"Ana Mendieta: A Retrospective"
November 20, 1987–
January 24, 1988
Curated by Petra Barreras del Rio and John Perreault (guest curators)

"The Great Goddess Debate: Spirituality Versus Social Practice in Recent Feminist Art"
December 8, 1988
Panelists: Lyn Blumenthal, Rosalyn Deutsche, Kate Linker, Arlene Raven, and Nancy Spero
Moderator: Judith Wilson

Window on Broadway: ACT UP: "Let the Record Show…"
November 20, 1987–
January 24, 1988
Curated by William Olander
This exhibition included the artwork *SILENCE=DEATH*.

1988

"Nitelife"
April 3–9, 1988
Curated by William Olander, Russell Ferguson, and Laura Trippi
Performers: Bill Callihan, Kimati Dinizulu and His Kotoko Society, Jeffrey Essmann (with Michael-John LaChiusa), Foreign Legion, Mary Hestand & Associates, Ishmael Houston-Jones (with Dennis Cooper), Maxine Lapiduss, Robbie McCauley with Ed Montgomery, Lee Nashville and Felicity (Dan Cohen and Bill Callihan), Nicky Paraiso (with Mark Bennett, Roy Nathanson, and Bill Ruyle), Reno, Mary Schultz (with Roy Nathanson), Doug Skinner (with Eddie Gray and Carol Benner), Carmelita Tropicana, Jim Turner, and Guy Yarden
Artists: Christian Marclay, Richard Prince, and Laurie Simmons

"The Ideology of the Margin: Gender, Race, and Culture"
Organized by Alice Yang

> **Introduction: "The Politics of Marginalization"**
> **April 27, 1988**
> **Speakers:** Luis Camnitzer, Abdul R. JanMohamed, John Jeffries, Renee Tajima, Marcia Tucker, Carrie Mae Weems, and Cornel West
>
> **"Culture and the Canon: The Institutions' Responsibility"**
> **May 4, 1988**
> **Speakers:** Fay Chiang, Kinshasha Holman Conwill, Douglas Crimp, Richard Powell, and Tim Rollins
>
> **"How We See Ourselves, How Others See Us"**
> **May 11, 1988**
> **Speakers:** Michael Callen, Martha Gever, Sharon Greytak, Adrian Piper, and Juan Sánchez
>
> **"Feminism and Third World Culture"**
> **May 18, 1988**
> **Speakers:** Alia Arasougnly, Jean Franco, Howardena Pindell, Barbara Smith, and Mitra Tabrizia
>
> **"Representation and Popular Culture"**
> **May 25, 1988**
> **Speakers:** Warrington Hudlin, David Henry Hwang, Hanif Kureishi, Greg Tate, and Judith Williamson

WorkSpace: "Félix González-Torres"
September 16–November 20, 1988
Curated by Laura Trippi

WorkSpace: "Girls Night Out (Femininity as Masquerade)"
September 16–November 20, 1988
Curated by Laura Trippi
Artists: Meg Cranston, Marilyn Minter, Rona Pondick, Tina Potter, Aimee Rankin, Alison Saar, and Susan Silas

"Impresario: Malcolm McLaren and the British New Wave"
September 16–November 20, 1988
Curated by Paul Taylor
(guest curator)

The Window: "An Installation by General Idea"
December 9, 1988–
February 12, 1989

"Christian Boltanski: Lessons of Darkness"
December 9, 1988–
February 12, 1989
Curated by Lynn Gumpert and Mary Jane Jacob, the Museum of Contemporary Art, Los Angeles
Exhibition traveled to other museums

1989

"Robert Colescott: A Retrospective"
February 24–April 16, 1989
Originated at the San Jose Museum of Art, CA, where it was curated by John Olbrantz

> **"Black to the Future: A Series on Contemporary African-American Aesthetics"**
> Organized by Kellie Jones, Visual Arts Director of the Jamaica Arts Center, New York

>> **"The Unedited Robert Colescott"**
>> **March 14, 1989**
>> **Speaker:** Lowery Stokes Sims

>> **"Alva Rogers in Performance"**
>> **March 21, 1989**
>> **Performers:** Charles Burnham, Lisa Jones, Alva Rogers, and Brandon Ross

>> **"African-American Aesthetics: Links to the Past, Directions for the Future"**
>> **March 28, 1989**
>> **Panelists:** Nelson George, Lisa Jones, Judith Wilson, and George C. Wolfe
>> **Moderator:** Kellie Jones

"Until That Last Breath: Women With AIDS"
February 24–April 16, 1989
Curated by Marcia Tucker
Artist: Ann Meredith

WorkSpace: "Overlooked/ Underplayed: Videos on Women and AIDS"
February 24–April 16, 1989
Curated by Alice Yang
Directors and Producers: AIDS Discrimination Unit; Jean Carlomusto; Gay Men's Health Crisis, New York; Amber Hollibaugh in conjunction with the New York Commission on Human Rights; Alexandra Juhasz; Carol Leigh (Scarlot Harlot); Maria Maggenti; Pratibha Parmar; and San Francisco AIDS Foundation

On March 18, 1989, William Olander, Senior Curator, dies of AIDS. In recognition of his rigorous and provocative curatorial vision, the William Olander Memorial Fund is established. The fund is used to purchase ACT UP's SILENCE=DEATH neon sign that was originally installed in the "Let the Record Show..." exhibition.

"Nancy Spero: Works Since 1950"
May 19–July 9, 1989
Originated at the Everson Museum of Art, Syracuse, NY, where it was curated by Dominique Nahas

"Strange Attractors: Signs of Chaos"
September 14–November 26, 1989
Curated by Laura Trippi
Artists: (Art)^n, Eve Andrée Laramée, Dove Bradshaw, Glenn Branca, Ellen Brooks, John Cage, Tony Cokes, Collins and Milazzo, Critical Art Ensemble, Steve DiBenedetto, Orshi Drozdik, Dana Duff, Laura Emrick, Diana Formisano, Paul Garrin, Ann Hamilton with Kathryn Clark, David Hammons, Carter Hodgkin, Jon Kessler, Zoe Leonard, Jill Levine, Christian Marclay, Steve Miller, Peter Nagy, Joseph Nechvatal, Alastair Noble, Cady Noland, David Nyzio, Dan Reynolds, Walter Robinson, Andres Serrano, David Smith, Leslie Thornton, Jon Tower, Sokhi Wagner, Oliver Wasow, James Welling, Grace Williams and Litina, and the Wooster Group

The Multicultural Internship Program is established in 1989, offering full-time, paid internships in the Director's Office and the Development, Registrar, Education, Curatorial, and Administration Departments. The program runs through 1993.

"Are You Angry Yet? Panel Discussion on Government Funding and Censorship of the Arts"
September 25, 1989
Panelists: Dean Amhaus, Carol Becker, Jim Fouratt, Joseph Papp, Faith Ringgold, and Ted Potter
Moderator: Russell Ferguson

Inaugural Day Without Art
December 1, 1989
Organized by Laura Trippi and Visual AIDS

1990

The third and fourth books in the Documentary Sources in Contemporary Art series are published: ***Discourses: Conversations in Postmodern Art and Culture***, edited by Russell Ferguson, Karen Fiss, William Olander, and Marcia Tucker, and ***Out There: Marginalization and Contemporary Cultures***, edited by Russell Ferguson, Martha Gever, Trinh T. Minh-ha, and Cornel West.

"Mary Kelly: Interim"
February 16–April 8, 1990
Curated by Gary Sangster
Exhibition traveled to other museums

"The Decade Show: Frameworks of Identity in the 1980s"
May 12–August 19, 1990
An institutional collaboration and multi-venue exhibition, curated by Sharon Patton, the Studio Museum in Harlem, New York; Julia P. Herzberg, the Museum of Contemporary Hispanic Art, New York; and Laura Trippi and Gary Sangster, the New Museum
Artists: Max Aguilera-Hellweg, John Ahearn, Carlos Alfonzo, Emma Amos, Ida Applebroog, Tomie Arai, Luis Cruz Azaceta, Jean-Michel Basquiat, Miriam Beerman, Louis Carlos Bernal, Dara Birnbaum, Joan Braderman, María Brito-Avellana, Fred Brown, Beverly Buchanan, Josely Carvalho, Shu Lea Cheang, Albert Chong, Ken Chu, Y. David Chung, Robert Colescott, Houston Conwill, John Coplans, Emilio Cruz, Jaime Davidovich, Judite dos Santos, Mel Edwards, Epoxy Art Group, Eric Fischl, Ismael Frigerio, Gran Fury, Leon Golub, Vanalyne Green, John Greyson, the Guerrilla Girls, Hans Haacke, Sachiko Hamada and Scott Sinkler, David Hammons, Maren Hassinger, Edgar Heap of Birds, Jenny Holzer, Reginald Hudlin, Alfredo Jaar, Martha Jackson Jarvis, G. Peter Jemison, Luis Jiménez Aranda, Philip Mallory Jones, Leandro Katz, Mary Kelly, Komar and Melamid, Barbara Kruger, Pok Chi Lau, Louise Lawler, Joseph Lewis III, George Longfish, Yolanda M. López, Chip Lord, James Luna, Margo Machida, Ana Mendieta, Amalia Mesa-Bains with Victor Zamudio-Taylor, Néstor Millán, Branda Miller, Sherry Millner, Yong Soon Min, Tyrone Mitchell, Tom Nakashima, Bruce Nauman, Catalina Parra, César Paternosto, Howardena Pindell, Adrian Piper, Liliana Porter, Richard Prince, Martin Puryear, Nick Quijano, Daniel Reeves, Faith Ringgold, Arnaldo Roche, Martha Rosler, Alison Saar, Betye Saar, Ben Sakoguchi, Juan Sánchez, Raymond Saunders, Andres Serrano, Cindy Sherman, Laurie Simmons, Coreen Simpson, Scott Sinkler, Jaune Quick-to-See Smith, Nancy Spero, Haim Steinbach, Kaylynn Sullivan TwoTrees, Jorge Tacla, Testing the Limits Collective, Rigoberto Torres, Sarah Tuft, Edin Vélez, Ethel Velez, Cecilia Vicuña, Christian Walker, Kay Walkingstick, Richard Ray Whitman, Pat Ward Williams, Krzysztof Wodiczko, David Wojnarowicz, Martin Wong, Bruce Yonemoto, and Norman Yonemoto

> **Broadway Window: "Cornered: Adrian Piper"**
> **May 12–July 12, 1990**
> Organized as part of "The Decade Show: Frameworks of Identity in the 1980s"

"The Decade Show":
Performance Series
June 6–16, 1990

June 6, 1990
Performers: Ana Castillo, Guillermo Gómez-Peña, Ishmael Houston-Jones, and Merian Soto and Pepón Osorio

June 7, 1990
Performers: Ethyl Eichelberger, Raphael Montañez Ortiz, Alva Rogers and Lisa Jones, and David Zambrano

June 8, 1990
Performers: Dan Kwong, Lydia Lunch and Emilio Cubeiro, Reno, and Kaylynn Sullivan TwoTrees

June 9, 1990
Performers: Kathy Acker, DanceNoise, Jimmie Durham, and John Kelly

June 15, 1990
Presented at the Studio Museum in Harlem, New York
Performers: Roger Shimomura, Carmelita Tropicana, Cecilia Vicuña, and David Wojnarowicz

June 16, 1990
Presented at the Studio Museum in Harlem, New York
Performers: David Chung, Robbie McCauley with Jeannie Hutchins, and Michael Smith

"From Receiver to Remote Control: The TV Set"
September 14–November 25, 1990
Curated by Matthew Geller (guest curator)

"Spent: Currency, Security, and Art on Deposit"
October 1–November 7, 1990
Curated by Luis De Jesus
Presented at the SoHo branch of Marine Midland Bank, New York
Artists: Ted Abramczyk, Jack Anderson, Ursula Biemann, Moyra Davey, Jessica Diamond, Devon Dikeou, Serge Kliaving, Corky Lee, Les LeVeque, Glenn Ligon, Donald Moffett, Paul Ramírez, Julia Scher, Irini Scocos, Gary Simmons, Carrie Mae Weems, and Chris Wilder

"Rhetorical Image"
December 9, 1990–February 3, 1991
Curated by Milena Kalinovska (guest curator)
Artists: Dennis Adams, Art & Language, Judith Barry, Lothar Baumgarten, Braco Dimitrijević, Rose Finn-Kelcey, Félix González-Torres, Tomislav Gotovac, Ian Hamilton Finlay, Thomas Huber, Ilya Kabakov, On Kawara, Jiří Kolář, Jarosław Kozłowski, Cildo Meireles, Tatsuo Miyajima, Muntadas, Barbara Steinman, Lawrence Weiner, and Krzysztof Wodiczko

---

1991

Broadway Window: "Love for Sale... Free Condoms Inside"
February 16–April 7, 1991
Gran Fury with PONY (Prostitutes of New York)

WorkSpace: "Carrie Mae Weems: And 22 Million Very Tired and Very Angry People"
February 16–April 7, 1991
Curated by Laura Trippi

"Africa Explores: 20th Century African Art"
May 11–September 18, 1991
Curated by Susan Vogel, the Center for African Art, New York
Presented concurrently at the Center for African Art, New York
Artists: Ajani, Sunday Jack Akpan, Kojo Anokye, Fode Camara, Sokari Douglas Camp, Dame Gueye, Kweku Kakanu, Tshibumba Kanda-Matulu, Seydou Keïta, Koffi Kouakou, Kane Kwei, Albert Lubaki, Gora M'Bengue, Kivuthi Mbuno, Middle Art, Mode Muntu, Iba N'Diaye, S.T. Ngui, Malangatana Valente Ngwenya, Nsedu, Tshyela Ntendu, Magdalene Odundo, Ouattara, Trigo Piula, S. Rufisque, Chéri Samba, Sim Simaro, and Samba Sylla

"The Interrupted Life"
September 13–December 29, 1991
Curated by France Morin
Artists: Gwen Akin, Hilton Als, Antonin Artaud, Joseph Beuys, Nayland Blake, Christian Boltanski, Victor Bouillon, the Burns Archive, Geneviève Cadieux, Sophie Calle, Mary Carlson, Sarah Charlesworth, Larry Clark, Hans Danuser, Jimmy DeSana, Eugenio Dittborn, Orshi Drozdik, Marlene Dumas, Jimmie Durham, Laura Fields, Adam Fuss, Peter Greenaway, Mona Hatoum, Ronald Jones, Tadeusz Kantor, John LeKay, Allan Ludwig, Amalia Mesa-Bains, Donald Moffett, Bruce Nauman, Elaine Reichek, Bastienne Schmidt, Jeffrey Silverthorne, Cam Slocum, Kiki Smith, Jolie Stahl, Mladen Stilinović, Darryl Turner, James Van Der Zee, Andy Warhol, Brian Weil, Frederick Wiseman, and David Wojnarowicz

"Seven Years of Living Art: Linda's Last Performance"
December 6, 1991
Curated by Marcia Tucker
Artist: Linda Montano

1992

"1+1+1: Works by Alfredo Jaar"
January 15–April 19, 1992
Curated by Alice Yang, as part of the touring exhibition "Alfredo Jaar," and Madeleine Grynsztein, the San Diego Museum of Contemporary Art, CA

"The Art Mall: A Social Space"
May 16–June 28, 1992
Curated by Brian Hannon
Artists: Doug Aitken, Vikky Alexander, Todd Alden and Steve Ausbery, Tamas Banovich, Diane Bonder and Elizabeth M. Stephens, Didier Canaux and Adam Cvijanovic, Lenora Champagne and Vivian Selbo, Marta Chilindron and Eduardo Costa, Devon Dikeou,

Judite dos Santos, Greg Drasler, Brenden Fitzgerald, Rinaldo Frattolillo, Ken Gonzales-Day, Bolek Greczynski with the Battlefields Crew from the Living Museum at the Creedmoor Psychiatric Center, Toby Lee Greenberg, Hit and Run Theatre, Ben Kinmont, Kwok, Chip Lord, Gen Ken Montgomery, Peggy Phelan and VRcades, Barbara Pollack and Grai St. Clair Rice, Teri Rueb, Ann Duncan Satterfield and Carol Irving, Kerri Scharlin, Jennifer Schlosberg, Jeffrey W. Schulz, Danny Tisdale, David Wells, and Shunsuke Yamaguchi

"The Spatial Drive"
September 27, 1992– January 3, 1993
Curated by Laura Trippi
Artists: Marina Abramović, Laurie Carlos, Lewis deSoto, Gretchen Faust and Kevin Warren, Fred Holland, Sonia Labouriau, John Lindell, Rei Naito, Marylene Negro, Laurie Parsons, Fiona Templeton, and the X-Art Foundation

"The Spatial Drive: Security and Admissions Project"
September 27, 1992–January 3, 1993
Artist: Laurie Parsons
Participants: Kimball Augustus, Bessie Bowens, Luis Burgos, Emily Ching, Judith Daniel, Dirk Glasgow, Adam Glickman, Shelley Goldberg, Elon Joseph, Tadeo Ortiz, Nondas Sable, Jonathan Schnapp, L. Daniel Vincent, and Alphonse Whitsett

"FluxAttitudes"
September 26, 1992– January 3, 1993
Curated by Susan Hapgood and Cornelia Lauf (guest curators)
Artists: Aaaart Guise Ink., Ricci Albenda, Eric Anderson, Ay-O (Takao Iijima), Guillaume Bijl, John Cale, Giuseppe Chiari, Tony Conrad, Philip Corner, Nancy Dwyer, Ken Friedman, Al Hansen, Sandra Hastenteufel, Geoffrey Hendricks, Georg Herold, Dick Higgins, Alice Hutchins, Ray Johnson, Alison Knowles, Petr Kotik, Liz Larner, Jackson Mac Low and Anne Tardos, Christian Marclay, Jackie McAllister, Jill McArthur, David Medalla, Vik Muniz, Maurizio Nannucci, Yoko Ono, The OParty!, Nam June Paik, Paul Ramírez Jonas, Michael Ross, Carolee Schneemann, Paul Sharits, Mieko Shiomi, Laura Stein, William Stone, Rirkrit Tiravanija, Danny Tisdale, Yasunao Tone, Marc Travanti, Wolf Vostell, Yoshimasa Wada, David Wells, and Martin Zimmerman

---

1993

"In Transit"
January 15–April 11, 1993
Curated by France Morin with Kostas Gounis and John Jeffries (guest curators)
Artists: Maria Thereza Alves, Bessie Bass, William Bosworth, Andrew Castrucci, Y. David Chung, Martha Cooper, Laura Cottingham, Matt Dibble, G. Roger Denson, Ernest

Drucker, John Fekner, Erik Freeman,
Aki Fujiyoshi, Mildred Howard,
Dorothy Imagire, John Jeffries,
Tadashi Kawamata, Don Leicht,
Helen Levitt, Glenn Ligon, Hung Liu,
Marlene McCarty, Santu Mofokeng,
Charles Moore, Margaret Morton,
Antonio Muntadas, Ramona
Naddaff, Lois Nesbitt, Gabriel
Orozco, the Parks Council Green
Neighborhoods Program, John Pitts,
Paul Ramírez Jonas, Larry Rogers,
Lee Quiñones, Martha Rosler,
Lorna Simpson, Camilo Vergara,
Simon Watson, Weegee, and
Krzysztof Wodiczko

**Broadway Window: "Face: Lyle
Ashton Harris"**
January 15–April 11, 1993

"The Final Frontier"
May 7–August 15, 1993
Curated by Alice Yang with Celeste
Olalquiaga and Lisa Cartwright
(guest curators)
Artists: Lawrence Andrews, Aziz
+ Cucher, Ana Barrado, Shu Lea
Cheang, Janine Cirincione, Brian
D'Amato, Elizabeth Diller, Michael
Ferraro, Michael Joaquín Grey,
Alexander Hahn, José Antonio
Hernández-Diez, Howard Hogan,
Michael Joo, David Kelleran, Middle
College High School/Roland Hayes
Intermediate School 291, Nela
Ochoa, Russell Country BBS, Julia
Scher, Ricardo Scofidio, Michael
Spertus, Fred Tomaselli, Willis
Tsosie, Lori Ann Two Bulls, and
Andrea Zittel

> **Broadway Window: "Andrea Zittel:
> Breeding Unit for Reassigning Flight"**
> **May 7–August 15, 1993**
> Organized as part of "The
> Final Frontier"

"Nari Ward: Carpet Angel"
May 7–August 15, 1993

**"Cross Talk: A Multicultural
Feminist Symposium"**

> **"In the Face of Violence"**
> **June 5, 1993**
> **Panelists:** Marina Alvarez, Anannya
> Bhattacharjee, Maria Milagros Lopez,
> Vanessa Jackson, Cynthia Newbille,
> and Ninotchka Rosca
> **Moderator:** Lisa Cartwright

> **"Negotiating Looks"**
> **June 5, 1993**
> **Panelists:** Coco Fusco, bell hooks,
> Lisa Jones, Carmelita Tropicana, and
> Kathleen Chiu Jaen Zane
> **Moderator:** Jacqui Alexander

> **"Imagining Alliances"**
> **June 6, 1993**
> **Panelists:** Rabab Abdul-Hadi,
> Inderpal Grewal, M. Annette Jaimes,
> Caren Kaplan, and Wahneema
> Lubiano
> **Moderator:** Chandra Talpade
> Mohanty

> **"The Invisible Hand of Censorship"**
> **June 6, 1993**
> **Panelists:** Shu Lea Cheang, Janet
> Henry, Maria Hinojosa, Josanne
> Lopez, Jolene Rickard, and Tricia Rose
> **Moderator:** Mallika Dutt

"Trade Routes"
September 10–November 7, 1993
Curated by Laura Trippi with Gina

Dent and Saskia Sassen
(guest curators)
Artists: Max Becher, Maria
Magdalena Campos-Pons, Benni
Efrat, Regina Frank, Jamelie Hassan,
Noritoshi Hirakawa, Soo-Ja Kim,
Koffi Kouakou, Laura Kurgan, Sowon
Kwon, Alan Michelson, Marcos
Novak, Rubén Ortiz-Torres, Miguel
Rios, Andrea Robbins, Allan Sekula,
Brian Tripp, Yukinori Yanagi, and
Vadim Zakharov

"Thornton Dial: Image of the Tiger"
November 17, 1993–January 2, 1994
Curated by Thomas McEvilley
(guest curator)
Presented concurrently at the
Museum of American Folk Art,
New York

1994

*The Astor Building is purchased,
and the floors above the New
Museum are converted into luxury
condominiums.* It is renamed the
New Museum Building. Trustee Saul
Dennison negotiates the acquisition
of the second floor as part of a plan
to increase the Museum's exhibition
and office space.

"Bad Girls" (Part I)
January 14–February 27, 1994
Curated by Marcia Tucker
Artists: Ann Agee, Xenobia Bailey,
Lynda Barry, Elizabeth Berdann,
Keith Boadwee, Lisa Bowman,
Barbara Brandon, Renée Cox,
Margaret Curtis, Jeanne Dunning,
Nancy Dwyer, Matt Groening, the
Guerrilla Girls, Jacqueline Hayden,
Maxine Hayt, Janet Henry, Amy Hill,
Mabel Maney, Portia Munson,
Chuck Nanney, Erika Rothenberg,
Veronica Saddler, Sybil Adelman
Sage, Beverly Semmes, Cindy
Smith, Elaine Tin Nyo, Cammie
Toloui, Dani Tull, Carrie Mae Weems,
Sue Williams, and Millie Wilson

> **Mercer Street Window:
> "Sistah Paradise's Revival Tent:
> Xenobia Bailey"**
> **January 14–March 10, 1994**
> Organized as part of "Bad
> Girls" (Part I)

> **"Bad Girls Music at the
> Knitting Factory"**
> **January 12–April 6, 1994**
> **Performers:** The Aquanettas, Blood
> Red Head, Blood Sugar, Cake Like,
> Cheese Cake, Chicken Milk, Double
> Zero, Judy Dunaway, Faith, Fluffer,
> Homer Erotic, Kate Jacobs, Tara
> Key of Antietam, Kissyfur, Kitten,
> Laito Lychee, Magic Hour, Maric
> Excommunikata, No Safety, Rebby
> Sharp, Ruby Falls, Sex Pod, Slant 6,
> Sugarshock, Sulfur, Thrust,
> and Vibraslaps

> **"Bad Girls Video (Program 1): She
> Laughed When She Saw It"**
> **January 14–February 27, 1994**
> Curated by Cheryl Dunye
> **Artists:** Jane Cottis, Heidi DeRuiter,
> Cecilia Dougherty, Sandi Dubowski,
> Elizabeth Beer/Agatha Kenar, Mary
> Patten, Alix Pearlstein, Suzie Silver,
> Kimberly Stoddard, Dawn Suggs, and
> Lee Williams/Angela Anderson

> **"GAG: An Evening of Bad Girls Xtra
> Bad Video"**
> **February 3, 1994**
> Curated by Cheryl Dunye
> **Artists:** Maria Beatty; ET, Baby,
> Maniac; Camera Obscura; Susan
> Muska; Jill Reiter; Suzie Silver;
> Greta Snider; Annie Sprinkle; and
> Jocelyn Taylor

"Bad Girls" (Part II)
March 5–April 10, 1994
Curated by Marcia Tucker
Artists: Gwen Akin, Laura Aguilar,
Janine Antoni, Xenobia Bailey,
Lillian Ball, Lynda Barry, Camille
Billops, Molly Bleiden, Andrea
Bowers, Lisa Bowman, Barbara
Brandon, Jennifer Camper,
Nancy Dwyer, Maxine Hayt,
Robin Kahn, Nina Kuo, Pat Lasch,
Cary Leibowitz, Lauren Lesko,
Rhonda Lieberman, Allan Ludwig,
Yasumasa Morimura, Monique
Safford, Sybil Adelman Sage,
Joyce Scott, Susan Silas, Coreen
Simpson, Cammie Toloui, Shari
Urquhart, Judith Weinperson,
and Pae White

> **"Bad Girls Video (Program 2):
> Female Friends"**
> **March 5–April 10, 1994**
> Curated by Cheryl Dunye
> **Artists:** Peggy Ahwesh, Lutz Bacher,
> Glenn Belverio, Sadie Benning, Diane
> Bonder, Mira Gelly, Cheng Sim Lim,
> Meryl Perlson, Liss Platt, Tom Rubnitz,
> Joyan Saunders, and Cauleen Smith

> **"Bad Girls Film at Anthology Film
> Archives"**
> **March 5–April 10, 1994**
> Organized by Jonas Mekas
> **Artists:** Peggy Ahwesh, Sadie
> Benning, Abigail Child, Amy
> Greenfield, Barbara Rubin, and
> Annie Sprinkle

"Bad Girls West," an "independent
sister exhibition" curated by Marcia
Tanner, runs from January 25 to
March 20, 1994 at the UCLA Wight
Art Gallery, Los Angeles.

**"Chinese Hand Laundry: Huang
Yong Pin" and "Field of Waste:
Chen Zhen"**
May 6–August 7, 1994
Curated by France Morin

**Window on Broadway: "Who Are
We? What Are We? Where Did We
Come From?: Rita Ackermann"**
September 23–December 31, 1994

**"Visiting Hours: An installation by
Bob Flanagan in collaboration with
Sheree Rose"**
September 23–December 31, 1994
Originated at the Santa Monica
Museum of Art, CA
Organized at the New Museum by
Laura Trippi

> **"An Evening of Readings"**
> **November 1, 1994**
> **Participants:** Ron Athey, Bob
> Flanagan, and Carol Queen

> **"Fight Sickness with Sickness: Bob
> Flanagan's Visiting Hours Online at
> Hot Wired"**
> **December 23, 1994**

1995

"Andres Serrano: Works 1983–1993"
January 27–April 9, 1995
Originated at the Institute of
Contemporary Art, the University of
Pennsylvania, Philadelphia, where it
was curated by Patrick T. Murphy
Organized at the New Museum by
Marcia Tucker

**"Temporarily Possessed: The
Semi-Permanent Collection"**
September 15–December 17, 1995
Curated by Brian Goldfarb, Mimi
Young, and Laura Trippi
Artists: ACT UP, Robert Colescott,
Janet Cooling, Gran Fury, Jamelie
Hassan, Kim Jones, Linda Montano,
and Martin Silverman

1996

The New Museum, in collaboration
with Routledge, publishes
*Contemporary Art and
Multicultural Education* by Susan
Cahan and art historian Zoya Kocur.

"A Labor of Love"
January 20–April 14, 1996
Curated by Marcia Tucker
Artists: Chelo González Amezcua,
Imogene Jessie Goodshot Arquero,
Alan Belcher, Robert Brady, Darren
Brown, Bette Burgoyne, Larry
Calkins, Rene David Chamizo, Dale
Chihuly, Pier Consagra, CPLY
(William N. Copley), Jacob El Hanani,
Tom Emerson, Dianna Frid, Carmen
Lomas Garza, Chuck Genco, Nöle
Giulini, Michael Harms, Bessie
Harvey, Mary Heilmann, Oliver
Herring, James Hill, Indira Freitas
Johnson, Jane Kaufman, Larry Krone,
Paul Laffoley, Dinh Q. Lê, Charles
LeDray, Liza Lou, Michael Lucero,
Raymond Materson, Josiah
McElheny, Sana Musasama,
Richard T. Notkin, Manuel Pardo,
Elaine Reichek, Faith Ringgold,
A.G. Rizzoli, Diego Romero, Richard
Rule, Alison Saar, Kevin B. Sampson,
Beverly Semmes, Judith Shea,
Kazumi Tanaka, Kukuli Velarde,
Margaret Wharton, Robin Winters,
Willie Wayne Young, and
Daisy Youngblood

**Broadway Window: "*Untitled
(Colored Water): Tony Feher*"**
April 18–May 2, 1996

"alt.youth.media"
September 6–November 5, 1996
Curated by Brian Goldfarb
Artists: Sadie Benning, Bent TV, Erik
Berglund, Don Bonus, Susan Boyle,
Gideon Bragin, John Carluccio,
Martha Chono-Helsey, Pamela
Cohen, D* Lab, Experimental Sound
Studio, Shepard Fairey, Cheri
Gaulke, Beverly Ginsburg, gURL,
Ice Censorship Project, Jubilee
Arts, Felipe Lara and Mary Phillipuk,
New Radio and Performing Arts,
Kimiko Roberts, the Safety Zone,
Adrienne Salinger, Kelvin Shawn

Sealey and the Obsidian Society,
John Serpentelli, Helen Stickler, Rio
Valledor, Video Machete, Visionary
Stampede, Marshall Weber,
Christian de Weever, Lucy Winer,
and Youth Radio
Youth Producers: Allegheny School
for Girls, Bell High School, Bushwick
Outreach Center, Cambridge
Community Art Center, Community
TV Network, Eagles Center Queer
Youth Video Workshop, Educational
Video Center, Episcopal High
School, Global Action Project,
Harvard-Westlake School,
Inner City Arts Video Workshop,
Jefferson High School Humanities
Students, John Jay High School,
KYTES, Minnesota Center for Arts
Education, Mirror Project, Out Loud,
Phillips Community TV, Rise and
Shine Productions, Stavros Center
for Independent Living, Video Butt
Crushers, VIDKIDCO, Vietnamese
Youth Development Center, and
many others

**"Carolee Schneemann: Up To
And Including Her Limits"**
**November 24, 1996–
January 26, 1997**
Curated by Dan Cameron

1997

**"Remota: Airmail Paintings by
Eugenio Dittborn"**
February 12–April 13, 1997
Curated by Dan Cameron

"Mona Hatoum"
**December 4, 1997–
February 22, 1998**
Originated at the Museum of
Contemporary Art, Chicago, where
it was curated by Jessica Morgan
Organized at the New Museum by
Dan Cameron

"Unland/Doris Salcedo"
March 19–May 31, 1998
Curated by Dan Cameron
Exhibition traveled to other
museums

**"Sweet Oblivion: The Urban
Landscape of Martin Wong"**
May 28–September 13, 1998
Curated by Dan Cameron and Barry
Blinderman, University Galleries of
Illinois State University, Normal, IL
First presented at University
Galleries of Illinois State University

"Urban Encounters"
July 16–September 20, 1998
Curated by Gregory Sholette
Participants: ABC No Rio, Bullet
Space, Godzilla, Guerrilla Girls,
REPOhistory, and World War III

**"Dancing at the Louvre: Faith
Ringgold's French Collection and
Other Story Quilts"**
October 1, 1998–January 3, 1999
Curated by Dan Cameron
Exhibition traveled to other museums

**"Xu Bing: Introduction to Square
Word Calligraphy"**
October 8, 1998–January 10, 1999
Curated by Dan Cameron

The New Museum publishes the
fifth volume in the Documentary
Sources in Contemporary Art series,
*Talking Visions: Multicultural
Feminism in a Transnational Age*,
edited by Ella Shohat.

1999

*Lisa Phillips becomes Director
of the New Museum, succeeding
Marcia Tucker. She formulates an
expanded vision for the Museum,
one that includes innovative
cultural and civic partnerships,
leading-edge art and technology
initiatives, and platforms to explore
a broadened idea of culture,
education, and the role of museums.
She conceives and realizes the
construction of the Museum's first
dedicated building at 235 Bowery—
as well as its expansion into 231
Bowery—and curates major surveys
of work by artists including Paul
McCarthy (2001), Carroll Dunham
(2002), John Waters (2004), and
Chris Burden (2013).*

**"Fever: The Art of David
Wojnarowicz"**
January 21–June 20, 1999
Curated by Dan Cameron

"The Time of Our Lives"
July 15–October 17, 1999
Curated by Marcia Tucker with
Anne Ellegood
Artists: Marina Abramović,
Ida Applebroog, Alan Berliner,
Chakaia Booker, Arlene Bowman,
Jean-Francois Brunet, Nancy
Burson, Geneviève Cadieux,
Alain Cavalier, Liz Cane, Bruce
Cannon, Harriet Casdin-Silver,
Consuelo Castañeda, Cho Duck
Hyun, Susan Hadary Cohen,
Sandi DuBowski, Karen Eaton,
Rebecca Feig, Film Board of
Canada, Peter Friedman, Neil
Goldberg, Joseph Grigely, Carol
Halstead, Jacqueline Hayden,
Heddy Honigmann, Keiko Ibi,
Yoshiko Kanai, Rachel Lachowicz,
Suzanne Lacy, Lisa Lewenz,
Micah Lexier, Brad Lichtenstein,
Kiti Luostarinen, Amanda Micheli,
Tracey Moffatt, Nigel Noble, Gail
Noonan, Jennifer Paige, Yvonne
Rainer, Jeffrey Saldinger, Joel Saxe,
Cynthia Scott, Cindy Sherman,
Alice Stone, Johnny Symons,
Susan Unterberg, Agnes Varda,
Jeff Wall, William Whiteford,
Lucy Winer Manabu Yamanaka,
Richard Yarde, Jacob Young, and
Lisa Yuskavage

"Cildo Meireles"
November 18, 1999–March 5, 2000
Curated by Dan Cameron and
Gerardo Mosquera
Exhibition traveled to other museums

2000

"Picturing the Modern Amazon"
March 30–June 25, 2000
Curated by Laurie Fierstein, Joanna
Frueh, and Judith Stein (guest
curators)
Participants: Barbara Allen,
Mariette Pathy Allen, Barbara Alper,
Matthew Barney, Claudio Bisca,
Simon Bisley, Björg, Mark Bodé,
Louise Bourgeois, Phyllis Bramson,
Jennifer Camper, Alain Celerier, Judy
Chicago, Janet Cooling, Renée Cox,
Robert Crumb, Lyman Dally, Diane
DiMassa, Bill Dobbins, Bailey
Doogan, Mary Beth Edelson, Nicole
Eisenman, Mary Fleener, Seth
Michael Forman, Kathleen Gilje,
Sidney Goodman, Roberta Gregory,
Barbara Hammer, Jane Hammond,
Oliver Herring, Joan Hilty, Chris
Hipkiss, John Howard, Miran Kim,
Aline Kominsky-Crumb, Krystine
Kryttre, Amelia Lavin, Annie
Leibovitz, Alfred Leslie, Bill
Lowenburg, Mary Ellen Mark, Susan
Meiselas, Pat Olliffe, Turtel Onli,
Jayne Parker, Harry G. Peter, Alberto
Ponticelli Herb Ritts, Alison Saar,
James Salzano, Debbie Schafer,
Andi Faryl Schreiber, Rhyan
Scorpio-Rhys, Andres Serrano,
Cindy Sherman, Clarissa Sligh,
Nancy Spero, Ann Sperry, Jocelyn
Taylor, Sarah Van Ouwerkerk, Anne
Walsh, Marnie Weber, Deborah
Willis, and Barbara Zucker

> **Window on Broadway:**
> **Performances by Bodybuilders**
>
> > **May 20, 2000**
> > **Performer:** Andrulla Blanchette
> >
> > **May 27, 2000**
> > **Performer:** Fran Ferraro
> >
> > **June 3, 2000**
> > **Performer:** Heather Foster

"Tiborocity: Design and Undesign
by Tibor Kalman, 1979–1999"
May 6–August 20, 2000
Originated at the San Francisco
Museum of Modern Art, where it
was organized by Tibor Kalman
(guest curator) in collaboration with
Aaron Betsky
Organized at the New Museum by
Lisa Phillips and Anne Ellegood with
Maira Kalman

"Martha Rosler: Positions
in the Life World"
July 15–October 8, 2000
Originated at Ikon Gallery,
Birmingham, UK, and the Generali
Foundation, Vienna

> **Window on Broadway: "Home**
> **Fronts: Between the Public and**
> **the Private"**
> **September 1–10, 2000**
> **Artists:** Nancy Buchanan, Susan
> Kleckner, Carolyn Potter, and
> Martha Rosler
> Organized as part of "Martha Rosler:
> Positions in the Life World"

"Adrian Piper: A Retrospective,
1965–2000"
October 27, 2000–January 21, 2001
Originated at the Fine Arts Gallery,
University of Maryland, College
Park, where it was curated by
Maurice Berger

"MEDI(t)Ations: Adrian
Piper's Videos, Installations,
Performances, and Soundworks
1968–1992"
October 27, 2000–January 21, 2001
Curated by Dara Meyers-Kingsley
(guest curator)

> **"Adrian Piper: Critical Impact I"**
> **November 3, 2000**
> **Speaker:** Greg Tate
>
> **"Adrian Piper: Critical Impact II"**
> **November 10, 2000**
> **Speaker:** Coco Fusco
>
> **"Adrian Piper: Critical Impact III"**
> **November 17, 2000**
> **Speaker:** Thelma Golden

The Media Lounge, New York's first
museum space dedicated to new
media exhibitions, is launched on
November 16, 2000. Designed by
LOT-EK, the architectural team of
Ada Tolla and Giuseppe Lignano,
the unique space integrates art,
technology, and architecture.
The initial round of programming
includes "Candice Breitz: Babel
Series," curated by Anne Ellegood,
and "rhizome@newmuseum.org,"
curated by Mark Tribe and Jennifer
Crowe of Rhizome.org.

2001

"Fresh: The Altoids Curiously
Strong Collection"
January 12–28, 2001
Curated by Dan Cameron and
Anne Ellegood

"Paul McCarthy"
February 24–May 13, 2001
Curated by Lisa Phillips and
Dan Cameron
Exhibition traveled to other
museums
Off-site projects for the exhibition
included *The Garden*, presented at
Deitch Projects, 18 Wooster Street,
New York, and *The Box*, presented
by the Public Art Fund at the public
atrium, 590 Madison Avenue, New
York. The exhibition also featured
works produced in collaboration
with Mike Kelley.

"William Kentridge"
June 2–September 16, 2001
Curated by Dan Cameron; Staci
Boris, the Museum of
Contemporary Art, Chicago; and
Neal Benezra, the Art Institute of
Chicago
Exhibition traveled to other museums

"Kristin Lucas & Joe McKay: The
Electric Donut"
July 13–September 16, 2001
Curated by Anne Ellegood

"Tom Friedman"
October 12, 2001–February 3, 2002
Originated at Southeastern Center
for Contemporary Art, Winston-
Salem, NC, where it was curated by
Ron Platt
Organized at the New Museum by
Dan Cameron

2002

"Wim Delvoye: Cloaca"
January 25–April 28, 2002
Curated by Dan Cameron

"Marlene Dumas: Name No Names"
February 23–June 2, 2002
Originated at Centre Georges
Pompidou, Paris, where it was
curated by Jonas Storsve

"Open_Source_Art_Hack"
May 3–June 30, 2002
Curated by Steve Dietz and Jenny
Marketou (guest curators) in
collaboration with Anne Barlow
Artists: Critical Art Ensemble,
Beatriz da Costa, Cue P. Doll, Harun
Farocki, Knowbotic Research, LAN,
Josh On, radioqualia, RSG, Superflex,
Surveillance Camera Players,
and Tenantspin

"Lee Bul: Live Forever"
May 17–July 7, 2002
The works in this exhibition were
created by the artist in collaboration
with the Fabric Workshop and
Museum, Philadelphia, and the San
Francisco Art Institute.

"Hélio Oiticica: Quasi-cinemas"
July 26–October 13, 2002
Originated at the Wexner Center for
the Arts, Columbus, OH, where it
was curated by Carlos Basualdo
Co-organized and presented by
the New Museum and Kölnischer
Kunstverein, Cologne
This exhibition included works
made in collaboration with
Neville D'Almeida.

"Carroll Dunham: Paintings"
October 31, 2002–February 2, 2003
Curated by Lisa Phillips and
Dan Cameron

The New Museum purchases an
empty lot at 235 Bowery, New York,
and in December 2002 announces
that it will construct its first
freestanding permanent home.

2003

On May 15, 2003, the New Museum
announces that Kazuyo Sejima and
Ryue Nishizawa of SANAA have
been selected to design the new
building. The design is unveiled in
November.

Lisa Phillips brings on Rhizome
as an affiliate of the New Museum.
Rhizome, an organization dedicated
to new media art, was founded by
artist Mark Tribe as a listserv in 1996

and now commissions, exhibits, preserves, and creates critical discussion around art engaged with digital culture. Rhizome is the leading international born-digital art organization.

"Black President: The Art and Legacy of Fela Anikulapo-Kuti"
July 11–October 19, 2003
Curated by Trevor Schoonmaker
(guest curator)
Artists: Radcliffe Bailey, Bili Bidjocka, Sanford Biggers, Klaus Bürgel, Sokari Douglas Camp, Brett Cook-Dizney, Victor Ekpuk, Timothy Evans, Kendell Geers, Ghariokwu Lemi, Barkley L. Hendricks, Satch Hoyt, Alfredo Jaar, Marcia Kure, Moshekwa Langa, Paul D. Miller, Adia Millett, Wangechi Mutu, Nanga-Oly Christophe, Aimé Ntakiyica, Odili Donald Odita, Olu Oguibe, Moyo Ogundipe, Moyo Okediji, Senam Okudzeto, Ouattara, Yinka Shonibare, Jason Stewart Smith, Pascale Marthine Tayou, Iké Udé, Obiora Udechukwu, Roberto Visani, Kara Walker, and Fred Wilson

"Trisha Brown: Dance and Art in Dialogue 1961–2001"
October 10, 2003–January 25, 2004
Curated by Hendel Teicher
(guest curator)
Originated at the Addison Gallery of American Art, Phillips Academy, Andover, MA, and the Frances Young Tang Teaching Museum and Art Gallery, Skidmore College, Saratoga Springs, NY
Artists: Trisha Brown, with Nancy Graves, Donald Judd, Fujiko Nakaya, Robert Rauschenberg, and Terry Winters

---

2004

The New Museum inaugurates the Three M Project in collaboration with the Museum of Contemporary Art, Chicago, and the Hammer Museum, the University of California, Los Angeles. Working collaboratively, the three museums combine their resources to commission and exhibit major projects by leading contemporary artists. Patty Chang, Fiona Tan, and Aernout Mik are awarded the first cycle of commissions. Their subsequent individual exhibitions, shown successively at each venue, represent the first major museum exhibitions in the US for each of these artists.

"John Waters: Change of Life"
February 8–April 15, 2004
Curated by Lisa Phillips and Marvin Heiferman (guest curator)

The New Museum sells its space in the Astor Building at 583 Broadway and moves to temporary quarters on the ground floor of the Chelsea Art Museum, 556 West 22nd Street, New York.

The New Museum publishes the sixth volume in the Documentary Sources in Contemporary Art series, ***Over Here: International Perspectives on Art and Culture***, edited by Gerardo Mosquera and Jean Fisher.

"East Village USA"
December 9, 2004–March 19, 2005
Curated by Dan Cameron
Artists: Charlie Ahearn, Alien Comic (Tom Murrin), Judith Barry, Jean-Michel Basquiat, Gretchen Bender, Ellen Berkenblit, Edo Bertoglio, Ashley Bickerton, Mike Bidlo, Sarah Charlesworth, Sue Coe, George Condo, Arch Connelly, Martha Cooper, Crash (John Matos), Debby Davis, Daze (Chris Ellis), Jimmy DeSana, Jane Dickson, Ethyl Eichelberger, John Epperson, Karen Finley, Luis Frangella, Futura 2000, Bobby G, Judy Glantzman, Nan Goldin, Rodney Alan Greenblat, Timothy Greenfield-Sanders, Peter Halley, Richard Hambleton, Keith Haring, Jenny Holzer, Becky Howland, Peter Hujar, Kiely Jenkins, John Jesurun, John Kelly, Richard Kern, Jeff Koons, Tseng Kwong Chi, Stephen Lack, Lady Pink (Sandra Fabara), Greer Lankton, Ann Magnuson, Frank Maya, Dona Ann McAdams, McDermott & McGough, Patrick McMullan, Frank Moore, Nicolas Moufarrege, Peter Nagy, Joseph Nechvatal, Klaus Nomi, Glenn O'Brien, Tom Otterness, Richard Prince, Lee Quiñones, David Robbins, Walter Robinson, James Romberger, Tom Rubnitz, David Sandlin, Hope Sandrow, Kenny Scharf, Peter Schuyff, Jim Self, Laurie Simmons, Jack Smith, Kiki Smith, Sonic Youth, Haim Steinbach, Nelson Sullivan, Philip Taaffe, Fiona Templeton,Paul Thek, Meyer Vaisman, Anton van Dalen, Tom Warren, Ande Whyland, David Wojnarowicz, Martin Wong, and Zephyr (Andrew Witten)

"Then and Now: The Gallery Scene"
December 16, 2004
Panelists: Lia Gangitano, Glenn O'Brien, and Magdalena Sawon
Moderator: Dan Cameron

"East Village Radio"
Interviewer: Dan Cameron

December 9, 2004
Guest: Sur Rodney (Sur)

January 20, 2005
Guest: Lee Quiñones

February 17, 2005
Guests: James Romberger and Marguerite Van Cook

February 23, 2005
Guest: Kiki Smith

March 17, 2005
Guest: Carlo McCormick

2005

"Fiona Tan: Correction"
April 9–June 4, 2005
Curated by Francesco Bonami and Julie Rodrigues Widholm as part of the Three M Project

"Aernout Mik: Refraction"
June 23–September 10, 2005
Curated by Dan Cameron as part of the Three M Project

"Patty Chang: Shangri-La"
July 8–September 10, 2005
Curated by Russell Ferguson as part of the Three M Project

In 2005, the New Museum institutes Global Classroom (G:Class), a new curriculum development program with a global emphasis. G:Class is an interdisciplinary museum education program that provides in-class and museum-based opportunities for high school teachers and students to work with professional artists and educators. It is designed to enhance critical thinking through peer-group discussions about critical issues that affect the lives of students and to foster the development of creative and professional skills. G:Class is the primary high school program at the New Museum through 2012.

"Brian Jungen"
September 29–December 31, 2005
Originated at the Vancouver Art Gallery, where it was curated by Daina Augaitis
Organized at the New Museum by Trevor Smith

In fall 2005, the New Museum breaks ground for its new building at 235 Bowery, between Stanton and Rivington Streets.

2006

"Andrea Zittel: Critical Space"
January 26–May 27, 2006
Curated by Trevor Smith and Paola Morsiani

Marcia Tucker dies of cancer at the age of sixty-six at her home in Santa Barbara on October 17, 2006. The lobby of the new building will be named in her honor.

2007

The New Museum opens its new 50,000-square-foot building to the public on December 1, 2007, coinciding with the institution's thirtieth anniversary. It is the first purpose-built art museum to be constructed from the ground up in downtown Manhattan. Designed by Kazuyo Sejima and Ryue Nishizawa of SANAA with Gensler, New York serving as Executive Architect, the eight-story structure is conceived as an open and dynamic form, with stacked rectilinear boxes shifted off a central core.

"Unmonumental: The Object in the 21st Century"
December 1, 2007–March 30, 2008
Curated by Richard Flood,
Massimiliano Gioni, and
Laura Hoptman
Artists: Alexandra Bircken, John
Bock, Carol Bove, Martin Boyce,
Tobias Buche, Carlos Bunga, Tom
Burr, Abraham Cruzvillegas, Aaron
Curry, Sam Durant, Urs Fischer,
Claire Fontaine, Isa Genzken,
Rachel Harrison, Elliott Hundley,
Gabriel Kuri, Jim Lambie, Nate
Lowman, Sarah Lucas, Matthew
Monahan, Kristen Morgin, Manfred
Pernice, Anselm Reyle, Marc André
Robinson, Eva Rothschild, Lara
Schnitger, Gedi Sibony, Shinique
Smith, Nobuko Tsuchiya, and
Rebecca Warren

**"Young-Hae Chang Heavy
Industries: Black on White, Gray
Ascending"**
December 1, 2007–March 23, 2008
Curated by Lauren Cornell and
Laura Hoptman
Artists: Young-Hae Chang and
Marc Voge

**"Sharon Hayes: I march in the
parade of liberty, but as long as I
love you I'm not free"**
**December 1, 2007–
January 27, 2008**
Curated by Jarrett Gregory and
Massimiliano Gioni

"Ugo Rondinone: Hell, Yes!"
December 1, 2007–November 2010
Curated by Laura Hoptman
Ugo Rondinone's large-scale
neon-lit installation is the first
artwork to be presented on the New
Museum's facade as part of the
ongoing Facade Sculpture Program.

**Founded in 2006, and initiated
by Anne Barlow, Museum as Hub
launches its programs at the
New Museum in December 2007
under the direction of Eungie
Joo.** Museum as Hub is a hybrid
education and curatorial platform
that explores art and ideas through
international collaborations. The
Museum invites four partner
organizations to participate in the
initiative: Insa Art Space, Seoul;
Townhouse Gallery, Cairo; Van
Abbemuseum, Eindhoven; and
Museo Tamayo, Mexico City. The
first round of programming centers
around the exhibition "Museum as
Hub: An Introduction," running from
December 1, 2007 through February
24, 2008 and co-organized by the
partner organizations.

Night School
January 2008–January 2009
Curated by Eungie Joo
Night School, a project by
Anton Vidokle, takes the form
of a temporary school with a
yearlong program of seminars
and workshops held on the last
weekend of each month. A group
of local and international artists,
writers, and theorists—including
Paul Chan, Okwui Enwezor, Hu Fang,
Liam Gillick, Boris Groys, Maria Lind,
Walid Raad, Raqs Media Collective,
Martha Rosler, Natascha Sadr
Haghighian, Rirkrit Tiravanija, Jalal
Toufic, and Zhang Wei—contributes
to the conceptualization and
facilitation of sessions.

**"Collage: The Unmonumental
Picture"**
January 16–March 30, 2008
Curated by Richard Flood, Laura
Hoptman, and Massimiliano Gioni
Artists: Mark Bradford, Jonathan
Hernández, Thomas Hirschhorn,
Christian Holstad, Kim Jones,
Wangechi Mutu, Henrik Olesen,
Martha Rosler, Nancy Spero, John
Stezaker, and Kelley Walker

"My Barbarian: The Golden Age"
February 6–March 30, 2008
Curated by Eungie Joo

**"The Sound of Things:
Unmonumental Audio"**
February 13–March 30, 2008
Curated by Lauren Cornell,
Massimiliano Gioni, and
Laura Hoptman
Artists: Vito Acconci, Sarina Basta,
Anthony Burdin, Trisha Donnelly,
Paul Elliman, Andy Graydon,
Language Removal Systems, Ulrike
Müller, Nautical Almanac, Keith
Obadike, Pauline Oliveros, Susan
Philipsz, Seth Price, and Stefan
Tcherepnin

"Montage: Unmonumental Online"
February 15–March 30, 2008
Curated by Lauren Cornell and
Marisa Olson, Rhizome
Artists: Michael Bell-Smith, John
Michael Boling, William Boling,
Charles Broskoski, Jessica Ciocci,
Petra Cortright, Chris Coy, Cao
Fei, Kenneth Tin-Kin Hung, Nina
Katchadourian, Oliver Laric, Olia
Lialina, Guthrie Lonergan, and
Paul Slocum

**Get Weird, a series of monthly
performances featuring
"experimental and freaky jams"
begins on February 21, 2008
with performances by Hisham
Bharoocha and Telepathe.** Initially
organized by guest curator
Alex Wagner, the series is later
programmed by Ethan Swan. It
continues through 2012 with
performances by Tarek Atoui, Mick
Barr, Deakin, Charles Gaines and
Terry Adkins, Sahra Motalebi, Prince
Rama, and Lee Ranaldo and Leah
Singer, among many others.

"SANAA: Works 1998–2008"
March 28–June 15, 2008
Curated by Lisa Phillips and
Karen Wong
Architects: Kazuyo Sejima and
Ryue Nishizawa, SANAA

"Paul Chan: The 7 ~~Lights~~"
April 9–June 29, 2008
Curated by Massimiliano Gioni

"Tomma Abts"
April 9–June 29, 2008
Curated by Laura Hoptman

**"Double Album: Daniel Guzmán and
Steve Shearer"**
April 23–July 6, 2008
Curated by Richard Flood

"After Nature"
July 17–September 21, 2008
Curated by Massimiliano Gioni
Artists: Allora and Calzadilla, Paweł
Althamer, Micol Assaël, Fikret Atay,
Roger Ballen, Huma Bhabha,
Berlinde De Bruyckere, Maurizio
Cattelan, William Christenberry,
Roberto Cuoghi, Bill Daniel, Nathalie
Djurberg, Reverend Howard Finster,
Nancy Graves, Werner Herzog,
Robert Kuśmirowski, Zoe Leonard,
Klara Lidén, Diego Perrone, Thomas
Schütte, Dana Schutz, Tino Sehgal,
August Strindberg, Erik van Lieshout,
Eugene Von Bruenchenhein, and
Artur Żmijewski

Museum as Hub: "Six Degrees"
**September 25, 2008–
January 11, 2009**
Curated by Eungie Joo
Artists: My Barbarian, Dave
McKenzie, Martha Rosler, Lisa Sigal,
Ginger Brooks Takahashi, and
Anton Vidokle

**"A.L. Steiner + robbinschilds:
C.L.U.E. (color location ultimate
experience)"**
October 8, 2008–January 11, 2009
Curated by Amy Mackie
Artists: A.J. Blandford, Kinski,
robbinschilds, and A.L. Steiner

"Live Forever: Elizabeth Peyton"
October 8, 2008–January 11, 2009
Curated by Laura Hoptman
Exhibition traveled to other museums

"Mary Heilmann: To Be Someone"
October 22, 2008–January 26, 2009
Originated at the Orange County
Museum of Art, Newport Beach,
CA, where it was curated by
Elizabeth Armstrong
Organized at the New Museum by
Richard Flood

"Daria Martin: Minotaur"
January 28–March 22, 2009
Curated by Dominic McIon as part
of the Three M Project

"Mathias Poledna: Crystal Palace"
January 28–March 22, 2009
Curated by Russell Ferguson as part
of the Three M Project

**"Naeem Mohaiemen: Young Man
Was No Longer A…"**
January 30, 2009
Commissioned by Rhizome
Speaker: Naeem Mohaiemen

"Jeremy Deller: It Is What It Is: Conversations About Iraq"
February 11–March 22, 2009
Curated by Laura Hoptman and Amy Mackie with Nato Thompson, Creative Time, New York, as part of the Three M Project

"New Museum Triennial: Younger Than Jesus"
April 8–June 14, 2009
Curated by Massimiliano Gioni, Lauren Cornell, and Laura Hoptman
Artists: AIDS-3D, Ziad Antar, Cory Arcangel, Tauba Auerbach, Wojciech Bąkowski, Dineo Seshee Bopape, Mohamed Bourouissa, Kerstin Brätsch, Cao Fei, Carolina Caycedo, Chu Yun, Keren Cytter, Mariechen Danz, Faye Driscoll, Ida Ekblad, Haris Epaminonda, Patricia Esquivias, Mark Essen, Ruth Ewan, Brendan Fowler, Luke Fowler, LaToya Ruby Frazier, Cyprien Gaillard, Ryan Gander, Liz Glynn, Loris Gréaud, Shilpa Gupta, Emre Hüner, Daniel Keller, Matt Keegan, Tigran Khachatryan, Nik Kosmas, Kitty Kraus, Adriana Lara, Elad Lassry, Liu Chuang, Guthrie Lonergan, Tala Madani, Anna Molska, Ciprian Muresan, Ahmet Öğüt, Adam Pendleton, Stephen G. Rhodes, James Richards, Emily Roysdon, Katerina Šedá, Josh Smith, Ryan Trecartin, Alexander Ugay, Tris Vonna-Michell, Jakub Julian Ziolkowski, and Icaro Zorbar

Stuart Regen Visionaries Series: Bill T. Jones
April 24, 2009

"Intersections Intersected: The Photography of David Goldblatt"
July 15–October 11, 2009
Originated at Fundação Serralves, Porto, Portugal
Organized at the New Museum by Richard Flood

"Dorothy Iannone: Lioness"
July 22–October 18, 2009
Curated by Jarrett Gregory

"Emory Douglas: Black Panther"
July 22–October 18, 2009
Curated by Sam Durant (guest curator) and Laura Hoptman with Amy Mackie

The Propositions series begins on September 25, 2009 and runs through 2013. As part of the Museum as Hub initiative and under the direction of Eungie Joo, Propositions is a public forum that collaboratively explores the developing ideas of artists and cultural thinkers. The inaugural Propositions session is led by Kara Walker, who considers: "The object of Painting is the subjugated Body. The Painter is the colonizing entity. How do Paintings understand the concept of liberty? And who will teach them?" Walker's invited guest on September 26, 2009 is Soniya Munshi.

"Trajal Harrell: Twenty Looks or Paris is Burning at the Judson Church (S)"
October 1–2, 2009
Curated by Eungie Joo

"Urs Fischer: Marguerite de Ponty"
October 28, 2009–February 7, 2010
Curated by Massimiliano Gioni

2010

"Skin Fruit: Selections from the Dakis Joannou Collection"
March 3–June 6, 2010
Curated by Jeff Koons (guest curator)
Artists: Paweł Althamer, David Altmejd, Janine Antoni, Assume Vivid Astro Focus, Tauba Auerbach, Matthew Barney, Vanessa Beecroft, Ashley Bickerton, John Bock, Mark Bradford, Maurizio Cattelan, Paul Chan, Dan Colen, Nigel Cooke, Roberto Cuoghi, Nathalie Djurberg, Haris Epaminonda, Urs Fischer, Robert Gober, Matt Greene, Mark Grotjahn, Adam Helms, Jenny Holzer, Elliott Hundley, Mike Kelley, Terence Koh, Jeff Koons, Liza Lou, Nate Lowman, Mark Manders, Paul McCarthy, Dave Muller, Takashi Murakami, Tim Noble and Sue Webster, Cady Noland, Chris Ofili, Seth Price, Richard Prince, Charles Ray, Tino Sehgal, Jim Shaw, Cindy Sherman, Christiana Soulou, Kiki Smith, Jannis Varelas, Kara Walker, Gillian Wearing, Andro Wekua, Franz West, and Christopher Wool

Symposium: "Art Museums, Private Collectors, and the Public"
March 13, 2010

"Public/Private Partnerships: The Development of the American Art Museum"
Panelists: Linda Nochlin, Inge Reist, and Sally Webster
Moderator: Richard Flood

"Crossing into the Future: New Models of Collaboration"
Panelists: Iwona Blazwick, Francesco Bonami, and Tom Eccles
Moderator: Lisa Phillips

Stuart Regen Visionaries Series: Jimmy Wales
April 8, 2010

Inaugural Seven on Seven
April 16–17, 2010
Conference organized by Rhizome
Founded by Lauren Cornell, Executive Director of Rhizome, in 2010, Seven on Seven is an annual conference that pairs leaders in the arts with visionary technologists and challenges them to make something new.
Participants: Tauba Auerbach and Ayah Bdeir; Jeffrey Hammerbacher and Aaron Koblin; Kristin Lucas and Andrew Kortina; Hilary Mason and Marc Andre Robinson; Matt Mullenweg and Evan Roth; Joshua Schachter and Monica Narula; and Ryan Trecartin and David Karp

"Rivane Neuenschwander: A Day Like Any Other"
June 23–September 19, 2010
Curated by Richard Flood
Organized by the New Museum in collaboration with the Irish Museum of Modern Art, Dublin

"Brion Gysin: Dream Machine"
July 7–October 3, 2010
Curated by Laura Hoptman

Museum as Hub: "The Bidoun Library Project"
August 4–September 26, 2010
Curated by *Bidoun* magazine

RE:NEW: RE:PLAY: "THEM AND NOW"
September 24–October 14, 2010
Curated by Travis Chamberlain
Director/Choreographer: Ishmael Houston-Jones
Collaborators: Chris Cochrane and Dennis Cooper

"The Last Newspaper"
October 6, 2010–January 9, 2011
Curated by Richard Flood and Benjamin Godsill
Artists: Judith Bernstein, Pierre Bismuth, Alighiero e Boetti, Andrea Bowers, François Bucher, Sarah Charlesworth, Luciano Fabro, Jacob Fabricius, Robert Gober, Hans Haacke, Karl Haendel, Rachel Harrison, Thomas Hirschhorn, Emily Jacir, Larry Johnson, Mike Kelley, Nate Lowman, Sarah Lucas, Adam McEwen, Aleksandra Mir, Angel Nevarez and Valerie Tevere, Adrian Piper, William Pope.L, Allen Ruppersberg, Dexter Sinister, Dash Snow, Wolfgang Tillmans, Rirkrit Tiravanija, and Kelley Walker
Partner Organizations: Joseph Grima and Kazys Varnelis/Network Architecture Lab; the Center for Urban Pedagogy; Latitudes (Max Andrews and Mariana Cánepa Luna); Slought Foundation; Jeffrey Inaba/C-Lab, Columbia University; StoryCorps; and Blu Dot; with special projects by Rachel Chandler and Jacob Fabricius

"Free"
October 20, 2010–January 23, 2011
Curated by Lauren Cornell
Artists: Liz Deschenes, Aleksandra Domanović, Lizzie Fitch, Martijn Hendriks, Joel Holmberg, David Horvitz, Lars Laumann, Andrea Longacre-White, Kristin Lucas, Jill Magid, Hanne Mugaas, Takeshi Murata, Rashaad Newsome, Lisa Oppenheim, Trevor Paglen, Seth Price, Jon Rafman, Clunie Reid, Amanda Ross-Ho, Alexandre Singh, Ryan Trecartin and David Karp, and Harm van den Dorpel

"Voice and Wind: Haegue Yang"
October 20, 2010–January 23, 2011
Curated by Eungie Joo

"Isa Genzken: Rose II"
November 13, 2010–
August 31, 2013
Isa Genzken's sculpture is the second artwork to be presented as part of the New Museum's ongoing Facade Sculpture Program.

RE:NEW: RE:PLAY: "Untitled Feminist Media Technology Show"
December 16–19, 2010
Curated by Travis Chamberlain
Writer and Director: Young Jean Lee
Collaborators: Becca Blackwell, Hilary Clark, Bianca Leigh, Katy Pyle, Regina Rocke, World Famous *BOB*, and Amelia Zirin-Brown

---

2011

The New Museum, in collaboration with Routledge, publishes *Rethinking Contemporary Art and Multicultural Education*, edited by Eungie Joo and Joseph Keehn II with Jenny Ham-Roberts.

"George Condo: Mental States"
January 26–May 8, 2011
Curated by Laura Hoptman and Ralph Rugoff

"Lynda Benglis"
February 9–June 19, 2011
Originated at the Irish Museum of Modern Art, Dublin
Organized in collaboration with Le Consortium, Dijon, France; the Museum of Modern Art, New York; the New Museum; the Rhode Island School of Design, Providence; and Van Abbemuseum, Eindhoven
Organized at the New Museum by Massimiliano Gioni

"The Now Museum: Contemporary Art, Curating Histories, Alternative Models"
March 10–13, 2011
Organized and supported by the New Museum; Independent Curators International, New York; and the CUNY Graduate Center, New York
Speakers: Bruce Altshuler, Richard Armstrong, Zdenka Badovinac, Carlos Basualdo, Ute Meta Bauer, Dara Birnbaum, Claire Bishop, Manuel Borja-Villel, Johanna Burton, Paul Chan, Beatriz Colomina, Kari Cwynar, Okwui Enwezor, Annie Fletcher, Kate Fowle, Massimiliano Gioni, Jessica Gogan, Saisha Grayson, Martin Grossmann, Alice Heeren, Anthony Huberman, Lu Jie, Eungie Joo, Michelle Jubin, Pamela M. Lee, Maria Lind, Natalie Musteata, Gabi Ngcobo, Gabriel Pérez-Barreiro, Lisa Phillips, Katy Siegel, Terry Smith, Philippe Vergne, and Dominic Willsdon

Ideas City Festival New York
May 4–8, 2011
Inaugural edition of Ideas City, an initiative cofounded by Lisa Phillips and Karen Wong
Keynote Speakers: Rem Koolhaas, architect and cofounder of Office for Metropolitan Architecture (OMA); Jaron Lanier, author, scientist, scholar, and founder of VPL Research; and Antanas Mockus, former President of the National University of Colombia and former Mayor of Bogotá

> "Cronocaos: An exhibition by OMA / Rem Koolhaas"
> May 7–June 5, 2011
> Organized as part of Ideas City

> "After Hours: Murals on the Bowery"
> March 7–July 7, 2011
> Copresented by Art Production Fund as part of Ideas City
> **Artists:** Judith Bernstein, Matthew Brannon, Ingrid Calame, Chris Dorland, Elmgreen & Dragset, Ellen Gallagher, Amy Granat, Mary Heilmann, Jacqueline Humphries, Deborah Kass and pulp, ink., Glenn Ligon, Adam McEwen, Barry McGee with Guess SKE, Richard Prince, Sterling Ruby, Gary Simmons, Rirkrit Tiravanija, and Lawrence Weiner

Seven on Seven
May 14, 2011
Conference organized by Rhizome
Participants: Michael Bell-Smith and Andy Baio; Ricardo Cabello (Mr doob) and Chris Poole (moot); Liz Magic Laser and Ben Cerveny; Zach Lieberman and Bre Pettis; Rashaad Newsome and Jeri Ellsworth; Emily Roysdon and Kellan Elliott-McCrea; and Camille Utterback and Erica Sadun

"Apichatpong Weerasethakul: Primitive"
May 19–July 3, 2011
Curated by Massimiliano Gioni and Gary Carrion-Murayari

"Gustav Metzger: Historic Photographs"
May 19–July 3, 2011
Curated by Massimiliano Gioni and Gary Carrion-Murayari

Stuart Regen Visionaries Series: Alice Waters
May 23, 2011

RE:NEW: RE:PLAY: "We Remember Stories, Not Facts"
June 10–26, 2011
Curated by Travis Chamberlain
Artist: Wu Tsang
Collaborators: Charles Atlas, Kingdom (Ezra Rubin), Ivan Monforte, NGUZUNGUZU (Asma Maroof and Daniel Pineda), Jonathan Oppenheim, Total Freedom (Ashland Mines), and Matt Wolf

"Charles Atlas: Joints Array"
July 14–August 28, 2011
Curated by Jenny Moore

"Ostalgia"
July 14–September 15, 2011
Curated by Massimiliano Gioni with Jarrett Gregory
Artists: Vyacheslav Akhunov, Victor Alimpiev, Evgeny Antufiev, Vladimir Arkhipov, Said Atabekov, Nikolay Bakharev, Miroslaw Balka, Irina Botea, Geta Brătescu, Anatoly Brusilovsky, Erik Bulatov, André Cadere, Olga Chernysheva, Chto Delat?/What is to be done?, Phil Collins, Neil Cummings and Marysia Lewandowska, Tacita Dean, Stanislav Filko, Hermann Glöckner, Ion Grigorescu, Andris Grīnbergs, Aneta Grzeszykowska, Tibor Hajas, Petrit Halilaj, Hamlet Hovsepian, Sanja Ivekcvić, Július Koller, Jiři Kovanda, Evgenij Kozlov (E-E), Edward Krasiński, Alexander Lobanov, Jonas Mekas, Boris Mikhailov, Andrei Monastyrski, Deimantas Narkevičius, Paulina Olowska, Roman Ondák, Anatoly Osmolovsky, Helga Paris, Pavel Pepperstein, Susan Phlipsz, Viktor Pivovarov, Dmitri Prigov, Anri Sala, Michael Schmidt, Thomas Schütte, Simon Starling, Mladen Stilinović, David Ter-Oganyan, Jaan Toomik, Andra Ursuţa, Andro Wekua, Workshop of the Film Form, Sergey Zarva, Jasmila Žbanić, and Anna Zemánková

Museum as Hub: "Steffani Jemison and Jamal Cyrus: Alpha's Bet Is Not Over Yet!"
September 12–December 4, 2011
Curated by Ryan Inouye and Ethan Swan

"Spartacus Chetwynd: Home Made Tasers"
October 26, 2011–January 1, 2012
Curated by Massimiliano Gioni and Gary Carrion-Murayari

"Carsten Höller: Experience"
October 26, 2011–January 22, 2012
Curated by Massimiliano Gioni, Jenny Moore, and Gary Carrion-Murayari

---

2012

Studio 231: "Enrico David: Head Gas"
January 18–April 19, 2012
Curated by Gary Carrion-Murayari

"New Museum Triennial: The Ungovernables"
February 15–April 22, 2012
Curated by Eungie Joo with Ryan Inouye
Artists: Mounira Al Solh, Jonathas de Andrade, Minam Apang, CAMP, Julia Dault, Abigail DeVille, House of Natural Fiber, Hu Xiaoyuan, Invisible Borders Trans-African Photography Project, Iman Issa, Hassan Khan, Lee Kit, Cinthia Marcelle, Dave McKenzie, Nicolás Paris, Bona Park, Gary-Ross Pastrana, Pratchaya Phinthong, Amalia Pica, Rita Ponce de León, the Propeller Group, Public Movement, Gabriel Sierra, Slavs and Tatars, Rayyane Tabet, Pilvi Takala, Mariana Telleria, Wu Tsang, José Antonio Vega Macotela, Adrián Villar Rojas, Danh Võ, Kemang Wa Lehulere, Lynette Yiadom-Boakye, and Ala Younis

Seven on Seven
April 14, 2012
Conference organized by Rhizome
Keynote Speaker: Douglas Rushkoff
Participants: Blaine Cook and
Naeem Mohaiemen; Michael
Herf and LaToya Ruby Frazier; Jon
Rafman and Charles Forman; Aaron
Swartz and Taryn Simon; Stephanie
Syjuco and Jeremy Ashkenas; Khoi
Vihn and Aram Bartholl; and
Anthony Volodkin and Xavier Cha

"Phyllida Barlow: siege"
May 2–June 24, 2012
Curated by Gary Carrion-Murayari

Studio 231: "The Parade: Nathalie
Djurberg with Music by Hans Berg"
May 2–September 2, 2012
Originated at the Walker Art Center,
Minneapolis, where it was curated
by Eric Crosby and Dean Otto
Organized at the New Museum by
Gary Carrion-Murayari

"Ellen Altfest: Head and Plant"
May 6, 2012–June 24, 2012
Curated by Jenny Moore

"Klara Lidén: Bodies of Society"
May 6–July 1, 2012
Curated by Jenny Moore and
Massimiliano Gioni

"Tacita Dean: Five Americans"
May 6–July 1, 2012
Curated by Massimiliano Gioni and
Margot Norton

Museum as Hub: "Carlos Motta:
We Who Feel Differently"
May 16–September 9, 2012
Curated by Eungie Joo

> **"Jeannine Tang and Reina Gossett**
> **with Eric Stanley and Chris Vargas:**
> **Love Revolution, Not State Collusion"**
> **June 7, 2012**

Stuart Regen Visionaries Series:
Maya Lin
May 30, 2012

"Pictures from the Moon: Artists'
Holograms 1969–2008"
July 5–September 30, 2012
Curated by Jenny Moore
Artists: Louise Bourgeois, Eric Orr,
Bruce Nauman, Ed Ruscha, and
James Turrell

"Ghosts in the Machine"
July 18–September 30, 2012
Curated by Massimiliano Gioni and
Gary Carrion-Murayari
Artists: Marc Adrian; Getulio Alviani;
Richard Anuszkiewicz; Marina
Apollonio; J. G. Ballard; Thomas
Bayrle; Emery Blagdon; Davide
Boriani; Robert Breer; Pol Bury;
Harley Cokeliss; Gianni Colombo;
Computer Center Boris Kidrič
Institute, Vinča; Toni Costa; Larry
Cuba; Homer Dudley/Bell Labs;
Harold Edgerton; Jean Ferry; Peter
Fischli and David Weiss; Alan Mark
France; David R. Garrison; Gego;
Karl Gerstner; Robert Gie; Rube
Goldberg; Jack Goldstein; João
Maria Gusmão and Pedro Paiva;
Hans Haacke; Richard Hamilton;
Pierre Hébert; Channa Horwitz;
Werner Huck and Paul Gysin in
collaboration with Harald
Szeemann; Jikken Kōbō/
Experimental Workshop (Shozo
Kitadai, Katsuhiro Yamaguchi, and
Kiyoji Otsuji); Joey the Mechanical
Boy; Fritz Kahn; Konrad Klapheck;
Jeff Koons; Emma Kunz; Mark
Leckey; Julio Le Parc; Ulf Linde,
Pontus Hultén, and Per Olof Ultvedt;
Heinz Mack; Mike Mandel and Larry
Sultan; Manfredo Massironi; James
Tilly Matthews; Herbert Marshall
McLuhan; Petar Milojević; Jakob
Mohr; François Morellet; Georg
Nees; Claes Oldenburg; Henrik
Olesen; Eduardo Paolozzi; Philippe
Parreno; Otto Piene; Seth Price;
Bridget Riley; Peter Roehr; Sylvia
Roubaud; Herb Schneider; Lillian F.
Schwartz; Paul Sharits; Robert
Smithson; Jesús Rafael Soto;
Julian Stanczak; John Stehura;
Larry Sultan; Jean Tinguely; Günther
Uecker; Stan VanDerBeek; Grazia
Varisco; Victor Vasarely; WGBH-TV
in collaboration with Allan Kaprow;
Nam June Paik; Otto Piene;
Aldo Tambellini; Ulla Wiggen,
Christopher Williams; Johanna
(Jeanne) Natalie Wintsch; and
Yvaral (Jean-Pierre Vasarely)

"Come Closer: Art Around the
Bowery, 1969–1989"
September 19–December 30, 2012
Curated by Ethan Swan
Artists: Barbara Ess, Coleen
Fitzgibbon, Keith Haring, John
Holmstrom, Curt Hoppe, Colette
Lumiere, Marc H. Miller, Adrian
Piper, Adam Purple, Dee Dee
Ramone, Joey Ramone, Marcia
Resnick, Bettie Ringma, Christy
Rupp, Arleen Schloss, Charles
Simonds, Eve Sonneman, Billy
Sullivan, Paul Tschinkel, Anton van
Dalen, Arturo Vega, Robin Winters,
and Martin Wong

"Haroon Mirza: Preoccupied
Waveforms"
September 19, 2012–
January 6, 2013
Curated by Jenny Moore and Gary
Carrion-Murayari

Ideas City Istanbul
October 11–14, 2012
Keynote Speaker: Amanda M.
Burden, Commissioner of the
New York City Department of
City Planning

"Judith Bernstein: HARD"
October 10, 2012–January 20, 2013
Curated by Margot Norton

"Rosemarie Trockel: A Cosmos"
October 24, 2012–January 20, 2013
Originated at Museo Nacional
Centro de Arte Reina Sofía, Madrid,
where it was curated by Lynne
Cooke in collaboration with
Rosemarie Trockel
Organized at the New Museum
by Lynne Cooke and Rosemarie
Trockel with Massimiliano Gioni
and Jenny Moore

Inaugural First Look: "Taryn Simon
and Aaron Swartz: Image Atlas"
Curated by Lauren Cornell
First Look, an ongoing series
of digital projects presented on
the New Museum's website, is
launched by Lauren Cornell in 2012.
Cornell selects *Image Atlas* by Taryn
Simon and Aaron Swartz as the
inaugural project. In 2014, Rhizome
begins to co-curate and copresent
the series with the New Museum.

2013

"NYC 1993: Experimental Jet Set,
Trash and No Star"
February 13–May 26, 2013
Curated by Massimiliano Gioni, Gary
Carrion-Murayari, Jenny Moore, and
Margot Norton
Artists: Janine Antoni, Ida
Applebroog, Art Club 2000, Lutz
Bacher, Alex Bag, Matthew Barney,
Sadie Benning, Lina Bertucci,
Nayland Blake, Gregg Bordowitz,
Lisa Bowman, Kathe Burkhart, Peter
Cain, Larry Clark, Patricia Cronin,
John Currin, Jessica Diamond,
Devon Dikeou, Cheryl Donegan,
Mary Beth Edelson, Nicole
Eisenman, Andrea Fraser, Coco
Fusco, Robert Gober, Nan Goldin,
Félix González-Torres, Renée Green,
Michael Joaquín Grey, Ann Hamilton,
Peter Halley, David Hammons,
Rachel Harrison, Todd Haynes,
Randolf Huff, Mike Kelley, Karen
Kilimnik, Byron Kim, Martin
Kippenberger, Derek Jarman, Jutta
Koether, Alix Lambert, Sean
Landers, Annie Leibovitz, Zoe
Leonard, Glenn Ligon, Sarah Lucas,
Kerry James Marshall, Daniel Joseph
Martinez, Paul McCarthy, Marlene
McCarty, Suzanne McClelland, John
Miller, Donald Moffett, Frank Moore,
Christian Philipp Müller, Cady
Noland, Kristin Oppenheim, Gabriel
Orozco, Pepón Osorio, Elizabeth
Peyton, Jack Pierson, Steven Pippin,
Charles Ray, Jason Rhoades, Julia
Scher, Andres Serrano, Cindy
Sherman, Gary Simmons, Lorna
Simpson, Kiki Smith, Rudolf Stingel,
Wolfgang Tillmans, Rirkrit Tiravanija,
The Thing, Lily van der Stokker, Nari
Ward, Gillian Wearing, Sally Webster,
Jack Whitten, Hannah Wilke, Sue
Williams, and Andrea Zittel

Museum as Hub: "How Do You Feel
(About Institutions)?"
April 12–13, 2013
Conference
Speakers: Naomi Beckwith, Tania
Bruguera, Johanna Burton, Lauren
Cornell, Anne Ellegood, Taraneh
Fazeli, Annie Fletcher, Vít Havránek,
Dóra Hegyi, Ryan Inouye, Eungie
Joo, Hyunjin Kim, Omer Krieger,
Jay A. Levenson, Michelle Marxuach,
Tobias Ostrander, Daniela Pérez,
Alexander Provan, Sarah Rifky,
Georg Schöllhammer, and
Ashok Sukumaran

Seven on Seven
April 19, 2013
Conference organized by Rhizome
Participants: Jeremy Bailey and
Julie Uhrman; Rafael Lozano-
Hemmer and Harper Reed;
Cameron Martin and Tara Tiger
Brown; Evgeny Morozov; Pfeiffer
and Alex Chung; and Jill Magid and
Dennis Crowley; Fatima Al Qadiri
and Dalton Caldwell; and Matthew
Ritchie and Billy Chasen

Ideas City New York
May 1–4, 2013
Keynote Speaker: Joi Ito, Director,
MIT Media Lab

"Adhocracy"
May 4–July 7, 2013
Curated by Joseph Grima
Organized as part of Ideas City
Participants: Advvt; Arduino, with
projects by Botanicalls, GROUND
Lab, Grathio Labs, and Tokyo
HackerSpace, among others;
AutLAB; Grégoire Basdevant; Josh
Begley; BlablabLAB; Thibault Brevet
in collaboration with Gianfranco
Baechtold, Laurent Beirnaert, Pierre
Bouvier, Raphaël Constantin, Lionel
Dalmazzini, Edina Desboeufs, Arthur
Desmet, and Thomas Grogan;
Defense Distributed; Yona Friedman;
Annika Frye; John Habraken; Garnet
Hertz; Jesse Howard; Markus
Kayser; Kickstarter; Minale Maeda;
Maker Faire Africa in collaboration
with Salma Adel/ICE Cairo,
Sannah Anwar, Alex Odundo,
Chika Okafor, Ugo Okafor/CcHub
Nigeria, David Olinayan, Elizabeth
Otieno, and Jennifer Wolfe + Esther
Adebayo; Enzo Mari; MINIMAL;
OpenStructures, with contributions
by Marie Caillaud, Riccardo Carneiro,
Christiane Hoegner, Tristan Kopp,
Thomas Lommee, Fabio Lorefice,
Lucas Maassen, Jeroen Maes, Juan
Montero, Eugenia Morpurgo, Unfold,
Artin Usta, Jo Van Boastraeten, Marijn
van der Poll, and Lukas Wegwerth;
Re-Do Studio; Orkan Telhan; Unfold
in collaboration with Alfred University,
Mustafa Canyurt, Larisa Daiga,
Eran Gal-Or, Ahmet Gülkokan, Eric
Hollender, Jonathan Keep, and Jen
Poueymirou; Johan van Lengen; and
Urban eXperiment

Museum as Hub: "Center for
Historical Reenactments:
After-after Tears"
May 22–July 7, 2013
Curated by Ryan Inouye
Participants: Kader Attia,
Khwezi Gule, Sohrab Mohebbi,
and Gabi Ngcobo

In the fall of 2013 the Education
Department establishes its
Experimental Study Program
(ESP), a semester-long program
for young people ages fifteen to
twenty. For each session, twelve
participants meet weekly on
Thursdays from 4 to 6 p.m. over
the course of three months. The
program offers teens the chance
to learn about contemporary
art, collaborate with artists on
new projects, and participate in
critical discussions about culture
through close work with peers
and interactive workshops. The
Teen Apprentice Program runs in
the summers, offering students
work experience and exposure
to contemporary art and ideas

through on-the-job training, career-
development talks, field trips, and
group projects that engage the
Museum's summer exhibitions. A
stipend is available for all selected
participants.

"Erika Vogt: Stranger Debris Roll
Roll Roll"
June 5–September 8, 2013
Curated by Jenny Moore and
Margot Norton

"Llyn Foulkes"
June 12–September 1, 2013
Originated at the Hammer Museum,
the University of California,
Los Angeles, where it was curated
by Ali Subotnick
Organized at the New Museum by
Margot Norton with Ali Subotnick

"Ellen Gallagher: Don't Axe Me"
June 19–September 15, 2013
Curated by Gary Carrion-Murayari

"XFR STN"
July 17–September 8, 2013
Curated by Johanna Burton, Tara
Hart, Jen Song, and Ben Fino-Radin
Artists: Alexis Bhagat, Alan W.
Moore, Taylor Moore, and the
artists of Collaborative Projects

Stuart Regen Visionaries Series:
Matthew Weiner in Conversation
with A.M. Homes
September 27, 2013

"Chris Burden: Extreme Measures"
October 2, 2013–January 12, 2014
Curated by Lisa Phillips with
Massimiliano Gioni, Jenny Moore,
and Margot Norton

First Look: "Xavier Cha:
Disembodied Selfie"
October 19, 2013–ongoing
Curated by Lauren Cornell
Originated at the 12th Lyon Biennale
and documented live online by the
New Museum

Ideas City São Paulo
October 25–27, 2013
Keynote Speaker: Paulo Mendes da
Rocha, architect

In the fall of 2013, under the
direction of Johanna Burton, the
New Museum's Department of
Education and Public Engagement
launches its R&D (Research &
Development) Seasons program,
which connects multiple platforms
around a single organizing theme.
Seasonal themes are generated
by artists in residence, and the
department's collaborations with
artists lead to exhibitions, performances, conferences, screenings,
publications, after-school programs
for teens, Family Day activities, and
archival research. The inaugural R&D
Season theme is ARCHIVES.

R&D Season: ARCHIVES:
"Performance Archiving
Performance"
November 6, 2013–January 12, 2014
Curated by Travis Chamberlain

Artists: a canary torsi, Jennifer
Monson, Julie Tolentino, and
Sara Wookey

2014

"Paweł Althamer: The Neighbors"
February 12–April 20, 2014
Curated by Massimiliano Gioni and
Gary Carrion-Murayari

"Laure Prouvost: For Forgetting"
February 12–April 13, 2014
Curated by Margot Norton

R&D Season: VOICE: "Jeanine
Olsen: Hear, Here"
April 22–July 6, 2014
Curated by Johanna Burton

"Hannah Sawtell: ACCUMULATOR"
April 23–June 22, 2014
Curated by Helga Christoffersen

"Roberto Cuoghi: Šuillakku corral"
April 30–June 29, 2014
Curated by Massimiliano Gioni and
Margot Norton

Seven on Seven
May 3, 2014
Conference organized by Rhizome
Keynote Speaker: Kate Crawford
Participants: Kari Altmann and
Aza Raskin; Ian Cheng and Jen
Fong-Adwent (Edna Piranha);
Anil Dash and Kevin McCoy;
Simon Denny and Nick Bilton; Avi
Flombaum and Hannah Sawtell;
Holly Herndon and Kate Ray; and
David Kravitz and Frances Stark

"Ragnar Kjartansson: Me, My
Mother, My Father, and I"
May 7–June 29, 2014
Curated by Massimiliano Gioni and
Margot Norton

"Camille Henrot: The Restless Earth"
May 7–June 29, 2014
Curated by Massimiliano Gioni and
Gary Carrion-Murayari

R&D Season: VOICE: "Brooke
O'Harra: I am Bleeding All Over the
Place: Studies in directing or nine
encounters between me and you"
May 16–24, 2014
Curated by Johanna Burton

"Here and Elsewhere"
July 16–September 28, 2014
Curated by Massimiliano
Gioni with Natalie Bell, Gary
Carrion-Murayari, Helga
Christoffersen, and Margot Norton
Artists: Abounaddara, Etel Adnan,
Rheims Alkadhi, Basma Alsharif,
Ziad Antar, Marwa Arsanios, Kader
Attia, Yto Barrada, Anna Boghiguian,
Fouad Elkoury, Simone Fattal,
Mekhitar Garabedian, GCC, Fakhri
El Ghezal, Tanya Habjouqa, Rokni
Haerizadeh, Rana Hamadeh,
Shuruq Harb, Susan Hefuna, Wafa
Hourani, Ali Jabri, Khaled Jarrar,
Lamia Joreige, Hiwa K, Amal
Kenawy, Mazen Kerbaj, Bouchra
Khalili, Maha Maamoun, Hashem El

Madani, Marwan, Ahmed Mater, Abdul Hay Mosallam, Selma and Sofiane Ouissi, Jamal Penjweny, Mohamed Larbi Rahali, Marwan Rechmaoui, Abdullah Al Saadi, Hrair Sarkissian, Hassan Sharif, Wael Shawky, Mounira Al Solh, Suha Traboulsi, Van Leo, Ala Younis, and Akram Zaatari

In September 2014, NEW INC is cofounded by Lisa Phillips and Karen Wong. It is the first museum-led cultural incubator dedicated to supporting innovation, collaboration, and entrepreneurship across art, design, and technology. NEW INC occupies eight thousand square feet of dedicated office, workshop, social, and presentation space at 231 Bowery. Each year, it selects an interdisciplinary community of one hundred members to take part in its twelve-month program, featuring business and entrepreneurial training sessions led by seasoned experts and mentors; group critiques; peer-to-peer learning; and critical discourse about the changing nature of culture, technology, and entrepreneurship.

Stuart Regen Visionaries Series: Darren Aronofsky in Conversation with Lynne Tillman
September 30, 2014

R&D Season: CHOREOGRAPHY: "Gerard & Kelly: P.O.L.E. (People, Objects, Language, Exchange)"
October 8, 2014–January 25, 2015
Curated by Johanna Burton

"Lili Reynaud-Dewar: Live Through That?!"
October 15, 2014–January 25, 2015
Curated by Helga Christoffersen

"Chris Ofili: Night and Day"
October 29, 2014–February 1, 2015
Curated by Massimiliano Gioni, Gary Carrion-Murayari, and Margot Norton
Exhibition traveled to other museums

> **"Fred Moten on Chris Ofili: Blue/r Vespers"**
> **January 29, 2015**

2015

"New Museum Triennial: Surround Audience"
February 25–May 24, 2015
Curated by Lauren Cornell and Ryan Trecartin with Sara O'Keeffe and Helga Christoffersen
Artists: Nadim Abbas, Lawrence Abu Hamdan, niv Acosta, Njideka Akunyili Crosby, Ketuta Alexi-Meskhishvili, Ed Atkins, Olga Balema, Frank Benson, Sascha Braunig, Antoine Catala, Aslı Çavuşoğlu, José León Cerrillo, Onejoon CHE, Tania Pérez Córdova, Verena Dengler, DIS, Aleksandra Domanović, Casey Jane Ellison, Exterritory, Geumhyung Jeong, Ane Graff, Guan Xiao, Shadi Habib Allah, Eloise Hawser, Lena Henke, Lisa

Holzer, Juliana Huxtable, Renaud Jerez, K-HOLE, Shreyas Karle, Kiluanji Kia Henda, Josh Kline, Eva Koťátková, Donna Kukama, Firenze Lai, Oliver Laric, Li Liao, Rachel Lord, Basim Magdy, Nicholas Mangan, Sophia Al-Maria, Ashland Mines, Shelly Nadashi, Eduardo Navarro, Steve Roggenbuck, Avery K Singer, Daniel Steegmann Mangrané, Martine Syms, Lisa Tan, Luke Willis Thompson, and Peter Wächtler

> *DISCOTROPIC* by niv Acosta
> **February 27, 2015**
> **Performers:** niv Acosta, Monstah Black, Alexandro Segade, and André D. Singleton

> **"DIS Whet Talks"**
> Various dates throughout the exhibition
> **Participants:** Casey Jane Ellison, Rob Horning, Chus Martínez, Robot Bina48 and Bruce Duncan, McKenzie Wark, and Sarah Watson

> **Symposium: "VISIBLE/INVISIBLE"**
> **March 7, 2015**
> **Panelists:** Karen Archey, Claire Barliant, Zach Blas, Heather Dewey-Hagborg, Nav Haq, Katherine Hubbard, Steffani Jemison, Carlos Motta, Jacolby Satterwhite, and Luke Willis Thompson
> **Moderators:** Johanna Burton, Lauren Cornell, and Alicia Ritson

> *If you wanna make the world a better place* by Geo Wyeth
> **April 11, 2015**

> **Launch of** *The Animated Reader: Poetry of Surround Audience*
> Presented at McNally Jackson, New York
> **April 19, 2015**
> **Panelists:** Yan Jun, Wayne Koestenbaum, Cory Tamler, and Mónica de la Torre
> **Moderator:** Brian Droitcour

Seven on Seven
May 2 2015
Conference organized by Rhizome
Keynote Speakers: Kate Crawford and Laura Poitras
Participants: Ai Weiwei and Jacob Appelbaum, with a film by Laura Poitras; Hannah Black and Thricedotted; Stanya Kahn and Rus Yusupov; Liam Gillick and Nate Silver; Camille Henrot and Harlo Holmes; Trevor Paglen and Mike Krieger with Adam Harvey; and Martine Syms and Gina Trapani

Ideas City New York
May 28–30, 2015
Keynote Speaker: Julián Castro, United States Secretary of Housing and Urban Development and Lawrence Lessig, Director, Edmond J. Safra Center of Ethics, Harvard University

"Albert Oehlen: Home and Garden"
June 10–September 13, 2015
Curated by Massimiliano Gioni with Gary Carrion-Murayari and Natalie Bell

> **"Albert Oehlen: Man in the Mirror,"**
> **Keynote Lecture by Mark Godfrey**
> July 9, 2015

"Leonor Antunes: I Stand Like A Mirror Before You"
June 24–September 6, 2015
Curated by Helga Christoffersen

"Sarah Charlesworth: Doubleworld"
June 24–September 20, 2015
Curated by Massimiliano Gioni and Margot Norton
Exhibition traveled to other museums

Stuart Regen Visionaries Series: Hilton Als
September 15, 2015

"Barbara Rossi: Poor Traits"
September 16, 2015–January 3, 2016
Curated by Natalie Bell
Exhibition traveled to other museums

"Wynne Greenwood: 'Kelly'"
September 16, 2015–January 10, 2016
Curated by Johanna Burton, Stephanie Snyder (guest curator), and Sara O'Keeffe
An earlier iteration of this project, "Stacy," was presented at the Douglas F. Cooley Memorial Art Gallery, Reed College, Portland, OR, in 2014 and was curated by Stephanie Snyder.

> **Release Party: Wynne Greenwood and Friends**
> **December 13, 2015**
> **Performers:** Morgan Bassichis, Joe DeNardo, K8 Hardy, Sara Jaffe, Fawn Krieger, and Emily Roysdon

"Jim Shaw: The End is Here"
October 7, 2015–January 10, 2016
Curated by Massimiliano Gioni and Gary Carrion-Murayari with Margot Norton

Documentary Sources in Contemporary Art, the New Museum's publication series that spanned 1984 to 2004, is relaunched as the Critical Anthologies in Art and Culture by the new series editor, Johanna Burton. The first volume to be published is *Mass Effect: Art and the Internet in the Twenty-First Century*, edited by Lauren Cornell and Ed Halter.

2016

"Pia Camil: A Pot for a Latch"
January 13–April 17, 2016
Curated by Margot Norton

R&D Season: LEGACY: "Cheryl Donegan: Scenes + Commercials"
January 20–April 10, 2016
Curated by Johanna Burton, Sara O'Keeffe, and Alicia Ritson

> **"Cheryl Donegan: EXTRA LAYER Fashion Show"**
> **April 7, 2016**
> Produced in collaboration with Print All Over Me

Open Score: Art and Technology
January 30, 2016
Conference organized by the
New Museum and Rhizome
Open Score is an annual conference
that explores the state of art and
technology today, convening
luminary artists, curators,
researchers, and writers to
discuss how technology is
transforming culture.
Participants: Simone Browne,
Adrian Chen, Jacob Ciocci, Simon
Denny, Kimberly Drew, Brian
Droitcour, Constant Dullaart,
Andrew Durbin, Ed Halter, Shawné
Michaelain Holloway, Rob Horning,
Juliana Huxtable, Zachary Kaplan,
Michelle Kuo, Laura McLean-Ferris,
Cathy Park Hong, Peter Russo, Jerry
Saltz, Emily Segal, and Colin Self

"Anri Sala: Answer Me"
February 3–April 10, 2016
Curated by Massimiliano Gioni,
Margot Norton, and Natalie Bell

"Who Owns Digital Social Memory?"
February 18, 2016
Organized by Rhizome
Panelists: Kimberly Drew, Dragan
Espenschied, Nathan Jurgenson,
Guadalupe Rosales, and Øs
Crunc Tesla
Moderator: Michael Connor

**Versions: "The Creative Landscape
of Virtual Reality"**
March 6, 2016
Conference organized by NEW INC
and Kill Screen
Versions is a conference on creative
practice and VR that explores VR as
an emerging medium.
Speakers: Gabo Arora, Monika
Bielskyte, Jessica Brillhart, Lauren
Cornell, Ela Darling, Gene Dolgoff,
Sam Dolnick, Shari Frilot, Katherine
Isbister, Julia Kaganskiy, Aaron
Koblin, Neil McFarland, Janet
Murray, Torfi Olafsson, Ken Perlin,
Skip Rizzo, Marte Roel, Rachel
Rossin, Jacolby Satterwhite,
Andrew Schoen, Lina Srivastava,
Rose Troche, Doug Trumbull, and
Jamin Warren

**R&D Season: LEGACY:
"Beatriz Santiago Muñoz: Song,
Strategy, Sign"**
April 20–June 12, 2016
Curated by Johanna Burton, Lauren
Cornell, and Sara O'Keeffe

Ideas City Detroit
April 25–30, 2016
Keynote Speakers: Theaster Gates,
dream hampton, Walter Hood, and
Amanda Williams

**"Cally Spooner: On False Tears and
Outsourcing"**
April 27–June 19, 2016
Curated by Helga Christoffersen

"Nicole Eisenman: AL-UGH-ORIES"
May 4–June 26, 2016
Curated by Massimiliano Gioni and
Helga Christoffersen

Seven on Seven
May 14, 2016
Conference organized by Rhizome
Participants: Trisha Baga and
Mike Woods; Ingrid Burrington and
Meredith Whittaker; Claire L. Evans
and Tracy Chou; Miranda July and
Paul Ford; Junglepussy and Jenna
Wortham; Jennifer Steinkamp and
Rana el Kaliouby; and Hito Steyerl
and Grant Olney Passmore

"Andra Ursuța: Alps"
April 27–June 19, 2016
Curated by Natalie Bell and
Massimiliano Gioni

"Goshka Macuga: Time as Fabric"
May 4–June 26, 2016
Curated by Margot Norton and
Massimiliano Gioni

**R&D Summer: "Simone Leigh: The
Waiting Room"**
June 22–September 18, 2016
Curated by Johanna Burton, Emily
Mello, and Shaun Leonardo

> **Care Sessions**
> **June 25–September 18, 2016**
>
> **"Lorraine O'Grady: Ask Me Anything
> About Aging"**
> **August 4, 2016**
>
> **Black Women Artists for Black Lives
> Matter**
> **Closed-Door Meetings: July 10–
> September 1, 2016**
> **Public Event: September 1, 2016**

"The Keeper"
July 20–September 25, 2016
Curated by Massimiliano Gioni,
Natalie Bell, Helga Christoffersen,
and Margot Norton
Artists: Hilma af Klint, Yuji
Agematsu, Korbinian Aigner, Levi
Fisher Ames, Ed Atkins, Hannelore
Baron, Wilson Bentley, Tong
Bingxue/Ye Jinglu, Arthur Bispo do
Rosário, Carol Bove/Carlo Scarpa,
Roger Caillois, Maurice H. Chéhab,
Oliver Croy and Oliver Elser, Howard
Fried, Peter Fritz, Olga Fröbe-
Kapteyn, Aurélien Froment, Richard
Greaves/Mario Del Curto, Ydessa
Hendeles, Susan Hiller, MM,
Vladimir Nabokov, Shinro Ohtake,
Henrik Olesen, Loretta Pettway,
Missouri Pettway, Quinnie Pettway,
Zofia Rydet, Harry Smith, and Vanda
Vieira-Schmidt

Ideas City Athens
September 19–25, 2016
Speakers: John Akomfrah, Sophia
Al-Maria, Tania Bruguera, dream
hampton, George Prevelakis, Nick
Srnicek, Hito Steyerl, and others

**Stuart Regen Visionaries Series:
Fran Lebowitz in Conversation with
Martin Scorsese**
September 27, 2016

"Cheng Ran: Diary of a Madman"
October 19, 2016–January 15, 2017
Curated by Helga Christoffersen
and Massimiliano Gioni

"Pipilotti Rist: Pixel Forest"
October 26, 2016–January 15, 2017
Curated by Massimiliano Gioni,
Margot Norton, and Helga
Christoffersen

The New Museum publishes the
second volume in the Critical
Anthologies in Art and Culture
series, *Public Servants: Art and
the Crisis of the Common Good*,
edited by Johanna Burton, Shannon
Jackson, and Dominic Willsdon.

**"Scamming the Patriarchy:
A Youth Summit"**
November 16, 2016
Co-organized by Brujas, By Us For
Us (BUFU), Discwoman, and House
of LaDosha

2017

"Jonathas de Andrade: O Peixe"
January 25–April 9, 2017
Curated by Natalie Bell

**"Raymond Pettibon: A Pen of
All Work"**
February 8–April 9, 2017
Curated by Gary Carrion-Murayari
and Massimiliano Gioni
Exhibition traveled to other
museums

Versions: "A New Reality"
February 25, 2017
Conference organized by NEW INC
and Kill Screen
Speakers: Cecilia Abadie, Drew
Bamford, Nancy Bennett, Drazen
Bosnjak, Chandler Burr, Leigh
Christie, Cory Doctorow, Judith
Donath, Jenn Duong, Claire L.
Evans, Charlotte Furet, Hector
Harkness, Adrianne Jeffries, Julia
Kaganskiy, Brenda Laurel, Lynn
Hershman Leeson, Victor Luo,
Robin McNicholas, Nick Montfort,
Opeyemi Olukemi, Jon Rafman, Adi
Robertson, Bijan Stephen, Marco
Tempest, Jamin Warren, Diana
Williams, Tim Wu, and Robert Yang

Seven on Seven
April 22, 2017
Conference organized by Rhizome
Participants: DIS and Rachel
Haot; Constant Dullaart and Chris
Paik; Olia Lialina and Mike Tyka;
Miao Ying and Mehdi Yahyanejad;
Jayson Musson and Jonah
Peretti; Bunny Rogers and
Nozlee Samadzadeh; and Addie
Wagenknecht and Cindy Gallop

"Carol Rama: Antibodies"
April 26–September 10, 2017
Curated by Helga Christoffersen
and Massimiliano Gioni

**R&D Season: BODY: "RAGGA NYC:
All the Threatened and Delicious
Things Joining One Another"**
May 3–June 25, 2017
Curated by Sara O'Keeffe
Artists: Jahmal B. Golden, Joey De
Jesus, Carolyn Lazard and Bleue
Liverpool, Tau Lewis, Shanekia

McIntosh, Maya Monès, Paul
Anthony Smith, Renée Stout, and
Christopher Udemezue

**"Lynette Yiadom-Boakye:
Under-Song For A Cipher"
May 3–September 3, 2017**
Curated by Natalie Bell and
Massimiliano Gioni

**"Kaari Upson: Good thing you are
not alone"
May 3–September 10, 2017**
Curated by Margot Norton

**"Elaine Cameron-Weir: viscera has
questions about itself"
May 3–September 3, 2017**
Curated by Natalie Bell

**Ideas City Arles
May 22–27, 2017
Keynote Speakers:** Rem Koolhaas,
architect and cofounder of, Office
for Metropolitan Architecture
(OMA), and Michel Bauwens,
founder of the Foundation for
Peer-to-Peer Alternatives

**R&D Summer: "Paul Ramírez
Jonas: Half-Truths"
July 5–September 17, 2017**
Curated by Johanna Burton, Shaun
Leonardo, and Emily Mello

**"Helen Johnson: Ends"
September 13, 2017–
January 14, 2018**
Curated by Gary Carrion-Murayari

**Ideas City New York
September 16, 2017
Speakers:** Ras Baraka, Tatiana
Bilbao, David Byrne, Majora Carter,
Mel Chin, Nadina Christopoulou,
Maurice Cox, Teddy Cruz, Fonna
Forman, Rosanne Haggerty, dream
hampton, Kemi Ilesanmi, Leslie
Koch, Eric Liu, Justin Garrett Moore,
Trevor Paglen, Gregor Robertson,
Jonathan Rose, Superflex, and past
Ideas City Fellows, among others

**"Kahlil Joseph: Shadow Play"
September 27, 2017–
January 7, 2018**
Curated by Natalie Bell and
Massimiliano Gioni

**"Petrit Halilaj: RU"
September 27, 2017–
January 7, 2018**
Curated by Helga Christoffersen

**"Trigger: Gender as a Tool and
a Weapon"
September 27, 2017–
January 21, 2018**
Curated by Johanna Burton with
Sara O'Keeffe and Natalie Bell
Artists: Morgan Bassichis, Sadie
Benning, Nayland Blake, Justin Vivian
Bond, Gregg Bordowitz, Pauline
Boudry/Renate Lorenz, Nancy
Brooks Brody, A.K. Burns and A.L.
Steiner, Leidy Churchman, Liz
Collins, Vaginal Davis, Harry
Dodge, The Dyke Division of the
Two-Headed Calf, Josh Faught,
ektor garcia, Mariah Garnett,
Reina Gossett and Sasha

Wortzel, Sharon Hayes, House of
Ladosha, Stanya Kahn, Carolyn
Lazard, Simone Leigh, Ellen
Lesperance, Candice Lin, Troy
Michie, Ulrike Müller, Willa
Nasatir, Sondra Perry, Christina
Quarles, Connie Samaras, Curtis
Talwst Santiago, Tschabalala
Self, Paul Mpagi Sepuya,
Tuesday Smillie, Sable Elyse
Smith, Patrick Staff, Diamond
Stingily, Mickalene Thomas, Wu
Tsang, Chris E. Vargas, Geo
Wyeth, and Anicka Yi

The New Museum publishes
the third volume in the Critical
Anthologies in Art and Culture
series, *Trap Door: Trans Cultural
Production and the Politics of
Visibility*, edited by Reina Gossett,
Eric A. Stanley, and Johanna Burton.

Acknowledgments

This book has been forty years in the making. Because the New Museum is always moving forward, we've rarely taken a retrospective look, but—after four decades—it is time. *40 Years New* is part of a larger scholarship initiative to mark our fortieth anniversary that includes the redesign and relaunch of our Digital Archive and the exhibition "Pursuing the Unpredictable," which contains materials drawn largely from our archives and incorporates the chronology that was the starting point for this volume.

The process of collecting and verifying the New Museum's history has been an enormous task that began seven years ago when we first started digitizing our archive and reconstructing the time line of an institution that never paid much attention to record-keeping or documenting things for posterity. This immense undertaking of creating the Digital Archive was initially led by John Hatfield, former Deputy Director, who had considerable first-hand experience of the institution's history. His efforts have been followed up more recently by an amazing team under the guidance of first Lauren Cornell, former Associate Director, Technology Initiatives, and then Karen Wong, current Deputy Director. Jasmine Lee, Digital Manager, and Amye McCarther, Archivist, have led the charge and managed an extremely challenging workflow with a dedicated group of research fellows and interns—who, over many months, meticulously verified each piece of information. We are greatly indebted to them all for creating an accessible archive that is a standout model for the field, brilliantly designed by Linked by Air.

This volume—*40 Years New*—and the work on the redesigned Digital Archive were undertaken in parallel and are intimately connected. Alicia Ritson, Marcia Tucker Senior Research Fellow, led the mammoth project of assembling the chronology and conducting photographic research, which were core elements of the Digital Archive and the starting points for this book and the exhibition "Pursuing the Unpredictable," mentioned above. I appreciate her lasting contribution to a project that will serve scholars and students alike for generations to come.

I would especially like to thank all of the contributors to this publication— Johanna Burton, Lauren Cornell, Massimiliano Gioni, Joseph Grima, Julia Kaganskiy, Ned Rifkin, Lynne Tillman, and Brian Wallis—whose essays and personal reflections illuminate our rich history around such topics as artists' collaborations, art and activism, alternative geographies, civic action, art and technology, and cross-disciplinary forms. Marcia E. Vetrocq, Managing Editor, worked closely with me as the book was taking shape and lent her expertise and insights to each of the authors' contributions. In addition, Olivia Casa, Copy Editor, and Sarah Dziedzic, Photo Researcher, contributed tremendous work over many months, and Maureen McElroy, Executive Assistant to the Director, provided additional assistance.

We are most grateful to the Andrew W. Mellon Foundation, Mariët Westermann, and Ella Baff for their multiyear support of scholarly initiatives that have nourished this entire project. We were fortunate to have Prem Krishnamurthy, Chris Wu, and Hyo Kwon from Project Projects design the book with great clarity and to have Phaidon and Keith Fox, CEO, as publishers who are committed to the New Museum's distinctive vision.

The history laid out in this book features a selection of our programs over four decades. It is not exhaustive, and there are many outstanding projects that we were not able to include. Moreover, there is so much that is invisible that makes the entire Museum (and its programs) run smoothly. These less visible forces are absolutely critical and include the staff and the Board of Trustees, who often work behind the scenes to keep the institution moving forward.

I want to thank Saul Dennison, former President of the Board of Trustees and current Chairman Emeritus, who has been my partner every step of the way over the past eighteen years and is always a beacon of pragmatism, good sense, and humor, and James Keith Brown, our current President, who has taken up the mantle and is a passionate champion of new art, innovation, and multimedia forms. They are a big part of this history, along with the entire Board of Trustees, who have put their faith in us and are our fellow adventurers. I also want to particularly acknowledge Massimiliano Gioni, *Edlis Neeson Artistic Director*, and Karen Wong, who have worked with me over the past eleven years and have lent their perspective and provided input on this book at critical junctures. The New Museum staff is without parallel, and they have created, and supported, programs and projects that have led the field and carried forward our founding ethos of embracing art that is often excluded elsewhere because it is difficult, unknown, or under-recognized.

Finally, this book would not have been possible without my family—Leon, Olivia, and Savannah—whose support over the past eighteen years has made them an important part of this history as well.

Lisa Phillips
Toby Devan Lewis Director

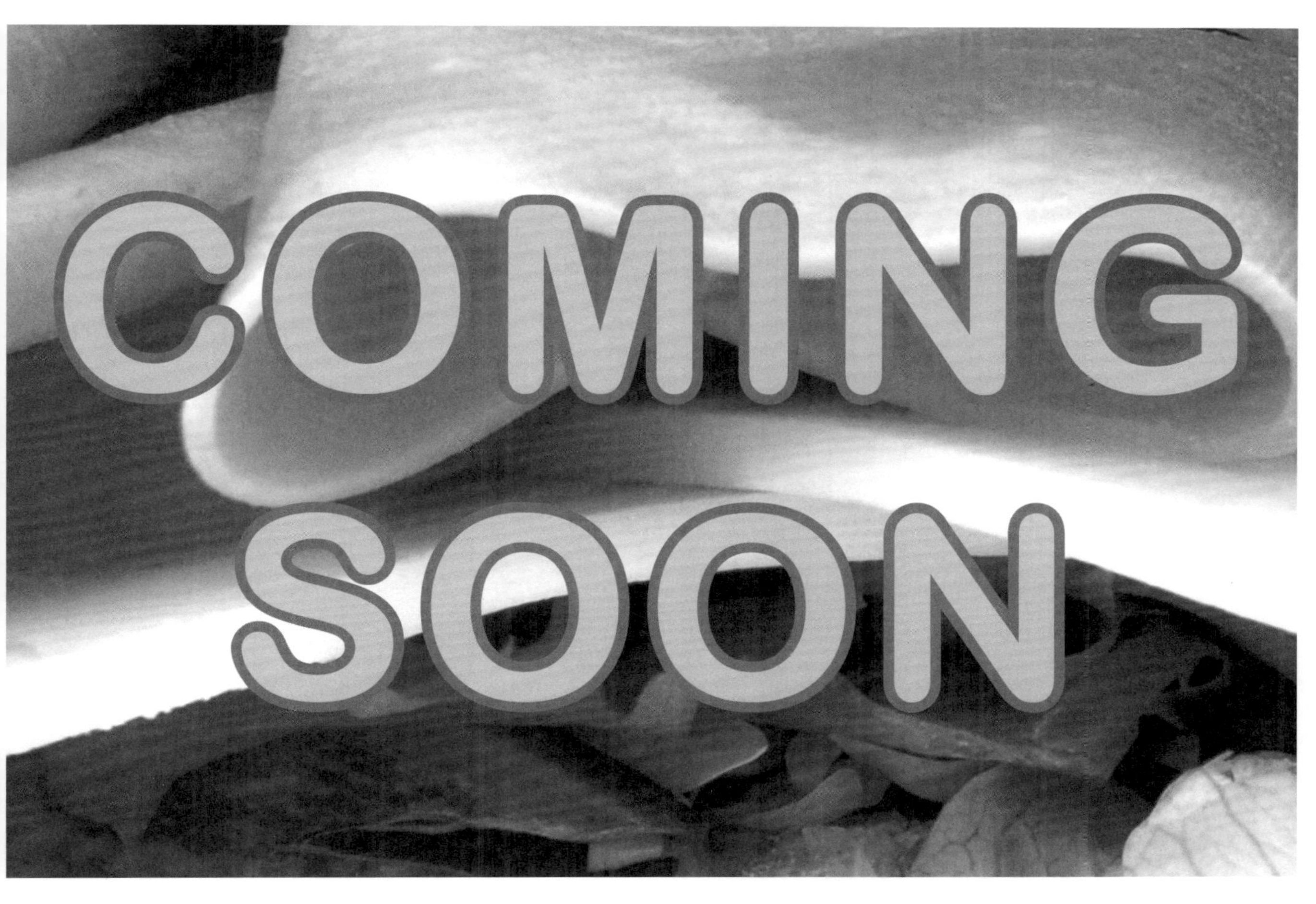

Alex Da Corte,
Fall 2020, 2017

Published by
New Museum
235 Bowery
New York, NY 10002

in association with

Phaidon Press Limited
Regent's Wharf
All Saints Street
London N1 9PA

Phaidon Press Inc.
65 Bleecker Street
New York, NY 10012

phaidon.com

On the occasion of the New
Museum's 40th anniversary

Editor: Lisa Phillips
Managing Editor: Marcia E. Vetrocq
Copy Editor: Olivia Casa
Research: Alicia Ritson
Graphic Design: Prem
Krishnamurthy, Chris Wu, and
Hyo Kwon, Project Projects
Image Research: Alicia Ritson
and Sarah Dziedzic
Typeface: Unica77 digitized by
Stephan Müller and MTA Mono
by Berton Hasebe
Lithography: Sebastiaan Hanekroot,
Colour & Books
Printing: Die Keure, Belgium

Major support for this publication
has been provided by the
Andrew W. Mellon Foundation.

Additional support has been
provided by Ydessa Hendeles
and by the J. McSweeney and
G. Mills Publications Fund at
the New Museum.

phaidon.com

978 0 7148 7525 5